The Soviet Empire: Expansion & Détente

The Soviet Empire: Expansion & Détente

Critical Choices for Americans

Volume IX

WITHDRAWN

Edited by

William E. Griffith

Lexington Books
D.C. Heath and Company
Lexington, Massachusetts
Toronto

Library of Congress Cataloging in Publication Data

Main entry under title:
The Soviet Empire: Expansion & Détente

(Critical choices for Americans; v. 9)
"Prepared for the Commission on Critical Choices for Americans."
Includes index.
1. Russia—Foreign relations—1953-1975. 2. Russia—Foreign relations—
1975- 3. Russia—Politics and government—1953- 4. United States—For-
eign relations—Russia. 5. Russia—Foreign relations—United States. I. Grif-
fith, William E. II. Commission on Critical Choices for Americans.
III. Series.
DK274.S65194   327.47   75-44727
ISBN 0-669-00421-9

Published simultaneously in Canada.

Printed in the United States of America.

International Standard Book Number: 0-669-00421-9

Library of Congress Catalog Card Number: 75-44727

Foreword

The Commission on Critical Choices for Americans, a nationally representative, bipartisan group of forty-two prominent Americans, was brought together on a voluntary basis by Nelson A. Rockefeller. After assuming the Vice Presidency of the United States, Mr. Rockefeller, the chairman of the Commission, became an ex officio member. The Commission's assignment was to develop information and insights which would bring about a better understanding of the problems confronting America. The Commission sought to identify the critical choices that must be made if these problems are to be met.

The Commission on Critical Choices grew out of a New York State study of the Role of a Modern State in a Changing World. This was initiated by Mr. Rockefeller, who was then Governor of New York, to review the major changes taking place in federal-state relationships. It became evident, however, that the problems confronting New York State went beyond state boundaries and had national and international implications.

In bringing the Commission on Critical Choices together, Mr. Rockefeller said:

As we approach the 200th Anniversary of the founding of our Nation, it has become clear that institutions and values which have accounted for our astounding progress during the past two centuries are straining to cope with the massive problems of the current era. The increase in the tempo of change and the vastness and complexity of the wholly new situations which are evolving with accelerated change, create a widespread sense that our political and social system has serious inadequacies.

We can no longer continue to operate on the basis of reacting to crises, counting on crash programs and the expenditure of huge sums of money to solve our problems. We have got to understand and project present trends, to take command of the forces that are emerging, to extend our freedom and wellbeing as citizens and the future of other nations and peoples in the world.

Because of the complexity and interdependence of issues facing America and the world today, the Commission has organized its work into six panels, which emphasize the interrelationships of critical choices rather than treating each one in isolation.

The six panels are:

Panel I: Energy and its Relationship to Ecology, Economics and World Stability;

Panel II: Food, Health, World Population and Quality of Life;

Panel III: Raw Materials, Industrial Development, Capital Formation, Employment and World Trade;

Panel IV: International Trade and Monetary Systems, Inflation and the Relationships Among Differing Economic Systems;

Panel V: Change, National Security and Peace;

Panel VI: Quality of Life of Individuals and Communities in the U.S.A.

The Commission assigned, in these areas, more than 100 authorities to prepare expert studies in their fields of special competence. The Commission's work has been financed by The Third Century Corporation, a New York not-for-profit organization. The corporation has received contributions from individuals and foundations to advance the Commission's activities.

The Commission is determined to make available to the public these background studies and the reports of those panels which have completed their deliberations. The background studies are the work of the authors and do not necessarily represent the views of the Commission or its members.

This volume is one of the series of volumes the Commission will publish in the belief that it will contribute to the basic thought and foresight America will need in the future.

WILLIAM J. RONAN
Acting Chairman
Commission on Critical Choices
for Americans

Members of the Commission

EDWARD TELLER
  Senior Research Fellow, Hoover Institution
  on War, Revolution and Peace,
  Stanford University

ARTHUR K. WATSON*
  Former Ambassador to France

MARINA VON NEUMANN WHITMAN
  Distinguished Public Service Professor
  of Economics, University of Pittsburgh

CARROLL L. WILSON
  Professor, Alfred P. Sloan
  School of Management,
  Massachusetts Institute of Technology

GEORGE D. WOODS
  Former President, World Bank

Members of the Commission served on the panels. In addition, others assisted
the panels.

BERNARD BERELSON
Senior Fellow
President Emeritus
The Population Council

C. FRED BERGSTEN
Senior Fellow
The Brookings Institution

ORVILLE G. BRIM, JR.
President
Foundation for Child Development

LESTER BROWN
President
Worldwatch Institute

LLOYD A. FREE
President
Institute for International Social Research

*Deceased

J. GEORGE HARRAR
Former President
Rockefeller Foundation

WALTER LEVY
Economic Consultant

PETER G. PETERSON
Chairman of the Board
Lehman Brothers

ELSPETH ROSTOW
Dean, Division of General and Comparative Studies
University of Texas

WALT W. ROSTOW
Professor of Economics and History
University of Texas

SYLVESTER L. WEAVER
Communications Consultant

JOHN G. WINGER
Vice President
Energy Economics Division
Chase Manhattan Bank

Preface

The rapid rise of the power and influence of the Soviet Union on a global scale raises new questions for the American people and gives a crucial dimension to Soviet-American relations. These superpower relations, with their major nuclear component, are complicated by the political and military balances in Europe and potential confrontation in the Middle East. Our interaction with the Soviet Union has a decisive impact on our relations with Western Europe, China, and Japan. Finally, there is the worldwide naval balance—freedom of the seas—which is vital to the United States economic interests.

The policy options for the United States and the choices that the American people must make in our relations with the Soviet Empire are all significant. How can we avoid open armed conflict and manage limited or fuller cooperation with the Soviet Union? Can we and the Soviet Union really develop parallel goals and joint endeavors beyond the manned space program? What should be our stance toward China, particularly since we are now trying to improve our relations with Peking? What priority should we give to Moscow over our relations with our allies and Middle Eastern problems? Can we afford not to maintain at least strategic nuclear and naval parity with the Soviet Union?

The Soviet Empire: Expansion & Détente is one of seven geographic studies (prepared for the Commission on Critical Choices for Americans) under the coordination of Nancy Maginnes Kissinger. Companion volumes cover Western Europe, the Middle East, China and Japan, Southern Asia, Africa and Latin America. It has been the Commission's belief that to limit our studies to only domestic issues would be examining only half of the problems confronting America in the remaining years of this century. Our neighbors to the north and south and across the oceans to the east and west are clearly a part of America's future as we witness daily the growing interdependence of all nations.

Forecasting any political future is not an exact science, but it is even more risky considering the secrecy characteristic of the ruling party in the Soviet Union. Yet, William E. Griffith's study provides the informed, analytical judgment that is of crucial importance in formulating our policy toward the Soviet Union.

W.J.R.

Acknowledgments

I am most grateful to all those who helped me in planning and editing this volume: to Nancy Maginnes Kissinger, Anne Boylan, and Charity Randall of the Commission staff; to the commentators on the first drafts of the chapters, Professors Gregory Grossman, Klaus Mehnert, Marshall Shulman, and Adam Ulam; to my research assistants, Paul Walker and Rada Vlajinac; to the typists, Edna Rindner, my administrative assistant, and Nancy Hearst; and last but certainly not least to the contributors, who responded so well to my predilections for conciseness and deadlines.

William E. Griffith

Contents

List of Tables

THE SOVIET UNION
and Eastern Europe

ARCTIC OCEAN

ALASKA

JAPAN

ARCTIC CIRCLE

• Novosibirsk

Irkutsk

• Khabarovsk

• Vladivostok

SEA OF JAPAN

• Ulan Bator

OUTER MONGOLIA

NO. KOREA
Pyongyang

JAPAN

• Seoul

SO. KOREA

Peking

CHINA

EAST CHINA SEA

0		1000		2000 MI
0	1000	2000	3000 KM	

I The Soviet Union and Eastern Europe: An Overview

William E. Griffith

Projecting the future, even more than writing the history of the past, is in my view not a science but an art. History is a web in which personalities and accidents play too great roles to justify more than an attempt to sketch some future possibilities.

Projection of the future is even more difficult in Communist-ruled areas such as the Soviet Union and Eastern Europe, because the secrecy which pervades their politics makes it so difficult to understand their past and present. Moreover, East-West détente has increased the interdependence between the Communist states and the rest of the world and therefore analysis of Communist policies has become even more difficult.

One can, however, perhaps foresee the future by studying Russia's past. The 1917 Bolshevik Revolution was indeed drastic. It brought to power a new, peasant-based, xenophobic Bolshevik elite, deeply suspicious of the West. But it was also a restoration—of the bureaucratic police state which by the 1880s Tsar Alexander III had fastened on Russia and which after 1900 began to be weakened by Tsarist decay, defeat in World War I, and the 1917 Provisional Government. Imperial Russia was historically a patromonial, bureaucratic state: the tsars saw themselves not only as autocratic rulers but also as the rightful owners of Russia, its land, and its people. Imperial Russia was ambivalent about the West. It had enjoyed neither Renaissance nor Reformation, neither private capitalism nor civil liberties, neither separation of church and state nor, until 1905, a legal political opposition.[1] One should not be surprised that Russia does not today. What would be surprising would be if it did—or the belief that it soon if ever will.

The rate of change in the Soviet Union and Eastern Europe is likely to be slower in the future than it has been since Stalin's death in 1953. The destructiveness of nuclear weapons and Soviet nuclear parity with the United States make general war, which was until 1945 the most compelling instrument for major change, most unlikely. They thus tend to freeze boundaries and spheres of influence, at least in the developed world. Moreover, the Soviet leadership has learned better how to control and check liberalization in its sphere of influence. Changes in the Soviet Union will probably continue to be gradual and result primarily from internal, not external developments. In Eastern Europe, despite probable waves of liberalization or flash risings in the future as in the past, Moscow will continue to use, probably successfully, whatever measures it deems necessary, including the Red Army, to restore its threatened hegemony.

It is also difficult to predict the future effects of the Soviet-American relationship on change in the Soviet Union and Eastern Europe. Unless the inflation and energy crises throw the non-Communist developed world into a prolonged worldwide depression, which in early 1976 seemed unlikely, the United States will probably remain technologically superior to the Soviet Union. But the American will for power abroad has declined and will probably not soon revive. While the current U.S. foreign policy crisis arises in part from temporary phenomena—the aftermaths of Vietnam and Watergate, a nonelected president of the opposite party from a fragmented and weakly-led Congress—there are longer-range tendencies at work as well—neo-isolationism and priority for domestic problems—which will delay if not impede the revival of a dynamic U.S. foreign policy. The Soviet Union, in contrast, will probably remain for the rest of the century, like Wilhelmian Germany, a young, *nouveau riche* expansionist imperial power, cautiously but firmly and globally moving outward. The most important and difficult problem to estimate, therefore, in the future of Soviet-American relations is not Soviet but American policy.

The Soviet Domestic Future

The Soviet political elite now has three policy choices in order the better to secure its rule: to maintain its present method of rule, to change it drastically, or to reform it gradually. The political elite has chosen gradual reform, and will most probably continue to do so, because the first option is economically too inefficient and because the second, it believes, dangerously threatens its monopoly of the commanding heights of political power. Soviet economic development and technological modernization will therefore probably not speed up, despite ample incentives to do so in order to maintain the high level of defense expenditures, to catch up with the United States in military and civilian advanced technology, and thus to fulfill the age-old Russian dream of overtaking the West. Indeed, the projected growth rate for the fifth Five Year Plan, confirmed at the Twenty-Fifth Party Congress, was remarkably lower than its predecessor's (1971-1975: 6.9 percent per year; 1976-1980, projected, 4.4 percent per year). This indicated that economic growth will continue to decline. Moreover, producer goods production is again, contrary to the previous plan, scheduled to grow more rapidly than consumer goods production.

Several factors continue to work against high Soviet economic growth: lower growth in the labor force, geographic and investment obstacles to raw material exploitation, lower agricultural productivity, and frequent bad harvests. Increased Soviet economic growth must therefore primarily be qualitative: the result of major economic reforms (à la Hungary: decentralization, a market economy, and rational prices), greater domestic innovation, and/or massive import of high-level foreign technology.

Major economic reforms are unlikely for political reasons. The Soviet political elite is unlikely to decentralize decision-making in industry or in agriculture and thereby to diminish its political control and to run the risk of managerial independence or, worse, autonomous workers' organizations. Greater domestic innovation is therefore unlikely. Soviet import of foreign technology will continue insofar as the OECD countries are willing to export it to the Soviet Union, but its stimulus to growth will be limited by the Soviet centralized planning system's built-in counter-incentives to technological dissemination and imitation. The centralized Soviet foreign trade system also produces counter-incentives against export, notably quality uncompetitiveness. Finally, although in purely economic terms the Soviets should continue to import food instead of producing raw materials for export, Moscow will probably continue to try to do the opposite, again for political reasons, because the Soviet leadership will try hard not to become permanently dependent on food imports.

Modernization and economic development do not inevitably produce political liberalization, pluralism, and "the end of ideology." Technological rationalization and modernization do push in these directions, and Soviet technological modernization will continue to erode the egalitarian and utopian aspects of its Communist ideology and thus to produce increasing skepticism among its technological and humanistic intelligentsia. The centralized, bureaucratic, secretive, police-oriented, and Great Russian nationalist characteristics of the present ruling Soviet elite, however, make it unlikely to introduce decisive reforms. For it will remain determined to preserve its own power; to keep the Soviet Union a superpower, which in its view requires the continued domination of its kind of Great Russian Communist elite over the Great Russians (that half of the Soviet population whose native language is Russian) and the increasingly restive other Soviet nationalities; and therefore to emphasize "progressive," "business-like" economic and technological development, Great Russian nationalism and cultural traditions, and military power, rather than, as Khrushchev unsuccessfully did, utopian social transformation.

Yet the Soviet Union will continue to change. The trend toward a more rational but still firm authoritarianism will continue. Post-Stalin Soviet reforms have been decreed from above. Indeed, in my view dissident pressures have not pushed them forward but slowed them down. Even since its formation the Soviet regime has been characterized by what (to adapt Marxist terminology) one may call "surplus repression." But Brezhnev has been trying, more systematically and less erratically than Khrushchev, to institutionalize the beginnings of a consultative role for some interest groups in Soviet society, notably the intelligentsia. For he is aware, as his successors probably will be, that mass terror of the Stalinist variety seriously and increasingly interferes with the efficient operation of a complex modern industrial society and that such a consultative role will satisfy most of the intelligentsia and not endanger the Communist party's monopoly of the commanding heights of power.

In the near future the present elderly, oligarchic, and, as the 1976 Twenty-Fifth Party Congress showed, remarkably stable Soviet *political elite* will go through a generational transformation. But it will probably not decisively change its policies as a result. It will reject the Stalinist variety of terror, Khrushchev's headlong reforms, and drastic liberalization, in favor of gradualist, reformist change. It will probably not give way to neo-Stalinist personalist autocratic rule—but it may: the history of the Roman Empire shows that a Claudius can give way to a Nero and a Titus to a Domitian. The role of personality, particularly in a centralized autocratic system, is often decisive and always unpredictable.

The rest of the century will probably see the further development of a "two-tiered" Soviet society. The average Soviet citizen, in the first tier, if he does not engage in what the regime sees as oppositional activity, will enjoy not only a rising standard of living but also something increasingly closer to the rule of law. The intelligentsia, in addition, will increasingly play a consultative role in the Soviet political process. The small minority in the second tier, those viewed by the elite as politically oppositional, will continue to be subjected to the police repression which has characterized almost all modern Russian history. Finally, the ruling elite will continue to determine the rules of the game: who belongs in which tier.

In my view the dominant characteristic of Soviet society over the rest of the century will be continued modernization and economic development without drastic, rapid political, economic, or social change. (I thus share the views expressed in this volume by Seweryn Bialer rather than those of Peter Reddaway, who foresees more rapid and drastic change.) The Soviet Union is the greatest modern example of revolutionary, forced, rapid economic and social modernization by centralized, hierarchic political coercion rather than by self-generating, self-regulating economic incentives. True, its political system is becoming an obstacle to the attainment of its main economic goal: economic growth for national security and power. But the Soviet elite, when it has to choose, will probably continue to give priority to maintaining its political control.

In the last ten years *intellectual dissent*, the most intense form of the post-Stalin repoliticalization of the Soviet intelligentsia, has gravely concerned the Soviet leadership and greatly impressed the West. This dissent is of much greater significance among non-Great Russians because there it combines nationalism with liberalization. Its members do not regard themselves as a counter-elite or even as primarily political, except in the most general sense of moral revulsion against the regime and opposition to its repression. Nor are they united in their views. Most of its prominent Great Russian figures are cosmopolitan and anti-Great Russian nationalist, in the nineteenth century "Westernizing" tradition. Others, such as Solzhenitsyn, are liberal, deeply religious Slavophils, distrustful of Western "demoralization," democracy, and détente. There is also an extreme right-wing fringe and a few "true Leninists." The anti-Great Russian nationalism of most of its prominent figures, plus the traditional passivity and strong nationalism of the Russian masses, the intelligentsia's fear that still they might explode, and regime policy repression will in my view continue to prevent the Westernizing dissident movement from gaining a significant mass base among Great Russians. Nor will the Slavophils probably achieve it either.

Determined by 1971 to crush the dissident movement, the regime has reacted by increasing repression and exile by voluntary forced emigration, but it has not reverted to mass terror and it is not likely to. Yet it has not yet, within its own self-imposed limits, totally crushed dissent. Indeed, although the dissident movement is at present at a low level of effectiveness, if one can judge from the similar developments in nineteenth century Russia it will revive again from time to time. In any case, it has already changed the style of Soviet intellectual life, for in it all the political trends—not only the Westernizing one—of pre-1917 Russia have reemerged.

Dissent among the (non-Great Russian) nations in the Soviet Union is and will remain different and for Moscow far more serious. (I call them nations, not nationalities, for that is what they are.) To all of them the Soviet regime has brought rapid, forced economic development and modernization. As always in modern history, this has produced an increasingly modernized, educated, and nationalist intelligentsia. Moreover, many republics, notably in the Caucasus, have developed a semi-legal "second economy," and their nationalism is accentuated by Moscow's attempts to bring this under control. Finally, some of them, notably the Baltic and Caucasian republics, see themselves with considerable reason as culturally superior to the Great Russians, whose domination seems to them, as it does to many East Europeans subject to Soviet hegemony, the more unjustified.

But the Soviet Communist elite will probably continue to contain national dissent. In so doing it will have, perhaps only less than for its anti-Chinese policy, the support of the overwhelming majority of Great Russians. For a

Soviet Union without its non-Great Russian nations, now almost one-half of its population, or paralyzed by national dissent and rebellion, would no longer be a superpower, and its external security, from the point of view of the Great Russians, would thereby be unacceptably menaced. The Great Russians, therefore, have an overriding motive to maintain the Soviet empire. Even so, for the rest of this century nationalist dissent will increasingly become *the* major single Soviet internal problem, and the non-Great Russian Communist leadership of the minority republics will be pushed by popular pressure to try to diminish Great Russian hegemony.

One other important and too often neglected point: the necessity for the Soviet Great Russian elite, and for Great Russians in general, to maintain firm control over national dissent makes it the more probable that the Soviet leadership will not allow serious national dissident movements in the East European countries which it controls. The Czechoslovak developments of 1968 had a significantly destabilizing impact not only in Poland and East Germany but also in the western Ukraine. In the nineteenth century the Russian tsars less and less allowed liberties to their rebellious subjects in Poland which they did not want to allow to their subjects in Russia. So it will be in the future.

In the Soviet Union as elsewhere those who want major change will have to choose either total opposition or gradual reforms "within the system." In my view the majority of the Soviet intelligentsia will continue to want reforms but not decisive changes. (They will, as the late Speaker Sam Rayburn used to counsel freshmen congressmen, "go along to get along.") The political elite will continue to meet them part-way. This "in-system" intelligentsia is professionally and ethnically differentiated. It does not yet seem very susceptible to the "revolution of rising political expectations," largely because the regime successfully coopts most of it. While it will continue to be prevented from organizing itself or from legitimately expressing decisively different options for Soviet politics and society, it will enjoy personal security, a rising standard of living, social status, recognition and consultation by the political elite, and a belief that its views, if not followed, will at least be heard. Thus the already increasing interaction between the ruling elite and the in-system reformist intelligentsia is likely to continue and intensify.

The same is likely to be true for the military, police, and intelligence bureaucracies, now more represented in the top political elite. Nor is the generalist, integrating Communist party elite likely to lose its commanding role. On the contrary, it will continue to combine national power, economic growth, acceptance of consumerism, and a simplified, progress-oriented, Great Russian ideology.

Of the Soviet workers and peasants less is known so less can be projected. To begin with the *peasantry*: the Soviet collective and state farm system is very inefficient. (American agricultural productivity is as much as ten times as high as that of the Soviet Union.) It does, however, fulfill the regime's minimal political requirement: the maintenance of political control over the peasantry so that they cannot interfere with elite policies by withholding their crops. As the disastrous 1975 Soviet harvest again showed, Soviet weather conditions are unpredictable and often bad, and Moscow will probably feel compelled to continue to compensate for them by massive purchases of U.S. grain. Efficient Soviet agriculture would release millions of peasants to industry and greatly raise the Soviet standard of living. (However, given the declining Soviet rate of economic growth, it might well also cause major unemployment, something anathema to a socialist society.) The world food problem may also be thought to demand greater Soviet agricultural productivity. One can therefore convincingly argue that from an economic viewpoint the Soviet collective farm system should be radically modified in the direction of more private initiative. In my view, however, political considerations will continue to override economic ones. It is therefore unlikely that the rest of the century will see any decisive Soviet agricultural reforms. On the contrary, the growing prosperity of some of the collective farms, particularly in the southern and Baltic minority republics, may well lead to their increasing conversion into state farms, probably increasing their productiveness but also accentuating national tensions. Even so, the peasantry seems likely to remain passive.

One cannot necessarily assume that the Soviet *working class* will also be passive. I know of no significant signs that their present political passivity will soon give way to active opposition. On the other hand, one should reflect carefully on the lessons of the December 1970 Polish seacoast riots. They were spontaneous. Their causes were economic, not nationalist. They were led by politically conscious workers, Communist activists, and some of the technological intelligentsia. Not only the new Gierek leadership in Warsaw but also Brezhnev and his colleagues reacted with deep concern and granted major economic concessions to the rebellious workers. While therefore it seems to me unlikely that Soviet workers will actively influence the political process before 2000, one cannot exclude the possibility of at least flash outbreaks, and the Soviet leadership would be especially reluctant to use force against workers, although it would to maintain its power. Again, much will depend upon the flexibility of the Soviet political elite.

One final point: the territorial structure of the Party, the increasingly strong regional economic interests, and the rise of ethnic nationalisms are likely, despite the Moscow center's resistance, to result in some greater regionalism, notably in economics, without, however, seriously imperiling the center's power.

The Future of Soviet Foreign Policy

In my view the rest of this century will probably see the continuation of the present political-military triangle which dominates the international scene today:

a limited conflict relationship between the Soviet Union and China, and between each of them and the West and Japan. The Soviet Union will also continue to try to recover its influence in the Middle East and to increase its influence in parts of the underdeveloped world, notably southern Africa. These attempts, however, are likely, as they have been under Brezhnev in comparison with Khrushchev, to be limited to areas in which the Soviet Union has strategic rather than only ideological interests. Overall Soviet strategy will remain cautious. Moscow will avoid major risk-taking, particularly with the United States, provided that overall arms parity is maintained between the two superpowers.

There is in my view no reason to believe that during the rest of this century the Soviets will abandon their conflict view of the world. They will continue to reject convergence with the West and to try to exclude "diversionary" and "counterrevolutionary" Western influence from the Soviet Union and from the East European area which they control. But they will continue to limit their conflict relationship with the West so as to lower the risk of nuclear war, limit somewhat arms expenditures, and therefore to improve superpower crisis management.

These three elements seem to be agreed by Moscow and Washington to be the minimum content of Soviet-U.S. détente. Both have had other, maximal expectations: for the Soviets, expansion of their influence, for example, in Western Europe and now in southern Africa, and politically and militarily to disarm the West. Nor do the Soviets conceal this hope. As Brezhnev said at the February 1976 Twenty-Fifth Soviet Party Congress:

. . . We make no secret of the fact that we see détente as the way to create more favorable conditions for peaceful socialist and communist construction . . . [2]

The U.S. wants more freedom of information in the Soviet Union and Eastern Europe, less Soviet influence in the Middle East, and the kind of crisis management which will limit the necessity for U.S. public opinion to support, if necessary, strong action in a crisis situation. Recently, U.S. public opinion has become disillusioned about détente because it sees Moscow succeeding in its maximum as well as its minimum aims while Washington, in its view, has gotten nowhere in its maximum aims and not done so well in its minimum goals. In this chapter, therefore, "détente" refers to the three minimal, agreed Soviet-U.S. factors set forth above.

The Soviets will probably wish to maintain minimal East-West détente as they define it—and as the United States should. Yet if the West were to fall into major economic or political crisis or become decisively inferior in military power, Moscow would be likely to return to a strategy of confrontation and higher risk-taking. If a major Sino-Soviet rapprochement, which I consider unlikely, were to occur, Moscow would probably also move in the same direction. The Soviet Union will continue to profit from Western weaknesses, which at least in the next ten years seem likely to be in their economies, energy, the Middle East and southern Africa. The Soviet political elite feels that the non-Communist developed world in general and the United States in particular are entering into major crises. Insofar as events in the next decades strengthen this Soviet view, Moscow will take more risks in East-West political competition.

The future of *Sino-Soviet relations* is the most difficult aspect of Soviet foreign policy to foresee, primarily because of the great difficulty of projecting future Chinese foreign policy. Since Brezhnev came to power in 1964, the Soviet Union has wanted limited détente with the West and improved state relations with China. The next decade will see a new, younger Chinese leadership. The death of Chou En-lai and the apparent resultant eclipse of his hand-picked successor Teng Hsio-p'ing show the near-impossibility of prediction about what future Chinese foreign policy will be. Moscow hopes, after Mao goes, to use its forty-five divisions on the Chinese border, and the Chinese desire to have more freedom of maneuver vis-à-vis the United States, in order to improve its relations with Peking so that the Soviet Union be under less pressure from Washington.

However, Moscow will probably not be prepared to grant China what Mao and in all probability his successors will demand: political, military, ideological, and economic equality with the Soviet Union. Although the recurring Soviet attempts, through international Communist conferences, to reassert Moscow's primacy over other Communist parties have been largely counter-productive, the Soviets will probably continue them. For to abandon the claim to Soviet primacy would be to surrender not only the ideological basis for Soviet primacy in the international Communist world but also for predominance of the Communist elite with the Soviet Union itself.

The post-Mao Chinese leadership is unlikely to accept anything less than complete parity with the Soviets. Moreover, the growing Chinese nuclear deterrent capability already has made a Soviet attack on China increasingly unlikely. By 2000 China may be well on the way to a stable second-strike thermonuclear deterrent, which will make it less likely still. For by then China may have become a major oil exporter, and therefore even more powerful and more able to buy and develop sophisticated weapons technology.

After Mao's departure Chinese hostility to the Soviet Union may decline somewhat. But conflict will probably continue to characterize Sino-Soviet relations. Moscow will continue to suspect the United States of moving too close to Peking, as Peking will suspect the United States of being too favorable to Moscow. The United States therefore can probably continue to pursue its present policy of "active neutrality" between the two Communist giants.

Rising Great Russian nationalism and military power, the probable downward economic, social, and political spiral of the non-raw material exporting under-developed countries (the "fourth world"), and tensions in such areas as the Middle East and Southern Africa will make continuing Soviet engagement in the *underdeveloped world* likely. Soviet policy there will continue to be directed defensively against Chinese and American influence. Maximally, it will try to increase Soviet political and strategic influence there, especially by obtaining military and naval facilities and bases. Sale and gift of arms will continue to be its main instrument.

Within the underdeveloped world Soviet priority will in my view continue to be in the *Middle East*, for geographic, strategic, naval, and oil resource reasons. Russia has historically long been interested in the area. For Moscow it is a strategic link between Europe and Asia. Its oil is a vital resource for the West and Japan and by 1980 the Soviet Union will probably be importing some of it itself.

While until recently Moscow needed air and naval bases there to counter U.S. *Polaris* deployment in the Mediterranean, future U.S. *Poseidon* deployment will be in the open ocean, and therefore the Mediterranean and the Middle East will be less important for Soviet naval strategy. However, Moscow will probably still view increased naval presence in the Mediterranean as a valuable source of political influence there.

The Soviet Union has recently lost most of its influence in the Arab East, almost completely in Egypt, and some in Syria and even in Iraq, and perhaps soon in South Yemen, but it will attempt to restore and if possible increase it. As long as the Arab-Israeli dispute continues, and unless and until they gain secure access to enough Western arms, several Arab states will need Soviet arms against Israel, and Moscow will therefore have a built-in source of political influence in the Middle East. If there is no Arab-Israeli settlement, and therefore another Middle Eastern war, the Soviet Union will probably for at least a time recoup some of its recently lost influence—only, it seems likely, to lose it once more when the Arabs again realize that only the United States, and not the Soviet Union, can enable them to achieve their major aim: Israel's withdrawal to its 1967 boundaries. Even so, the Soviet Union will probably be prepared to accept a Middle Eastern settlement to which the Arabs would agree and will not go all-out to sabotage it. In the Gulf, however, Soviet-U.S. competition will continue. Moscow will not abandon its support for the few radical Arab states left, such as Libya, and for those radical elements of the Palestine guerrilla movement who will continue to reject any settlement with Israel. The Soviet Union is therefore unlikely to agree to any overall limitation of arms shipments to the Middle East.

Moscow's greatest concern in the area will increasingly be the rising power of *Iran.* As long as the Shah rules and his strategy continues to be successful, Moscow will confront rising, anti-Soviet, Iranian influence to Iran's west, south, and east. Moreover, the Iranian-Iraqi rapprochement and Iraq's large oil revenues have contributed to the recent sharp decline of Soviet influence in Baghdad.

India will be another major area of the underdeveloped world on which the Soviet Union will probably continue to concentrate. But India's intractable problems will probably continue to get worse, and Moscow will hardly be prepared, or perhaps even able, to supply sufficient economic aid to contain them. Nor is Mrs. Gandhi's recent imposition of authoritarian personal rule likely to improve the situation. New Delhi will not want to be wholly dependent on Moscow, which cannot supply it, as Iran and the United States can, with the oil and grain which it will increasingly and desperately need. But neither Washington nor Tehran is likely to relieve Moscow of most of the burden of propping up India. Furthermore, the August 1975 coup in Bangladesh, followed by its new rulers' move away from India and the Soviet Union toward Pakistan and the Muslim world, may nullify much of Moscow's gains in the 1971 Indo-Pakistani war, to the benefit of the United States, Pakistan, Iran, and China, all of whom Moscow rightly sees as its opponents.

With respect to *Western Europe*, the Soviets have conflicting and incompatible aims. Moscow will fear Atlanticism less because of Soviet-U.S. détente, which it will not want to endanger. However, it will still try to decrease the effectiveness of NATO and to lower U.S. military, economic, and political influence in Western Europe, and it will therefore favor a more independent but not West German-dominated Western Europe. Moscow will therefore try to slow down and if possible to reverse progress toward West European political unity, and even more military or, worst of all for the Soviets, thermonuclear unity. The Soviets will also try to prevent West German domination of a united Western Europe and any future alliance of it with China. Therefore, even though West European unity is the main prerequisite for a more independent policy of the region vis-à-vis the United States and for the kind of economy of scale which would be of foreign trade advantage to the USSR and would enable Western Europe to challenge the U.S. economically, its potential dangers make support of it an unlikely Soviet policy. Secondly, Moscow will continue to favor détente *inter alia* because it will hope that détente will destabilize Western Europe while not damaging East European stability. Thirdly, Moscow's maximal aim in Western Europe will continue to be the "Finlandization" of as many West European states as possible.

Whether or not the Soviets will want either popular front governments or Communist ascendancy in the unstable states in Southern Europe, Portugal, Spain, Italy, and France, is another question. The Soviets anticipate more instability in Southern Europe because of the economic and political crises there, their inflation and capital transfers to OPEC, and the possibility of a new Middle Eastern war and another limitation of Arab oil production. Yet Moscow fears that pushing for such developments would alarm the United States, endanger Soviet-U.S. détente and, worse, bring right-wing military or fascist regimes into power in Southern Europe.

There has recently been a debate in Moscow about how best to react to these new opportunities. The debate centered around the confused developments in Portugal. In retrospect, given the recent setbacks to the Portuguese Communists in Lisbon, it appears that Moscow and the Portuguese Communist leadership at first overestimated the chances for communism coming to power in Lisbon and underestimated the negative impact of their push for power there on communism elsewhere in Western and Southern Europe and on Communist-Social Democratic relationships. After the Portuguese Communists lost out in the second half of 1975, the Soviets, realizing their miscalculation, took a more moderate line. But their hostility to Peking increased and their project of a European and/or international Communist conference antagonized the Italian, Spanish (and the Yugoslav and Romanian), and later the French Communists.

For the Soviets Portugal was peripheral compared to France, Italy, and Spain. The Italian and Spanish Communist parties—the latter, still formerly illegal, can now more easily operate in partially liberalized post-Franco Spain—now oppose the Soviets on several important domestic, inter-party, and international issues. They have abandoned the Leninist doctrine of the "dictatorship of the proletariat" for a popular front electoral strategy including Christian Democrats as well as Socialists. They reject the primacy of the Soviet party and, although they oppose most of Chinese ideology, they reject the Soviet desire to excommunicate the Chinese. In late 1975 and early 1976 the French Communist party also rejected the dictatorship of the proletariat and began to oppose the Soviet position in the still stalled negotiations for a European Communist conference. To be sure, these parties' motives were initially tactical and electoral, but the Italian and Spanish parties have now clearly moved away from Soviet ideological positions, for what begins as tactics becomes consolidated as strategy.

The 1976 25th Soviet Party Congress cast into public and stark relief these differences—indeed, their highlighting was its main event. Suslov's subsequent March 1976 speech indicated that Moscow continued to harden its line with respect to them. Are these Soviet-West European Communist tensions likely to make Moscow precipitate a third great Communist schism, after the Soviet-Yugoslav and Sino-Soviet splits?

In my view it is too early to give with much confidence an answer to this question. It seems to me likely that within the next few years the Italian Communist party will enter the government, and that it will perhaps even be the strongest single party in it. The French Communist party may do the same, but the French Socialists are far stronger than it. The Spanish Communist party is important but still a relatively small minority, and illegal to boot. I agree with Robert Legvold's estimate, in this volume, that Moscow still wants the west European Communist parties to enter their governments and this would at least at first help the Soviets and hurt the United States.

The Soviets probably still regard West German *Ostpolitik* as a great triumph for Soviet *Westpolitik*. The agreements on the German question have defused, in their view, West German "revanchism," stabilized East Germany, made West Germany even less likely to become a nuclear power, and particularly because of the defusing of Berlin, thus become a major cornerstone of East-West détente. Yet the returns on *Ostpolitik* will not soon be in for Moscow or for Bonn, and

Moscow will continue to try to block Bonn's desire to "maintain the substance of the German nation" by increasing its contacts with East Germany.

At first Moscow believed that the Conference on Security and Cooperation in Europe (CSCE) would stabilize its hold over Eastern Europe, bar Western ideological influence from penetrating there, and help limit West European unity and West German influence in it. These Soviet expectations were largely disappointed. Although the Conference's Final Act may perhaps further cement the Soviet hold over Eastern Europe, that hold is due much more to the Red Army than to declarations. On the other hand, the daily coordination at the Conference of the foreign policy of the nine EEC members, thereafter with the United States and Canada and to a considerable degree with the neutrals; the Romanian and Yugoslav obstruction of Soviet wishes; and finally the negative reaction of much of U.S. public opinion to the Conference's results probably gave the Soviet leaders the impression that their losses were almost as large, if not larger, than their gains. It is not surprising, therefore, that before the Conference ended the Soviets abandoned their desire to institutionalize it. (Mutual force reductions [MFR] are treated below.)

Soviet policy toward Western Europe will continue to be cautious. It will give priority to its minimum aims and will be unwilling to take serious risks to obtain its maximum ones. Its success will be primarily determined by Western European and Atlantic strength and unity, or the opposite, and by the degree of domestic instability in Southern Europe, rather than by its own efforts.

With respect to *Japan*, the Soviet Union will continue to have two minimum objectives: to prevent the conversion of Japanese economic and technological power into political and military power and to prevent Japan from having closer relations with China than with the Soviet Union. Although Moscow also would like to lower U.S. influence and military presence in Japan, it will prefer it to remain rather than to face a fully rearmed and/or pro-Chinese Japan. The Soviet Union will also continue to try to obtain Japanese technology and credits for the development of Siberian natural resources and in order to prevent Japan from concentrating on technology transfer to China instead, but it will probably not succeed unless it makes the former more economically attractive to Japan and returns to Japan the four southern Kurile Islands. The January 1976 visit of Soviet Foreign Minister Gromyko to Tokyo was a fiasco, for he refused to make any concessions to Japan on the Kuriles, and Prime Minister Miki then indicated that Japan will sign a friendship treaty with China including the so-called "hegemony in Asia." (Whether Tokyo will do so is not yet clear.) In any case, Japan will probably move closer to China, in part in order to get more Chinese oil, even if its relations with Moscow suffer thereby. The Soviet attitude toward the extension of Japanese economic and therefore political influence in East and Southeast Asia will remain ambivalent, since Soviet dislike of it will be counterbalanced by greater Soviet fear of its Chinese equivalent. Moscow will, probably without success, use its naval presence in the West Pacific and Indian

Oceans to try to influence Japanese foreign policy. In sum, Soviet policy aims toward Japan are likely to remain incompatible and therefore unsuccessful.

In *Southeast Asia* the United States exit from Indo-China and the subsequent replacement there of non-Communist by Communist governments had six lessons for Soviet-American relations. First, as de Tocqueville long ago remarked, the successful conduct of a long-term foreign policy is the most difficult task for any democracy, for public opinion is, rightly or wrongly, impatient. Second, when Moscow (and/or Peking) support indigenous, national-Communist guerilla movements and the United States supports non-Communist ones not identified with nationalism, the nationalist ones will win. (Conversely, when the Soviet Union supports Communist parties, such as it did in Iraq and the Sudan, which reject at least the Islamic aspects of Arab nationalism, Moscow will lose and Washington will gain.) Third, the major initial motive for massive U.S. troop deployment to South Vietnam in early 1965, Washington's belief that its fall to Hanoi would be a decisive and for the United States a disastrous gain for worldwide revolutionary Chinese aims, and Washington's subsequent belief that the Soviet Union could and would help the United States to bring Hanoi to a compromise peace, were, in the easy light of hindsight, both wrong. For Chinese revolutionary strategy was bound to meet, as it did, effective Soviet resistance, and after the coup and counter-coup in Indonesia in September 1965 Peking lost its principal allies, Sukarno and the Indonesian Communist party. Moreover, the Soviet Union, not China, gave Hanoi the modern weapons technology which finally enabled it to crush Saigon. Fourth, Hanoi has never been controlled by Moscow or Peking and is unlikely to be so in the future, at least as long as the North Vietnamese can continue to manipulate the Sino-Soviet split to assure their independence. Fifth, the United States exit from Indochina has and will intensify Sino-Soviet competition in the area and in Asia in general. Since Moscow's competition with Peking is far fiercer than with Washington, it will also intensify the Soviet naval buildup in the area. For in East and Southeast Asia outside of China, the Soviet Union is, like the United States, primarily a sea and air power, not a land power, as it is elsewhere. Sixth, the Chinese rapprochement with Iran, to which Moscow, not Peking, is the main danger, and Moscow's losses in Bangladesh restrict predominant Soviet influence in the area only to India, while Iran, Pakistan, and Bangladesh are anti-Soviet, therefore pro-American and pro-Chinese, while Vietnam will retain a policy of "active neutrality" vis-à-vis Moscow and Peking.

So will *North Korea*, and for the same reasons: it will continue to profit from Sino-Soviet competition for its favors and to need Soviet and Chinese arms for its security. Moscow and Peking seem after the fall of Saigon to have cautioned North Korea against attacking South Korea, and one can assume that both will continue to do so as long as Soviet-American détente and the Sino-American rapprochement do not deteriorate.

In *Africa* the recent Soviet (and Cuban) successes in Angola occurred after a long series of Soviet failures to the north, in the ex-Belgian Congo, Ghana, Algeria, and the Sudan. Thereafter, sharp Sino-Soviet rivalry developed for influence in the black guerrilla movements in southern Africa. The causes of the Soviet and Cuban victory in Angola included the coup in Lisbon, the Portuguese withdrawal from their African colonies, black African hostility to white minority rule in southern Africa, the splits in the Angolan liberation movement, the long-time Soviet ties with the urbanized, largely mulatto and Marxist-led MPLA, the much greater Soviet air- and sea-life capability, and, most of all, Castro's dispatch to Angola of a large Cuban expeditionary force. Their victory was not counterbalanced militarily—indeed, it was aided politically, by U.S. arms and financial support to Roberto's FNLA, especially because it paralleled in time and hostility to the MPLA the South African military intervention to aid Savimbi's UNITA, which turned much of black Africa toward the MPLA. U.S. involvement in Angola, despite the fact that Zaire and Zambia urged the United States to intervene, thus played into Brezhnev's and Castro's hands. Globally, however, Soviet and Cuban intervention in Angola greatly intensified U.S. public disillusionment with Soviet-U.S. détente, with results which at least before the 1976 U.S. presidential election could not be foreseen.

The independence of Angola and Mozambique gave direct access to Rhodesia and Namibia (Southwest Africa) to the black guerrilla movements. But, although Rhodesia will likely soon come under black majority rule, the great power and determination of South Africa make it difficult to see how the guerrillas can soon succeed in Namibia if South Africa decides to hold it, and far less so in South Africa itself. The Soviets have long aided the African National Congress (ANC), the main South African guerrilla movement, while it is doubtful that the United States or the United Kingdom will support it or other guerrilla movements. South Africa faces a prolonged guerrilla struggle during which Soviet influence in Southern Africa will probably increase.

In *Latin America* the Soviet Union long supported the traditional Latin American Communist parties, which usually collaborated with those govern-ments in power which would accept them, but which recently, notably in Chile, have been broken by right-wing military dictatorships. Soviet influence in Latin America now remains great only in Castro's Cuba. It is now much greater there than it was in the 1960s, when Soviet-Cuba relations were strained by Castro's radical ideology, his support of Latin American Communist parties, and by Soviet-American détente. His guerrilla failures in Latin America and Cuba's economic crisis led him in the 1970s to align himself closely with Moscow; and after his guerrilla failures he pragmatically took over, with some initial success, Moscow's preferred strategy of improved state-to-state relations with the rest of Latin America particularly in the Caribbean.

Castro never stopped trying to expand his influence abroad. Cuban troops have for some time been in Guinea, Congo-Brazzaville, Syria, and South Yemen. Cuba's large troop presence in Angola was much more massive and decisive than elsewhere but it was not new in principle. While Castro needs Moscow, Moscow also needs Cuban troops—as their Angolan victory showed—to give effective proxy aid to, and thereby to acquire influence for Moscow and Havana over black guerrilla movements in Southern Africa. Castro became a valued Soviet (and MPLA) ally in Angola, and he can reasonably hope thereby to increase his influence over, and autonomy from, Moscow.

The Military Field

The three main recent developments in Soviet military policy have been Soviet achievement of effective strategic parity with the United States, the great increase in, and global deployment of, Soviet naval power, and the massive Soviet conventional and nuclear deployment on the Chinese border. Moscow clearly, and in my view correctly, believes that it has gotten substantial political payoffs from these, from the first two by improving its position in the worldwide "correlation of forces" with the West, and from the third by containing China (e.g., stopping border incidents) and increasing potential Soviet influence on the post-Mao scene. Moreover, since Soviet ideology and the Soviet economic model no longer are attractive abroad, Moscow must rely all the more on increased military power to increase its global influence.

The Soviets signed the SALT I agreement because of Soviet-U.S. détente and to limit the qualitative technological leap forward in the strategic arms race (e.g., MIRV), in which the United States has the advantage. (I do not find sufficiently convincing the charges that they have violated it, although they have acted contrary to the U.S. unilateral statements made at its signing—as they had the legal right to do.) Recently, the United States has moved away from its previous public mutual assured destruction ("MAD") strategy, i.e., deterrence through threat of nuclear destruction of cities, toward more nuclear options in a limited nuclear war (the "Schlesinger doctrine"), i.e., more accurate missiles to avoid destruction of cities. The Soviets have never accepted MAD, despite what many in the United States argue is its contribution to strategic stability and arms control by rendering nuclear war inevitably so destructive as to deter it. Its U.S. opponents argue that MAD risks city destruction and provides no other nuclear response to a U.S. president except such an apocalyptic counter-city strategy. Moreover, the U.S. qualitative technological leap forward in the strategic arms race (especially in the accuracy of MIRV, MaRV, and cruise missiles) and, conversely, the Soviet advantage in quantity (throw-weight) and in less budgetary constraints and effective public pressure for arms control, have made more difficult a mutually acceptable definition of "essential strategic equivalence" and therefore encouraged the qualitative arms race.

Continued progress in SALT will require, first, mutual realization that the Soviets see the U.S. qualitative lead as destabilizing while the United States sees the potential Soviet quantitative lead as destabilizing: second, an agreed judgment as to whether, and if so when, and how much increased accuracy becomes qualitatively more important than increased throw-weight and how its destabilizing effects can be verifiably limited; and effective U.S. linkage of Soviet concessions in SALT II with U.S. concession on agricultural exports and trade technology transfers. The November 1974 Vladivostok Soviet-U.S. agreement on Salt II principles gave hope for continued progress, but in some form, however limited, the qualitative race seems likely to continue. There is some prospect for slowing it down and, by institutionalizing SALT, for contributing to Soviet-U.S. political détente. But this will require that disillusionment in the United States and the Soviet Union about Soviet-U.S. détente in general, and SALT results in particular, be countered by continued mutual emphasis on the three minimal factors requiring Soviet-U.S. détente: avoidance of nuclear war, limiting the arms race, and crisis management.

Some gradual progress will probably be made on mutual force reductions (MFR) in Europe. This will require that the United States government not be forced by domestic political pressures into major unilateral troop reductions. It will also probably require that all conventional and nuclear arms in Europe (i.e., including U.S. FBS—"forward-based systems," i.e., nuclear-armed airplanes) be included in it. The impact of new conventional arms technology (anti-tank and anti-aircraft precision-guided munitions, PGM's) on the balance of forces in Europe is important, but still unclear. The effect that an increasingly politically and militarily united Western Europe, an unlikely but possible development, might have on continuing MFR negotiations is also uncertain. In my view the major Soviet motive in MFR is not to bring troop levels down for the sake of lowering Soviet defense expenditures. Rather, it is, in addition to contributing to détente in general and in Europe, to enable the Soviets to get some kind of influence or control, if possible in an institutionalized form, over West German military power, and thus to limit it and impose on the Federal Republic a military status inferior to that of the other West European states. Moreover, although Moscow likely still wants some scaling-down of U.S. troop strength in Europe, it is probably so concerned lest that result in a build-up of West German forces and eventually a West European defense community, and even a nuclear one, that the Soviet Union now seems to prefer that the United States only slowly reduce its forces in Europe and sees MFR negotiations as a useful means for assuring against any rapid, unilateral U.S. troop withdrawal.

The global buildup of the Soviet navy will probably continue. In my view the Soviet Union is trying to reach worldwide naval parity with the United States. One may argue that this is not necessary for Soviet national interests, since the Soviet Union is primarily a land power while the United States is primarily a sea and air power. But the lessons of history, notably that of the Imperial German naval buildup before World War I, indicate that major powers tend to build navies for the sake of the political influence which they believe, and in my view correctly, that big navies will give them.

Here again the American response will greatly influence Soviet naval policy. If the United States accepts naval parity with the Soviet Union but remains determined to deny its superiority, the Soviet Union will probably settle for parity. If the United States insists on maintaining naval superiority and outbuilding any Soviet attempt to achieve parity, the Soviet Union will probably not decisively interfere with overall Soviet-American détente. If the United States seemed prepared to accept Soviet naval superiority, in all probability the Soviets will try for that.

Soviet-American Relations

In my view for the rest of this century the Soviets will continue to follow a strategy of limited conflict with the United States. (The consequences of this for U.S. policy I discuss at the end of this volume.) The Soviet leaders will probably view their policy toward the United States as largely reactive to American power, just as the United States will view its policies as reactive towards Soviet power. The continuing rise of Soviet military capabilities, the young, intensifying nature of the Soviet will to power, and the residual Soviet ideological commitment to the belief that history is on its side and is primarily determined by the capitalist-Socialist conflict will probably continue to give to the Soviet leadership the dynamism necessary to try to expand its influence, provided that it can do so without serious risk of a military confrontation with the United States. (Indeed, this has been the policy of the Great Russian ruling elite throughout modern history.) Much will therefore depend on the U.S. response.

The Soviets will try to benefit more from détente than the United States and thereby to obtain their maximum objectives: the weakening of the U.S. military and strategic position, its alliances, and its relations with China. They will try to get U.S. trade and technology for as little in return as possible and to engage U.S. investment in the development of Soviet natural resources. They will probably continue to try, as they put it, to "institutionalize and make irreversible" Soviet-U.S. détente while simultaneously maintaining a limited conflict relationship with the United States. (The United States will probably also do the same, but to a lesser degree.)

Some partial improvement of Sino-Soviet state relations after Mao is possible, but no major Sino-Soviet rapprochement is likely. The United States can therefore probably continue to use Sino-Soviet hostility to pressure the Soviet Union toward more Soviet-U.S. détente. The other factors which favor détente, particularly trade and technology, are likely to remain effective. The Soviets will therefore have the same motives which they do now for their concept of détente with the United States and will give it continuing priority.

What seems to me less certain is whether this motivation will be equally true for the United States. In the near future American foreign policy priorities are likely to be more in the economic, energy, and food areas than with respect to the Soviet Union. These problems center primarily in the Middle East because for at least the next decade the United States will become increasingly dependent on Middle Eastern oil, and Western Europe and Japan even more. The main U.S. problems in this respect are two: security of supply, which could be seriously endangered by another Middle Eastern crisis, and high prices, the impact of which on the U.S. and OECD economies will continue to be great. Even if by 1985 the United States develops extensive energy substitutes, which it shows no sign of doing, Western Europe and Japan cannot. In order to meet the problems of inflation and the high price of energy the United States will have to form and maintain a coordinated Western-Japanese position. The Soviet Union, on the other hand, will hope to benefit economically and politically from the destabilizing effects in the OECD area of inflation and the energy crisis.

These new priorities may lead the United States to downgrade its present priority for bilateral Soviet relations. This "objective" factor limiting U.S. priority for relations with the Soviet Union has been recently reinforced by another, interacting one: disillusionment in major sectors of U.S. public opinion with the overall results of Soviet-U.S. détente. Its causes range from resentment of the Soviet "great grain robbery" (due, it must be said, to American blunders, not Soviet duplicity) to the belief that U.S. technology transfers and credits have been one-sidedly beneficial to Moscow, allegations that the United States lost out in SALT I and that even so the Soviets have violated its terms, and disillusionment, particularly in the U.S. intellectual and Jewish communities, over Soviet domestic repression against dissident intellectuals and Jews, allegations (in my view incorrect) that Moscow planned and started the 1973 Arab attack on Israel, and most recently to Soviet and Cuban involvement in Angola. (That no such equivalent U.S. public opposition to détente with China exists must make the Soviets all the more concerned about this trend.)

This disillusionment supported the initially successful pressure on Moscow by Senator Jackson for expanded emigration of Soviet Jews. More important from the Soviet viewpoint, for Moscow is probably glad to get rid of some of the politically activist Soviet Jews, it also resulted at the end of 1974 in sharp congressional restrictions on U.S. government-guaranteed credits to the Soviet Union. Thereupon Moscow denounced the U.S.-Soviet trade agreement. The Soviet leaders are seriously disturbed by these developments. As long as Sino-Soviet hostility remains, however, they will probably not be sufficient to turn Moscow away from détente. Indeed, whatever one may think of the relative priority for U.S. foreign policy of the issue which he chose, it may be argued, and in my view with considerable reason, that the initial success of Senator Jackson's pressure showed that the United States could have more successfully linked technology transfer and credits to the Soviet Union with other issues, e.g., arms control arrangements, and can do so in the future. Conversely, his ultimate failure showed the limits of such U.S. pressure.

In the future the Soviet Union will probably try to keep Soviet-U.S. relations central in U.S. foreign policy, in large part as now to limit U.S. relations with and transfer of technology to China. The U.S., in contrast, may make its relations with the Soviet Union less central to its foreign policy. U.S., not Soviet, policy will therefore probably become a greater factor for change in the Soviet-American relationship.

Eastern Europe

"Eastern Europe" is an un-area. It is simply the territory which in 1945 came under Soviet control, including those areas, Yugoslavia and Albania, in whole, and Romania in part, which have since escaped from it. Its differences in religion, culture, history, and levels of political and economic development are enormous. To compare East Germany or the Czech lands, which are Central European, with Albania, which is more Middle Eastern than Eastern Europe, makes little sense. Within the space of this brief overview, therefore, it is impossible to do anything like complete justice to the complexity of East European affairs. I shall therefore limit myself to some general remarks.

For the rest of this century, barring the very unlikely event of decisive weakening of the Soviet regime itself, Soviet control over Eastern Europe is likely to remain at or above, or at least probably not much below, its present level. The Soviet Union will not soon reconcile itself to its present low level of influence in the Balkans. Indeed, after Tito goes, Moscow will probably try to regain its lost influence in Yugoslavia, Romania, and Albania. This is the more likely because the Balkans are becoming more important to the Soviet Union because of its involvement in the Mediterranean and the Middle East and its hopes of gains in unstable Southern Europe. Moreover, Eastern Europe's need for Soviet credits to buy more expensive oil will increase Soviet leverage over the area, but also Eastern European popular resentment of Moscow, with resultant increased political instability.

The part of Eastern Europe now under Soviet control will not necessarily remain as quiet as it now seems. The lesson of the 1956 crises in Poland and Hungary, of the 1968 crisis in Czechoslovakia, and of the 1970 Polish seacoast revolts is the same as that of the nineteenth century Polish risings: nationalistic and libertarian discontent will remain endemic in Eastern Europe for Moscow's hegemony there means national humiliation, economic inefficiency, and cultural repression. Instability in Eastern Europe will therefore remain one of the most serious Soviet foreign policy problems. It is likely to be made more serious by economic modernization and political mobilization in the area, for these intensify East European nationalism and threaten to spill over to the Soviet minority nationalities.

Because of the continuing thrust forward of Soviet foreign policy, and because instability in Eastern Europe automatically tends to produce instability within the Soviet Union, particularly among those nations bordering on Eastern Europe, Moscow will therefore remain determined, if all else fails, to use military force to suppress either flash risings or longer-range movements towards liberalization and national independence in its hegemonic area in Eastern Europe. The 1968 Soviet invasion of Czechoslovakia made clear that the Soviet Union will not only not tolerate withdrawal from the Warsaw Pact and dissolution of the Communist party, as happened in Hungary in 1956, but also the kind of liberalization which, Moscow rightly believed, threatened in Czechoslovakia Communist party monopoly, rigid control of the communication media, deviation from Soviet foreign policy, and destabilization of Communist rule in·Poland, East Germany, and the Soviet Ukraine.

In the *present Soviet sphere of influence*, East Germany, Poland, Czechoslovakia, Hungary, and Bulgaria, the East European party elites will therefore maintain control of the commanding heights of power. The far-reaching economic reforms adopted in the mid-1960s in Hungary, and the lesser ones in East Germany, to say nothing of Yugoslav decentralization, market economy, and workers self-management, may eventually spread to the rest of Eastern Europe, for they reflect a general tendency, once regime power is established, to give some priority to expertise instead of only to political mobilization. Yet the fear for their power of technologically incompetent Communist party officials, and the opposition of unskilled workers to greater financial rewards to skilled workers and especially to managerial personnel, have frequently braked or blocked the former trend toward bureaucratic efficiency. The tension between the two is likely to continue in the future.

Indeed, except for the special case of Gierek's Poland, the early 1970s saw economic recentralization in Eastern Europe. While the Hungarian recentralization was largely domestic in origin, arising primarily from egalitarian working-class discontent, Moscow probably feared that the Hungarian reforms might infect the Soviet Union and encouraged the Hungarian leadership to roll them back somewhat. Moreover, the quadrupling of world oil prices will make Eastern Europe far more dependent on the Soviet Union, its main source of oil, for credits to buy it. Finally, major economic reforms would require greater opening of the East European economies to the world, which would result in the import of Western inflation as well as of political and cultural influence. Neither Moscow nor the East European leaderships feels that they can or should allow either. The Soviet Union will probably continue to prefer, if satisfied with its reliability, indirect rather than direct rule in Eastern Europe. The attraction to East Europe of Western Europe, and especially of West Germany, will probably continue to increase, but the Soviet and East European party elites, including the East German leaders, will prevent it from seriously endangering their rule.

If détente and Sino-Soviet hostility continue, *Romania* can probably maintain its present degree of autonomy from the Soviet Union. Internal liberalization there is extremely unlikely, for Romania's traditions are not of democracy but of Byzantine-Ottoman-Phanariot autocracy. The Soviets will continue to meddle in Romanian politics but will probably not intervene militarily. However, if Yugoslavia became seriously destabilized and the Soviets were to decide to obtain dominant influence there, by military means or otherwise, they would also be likely to intervene, including militarily, in Romania.

Yugoslavia is the major single area of potential destabilization in Eastern Europe, indeed in Europe as a whole. Tito will soon leave the political scene. He has not solved the national problem, *the* problem of the country, but only suppressed it. Even so, it is unlikely that after him Yugoslavia will break up. As serious as post-Tito national tensions will become, the perceived threat to Yugoslavia from the Soviet Union, and the unlikelihood that any of the constituent republics of Yugoslavia could maintain effective independence alone, will probably keep the Yugoslav state in existence and keep it controlled by the Communist party. (Indeed, quite possibly, only Communist rule can keep Yugoslavia united.) Nonetheless, Yugoslavia's domestic instability will make foreign policy much less effective.

National tensions in Yugoslavia may produce something like a Turkish situation: While the Communist party will remain in theory in control, the army, the only centralized organization left in the country, will dominate the Party much more than it already does. Finally, the degree to which the Soviets will take risks to renew their pre-1948 domination over Yugoslavia, especially by military means, will to a great extent be determined by their view of the probable reaction by the United States, and to a lesser extent by Western Europe, in particular, by West Germany, as well as by the opportunities they will see in increased post-Tito instability in Yugoslavia. To the extent that the United States continues to try to deter Soviet intervention in Yugoslavia, the Soviets will probably continue to feel that it would strike a serious, perhaps fatal blow to East-West détente, and this will probably continue to deter them from doing so.

Albania will most likely remain a Chinese satellite as long as Hoxha is in power and probably for some time thereafter. Were China to abandon Albania, which seems unlikely in the near future, the Albanian leadership might then turn toward Western Europe. Internally, the country will probably remain neo-Stalinist.

In sum, Eastern European foreign and domestic affairs will continue to be determined primarily by developments in the Soviet Union and by Soviet relations with the West. The nuclear stalemate and détente in Europe make decisive change in Eastern Europe, except perhaps in Yugoslavia, unlikely for the rest of this century.

Notes

1. Richard Pipes, *Russia under the Old Regime* (New York: Charles Scribner's Sons, 1974) and Zbigniew Brzezinski, "Soviet Politics: From the Future to the Past?" Columbia University Research Institute on International Change, mimeo., March 1975.

2. *Pravda*, February 25, 1976, p. 4.

II The Soviet Political Elite and Internal Developments in the USSR

Seweryn Bialer

It is generally agreed that at the present time the Soviet Union has serious difficulties maintaining dynamic economic growth and securing rapid technological progress. The Soviet political system, while considerably different from Stalin's, has failed to keep pace with social change and increasingly conflicts with the needs of a rapidly modernizing society. This says little, however, about the likelihood of significant changes in the system, for it identifies only *sources* of pressures for change caused by economic growth and a much higher level of aggregate performance and technology. To explore the *likelihood* of change requires an assessment of the strength and political expression of these pressures and especially an assessment of the responses of the political elite to them. This moves the focus of attention from socioeconomic inputs to the internal structure, process, and policies of the Soviet political system. The critical question is not to identify major alternative paths of development but rather to determine by whom, how, and under what restraints paths of development will be selected.

Of the questions "who" and "how," it is easier to answer the first—that is, to identify the groups or institutions within Soviet society which have or are developing the political resources and the ability to bring about change. This identification, if it is not to be purely speculative and based solely on what may happen, has to come from an assessment of the sources of change in the two post-Stalin decades. Their most striking aspect is that their decisive stimuli have come from incumbent leaders and elites. This is not to say that pressures from outside the official framework, especially those originating in

25

the intelligentsia, were not at times influential in policy formation. Yet their intensity and cumulative effect have fallen far short of generating a serious shift in the traditional closed decision-making process.

The post-Khrushchev decade has shown, moreover, not only the narrow base of extra-official pressure but also disclosed the leadership's determination and ability to resist it. The best example of this is the unprecedented Soviet dissident movement, which is as notable for its ability to establish its presence and to survive as it is for its inability to broaden its base and to influence official Russia to meet any but a few of its minimal, tactical demands. The process of change in post-Stalin Russia, liberalizing or restrictive, fundamental or mildly reformatory, has basically been brought about by initiative from above or, at least, from the strongest factions with the Soviet leadership and elites.

But the real difficulty, is not to identify "who" but "how"—that is, to evaluate the potential for internal transformation of politically significant groups. It is here, as Jeremy Azrael points out,

where the critical unknowns lie; here, above all, one must penetrate in order to estimate the forces of continuity and change that will shape the development of the Soviet system for the foreseeable future. In the short and medium run, at least, the decisive variable is not the disembodied 'logic' of socio-economic maturation but the character of the emergent political leadership.[1]

This chapter will address these questions: the character of the existing and emergent political leadership, the actual changes in the composition, structure, and behavior of the Soviet political elite in the last decade, the post-Khrushchev period.

Significant changes in the Soviet political elite do not occur often and are not readily detected in the short and medium term. We will examine to what extent and for what reasons such changes have taken place, in four essential dimensions: in the composition of the Soviet leadership and political elite, in its structure and group relations, in its responsiveness to social pressures, and in its perception of reality and outlook; and in two time frames: the pattern in the post-Khrushchev period and its implications for the future.

Changes in Composition

The most visible and comprehensive elite change occurs when a new generation with different styles and standards of conduct enters the elite in high numbers. While this may result from dramatic, wholesale purges, it also takes place from the gradual turnover of personnel, which may seem inconsequential in short-range effects but may be crucial in long-range cumulative influence. The present Soviet political elite appears to be distinguished by its unprecedented stability, not only in the highest councils of the Soviet Party-state but also in the various central and local administrative structures. For example, between the first two Party congresses of the post-Khrushchev period (1966 and 1971), 82 percent of the living members of the Central Committee of the CPSU retained their membership in this elite institution; and at the Twenty-Fifth Party Congress in March 1976 over 90 percent of the living key leaders and executives who held the position of full membership in the Central Committee were reelected.

Since the selection of Central Committee members and the appointment of high-level officials depend ultimately on the top Soviet leadership, the Politburo and Secretariat, the ratio of turnover in the broad strata of leadership—except by natural causes—reflects the situation in that top leadership. It is a function of a conscious personnel policy preferred by the top leaders or forced upon them by the circumstances of their own political situation. The continuity of the leadership strata in the last decade and especially at the beginning of the post-Khrushchev period when a high turnover might have been expected to accompany the succession, shows the leadership's overriding concern for the stabilization of the regime.

After Stalin's death, his successors saw that the major long-range danger to the efficacy of the regime was stagnation caused by politically redundant and economically counterproductive policies and methods of rule. If the cycle of post-Stalin reforms and revisions was a response to and a reaction against the consolidation, tighter controls and petrification of the political system in Stalin's postwar Russia, the post-Khrushchev leadership's attempt to stabilize and consolidate the system politically and ideologically has been a response to and a reaction against the cycle of organizational, political, and ideological fluidity in the Khrushchev era, which produced near-chaos. Yet this is only part of the explanation; the more important factor, the structural arrangements and political balance within the elite, will be discussed below.

Whatever the reasons for the lower rate of change in elite personnel, however, the replacement of elite members by individuals with different attitudes and behavior occurs even when the ratio of personnel turnover is low. The evidence for the last decade, however, argues that elite replacement has not been a major channel of elite change. The established Soviet elites which control recruitment of new elite members and their advancement tend, as in every society, to select those individuals who share their own behavior patterns and commitment to the basic values of the established system.

The bureaucratization of the career status of the potential and actual elite members, the limits on their professional autonomy, the high penalties of nonconformity even when terror is absent, as well as the highly centralized policy and control of recruitment and advancement at all levels of leadership make the tendency toward self-replication, common to elites everywhere, particularly pronounced in the Soviet Union.

Yet, even so, the strength and vitality of this mechanism may gradually erode.

We must therefore look more closely at who comprise the elite and how they advance. Are there any major signs that a change *in* the pattern of elite recruitment is taking place which is conducive to a change of the elite *through* the recruitment of new members? The limited evidence suggests that with minor exceptions there has been little erosion of the mechanism of self-replication but that there exists a high potential for erosion in the coming decade.

First, the statistics of political elite turnover, while very low, conceal a pattern that increases the effect of such low turnover on changes of the elite. The turnover of incumbents in a great number of high executive positions represents not an influx of outsiders but rather a rotation system that, in the post-Khrushchev period, has substituted demotion for earlier purges. Shifts of power and function within the leadership do not reflect a comparable change in the membership of the elite as a whole.

Second, recruitment into the elite and advancement show remarkable, traditional gradualism especially in economic administration and middle-level party bureaucracy. There have been few meteoric careers and even fewer seizures by elite newcomers of elite positions. The traditional party formula of strictly "combining old and young cadres" has been consistently pursued. Consequently the age spread between groups occupying different levels of elite positions has remained almost unchanged in the last decade. And while the "old" become older, the "young" do not remain so young. The aging of the leadership in the two top decision-making bodies, the Politburo and the Secretariat, in the post-Khrushchev era can be seen clearly in Table II-1. Moreover, in the top leadership group, the Politburo, the members with the shortest tenure are in some cases actually older in average age![a]

Third, Soviet political elite are today more homogeneous than formerly.

Table II-1
Average Age of Politburo Members

	1966	1971	1976
Politburo Full Members	59	61	66
Politburo Alternate Members	53	58	60
Central Committee Secretariat	55	59	64

[a]Politburo Member, March 1976:

	Tenure in Politburo	Average Age
Full Members:	Over 10 years	70.2
	5 - 10 years	63.8
	less than 5 years	64.6
Alternate Members:	Over 5 years	58.3
	5 years or less	62.3

Their major background characteristics, understood in the formal, traditional sense of class origin, education, learned skills, job experience, etc., are similar. Newcomers and established groups are characterized by similarities in education, and social background. Thus distinction in background between the *apparatchik* and the technocrat has been largely blurred.

To stress formal characteristics in elite background, however, may well obscure another, possibly more significant aspect of a study of old and newer membership. This aspect—identification with political generations—already plays some role and will surely prove even more important in the near future. It suggests that even some groups sharing basic formal characteristics, such as career patterns, may nevertheless differ markedly in their actual life experience, since identical jobs pursued in periods with different political atmospheres, priorities, and rewards and sanctions can produce different styles and encourage divergent habits and different mentalities, outlooks, and perspectives. Those differences are especially important when they affect an individual's formative years, that is, for the Soviet elite members, when they joined the Party and began their administrative careers. Political generations, though directly correlated to age, involve discontinuities. An age difference of a very few years, coming at a break-point between political generations, can prove infinitely more important than that of an entire decade located within a single political generation.

The Soviet case involves three relevant political generations—the prewar, the World War II, and the post-war Stalinists. The overwhelming majority of the present top leadership belongs to the first category. Their generational homogeneity and successful resistance to rejuvenation has been conditioned by two facts: they entered the elite simultaneously in very large numbers during and as a consequence of the Great Purge, and they were the youngest political elite in any modern nation-state. Throughout the entire postwar period this generation has maintained a unified front against younger generations.

Already present in significant numbers at a level directly below the top leadership is the second generation, whose politically formative years coincided with World War II and who, together with the third generation, constitute the great majority of new appointees to middle level positions. The formative experience of their wartime administrative careers, as Jerry Hough has suggested, may well have set many of them apart from the preceding generation in attitude and outlook, by inculcating indifference toward formal "ideological" questions, by placing emphasis on patriotism as a major basis of legitimacy, by stressing considerable freedom of action in daily decision-making, by increasing responsiveness to popular aspirations for improved material conditions, and by developing respect for the need to maintain popular discipline without recourse to terror. Such a suggestive proposition, while of course speculative, has special relevance for the near future, when this group will surely enter the central leadership in great numbers and establish its strength at middle levels.

The war generation, however, is a relatively small one, spanning only five years, and has little chance, therefore, of dominating any elite group, let alone the top leadership. The impact of its different formative experience will be reduced by its numbers but also by the character of the somewhat larger generation which follows it, those who learned their political trade in the 1945-1953 period, the most stultifying if not the most harsh period of Stalin's rule. Thus the real turning point may occur only when the post-Stalin political generation enters the elite. (Its members are still almost totally absent from even middle leadership levels.)

The evidence argues that elite replacement has not been a major channel of elite change in the last decade, because it has been blocked for so long. Therefore the importance of this factor in the near and intermediate future may be very great. (Two-thirds of Politburo members and alternates are men in their sixties—about half are 65 and over; half the members of the Presidium of the Council of Ministers are in their sixties.) Not only will the future replacement ratio be very high, but the time span into which replacement of a large number of individuals is condensed may be relatively short. Almost certainly massive replacement would mean a generational break in continuity and increasingly involve the potentially very important difference between the Stalinist and post-Stalinist generations.

Changes in Structure and Group Relations

In order to evaluate change in the structure of the Soviet political elite and the potential for further change, it is especially important to examine two specific aspects of Soviet political life—"collective leadership" at the top of the decision-making structure and the pattern of relationships between the major administrative hierarchies.

Collective Leadership

The centralization of the Soviet system of administration, the lack of institutional arrangements for tenure and removal from high offices, the weakness of legitimate channels of control directed upward from lower elites, let alone from outside the elites, and the secrecy affecting decision-making and the political process have all in the past, and, to the extent that they are present today, continued to cause concentration of individual power within the top Soviet leadership. It is clear, however, that when compared not only to Stalin's dictatorship but also to Khrushchev's directorship, the pattern of the distribution of power, of conflict and accommodation, prevalent today is different and shows no signs of radical change. Khrushchev's Presidium was "collective leadership" as opposed to Stalin's one-man rule. Brezhnev's Politburo shows this kind of leadership in a much more pure and stable version, one much less prone to become only a transitional stage between periods of one-man rule. In the last decade those competing tendencies, toward oligarchy and a dominant leader, which have been evident from the beginning of the post-Stalin era, were, if not resolved, then settled at least more clearly in favor of the former.

Before examining the roots of this oligarchic development and the likelihood of its persistence, let us set forth the most significant traits of the oligarchic pattern and contrast them with the preceding period. In the last decade Brezhnev undoubtedly became the single most powerful and prominent member of the Soviet leadership, not only as spokesman for the leadership but as the most forceful initiator and critic of foreign and domestic policies within it. Yet his colleagues have succeeded in placing a number of controls on his power and authority, with the object of preventing a new drift to one-man rule.

The most important differences with Khrushchev's leadership cannot be expressed adequately in such terms as "less" or "more," however; they are concerned rather with the question of "power for what." The powers of a leader are static; their limits and scope can be evaluated primarily in their actual use. In this perspective Brezhnev's powers differ from those of Khrushchev and are differently used. Khrushchev's power was expended most notably in efforts to change institutions and policies, and its limits tested most visibly in alternate advances and retreats before opposition among the leadership. Brezhnev's power has never really been tested in those terms and has been expended primarily in assuring the continuity of Soviet institutions and in gradual adjustments of policies. Within the context of these aims his position has been very strong and stable. While Khrushchev often tried to form a new consensus within the elite or to undermine an existing one, Brezhnev has been concerned primarily with maintaining consensus.

Below Brezhnev we can identify a core of senior leaders who are accorded more respect and exposure, who carry more weight in decision-making across a broad spectrum of policy issues, and who have primary responsibility in a number of policy areas. Their importance and influence fluctuates. However, their demonstrated conflicts over power and policy have not usually led to the expulsion or disgrace of the losers (with the few recent exceptions—e.g., Shelest, Shelepin, Polyanski).

Another trait of the present leadership is that all major specialized hierarchies of the Soviet Party-state have their chief executives represented in the Politburo, unlike Khrushchev's Presidium. (The most notable expansion in this direction occurred in 1973 when the head of the armed forces, the chief of the Secret Police and Intelligence, and the foreign minister were co-opted to full membership.) Moreover, among the full membership of the Politburo there is a somewhat greater representation than previously of leaders not directly associated with the central Moscow establishment. Finally, in the last decade neither

of the other two major institutions of the top leadership, the Party's Central
Secretariat or the Presidium of the Council of Ministers, has placed enough of its
members in the Politburo even to approach a majority, as was the case, for
example, with the Central Secretariat in various periods of Khrushchev's
leadership.

Why has this leadership pattern developed and persisted in the last decade and
what are its consequences for the system? After Khrushchev's ouster, the unity
of the new leadership survived initially thanks to a minimum common denominator of political preferences, the negative task of dismantling Khrushchev's
so-called hair-brained schemes (e.g., deStalinization, the abolition of the regular
country Party committees, the bifurcation of the Party apparatus into industrial
and agricultural, the administration of the economy through regional councils,
and the multiplication of numerous high-level committees and commissions that
bypassed the regular Party and governmental channels).

The prospects for open splits, factional struggle, and the elimination of the
weak at the top, with repercussions on the lower strata of leadership, were
minimized because the personal power positions of the probable contenders
were at the beginning apparently more evenly balanced than in the past and their
personal following much less crystallized. Moreover, the policy stimuli for such
splits lacked the urgency of previous periods of succession: the division of
opinion among the leaders seemed less polarized and the distance between
divergent opinions narrower. In part this reflected elite reaction to the fluidity
of the Khrushchev era and the commonly recognized need to stabilize the
regime.

The lessons of Khrushchev's ascent (and descent) have probably not been lost
on the present Soviet leaders, just as the danger of terrorist methods to settle
internal struggles were not lost on Stalin's successors. A leader who would like to
imitate Khrushchev's rise to power through the gradual elimination of his
opponents would now encounter much less enthusiastic support among his
followers and much greater defensive unity among his nonsupporters and
outright opponents.

The pattern prevalent in the Soviet leadership emerged from the desire for a
"return to normalcy" through policies of institutional continuity, gradualism,
accommodation, and reassurance of the elite. Once established and relatively
stabilized, this pattern provides a structural base for the continuation of such
policies. It puts a premium on compromise and is ill-suited to accommodate
innovative ambitions which stray much beyond the existing consensus and to
mobilize support for them. The increased security of all leaders, the greater
diffusion of their everyday influence, the stability of the position of the top
leader himself are paid for by narrowing the range of accepted alternative
solutions in internal policies, by stressing the managerial as counterposed to the
political dimension of decisions (i.e., the question of "how" rather than "what"
to do), and by increasing the making of "nondecisions."

The post-Khrushchev leadership has shown its durability. It has minimized the danger to the oligarchy "from above"—the accumulation of autocratic power and domination by one leader—and the danger "from below"—the dispersal of prerogatives to lower and broader segments of the political establishment, which then go out of control. The leadership withstood, though with visible strains, the difficult task of dealing with the Czechoslovak crisis; it took the Soviet Union through a major turn towards détente and thereafter the setbacks to Soviet aims in it; and it survived very bad crop years in 1972 and 1976 and a decline in industrial growth and productivity. The existing leadership pattern has a very good chance to continue unchanged in the near future.

Yet within the next few years the inevitable succession will have to occur. And with no established strong rules for orderly succession a crisis may occur. Can the existing pattern survive the test of the coming succession?

Were the approaching succession "simply" a question of replacing Brezhnev, one could well argue that as far as *internal* factors are concerned a continuation of the present pattern can be expected. The strong elements of what T.H. Rigby perceptively calls a "self-stabilizing oligarchy" make the composition of the Politburo more predictable and stable, its politics more balanced, its operation more bureaucratic, and the position of the top leaders less personalized than ever before. This provides a significantly different base for the succession than before. Of course the specific circumstances of Brezhnev's departure—whether he retires voluntarily, dies, or is ousted—will affect how orderly the succession will be. Still the existing arrangements are probably sufficiently self-regenerating to handle it.

The stability and longevity of the existing pattern, however, have been conditional on two internal structural factors: gradualism in major policy changes and gradualism, to say the least, in personnel replacement. We do not know whether the first condition will still obtain in a succession or whether, after the cycle of cautious readjustments and traditionalism of the last decade, the mood of the leadership and the elite will swing towards revitalization and major reforms, just as the frozen conditions of Stalin's Russia were replaced by the flux of the Khrushchev period. The key determinant of what will be the dominant tendency in this respect during the succession will be whether there is a major increase in the perception by Soviet leaders and the elite of pressures and frustrations stemming from failures or dangers at home or abroad.

What we do know, however, is that the second condition—gradualism in personnel replacement—will most probably not occur. The coming decade will almost certainly see the replacement of almost the entire core group of the leadership, a replacement that, considering the vagaries of nature, may occur almost simultaneously. Much of this core group will leave within five to seven years. It is virtually impossible to predict how the impressive but still precarious, unformalized and relatively recent leadership arrangement in the Soviet Union will withstand the test of the strains created by these circumstances.

Pattern of Relations within the Political Elite

The increasing outspokenness of group alignments was a centrifugal force within the Soviet political elite under Khrushchev. The elimination of terror from intra-elite relations and the disappearance of the institution of the absolute "leader" transformed divisions within the elite from a secondary phenomenon in the Soviet political process, susceptible to manipulation in the interest of centralized leadership and uniform policies, into a primary fact of Soviet political life. The ouster of Khrushchev, if anything, strengthened the translation of diverse opinions and interests within the Soviet political elite into political pressures.

A consideration of the changes made in the structure of the Soviet Party-state over the last decade, together with the policies pursued by the post-Khrushchev leadership and with the general political mood in the Soviet Union, can support a conclusion which at first glance appears somewhat paradoxical. The establishment of a collective leadership and the policies of this leadership in organizational, political, economic, and ideological matters led in its first few years to an improvement in the power position or in the satisfaction of the group interest of almost all institutional segments of the Soviet political elite, and in the years that followed did not noticeably undermine their positions. While probably no elite group welcomes all changes or all policies, a rare situation has emerged where the fears of almost all elite groups have been to some extent allayed and their desires to some extent satisfied.

The elite as a whole became more secure in office, as was symbolically underscored by the repeal of the article in the Party Statutes which required periodic turnover of membership in Party organs. The disappearance of the "catch-up-and-surpass" slogans, the dampening of the "campaign" spirit, and even the simple expedient of lowering exaggerated and chronically unfulfilled plan targets diminished the pressure on those Party and state officials responsible for the economy. The sober, more realistic, task-oriented and present-oriented style of leadership is much closer to the preferred style of almost all segments of the elite. The sensitivities of the political elite to the horrors of Stalinist terror and to the embarrassment caused by disclosures about the Stalin era have been gratified.

The Party apparatus more than any other group could hail a return to normalcy. The "generalist" first secretary, the personification of the all-inclusive responsibilities of the Party apparatus, again returned as the backbone of the Party hierarchy. The decline in the numerical strength of the apparatus has been reversed. (By some estimates the party bureaucracy grew under Brezhnev by 15-20 percent.) Stress is again placed on being "engineers of the human soul" and not only on engineers, on experience in party work and not only on a simple technical diploma. The distinctiveness of the apparatus as a political and not merely a managerial-administrative organization has reemerged, and its organizational cohesion has been strengthened.

The gains of the primarily economic state administration are symbolized (if sometimes exaggerated) in the division of the crucial offices of general secretary and prime minister. The economic administration under Kosygin is today a bureaucratic complex more directly controlled through its own channels and with greater authority over industry *and* agriculture than in Khrushchev's day. The creeping economic centralization of the last years of Khrushchev's leadership has been replaced by an open reestablishment of the Moscow-based ministerial administration, in which the authority of the ministries substantially exceeds that of Khrushchev's state economic committees. While the power of the central bureaucracy has increased, at the same time the degree of nominal and real autonomy of the plant manager is greater than in the Khrushchev era. Khrushchev's stress on the build-up of the intermediate level of economic administration impinged on the relative autonomy and prerogatives of both the highest administrative bodies and the low-level economic institutions.

The decision to leave the essentials of the Soviet system of planning and incentives unchanged and to concentrate on its improvement through better management and the stress on the greater efficacy of the "visible hand" as against economic mechanisms have placed the high level economic administrator in the center of attention and action and left him and the lower level manager in a situation with which they are familiar and where they have experience. Innovations in the centralized economic administration which added to its complexity contributed to the expansion of an administrative bureaucracy the ranks of which increased by over one-third since 1965. The rediscovery of the "managerial sciences," the outpouring of Western and native managerial manuals, and the establishment of training facilities modeled after Western business schools in a society where both the elite and the population are awed by technology and science have upgraded the managerial profession. The managerial profession is more prestigious, more visible, more deferred to at present than it ever was before.

The gains of the military establishment are visible and formidable. In the last decade the impressive modernization of the Soviet armed forces has taken place and the long-sought strategic parity with the United States has been achieved. The professional, as opposed to political, autonomy of the Soviet high command is greater than in any period of Soviet history. As John Erickson has remarked, while Khrushchev, by removing the stain of treason placed on the military by Stalin, restored the honor of the military, the present leadership has restored its professional pride. The Soviet military is an expanding, prestigious, and far from frustrated institution, in absolute terms and especially in comparison with the Western military.

The police apparatus has also not been denied its rewards. While its achievements are less tangible (or for that matter visible to the outsider), they appear to be real. The morale and self-confidence of police officials, no longer burdened by *official* accounts of the crimes of their predecessors, have been largely restored.

The role of the police in Soviet society undeniably has become more visible and pronounced in the last five years. The publicized trials and arrests of dissenters are only one of its expressions. The recentralization of the police apparatus and the reestablishment of the Ministry of Internal Affairs also point in this direction. Yet it is very difficult to evaluate the role and influence of the police within the elite establishment.

The cooptation to membership in the Politburo of the head of the police *and* intelligence establishment, Andropov, may and in part at least must reflect realities of power. In its symbolic aspect—the first time since the Stalinist period when an active head of the police has occupied such a seat—it clearly upgrades the respectability and the political weight of the service. The unprecedented growth and activism of anti-regime dissent and the fear of undesired political fallout from the increased openings to the West which détente makes inevitable have heightened the importance of the police *for* the political elite. An additional element of elite fear that contributes to the importance of the police arises from the uncertainties and concern regarding the non-Russian and especially the non-Slavic republics. However, there are no signs that mass police terror is returning or that police methods are being in any way introduced into relations *within* the elite. The role of the police in everyday social management, while more pronounced, does not transgress the functions and lines of authority traditional for the post-Stalinist period. We have too little and too tenuous evidence to declare, as some do, that the police has attained a veto over the policies of the present leadership.

For the analyst, the Soviet decision-making process resembles the famous "black box," with the difference that in this case we not only do not know or have only a glimpse of what goes on within it, but we know very little about what goes into it; we know a great deal only about what comes out of it. The process must therefore be judged by its persistent and patterned results. From this point of view, what conclusions can one reach from an overview of the last decade? To what pattern of relations within the Soviet political elite does it testify? With what structural characteristics is it consonant? Our basic conclusion is that the major institutional hierarchies in the Soviet Union have been granted or have achieved in fact a greater degree of operational autonomy and have developed greater ability to influence the major decisions of the Soviet leadership.

In part this reflects the conditions within the top leadership: the balancing of countervailing forces and views within it, where no one leader is in a position to translate his outlook into the general policy line, and where their only commitment as a group is to a broadly acceptable middle-ground policy that will not diverge too far from most respected views but will incorporate elements of many of them.

In part it expresses the enormous expansion of the scope and increase in the complexity of running Soviet society and an implicit acknowledgment that total control of operation and total concentration of decision-making are difficult to reconcile with the attainment of the regime's goals, especially economic ones. The Soviet leadership, and the top leader in particular, in order to preserve their power have to share it more widely with, and use it with greater consideration for, major institutional interests. Authority *to order* is undiminished but becomes illusory when not translated into authority *to do*.

No major institutional interest therefore seems able to push its position to the limits, to override completely other interests. This conclusion leaves open, however, the question of the relative weight of specific interests. There are two important elite interests to be considered. The *first*, associated with the defense-heavy industry complex (and discussed in detail in another chapter in this volume), has above anything else a policy orientation that cuts across the organizational lines of the elite establishment. The *second* concerns primarily the strategic location of the Party bureaucracy within the Soviet elite.

The Defense-Heavy Industry Complex

It is only partly in jest that one says "the United States may *have* a military-industrial complex but the Soviet Union *is* a military-industrial complex." Tradition and the present international status and ambitions of the Soviet Union; the lingering insecurities of the past and the new insecurities of the present; the commitment to hold at any price a potentially explosive empire in Eastern Europe; the pride in the accomplishment in the defense-heavy industry area, by far the single most important area of the real achievements of the Soviet regime; the fact that it is the most efficient and modern societal sector with a greater concentration of scientific, technological, managerial talent, and labor skill than all other sectors combined; the relative effectiveness, as compared to traditional ideological themes, of mobilization of support through patriotism tied in with the glorification of the past and present defense complex; the presence of those associated with or even "graduated" from the defense complex within all segments of the elite and leadership—all these combine to make the weight of the interests of the defense complex much greater than the weight of the representation of the military-heavy industry elite segments in the leadership institutions and policy-making bodies. The role of the defense *factor* in Soviet policy-making is much greater than the direct political weight of the military and the heavy industry *sector* of the elite. The policy orientation characterized by an almost automatic first priority responsiveness to defense-heavy industrial needs seems almost to be a component part of Soviet political culture.

The Party Apparatus

The position of the professional Party bureaucracy, the Party apparatus, in the Soviet power structure underwent historically a number of changes. From being one of the several channels through which Stalin communicated his commands, the Party apparatus achieved, in the years following Khrushchev's defeat of the "anti-Party group" in 1957, an institutional preeminence greater than ever before or after. In the last years of his rule Khrushchev became increasingly the spokesman not of the Party apparatus but of his ambition to gain unrestricted leadership. After he was ousted, his disregard of the Party apparatus was quickly reversed and in the whole post-Khrushchev decade no significant changes took place in its structure and official prerogatives. With the restoration of central ministries and the stress on vertical control within the specialized bureaucracies, the uniquely favorable conditions for primacy of the party apparatus no longer obtained, yet its central position in the Soviet political process remains in our opinion unquestionable.

It is sometimes suggested, however, that the core role of the Party organs and Party bureaucracy, especially on the territorial level, has switched or is switching from policy guidance to policy brokerage—that is, to the role of an intermediary which brings together, and mediates between, specialized officials in what is basically *their* decision-making.

It is much too early to say whether this is really taking place. There are a number of qualifications and reservations that come to mind, such as that of the broker's image, which, if at all valid, would refer primarily to the economic field (in our opinion this view is totally unacceptable in other fields, such as culture for example); or that the image that the Party tries to project to the public and for its own communications is exactly that of policy guidance, not of brokerage, and that therefore this view is at most the depiction of a state of affairs as it sometimes exists but not of the desired state of affairs; or that the whole image of the Party-broker suggests or implies a situation that is not true for any bureaucratic hierarchy in the Soviet Union, namely, neutrality. Those reservations and objections notwithstanding, the image of the Party apparatus as a broker does describe a tendency in Soviet decision-making for which examples can be provided, and one not inconsistent with the general situation within the post-Khrushchev Soviet elite era.

The main fault in this image of the Party apparatus is different: its overconcentration on one dimension of the decision-making process and its neglect of a second one. The first concerns the choice among conflicting and competing solutions advocated by the officials of diverse specialized bureaucracies. Here too the Party functionary's role is not as neutral and his preferences more weighty than the role of broker implies. Yet there seems to be a real decline in the activist role of the Party apparatus in this dimension of decision-making.

The decision-making process has however a second dimension—the delineation of the range and limits of acceptable alternative solutions. The power to influence the agenda of decision-making and to decide the range of solutions to be considered is a core political function and has more direct repercussions on the direction of change of the system than the first dimension. Here, in our view, the role of the Party apparatus is still dominant, its prerogative undiminished, and its effectiveness not eroded.

Changes in the structure of relations within the Soviet political elite were a more important channel for elite change in the last decade than elite replacement. The greater assertiveness of institutional interests, the increase in the operational autonomy of elite organizations, the diffusion of influence from the top leadership, and the relative stability of the balance of countervailing forces within the top leadership stopped, however, very short of institutionalization. They may therefore be partly reversed, even if with difficulty, in the coming succession.

The post-Khrushchev structural innovations may satisfy the present generation of officeholders. But they may not satisfy the next one, which may want not only to broaden its operational autonomy but also to influence the agenda of decision-making. Response to social reality always involves a lag: not only individuals but also groups respond to new conditions on the basis of attitudes and habits developed in the old conditions. The situation which future Soviet leaders will face with regard to their major elite institutions will be very different from the ones faced by Stalin's successors. Stalin did not simply control the Party, the military or the planners—he crushed them. Ironically, only now, when Stalin is again becoming an officially "respectable" figure, is the delayed impact of Stalinism on the character of Soviet bureaucracy dissolving. Soviet administrators display today more self-confidence and professional pride than ever before. These qualities are easily reconcilable with an authoritarian outlook toward the society at large but are difficult to fit into a highly restrictive elite structure without endangering its effectiveness.

Change in Elite Responsiveness

The patterns discussed so far have concerned changes which originated within the elite system itself or were primarily concerned with relations within the elite. We must also consider, however, possible changes in relations of the political elite with other strata and groups of Soviet society. Such changes would primarily result from significant shifts in the opportunities of various social groups to gain access to the elite and a corresponding increase in elite responsiveness to outside pressures.

It has already been maintained that pressures from outside the official framework have not determined changes in the post-Stalinist era but that, rather, the key stimuli for these changes have come from incumbent leaders and elite groups. When pressures for change from outside the official framework are considered in other than abstract terms they basically can take the following three forms under Soviet conditions:

1. Organized group pressure, which is considered illegitimate by the regime even when it remains within legal limits. This type of pressure, which rejects core beliefs and proposes major systemic changes, was created by the dissident movement. (It is treated in greater detail in another chapter in this book.) While it has been a great embarrassment to the regime and has had very negative repercussions on the Soviet image in world opinion, in our view its actual effect on Soviet domestic policies—its potential future importance notwithstanding—has been minimal and, if anything, has furthered greater ideological and cultural rigidity. Dissent epitomizes for the political leadership the danger of instituting changes in the system but in its present isolated state it is not strong enough to produce any such changes.

2. Pressure from segments of specific occupational and professional strata (writers, jurists, economists, engineers, scientists). Members of these high status occupations and professions can use professional channels of communication, and in policy areas requiring expertise have gained access to the decisionmakers.

Some of these professional strata, for instance the engineers, are so large, and diffuse, and enmeshed in the regular administrative structure, that it is very difficult to speak about group pressure at all. With regard to the other strata, centers of opinion and interest communities are discernible. Most publicized in the West is the prestigious Soviet scientific community, whose indispensibility to the political elite is unquestionable. That these groups or their segments try to influence official policies is amply documented. That they are sometimes successful can also be demonstrated.

The question is, however, when are they successful and what policies do they try to influence? First of all, as a rule the closer their profession is to the technological sphere and the more removed from the ideological one, the less ignored are their interests and pressures. Writers on the one extreme and scientists on the other represent the two poles of permissible freedom and influence. (The gravitation of economists from identification with cultural toward scientific spheres is important here.) Second, the main policy pressures emanating from these groups concern the status of their profession, allocation of resources to it, and their right to professional autonomy and integrity. In these concerns the scientific and technological groups have been by and large very successful in the last decade.

Yet one should beware of confusing the importance to the Soviet system and society of science and scientists (let alone other professional groups), their success in developing professional integrity and autonomy in basic research, and their proximity to men of power, with their general political influence. While respecting their expertise and responding to their needs, the Soviet politician is unlikely to attribute to them superior insight and wisdom. Since 1968, under the impact of the Sakharov Manifesto and the subsequent defense of his person and position by a number of scientists, the Party has shown increased anxiety about the political and social attitudes of scientists, has considerably tightened supervision over personnel policy in the scientific establishment, and has tried to denigrate by propaganda the expertise of scientists in social and political matters.

The Soviet professional communities are politically fragile groups. Each "group" is not only politically heterogeneous, but it also displays a very broad range of views and opinions concerning matters on which advice is given to political authorities. It is composed of individuals of different generations with different training and diverse institutional associations and career orientations. The choice between conflicting advice and pressures remains the politician's. To what extent the choices made by politicians between different expert advice and pressures will gravitate from those accepted today to those today rejected (e.g., market-oriented economic reform versus mathematization and computerization of centralized planning, civilian versus military stress in scientific research, or restriction or flow of scientific information across institutional and national borders) may have very important systemic consequences. But this choice depends only marginally on what goes on within, or is influenced by, the professional groups. It depends decisively on what goes on within the political elite, and it is influenced by elite goals, by elite perception of internal and international successes and failures, and by the elite's quest for self-preservation. The greatest influence of scientists *and* science, David Holloway has remarked, "may have been felt in ways that are most difficult to discern: in the changing of social values through technological process and in the erosion of the party's legitimacy as a result of the disjunction between political authority and scientific truth." But his is a different matter, very long-range in its implications, which in our view will have no political effects in the short and intermediate run as long as science advisers are basically the presenters of contingency plans, without the right or the ability to take a stand on the moral and social consequences of proposals under consideration.

3. Shapeless and inchoate pressure from broad strata of the population— Soviet "public opinion." Our knowledge of this "public opinion," necessarily very impressionistic, although enriched lately by information gained from recent Soviet emigrés, points to the following conclusions:

a. The Party authorities are attentive to the moods of the population, especially as expressed in complaints and petitions, and are kept informed about its direction and intensity through various official channels, to which the new instrument of empirical sociological research has recently been added.

b. In addition to very effective control instruments, of which the police, with its enormous net of informers, is only one, the Soviet system incorporates a number of effective safety valves which counteract dissatisfaction in forms dangerous to the regime. The two most important are: (i) the encouragement and actual expansion of citizens' demands on and participation in local government (the soviets). These demands concern limited and usually individual or neighborhood needs; and their main function is to expose and therefore inhibit official misconduct at lower administrative levels, and thereby to diffuse popular discontent and direct it away from the center toward local officials. (ii) The existence of the extensive subterranean, semi-legal and illegal market of goods and services in which local officials and managers also participate, and which amounts, as a communist official expressed it, to a "secondary redistribution of the national income."

c. The Soviet Union is one of the very few countries which in the last decade has avoided youth and especially student turmoil. Career orientation still seems dominant among Soviet students, and the students' hope for change, so often expressed to Western visitors, rests on what their generation will do when it takes over the reins of government but not on what it is able or willing to do now.

d. Major dissatisfaction and demands within Soviet "public opinion" have very different priorities. They are not expressed jointly. They do not necessarily reinforce and, indeed, very often counterbalance each other: for example the aspirations of nationality groups versus those of the Russians, particularly the large Russian minorities in non-Russian areas and the intellectuals' anti-authoritarianism and desire for creative freedom versus the managerial desire for greater autonomy for themselves and for greater discipline for the workers, and both versus the workers' egalitarian aspirations and anti-intellectualism.

Those multiple cleavages between Party and society, which have direct political implications for the present and disruptive potential for the future do not overlap. Thus the Party has ample room for maneuver. The Party does not face "society," or generalized demands, but separate segments of society with specific demands, which the Party can mobilize against each other, or at least neutralize, and thus strengthen its own position.

e. A very important question about Soviet "public opinion" concerns the level of its expectations. The material aspirations and expectations of Soviet citizens have risen noticeably in the last decade. What is more striking, however, especially when compared to the situation in the West, is that, first, in absolute terms these expectations are very modest for an industrial nation and, second, that they are not far removed from what is realistically possible, though often unrealized, in Soviet conditions. To put it differently, although material expectations are ahead of reality, one doubts whether there is a widening gap between expectations and reality. This situation, striking in a system which for decades overindulged in utopian promises, suggests a restraint in popular expectations related to past experiences. Visible and significant improvements in the material condition of the Soviet population have not yet resulted in that familiar phenomenon in other industrial societies: a self-generating spiral of expectations which cannot be realized. The intensity of popular pressures to which the Soviet authorities are exposed is very limited and as long as some improvements continue to occur, the situation will probably remain stabilized in this respect.

But however we evaluate the amorphous pressures in Soviet society, responsiveness by the Soviet leadership to some of these aspirations is clearly much greater now than in the past. However, it is selective, and it concerns primarily material aspirations. While Soviet living standards and consumption levels are still far behind those of the developed industrial societies, in the last ten years the production of consumer goods, housing construction, and real wages have increased very much by any standard. The welfare function of the Soviet state including, for the first time, the rural population, has also expanded considerably. Moreover, the special stress on increasing minimum wages has significantly reduced the gap between the pay of administrative and blue-collar workers.

To what kind of pressures is this behavior of the Soviet leadership responsive? In part, of course, it is responsive to changes in the distributive sector of the Soviet economy, where the population acquired for the first time in Soviet history a limited possibility to express its demands through selective buying. A thousand complaints of irate citizens to local soviets or newspapers will probably improve the quality of consumer products less than a large inventory of unsold goods. In part, it has to do with the importance that the Soviet leadership attaches to material incentives in its economic programs. But in large measure, this responsiveness can be described as an anticipatory reaction, that is to say, not a response to the actual behavior of workers but to the leadership's fear that if the interests of the workers are not sufficiently considered, their behavior might become disruptive and dangerous. The lessons of the dangers of workers' dissatisfaction in East European countries, and especially the workers' uprising in Poland in December 1970, have not been lost on Soviet leaders. Where such a high premium is placed on stability, an organized dissent movement is active, mass terror is absent, popular expectations have long been encouraged, and the opening of Soviet society to foreigners has made material comparisons possible, the Party must pay more attention to the material satisfaction of the population so that it can continue to curtail cultural freedom, withhold political freedom, and preserve political stability.

The primary pressures which produced institutional and policy innovations in the post-Stalin era have not been the actual pressures of social groups or strata but changing material conditions in the society and changing political circumstances within the elite. In the future, tensions between political authority and social strata may generate politically significant pressures for change, but this is uncertain. In this respect the widening cleavage between the two halves of Soviet society—the dominant Great Russians and the other nationalities—is by far the most important tension.

The increasingly assertive non-Russian ethnic nationalisms are directed not only against specific aspects of what they see as discriminatory Soviet political, economic, demographic, and cultural policies, but against the very principle of Soviet federalism—the political and economic centralization of the Soviet Party-state, which concentrates decision-making for the entire Soviet Union in

Moscow while retaining an administrative framework which safeguards the territorial boundaries and formal ethno-cultural institutions of non-Russian nationalities.

There are many reasons why the nationality problem should be singled out for attention from the point of view of its potential political significance for the future:

1. Its aggravation threatens the most potent unifying and legitimizing systemic force within Soviet society—great power nationalism, which primarily accounts for the political stability of the Soviet state in the last thirty years as opposed to the instability of East European Communist regimes.

2. The polarization of the Soviet peoples along ethnic lines is increasing faster than their identification with, and consciousness of, a new Soviet nationhood, and it is nourished both by tradition and by socioeconomic progress. The leadership's earlier hopes that ethnic nationalism would wither away in the "natural" process of Soviet development have not materialized.

3. The nationality problem and the danger of its intensification adds another dimension to, and greatly complicates, many of the administrative and political dilemmas which the Party faces. Most important in this respect is the superimposition of the ethnic dimension over the Party's dilemma in the field of economic organization. There the need for greater economic effectiveness generates pressure for decentralization, which in turn, however, clashes with the Party's fear that it will lead to loss of political control.

4. The concept and reality of Soviet federalism contains a potentially dangerous dualism: in theory and in practice it denies any but the slimmest margin of autonomy to the federated nationalities, but at the same time its symbolic institutions and administrative framework provide a base from which the struggle for national autonomy can be waged.

5. Ethnic identification and aspirations could, and to some extent today already do, bridge the social divisions of occupational interests and class distinctions. Moreover, already today they are the only example of where the interest of one segment of the Soviet political elite corresponds with that of a Soviet social stratum and therefore leads the former to represent the latter. This representative function by segments of the minority political elites for their native social groups is still very limited and tenuous, but in the eyes of the central, primarily Great Russian political elite, it is probably the most dangerous trend because in many respects it repeats the nationalist threats to them in Eastern Europe.

The Soviet Communist elite has so far been unable to design a program to meet the challenge of ethnic nationalism, that is, one which could reverse the trend or respond positively to these national aspirations. By all accounts, it is exactly because of the lack of agreement on such a long-range program that the promulgation of the new Soviet constitution, to replace the 1936 one, has been delayed so many times. In the meantime the Party holds the line, fighting against the tolerance often exhibited by native Communist cadres with regard to their own minorities, and hoping that the migration of Russians to minority republics (especially the Central Asian and Baltic republics) will achieve what industrialization alone has been unable to do.

The Soviet Union is almost the only state which after World War II has been able to hold the line against the successful global trend of national and ethnic self-assertiveness against central authority. However, the growing autonomous aspirations of the minority peoples of the Soviet Union and of the minority segments of the political elite may become at some time in the future the major factor contributing to change of the system. In any case, in the foreseeable future, the nationality problem, and the resultant fear of the central elite and most other Great Russians for their power, is one of the major brakes on the evolution of the Soviet system away from authoritarianism and on innovative impulse of the Soviet political leadership.

Change in Elite Beliefs

Basic continuity of elite composition and, initially at least, of the structure of elite positions is sometimes accompanied by enormous changes in the style and direction of politics and decision-making, which result from transformation in the beliefs and values of the established elite. The transformation of the Yugoslav system after 1948 and the developments in Communist Eastern Europe after 1953 (particularly the 1968 events in Czechoslovakia) are examples of this process. How applicable is this pattern in the case of the Soviet political elite?

The question of change in perception and outlook of the Soviet leadership and political elite inevitably raises the entire complex of problems expressed by the concepts of "erosion" and even "end of ideology." The "end" of Soviet ideology has occurred so many times in the past fifty years that its burial should long since have been forgotten. If one is waiting for the end of ideology, and not for its change, the warning of Clifford Geertz, that one may wait for it as long as the positivists waited for the end of religion, is very timely. The end of ideology theme is misleading insofar as it implies that the political realism dominant in the thinking of the contemporary Soviet elite is devoid of ideology because it is not associated with, and is even averse to, serious theorizing.

To look at the Soviet political elite today as revolutionary fanatics whose every concrete act is colored by the ultimate ends as prescribed by Marxist and Leninist holy writ is as nonsensical as it is to see them only as cynical manipulators who simply drift toward undefined goals and whose response to reality is not influenced by their intellectual and political revolutionary origins. The question is not whether their beliefs have changed, but which beliefs, how much, and in what direction; not whether they have an ideology but to what ideology they subscribe.

Let us first distinguish various dimensions and levels of ideology. The most basic of these is doctrinal, what Franz Schurmann terms "the pure ideology." Whatever distortions of selectivity, interpretation, or addition were performed in the process of Soviet development on Marxian theory and the original Bolshevik ideas, Marxism-Leninism is still the core of this pure ideology.

What has happened to the "pure ideology" in the last decade may best be evaluated by comparing it with the Khrushchev era. Both saw, in comparison to the Stalinist period, a pronounced expansion of the output of ideological literature, much greater attention to its mass dissemination, and greater stress on ideological training and Party schooling. Their similarity reflects in both cases a conscious response to the disappearance of mass and elite terror, through the upgrading of the role and weight, if not the effectiveness, of ideological (and economic) social controls.

Although in the last decade the volume of ideological literature and the scale of propaganda of "pure ideology" has increased, the key doctrinal tendency of these two post-Stalinist periods differs. The association of the Khrushchev period with "goulash communism" and with an attempt to reorganize the Party along functional economic lines sometimes conceals what appears to be on the whole the dominant tendency of this period, that of an (unsuccessful) ideological revival. The reformatory zeal and flux of the Khrushchev period found a reflection and a base in ideological innovations and in a belief that ideological truths can impress and inspire the masses. In the last years of Khrushchev's rule this manipulation of ideological symbols was increasingly intended to link the leader directly with the Party and masses, over the heads of the bureaucracy.

The basic tendency of the post-Khrushchev period has been that of *ideological retrenchment* and *partial retreat*. The retrenchment finds its expression in the disappearance of ideological innovations, in the very dogmatic, uncritical, monotonous tenor of the textbooks, pamphlets, etc., used in mass and Party indoctrination, and, most importantly, in the lack of any serious effort to go beyond routine in the attempt to propagate the doctrine to nonbelievers or doubters, but rather to stress resistance to, and defense against, "alien ideas."

The partial retreat is clearly expressed in drawing a line between science and doctrine. The issue of possible incompatibility between the substance of certain scientific thought and ideology has simply been dropped, and with it the attacks, reinterpretations, and even suppressions of specific scientific theories. The Party philosophers have ceased to be the ideological watchdogs of scientific research: their main function now is to provide a justification for the accommodation between science and ideology. The other expression of the partial retreat, ambiguous, uncertain, and much less clear, is the debates in nonprofessional journals and at conferences on policy issues concerning a wide range of social, ecological, and economic issues. The participants do not try and are usually not pushed to link their factual analysis and recommendation to doctrinal truths. The doctrinal position on policy issues is ambiguous, nonauthoritative, and ill-defined. The discussion, therefore, is conducted neither against a doctrinal prescription nor in support of it, but parallel to doctrine. Doctrinal entrenchment takes place on one level, where rigidity and dogmatism is very pronounced—in mass propaganda and mass culture, general education and Party schooling, and with regard to the central questions of Soviet history. At the same time direct doctrinal intervention in expert deliberation is limited, and thereby the desire to issue binding verdicts on policy questions which are unresolved or unclear in practice is curtailed.

Thus the doctrine can retain a semblance of consistency and minimize disagreements about its meaning and consequences for action by keeping increasingly aloof from social practice, i.e., by its increased ritualization. The staying power of the doctrine depends, however, not only or mainly on its logical coherence and consistency but on the social functions that it performs. And it is the long-range importance of these social functions in the Soviet Union today, together with other more immediate reasons, that explains the ideological retrenchment and orthodoxy.

One of the more significant immediate reasons for the entrenchment is the process of détente with the West. While the long-range consequences of détente may increase access to competing ideas and world views in the Soviet Union, its immediate effects on official policies are just the opposite. Concern over the possible destabilizing effect of détente on the internal (and East European) situation inspires a tough cultural line and ideological vigilance and orthodoxy.

One of the very important long-range functions of doctrinal orthodoxy and retrenchment concerns the Soviet imperial position in Eastern Europe and the Brezhnev doctrine of limited sovereignty which safeguards it ideologically. The doctrinal orthodoxy provides its sole possible legitimization in the eyes of the Soviet political elite, among some segments of the East European Party elites, and in parts of Communist parties outside the Soviet bloc. Soviet dominance of Eastern Europe rests of course primarily on Soviet military power, but the ability to contemplate its use, let alone actually to use it, requires not so much for the population as for the elite itself the evocation of the doctrine right which makes it "just."

But the most important function of the doctrinal orthodoxy is to legitimize the Party's and Party apparatus' dominant power position *within* the elite. Not that the Party's administrative role is parasitic—its coordinating function is a necessary one. But it is not the only institution which can perform this function and the way in which it performs it is not the only one. The effective legitimizing base of Party and regime is nationalism, but to nationalism the Party has no unique claim: only when nationalism is combined with doctrinal orthodoxy does the position of the Party and its apparatus become unique.

Analysis of the changes in the perception and basic political outlook of the Soviet political elite should concern itself not with "pure" but with "practical" ideology—the ideas, principles, and preferences which provide the dominant perceptual *framework* of elite behavior and action, the matrix of its collective conscience. "Practical ideology" has been and continues to be influenced by doctrine, not only in its symbolic expressions (language, terminology, emotive meanings) but also in substance. Increasingly, however, its influence is mainly negative: it rules out certain options in decision-making and reinforces or weakens the arguments against others. But doctrinal influence is only one influence on "practical ideology." Its dominant source is the tradition of the Soviet system, the historical experience of the political elite itself. This is especially true with regard to those elements of "practical ideology" addressed directly, or directly relevant, to the political process.

We propose to identify some of the most important elements of the Soviet political elite's "collective conscience" and to indicate wherever possible the direction of its evolution in the post-Stalin era.

1. The withering away of utopia and utopianism in the thought and practice of the political elite has been accelerated. This utopianism, the strongest and closest derivative of the doctrinal tradition, still constituted under Khrushchev one part of the vision of the future within which the elite operated. Incorporated in the Party program of 1961, the promise of the leader read, "The Party solemnly proclaims: the present generation of Soviet people shall live in communism." The present Soviet leadership dislikes and discourages this kind of fantasy. *Delovitost'*, business-like behavior, has become their ubiquitous slogan, the leadership quality most praised in the written and spoken world. The *delovitost'* of the top leaders, however, is that of businessmen concerned with the rationalization of means rather than the definition of ends.

2. The elite impulse to *re*shape society has radically declined. On the contrary, for the ruling elite Soviet social structure has found its permanent shape—at least for the foreseeable future. What the Party proposes to the Soviet population is nothing but the indefinite continuation of the basic existing social relations and material progress. The innovative impulse of the political elite is focused entirely on functioning, not on restructuring innovations.

3. If nothing else, generations of Soviet leaders have assimilated from the Marxian tradition the dimension it shared with Western rationalism: the belief in progress. The decline in the West of the attractiveness of the affirmative, optimistic idea of progress is not duplicated in the Soviet Union. True, one can discern for the first time some elements of doubt and devaluation of expectations. The optimism of the Khrushchev era has been replaced by a more somber assessment and by much greater realism about what can be achieved in the short and intermediate term. The old attitude, which looked at nature as a fortress to be conquered, is being complemented by reflections and fears about the ecological dilemma. The future looks less like unilinear, unbridled progress. But what has changed very little or not at all is the deeply entrenched belief in, and commitment to, continuous economic growth, the all-pervading technological

ethos, the faith in science, and the lack of recognition that scientific knowledge is an instrument, not an end in itself.

4. The persistent centrality of the belief in progress and its almost total equation with material growth are associated with and supplemented by a deeply rooted attitude of evaluating one's own performance in "progressing to progress" by the standards of Western industrial nations. Only in this sense is the Soviet political elite still "internationalist." The sources of this "comparative" mentality are many: justification of the past history of sacrifice and denial, ultimate legitimization of the superiority of the system, and the assurance of the security of the system from alien and hostile external forces. The most important point, however, is that regardless of its specific sources, this way of thinking has taken hold of and pervades all segments of the elite and thus acquired an existence of its own. This mentality infuses into the political elite a sense of urgency and stress on mobilization even in times of notable achievement. Its systemic effects are somewhat contradictory. On the one hand it promotes taut planning, mobilizational atmosphere, social discipline, etc. On the other it is probably the single most important incentive to functional innovations, to performance-oriented reform, once the performance according to old methods becomes unsatisfactory according to the standards of Western competitors. The tendency that emerges from this internal contradiction is to opt for reforms which improve performance but preserve mobilizational atmosphere and social discipline.

5. The mainstay of the awareness of common purpose within the political elite is provided more than ever by nationalism. Partly in its great-power Soviet variety and partly in its cultural, traditional Russian variety, it constitutes the major effective, long-lasting bond within the political elite and between the elite and the masses. The old conservative theme—the cult of national unity and the condemnation of individuals and groups who threaten to impair it—provides the emotional base for an authoritarian political outlook and is in turn reinforced by it.

6. Lastly, there is an entire set of beliefs and attitudes dominant within the Soviet political elite which expresses deep-seated fear and mistrust of spontaneity in political and social behavior, induces an interventionist psychology, and stresses the need of strong central government, organization, and order.

The Soviet political elite is of course not homogeneous; it includes varying interests, outlooks, and sympathies. It tends to divide in times of internal crisis and severe stress. Yet the core sets of attitudes and beliefs discussed above are strong and persistent in the elite stratum as a whole.

When analyzing groups and interests in Soviet society, there is an understandable tendency to concentrate on conflict relationships among them, which gives them uniqueness and variety. But the context of elite group activity in the Soviet Union is that of a relationship between groups who fundamentally accept the system but compete for advantages within it.

The difference between the Soviet political elite and the Communist elites of Eastern Europe is as striking as the difference between the Soviet and East European societies. When we speak about a regime's legitimacy we stress too often and too much its popular, mass dimension. But its elite dimension is more crucial from the point of view of the stability of the system and especially its potential for transformation. For the decline or disintegration of elite legitimacy either leads to the decline of mass legitimacy or transforms the lack of popular support into an effective popular opposition. The revolutions, revolts, and bloodless "springs" and "Octobers" in Eastern Europe were first and foremost basic crises of legitimacy within the Communist elites. In contrast, the changes in outlook of the Soviet elite that occurred in the post-Stalin era and their internal conflicts did not take the shape of a basic crisis of legitimacy among a majority or a crucial segment of the elite.

Assessments of the existing trends in the Soviet Union, let alone projections into the foreseeable future, differ considerably. Some postulate a prerevolutionary situation in Russia. Some at the other end of the continuum project an inexorable evolutionary transformation of the Soviet system. The basic common denominator of both views is the assumption that the various parts of any social system are interdependent, so that changes in one sector will be followed by strains which necessitate adjustive changes in other sectors if the social system is to maintain its viability. The adherents of these two views differ in assessing the consequences of their projections. In the first case they argue that resistance to necessary adjustments and the narrowness of these adjustments are likely to lead to a revolution. In the second case they think that the cumulative effects of even small enforced adjustments will lead to systemic transformation; i.e., that modest changes will set in motion a process which will have final effects quite out of proportion to the original push.

The major concern of this chapter is not with the ultimate effects of an existing pattern of change in the Soviet Union but with ascertaining the existence of such a pattern, with what the trend is now and not what may happen eventually. But in my view the present probably points neither to revolution nor to transformation, but rather to the sharp limitation of innovative pressures—in short, to continuity.

Even so, while stressing gradualism, stability, and continuity as dominant we have also identified a number of issues, problems, and structural characteristics which contain tremendous destabilizing potential. They range from the coming succession and the approaching replacement of the whole core leadership group to the potentially extraordinarily explosive national problem, which may be contained in the coming decade but seems insoluble within the existing political framework. The failure to deal successfully with any of these problems, and especially their simultaneous aggravation brought about by or combined with an internal economic crisis or external shock, can become a departure point for a profoundly destabilizing chain reaction within the system.

In some areas the stability of the Soviet system is very narrowly based. It over-relies on the "visible hand" of political controls, administrative organization, and conscious manipulation and interventionism; and it is still based too little on the "invisible hand" of socialization, tradition, and internalized controls. One is reminded of the remark of Trevelyan when he tried to account for the discrepancy between the fact that the rise of population which occurred in England after 1790 was attributed to developments in industry and agriculture while a similar population increase occurred in Ireland in this period without such economic improvements: "The decisive factor seems to have been the absence of a potato famine in the 18th century. The potato is the easiest method of supporting life at a very low standard—until a year comes when the crop completely fails."

While a failure of will and effectiveness of the political elite seems unlikely in the coming decade, what seems even less likely in the foreseeable future is a transformation of the Soviet political system in a democratic direction in a peaceful, evolutionary, "painless" way. The nature of the Soviet political elite, the way in which the Soviet system was established, and the way in which it is now run argue forcefully against the effectiveness of incremental changes in breaking the vicious circle of tradition, elite self-replication, bureaucratization, and autocratic societal controls. It may well be that only a crisis of major proportion, an open struggle within the leadership or the emergence of a dominant leader can provide conditions under which an initial push of sufficiently high magnitude to start such a change can occur, and that the stimuli for breaking the circle or reversing its direction must appear simultaneously at various points of the system.

To those who think in terms of a historical process which *has* to transform the Communist societies, the confluence of conditions that may be necessary for such a transformation may seem too restricted and exaggerated. Perhaps, as Gregory Grossman has suggested, we fail fully to appreciate the complicated conjuncture of favorable circumstances necessary for a successful transition of the Soviet system beyond its traditional mold.

Internal Soviet Situation and U.S. Policy:
Problems and Options

To discuss policy options of the United States in its relations with the Soviet Union from the point of view of their impact on internal Soviet development, and particularly their influence on the evolution of the Soviet system away from its Stalinist past, is quite a different, and much less fruitful, exercise than to discuss them with respect to specific areas of U.S.-USSR confrontation, competition, or cooperation on the international arena. Only an incorrigible believer in historical inevitability can possibly pretend to know what the long-range effects of the rapidly and fundamentally changing international environment, of which U.S.-USSR détente is only a small part, will be on the political, economic, and above all social and psychological processes in the major nation states and specifically in the Soviet Union. Let me, therefore, limit myself to a few general propositions concerning U.S. policies with regard to the Soviet Union, which may indicate the range of U.S. options and the limits on their effectiveness. Our starting assumption, and in our opinion the only viable one, is that American-Soviet relations in the coming decade will remain within the framework of what is loosely defined as "détente," i.e., lowering of tensions, decline in the apocalyptic vision of a final confrontation, negotiations as the basic form of conflict-management, and increased areas of cooperation; and that therefore the problem is the substance and direction of détente policies themselves.

In its efforts to maximize through its own policies the chances for internal Soviet evolution in a desired direction, or at least to minimize the possibility that its policies will cater to the most authoritarian policies of the Soviet elite, the U.S. possesses some leverage. The most important points of this leverage are:

1. The Soviet need for Western technology and the commitment in Soviet intermediate-range planning to a transfer of technology from the West, which may have reached a point where a failure to expand such transfer may involve painful dislocations in Soviet economic development.

2. The Soviet need for major credits from the West, and especially from the United States, without which large-scale expansion of East-West trade is almost impossible. The size of such credits places U.S.-Soviet economic relations outside the framework of simple commercial transactions.

3. The question of Western credits both for the Soviet Union *and* Eastern Europe is particularly crucial because of its direct and indirect significance for Soviet relations with its East European empire. Import of Western technology by the Soviet Union without a major expansion of long-term investment credits would limit Soviet ability to supply Communist Eastern Europe with industrial raw materials and therefore would produce potentially dangerous tensions in Soviet-East European relations.

4. Continued Soviet perception of the Chinese danger, on the assumption that the asymmetry in Sino-Soviet-American relations which favors the United States will survive Mao's departure and will continue to be institutionalized at the level of "neither peace nor war."

5. The very Soviet commitment to détente with the West, which stems from the recognition of the danger of any other policy and from the belief of the Soviet leadership that they will be better able than the West to minimize the vulnerability of their social system to the impact of détente and to maximize the opportunities which détente may provide internal growth and external influence. The danger of the reversal of détente or of its losing its momentum at its present initial stage may provide in itself a very important point of leverage for the United States in pressing for Soviet restraint on particular issues and areas.

6. An important extension of this proposition is the potential leverage produced by commitment to détente on Soviet leadership politics. The dominant group within the Soviet leadership, led by Brezhnev, has in our view staked its political fortunes on the continuation and expansion of the détente with the West.

Past experience and our knowledge about the present Soviet ruling elite and the Soviet system indicate, however, that despite these elements of leverage the actual and potential influence of U.S. policies with regard to the Soviet Union on the latter's internal development is and can be expected to be very limited, and that the range of U.S. policy options in this respect will continue to be quite narrow. At the same time, however, the actual and potential influence of U.S. policies on Soviet international behavior is and can be expected to be quite considerable.

The broadest and most fundamental questions about U.S. policy options with regard to Soviet internal developments are, therefore: should internal change of the Soviet system be a *direct* consideration of U.S. policy only marginally, while the priority of U.S. concern should be actual Soviet international behavior: its position on, limitation, and regulation of the armament race, its restraint or aggressiveness in pursuing Soviet interests in such danger spots as the Middle East and the Balkans, its willingness to expand cooperation in solving global ecological and economic problems, etc.? Should the United States strive for overall balanced reciprocity in its political, arms, scientific, and economic agreements with the Soviet Union without permitting considerations about long-range effects of these agreements on the possible transformation of the Soviet system to influence the United States into a position where an overall imbalance in certain or probable gains from such agreements in Soviet favor is recurrently traded off for their possible impact on long-range processes in the Soviet Union?

While U.S. leverage can be, in our opinion, more effective when utilized to influence Soviet behavior on the international arena than to induce internal changes, it also can, to a limited extent, be used to influence internal Soviet developments in several respects.

The first dimension concerns U.S. policies calculated to bring directly a desired change in Soviet internal behavior as a price for expected Soviet gains in other areas. The main example is the attempt to liberalize Soviet emigration policies in return for the liberalization of the terms of Western trade with the Soviet Union.

Opponents of these attempts point out that this kind of pressure on the Soviet Union may endanger détente in general, or at least may minimize U.S. ability to reach meaningful agreements with the Soviet Union in such areas as arms control or international cooperation, which after all are the primary goals of détente. The proponents of such efforts argue that U.S. policy must also further fundamental human rights. They argue, moreover, that the Soviet Union, through its dealings with U.S. corporations, through its broad access to

American elites and opinion-makers, through its almost unrestricted ability to learn and report about the United States, through its freedom to lobby in the United States and among U.S. citizens for particular U.S. policies, *already* intervenes in the "domestic affairs" of the U.S. continuously, purposefully, and sometimes successfully.

In either case, one has to be conscious of the narrow limits of what can realistically be expected from U.S. efforts to influence directly Soviet domestic behavior. It would be fatuous to expect that the limited U.S. leverage could achieve any concessions that in the eyes of the Soviet leaders would seriously endanger their rule or their system.

The second dimension of the possible impact of specific U.S. policies on the Soviet internal scene concerns its potential influence on Soviet leadership politics. Political logic and past experience suggest that U.S. policies, whether they stress a desire for reconciliation and willingness to grant concessions or firmness in defence of what the U.S. considers its vital interests, are an important input in Soviet internal leadership politics.

The oligarchic nature of the present Soviet leadership and the increased importance of pressures and counterpressures exerted by elite factions and interest groups on Soviet policy formation suggest a potentially important influence of specific U.S. policies and behavior, of timely concessions or firm stands, on the strength and success or weakness and decline of particular Soviet leaders and leadership groups. The United States obviously is and should be interested in the survival and success of these leadership groups whose views and behavior it deems most favorable to détente. Yet the question remains whether, with the exception of specific, more or less clear-cut cases, the United States can and should put great stress on indirect participation in Soviet leadership politics.

First, we really do not know much about the changing and changeable internal divisions of views and the specific balance of power on particular issues within the Soviet leadership. We are able very often to determine the existence of a division of opinion or of a struggle, but we are uncertain who belongs to what groups and how strong an opposition to a particular view is.

Second, in an ambiguous situation where "hard" data are lacking one tends to ascribe to the other side the division of views and the balance of influence one knows from one's own side (e.g., military vs. civilian), a method of analysis which often is exaggerated or even irrelevant.

Third, inertia and uncertainty tend almost always to favor in the eyes of the foreign partner the leadership group in power over its challengers, to overvalue the known, "good" qualities of an existing arrangement over the less known alternatives which are therefore likely to be seen as dangerous.

Fourth, Soviet leaders themselves can and do play the game of raising the spector of the "bad guys" in the background in order to press for concessions from their foreign partner.

The third dimension of the impact of U.S. policies on Soviet internal development concerns its possible long-range consequences, ones unintended by Soviet policymakers, and hoped for by Western policymakers.

The long-range consequences of some direct concessions attained from the Soviet leadership may have an importance for Soviet internal development much greater than their immediate impact would indicate. But it is not specific Soviet concessions or specific American efforts directed towards their attainment which are the most important, but rather the intermediate and long-range effect of the détente policy in general. Reduced external tensions and the declining possibility of invoking the danger of "American (or German) imperialism" provides the most favorable long-range conditions for Soviet evolution towards a less repressive, regimented, and mobilizing regime, apart from any conscious U.S. policies directed toward bringing about such changes. These prospects and perspectives will not, however, come to pass automatically. Only under certain crucial conditions can changing Soviet relations with the West, and especially with the United States contribute significantly to internal Soviet transformation.

One such condition is the American ability to contain Soviet ambitions on the international arena, that is to say, to maintain a balance of forces and will vis-à-vis the Soviet Union which while recognizing Soviet interests would prevent the expansion of Soviet domination over crucial areas (e.g., the Middle East), and would radically minimize the temptations to the Soviet leadership, which are bound to increase in the coming decade, to exploit opportunities for changing the international status quo, e.g., in Yugoslavia or Portugal.

Finally, the greatest influence that the United States can have over internal Soviet evolution in the intermediate and long run will come not from its specific policies, but will be a result of how successfully the United States will face the problems of its own internal stability and of its economic, social, and political dynamism. The key to evolutionary change of the Soviet system, to the extent that it can be influenced by the United States, lies less in U.S. relations with the Soviet Union than in U.S. internal policies and U.S. relations with the major industrial democracies.

Note

1. Jeremy Azrael, "The Party and Society," in Allen Kassof (ed.), *Prospects for Soviet Society* (N.Y.: Praeger, 1968), p. 71.

III The Development of Dissent in the USSR

Peter Reddaway

Introduction

Under Stalin Soviet society was effectively atomized by the prolonged application, over two decades, of mass terror. In an important if paradoxical sense, it was depoliticized. Since his death in 1953 a process of incipient repoliticization, or incipient pluralization, has begun, affecting both the *apparat* which rules the country and many groups outside it. The process was encouraged in various deliberate and nondeliberate ways by Khrushchev, but has developed much faster under his successors. This has been partly in reaction to their tendency to try to *discourage* it and, in important respects, to reverse it. One could also perhaps say that in the absence of a return to mass terror such a process has been inevitable. In any case, most of the groups outside the *apparat* have developed increasingly dissenting features, a trend which seems sure to continue.

Today the leadership of the *apparat* possesses enormous power—both internally, through the Committee of State Security (KGB) and other control mechanisms, and externally, through nuclear weapons and other forms of military might—but, probably, decreasing authority (at any rate at home). A similar situation, with similar potential dangers, existed, we might note in passing, in the last decades of the tsarist system, with which remarkably many parallels can be drawn before one risks incurring the charge of historicism. Today's leadership cannot, however, try to increase its authority by adopting a new ideology or seriously atoning for the past, as such a course appears to it much more risky—cf. Khrushchev's partial attempts—than "clinging on."

57

Why is this so? First, perhaps, because the post-Khrushchev leadership has systematically suppressed the issue of the mass crimes of Stalin, which involved, among other things, the death of some twenty million Soviet citizens through shooting, concentration camps, deportations, and artificial famine in the period 1930-1953. The leadership is therefore widely, if often subconsciously, linked with those crimes and with all the personal, social, and economic suffering which accompanied them, some of which persists to this day. A second reason is that Soviet Marxism-Leninism has become ossified, ritualized and almost universally— except within the Party apparatus, where it is the obligatory language—discredited or ignored. In this way an ideological vacuum has been created in society and even, potentially, within the *apparat*. It is this vacuum which the dissenting forces show some signs of beginning to fill, much to the alarm of the *apparat*.

Not surprisingly, therefore, the Soviet leaders continue firmly to reject the idea of "ideological coexistence" (as opposed to "peaceful coexistence"), as such coexistence would tend to facilitate and, even worse, legitimize the growth of a domestic opposition. Also, however moderate such an opposition's aims might in fact be, if it were "extra-systemic" its activities would always be liable to be regarded and branded by the regime as organized subversion.

Definitions of Dissent and Opposition

This brings us to the problem of defining dissent and opposition. Broadly, opposition implies an aspiration to rule in place of the existing rulers, whereas dissent indicates no such aspiration, just an objection to certain of the rulers' actions or policies. Thus Trotsky and his followers openly called themselves an opposition, even when exiled abroad. But the 2,000-odd documents and books of *samizdat* (underground press; lit: self-publishing) which have reached the West in the last decade from extra-systemic sources contain very few references to any "opposition" in the USSR today. Their authors use most frequently about themselves and their colleagues the word dissenters (*inakomyslyashchie*). And such people are usually regarded as expressing dissent (*inakomyslie*), either in their writings or by their "actions in defence of human (or national) rights."

Nonetheless, Soviet dissent should still be viewed as a seed-bed for opposition, and some of the dissenters as proto-oppositionists. For although most dissenters do not form conspiratorial groups or draft political programs, and thereby at least imply a desire to change the system and play a leading part in a new one, there are some who do, and the borderline between the two categories is often blurred. Also, there is the ambiguous phenomenon of those writings— like some of Sakharov's, Solzhenitsyn's, and Roy Medvedev's—which virtually amount to oppositional programs, but whose authors have shown little or no inclination to participate in collective oppositional (rather than dissenting) activity. This phenomenon could, perhaps, be called intellectual opposition.

Opposition Within the Apparat

Although the regime's greatest weakness is the inflexibility of itself and its *apparat* (terror no longer being available to cut through the various powerful vested interests), opposition can and does, as Conquest and others have shown, exist at the higher levels. It occurs on particular issues and groups of issues, but, as with the "anti-Party group" in the mid-1950s, it can quickly develop and embrace broad trends of policy. It is especially likely to appear when a power struggle is producing instability in the leadership.

Opposition within the *apparat* is, when it occurs, the only significant and fully political opposition to exist in the contemporary Soviet Union. But it exists only sporadically and is not usually easy to document. (In this volume it is discussed by Seweryn Bialer.) So this chapter will confine itself to a few comments about where Party leaders might in the future look if, as can be expected, they feel compelled to seek elsewhere for new ideas.

Already one can infer that certain sorts of unorthodox ideas attract, at any rate, small sections of the *apparat*. Roy Medvedev, although a rather isolated figure among the active dissenters, has evidently enjoyed enough protection from *apparatchiki* sympathetic to his brand of "socialism with a human face" to enable him to continue writing and publishing abroad. Sakharov's ideas about the interdependence of economic reform and political reform must have at least some potential advocates in the more intelligent sections of the central *apparat*. And, probably of greater significance, the Russian nationalist dissenters outside the *apparat* clearly enjoy high-level protection, as they have so far been virtually immune from arrest.

Soviet Law and KGB Practice in the Area of Dissent

The traditional Soviet tendency has been to see, or pretend to see, actual or potential opposition in almost all forms of persistent dissent. Yet it should be stressed at this point that the Criminal Code, in defining different types of political offense, does make a distinction between dissent and opposition, even though not in those terms. Opposition is punishable under, notably, articles 70 and 72, which concern "anti-Soviet agitation and propaganda" and "anti-Soviet organization," both conducted with the aim of weakening or overthrowing the Soviet system as a whole. The penalties are correspondingly severe. Article 190-1, by contrast, in practice concerns dissent. It penalizes the possession or propagation (in written or oral form) of "deliberate fabrications which discredit the Soviet political and social system." It is not concerned with agitation against the system as a whole, and so the penalties are relatively light (up to three years imprisonment or five years exile).

The fact that "deliberate fabrications," rather than "views objectionable to the state," are specified in article 190-1 can presumably be explained by an official desire not to contradict too blatantly the constitutional guarantee of freedom of conscience. Yet, partly due to the dissenters' efforts, this fact has a definitely inhibiting effect on the KGB in some cases. In others, however, the well-documented pleas of defendants that they have propagated no fabrications, let alone deliberate ones, are simply ignored by the courts (acting on Party or police instructions), which sentence them regardless. The dissenters' only satisfaction then is that they have clearly revealed the kangaroo nature of the proceedings.

Similarly, the KGB has to consider carefully, in some cases, whether it has enough evidence to prosecute under, say, article 70, or whether it must content itself with article 190-1. The strength or weakness of their inhibitions in any particular case depend on many factors: are they operating in Moscow (under the eyes of activists and foreigners), or in the provinces (where arbitrariness knows fewer restraints)? Is the defendant skillful in his own defence and would he be able effectively to expose evidence they might fabricate? Has he managed to outmaneuver them and secure the services of one of the few lawyers who will vigorously defend him? And what are the operational guidelines of the moment from their political masters?

The KGB is, then, subject to certain political and legal restraints in its handling of dissent. More than this, ever since the arrest of Beria, the reduction of his empire, and this empire's subordination to close Party control, the regime has taken pains to bureaucratize the KGB, and thus to ensure that it can never again be used to destroy the Party leadership as it did in the 1930s. The regime has achieved this partly through introducing (in the 1950s) laws to limit the KGB's powers, and partly through appointing men from the Party apparatus to head the organization, follow Politbureau guidelines, and prevent the reemergence of any tendencies to autonomy.

The dissenters, too, impose restraints. As discussed above, they try to take full advantage of the more liberal laws. They also, with equal skill, use the weapon of publicity through *samizdat*, foreign news media, and Western radio stations broadcasting to the USSR. In this way they increase the political cost of planned KGB repressions and sometimes mitigate or even prevent them.

Mainstream Dissent Outside the Apparat

Manifestations of "mainstream" dissent first appeared in the mid-1950s. But a genuine human rights movement, in which different groups consciously cooperated with each other, began to emerge only in 1965-67. The main catalyst was the Ukrainian and Moscow arrests of 1965. These alarmed the more critical minds among the professional classes, which had become accustomed, since 1953, to a significant degree of security and stability in their lives, to an at least embryonic rule of law. These minds had also been pondering for some years the phenomenon of Stalinism and drawing the lesson that unless one resists tyranny firmly from the start, the tyrant will soon eliminate the chance of any resistance at all. They therefore felt that the 1965 arrests, coming at the same time as the tightening of the censorship and the banning of public discussion of Stalinism, might well signal a regeneration of Stalinism and that they must resist at once before it was too late.

This attitude of "Never again!", stimulated by further political arrests in 1967 and the trial of the young intellectuals Galanskov and Ginzburg, brought the human rights movement to maturity in 1968. In this year the *Chronicle of Current Events* began to appear, every two months, and to act as a forum and "information center" for all the main groups.

The most important prerequisite for this achievement by the dissenters—and also for all others—was the breaking of a series of social and political taboos, which were several decades old, and the creation of a certain atmosphere among a small section of the intelligentsia in various large cities. In this atmosphere people dared to think and act independently of the authorities, to create formal and semiformal associations, to intercede for persecuted individuals and groups, to send information and texts of intercessions to the editors of the *Chronicle* in Moscow, to give similar material to foreign journalists, tourists, and diplomats, to listen systematically to foreign radio stations and then circulate the information obtained, to turn *samizdat* into a large-scale cottage industry, to stage demonstrations, to propose to the authorities carefully drafted proposals for law reform and so on. In this atmosphere the *Chronicle* could appear and, with luck, survive.

What have been its editorial principles? It avoids value judgments, it reports factually and objectively on events connected with human or national rights, and it summarizes new works circulating in *samizdat*. Its liberal political position is implied by the article of the "Universal Declaration of Human Rights (No. 19)," which it carries regularly on its masthead: "Everyone has the right to freedom of opinion and expression; this right includes freedom to hold opinions without interference and to seek, receive and impart information and ideas through any media and regardless of frontiers." Its economic position is not stated, but its overall attitudes showed clearly enough in the atmosphere of enthusiasm (and then mourning) for the "Czechoslovak Spring," which some of its pages reflected.

The *Chronicle*'s editors were, and still are, anonymous, as are the news items and articles, but not usually the documents, which it carries. But much is now known of its methods of compilation. Its editors have changed and rotated quite often, and very few people have known for sure who they were at any particular moment. Material for inclusion has been passed to these few people along chains which have developed on the basis of personal friendship and trust. The method of distribution has been the standard one for *samizdat*: typescripts passed from hand to hand, constantly being retyped in ten copies on onionskin paper.

Throughout its first two or three years the *Chronicle* steadily expanded its geographical coverage and its size. By 1971 it had published material from most of the major population centers of the European and Central Asian areas of the Soviet Union, as well as from a few labor camps and cities in Siberia. The most prominent cities over the years have been Moscow, Leningrad, Kiev, Lviv, Vilnius, Kaunas, Riga, Tallin, Gorky, Novosibirsk, and Tashkent.

The *Chronicle*'s subject matter, apart from the *samizdat* summaries, can be categorized as information on: the judicial or extra-judicial persecution of individuals for expression of their views; on the severe conditions in the labor camps and mental hospitals used to imprison dissenters; on the persecution of minority nationalities and religious believers; on the activities of the censorship and a few other oppressive institutions; and on reactions to the dissenters' situation in the outside world. Underlying all the *Chronicle*'s reporting has been an insistent concern for legality, for the observation of Soviet laws (in their more liberal interpretation), and for subtly educating its readers in how to use their legal rights to promote the democratization of society. Other notable features have been the *Chronicle*'s size and the accuracy, concreteness and detailed nature of its information: an average issue is 10-15,000 words long; the first thirty-two issues contain nearly 4,000 different names (about half belonging to dissenters and a third to officials and their collaborators). It has made no reporting errors of substance; and it has corrected most of its minor errors in subsequent issues. In the underground conditions of its compilation and editing, clearly unusual care has been needed to attain this level of accuracy.

The "mainstream" dissent movement, as opposed to the related but largely separate national and religious movements, has so far been supported at various times by only some two thousand people whose names we know. However, it has a considerably larger number of sympathizers, who read *samizdat* publications and help it in various ways, but prefer not to put their names to documents or protests. Socially, the movement is overwhelmingly middle-class. Among its informal leaders are a high percentage of people from research institutes, including a disproportionately high number of mathematicians and physicists. Other leaders and supporters are engineers, teachers, lawyers, writers, artists, journalists, and students, with a very small number of workers and military men.

The movement has only been organized in the loosest sense, through personal contacts and a feeling of common purpose in difficult and often dangerous circumstances. That it would lose much of this unity if the regime were one day to liberalize and to ease the pressures on it is certain. The moral concerns which hold it together are a common humanitarianism, a common insistence on legality, and a common moral opposition to the oppressive methods of the regime. Hence it views itself not as a political but as a human rights movement, a movement which asserts the worth of the individual vis-à-vis the omnipotence and frequent brutality of the state.

This said, we may now look more closely at the main political, ideological and philosophical tendencies within it.

Neo-Leninists and Neo-Marxists

A small and apparently declining sector consider (or considered) themselves neo-Leninists or neo-Marxists. Some of these have formed groups with names like "True Communists," which the KGB has usually broken up without much difficulty. People such as the late writer Alexei Kosterin and ex-Major-General Pyotr Grigorenko have tried to promote a return to Leninist ideals within the Party, but have found little response and been expelled. Kosterin died in 1968, and Grigorenko was imprisoned in a psychiatric hospital. The historian Roy Medvedev has pursued a similar line in a very different and less idealistic style, but also with little apparent success. The absorbing *Political Diary*, produced in his circles, shows in some detail how the *apparat* reacted over the years 1964-70 to this political trend, and how it moved against it with increased decisiveness after seeing what a similar (if much stronger) trend could produce in Czechoslovakia in 1968. Nonetheless, Medvedev has so far been allowed to keep the small flame of liberal communism alight in the USSR, perhaps because elements in the *apparat* believe that the regime might one day need to turn in that direction.

Liberals and Humanitarians

The second trend in the mainstream, and much the most important, can be described as liberal and humanitarian. Many people in it would call themselves apolitical supporters of ordinary human decency. Their more politically minded colleagues would probably not reject the Western labels liberal, liberal Socialist, or, in the case of the Orthodox layman Anatoly Levitin, Christian socialist. This is the trend which is evident in the *Chronicle of Current Events* and which includes people like Pavel Litvinov, Larissa Bogoraz, Natalya Gorbanevskaya, Victor Nekrasov, and Andrei Sakharov.

Sakharov is one of the more politically minded adherents of the trend, who regards himself as having moved from neo-Marxism to Liberalism since the mid-1960s. But he is typical of it in his tactics and his values. Skillfully using his semi-protected position as a famous scientist, he has done more than anyone else to legitimize in practice the constitutional right to communicate truthful information at home and abroad. Such communication has now been performed so often with impunity by Sakharov, and by others operating to some extent under his wing, that it has become increasingly difficult for the KGB to prosecute producers of the *Chronicle*, which regularly publishes truthful information. (Naturally the KGB's guidelines could always be changed in the future, to obviate the dilemma.)

The humanitarians believe in the liberal principle of helping any individuals or groups which are being persecuted for their beliefs. Thus they maintain links with a wide variety of national, religious, and cultural groups. They study the problems of these groups, transmit their petitions, journals, and appeals abroad,

give these documents to foreign visitors and journalists, and publish them in full
or in summary in the *Chronicle*. They also run an unofficial Red Cross system of
welfare and support for political prisoners and their families. Money and
clothing are collected from well-off sympathizers and distributed to those in
need. Money also comes from Sakharov and Solzhenitsyn, out of funds they
have set up abroad, using income from their publications and from literary and
humanitarian prizes. In addition to much ad hoc activity, regular meetings are
held in Moscow flats, where relatives of political prisoners congregate, often
from distant corners of the country, to exchange information and experiences,
obtain legal advice, and, as their family incomes have often dropped to zero,
communicate their material needs.

Liberal Russian Nationalists

The third and last broad trend can be labeled liberal Russian nationalist. This
label distinguishes it from the chauvinistic variety, which will be discussed later
in a broader review of recent forms of dissenting Russian nationalism. This trend
is not particularly strong or influential, but the presence in it of one man,
Solzhenitsyn, however uncomfortably he fits, suggests that it may become
stronger. Solzhenitsyn belongs in part, in fact, in the previous category, to which
many of his friends also belong, since humanitarianism and human rights
(especially opposition to censorship) figure strongly among his preoccupations
and exist alongside his predominant concern: the moral regeneration of the
Russian nation and the rebirth of Russian culture; but his "Open Letter to the
Soviet Leaders," published in 1974, clarifies matters and puts him indisputably
among the liberal nationalists.

Vladimir Osipov, for three years the chief editor of the *samizdat* journal
Veche, calls himself a "liberal patriot." He has friends among the liberals, but
strongly supports Solzhenitsyn's political position, and has consistently propagated in *Veche* the virtues of the nineteenth century Slavophiles, whom
Solzhenitsyn also admires. In early 1974 Osipov was ousted from the *Veche*
editorship by apparently less liberal elements, but soon founded a new journal of
his own, *Zemlya* (Earth), only to be arrested in November of that year. It
remains to be seen how strong support for his position will be, and also whether
the KGB will ultimately regard the liberal or the right-wing nationalists as more
dangerous. The question of why it regarded Solzhenitsyn as more dangerous
than any other dissenter, and therefore deported him abroad by force, is clearer.
His *Gulag Archipelago*, in particular, undermines the regime in passionate
language at what are probably two of its most vulnerable points: its past record
of mass crimes and its now widely discredited ideology.

The Relation of the Mainstream Dissenters to the West

The values of the dominant trend in the mainstream dissent movement are, broadly speaking, similar to Western democratic ideals. The dissenters have therefore, with one or two exceptions, expected that the Western democracies will support them, and have sent a continuous stream of appeals to them to do so. The response of the West has been much less than the dissenters hoped, but it has been more than nothing. The West's most important responses have probably been, first, the contribution of Western radio stations (especially Radio Liberty, which devotes up to a quarter of its broadcast time to *samizdat*) and, second, the determination of some governments and newspapers to try to defend the limited rights of Western journalists in the USSR. However, "détente" has worried some dissenters, notably Sakharov, because while they support it fully in principle, they fear that the regime will succeed in conducting it on its own selfish terms, and in exploiting what they see as Western opportunism and naïveté. In this way, they fear, the West may be lulled into a false and dangerous sense of security, and the regime may be able both to postpone reform (especially economic) at home and to suppress more easily the growth of democratic trends.

To some extent their fears may, so far, have proved justified. Governments which have publicly criticized the South African, Brazilian, Greek, Spanish, Chilean, and other authoritarian regimes have preferred not to criticize publicly (or even, apparently, privately) the USSR's suppression of human rights and its treatment of political prisoners in forced labor camps and mental hospitals. In particular, the deliberate silence of the Nixon-Kissinger administration on these issues probably enabled the KGB to be considerably more repressive than the Politbureau would otherwise have permitted.

The one occasion on which a few governments (but not the American) spoke up was in the autumn of 1973, when a virulent campaign against Solzhenitsyn and Sakharov was launched in the Soviet media. This episode did however see a certain breakthrough in nongovernmental, liberal opinion in the West, which opinion, by its interventions, succeeded in acting as an at least temporary brake on KGB repression. An important lead was given by a statement of America's National Academy of Sciences in defence of Sakharov, and much liberal opinion—in the press and in organizations like the International PEN Club, the American Academy of Arts and Sciences, Amnesty International, etc.—followed suit. Thus, we might note, the situation of the late tsarist period may have been recreated. At that time equivalent opinion was strongly critical of the autocracy, while Western governments generally held their fire, not apparently realizing sufficiently that the noble causes of constitutional government and international stability would not be served if the autocracy reformed itself too little and too late.

Mainstream Dissent and its Impact on the Regime

The dissenters have not claimed that they constitute a powerful pressure group, nor that they make a continuous impact on the regime's policies. Yet we have seen the danger which the regime ascribes to Solzhenitsyn's writings, and the Politbureau must often have taken the dissenters into account when deciding, for example, how much to rehabilitate Stalin, how far it could afford to tighten political control, whether to make the censorship more severe (which would divert still more works into *samizdat*), whether to continue its internment of dissenters in mental hospitals (a convenient device internally, but politically embarrassing abroad), whether to ease its emigration policy, and so on.

Above all, perhaps, the mainstream dissenters have had an impact on the regime in two indirect but powerful ways. First, their writings and their example have probably had a considerable impact in persuading Western opinion of the continuingly oppressive nature of the Soviet system. In a period when, in reaction to the prolonged tensions of the cold war, some Western opinion has felt inclined to take Soviet assurances and intentions at face value, this role could probably not have been filled as effectively by anyone else. And second, the dissenters have, by breaking out of "the inertia of fear," provided a powerful example of behavior to other oppressed groups in Soviet society. Their books and protests, and the *Chronicle*, have been systematically sent abroad and then broadcast back to the USSR on Radio Liberty and other stations and listened to by several millions of people. Some of the latter have belonged to a wide range of groups which, as we shall see below, have gradually found the means and the resolution to imitate the dissenters' methods and take advantage of their services.

Mainstream Dissent and its Prospects

But however much impact the dissenters have or have not made, in late 1971 that impact became too much for the regime to continue tolerating at the then existing level. A high-level decision was taken to suppress the *Chronicle* and other major *samizdat* activities at all costs. A contributory factor in the decision, many dissenters believe, was an assurance allegedly given by the Nixon administration, as it laid the groundwork for "détente," that it would not make a public issue, or even protest, about the Soviet suppression of dissent. There is no evidence that such an assurance was given, but, as mentioned above, no protests were in fact made. Indeed, President Nixon and Dr. Kissinger on several occasions in my view appeared to imply that protests should not be made by nongovernmental bodies either.

In any case, in January 1972, as preparations were being made for Nixon's first visit to Moscow as president, the KGB struck at the *Chronicle* and its

Ukrainian equivalent, the *Ukrainian Herald*. In the course of 1972 several hundreds of flat-searches and interrogations were conducted in the case against the *Chronicle*, in a variety of cities, and a dozen or so arrests were made. The breakthrough came late in the year, when two well-known Moscow dissenters, Pyotr Yakir and Victor Krasin, began to collaborate with the investigators after several months in prison. With a mass of detailed information from these men the KGB eventually succeeded in silencing the *Chronicle*, driving some of their associates into emigration under threat of long-term imprisonment, imprisoning others, and intimidating yet others. Much of the intricate network of *Chronicle* correspondents and distributors was uncovered, and 1973 was a year of reduced and less coordinated activity. Indeed, the movement per se sank to a low ebb, as the *Chronicle* had, in effect, been its principal collective expression. Nonetheless, many networks continued to function, funneling information and documents to the outside world in as large quantities as before, partly perhaps in response to the founding of the "substitute" *Chronicle of Human Rights in the USSR* in New York.

In September 1973 the KGB launched its media campaign against the two most formidable dissenting figures, Sakharov and Solzhenitsyn, presumably planning to arrest or deport them and thus acquire greater control over the movement. At this moment, however, when, ironically, mainstream dissent was in considerable confusion, Western opinion at last spoke up. As a result, over the next few months, the KGB presumably received new guidelines from the Politbureau, the remaining dissenters took courage, a new coordinated network gradually took shape, and, in May 1974, the *Chronicle* reemerged with four large issues to fill in most of the backlog since its suppression.

To sum up, at least half the leaders of the "first generation" of mainstream dissent had, by the end of 1974, been more or less neutralized through imprisonment, emigration, exhaustion, intimidation or death. But a second generation had begun to appear, and it seemed to be heartened by the increased vigor and cooperation of a wide range of dissenting groups outside the mainstream. If, though, as may be surmised, the humanitarian mainstream is too Western-oriented, too apolitical, and too rational ever to develop widespread support in the USSR, then, if the politicization of society should gather speed, more politically minded dissenters may divert an increasing amount of their energies elsewhere. But the services of a basically humanitarian movement seem likely to be needed for the foreseeable future, and the moral strength of the present movement will probably prove to be more than the KGB can break.

Dissent Among the National Minorities

It is questionable whether the KGB has become more concerned over the last decade about mainstream or nationalities dissent. For the latter might eventually, as Amalrik has predicted, lead to the fragmentation of Russia's borderlands, as happened in 1917-21.

The evidence suggests that significant and growing currents of opinion in a number of the Union republics feel that their nations did not achieve after 1917 (or 1944) the liberation from Russification and Russian imperialism which the Bolsheviks appeared to promise them and which was justified by their growing national consciousness (similar to that of many other peoples in the world's disintegrating empires). Such currents of opinion have been strongest in those republics and areas which the USSR annexed during World War Two: here the brutality of the annexations ensured that there were fewer illusions about Soviet intentions.

National dissent in the republics has opposed, mainly, two separate but interconnected policies: first, the camouflaged but persistent policy of Russification, which manifests itself in the promotion of things Russian and in discrimination against minority languages, traditions, literatures, cultures, and religions, and also in the officially sponsored settlement of minority areas with Russians (or other Slavs). And second, this dissent has opposed the policy in practice—despite the facade of a federal structure which enshrines the sovereignty of the national republics—of dictating all important political and economic policies from Moscow.

The national dissenters have based their protests and demands on the law and the constitution and thus, not surprisingly, have had common interests and regular contacts with the mainstream dissenters. They have also found sympathy on occasion from the local Party leaders, whose loyalty to the center—particularly over economic exploitation by Moscow—has apparently sometimes become weaker than their loyalty to their nation. If this last phenomenon should become more common in the future, involving, as it does, a major potential vulnerability of the Soviet system, then it could probably be said that the nationalities problem would become the regime's first preoccupation in the area of dissent. Already it is a major factor inhibiting potential liberal reforms by the regime, although it is also possible that, for example, the Lithuanian Catholics might eventually, by the militancy of their dissent, induce the regime to revise the whole of its elaborate antireligious policy.

The Ukraine

Ukrainian dissent has a long and complex history, but stems, in its contemporary form, mainly from Khrushchev's policy of increased Russification, introduced at the end of the 1950s. This stimulated dissent in literary and other circles, but, although several groups were arrested each year and their members sentenced (in a few cases to death), little suppression of socially more established dissenters occurred until 1965. Then, concurrently with the arrests of Sinyavsky and

Daniel in Moscow, twenty Ukrainian intellectuals were also arrested and sentenced to up to six years each. Their cases were documented in *The Chornovil Papers*, the compilation of a young Lviv journalist, Vyacheslav Chornovil. In his long introduction, written in early 1966, Chornovil used to great effect the juridical approach developed in subsequent years by the mainstream dissenters. As the Ukrainian dissenters have maintained regular ties with the latter, their problems have been well covered in the *Chronicle*.

For his book, Chornovil served eighteen months in a labor camp, but with this and one other exception there were no arrests of well-known people in the Ukraine from 1966 until December 1971. This was the period when the first Party secretary, Petro Shelest, tried to establish a *modus vivendi* with the Ukrainian intelligentsia. The other exception was the historian Valentyn Moroz, who was imprisoned for four years (1965-1969), and was resentenced in 1970 to fourteen years of prison and exile for his writings. These powerful essays concern human and national individuality and concentrate especially on the rebuilding of Ukrainian nationhood.

But, as noted above, the KGB's major move came in January 1972. At this point, with Shelest's political position slipping fast and Shcherbytsky replacing him in May, the KGB arrested at least fifty dissenters and sentenced each to an average of nearly ten years of prison and exile. In this way the *Ukrainian Herald*, which had published six large issues in *samizdat* over two years, was soon suppressed, and with it, for a period, articulate national dissent. In 1974, however, soon after the reappearance of the Moscow *Chronicle*, it reemerged. Nonetheless, Ukrainian dissent sustained in 1972 the heaviest single KGB assault since 1953 of any dissenting group, and so it remains to be seen how quickly it will recover. When it does so, it will probably be stronger as a result of its new martyrs and it will have more chance of extending its roots from the intelligentsia into the working class, which may, especially in the west Ukraine, prove to be more fertile soil than can at present be demonstrated in documents.

Lithuania

For whatever the potential strength of Ukrainian dissent, it has at no stage (since the 1940s) been a mass movement. The only republic whose national movement has achieved this status so far is Lithuania. Here the interlocked national and Catholic traditions, reminiscent of Poland, and the relatively small number of non-Lithuanians in the population of three million have facilitated the growth of a movement which the KGB seems powerless to stop. The movement began in the late 1960s among groups of Catholic priests, who protested against the restrictions imposed on the printing of Bibles and religious literature, on the admission of students to seminaries, and on the freedom of action of the hierarchy. In 1971 the arrest of two priests stimulated unrest and, although they received only one-year sentences, in early 1972 the *Chronicle of the Lithuanian Catholic Church* began to appear in *samizdat* and 17,000 signatures were collected for a petition to appeal to Dr. Waldheim to intervene and bring religious persecution to an end. In May 1972 riots broke out in Kaunas, Lithuania's second city, after a student had burned himself to death in protest against the persecution of religion and of national traditions.

Since then the situation has remained tense, with the *Chronicle of the Lithuanian Catholic Church* appearing regularly and with occasional arrests and trials. By early 1976 twenty large issues of the *Chronicle* had come out, edited in a more militant style than most other *samizdat* journals and calling repeatedly for support from the Vatican and Christians abroad. The most determined KGB drive against it was launched in November 1973 with a large wave of searches and interrogations, and some arrests, in various cities and villages. To date, though, evidently in deference to the mass nature of the dissent, the authorities have refrained with few exceptions from imposing long sentences at political trials.

Armenia, Latvia, Estonia, Georgia, and Moldavia

In Armenia, Latvia, and Estonia national movements clearly exist, but are much weaker than those in Lithuania and the Ukraine. Their exact strength is still difficult to gauge, as few documents are available. Those at hand suggest that the Lithuanian example may have started to infect Latvia and Estonia, where small dissenting groups have been arrested, but the results are unlikely to be as dramatic as in Lithuania. Neither of these two republics is united around a single national religion, and each has a higher proportion of Russian settlers.

In Armenia national and religious traditions are intertwined, as in Lithuania, but memories of the Turkish massacres appear to have acted as something of a brake on the growth of the national movement. The latter seems to have developed at the end of the 1960s. Major arrests and trials of dissenters occurred in 1968-70 and 1973-74. The KGB's "clamp-down" of 1973 was launched on the same day, November 19, as its parallel operation in Lithuania.

In Georgia documentary *samizdat* evidence of national dissent began to appear only in 1973. One catalyst appears to have been the removal, in 1972, of First Party Secretary Mzhavanadze and the drive of his successor, Shevardnadze, against corruption. Another catalyst was a revolt by laymen and priests against the serious corruption of the hierarchy of the Georgian Orthodox Church. But although the Armenian example may prove infectious, the contribution of the church revolt to the national stirrings is likely to be limited, as the church is in general much weaker in Georgia than in Armenia, let alone in Lithuania or the western Ukraine. There is, however, interesting evidence of the influence on some Georgian dissenters of the mainstream dissenters in Moscow. In Moldavia national stirrings favor, as might be expected, the return of the republic to the Romanian motherland which, with its militant nationalism, has not refrained from hinting that it would also favor Moldavia's reunion with it.

Belorussia and, even more, Azerbaidzhan, it should be noted, show little sign of nationalist stirrings. The Central Asian republics are a more complex phenomenon; they have not yet produced any *samizdat* documents except those by the exiled minorities to be discussed below. Anti-Russian nationalism and pan-Islamicism clearly exist, but they have not yet progressed, apparently, beyond moods and attitudes, occasional minor riots, and what dissenting scholars can convey between the lines of their writings.

The Dissent of National Minorities Without Their Own Republics

Attention will now be turned to a different source of national dissent, those peoples who wish, in large numbers, to emigrate from the USSR or to return from their places of internal exile to their homelands inside the USSR.

The Jews

The best known of these peoples are the Jews, whose national movement has, since 1969-70, received wide publicity. The movement's development is of special interest and importance, as the Jews are not tucked away in a corner of the Soviet Union like all the peoples described above except the Ukrainians. They are, on the contrary, scattered in many parts of the country, especially in its large cities, where some of them occupy important positions in the economy, the arts, higher education, research, and the professions.

In the late 1960s the still extant traces of the Russian Zionism of forty years earlier received a boost from the Israeli victory in the Six-Day War and the emerging human rights movement, in which many Jews participated. The result, especially as the KGB pressed down increasingly on the human rights movement, was the rapid development of a movement to emigrate to Israel. The movement spread quickly from Kiev, Moscow, and the Baltic to Georgia, Leningrad, Kharkov, Novosibirsk, Sverdlovsk, and Central Asia. Imitating the methods of the mainstream dissenters, the Jews produced a *samizdat* journal, *Exodus*, adopted the juridical approach in appealing to the authorities, staged demonstrations and sit-ins, and passed news and other materials to foreign journalists. The Jews also pioneered a new method, soon imitated by the dissenters, of communicating regularly with the West by international telephone, dictating whole documents onto tape recorders in London, Paris, New York, and San Francisco.

At first the authorities resisted. But in 1970-71, as the Jewish lobby in the West began to operate and as the thwarted would-be emigrants resorted to increasingly militant methods, including the planned hijacking of a plane, the KGB had little choice but to yield. The other options were presumably unacceptable. To put thousands of Jews in camps was impossible for reasons of foreign policy, and was anyway no longer, for a fully bureaucratized KGB, an easy task. But to tolerate the status quo, in which the Jews were, with virtual impunity, providing an example of militancy to many other oppressed groups in various cities, at the same time that anti-Soviet publicity was building up abroad, was also impossible.

So the gates were unlocked and in 1974 the one hundred thousandth Jew pushed through them. A radical change in emigration policy had been forced on the regime, a change which the "Jackson Amendment" capitalized on, but in no way initiated. However, the Soviet abrogation in January 1975 of the U.S.-USSR Trade Agreement of 1972 did result in a sharp decline in Jewish emigration. Were it to rise again, the major limiting factor in the future might turn out to be the capacity of Israel and the West to absorb it. At the same time, the regime can be expected to detain various Jewish scientists and other economically valuable people for considerable periods before letting them go. Meanwhile some of them will probably continue to give support of various kinds to the mainstream dissenters, especially in Moscow.

The Soviet Germans

The Soviet Germans, at present almost two million in number, were deported by Stalin after the Nazi invasion of 1941, and as a result lost their Autonomous Republic on the Volga. In 1955 the punitive exile regime imposed on them was lifted, but not until 1964 were they legally exculpated of the alleged crime of having helped the Nazi invaders en masse. These easings of their position were closely connected with the evolution of Soviet-West German relations. But their long campaign for permission to return to their homeland and to have their Autonomous Republic restored had still, in 1976, been unsuccessful. Many decided in the early 1970s that the struggle was hopeless and were impressed by Jewish emigration.

Thus a German emigration movement emerged, using the same militant tactics as the Jews. In 1974 close links were established with the mainstream dissenters, demonstrations were staged in Moscow and Tallin, and a *samizdat* journal, *Re Patria*, began to appear.

Again, militancy, helped by the conjuncture of Brandt's *Ostpolitik*, appears to have paid off. In the years 1972-74 some 10,000 Germans reached West Germany, and the rate rose steadily to some 4,000 per year. Few Germans seem to have gone to East Germany. As with the Jews, though, Soviet policy has been two-pronged: some forty Zionist Jews were, in late 1974, in labor camps, along with about twenty-five activists of the German movement. Although the Soviet Germans number about a million fewer than the Jews, their movement seems likely to have become a strong one and is supported with growing resolution in West Germany. Thus, the emigration of Soviet Germans has figured increasingly prominently in negotiations between the Soviet and West German governments.

The Meskhetians

The Meskhetians are a small Turkic people, of probably less than 200,000 people, on the south Georgian border with Turkey. In November 1944 they were deported by Stalin to Central Asia, evidently to clear possible opposition from the path of a planned Soviet advance into Turkey. No charges were preferred against them and, in the mid-1950s, the punitive regime imposed on those who survived the deportation was lifted. At once they began a campaign to be allowed to return home, organizing "congresses of the people" at which, in the mid-1960s, 6,000 delegates elected campaign committees. They also sent emissaries to Moscow to lobby both official bodies and, to greater effect, the circles which produced the *Chronicle*.

In 1971 they began to demand the right to emigrate to their brothers and fellow-Muslims in Turkey if the authorities would not let them return home. By 1976 the Turkish government had shown no public readiness to accept them and apparently none of them had received exit permits. As the regime has apparently opposed their return home for strategic reasons, the problem they present will presumably fester until such time as emigration is allowed.

The Crimean Tatars

The recent history of the Crimean Tatars has certain similarities to that of the Meskhetians. Their deportation in 1944 was, however, punishment for their alleged wholesale collaboration with the Germans, and not until 1967 did they win the removal of this charge from the record. Nearly half of them had died as a result of the deportation to Central Asia and elsewhere, and the survivors had undergone a punitive exile regime until 1956. From that point on a powerful, democratically organized campaign to return home was launched, with similar features to that of the Meskhetians. The Moscow dissenters, led by Kosterin and Grigorenko, took up the Tatars' cause with vigor, but to no avail. Between 1956 and 1974 over 200 members of their movement were imprisoned, and thousands who returned to the Crimea without permission were expelled.

Presumably, again, strategic reasons have inhibited the regime from allowing them home. And presumably the problems of this notably united people of nearly half-a-million will continue to generate dissent until the authorities relent. If the government refuses to relent, the Tatars, too, may be driven to demand emigration to Turkey, their traditional haven for over two centuries when times have been bad in Russia. But the mere demand, as is true of the Meskhetians, may not produce any satisfaction.

Nor have the numerous Crimean Tatar appeals to the UN and other bodies abroad helped them much as yet. World opinion has been as indifferent to their situation as it has to the Meskhetians', in contrast to its response to the Jews.

Russian Nationalist Dissent

Russian nationalist dissent of the variety less liberal than Solzhenitsyn's or Osipov's is an important, but still little studied sector in the spectrum of dissent. To put it in perspective a brief review of the full range of semi-legitimate and extra-system Russian nationalism since the early 1960s may be useful. Its emergence at that time was probably provoked in part by Khrushchev's orthodox Marxist-Leninist position on the nationalities and religious questions, as embodied in the new Party program of 1961. This position tended to injure those Russian as well as Ukrainian (and other) national feelings which had been developing during the gradual de-atomization of society in the 1950s. Hence the emergence in 1964 of both the officially approved "Motherland" (*Rodina*) clubs and the liberal nationalist underground group of Leningrad Social-Christians and, in 1965 of the "All-Russian Society for the Preservation of Historical and Cultural Monuments." The blossoming of this society, whose membership reached three million in a year and seven million by 1972, suggested that the new Party leadership hoped to gain popular support by making concessions to national feelings. Further evidence of benevolent tolerance, or even support, in high places were the thinly disguised neo-Slavophile writings which appeared in a leading Komsomol organ, *Molodaya gvardiya*, in 1967-70, discreetly propagating disapproval of industrialism and proletarian internationalism, while approving of various traditions and qualities associated with the Orthodox Church and the Russian nation.

But official tolerance declined in 1970. In November *Molodaya gvardiya*'s chief editor, Anatoly Nikonov, was dismissed and replaced by a Central Committee apparatchik and a few months later one of his neo-Slavophile contributors, Yury D. Ivanov, was fired from his post at Moscow University. The main response to this came within two months of Nikonov's removal, when Osipov and others founded the *samizdat* journal *Veche* for Russian patriots loyal but not subservient to the regime. Almost at once, from the summer of 1971, the KGB reacted by threatening Osipov with arrest and harassing him and his wife. But soon the 1972 campaign against the *Chronicle* and the *Ukrainian Herald* took precedence, and only in 1973 did the KGB go beyond harassment of *Veche.* This was done by sponsoring efforts to "coopt" the journal to assume a position more acceptable to the regime; *Veche* would disown Orthodoxy and anti-industrialism in favor of neo-paganism, virulent anti-Semitism, and recognition of the Party as the preserver of national unity and stability against the many threats of disintegration which faced the country. When this attempt foundered on the issue of Orthodoxy which apparently united the producers of *Veche,* the KGB opened a criminal investigation against *Veche* and its numerous supporters and in this way forced Osipov at last, in March 1974, to close it down after nine book-length issues. Soon, though, a different *Veche* faction, accused by Osipov and his supporters of unsavory collaboration with the authorities, revived it. The new group put out a tenth issue, denounced Osipov for alleged personal misdemeanors, and, while showing some signs of a shift "to the right," asserted its intention to continue the established line. But in July this group, too, closed *Veche* down under pressure of an investigation by the KGB. When Osipov, who described himself in 1974 as a "liberal patriot," then started *Zemlya (The Earth),* his arrest, as noted above, swiftly followed.

All this suggests that in late 1974 the regime was trying, by neutralizing the most independent figures, to bring the dissenting Russian nationalists as closely into line as possible, but, by largely avoiding arrests, to keep their alienation to a minimum. However, as a number of *Veche* collaborators, including several of the Leningrad Social-Christians, had remained unbroken by their camp-terms, and as one of these, Leonid Borodin, started another new publication, *Moscow Almanac (Moskovskii sbornik)* in September 1974, it seemed doubtful whether the KGB would achieve any easy *Gleichschaltung.* At the same time the patrons of the *Molodaya gvardiya* line of 1967-70, whoever they may have been, had clearly retained considerable power since 1970. The first detailed, high-level rebuttal of this line (which began to reappear in *Nash sovremmenik*) had reportedly been barred by them from publication for nearly a year, prior to its appearance in late 1972, and shortly thereafter its author, A. Yakovlev, acting head of the Propaganda Department of the Central Committee, was removed from his post and "exiled" to Canada as ambassador. The notably defensive tone of his article made this development less surprising than it would otherwise have been.

Veche was concerned primarily with the thought of Slavophils, nationalists and neo-Slavophils; the Orthodox Church and religious thought; Alexander Solzhenitsyn; problems of ecology and the preservation of old Russian architecture; literary and musical themes; and the collapse of moral standards, genuine culture, and self-respect in the Russian nation. Broadly speaking, *Veche* may be said to have represented all the main Christian tendencies—liberal, centrist, and rightist—within dissenting Russian nationalism, with its editorial position more on the liberal side. The word "liberal" implies, in this context, not a commitment to classical political liberalism and a multiparty system, but rather a desire for a liberalized, benevolently authoritarian regime incorporating the best traditions of the Russian nation as well as a liberal attitude on issues such as political censorship, anti-Semitism, the right of minority republics to secession, and the permissibility of publicly criticizing the Orthodox Patriarch and the Hierarchy. In these terms, Solzhenitsyn and Osipov are liberal nationalists and can be distinguished from centrist and right-wing tendencies. This said, though, it is worth noting the view (however debatable) of A.M. Ivanov, writing under his pen-name A. Skuratov in *Veche* No. 10, that *Veche*'s supporters completely share the basic position of Solzhenitsyn as expressed in his "Open Letter to the Soviet Leaders."

In any case, the right-wing fascistic tendency is relatively weakly expressed in *Veche*. This tendency is more often atheistic or pagan, it glorifies strong leaders like Stalin and even (for his Jewish policy) Hitler, and it has a world view permeated by belief in a world Jewish conspiracy as set forth in "The Protocols of the Elders of Zion." By 1976 only a few documents of this tendency were as yet available, although some had, in disguised form, achieved official publication. It was still impossible to gauge the strength of the support in regime circles for either this tendency or the *Veche* tendencies. Even more unclear was how much this support was based on any belief in the ideas themselves, and how much on the view that they might prove a useful instrument in intra-Party struggles, in the way that anti-Semitism was used by the Polish leadership during the struggles of the late 1960s. It should be remembered, though, as Seweryn Bialer points out, that the "take-over" generation of *apparatchiki*, now in their mid- to late 50s, was formed politically during the ultra-patriotic years of the Second World War.

Religious Dissent

Religious dissent has a somewhat marginal political element to it, as most religious dissenters—of whom there are many varieties, including even Buddhists—simply want greater freedom for religion and are not concerned much about politics (except where religion is intertwined with it, as in Lithuania, the western Ukraine, Armenia, Georgia, and, incipiently, Russia itself). But the persecution of those desiring religious freedom naturally tends to alienate them from the regime. Also, their causes have often been taken up by mainstream dissenters; some of the latter belong to a church or faith and act as "link men." The dissent movements among the Baptists, the Lithuanian Catholics, and some communities of Russian Orthodoxy are of a mass character.

Most persistent among the denominations in their efforts to oppose persecution and widen religious freedom, yet simultaneously the most apolitical, have been the Baptists. Nearly a thousand of them have been sentenced since Khrushchev intensified antireligious activity in 1960. Now a few Baptist and Pentecostal communities, mainly German in composition, have begun to seek emigration. The Orthodox have lacked the Baptists' persistence but have had a number of people, such as Anatoly Levitin, Dmitry Dudko, and the Pskov priest Sergei Zheludkov, closely involved in mainstream dissent. They also have a growing number of people active in the Russian nationalist dissent movement.

Working Class Dissent

Some reports indicate that discontent is quite widespread among workers and peasants, but except for frequent "go-slows" and rather rare strikes as well as the mass participation in certain national and religious dissent movements, it is not yet organized. It may well become more so in the future, especially if the example of other groups asserting their right to voluntary association leads to the appearance of free, unofficial trade union groups—a development which would please the mainstream dissenters. In due course such a tendency might develop and link up in certain ways with the mainstream of dissent. The regime clearly fears this, partly because a "link-up" of that sort was a critical factor in the growth of opposition in the period 1900-1917; consequently, the government has tried hard over the last decade to raise steadily the real incomes of the working class. The government must also fear the working class as a potentially destructive force in the long tradition of elemental Russian revolt "from below," and it remembers well the serious south Russian riots of 1962 and the Polish riots of 1970. How easily the government can manipulate the Russian working class against Jews and other rebellious minorities, as Seweryn Bialer suggests it can, seems uncertain. Such exercises may strike it as too risky, for they could easily get out of control and turn in the wrong direction. It is notable that the regime has not yet, despite the "availability" of widespread anti-Semitism, unleashed any programs against Jews.

However, the evidence easily available on this critical subject is as yet of low quality; thus only very tentative speculations can be advanced.

Conclusions

How Strong or Weak are the Dissenting Groups?

It is difficult to answer this question with confidence, as most of the groups concerned have dissented actively for less than a decade: the whole phenomenon is very new. It can, however, be said that dissent in its many forms is deeper rooted in the USSR than most Westerners realize, and carries a much stronger emotional charge to it than the majority of Western dissent. It would not survive otherwise, under such an oppressive regime. This is especially true of minority nationalism, which has continued to advance in many parts of the world for over a century, but has received repeated setbacks in Russia and the USSR. At present the various groups have reached a stage in which they represent dissent rather than political opposition. But the process of the pluralization and repoliticization of society is likely to continue, and possibly accelerate, whatever the KGB does, just as the authority of the Communist party is likely to decline.

In 1965 no organized dissent existed on any significant scale, except among the Crimean Tatars, Meskhetians, Germans, and Baptists. But even in these cases it was (apart from some isolated Baptist efforts) completely unpublicized. Ten years later the situation is radically different. The de facto freedom of expression of a steadily increasing number of groups has increased from virtually nil to a very significant level. The media involved—*samizdat* and foreign publications and radio stations—have been either semi-legitimate or illegitimate: the regime has not, even occasionally, allowed access to its own media. But it has also not been willing, or able, to practice oppression severe enough to curtail the newly won freedom.

The exact degree of oppression of any particular group or individual has depended on many factors, including: the amount of support it (or he) has in the USSR and, often more importantly, abroad; the relevance of its (or his) foreign support to the Soviet economy; the importance of it (or him) to the economy; and how vigorously it (or he) is likely to practice self-defense. These sorts of considerations have, taken together, meant that Solzhenitsyn can be dealt with at least cost by deportation, as adverse foreign literary opinion does not affect the economy, whereas similar treatment of Sakharov might seriously affect Soviet-American scientific and even trade agreements and must therefore, be eschewed. Also, of course, Jews need to be granted concessions, but not Meskhetians or Crimean Tatars: these peoples have no foreign lobby at all, let alone one in a position to influence matters affecting the Soviet economy.

It can be argued, correctly, that the mainstream liberals are numerically weak and that their values, taken as a whole, are unlikely ever to receive mass support in the USSR. But that is not the main point here. Their example—in persistently asserting their right to free speech and free association and in publicizing similar acts by many other groups—has had a great influence in broadening the base of dissent. Mutual awareness and even, in some cases, coordination has been created between not only the groups mentioned in this chapter, but also others, including, for example, dissenting artists, parapsychologists, and Buddhists.

Another source of the dissenting groups' strength is their belief that an ideological vacuum exists in Soviet society, that there is little positive, internalized support for the regime inside most citizens and that the widespread desire to avoid war and social upheavals is a poor substitute for such support, although it can be exploited by the regime for quite a long time, as it has been since 1953, but not forever. They also sense that the regime is at least inwardly aware of this situation and of the opportunities it provides for expanding the dissent movement, for emerging from their isolation, and for challenging the regime's claims to infallibility and an ideological and spiritual monopoly.

The Future of Dissent

None of the above implies that the dissenting groups will evolve rapidly into a political opposition, let alone that such an opposition would in due course introduce liberal democracy into the USSR. It does however imply that dissent is now not only ineradicable, but likely to develop steadily in the future. The forms it takes will doubtless become even more varied than at present, and only some of them will affect political developments. Some movements will probably be nationalist and chauvinist and could eventually help to trigger off sudden changes in the regime by, for example, drawing the military into politics as a semi-autonomous force. But no such sudden changes seem, to this writer, likely before the 1980s. Until then, if not longer, the reasonable stability which has existed within the regime since the execution of Beria in 1953 appears likely to continue.

The various sources of this stability are discussed illuminatingly by Seweryn Bialer. While he notes the many potential crises which face the regime in the medium term, he believes that it will generate sufficiently effective reforms to overcome them and maintain political stability. His analysis gives much weight to the crucial role in this of the coming "takeover" generation of Party leaders. He may be proved correct, but this writer leans more, if not completely, towards the assessment of Soviet historian Andrei Amalrik, who in 1969 forecast serious political upheavals in the mid-1980s. *Inter alia*, he wrote:

The regime ... has no wish to change its ways either of its own free will or, still less, by making concessions to anyone or anything. The current process of "widening the area of freedom" could be more aptly described as the growing decrepitude of the regime. The regime is simply growing old and can no longer suppress everyone and everything with the same strength and vigor as before.[1]

How Much Influence Can the Outside World Exert on Soviet Internal Politics?

Before tackling this question it may be useful to give a brief interpretation of the Soviet leaders' probable assessment of their own present situation and of their medium-term aims. When they look back over the last fifty-seven years they must see them filled with many successes, as Bialer suggests, but, also, with many disturbing setbacks and failures. Internationally, communism has not spread where it should have and, where it *has* succeeded, it has escaped, either wholly or in part, from Soviet control. Internally, the economy shows few signs of closing the gap with the West; the bureaucracy is proving incapable of greater flexibility, social problems such as drunkenness, petty corruption, criminality, and teenage indiscipline seem to increase rather than decline, and dissent movements appear in increasing numbers and prove impossible to suppress.

At home, therefore, the leaders' main medium-term priority appears to be a steady and impressive economic development which they hope will eliminate all discontents by (a) satisfying the revolution of rising expectations which they see beginning, (b) removing the causes of the social problems listed above, (c) compensating for the decline in social mobility and the perpetuation of dull, oligarchic leadership (which the present writer, like Bialer, anticipates), and (d) isolating the dissenting groups by making the spiritual vacuum, in the face of economic plenty, seem irrelevant. They also hope that it will ensure a steady build-up of all forms of military might, both defensive and offensive. Abroad, the main aim is apparently the development by the mid-1980s of a strong military presence in many parts of the world, which will greatly strengthen the USSR's capacity to intervene diplomatically and, if necessary, militarily, wherever its great-power interests indicate.

In pursuing these aims the Soviet leaders will undoubtedly seek to keep the often seriously conflicting demands of economic rationality and political control in a tolerable balance. This they have done consistently—*pace* Bialer, who implies that economics has always had priority.

Against this background, then, what influence can the outside world exert vis-à-vis the regime itself, the in-system intelligentsia, the dissenting groups, and the interaction of all three with each other? First, and obviously, much depends, especially in respect to the regime, on the moment, the circumstances, and the personalities involved, i.e., "the conjuncture." In times of crisis for the regime—over the succession, an East European revolt, tension with China, a disastrous harvest, or internal riots—the outside world's opportunities will almost invariably increase until the crisis is resolved. But in normal times the outside world's influence is not substantial. Naturally it cannot be quantified, and it varies greatly depending on the issue, but let us suggest for the sake of argument that on issues where foreign opinion is relevant an average weight of 10-15 percent is given to it in Politbureau discussions.

Now let us take two issues where important changes specially affecting dissent groups have occurred in recent years: emigration and freedom of speech in *samizdat*. Here Bialer's pattern of the stimulus for changes almost always coming from the political leaders and the elite cannot be observed: the stimulus clearly came from the dissenting groups. It was then supported in various ways by external forces, and these in turn reinforced the internal pressures. On both issues the in-system intelligentsia, too, played a role as a transmission belt: people in the section of it with close ties to the mainstream dissenters began to read *samizdat* and/or listen to it on foreign radio stations, and the same people also tended to feel that emigration policy should be eased, and in some cases applied to emigrate themselves. Another section—less humanistic and more technocratic in outlook—probably had little or no sympathy for the dissenters, but nonetheless felt that rationality and the best interests of the system demanded changes. Militant Jewish malcontents were best got rid of to Israel and, while the ruling oligarchy continued to insist on a tight censorship policy, *samizdat*, though undesirable in many ways, would at least stimulate badly needed new thinking and also facilitate freer discussion by the in-system intelligentsia through the medium of semi-official, duplicated publications in restricted editions.

On both issues, therefore, for the reasons indicated here and also earlier in the chapter, the regime found its hand forced. In early 1971 it made the momentous decision to allow a significant measure of freedom to emigrate, a decision which is, in this writer's opinion, within certain margins irreversible. Second, in the years after 1966 the regime decided that it could prosecute only a small fraction of the people who wrote, signed, edited, and circulated *samizdat*. In 1973 it took a related decision, which may have been more hotly debated in the Politbureau: to cut back the jamming of foreign radio stations to roughly the pre-1968 level. Here, these considerations probably counted: the substantial energy saving involved; the relative ineffectiveness of much of the jamming, especially outside the big cities; the Western pressures over "Basket 3" at the European Security Conference; and the limited impact of the proposed cut-back, provided that Radio Liberty remained, as it did, on the jamming list.

Again, one might postulate for the sake of argument, and with all due diffidence, that some 70 percent of the effort required to get these various changes implemented came from the dissenters, some 15 percent from external forces, some 10 percent from the in-system intelligentsia, and some 5 percent from those who proposed the reforms in the Politbureau.

U.S. Methods of Influencing Soviet Internal Politics from Outside

Among these methods are long-term, "defensive" ones such as maintaining American military strength and will, and—a point given an unusual and overwhelming importance by Bialer—ensuring the success of the Western political and economic system. But there are also more "activist" methods like the operation of radio stations whose broadcasts the Soviet regime regards as ideological subversion, and the granting or withholding of Western technology and trade credits, of scientific exchanges, and of presidential visits or presidential participation in summit conferences.

Of these methods the most constantly and deeply effective, in a country subject to a draconian censorship of all the legitimate media, is the operation of radio stations. These are listened to by every social stratum in the USSR, but they have a special significance for the dissenting groups. The Muscovite Vladimir Bukovsky expressed the view in 1970 that the dissent movement expanded in proportion to the spread of *samizdat* throughout the country, and that "That depends on the outside world, on the western radio stations."[2] Among these, Radio Liberty, as the only station which broadcasts *samizdat* systematically in the main languages of the USSR, is considerably the most important.

In trying to obtain Soviet concessions by the "activist" methods listed above, the U.S. government uses "linkage" as a normal tool of diplomacy. What has been unusual about the "Jackson Amendment" (credits in return for freer emigration) has been only its very public and also very specific character. It would be surprising if the West German government had not recently been practicing some form of linkage in a similar context vis-à-vis the Soviet German emigration movement, but in unpublicized negotiations, not publicly.

The public and specific nature of the Jackson Amendment made it easier to generate public American pressure on the U.S. and Soviet governments to negotiate the terms Jackson proposed. It also strengthened the Soviet Jewish movement, encouraging more Jews to apply to emigrate, and it gave an incentive to the Soviet government to "prove its *bona fides*" in advance by letting Jews out at a probably somewhat greater rate than it would have done otherwise. In 1974 the deal was eventually negotiated, and in October an awkward method was devised to record it, by at the same time not publishing the agreement with the Soviets' signature. The Trade Bill, the object of the whole exercise from the Soviet viewpoint, was then passed. The bill contained huge trade credits, subsidized by the U.S. taxpayer, but these were denied by the U.S. Congress, which voted to reduce drastically the total of credits available to the USSR. At this point the game was no longer worth the candle and in January 1975 the Soviet government bowed out.

Linkage could clearly be practiced in other contexts, e.g., credits in return for a Soviet arms control agreement. To make any such linkage public might well benefit the U.S. government, *if* a body of opinion could be mobilized behind it in America (and preferably in the USSR as well). If the issue were one on which an extra 10-15 percent of pressure on the Soviet government from public opinion was enough to swing it, i.e., if the Soviets were moderately predisposed in favor, then this tactic could possibly help to get the United States better terms than it would otherwise have.

U.S. Policy Options

In the following discussion of U.S. policy options, certain broad policy aims are taken for granted. These are (a) that ideally the Soviet regime would be preoccupied with its own internal development, so that world war would be easier to avoid; (b) that the United States would always be militarily strong and purposeful enough to resist any Soviet aggression should the Soviet leaders for some reason launch a war, e.g., to divert attention from internal problems; and (c) that ideally the Soviet regime would gradually democratize itself so that it became a more reliable partner in helping to stabilize a dangerous world, and so that the peoples of the USSR and Eastern Europe could enjoy a freer life.

In the foreseeable future Soviet policies towards dissent seem unlikely to harden or soften dramatically. Thus we may delineate no more than three U.S. policy options on the subject, an activist one of the type associated with the Congress and Senator Jackson, an ambivalent one of the type pursued by the Nixon and Ford administrations, and one of strict noninvolvement, as advocated by Senator Fulbright. From these descriptions it is at once clear that recent U.S. policy has tended to be contradictory, with different branches of government (and different senators within the legislature) pursuing conflicting policies.

First Option

An activist policy on dissent could be expected (a) to aid the frail shoots of democracy in the USSR by supporting through Radio Liberty, etc., all the basically democratic trends (but not putting excessive emphasis on freedom of emigration, which has only a limited liberalizing effect on the regime and which can also lead to absorption difficulties for the emigrants); (b) to warn the Soviet leaders of what may well be their own ultimate need, i.e., in their own interests to accommodate the dissenters in some degree; and (c) to increase the currently very limited constraints of domestic opinion on the conduct of Soviet foreign policy. An activist policy would be unlikely to discourage the Soviet leadership from negotiating on arms or trade issues and could even encourage it to do so more vigorously. Phases of Soviet displeasure and "withdrawal" would be quite possible, associated perhaps with Soviet leadership changes. But as both economically and diplomatically (against the Chinese) the Soviet leaders will *need* the United States, and have neither isolationism nor any other great power to turn to, they would be likely soon to curb their displeasure.

Second Option

If, on the other hand, U.S. policy became one of strict noninvolvement on dissent, the corollary of what is said above would be likely to occur. The Soviet dissenters would feel let down, the regime would feel less need to reform and liberalize itself, and it would also, probably, feel less constrained in pursuing an activist foreign policy. Trade with the United States might expand more rapidly, but arms control negotiations could become either easier or more difficult. Here, as in other areas of policy, much might depend on the emergence or nonemergence of a strong Soviet leader with some vision of how to tackle the regime's formidable internal problems.

Third Option

The third option, of an ambivalent, midway position, would probably have effects somewhere between those outlined above. If conducted as by the Nixon and Ford administrations, it would also involve some confusing of public opinion in East and West, as the involvement component—most importantly, the operation of Radio Liberty and Radio Free Europe—was publicly ignored by both U.S. and Soviet leaders and therefore functioned largely in the shadows.

Notes

1. Andrei Amalrik, *Will the Soviet Union Survive Until 1984?* (New York: Harper and Row, 1970), p. 30.
2. *Survey*, London, No. 77, 1970, p. 145.

IV

The Soviet Economy: Domestic and International Issues

Joseph S. Berliner and
Franklyn D. Holzman

In the half century since the October Revolution the USSR has been transformed from a predominantly peasant nation into a mighty industrial power. On the face of it one would expect the leaders of the nation to be rather satisfied with that notable record of economic growth. But they are not. On the contrary, the intensity of the preoccupation with economic growth is perhaps unrivaled among nations, and it is the key to most of the domestic and international issues discussed in this chapter. The reasons therefore require some explanation.

Most governments are concerned to some degree with the promotion of economic growth, for the familiar reasons: to provide rising levels of consumption for their population, to ease the burden of labor, to raise the standards of health and education, to support foreign policy and defense objectives, and to contribute to the nation's prestige and self-esteem. These reasons the USSR shares with other countries. There are two other reasons that are distinctive of the USSR, however, and it is they that explain the greater commitment to economic growth.

The first is the heavy burden of defense expenditures on the Soviet economy. The USSR must match the military power of the United States, the major industrial nation in the world. It must maintain in addition a force capable of securing its political hegemony over a group of small nations in Eastern Europe, several of which have challenged that authority at various times. And most lately it has had to divert its forces to the defense of its long border with its former Eastern ally China. With a per capita GNP less than half that of the United

States, it maintains a defense establishment roughly equal to it. No nation not actively engaged in war or living in its shadow supports so large a burden of defense. Hence the pressure for increasing output to ease that burden is greater than in other countries.

Even in a world of peace, however, the Soviets are uncommonly occupied with economic growth. The second reason derives from the historic Soviet commitment to the goal of "overtaking and surpassing" the advanced capitalist countries. The roots of that goal go back half a century to the October Revolution and to the deeply held Marxian conviction about the inevitable course of history. A fundamental tenet of that conviction is that the capitalist nations are destined to stagnate under the weight of the growing contradictions of a class society, while the socialist nations will release the energies of the masses and generate an unparalleled burst of economic progress. The rightness of the Soviet course will be evident to all when the day arrives that the Soviet people will live in prosperity and justice while the masses in the capitalist countries languish in exploitation and poverty. The approach of that day is the justification of the great travails endured by the Soviet people in the years of revolution, collectivization, and rapid industrialization.

Because of this profound commitment to overtaking the capitalist countries, however, the Soviet investment in economic growth differs from that of other countries. The adequacy of the nation's growth performance is judged not only by domestic economic and political considerations, but by the growth performance of the countries they are dedicated to surpass. A given rate of growth may be deemed entirely satisfactory if other countries are growing very slowly. But that same growth performance may be quite unsatisfactory if the other countries are growing very rapidly. Perhaps the leaders of all governments are concerned to some extent with the growth performance of certain others. But no government evaluates the economic performance of its own economy so heavily in terms of the performance of others as the government of the USSR. Soviet economic policy cannot be fully comprehended except in the light of this other-directedness in their approach to growth.

There was a time, in the nineteen-thirties, when history seemed indeed to be moving in the direction prophesied by Marxian theory. The capitalist world was languishing in a deep depression while Soviet industry forged ahead at an awesome pace. But in the postwar world the goal began to recede. The advanced capitalist countries exhibited an unexpected resurgence of technological and economic vitality, joined now by that astonishing newcomer—Japan. That development alone would have diminished the satisfaction that the Soviet leaders derived from the growth performance of their own economy, which was still substantial. But in the late fifties the growth rate of the Soviet economy began to decline, and the decline has not yet been reversed. The consequence is a profound dissatisfaction with the performance of the Soviet economy. There is not much that Soviet policy can do about the growth rate of the capitalist world. The full burden of the commitment to overtake the capitalist countries must therefore fall on the capacity of the Soviet economy to accelerate its own rate of growth.

The first part of this essay will examine the sources of Soviet growth. The second part will consider options available for accelerating the rate of growth by drawing on domestic resources alone. The three parts following deal with Soviet international economic relations and their potential as a source of increasing growth. In the last part we consider various options that the United States may choose in shaping its economic relations with the USSR.

The Sources of Economic Growth

The total output of the Soviet economy has grown at the rather respectable rate of about 5.7 percent per year in the postwar period. Table IV-1 presents the results of the research of Professor Abram Bergson on the growth rates of total output in a variety of industrial countries.

Japan is in a class by itself, with the remarkable growth rate of 10.3 percent per year in the period 1955-1970. But the Soviet economy has done as well as the major continental countries of Western Europe, all of whom have grown at about 5.5 percent per annum. And compared to the growth performance of the United States and the United Kingdom, the Soviet economy has done very well indeed. No government would fall on that record.

It is not a record about which the Soviets are very happy, however. The first reason is that noted above: for a government devoted to the objective of overtaking and surpassing the leading capitalist countries, there is little comfort in a growth performance that merely keeps abreast of the rate of growth of most of them. Moreover, the remarkable record of Japan attests to the presence of a

Table IV-1
Annual Average Percentage Growth Rate of Various Industrial Countries (1955-1970)

	Total Output	Total Factor Productivity
United Kingdom	2.5	1.8
United States	3.4	1.6
West Germany	5.6	3.4
France	5.4	3.9
Japan	10.3	5.9
Italy	5.6	4.4
USSR	5.7	2.4

certain uncommon dynamic for growth under non-Soviet conditions, the source of which the USSR has not succeeded in tapping. The United States and United Kingdom growth rates have been much lower than that of the USSR, but the per capita level of output of the former at least is still so much larger than that of the USSR that the day of overtaking is very far in the future.

More disconcerting is the time trend in Soviet growth rates during this period. The trend has been distinctly downward, particularly in the industrial sector. Nonmilitary industrial production grew at an annual rate of 9.8 percent in the period 1951-1960. In the next two five-year-plan periods it declined to 6.9 percent and 6.8 percent respectively. Preliminary results for 1971-1972 place the rate at 5.6 percent. Unless the economy can recover the growth-rate levels of the earlier postwar period, relative Soviet performance may prove to be even less satisfactory than that of earlier years.

Turning to the sources of growth, it is customary to distinguish what may be called quantitative and qualitative sources of growth. The quantitative sources of growth are those due to increasing quantities of the basic factors of production like labor and capital. The qualitative sources of growth are those due to the improving quality of the factors of production or of production methods; better machinery rather than simply more machinery, for example. Ordinarily a growing economy benefits simultaneously from both sources of growth; as the years go by it has better machines as well as more machines. The qualitative sources of growth are summarized in an index known as "factor productivity," which measures the extent to which the growth of output has been due not to the mere increase in the quantities of labor and capital available but to the increase in the quality or "productivity" of the factors of production and of production methods. For example, if one supposes that the labor supply and the stock of capital were growing at the same rates in two economies and that there was no change in factor productivity, output would be expected to grow at the same rate in both economies (under various commonly made assumptions). But if factor productivity grew more rapidly in the first economy, its output would also grow more rapidly than that of the second economy. Increasing factor productivity is therefore a way in which an economy can break through the limits on growth, as it were, imposed by the available supplies of labor and capital.

Professor Bergson's estimates of the comparative growth rates of factor productivity are presented in the second column of the table above. The first point to be noted is that relative Soviet performance in raising its factor productivity is somewhat poorer than its performance in increasing output. Though still somewhat better than the United States and the United Kingdom, it is substantially lower than that of the other countries. Moreover, increasing factor productivity has contributed less to the growth of output in the USSR than in all the other countries. The annual increase in factor productivity in the USSR (2.4 percent) accounts for less than half (42 percent) of the annual growth of output (5.7 percent). In every other country increasing factor productivity accounts for a larger percentage of the growth rate of output than that. The Soviet economy is thus distinctive in the extent to which it has depended on increasing labor and capital rather than on the qualitative sources of growth—on pouring more machines into the economy rather than better machines.

Second, in evaluating the growth performance of nations it is customary to take account of what Alexander Gerschenkron has called the "advantages of backwardness." One of those advantages is the opportunity available to newly developing countries of borrowing advanced technology from more developed countries. Because of that advantage one expects the former to enjoy higher rates of growth of factor productivity than the latter. The "other countries" listed in the table conform roughly to that expectation. They are listed in order of the percentage of the labor force engaged in nonfarm sectors, which may be taken as a rough indicator of level of development; the United Kingdom has the largest proportion of its labor force engaged in nonfarm pursuits and Italy has the smallest. On casual inspection it is evident that as the percentage of the nonfarm labor force declines, the annual increase in factor productivity tends to rise; Bergson indeed found the correlation to be highly significant. Now the percentage of the labor force in nonfarm activities is lower in the USSR than in all the other countries. Therefore if the Soviet growth pattern were consistent with that of the other countries, its growth rate of factor productivity should be higher than that of any of the others. Looked at in this perspective, the Soviet rate of 2.4 percent is dismally low. One cannot conclude with any confidence that this result signifies that there is some serious defect in the way the Soviets manage their economy. Each country is unique and there may be perfectly good reasons why Soviet performance may be expected to differ from that of other countries in this respect. Whatever the reasons, however, it is clear that there are certain sources of economic growth from which the Soviets do not benefit to the same extent as other countries do.

To accelerate the rate of growth, the Soviets must find ways of either increasing the annual supplies of new labor, capital, and other productive resources, or of increasing the productivity of their resources, or both. In the next section we shall consider the prospects for accomplishing that by relying on domestic policy alone. Subsequent sections will deal with the contribution that foreign economic relations can make toward those two sources of growth.

Domestic Sources of Growth

The industrialization of the USSR was accomplished primarily by drawing on the quantitative sources of growth. The essence of what has become known as the "Soviet growth strategy" consists precisely of a rapid expansion of the industrial labor force drawn out of agriculture and out of the home, an intense exploitation of the untapped natural resources of the country, and a large annual increase in the stock of capital based on a high rate of investment. With this pattern of industrialization high rates of growth can be attained by the large annual increases in the quantities of the factors of production alone, even if the productivity of the factors does not increase rapidly. In the course of time, however, the possibility of maintaining past rates of increase of the quantities of the factors tends to diminish. Unless the managers of the economy are able to find ways of offsetting the decline in the availability of the factors of production by a rise in their productivity, the rate of growth of output will decline. That is the origin of the current intense Soviet preoccupation with issues of productivity.

Labor, Natural Resources, and Capital

In the postwar period, as we have seen, the Soviets continued to rely more heavily than other industrial countries on quantitative sources of growth and less on rising productivity. However, the forecasts of future prospects for growth from that source are not hopeful.

First, demographic projections all point to a decline in the growth rate of the labor force. Total civilian employment grew at an annual rate of 1.9 percent in the years 1950-1970. However, the current five-year plan (1971-1975) provides for an increase of 1.6 percent, and the forecast for the following five years is 1.5 percent. The pool of underemployed agricultural labor, which formerly provided large annual increments to the industrial labor force, is now largely exhausted, and as long as the present collectivized organization of agriculture prevails industry can no longer expect the large annual supplies of new labor it obtained in the past. Further, female labor participation is close to the practical maximum—the home can no longer be drawn upon for labor. The annual increase in the industrial labor force declined from a substantial 4 percent in the period 1950-1965 to the modest rate of about 3 percent in 1965-1970. In the current five-year plan it is scheduled to grow at only 1.3 percent per year, and the same rate is forecast for the following five years. Hence economic growth will no longer benefit to the same extent as in the past from large annual increments of labor.

The second primary factor of production is the quality and availability of natural resources. An expanding economy requires increasing quantities of energy, minerals, and agricultural products. The higher the quality of the natural resources, the smaller the quantities of labor and capital required to make them available. In the rapid industrialization of their country the Soviets benefited greatly from the availability and accessibility of abundant natural resources. In all industrializing countries, however, the richest resources are eventually fully exploited and continued development requires moving into more remote areas, opening up less productive mines, bringing more marginal lands under cultivation and so forth. Occasional discoveries of new mineral or fuel reserves temporarily delay the process, but do not reverse it. The USSR has been no exception to this pattern.

The major natural resources necessary to industrialization are energy, minerals, and agricultural and timber lands. The USSR has vast reserves of all the principal energy resources: gas, oil, coal, and water power. The sources closest to the centers of population, however, have been largely exploited, and the reserves for future exploitation are heavily concentrated in remote and often inhospitable locations in Siberia and Central Asia. The pipeline system that supplies European Russia with most of its natural gas, for example, is over 4,000 miles long, originating in central Asia. The largest reserves of hydroelectric power are in the great rivers of Siberia. The long-term strategy used for minimizing the cost of bringing those resources into use has been the movement of capital and labor to the sources of the energy and the building up of the industry and population of those areas. The results have not been particularly successful, largely because of the difficulty of attracting people to the regions and inducing them to remain permanently. It is always possible, of course, that new discoveries will reduce the cost of increasing energy supplies. Large regions of the vast country have not yet been explored and the offshore areas of the Caspian, Black, and Baltic seas may yield new sources of oil and gas. But the cost of bringing new energy sources into production is likely to be higher than in the past.

The third quantitative source of growth is the stock of productive capital. In the period 1950-1967, the capital stock increased fairly uniformly at an annual rate of about 9 percent. If that rate could be increased further it would help offset the diminishing increments of labor and the declining quality of natural resources. It is more likely, however, that the annual increments in capital will also fall below the 9 percent of the past. The chief evidence for this expectation is that the annual rates of increase in the volume of new investment have declined steadily. The Soviets report that the volume of investment increased 12.9 percent per year in 1950-1958, but by only about 7.6 percent per year in 1958-1970 and 6.9 percent per year in 1971-1975. The draft Tenth Five Year Plan provides for a further sharp decline, to 4.4 percent per year during 1976-1980. These declining annual rates of increase in investment are bound to cause eventually the annual increase in the stock of capital to decline below the healthy 9 percent of the past. That decline could conceivably be arrested if it were possible to reverse the decline in the annual rate of increase in the volume of investment, but such a reversal would require that growing shares of each year's total output be allocated to investment. Bergson has shown that to maintain a 9 percent annual increase in the capital stock would require the rate of investment to rise to a level of 36-40 percent of total output in 1975, and 39-48 percent of total output in 1980; the precise figures depend on various assumptions about the growth rate of factor productivity.

The prospects for increasing the supply of agricultural land are also dim. Despite the great land mass of the country, the area of high quality agricultural land is quite limited. Most of it was already in use at the time the industrialization drive began. The industrialization process placed heavy demands on agriculture to increase supplies of raw materials at the same time that the growing population had greater incomes and demanded more foodstuffs. Most of the increasing agricultural output was satisfied by capital investment in the traditional agricultural areas; less was accomplished by bringing new areas into cultivation. By the mid-fifties, however, the Soviet leaders judged the returns to further investment in traditional land to be less than could be attained by opening up new lands. The vast virgin lands opened up in Kazakhstan and Western Siberia were known to be marginal, primarily because of uncertain rainfall and the short growing seasons. It is still a matter of debate whether the resources invested in these lands would not have been better employed in the form of increased capital expenditures on the older lands. The same question has now come to the fore again with the announcement of a program opening another large new area for agricultural exploitation, described in the draft Tenth Five Year Plan as the "comprehensive development of agriculture in the Non-Black-Earth Zone of the Russian Republic." While the rainfall conditions in these northern regions are favorable, the length of the growing season is shorter and the soils are of poorer quality than those of the traditional agricultural regions. The draft plan provides for the irrigation of 5.7 million acres of these new lands, for the draining of 5.7 million acres of swampland, and for bringing water to 13 million acres of pasture. The cost of increasing inputs into agricultural resources, like that of energy resources, is therefore likely to rise.

While it is not unimaginable that the Soviets may manage to allocate such large shares of each year's output to investment, competing pressures for rising living standards make such a course unlikely. Since the death of Stalin, the regime has come to rely increasingly on monetary rewards to stimulate agricultural output, to maintain labor discipline, and to support managerial incentives. The rising monetary incomes must be balanced by a growing volume of consumer goods and services if inflationary pressures are to be avoided. The fact that the savings deposits of the population have been rising considerably more rapidly than the volume of consumer goods in recent years suggests problems in achieving a noninflationary balance. Apart from the incentive system, however, the regime has increasingly solicited public support for its policies by relaxing the harshest police controls of the past and by promising rising living standards. The present government has eschewed Khrushchev's incautious boasts of imminent abundance, but it remains heavily committed to a program of increased consumption levels. The huge imports of grain in the nineteen-seventies stand in sharp contrast to the export of grain in the nineteen-thirties during the famine following the collectivization of agriculture. With the memory of the Polish food riots of 1970 still fresh, the government could ill afford to risk the unrest that a decline in the food supply might entail. The commitment to rising consumption levels is also manifest in the importation of foreign manufacturing facilities for passenger cars, soft drinks and other consumer items.

When the Ninth Five Year Plan was adopted in 1971, it was heralded as a new departure, for the rate of growth of consumer goods industry was planned to be larger than the rate of growth of producer goods industry. This was the first time in the history of Soviet planning that consumer goods industry received that degree of priority. It is instructive to note, however, that this feature of the plan was not carried out. At the termination of the five-year period the old pattern had prevailed and producer goods had continued to grow more rapidly than consumer goods as in all past plans. The draft of the current Tenth Plan, moreover, confirmed at the Twenty-Fifth Party Congress, reasserted the traditional pattern and once again producer goods industry is planned to grow more rapidly than consumer goods. That brief flirtation with a slight reordering of priorities is a sobering caution that in the tight competition for resources the government may not always succeed in fulfilling completely its commitments to raising consumption levels. It is clear nevertheless that consumption has a higher claim on resources than it had in the past and its size can no longer be treated as a residual, to be determined after the desired rate of investment has been attained. Under these circumstances there is a serious question about whether the rate of investment can be pushed to the levels required to maintain past rates of growth of the capital stock.

In the case of all three factors of production, then, the prospects of drawing on the quantitative sources of growth are less favorable than they were in the past. Factor productivity has therefore become more important in Soviet policy.

The prospect of declining rates of increase in the quantities of the factors of production places a double burden on factor productivity. To keep the growth rate of output from falling below its current level, the annual rate of increase of factor productivity will have to rise merely to offset the declining rates of increase of the quantities of the factors of production. But the Soviet leaders will hardly be content to maintain the current growth rate of output. Their goal is to regain, to the extent possible, the higher growth rates of the past, which will require an even greater increase in factor productivity.

Two main lines of effort can increase factor productivity. One is an increase in the general efficiency of the economy. The other is the promotion of technological progress.

Increasing Efficiency

Efficiency refers to the amount of output that a society succeeds in producing with a given volume of resources. Most economies fall short of perfect efficiency, in the sense that the potential output is generally much larger than the output attained. Inefficiency in capitalist economies is the result of unemployment of labor, tax policies that distort the allocation of resources, monopolistic markets that have similar effects, and so forth. The causes of inefficiency in socialist economies are somewhat different, but they are substantial nevertheless. Indeed, the analysis of the sources of inefficiency and the search for methods of eliminating them are a major preoccupation of Soviet economists.

The relationship between inefficiency and factor productivity may be illustrated by an example. Suppose an inefficient economy produced 60 percent of its potential output with given resources. Assume further that a way were found to raise the level of output to 80 percent of potential in the course of ten years. During those ten years, factor productivity would be increasing at an annual rate of roughly 2 percent. If the level of efficiency then stabilized at 80 percent, factor productivity would cease to grow thereafter, although it would be at a higher level than in the past. The reduction of inefficiency is therefore a somewhat limited source of rising factor productivity, for the more rapidly the economy benefits from it, the sooner it is exhausted. Nevertheless, rising efficiency can contribute significantly to the growth of factor productivity for a substantial period of time. Moreover, somewhat paradoxically, the greater the inefficiency of an economy, the greater the potential increase in factor productivity from that source.

The sources of inefficiency in the Soviet economy have been extensively studied, both in the USSR and elsewhere. They are to be found in the methods of pricing, in the incentive system, in the techniques of planning and enterprise administration, and so forth. In the past two decades there have indeed been a number of major reforms intended to eliminate the major sources of inefficiency. Each was heralded at the time as the breakthrough to a large increase in efficiency. In 1957, for example, Khrushchev pushed through the Territorial Reorganization Reform. Under the preexisting industrial ministries, neighboring enterprises often found it very difficult to cooperate with each other if they belonged to different ministries, and that was thought to be the crucial source of inefficiency. The remedy adopted was a massive reorganization of industrial administration, in which the ministries were abolished and all enterprises in a single region were thereafter administered by a regional economic council. Seven years later, following Khrushchev's removal from office, that reform was judged to have helped little if at all. The regional councils were dissolved and the old ministry system restored.

The new regime of Brezhnev and Kosygin had its own idea of the locus of inefficiency. It was the "petty tutelage" of the enterprises by the organs of government. If enterprise managers were given more autonomy, most of the wasteful practices of the past could disappear. That view was incorporated in the celebrated 1965 Economic Reform. The results of this reform were probably positive, but they were not of substantial magnitude. Again the reform was disappointing, and while it has not been reversed, one reads little more about it in the Soviet sources today. The current focus of attention is a new wave of changes known as the Corporate Merger Reform. This reform is geared more to the promotion of technological progress than to the improvement of efficiency, and will therefore be discussed below.

In addition to these organizational reforms, there have been numerous other reforms of the incentive system as well as the price structure. Their net result may well have been some gain in efficiency, but it has not been of dramatic proportions. The chief lesson is that it is not an easy matter to raise the efficiency of an economy. Past failures do not, of course, preclude the success of some future reform. But the recent history of those efforts offers little basis for anticipating that the key will soon be found.

In retrospect, the past reforms did not introduce fundamental changes in the economy. Generally they dealt with specific features, or clusters of features, of the economy, although some were regarded as making fundamental changes at the time. We have therefore had no test of the extent to which efficiency might be raised by a truly fundamental reform. The one that comes first to mind, of course, is an extensive decentralization of economic activity, in the manner of the "market socialism" of Yugoslavia, for example. Such a reform is highly threatening to the present political structure, however, for it would very likely lead to a weakening of central political power. Moreover a large class of managers, government officials, and party functionaries have interests vested in the present form of economic organization—interests in the form of income, status, and power that would be undermined by a genuine reform. As long as the economy continues to perform unsatisfactorily, however, that solution will always be waiting in the wings. An alternative approach that offers the possibility of increasing productivity would therefore be highly welcome to the Soviet leaders, as a means of avoiding the necessity to confront the prospect of genuine economic decentralization. The alternative most diligently pursued at present is the promotion of technological progress.

Technological Progress

Technological progress generally refers to the introduction of new and improved products and processes. It must be clearly distinguished from an increase in efficiency. An economy experiencing no change in efficiency (for example, a perfectly efficient one) could nevertheless advance technologically, and an economy with an unchanging technology could conceivably increase its efficiency.

As a source of increasing factor productivity, technological progress is not limited in the way that increasing efficiency is. In principle, it is limited only by the imagination of the nation's scientific and technical personnel. As each reform designed to increase efficiency proved to accomplish very little, more and more hope has been invested in technological progress as the solution. It has become something of a *deus ex machina.*

The Soviet economy has not been noted for technological innovation, although in special fields such as space and military technology it has scored a number of dramatic successes. Those fields, however, are largely insulated from the economic processes of the normal civilian economy. In most sectors of the civilian economy there are rather extensive obstacles to innovation that are widely reported and analyzed in the sources.

The core of the problem is that all the economic institutions of the society are geared to the major objective of fulfilling the targets of the national economic plan. There is a certain logic to those arrangements, since national planning is thought to be the great advance of Soviet socialism over the "anarchy of the market" that prevails in the capitalist world. And if planning is to work properly, it is vital that enterprises bend their efforts primarily to the fulfillment of the tasks assigned to them as part of the plan. Innovation, however, increases the degree of uncertainty in planning. In all economies new products and processes upset the production schedules of enterprises, costs of production are difficult to plan in advance, and "cost overruns" are a normal part of the innovation process. The Soviet manager who undertakes an innovation, therefore, faces the prospect of underfulfilling his plan more often than the manager who sticks to an established product line and to safe and familiar manufacturing processes. Innovation increases the risk that the central planning bureaucracy may not manage to provide the enterprise with the materials and equipment required and may not succeed in finding customers for new and untried products. The methods of pricing are such that the producer of a new product generally earns a smaller profit than the producer of an established product. The incentive system is geared heavily to plan fulfillment, and since innovation tends to upset short-run production schedules, the personnel of innovating enterprises often earn smaller incomes than they would if they avoided innovation.

This is not to deny that there are other forces that promote innovation. A certain volume of technological advance occurs each year through the process of innovation-by-order; when the ministry directs an enterprise to produce a new product, it may drag its heels but it must eventually follow the order. Among the hundreds of thousands of competent engineers and managers there are many who respond to the instinct of workmanship and who regard innovation as a personal challenge. These and other forces account for a certain steady rate of technological advance. But for the civilian economy as a whole there remain powerful deterrents to innovation.

With the growing attention to technological progress as the most hopeful source of rising factor productivity, a variety of efforts have been made to increase the hospitality of the economy to innovative activity. The methods of pricing have been altered in ways intended to increase the profitability of new products relative to older ones. Special incentive arrangements have been introduced to offset the losses of income borne by innovations. The most celebrated, however, is a major new reform of the system of industrial organization—the Corporation Merger movement.

A corporation—or "production association"—is a merger of a number of previously independent enterprises. In most cases the merger is a form of vertical integration. Its chief purpose is to provide greater stability in the producer's sources of supply. In the past, one of the most troublesome problems faced by innovators was the supply of research and development services. Those services were generally supplied "out-of-house" by research and development (R&D) establishments that were independent of the enterprises. Under that arrangement the R&D establishments confined their efforts to the fulfillment of "their" plans, and had little interest in the subsequent history of the new products and processes they designed after they were turned over to the enterprises for adoption. The innovating enterprises, for their part, found it difficult to interest the R&D establishments in providing the back-up services they needed for "their" innovative efforts. Many of those R&D establishments are now to be merged with several enterprises into a single corporation, so that the R&D services will be supplied in-house. It is hoped that innovation lead-times will be reduced and the quality of R&D services improved.

The Corporation Reform was announced in 1973 and the merger movement was to be completed in 1975. Earlier experiments with the corporate form of industrial organization are reported to have been quite successful, and the reform will very likely improve matters as far as it goes. But it will take some years of experience before a judgment can be rendered. The 1965 Economic Reform, it must be noted, was also preceded by experiments which were heralded as models of success. When that reform was extended to all industry, however, its long-run effect proved to be less than dramatic. That indeed is one of the problems in the implementation of economic reform in the USSR. When a new idea appears to work well in some selected cases, there is an irresistible urge to apply it uniformly everywhere. The Corporation Reform appears to require that every enterprise be merged into a corporation, and in the process of universalization it is likely that some—perhaps many—inappropriate mergers will be made. Some Soviet economists, for example, have been urging for some time that the size distribution of Soviet enterprises is too heavily skewed toward large size, and the economy has lost some of the advantages of flexibility that the large number of small enterprises provides in economies like Japan, West Germany, and the United States. If they are right, the Corporation Reform will not be an unmixed benefit.

The central question, however, is whether the Corporation Reform cuts to the core of the obstacles to technological innovation. Our best guess is that it does not. It may improve matters with respect to the specific problem of the supply of R&D services. But it is still fundamentally a centrally planned economy and the new corporations, no less than the older enterprises, must depend on the central planners to provide them with materials and equipment and, thereafter, to sell their output. The reforms in incentives and prices have reduced the degree of discrimination against innovation, but they do not appear to have converted the decision to innovate into a much more attractive alternative than the decision to keep things unchanged and to concentrate on fulfilling the plan.

We conclude that the prospects for increasing factor productivity by economic reform are not great. Past reforms that sought either to increase efficiency or advance technological progress have not been notably successful. The Corporation Reform is too recent to judge, but its scope is not so broad as to suggest that it may entail a fundamental change in economic structure. It follows that a sharp increase in the rate of economic growth on the basis of domestic economic policy alone is not very likely.

But if the domestic sources of growth are limited, there remain foreign sources of growth. Indeed, the intense current Soviet interest in foreign economic relations may well reflect a certain doubt that the domestic economy by itself can generate a sufficient increase in growth. The question then is the potential for growth in foreign economic relations.

Soviet Foreign Economic Relations: The Record

The Soviet Union is one of the few relatively self-sufficient giant nations in the world. Like the United States (in particular) and the Peoples Republic of China, it occupies a large area, has a large population and therefore a large domestic market, and is wealthy in natural resources. This combination of factors naturally leads to a relatively small participation in international trade. Most of the nation's trade takes place internally; exports are a small percentage of output, imports a small percentage of consumption. While international trade is relatively less important to the giant nations, it nevertheless does raise the level of economic possibilities. There are always some products which the giants can buy more cheaply from foreign nations by exporting products in which they have a comparative advantage. While the trade of a large nation is too complex to be described in a few sentences, there have been a number of constants in Russian-Soviet trade dictated by the great Soviet natural endowment in resources on the one hand, and the fact that it has never caught up technologically with the advanced Western nations, on the other. As a result, imports have always included a significant percentage of machinery and equipment, financed by exports of, among other things, a good share of food and raw materials.

A number of stages may be distinguished in the history of Russian trade with the West. At the beginning of the eighteenth century, Peter the Great opened commerce with the West to develop his nation's industry and further its military ambitions. The country imported machinery and equipment, Russian students were sent abroad, and thousands of foreign technicians were brought into the country. A second attempt to modernize the economy began in the 1880s, through imports of machinery, equipment, and technicians. These imports were financed by exports of foodstuffs and raw materials and an enormous inflow of financial capital from the nations of Western Europe. Trade with the West ceased for several years after the Russian Revolution of 1917. The third major phase began in the late 1920s and early 1930s, at which time the Soviets relied very heavily, once again, on imports of foreign machinery and technology to launch their First Five Year Plan (1928-1932), which was designed to transform the nation into an industrial power. Soviet GNP grew rapidly during the First Plan and imports contributed substantially to that growth. Trade dried up in the subsequent five years and by 1937 amounted to only one-half of one percent of GNP—practically a state of autarky.

The present stage of Soviet trade with the West may be dated from World War II. The Nazi attack in 1941 brought the USSR into close economic contact with the United States which endured until some time shortly after World War II ended. As part of its general policy of exporting all forms of material and supplies to allied nations doing more of the fighting in Europe than we were, the United States exported roughly $11 billion worth of goods to the USSR under the Lend-Lease program. These exports to the USSR were certainly one of the best investments this nation ever made and undoubtedly shortened the war in Europe. While Soviet leaders have at one time or another expressed appreciation of Lend-Lease, they have been much more interested, and perhaps justifiably so, in pointing out that it was not Lend-Lease but more than twenty million Russian lives and enormous suffering and destruction that was crucial in finally repulsing the Germans on the eastern front.

The hot war had hardly ended when the cold war began, with sharp adverse effects on East-West economic relations. The cold war was most intense in its economic manifestations between the United States and the USSR, much less intense so far as Western and Eastern Europe were concerned. In fact, trade between Eastern and Western Europe reached 1938 levels (in real terms) by 1948, even though output in those nations had not recovered to prewar levels. The fact of the matter is that the nations of both Eastern and Western Europe are all relatively small and fairly heavily dependent on international trade, with trade/GNP ratios ranging from 15 to 50 percent. Furthermore they are used to trading with each other; it would have been costly to them to break off their mutual trade. The United States and the USSR, on the other hand, are much less dependent on trade and can turn their backs on it at a much lower economic cost. They are therefore much less averse to using trade as an instrument of political policy than the smaller nations, which have more to lose.

One of the first confrontations between the United States and USSR occurred over the Lend-Lease settlement. The U.S. demands and Soviet offers were never close, and no agreement could be reached. Then came the Marshall Plan in 1947 in which the United States offered financial assistance toward the reconstruction of Europe, including the USSR in the original offer. The Russians and Czechs attended preliminary meetings in Paris in June 1947 and for a short while it looked as if an East-West economic détente was in the making. However, after a few days the Russians left, claiming that the controls that the United States planned to exercise in connection with the use of their aid would have the effect of subjugating Eastern as well as Western Europe. In retrospect, it is clear that these claims were excessive. The Russians also objected to the inclusion of Germany, fearing its restoration as a great power. The Czechs were forced to withdraw and other Eastern European nations were forbidden to participate. On the purely political level, the cold war was progressing even more intensely. The 1948 takeover in Czechoslovakia, the Berlin blockade, and the Allied airlift to that beleaguered city were probably the most decisive confirmations of the intractability of the conflict.

In 1949, the Soviets formed their own economic bloc—the Council for Mutual Economic Assistance (CMEA)—largely as a reaction to the Marshall Plan. At the same time, the CMEA nations began to trade much more heavily with one another than ever before, although CMEA as an instrumentality toward this end was fairly ineffective until at least 1960. As a group of Communist economies, all of which ran their systems by central planning with direct controls, it was natural for these monopolies to plan bilaterally their trade with each other each year. This institutional affinity provided the device by which they redirected their trade away from Western Europe and toward each other and, in particular, toward the Soviet Union. In fact, it was clearly Soviet policy in this regard which dominated the decision-making, for reasons mentioned above. The result was that a group of nations which conducted about 15 percent of their trade with each other before World War II, by 1953 achieved a level of intrabloc trade approaching 75 percent.

Not all of this violent shift in trade patterns can be attributed to Soviet policy alone, however, for it was in part a response to American policies. Beginning in 1947, the United States began to construct a network of controls over and impediments to East-West trade which probably contributed to the reduction of that trade to a smaller trickle than even Stalin had anticipated. The major instrument of U.S. economic warfare was the 1949 Export Control Act, which replaced a number of ad hoc measures used immediately after the war. Under this Act, the United States exercised control over exports of "strategic" products—those either in short supply at home or which might contribute to the military-industrial potential of unfriendly nations. The latter category rapidly assumed primary importance and exporters to the Eastern European nations and the USSR found that they were unable to obtain licenses for the shipment of literally thousands of so-called strategic products.

Needless to say, export controls exercised by the United States alone would have had little effect if the USSR and Eastern Europe had free access to Western European markets. Therefore Congress passed the Foreign Assistance Act in 1948 and the Battle Act (Mutual Defense Assistance Act) in 1951 in attempts to enlist the cooperation of the North Atlantic Treaty Organization (NATO) powers and Japan in making our embargo effective. Under persuasion from the provisions of the legislation, these nations jointly established lists of strategic commodities, similar to but usually less comprehensive than the U.S. lists; listed commodities were not to be shipped to "nations threatening the security of the United States, including the USSR and the countries under its domination." The "persuasion" provided by the Battle Act was the discontinuation of American aid, at that time substantial, to any nation which broke the embargo.

A third body of legislation which obstructed trade with the East was the Johnson Debt Default Act of 1934. This Act prohibited the extension of credits or any other kind of financial assistance by private business or banks to any nation in default on its obligations to the United States. The Act was passed in response to the wholesale defaults by European nations on World War I debts. After World War II, the Act was modified to exclude from its provisions all nations which joined the International Monetary Fund (IMF) or International Bank for Reconstruction and Development (IBRD). At that point, the Act continued to apply only to the USSR, on the basis of World War I and Lend-Lease debts (which remained unsettled but not defaulted), and to most of the nations of Eastern Europe. Under the circumstances, it was clear that the Johnson Act was no longer being used for the purpose for which it was legislated but as an instrument of East-West economic warfare. It certainly was unrelated to the credit-worthiness of governments, particularly of the post-World War II vintage; and World War I debts had faded into the statute of limitations.

The final major weapon used by the U.S. arsenal was the withdrawal of most-favored-nation (MFN) treatment from all of the nations of Eastern Europe and the USSR; this was done in 1951 under the stress of the Korean War. This meant that in order to export products, mostly manufactured, to the United States, Communist exporters had to climb over the 1930 Smoot-Hawley tariffs which were much higher than those negotiated since under MFN arrangements. This made it less profitable for the Eastern nations to export to the United States and harder for them to compete in our markets. Western Europe did not join the United States in this act but for the most part continued to extend MFN.

The sum of all of these acts amounted to a policy of economic containment. We controlled exports and credit to, and imports from, the USSR and its allies. We put pressure on our own allies into joining with us in most of these efforts. The USSR, which desired to insulate Eastern Europe from the West, found its job made easier by American policies—perhaps too easy. Western Europe went along with U.S. policies—but not all the way. So, for example, while American exports to the USSR and Eastern Europe fell from $400 million in 1948 to $2 million in 1953, Western Europe's exports declined only from $1.3 billion to $0.9 billion.

With the end of the Korean War and the death of Stalin in 1953, and the Indo-China Armistice in 1954, not to mention the sharp decline in American aid to Europe following the closing of the books on the Marshall Plan, the United States began to run into increasing difficulties in holding Western Europe in line on East-West trade policy. Further relaxation of tensions between Eastern and Western Europe developed after the four power Conference in Geneva in 1955 and the widely heralded "Geneva Spirit." Relaxation of political tensions finally spilled over into economic policies and the nations of Western Europe began to reduce their embargo lists. The lists were progressively reduced virtually every year and by 1960 had become a much smaller impediment to trade. The United States strongly opposed these and other relaxations of economic policy; for example in 1957 Western Europe eliminated the so-called Chincom differential, which meant reducing export controls on China to the level of the USSR at the same time that the United States maintained a complete embargo. The United States did reduce its control list slightly, but year by year the difference between our list and those of our European allies grew.

To the extent that West European controls were much less extensive than U.S. controls, the latter were ineffective except in the occasional commodities in which the United States had a complete monopoly. The result was that Eastern Europe and the USSR received the products they wanted, Western Europe got the business, and American businessmen were debarred from a profitable market. So, over the decade ending in 1963, while U.S. exports to the Eastern bloc rose from almost zero to roughly $150 million—much of it grain—Western European exports rose from $0.9 billion to $3.2 billion. Western Europe, more dependent on foreign trade than the United States, was naturally more interested than America was in breaking down the trade barriers. But aside from this matter of self-interest, it was certainly apparent that the embargo was not having its desired effect. The Russians did, after all, develop their own H-bomb. The nations of Eastern Europe and the USSR were growing very rapidly and if they were being adversely affected by the embargo, the effect was not so large as to be regarded as obvious.

The rise in East-West trade with the reduction in European export controls implied a readiness on the part of the Eastern bloc to engage in more trade. This was certainly true after 1955. This interest in more trade with the West should not be taken to imply an interest, on the part of the USSR at least, in eliminating all barriers to trade between the two blocs. Not at all. It simply indicated that the barriers were higher than Moscow deemed desirable and that, at the margins at least, there were gains to be had from East-West trade of which the Soviet Union wanted to take advantage. The additional desired East-West trade, while significant, would nevertheless not be pursued on a scale which threatened the economic interdependence among the CMEA nations. In implementing this policy, the Eastern nations each signed many trade agreements with the nations of Western Europe beginning in the late 1950s. In 1958, Khrushchev proposed to Eisenhower an agreement which foresaw a large expansion of trade in what he called "peaceful" goods. This proposal was "cold-shouldered" as were subsequent proposals made the following year by Khrushchev and Mikoyan on their visits to the United States. Soviet and East European policies toward East-West trade grew more favorable as time went on. Economic difficulties at home, epitomized by the general slowing up of growth rates, interest in importing technology, interest in borrowing capital, and grain crises were among the economic factors contributing to this. Politically, progress was impeded by the U-2 incident, the Cuban Missile Crisis, the Berlin Wall and the war in Vietnam.

Despite these and other impediments, East-West trade began to be viewed differently in the United States during the 1960s, although in this respect the Congress lagged far behind Presidents Kennedy and Johnson and a good section of the business community. There were a number of factors behind the change in opinion. The United States began to catch up with the Europeans in realizing that our controls were not greatly hurting the Russians, particularly in view of the crumbling West European control system: in addition, the restrictions did not significantly enhance our security. American businessmen, moreover, were becoming more and more aware of the growing opportunities in Eastern Europe. Correspondingly, American administrators, worried about the seriously deteriorating U.S. balance of payments situation, could not help but be aware that by our controls we were voluntarily relinquishing hundreds of millions of dollars in foreign exchange earnings annually to Western Europe. It had also been clear for some time that the Communist bloc is not "monolithic," that there is a genuine Sino-Soviet split and, as with Yugoslavia after her break with the USSR a decade earlier, differentiated policies toward the various Eastern nations were a much more promising strategy than that which had been espoused in the 1950s and early 1960s.

Despite the wide recognition of the factors just mentioned, congressional opinion was sufficiently opposed to change because of the Vietnam War; therefore major changes in policy could not be implemented. Export controls were broadened again and credit controls were strengthened against nations which were helping North Vietnam. At the same time American trade with the USSR began to increase, and by the mid-sixties the United States began again to remove commodities from the export control list.

In the meantime, trade and investment flows between Eastern and Western Europe proceeded apace. Agreements were signed which facilitated not only trade but cooperation in many other fields including science and technology. Trade controls were virtually dismantled. MFN status was universally granted. Credit was extended without discrimination. During this period the Eastern nations demonstrated the strength of their interest in more intimate economic relations by making various institutional arrangements and adjustments which were quite substantial. Western companies were wanted to construct factories in their countries (e.g., Fiat in the USSR). The governments of Eastern Europe agreed to work with Western companies in co-production and co-marketing arrangements and to allow joint ventures in which the Western partner was allowed to own, in some countries, up to 49 percent of the stock. These were long steps for nations whose basic ideology forbids private ownership of the means of production.

In the past few years, American policy has come abreast of the rest of the world, although a few snags do still remain. The policy of détente, which viewed economic ties as one link in a chain of problem areas including the arms race, peace in Vietnam, and the Middle East, and so forth, led to a sharp relaxation of controls over East-West trade and investment and, in fact, to many measures to facilitate that trade. These measures included an end to the embargo on China and the relaxation or removal of almost all controls over trade with the USSR under the U.S.-USSR Trade Agreement of 1972. The Trade Agreement also provided for a final settlement of the Lend-Lease debt. Because of Soviet dissatisfaction with various provisions of the 1974 Trade Reform Act as enacted by Congress, the Agreement has been annulled. Specifically, the Soviets objected to the Stevenson Amendment, which limited Export-Import Bank credits to them to $300 million over a four year period, and to the Jackson-Vanik Amendment which tied MFN to Soviet emigration policies.

This record of Soviet foreign economic relations reflects in part the policies of other countries. But it also reflects certain of the characteristics of Soviet economic institutions and the views of the country's leaders about the role of foreign commerce in the nation's development.

Soviet Bloc Institutions and Views of Foreign Trade in General

In order to develop informed foreign economic policies toward the Soviet Bloc nations, it is essential to understand the ways in which their institutions and conduct of foreign trade differ from those which prevail under capitalism. The techniques and institutions by which foreign trade is conducted among Western nations are largely determined by the fact that the domestic economies of these nations operate primarily on a basis of private enterprise, free markets, and decentralized pricing. One does not usually think about it in these terms because this is the way it is and always has been in the West. Basically, foreign trade is simply an extension of domestic trade with certain added institutions to take care of the fact that each country has a different currency (hence the need for exchange rates, foreign exchange markets, the IMF), each country is "sovereign" and may want to protect some industries (hence tariffs, quotas, the GATT), and so forth.

The USSR and the nations of Eastern Europe use an entirely different set of institutions to operate their economies. Their means of production are nationalized and belong to the state, the allocation of resources is determined in the government's central plan, and the plans are implemented by direct controls. Prices are also set centrally and have little to do with allocation. Under this set of arrangements, the institutions for conducting foreign trade are quite different from those under capitalism and are largely understandable only if one has knowledge of internal institutional arrangements. We therefore present, first, a brief review of internal institutional arrangements, concentrating, however, on three features which are most important in determining their impact on foreign trade behavior. We then set forth some of the distinctive features of Communist foreign trade. The descriptions which follow will, for simplicity's sake, represent a rather extreme "Stalinist" model of a Communist economy. This model is no longer fully applicable to any of the Communist nations because of the recent economic reforms. However, with the possible exception of Hungary, it is accurate enough in essentials to be used for our purposes. The three domestic features of the centrally planned economies (CPEs) on which we concentrate are: use of direct controls instead of the market, overfull employment or "taut" planning, and irrational pricing.

Planning With Direct Controls

Market forces are employed in the CPEs to allocate labor and to distribute consumer goods among the population. Higher wages and better living and working conditions are used to attract labor into needed areas of employment. Consumers are free to spend their incomes on products of their choice in the various state stores. True, wages of labor and prices of consumers' goods are set by central planners and are usually fixed for long periods of time. Nevertheless, within this constraint, the allocation and distribution of labor and consumers' goods is accomplished largely via market mechanism.

There is, however, a very large sector in which direct controls, not market forces, determine allocation. This is the intermediate products sector, which includes all transactions between enterprises and between enterprises and state organizations. In this sector the planners set output, sales, and profit targets as well as prices for most enterprises; they determine delivery dates and inform all important enterprises from which they buy their principal nonlabor inputs and to whom they ship their outputs. Since there is no real market through which supply and demand can adjust automatically, this chore must be handled explicitly by central planning organizations in a laborious process which requires the establishment of "material balances" for thousands of products. A "material balance" lists all sources of a commodity on one side and all uses or shipments on the other. If the two sides do not balance, either because of some unpredictable event or because, initially, potential supplies and desired demands are not equal, then substantial difficulties are encountered because of the complexity of interindustry relationships. If, for example, the steel balance shows a one million ton deficit, and the decision is made to increase steel output by this amount, that steel industry will have to be allocated more coal, limestone, machinery, labor, and so forth—upsetting the balance of each of these products as well as of labor. Further, in order to produce more coal, limestone, and machinery it is necessary to have more steel (and machinery, labor, etc.) than the original million extra tons desired, and so forth; thus there is a many-staged regress. Alternatively, if it had been decided to solve the balance problem by reducing shipments of steel (rather than increasing outputs), similar adjustments would have had to be made as various enterprises found themselves with less steel than anticipated, and were, thereby, forced to cut back their own outputs and, consequently their shipments to other enterprises, and so on. In so complex a process it is inevitable that demand and supply are imperfectly balanced and shortages and surpluses occur.

Overfull Employment Planning

In practice, central planning has always been overfull employment planning. As some scholars have put it, the plans are too "taut," envisioning higher levels of economic activity than can possibly be sustained given available resources, labor, and given potential productivity increases. Enterprises are assigned targets which cannot all be fulfilled despite the fact that managers have strong incentives in the forms of bonuses to reach their targets. The result is that the demand for goods generally exceeds the quantities available (both intermediate and final products), sellers' markets are pervasive, inventories are inadequate and poorly distributed because of hoarding, planners' balancing problems are aggravated, and repressed inflation prevails—too much money chasing too few goods.

Irrational Prices

Partly as a consequence of central planning with direct controls, prices in the CPEs have always been disequilibrium prices which would not equate supply and demand if the economy were freed and which do not bear rational relationships to each other or to costs of production. Prices do not, of course, have to equate supply and demand, particularly in the internal intermediate products markets, since this is accomplished directly by the planners through the method of balances. There are other factors behind price irrationality. Until recently, enterprise accounts have not included proper charges for rent, interest, and profits—only labor has been adequately accounted for. Furthermore, many enterprises have received subsidies and have sold their products below cost;

others, mainly in the consumer goods industries, have had very large excise taxes levied on their products. The overall picture is one of great confusion. This is frankly admitted in the Bloc, as the following statement in 1971, by three Polish economists testifies:

... Because of the autonomous system of domestic prices in each country, an automatic and purely internal character of the monetary system and arbitrary official rates of exchange which do not reflect relative values of currencies, it is impossible to compare prices and costs of production of particular commodities in different countries.[1]

The three basic features of central planning outlined above have side ramifications for foreign trade behavior and relationships, some of which are now briefly described.

Trade Aversion

It used to be contended that Soviet bloc nations were autarkic—that they tried virtually to do away with trade. This may have been true of the USSR in the mid-thirties, but it is certainly no longer true for that country nor for the other Eastern nations. Nevertheless, there are practices related to central planning which tend to reduce trade below levels that would obtain under capitalist institutions. First, use of the method of balances and direct controls to implement planning causes an "aversion" to foreign trade on the part of the planners because of the difficulties which result if any of the balances are upset. Psychologically, they appear to be unwilling to depend on foreign sources of supply which are outside of their direct control if they can do so without too great a cost. This is especially true of trade with capitalist countries because of fears of disruption due to military or political factors, but is less the case in trade with their Socialist partners. It is worth noting, however, that this aversion is offset in part by a dependence on emergency or crisis imports to patch up the plan when domestic targets are not fully achieved.

Irrational pricing contributes to trade aversion by making it difficult for the planners to determine what can be profitably imported and exported. To cope with this problem, a number of ad hoc devices called "foreign trade efficiency indexes" have been developed. These indexes are usually used with prices which have been adjusted for some of the more obvious irrationalities. These adjusted prices are purely notional and are not used in transactions.

As we shall see below, central planning leads to rigidly bilateral trading patterns among the CPEs—trade that is virtually always bilaterally balanced. Bilateral balance is usually accomplished by reducing both sets of exports (imports) to the lower of the two desired levels. Roughly speaking, this practice reduces intrabloc trade by anywhere from one-sixth to one-quarter of its potential level.

Finally, to understand generally why it is likely that trade will be a smaller percentage of GNP under central planning than under capitalist free markets, it is worth noting that under the former, trade requires an explicit decision and action on the part of the government authorities whereas under the latter trade takes place "naturally" unless inhibited by explicit government-imposed barriers.

Inconvertibility and Bilateralism

The CMEA nations have striven without success for twenty-five years to eliminate the inconvertibility of their currencies and to multilateralize intrabloc trade. One factor behind inconvertibility is overfull employment planning. This affects a CPE's balance of payments in the same manner that inflation operates on the balance of payments under capitalism, i.e., it causes excess demand for imports. Eventually excess demand for imports leads to controls over imports and usually to restrictions on the freedom of residents to convert their own currencies into foreign currencies for the purposes of importing goods and services, traveling abroad, investing in the stocks and bonds of foreign nations, and so forth. This has always been called "currency" inconvertibility.

The CPEs have another type of inconvertibility as well, which appears to be quite unique to them: "commodity" inconvertibility. Commodity inconvertibility is caused not by inflationary pressures but by central planning with direct controls. Under central planning with direct controls, foreigners are not allowed to come into the country and shop around indiscriminately for goods (aside from consumers' goods and services bought by tourists, diplomatic personnel, etc.). Basically, they are restricted, usually under long-term agreement, to the commodities offered by the state foreign trade monopoly and its combines as established in the state plan. This is because unplanned purchases by foreign importers would disrupt the carefully drawn fabric of the plan. Further, given irrational domestic prices, foreigners, if free, might purchase commodities at prices below cost of production—heavily subsidized commodities, for example. For these reasons, the Communist nations do not allow foreigners to hold their currencies or to take them outside of the country. If they did, however, there would not be many takers because of the considerable uncertainties as to what the money would be allowed to buy and at what price.

Inconvertibility always leads to bilateralism and CPE trade is no exception. Bilateralism is particularly prevalent in intrabloc trade. Since no nation is willing or allowed to hold another's currency, trade must be bilaterally balanced, and it is. All efforts to introduce multilateralism have failed, including the introduction of a Bank for International Economic Cooperation (BIEC) and, through this bank, the creation of a so-called transferable ruble. East-West trade is much more multilateral than intrabloc trade because it is conducted in western convertible currencies. Since foreign currency earned in trade with one Western nation can be spent in any other, there is no need for bilateral balance. Unfortunately,

Western currencies are not used to multilateralize intrabloc trade because any nation which holds convertible currency prefers to spend it in western markets where products are generally more available and of higher quality.

Foreign Trade Monopoly

In the Communist countries the conduct of foreign trade is assigned to a state monopoly. This is almost inevitable given the centralized nature of all other economic activity and the problems faced by the central planners in dovetailing imports and exports into their commodity balances. The Ministries of Foreign Trade are assisted in their operations by twenty to fifty subministries or combines which administer the exports and/or imports of particular groups of commodities. These combines act as intermediaries between the producing or consuming enterprises within the country and the foreign export or import firms, a process which reduces efficiency and discourages foreign trade. As a result some of the East European nations have allowed some of their enterprises to deal directly with foreign enterprises.

The existence of foreign trade monopolies has led many Western economists to hypothesize that Communist nations thereby exert monopoly power in foreign trade with the West and as a result extract exorbitant gains from trade. This view results from the confused assumption that because the foreign trade monopoly completely controls its own nation's trade, it must also have monopolistic powers on the world market. This does not necessarily follow. It is true, of course, that when the Soviet Union enters the market to purchase $1 billion worth of grain or indicates that it is prepared to buy a fertilizer factory, it is able to exert some monopolistic or, rather, monopsonistic power. But in the ordinary day-to-day transaction in East-West trade, there are usually many buyers and sellers; and East as well as West have alternative transactions available to them. Under these circumstances little if any monopoly power exists on either side. Our previously cited example, it should be noted, was one in which the USSR acts as a large buyer. It undoubtedly exerts much less power as a seller. In fact, experience has shown that generally speaking the Communist nations often have to undersell world market prices in order to dispose of their exports.

The reasons which explain the existence of foreign trade monopolies also are responsible for the tendency to try to conduct trade within the framework of annual and longer term agreements. These agreements are used to ensure that foreign trade conforms as closely as possible to the plans and "balances" of the central planning board.

Tariffs and MFN

With nationalized industry and a state monopoly of foreign trade there is no need for a tariff system. Import decisions are made by the state directly, obviating the need for the intervention of tariffs. These import decisions constitute, in effect, implicit quotas. Also any profits on trade go directly to state organizations and the state budget, obviating the need for the tariff as a financial instrument.

This system creates problems for the CPEs regarding MFN (most favored nation) status. While MFN deals with all impediments to trade, the major area of negotiation is the reduction of tariffs. In order to enable themselves to bargain for MFN status, several of the CPEs introduced two-column tariffs in the 1960s, the lower set of rates being reserved for those nations which granted them MFN status. Unlike Western tariffs, the lowering of these so-called tariffs does not affect the amount of the product imported (since this decision is contained in the plan) nor does it affect price (also set in the plan). In this sense, it does not reduce "protection." However, it may well redistribute imports, since the foreign trade combine has a financial incentive to buy from the Western nation which has lower tariffs. Granting MFN status in terms of a set of tariffs which cannot affect the price or volume of imports is not particularly in the spirit of MFN, which was partly conceived to reduce protection and increase trade. It is difficult to say whether it is in the spirit of "nondiscriminatory trade," another goal of MFN, particularly since it seems a reasonable presumption that in the big bilateral negotiations in which trade between bloc nations is contracted for annually (and longer), the tariffs are quite irrelevant.

Because of the artificiality of CPE tariffs, a practice has developed in which CPE nations reciprocate MFN status by guaranteeing to increase their imports each year by a certain percentage. This, in effect, simulates the trade-increasing effects of lower prices through lower tariffs. Poland and Romania have agreed to such arrangements through GATT. In fact, of course, such arrangements are hardly necessary these days because of the hard currency shortages which the CPEs are experiencing: any increase in their hard currency earnings from MFN or any other source is bound to be spent very rapidly in Western markets.

Foreign Trade Pricing and Exchange Rates

The CPEs' trade at world prices is unrelated to their domestic prices. These governments do not use their exchange rates as real prices of their currencies in foreign trade. These bizarre practices are made necessary by their irrational internal pricing systems and the existence of commodity inconvertibility. Given a set of seven or eight different irrational pricing systems, the CPEs have been hard put to find a meaningful and objective set of relative values at which they could fairly trade. As a last resort they have had to trade at world prices. Although they have had to adjust these prices to fit some of their idiosyncrasies, they have maintained their stability over a number of years, despite changes in actual world trading prices.

Exchange rates typically link the average price levels of tradeable goods in different countries. Prices in pounds in England are lower than prices in dollars of the same products in the United States; hence the pound is worth more than the dollar and this is reflected in the exchange rate of the two currencies. What meaning can an exchange rate between two nations have if their price systems are irrational? The answer is: no meaning, and this is why the exchange rates serve no function. The problem of not having an exchange rate is gotten around in different ways in intrabloc and East-West trade respectively. The annual trade between two bloc nations is exactly balanced (in world prices) for the very purpose of avoiding the necessity of having to exchange currencies. If it were not for commodity inconvertibility, one nation might accept the currency of the other and use it eventually to buy something—but this is not permitted. East-West trade is also conducted at world prices but also in world currencies—dollars, pounds, gold, etc. Trade is not balanced bilaterally. Rather each CPE nation is free to spend its earnings of convertible currency in any other Western country. Since the CPE's trade is limited to dealing in convertible currency, there is never any question of having to use the official exchange rate for conversion of their domestic currency into a Western currency.

A major consequence of the fact that the exchange rate is not a real price and cannot be used as such is that devaluation of the currency is not available to the CPE as an instrument for rectifying balance of payments problems. It does not matter what the official exchange rate of a currency is for the exchange rate does not relate domestic to world prices—and the price at which a product is traded remains the world price.

Dumping

The CPEs have often been accused of "dumping" in Western markets. Given irrational domestic prices and nonfunctioning exchange rates, it is almost impossible to prove a "dumping" charge in the usual way, i.e., that products are or are not being sold abroad at below the domestic cost or price. Most cases of alleged "dumping" which have been studied have turned out not to be cases in which the Communist country has been out to disrupt the importer nation's home market or alternatively to destroy the competition by low or loss prices only to raise prices later and reap large profits. Mostly, low prices have been charged through ignorance or because there has been no other way to gain entry into markets which have otherwise discriminated against imports from Communist nations.

Balance of Payments Pressures in East-West Trade

The CPEs have long experienced serious hard currency shortages. These shortages do not always show up explicitly or fully as deficits and debts because of stringent foreign trade controls. Nevertheless, despite controls, CMEA's hard currency indebtedness has risen steadily since 1960, relieved only briefly in the case of the USSR in 1973-1974 as a result of the rise in oil, gas, and gold prices. Since then, as a result of the Western recession and the disastrous 1975 Soviet harvest, CMEA's hard currency indebtedness increased sharply again and is believed to have passed the $30 billion mark by the end of 1975. Over the longer run, the secular balance of payments pressures with the West stem primarily from the features of central planning described above.

Overfull employment planning is—and has an impact like—inflationary pressure. Demand exceeds supply, which leads to rising domestic prices, more imports, and fewer exports (as domestic buyers compete with foreigners for exportable goods). Rising domestic prices themselves reduce the country's competitive position in world markets.

Overfull employment at home also means the existence of perennial sellers' markets. Sellers' markets tend to dampen the competitive instinct since buyers will accept whatever is put on the market. Products tend, therefore, to be of poor quality, relatively unadvertised, serviced poorly, not adapted to special needs, and so forth. Even if central planning were not characterized by such "tautness," many of the same characteristics would hold because under central planning, particularly in the intermediate product markets, products do not have to be "sold"—they are distributed by the plan. All of these factors breed into plant managers an approach to business which is not calibrated for success in capitalist markets. They cannot compete in the markets of the advanced Western nations in manufactured goods, in many of which they should, by any other token, be very competitive. This explains, for example, why such a high percentage of Soviet exports consist of raw materials. Raw materials like oil and gas are homogeneous and do not require "selling," servicing, and so forth. Unfortunately, the smaller Eastern countries cannot rely on exports of raw materials to finance their needs from the West.

Many advanced nations depend on new technological developments and new products as an important source of exportable goods. Other nations, not quite so advanced, are able quickly to master new techniques and duplicate new products and then rapidly outcompete the innovators in world markets. Japan is the classic case. We indicated earlier that for systemic reasons the CPEs have had great difficulties in innovating, imitating, and diffusing new technologies and products. Relatively speaking, they have less technology to export and they are not good at exporting the products which they copy. Further, as is now well known, they (particularly the USSR) are presently engaged in large-scale import of technology and this is a source of current balance of payments problems.

The Communist nations conduct much more than half of their trade with each other. This is done not because they can produce so many products as cheaply as other nations but on political grounds. As a result they are a relatively high cost enclave in the world economy. This implies that as restrictions on

East-West trade are removed, the East will have more of an incentive to import from the West than West from East. Until all restrictions are removed, this tendency will be another factor causing the Eastern nations to have balance of payments problems.

Some of the above problems could be ameliorated or cured by currency depreciation—if Communist currencies could be meaningfully devalued. As we have noted, devaluation is meaningless under existing conditions. The USSR cut the value of the ruble to less than 25 percent of its previous value on April 1, 1936, and to less than one-half of its previous value on January 1, 1961. Neither devaluation, and these were enormous ones, had the slightest impact on their exports or imports.

Potential Benefits from Expanded Foreign Economic Relations

The differences between the economic institutions of the CPEs and the West create certain difficulties in the expansion of foreign commerce. New institutional arrangements could be developed to minimize those difficulties, however, if both sides saw substantial benefits in the expansion of economic relations. From the Soviet point of view, there are three kinds of potential benefits. First are the normal gains from commodity trade that accrue to all nations involved in the international specialization of labor. Second, expansion of foreign commerce would contribute to an increase in the rate of technological progress. And third, an increase in East-West trade would help alleviate certain problems encountered in the conduct of East-East trade.

The Gains from Trade

Two groups of commodity imports offer the largest potential gains from trade: agricultural products and machinery and equipment. The Soviets could, if they chose, continue to expand agricultural output to meet the requirements of their own economy and those of their political allies, but it would be a costly policy. The primary reason is the increasingly marginal quality of new agricultural land alluded to earlier. In addition, the organizational and incentive principles of the Soviet economy operate more successfully in industry than in agriculture: they are particularly applicable to the collective farms. Because of these natural resource and organizational limitations, expansion of agricultural output would absorb large volumes of capital investment. Following the familiar economic argument, if that capital were used instead to expand the output and exports of those fuels, minerals, and manufactures in which the Soviets are relatively efficient, they could provide themselves with agricultural products more cheaply by import. The case for this policy has become stronger in the last two years with the sharp increase in world prices of such commodities as fuels and gold.

There is a powerful strategic argument against this policy, however. The larger the percentage of imports in total agricultural consumption, the greater the vulnerability of the country to political pressures from abroad. A program of stockpiling could reduce the country's vulnerability to short-run difficulties in access to foreign supplies, but any substantial dependence upon foreign sources would weaken the political and strategic position of the USSR. The mounting prospects of worldwide food shortages make the case even stronger. If the USSR had to take its place alongside India, Africa, and other possible food-deficit areas in the sharing of surpluses produced elsewhere, its international political weight would be greatly decreased.

The announced intention to bring a large mass of north Russian agricultural land into production shows that the decision has now been made. The program will clearly require a large volume of capital investment, which could be used much more productively in the development of oil and gas production. It is a clear trade-off of economic growth for strategic gains, but it is difficult to imagine that any other choice could have been made. Even with this massive forthcoming effort, it is by no means certain that the Soviets can become self-sufficient in foodstuffs. But they are determined to minimize their long-run dependence on the world's food exporters.

Among manufactured products the Soviets could gain from expanded imports of specialty consumer goods like processed foodstuffs, clothing, and hardwares. These goods could be sold domestically at relatively high prices and would increase the effectiveness of the money incentive structure and reduce inflationary pressure. Since they have no strategic significance, Soviet purchasing agents could take maximal advantage of world price fluctuations. But the Soviets are more interested in importing advanced technological products like electronic equipment, chemicals, and specialized machinery, particularly those in which their domestic technological capability trails furthest behind that of other countries.

To the extent that expanded imports of these products are financed out of current export earnings, the gains to the Soviets—and to their trading partners— are the normal gains from trade. Other countries will benefit from the diversion of Soviet resources to the expanded production and export of fuels, steel-making equipment, turbines, earth-moving machinery, and other commodities in which the USSR is relatively efficient. And the USSR will benefit in the same fashion. It is impossible to foretell how the total gains from trade expansion will be divided between the USSR and her partners. But since national product per unit of resources will rise in both, the relative position of the USSR may not change greatly. (Some estimates of the potential Soviet gains from East-West trade are presented below.)

The rate of expansion of commodity trade will be limited by the Soviets' ability to increase their export earnings. That increase depends on the rate of growth of the Soviet capital stock and labor force, Soviet willingness to increase the allocation of those resources to the export industries, and Soviet ability to compete effectively in Western markets. In none of these respects is the prospect very bright. The rate of growth of both the capital stock and the labor force is likely to decline, as we have shown. The massive program of agricultural expansion will absorb a substantial volume of investment in the next few years. And in the absence of radical economic reform the competitiveness of Soviet manufactures in Western markets is not likely to increase substantially. Because of these limitations, in the absence of other sources of financing, the rate of trade expansion will be rather restricted, and so will be the magnitude of the gains. That is one source of the intense Soviet interest in obtaining credits from abroad.

The Acquisition of Foreign Technology

The international transfer of technology has been a major contributor to the rapid rate of technological progress in the postwar world. One can only imagine how great the loss would have been if each nation had sought to keep secret all the new scientific and technological knowledge generated within its borders, and had forbidden the export of machinery and other products embodying that knowledge. Each nation's progress owes a heavy debt to that of others.

There are three major channels of international transfer of technology. One is through the medium of publications: scientific and technical books and journals primarily. The Soviets have long made full use of this channel. They have an extensive program of acquisition of foreign published materials and a highly developed apparatus for abstracting, translating, and disseminating the material acquired. Since this form of technological transfer poses few political problems, it has been heavily exploited. However, while it is a vital part of the whole process of technological transfer, it is of limited value. A large part of the technological knowledge contained in any country is not committed to print, or not fully, particularly the knowledge of the most advanced techniques, including those still in the stage of research and development. Hence a nation that relies primarily on published materials for the import of technological knowledge is bound to lag behind the world technological level. In fields of rapidly advancing technology the gap will be particularly large.

The second channel of technological transfer is international travel, which occurs in many forms. Students study in the technical schools of other countries, visiting professors teach in the classrooms and conduct their research in the laboratories of other nations, immigrants reside for long periods of time in other countries and work in the factories, both bringing and acquiring technology. Scientific, professional, and industrial associations conduct national and international meetings, both of which are often visited by interested persons from other countries. The technological knowledge embodied in products is widely disseminated through the travel of the sales forces of business concerns. The sales engineer going abroad to sell conveys, in his sales catalogs and his promotional offers, a great deal of technological information to the firms to whom he seeks to sell. If performance guarantees are to be given, he examines closely the production facilities and techniques of the prospective customer, thus obtaining a certain amount of new technological knowledge. In the search for new and cheaper sources of supply of materials and components the businessman combs the enterprises of other lands both giving and receiving technological knowledge. It is indeed a vital part of the competitive position of many firms to be completely current on the most advanced state of the technology in other parts of the world against which they must compete.

This important channel of international transfer of technology has been accessible to the USSR to only the most limited extent. The borders of the nation are so difficult to penetrate, in either direction, that it is difficult to imagine that the USSR can ever attain the wide diffusion of world technological knowledge characteristic of other countries. One of the Soviet innovations in international science and technology, as well as in the arts, is the "cultural exchange agreement," in which governments contract to supply to each other so many scientists or engineers for a specified number of man-months in specified fields. Some knowledge does manage to pass through the borders of the country by this technique, but it is a most clumsy method and does not foster the long-term ties that lead to fruitful communication. Some Soviet scientists and engineers are permitted to attend international meetings abroad, but their number and the form of their participation is far below those of other countries. Most important, the droves of Japanese, American, German, and other business-men who fan out among the enterprises of other countries seldom appear in the offices of Soviet enterprises to give and to receive information, nor do many Soviet engineers and industrialists have the opportunity to travel in the same fashion in other countries. The typical Soviet industrial executive or designer therefore probably has far less knowledge of the most advanced techniques, present and prospective, available in other countries than do their opposite numbers abroad.

An effort has been made in recent years to expand this channel of technological transfer. The numbers of people involved in cultural exchange agreements have been rising. Soviet scientists and scholars attend international meetings somewhat more often and in somewhat greater number than in the past. Some foreign firms have been permitted to establish offices in Moscow, and occasionally to visit the Soviet enterprises with whom they deal or wish to deal. And some Soviet industrial executives have been allowed to travel abroad with purchasing missions. But barring a fundamental political change, it is impossible to imagine that the personal transfer of technology can ever approach the significance that that channel has in · the case of other countries. In any assessment of the prospects for technological advance in the USSR, this factor must be considered a permanent handicap that the Soviets have got to contend with.

The third channel of international transfer of technology is trade in the products that embody that technology. Much of it occurs in the ordinary commodity trade discussed above—in the import of specialized materials, components, machinery, and so forth. Another form is the importation not of the products but of the manufacturing or processing facilities for producing the products—whole factories or production installations. Both forms were extensively used during the large import program in the first two five-year plans. In the postwar years advanced technology continued to be available from some of the CMEA countries, but the supply from the capitalist world was greatly reduced. Western strategic controls on exports to the USSR were never so tight as to prevent the acquisition by the Soviets of a few models of advanced machinery and other products. In many instances these models were copied by Soviet designers and a Soviet version of the product put into production. The copying of foreign models was for many years the principal form of the import of advanced foreign technology from the capitalist world.

That method became increasingly unsatisfactory for a number of reasons. One is that because of the long lead times, the products incorporating technology so obtained were always already obsolete by world standards. The second is that with the increasing importance of petrochemical and electronic technology, copying became less feasible. In mechanical equipment most of the technology is evident in the physical product itself; "the technology is transferred with the product," in engineering terminology. But the physical possession of an integrated circuit conveys no information at all regarding its manufacturing technology. Third, a growing number of Soviet technological developments had licensing potential which would be lost unless the USSR entered into international patent agreements, which they have now done. The possibility of acquiring foreign technology by direct copying is therefore no longer available. If it is to be acquired at all, it must be done through commercial arrangements. Some of it can be acquired through the expansion of commodity trade. But the major source is the acquisition of entire plants or production installations. The prototype of these arrangements is the construction of an automobile plant in the USSR by the Fiat company. Perhaps the largest of the deals sought by the USSR is the construction of a natural gas pipeline and gas liquefication and transportation facilities by a consortium of United States firms.

To evaluate the contribution of acquired foreign technology to the promotion of technological progress, imagine that there were created in the USSR a new science-based corporation, of the kind currently being formed, called "The Outside World." The corporation produces more advanced designs than those in the rest of the economy, and it constructs the manufacturing installations incorporating those designs. The consequence of the activity of this corporation would be an increase in the rate of technological progress. In the same way the acquisition of foreign technology may be expected to increase the rate of technological progress. The magnitude of the effect depends, however, on the relative weight of The Outside World in the total economy. If the production of industrial technology is dominated by the older, less progressive corporations, then the addition of one progressive new one will make a positive difference but it will be relatively small. As applied to the Soviet case, the size of the economy is so large that imported technology cannot be expected to make a very large difference, although it will be a positive one.

In market economies, imported technology tends to diffuse through the system and to become quickly incorporated into the domestic technology. If this happens in the USSR, the benefit of the policy will be greater. But the diffusion process appears to be closely related to the state of competition. In market economies new technology is quickly adopted by other firms which fear the loss of their share of the market. The presence of advanced foreign products also imposes a certain technological discipline on all producers. The presence on the market of fine Japanese hand calculators and well-built small German cameras obliges domestic producers either to adopt the new technology or leave the market entirely. That pressure for diffusion is much weaker in the USSR where the state regulates the quantity of output, so that the producer of an inferior product generally can expect that it will eventually be sold. The superior product does not invade and take over a market, forcing other producers either to conform or to leave the business. Hence the effect of the imported technology will be largely confined to its own sphere and it is not likely to have a strong technology-enhancing effect on the rest of the economy. Imported technology is no substitute for the kinds of organizational reforms that may be needed to spur technological progress in the economy at large, including the efficient absorption of imported technology.

Finally, the imported technology is generally financed by credits extended by the seller. The effect of the credit-financing is to increase the stock of capital at a faster rate than it could be increased on the basis of domestic investment alone. The package thus tends to increase both the quantitative and the qualitative sources of economic growth. The credits increase the quantity of capital, and the imported technology financed by the credits raises the quality of the capital.

Summarizing the argument, of the three channels of international transfer of technology, published materials have long been fully exploited by the Soviets and little more is to be expected from that source. Some small increase may be expected from the personal transfer of technological knowledge, but because of political restrictions on the movement of people its contribution will remain far short of that enjoyed by other countries. The greatest gain is likely to come from the credit-financed purchase of foreign plants and production facilities, which will increase both the quantity and quality of the capital stock.

East-East Trade Problems

The rigidity and other problems of central planning with direct controls have been described. Plans are never perfect; often there are unplanned deficits (as a result of excessive tautness) and sometimes surpluses of certain products. The problems which face the central planners in adjusting to unplanned deficits are often serious because of the way in which an unplanned deficit in one product, if it is an input, can cause unplanned deficits in a whole succession of other products, as described earlier. Many ad hoc devices have been developed by the planners to deal with these problems. One such device is through foreign trade—to try to export unplanned surplus commodities and import unplanned deficit commodities. Unfortunately, this is very difficult to do in intrabloc trade because of the tautness of planning and commodity inconvertibility. None of these nations has any slack in its plan with which to help out a neighbor. For nation B to help nation A, which has an unplanned deficit in commodity Y, B would have to just happen to have an unplanned surplus in the same commodity, an unlikely coincidence. East-West trade provides much more flexible markets for both covering unplanned deficits and selling unplanned surpluses. Needless to say, it functions much better with regard to the former than the latter problem because of the difficulties the CPEs have (described earlier) in selling in the West.

Another problem from which intrabloc trade suffers is rigid bilateral balancing. Rigid bilateral balancing of trade implies either a loss of possibly one-third of the potential volume of trade *or* unprofitable trade of roughly the same amount. These rough figures are arrived at as follows. Suppose A wants to import 100 units from B but B only wants to buy 65 from A. If B insists on bilateral balancing at his level of imports, then trade will be balanced at 65 and A will be unable to import 35 worth of desired goods. If A prevails upon B to balance at a higher level, say at its desired level of 100, then B will have acquired 35 worth of A goods which it does not want. The first case is one in which trade is reduced below its most profitable level; the second involves unprofitable trade. The hypothetical figures in the example presented are not too far from those experienced in western free trade. It has been shown that if one calculates the percentage of the total trade of a nation that is represented by bilateral surpluses and/or deficits, it usually turns out to be somewhere between 25 and 40 percent.

Under these circumstances, East-West trade can serve two functions. First, to the extent that it replaces intra-bloc trade, it also probably expands it (and the gains from trade), since the bilateral balancing constraint no longer exists. Second, to the extent that the potential surplus nations in intra-bloc trade accept imports which they do not want, they are motivated to reexport them.

(Hungarian reexports as high as 15 percent of total annual imports have been reported.) The Western world market probably provides for easier disposal of many of these goods than the other intra-bloc markets. Unfortunately, it is impossible to estimate the gains from East-West trade which may be attributable to these sources.

We have already indicated that the CPEs might benefit from improved economic relations with the West through loans and credits to finance imports of plant, equipment, technology, and so forth. The urgency of these credits is underscored by the hard currency balance of payment problems which normally beset these economies because of central planning. These factors (difficulties in "selling," inability to devalue effectively the currency, etc.) were discussed in the preceding part.

The part "Soviet Foreign Economic Relations" also indicated that the Socialist nations are, in effect, a trade-diverting customs union, in which they buy goods from each other which could be, in many instances, bought more cheaply in the West. Further, the Western products would also often be of higher quality. Any shift from intra-bloc to East-West trade will lead to gains from this source.

The USSR and the nations of Eastern Europe have revealed their strong interest in Western products, technology, and investment by the large debts which they have incurred over the past decade and by their continuing search for additional credits. In fact, this visible evidence of demand for Western products is but the tip of an iceberg. There exists in these nations an enormous repressed demand for hard currency imports which must be and is controlled to levels dictated by hard currency exports and available credits. The existence of repressed demand for additional commodity imports from the West is inferred from studies which have concluded that the USSR (and the other CPEs) engages in less foreign trade than it did when it was a capitalist country and less than a comparable capitalist country would trade today. Soviet exports and imports are each presently in the neighborhood of 3 percent of GNP. For the United States, which is certainly as self-sufficient as the USSR, if not more so, the comparable percentage is about 5-6 percent. For Imperial Russia the ratio was 10 percent, and statistical studies suggest that the present-day USSR could benefit from exports and imports which each amounted to between 5 to 10 percent of GNP. Soviet trade is relatively low partly because of central planning and trade aversion, partly because of its policy of conducting the preponderance of its trade in the limited markets of Eastern Europe, and partly because it cannot generate the hard currency earnings or secure the credits to expand its imports from the West. It is well worth noting that an increase in the percentages of exports and imports to GNP from 3 to just 4 percent would increase the value of each by $6½-7 billion! Clearly, if the USSR could increase its exports to the West by this amount or more, the receipts would not be spent in Eastern Europe, with whom they now overtrade, but would be spent on imports from the West.

U.S. Policy: Problems and Options

The benefits that the USSR derives from an expansion of foreign economic relations depend in part on the policies that the United States adopts toward trade expansion. If détente continues, there is a substantial potential for an increase in U.S.-Soviet bloc trade, which could come from a number of sources. First, as American controls on trade with the Eastern nations are equalized with those of Western Europe, Japan, and Canada, America will regain a more normal share of that trade. In 1938 and 1948, American exports constituted 16 and 31 percent respectively of the trade of this group of nations with the Eastern nations. In 1953, it amounted to only 0.2 percent and in 1970, though rising, it was still less than 5 percent. By 1973, the United States share of exports was about equal to the 1938 share but this was the result, in part, of the extraordinary level of grain exports to the USSR in that year. So there would appear to be considerable room for further expansion of nonagricultural exports at the expense of other advanced Western nations. The U.S. Department of Commerce has estimated the 1978 levels of U.S. exports as shown in Table IV-2. The USSR figures do not include grain exports, which could obviously be expanded significantly in any year should the Russians have a bad crop.

Over the longer run there are two other potentially important sources of trade with both the USSR and Eastern Europe. First, we have already noted that the CMEA nations overtrade with each other and undertrade with the West, for primarily political reasons. Should the political climate change enough to loosen the economic bonds of CMEA, there might be a fairly rapid shift from intra-bloc to East-West trade. Romania, for example, in the period of its strain with CMEA policies, reduced its share of intra-bloc trade from about 70 to 50 percent in a few years. A decline of this magnitude today for CMEA as a whole could involve an increase in East-West trade of some $6-7 billion, of which at least $1 billion, and probably more, would be diverted to the United States. It is difficult to predict the probability of significantly more diversion from intra-bloc to

Table IV-2
Estimated 1978 Levels of U.S. Exports
(in millions of dollars)

U.S. Exports to:	If 1972 Shares Are Maintained	If U.S. Trade and Credit Controls Are Removed
Eastern Europe		
high	607	1,550
low	356	888
USSR		
high	357	1,051
low	232	684

East-West trade. The probabilities of an increase in USSR-West trade would increase sharply if the USSR should decide that, in order to meet its hard currency needs, it would have to divert petroleum and other raw material exports from Eastern Europe to Western nations. The increased hard currency earnings would lead to increased Soviet imports from the West. However, the Eastern European nations would be forced to buy their petroleum, at least, from the Middle East so that little East-West trade would develop on this account.

Second, we have indicated above that central planning leads to trade aversion and that most CPEs trade below the levels appropriate to similar capitalist nations. This is particularly true of the USSR. Several factors could lead to increased trade participation ratios and, therefore, to an increase in East-West trade. One of these is détente. Certainly, in the case of the USSR, one important factor in the low trade participation ratio is an unwillingness to be dependent on potential enemies. A second factor is economic reform. If the Communist nations reform and decentralize their economies, many inhibitions regarding trade would disappear. Reform would also remove some of the causes of the persistent hard currency problem and by this token also enable trade to expand with the West. While potentially considerable East-West trade could develop from greater Eastern trade participation, the possibilities that this will happen in the near future appear small.

The preceding paragraphs have spelled out the possibilities of greater U.S. exports to the USSR and to Eastern Europe while ignoring a major constraint: the ability of these nations to finance such an increased level of imports. As indicated earlier, the CPEs have serious hard currency balance of payments problems and are in no position to expand imports from the West. In fact, the high figures for U.S. exports to Eastern Europe and the USSR presented in the above table assume that the Eastern nations have been granted MFN and have access to long-term credits equal to that of other industrial nations. While it seems likely at this juncture that trade will be normalized in these respects, it is not certain. If the USSR diverts hard currency exports (gas, oil) from Eastern Europe to the West, this will by itself finance larger imports from the West. Some relief from the hard currency problem may also result from the various co-production and co-marketing schemes and joint ventures which have been springing up between East and West. The single potentially most important factor in increasing trade and investment will be the willingness on the part of advanced Western nations to make more credit available, particularly for long-term investments, than has hitherto been the case. In a sense a real case of comparative advantage exists and is taken advantage of when the rich capitalist nations which are short of raw materials invest in technology and raw materials resources in the capital-short USSR. Almost unlimited investment is possible; how much is economically and politically desirable is the central question for U.S. policy.

To Trade or Not to Trade

The expression "trading with the enemy" summons up visions of treason and cuts close to the patriotic nerve. When nations define their relationships to others in terms of friendship or enmity, the policy options tend to be posed simply and starkly. To many people the issue has always been and continues to be one of whether we ought to permit any trade at all with Communist countries. The option not to trade does not command widespread support today but it continues to lurk in the background of the current debate over the appropriate volume and type of trade and therefore merits brief consideration.

We may assess the consequences of the choice of that option by a review of our economic policies toward Communist nations in the period since World War II, as set forth above. These policies can be characterized basically as pure economic warfare, designed to deprive the USSR and its allies of commodities, credits, markets, and anything else that might contribute significantly to its military or economic strength. These policies were implemented by the Export Control Act of 1949 and its successor Acts, the Mutual Defense Assistance Act of 1951 or Battle Act, the Johnson Debt Repayment Act of 1934, denial of MFN status to the Communist nations in 1951, Trading With the Enemy Act, and various other laws.

On the whole these policies must be judged to have been a failure. They were largely ineffective from economic and military standpoints, were often implemented badly, and took little account of changing political realities. Perhaps the most fundamental mistake was the assumption that by placing an embargo on the USSR, even with the collaboration of Western Europe, we could significantly reduce its economic and military strength. While there may have been some slight warrant for this assumption immediately after World War II, there was none by 1953, by which time wartime destruction of productive facilities had been more than made good and an H-bomb had been independently developed. For an embargo to succeed, the target nations must be heavily dependent on external sources of supply for strategic products and must be effectively cut off from these sources by the embargo. Such conditions sometimes exist in the short run; a nation suddenly subjected to an effective embargo at the outbreak of a war, for example, may experience critical shortages of certain vital commodities, particularly if it is a small nation. But the conditions for a successful long-run embargo of the USSR do not exist and never have. Like the United States, and possibly even more, the USSR is virtually self-sufficient and has been since the late 1930s when it began to produce synthetic rubber and to mine enough nonferrous metals to meet almost all of its domestic requirements. By 1937, the USSR was importing no more than one-half of one percent of its GNP, a level of trade dependence less than one-tenth that of the United States, the least dependent of Western industrial nations. One could hardly embargo such a nation—it was already existing practically without foreign trade. Even during the early thirties when trade was used as a device to expedite the industrialization drive, imports rose for a year or two to a peak of only about 4 percent. After World War II, when the United States launched its economic warfare effort, the USSR was trading no more than one or one and one-half percent of GNP at most—which hardly leaves much room in which an embargo might be effective. It might be argued that the embargo can be effective by denying the USSR the product that it appears to want most from us today, namely technology. An effective embargo could deny the USSR technology in many areas in which it is lagging. However, in those areas which are most crucial from a military standpoint, namely in the military and aerospace industries, the Soviet Union has shown itself capable of keeping within a reasonable distance (perhaps at high cost) of the most advanced Western nations. This suggests that the depth of possible damage of an embargo on technology is strictly limited if reduction of military potential is the ultimate target. It is also worth considering, at this point, that the advent of nuclear weapons and rockets to deliver them pretty much divorces the ultimate military capability of any nation from all technology but that directly related to the production of military and military-related products.

The United States attempts at economic warfare were misguided in other respects. For one thing, this nation never received full cooperation from its NATO allies despite the passage of the Battle Act of 1951 and despite the establishment of the elaborate machinery of COCOM (the Coordinating Committee composed of all the NATO allies except Ireland and including Japan) to insure that products which the United States embargoed would not reach the USSR via other Western nations. Not only did the COCOM nations eventually refuse to make their embargo lists as comprehensive as ours, but implementation of their controls apparently was much less rigorous than our own. They also refused to go along with our complete embargoes on shipments to China and Cuba, with strict limitations on medium- and long-term credits to the Eastern bloc nations, and with denial of MFN status. At this point in history it seems a little difficult to understand why we persisted in maintaining stricter controls than our NATO partners when their unwillingness to cooperate doomed our extra controls to failure!

Much of the time our export controls have been directed at preventing the Eastern nations from reaping the gains from trade; in fact, a renewal of the Export Control Act in 1962 explicitly so stated. Observed strictly, of course, such a policy would have the effect of cutting off all trade with the Eastern nations since, presumably, they would not trade if there was nothing to be gained from trade. Pursuit of this kind of policy did lead those administering our export controls to prohibit the export of all sorts of industrial products without the slightest military value (e.g., mechanical potato pickers) at the same time that shipments of many nontechnical products such as wheat were allowed. The fallacy of such a policy was well put by Harvard Professor Thomas Schelling before the Senate Committee on Foreign Relations in 1964:

Wheat shipments may have the same effect on military programs as jet engine sales. Wheat shipments may permit the Soviets to keep chemical industries oriented toward munitions rather than fertilizers; jet engine sales may permit the Soviets to allocate engineering resources to consumer goods rather than jet engines.

One might go even further and add that wheat shipments probably save the Russians more in resources than most shipments of most industrial products because agriculture is the least efficient sector of their economy—that is, the sector in which they have the greatest comparative disadvantage.

Our policies have been marred also by misconceptions relating to the difference between economic warfare goals which are geared to short-run and long-run objectives respectively. The effective method of weakening a potential enemy over the long run is to allow him to buy whatever he wants (with the exception of the most highly strategic weapons) and thereby make him as dependent as possible on one's own country. A policy of denial and embargo has just the reverse effect: it forces the potential enemy to become independent so that should hostilities ever develop, he would be relatively invulnerable to further economic warfare. In reverse, this is one of the arguments which has been raised against future American imports of oil and gas from the USSR, an argument we consider below. We would like to stress that while a long-run embargo precludes a nation from taking advantage of another nation's dependency, we are not advocating that the United States trade with the USSR for purposes of pursuing economic warfare at some future date. As noted earlier, it is our belief that the United States can neither significantly strengthen nor weaken the USSR by *any* economic policy that it adopts. On the other hand, by refusing to consider relaxing controls against trade with the Communist nations over the 1950-65 period, the United States was unable to take advantage of the fact that they would have liked a higher level of trade with us.

Finally, American policies toward the Communist nations suffered from a failure to differentiate among those nations and to take advantage of differences which did exist between them. True, there were exceptions, such as our early assistance to Yugoslavia and extension of MFN status to Poland in the late 1950s. But how long did it take us to recognize that there was a Sino-Soviet conflict? And why did it take ten years before Romania's attempts to loosen its ties with CMEA were assisted in 1975 by extension of MFN status? Under the détente of the past few years, our policies have taken a quantum jump toward rationality. Hopefully this trend will continue.

Strategic Options

Many people have long been convinced of the absurdity of the effort to maintain a permanent peacetime embargo on the USSR, but are anxious about the strategic implications of the increase in trade that will ensue. They fear that a policy of expanded commerce will strengthen the USSR and weaken the United

States in the course of time. If the spirit of détente should someday be replaced by one of active military rivalry, we will then be weaker strategically than we would have been had we never succumbed to the lure of détente—so the argument goes.

There is no doubt that expanded trade and credits will provide the USSR with certain economic benefits and will contribute to a rise, however small, in the growth rate. Indeed it is the prospect of such gains that fuels the Soviet interest in expanded trade. It must be remembered, however, that the gains from trade are shared by the trading partners, though not necessarily equally. U.S. exports to the USSR add to the income produced in the United States in the same way as exports to any other country. And U.S. imports of oil, gas, and other commodities from the USSR provide benefits similar to those derived from imports generally. From a strategic point of view the Soviet leadership might be charged by their own hardliners with having strengthened the United States by relieving unemployment in the U.S. export industries and easing the fuel problem in the United States by the export of Soviet oil and gas.

While both the USSR and the United States will gain from an increase in trade, the size of the gain to either side is not likely to be large relative to the size of their economies. A few rough calculations will illustrate the point. Total Soviet trade was recently (1972-1973) about $18 billion each way. Trade with the industrial West is about $4 billion. Suppose that the latter is doubled overnight to $8 billion. How much do the Soviets gain from an increase of $4 billion in commodity trade with the West? Suppose that their gain, from being able to exchange their exports for imports of superior goods and/or some at lower prices, is 75 percent. The total gain to the Soviets under this favorable assumption is $3 billion. This figure must be judged in the perspective of an annual GNP of close to $700 billion! The relatively small size of the total gain figure, it should be noted, is due to the fact the USSR trades such a small percentage of its GNP and is not dependent on imports for any vital necessities in the way, for example, Japan and Western Europe are dependent on petroleum.

Suppose now the USSR receives $10 billion in credits over a five-year period—or $2 billion a year. Since annual gross investment is presently close to $200 billion, these credits would increase Soviet capacity to invest by a little over 1 percent a year. With GNP increasing by more than $35 billion a year (roughly $650 billion times 5.5 percent), with all other things equal, a 1 percent increase in investment could at most increase output by less than $0.4 billion a year for each of five years and thereafter until depreciated. We say "at most" because this calculation ignores the contribution to output of labor and other factors. Further, it does not take into account the repayments of the credits, which eventually have to be subtracted from output in calculating net benefits.

Suppose now that the USSR uses the proposed credits not to increase its rate of investment but to import technology. In other words, instead of building its own automobile factory or its computers, or laying its own pipeline, Moscow imports Western know-how and equipment. How much does the Soviet Union stand to gain? Certainly the $2 billion a year invested in this manner will yield more than the average increase in output from investment of $0.4 billion calculated above. Suppose imported technology yields three times as much output or an additional $1.2 billion a year. This comes to a maximum increase in the growth rate of 0.3 percent a year. From this, one would have to subtract repayments of principal plus interest on the credits, not to mention other (domestic) factor inputs, in order to pinpoint that part of the growth due to the new technology.

Under the very favorable conditions assumed above, the projected gains to the USSR from increased trade and investment with the West are certainly worth striving for. These gains are measured in the billions of dollars and cannot be ignored. On the other hand, the fundamental economic situation in which the USSR finds itself will not be changed by this increased contact with the West. Increased trade will add no more than one-half percent to GNP in any given year. Higher rates of investment through credits can hardly increase the rate of growth by more than 0.1 percent per year. Only imports of technology could change trends. Under our very favorable assumptions, the rate of Soviet growth might be increased by from, say, 5.5 to 5.8 percent. In the perspective of a Soviet growth rate declining from about 7-1/2 percent in the 1950s to about 5-1/2 percent in the 1960s, it could be argued that a substantial infusion of foreign capital "might" recoup, say, one-sixth of the loss. If it did, however, the economic position of the USSR would still not be changed in any fundamental way. Recovery to the former rates of growth, if possible at all, would require radical reforms which would encourage faster technological change throughout the economy. The economy of the USSR is too large and varied to be significantly transformed by selected imports in particular industries. One may wonder why, if the potential gains are as modest as all this, the Soviet leaders have banked so much on expanded economic relations with the West. A possible answer is that they may have overestimated the gains.

One source of concern is that the political pressure for détente may lead the United States to accept conditions of trade and credits that would greatly increase the Soviet benefit relative to that of the United States. This is not likely to happen in the case of commercial trade, despite the unfortunate case of the large Soviet grain purchases. Future Soviet grain purchases are likely to be much more closely monitored by the U.S. government, so that the Soviets will not be able so easily to prevent prices from rising as a consequence of their own massive purchases. In ordinary commercial trade, however, the volumes are neither that large nor concentrated, and the Western traders are private companies operating without the large government subsidies involved in the international grain trade. Prices of purchase and sale are therefore likely to be close to world prices.

It is in the extension of credit that the pressures for concessions are likely to be concentrated, and it is here that the major options for U.S. policy lie. Three options may be distinguished. One is to offer no U.S. government credits. A second is to offer government credits to the USSR in the same relative volume and on the same terms as are offered to other nations with whom the United States trades. A third is to treat the USSR more favorably than other countries, both with respect to the volume of credits and perhaps with respect to terms as well.

If we selected the first option, the volume of trade would depend on the credits that U.S. industry and commercial banks are prepared to offer and on the terms on which the USSR or its American exporters can borrow on the world's money markets. Assuming that the trade restrictions of the past have been abolished, the volume of U.S.-USSR trade would increase but by a modest amount. This option must be regarded as contrary to the spirit of détente, for since U.S. government credits are available for the financing of trade with other countries, the USSR would continue to be discriminated against in U.S. policy.

The instrumentality of the second option is the Export-Import Bank. The United States, like most large trading nations, offers a certain volume of credit at subsidized interest rates for the purpose of assisting its exporters in competition with the exporters of other countries. The Export-Import Bank, which administers that program, could make available to American firms exporting to the USSR a volume of credit roughly equivalent to that offered to the other countries to whom we export. Like all recipients of subsidized credits, the USSR would benefit from the lower cost of its imports relative to what the cost would be if the credit were financed at commercial rates. The volume of trade is therefore likely to be greater than it would be if only commercial credit were available. This option was evidently favored by the Nixon and Ford administrations and, between the fall of 1972 when the U.S.-USSR Commercial Agreement was signed and the fall of 1974, Export-Import Bank credits were extended and were used to finance transactions with the USSR. The Congress, on the other hand, in passing the Stevenson Amendment to the Trade Reform Act in January 1975, which limited Export-Import credits to the relatively small sum of $300 million over a four-year period, clearly indicated its disagreement with the Administration's judgment on this matter. Soviet leaders have expressed their keen dissatisfaction with that limitation and the Stevenson Amendment was certainly a major factor behind their subsequent decision to withdraw from the 1972 Commercial Agreement.

Soviet dissatisfaction with regard to the limitation on credits has two dimensions. First, the Stevenson Amendment is the first instance in which a credit ceiling has been placed on the Export-Import Bank credit available to a specific nation. It thereby denies the USSR "equal treatment" with other nations, a status it has long felt entitled to and have in the past fought for, primarily in connection with MFN treatment on trade barriers. Second, apparently part of the *quid pro quo* involved in the Soviet understanding of détente was that they would receive a larger volume of credits, and at lower interest rates, than is normally extended under U.S. credit policy. No specific amounts have been formally stated, but the projects in which the Soviets have expressed interest suggest that they are prepared to place contracts involving credits totaling billions of dollars rather than millions. This is, in effect, a third U.S. policy option—to offer at subsidized Export-Import Bank interest rates a volume of credit substantially in excess of that extended to our traditional trading partners.

A fourth possible policy option would be for the United States to extend to the USSR through the Export-Import Bank a larger amount of credit than is usually available but require that the USSR borrow all or part at commercial rates of interest. This would undoubtedly also be viewed by the USSR as discriminatory unless, perhaps, it was allowed to borrow very large amounts at subsidized rates before being obliged to pay commercial rates.

The choice among these options depends on an assessment of the political benefits to be gained; the more we are prepared to give the larger the political benefits we may expect to enjoy. But in making the choice it is to be hoped that full account will also be taken of the consequences for the United States of the various levels of credit.

Some critics object to a large volume of credit on the grounds that it would expand the volume of trade well beyond that which would be reached under normal economic relationships. The gains from trade which the Soviets would derive from normalized trading relationships may be quite acceptable, but it is conceivable that the volume of U.S. exports could be artificially expanded by subsidized credits to an extent that might begin to make a significant difference in the Soviet growth rate and in its military capabilities. The point must be conceded in principle, but on the basis of the rough estimates presented above, the volume of credits that have any reasonable prospect of being offered is not likely to have that large an effect on Soviet growth.

The point is sometimes made that credits give the recipient immediate command over a larger volume of output than could be obtained on the basis of ordinary commercial trade. The distinction between trade and credits is not that sharp, however. Ordinary trade also increases the volume of current output, for it enables the trader to shift resources from activities in which the country is relatively inefficient to more efficient ones. Hence if one objected to the offer of credits for this reason, he ought also to object to the expansion of trade as well. Trade and credit are, in a sense, alternative ways of increasing the volume of available current production. The argument therefore boils down to the preceding one, that subsidized credits will expand the volume of trade by an indeterminate amount beyond that which emerges on the basis of commercial relations alone.

In evaluating the cost of a program of subsidized credits, it must be borne in mind that credits extended to the USSR generate a flow of capital that would otherwise have gone to other countries, or perhaps to other uses in the United States. If Soviet oil and gas resources were developed by U.S. firms with capital raised in the money markets at prevailing interest rates, there is a higher probability that the long-run gains to the United States from the future imports of Soviet oil and gas would be greater than if the same resources were invested in U.S. oil and gas development. But if the Soviet developments are financed by credits subsidized by the U.S. government, one can be less certain. It is very possible that at commercial rates the resources would have been better used in developing our domestic resources than those of the USSR. It is therefore important that in the progress of détente the United States not be so carried away by the lure of political gains that it offers incommensurably large economic benefits to the USSR at the expense of our own economy.

Much of the anxiety about the expansion of our economic relations with the USSR derives not so much from commodity trade and credits but from the more general technological gains that the Soviets would make. Is the United States not simply turning over its advanced technology to the Soviets, thus enabling Moscow to catch up with America quickly and possibly to overtake the United States? There is no doubt that the import of foreign machinery and production facilities and the purchase of foreign production licenses will advance the level of Soviet technology. The United States will gain from the commodities imported in exchange for that technology, but there will be no equivalent U.S. gain from the import of Soviet technology.

How significant the Soviet gain will be is not easy to assess. The Soviet leaders evidently expect it to be very large indeed. One suspects that some look upon the import of foreign technology as the solution to the most pressing economic issues—the decline in the growth rate and the lag in Soviet technology behind that of the advanced industrial nations. For the reasons set forth above, we think that such hopes are unrealistic. An underdeveloped country, as the USSR was in the 1930s, can make large gains on the basis of imported technology in the process of transformation into an industrial economy. But that transformation is now largely completed. The closer a developing nation comes to the technological level of the most advanced nations, the more its rate of technological progress depends on its own innovative capacity rather than on the acquisition of technology from abroad. One can found a machine tool industry or a computer industry by importing foreign equipment. But one cannot in that way overtake or even rival the nations that supply the technology, particularly in the fields of the most rapidly advancing technology.

Contractual agreements are often based on different assessments by the parties of what they stand to gain. Our judgment is that the Soviet leaders expect much larger benefits from the importation of foreign technology than they will succeed in realizing. The imported technology, and the accompanying technological knowledge, will raise the level of productivity in the sectors in which they are employed and there may well be some limited spillover into other sectors. But the volume is not so great, relative to the size of the Soviet economy, as to make a massive impact, nor can foreign technology make up for the deficiencies in the innovative capacity of the domestic economy.

If this assessment is correct, the current Soviet enthusiasm for imported technology may one day change to disillusionment. That ought not lead to a reaction against the import policy, for the gains are still positive. But the policy will then be seen simply as a rational way of allocating the nation's resources and not as the means of making the quantum leap to the level of technological leadership. For that there is no alternative to fundamental economic reforms.

While the Soviet leaders may currently anticipate large technological gains from the acquisition of American plant and equipment, it can be argued that their interest lies not only in the technology but in the favorable credit terms under which they hope to acquire it. If the former were overriding, one would expect that the Soviets would be interested in large-scale imports of that technology even if they had to be financed either under the terms of credit available in the world capital markets or through the sacrifice of all other imports from the West. Evidently that is not the case. The value the Soviet leaders place on the strictly technological gains from American machinery and equipment apparently is not so great as to make it worth paying the full market price or to give up other imports. But they would buy large quantities if they could buy it at cut rates. If this is their assessment, they are probably right. A large volume of capital imports at favorable interest rates would help cushion the anticipated decline in the growth rate of the capital stock and thus shore up the rate of economic growth. They seek American technology but only in combination with cheap American credit.

We conclude that while the Soviets will enjoy certain substantial gains from expanded economic relations with the United States, the magnitudes are not such as to pose a significant strategic problem for the United States. Moreover, the United States also stands to gain economically from the expansion of trade. The first part of this conclusion may have to be modified if the third option with respect to subsidized credits is adopted. One can always imagine a volume of credit so large as to make a significant difference, but it is doubtful that an amount of such size would be forthcoming.

The strategic issues extend further than the question of the direct economic benefit to the USSR, however. There are other ways in which the position of the United States may be weakened as a consequence of a significant expansion of trade and credits. One is the possibility that we may grow increasingly dependent on the USSR as a source of supply of some vital commodities. The second is that our freedom of action will be curtailed as increasing quantities of U.S. capital are invested in the USSR.

All trade involves some degree of mutual dependence which in normal times is not a matter of concern. The Arab oil embargo drove home the lesson that these are not normal times and that oil, in particular, is a commodity of peculiar strategic importance. For the United States, indeed, the issue of dependence is primarily one of oil. For the USSR it is food.

We have suggested above that the Soviets have already made their decision at what is likely to be a very high cost; they have undertaken a considerable expansion of agricultural output in the northern lands that is designed to render the nation largely self-sufficient in food production. If they had greater confidence in the durability of the present détente, perhaps they would not have made the decision. There may, however, be an economic as well as a strategic motivation. World food prices may well rise in the next decade and the spread between high Soviet domestic costs and world prices will narrow.

In any case, if the direction of trade expansion had taken the form of growing Soviet food imports from the United States and growing U.S. fuel imports from the USSR, there would have been a certain balance of strategic risk. The prospect now is that Soviet imports will consist of such commodities as machinery and production facilities, a sudden cessation of which would impose no short-run hardships. The larger the share of Soviet fuels in U.S. imports, however, the greater the short-run U.S. vulnerability to a sudden cessation of trade. It is true that the USSR is not a member of the Organization of Petroleum exporting Countries (OPEC) and has had no formal collaboration with that organization. It has also been argued that the United States would be wiser to import oil from both the USSR and the OPEC countries than to import only from the latter. That may well be true, but it takes no great feat of imagination to foresee circumstances in which the USSR may find it expedient to associate with OPEC.

The most ambitious of the Soviet proposals for expansion of trade involves the supply of U.S. capital equipment and technical expertise to develop Soviet oil and gas resources. The investment is to be repaid in the form of Soviet exports of oil and gas over an extended period of time. In evaluating the proposals it is vital to the U.S. national interest to consider seriously whether the volume of fuel imports from that source conflicts with the objective of Operation Independence. If it does, strategic considerations may dictate a limit to the expansion of Soviet-U.S. economic relations.

The second concern is that, apart from dependence on specific imports like oil and gas, the expansion of trade and credits will limit the flexibility of U.S. policy. The larger the proportion of U.S. business and labor involved in trade with the USSR, the greater the potential leverage of the USSR on U.S. policy. When jobs and profits have been invested in trade with the USSR, the public debate on issues of foreign policy may be heavily influenced by that fact. More serious, however, is the volume of investment in facilities in the USSR. The company that loses an export contract with the USSR can hope to find other customers. But the company that has built production facilities in the USSR faces a much larger potential loss and will have a keener financial interest in U.S. policies toward the USSR.

The capital exporter gives a hostage to the recipient of the capital. As Professor Gregory Grossman has argued, a large Soviet indebtedness to the United States may complicate the political relations between the two countries. A volume of credits of the magnitude the Soviets sometimes appear to have in mind, amounting to billions of dollars, will eventually require a large stream of Soviet exports to pay the interest and the amortization of the loans. It is possible to imagine circumstances in which the Soviets may find it difficult to generate the required volume of exports, which could lead to political tensions.

These are legitimate concerns in evaluating the U.S. economic relations with the USSR. But their significance should not be exaggerated. It should be recognized that the USSR has always paid its commercial debts and would probably try to avoid jeopardizing its favorable credit rating. Further, through the rigid controls it exercises, the Soviet government can always cut back its hard currency imports if necessary to meet a debt repayment schedule. It should also be recognized that the debt repayment problem, if it becomes one, is a problem for the distant future. In view of the many uncertainties of the distant future, we feel that not much weight should be assigned to this potential risk. For another, the volume of Soviet trade is never likely to be so large a proportion of our total trade as to generate a major political lobby. And for most of the large and multinational corporations involved in the trade the volume of their Soviet business is likely to be a small proportion of their total. Nor is Soviet politics completely immune to the influence of its industrial interests. Sections of Soviet industry will also become increasingly dependent on trade with the United States, although perhaps not in strategic commodities. While Soviet officials do not exert political influence in the same manner as private U.S. lobbies, that dependence may well reduce to some degree the flexibility of Soviet policy as well. Hence these concerns do not constitute a decisive case against détente or against the expansion of trade. But they do suggest that, with the end of the embargo, U.S.-USSR economic relations ought not to be permitted to grow in whatever directions and to whatever levels might be dictated by the interests of U.S. business and the Soviet government. The U.S. has a national interest in keeping the expansion of trade under careful surveillance.

Political Options

Most people would regard strategic issues of the kind discussed above as proper considerations in matters of international trade policy. The use of trade as a political instrument, however, is generally regarded as inappropriate, and rightly so. One need only imagine a world in which that principle were generally ignored, to recognize the good sense behind it.

Yet like all such principles, it is not absolute. There are circumstances in which it ought not to be applied, as the principle of free speech ought not to be applied to the cry of "fire" in a crowded theater. Even in trade among friendly nations with similar social systems, circumstances sometimes arise in which trade restrictions are properly used as political instruments. In Soviet-U.S. trade, however, such circumstances are always present. In a centrally planned economy it is impossible for the government not to consider the political implications of its foreign trade decisions, much as a monopolist can hardly ignore the effect of the volume of his output on the price that he can charge. The Soviets do not even regard this as a matter of dispute, and are quite forthright in declaring that trade is an arm of Soviet foreign policy. Second, because of the differences in social systems, circumstances are bound to arise in which each side might consider that by its trade with the other it becomes a party to social practices regarded as repugnant. In the nineteen-thirties, for example, American long-shoremen refused to unload Soviet cargoes of timber alleged to have been cut by prisoners of the labor camps. The strike started, according to legend, because of the discovery on some logs of the words "Help Us" written in Russian blood. Apocryphal or not, the legend illustrates a prevailing circumstance in trade among highly dissimilar societies. It is therefore not very helpful to approach the question of U.S.-USSR trade from the universal proposition that political considerations should not enter into the options we may properly entertain in the formulation of our policy toward the USSR. The question is rather the substance of the political considerations.

Two major options have emerged involving political conditions on trade policy. One involves the use of trade policy as an instrument in securing Soviet participation in an arms control agreement. The other concerns Soviet restrictions on emigration. With respect to the first, it would be idle to question the propriety of using trade and credit expansion to facilitate a general agreement involving arms control. The appropriate question is rather whether it will work, and indeed the policy of détente is based on a judgment that it will. It is argued that by the elimination of past trade restrictions the United States can contribute to the reduction of the level of mistrust between the nations which would in turn make it possible for both to take certain risks involved in arms agreements that they would not take in a regime of economic warfare. The question, then, is not whether America should, in principle, tie trade expansion to arms control but whether in practice there are political and economic benefits to be gained.

It is not an easy game to play. It is unimaginable that the USSR would accept arms control conditions that would gravely jeopardize its military security for the sake of economic benefits in the form of trade and credits. The Soviet leaders are realists, however, and are prepared to strike bargains at the margins. If trade and credit concessions are part of a package agreement that increases the military security of the United States, they may well be worth the while. One need only be sure that the full costs of the concessions are understood by the political authorities and weighed alongside the strategic benefits secured.

The other major political issue is the link between trade expansion and the denial of the right of emigration from the USSR. Again, there is no question of general principle here. No nation is bound to ignore absolutely the political and social conditions of its trading partners and to act as if its trade policies had no influence on those conditions. National sovereignty is no longer held to be so absolute, if it was ever so held, as to oblige other nations to accept whatever treatment it accords its subjects, of whatever nationality or race. The post-Nuremburg world has been groping toward a definition of the notion of human rights, a concept that implies a limitation of the sovereignty of nations over their own citizens. Many would hold that slavery and racism, for example, are not matters of "internal policy" with which other nations have no right to interfere. The United Nations has recognized the right to interfere, in voting economic sanctions against Rhodesia, and the United States has recognized it in its embargo of arms sales to South Africa.

The Jackson-Vanik amendment ought therefore not be approached as an issue of the general principle of whether the United States has the right to interfere in the internal affairs of the USSR. Two other questions ought rather to be asked. The first is whether the denial of the right to emigrate is an abridgement of a fundamental human right so repugnant as to oblige other nations to take measures to seek to change that Soviet policy. The second is whether the use of trade policy, in this case the denial of most-favored-nation (MFN) status, is an effective instrument for attaining that end.

On the first question, the United Nations has declared the right to emigrate as a fundamental human right, in a document to which the USSR is a signatory. The case for that declaration is compelling. One might concede that a nation may adopt laws that are highly discriminatory or offensive to some portion of its population, laws that forbid the practice of certain religions, for example, or that impose certain educational requirements on all children that are offensive to their parents, or that allow certain liberties and deny others, or that impose measures of racial or ethnic or social discrimination. If people who regard their humanity as denied by such laws are free to leave the country, there is a certain mitigation of their condition. But if they are both denied the right to an ethical and dignified life and at the same time compelled to tolerate that condition forever by denial of the right to leave, their condition is insufferable. These are the terms in which the supporters of the Jackson-Vanik amendment express the case that the right to emigration is not a matter of the internal affairs of the USSR but a fundamental human right with which others have an obligation to be concerned.

Some opponents of the amendment reject this position, and regard the right to emigrate as an internal affair of a country in much the same way as its property and criminal laws are internal affairs. Other opponents accept the human rights argument but question the effectiveness of the amendment as an instrument for securing a modification of Soviet policy. Effectiveness is properly a concern in policy issues of this sort. The critique of the peacetime trade embargo is indeed based in part on the argument that it has been ineffective in attaining the stated goal. And people generally tolerate the violation of human rights in their own countries and elsewhere when there are no known instruments that may be effective in securing a change in policy.

Up to the moment of passage of the 1974 Trade Reform Act, one could only speculate on the effectiveness of the Jackson-Vanik amendment. Since the Soviet rejection of the conditions contained in that Act, many analysts have concluded that the question has been decided—in the negative. For reasons to be set forth below, we believe that the evidence is not yet decisive, although as an option for U.S. policy the emigration issue may no longer play as prominent a role in the trade discussions. Nevertheless the issue merits attention because it is highly instructive on the questions that arise in the effort to establish political conditions on the expansion of commerce.

The reasons for expecting that the denial of MFN status might be an effective instrument for eliciting Soviet concessions in the matter of emigration policy originate, as in all such cases, in a set of special historic conditions. The end of the Stalinist terror in the USSR has made it impossible for the present leadership to suppress dissent with the thoroughness of earlier years. Consequently various forms of dissent have begun to emerge publicly. Writers and other intellectuals—like Sakharov and Solzhenitsyn—have openly denounced the denial of human rights. Religious groups like Baptists and Jews have demanded the right to practice their religion. And national and ethnic groups like Ukrainians, Jews, and Lithuanians have protested the suppression of their national cultures. The Jackson-Vanik amendment refers to the right to emigrate generally, and therefore applies to all persons, including these dissident groups. In the case of the Jews, however, other special conditions have combined to generate the strongest pressure for emigration: the establishment of the State of Israel, the revival of anti-Semitism in the USSR, and the strong support from Jews abroad have encouraged a substantial number of Soviet Jews to take the risk of open struggle for the right to emigrate. It is the combination of all these conditions that has thrust the issue of emigration to the fore. In the absence of these conditions, the right to emigrate would be one more human right denied in one part of the world with little prospect of effective action elsewhere to restore it. It is the events within the USSR that have forced this particular issue on the political agenda of other nations. At the same time the economic pressures within the USSR have created conditions in which the country's leaders appeared prepared to make some unpleasant concessions for the sake of the anticipated gains from trade and credits.

Some commentators who are prepared to entertain options involving political conditions on trade expansion nevertheless question whether the emigration issue is the appropriate option for U.S. policy. On a full review of U.S. policy objectives, other issues might be identified as more important; or one might argue that the condition ought to be general Soviet good behavior rather than some specific form of behavior like free emigration. Certainly the design of policy ought to be based on such broad review. But in a democracy it is not possible to fine-tune foreign policy in insulation from domestic political forces. There was widespread sentiment around the country that the Soviets were prepared to grant much greater concessions than had been extracted by our Administration which had so committed its prestige to the success of détente that it was giving away more than it was getting. Various members of Congress were searching for ways to stiffen the Administration's bargaining posture, but as one observer put it, the Jackson-Vanik amendment "was the only amendment in town." Moreover, powerful sections of the labor movement continue to oppose trade concessions to the Soviets, which they regard as a form of support for "slave labor." If a wave of strikes or other instances of labor unrest should erupt in the USSR, it is likely that American labor would seek to push another amendment on to the trade bill. Similarly, the rise and suppression of religious activity in the USSR would kindle analogous demands for political restrictions on trade expansion. It happens at the moment that emigration holds the political stage, and in the reality of democratic politics that has determined the form of our option.

In assessing the likelihood that the Soviets will agree to permit more of its citizens to emigrate in exchange for an expansion of commerce, we have two pieces of evidence. First, while publicly deploring what they regard as interference in their domestic affairs, they had quietly agreed to a substantial increase in emigration. Second, after the passage of the 1974 Trade Reform Act, the Soviets reversed their position and annulled the 1972 Trade Agreement. Four factors may account for this reversal. First, the Soviet leadership may be divided on the question and the constellation of political forces may have changed. Second, the international publicity given to the issue may have made it impossible for them to accept openly what they had earlier agreed to quietly. Third, the Trade Reform Act contained not only the Jackson-Vanik Amendment but also the Stevenson Amendment, which limited the volume of Export-Import Bank credits to $300 million over a four-year period. Fourth, the recent rise in the prices of petroleum, gas, and gold had increased Soviet hard currency earnings, thereby reducing the value to them of the benefits to be received under the Act. (This could have been one reason for a change in the constellation of domestic political forces mentioned first.)

Perhaps all four factors played a role in the Soviet decision to reject the terms of the Act. If the fundamental Soviet interest was in a large volume of subsidized credits, the Stevenson Amendment may have been decisive. Not only did it single out the USSR for discriminatory treatment, but it also greatly reduced the size of the potential benefits that the Soviets had expected to derive from the expansion of commerce. It is therefore a reasonable conjecture that the potential availability of a large volume of Export-Import Bank credits might have overcome their distaste for the Jackson-Vanik amendment. On the other hand, it could well be argued that the dramatically changed balance of payments situation in 1974 may have reduced the Soviet need for credits sufficiently so that it would have balked at the Jackson-Vanik amendment anyway. While this may well have been one of the factors which was weighed by them in the balance, the timing of events leaves doubt about its importance. The balance of payments implications of the rise in energy and gold prices were certainly clear to the USSR by the early spring of 1974, if not earlier. The annulment of the Trade Agreement, on the other hand, followed closely on the heels of the Stevenson Amendment, not to mention the extra dose of publicity on the emigration clause of the Act.

In both arms control and emigration policy, there is always the danger of overplaying a strong hand. In both cases there are limits beyond which the USSR will not go; they will obviously not agree to terms that would substantially weaken their military position or threaten the system of political control over the population. Within those limits, however, there are real options for the United States to influence the political conditions under which trade and credits are allowed to expand.

Economic Options

Finally, the expansion of trade requires a certain amount of institutional adaptation on the part of the United States and the USSR, as well as consideration of the policies to be adopted toward Soviet and East European membership in such international trade organizations as the General Agreement on Trade and Tariffs (GATT) and the IMF.

For the most part, we feel that the now annulled October 1972 Trade Agreement between the United States and the Soviet Union was a significant first step in the direction of eliminating many of the problems which have stood in the way of improved economic relations. Since the provisions of the Agreement are well known, only a brief outline of major points is necessary here:

1. A settlement was reached on the Lend-Lease Debt. This cleared the way for the USSR to receive MFN treatment subject to congressional approval. It also allowed the USSR to receive medium- and long-term credits on a par with other nations since it was no longer considered subject to the terms of the Johnson Debt Default Act of 1934.
2. Both countries have agreed to withhold exports to the other in situations which might lead to domestic market disruption. This is the solution to American fears of Soviet "dumping." It is, in fact, a fairly extreme solution, since it effectively prohibits Soviet competition with U.S. domestic industry.

3. The Agreement encourages the settlement of commercial disputes in third nation arbitration courts because of the American reluctance to have disputes adjudicated in Soviet courts.
4. Both nations agree to provide expanded and improved commercial facilities to the governments and private trading enterprises of the other nation. Each nation has set up an official commercial office on the territory of the other.
5. Each nation commits itself to facilitating mutual bilateral trade.

Thus the Trade Agreement managed to resolve a number of the institutional problems that complicate the conduct of trade between the two systems. Presumably similar solutions will be incorporated in a future agreement, if there is one. But a variety of problems remain to be solved. For example, while U.S. access to the Soviet market in both the physical and informational senses has been improved, it is far from the level which prevails in Western countries or which appears possible in the USSR. There are also questions regarding the effectiveness of the other provisions of the Agreement until they have been tested in practice.

Perhaps the major option facing the United States with regard to its domestic institutions is whether or not to introduce institutions to prevent another "grain deal." Actually, the case of the grain deal embodies two separate issues. First is the question as to whether the United States government should allow American private enterprises to export, without government intervention, large quantities of commodities that have become scarce or are regarded as strategic. This is not a peculiarly Soviet problem but simply one that happened to surface in the recent large Soviet grain transaction. This problem is more appropriately studied as a question of general international economic policy rather than of East-West policy. It seems clear, however, that the trend of thought and of action on this matter is for the U.S. government to intervene in such cases.

For example, a few years earlier, given some warning, our government intervened to stop exports of soybeans when it appeared that further exports would lead to a domestic shortage. Prohibition of export in the case of soybeans caused considerable distress among our traditional customers, particularly Japan, which had become dependent upon the United States as a supplier. The grain and soybean cases point up the dilemma of finding a satisfactory position on this issue. On the one hand, the national interest requires that the United States government maintain some supervision over the export of scarce or strategic commodities. On the other hand, good relationships, particularly with friendly nations and traditional customers, require that due consideration of their needs also be weighed in the balance.

An apparent solution to the Soviet grain deal problem was reached in 1975. First, American exporters are now required to disclose to the government within twenty-four hours any anticipated large-scale exports to the USSR. Second, in October 1975, the two governments signed a Grain Agreement precipitated by the Soviet crop failure of that year and Russian attempts to purchase again enormous quantities of grain from the United States. In August President Ford had halted all grain shipments to the USSR until it could be determined whether or not such sales would be inflationary as they were in 1972. Subsequently discussions with the Soviets led to a five-year Agreement which committed the United States to sell and the USSR to buy from six to eight million tons of grain annually. This is designed to stabilize the grain market and also to shift some of the storage costs to the USSR. Additional purchases by the USSR, if desired, are allowed but *only if* U.S. grain supplies do not fall below specific levels.

The second issue brought up by the grain deal is that of the monopoly power of a state trading organization facing private enterprise. This problem was considered briefly in the Part "Soviet Bloc Institutions" above. It is our judgment, stated there, that the monopoly powers of the state trader in the world market are overestimated, granting, of course, that exceptional instances like the "grain deal" do occur. To the extent that private enterprises feel handicapped in entering into negotiations with state trading organizations, there may be warrant for the establishment of some kind of organization through which these enterprises can approach the state traders. Such an organization could serve important informational functions as well which, because of the high prevalent level of ignorance, might significantly advance U.S.-USSR trade. The options which face us, then, are first whether or not to establish organizations which American enterprises can use (if they desire) to facilitate their trade with the USSR; and second, if such organizations are considered desirable, to decide whether they should be established and managed by a U.S. government bureau or left to the business community to handle. It is worth noting that in a number of European countries and in Japan, private consortia have been developed for this purpose, in some instances with government encouragement in the early stages.

A somewhat related issue is raised by the concern that has been expressed that American enterprise may sell technology to the Russians at too low a price. This concern has led to proposals that the United States government establish an agency or "screening committee" or develop some other technique for guarding against such contingencies. These fears are apparently engendered by a number of special characteristics of the "technology market." Most important seems to be the fact that the United States government does finance a large part of the R&D in this country and much of the technology which is sold abroad by private enterprises may be sold at prices which do not reflect these government subsidies. To the extent that technology purchased by the USSR is financed by Export-Import Bank credits, they contain an additional subsidy in the form of low interest rates. Finally, technology sold abroad is usually both unique and a sunk cost. Under these circumstances, the problems of establishing a "proper" market price—if there is such a thing—are substantial.

The fears which have been expressed that technology is being sold to the

USSR at a price below its social cost could reflect either a general concern that such burdens should not fall on the American taxpayer or a specific concern that the USSR should not receive unpaid-for benefits. It seems fairly clear that the latter concern is the one at issue or else the problem would have been raised a long time ago with regard to our much larger exports of technology to other Western nations.

Our feeling about the possibility that the USSR may receive unpaid-for benefits in buying technology is conditioned by what has already been stated above in connection with technology transfers to the USSR. To repeat, there appears to be little probability of technology transfers on such a scale that the economic positions of the two nations could be significantly altered by the prices placed on technology sales. Further, we have seen no evidence that American businessmen are prepared to bargain for less than they think they can get in trade with the USSR or that technology has in fact been sold at bargain prices.

The possible instance in which a screening committee might appear to serve a useful function is one in which the USSR is attempting to buy a type of technology owned by a number of U.S. enterprises which are competing for the sale. Because of government research subsidies, competition could lead to what might be viewed as too low a price. It is only fair to point out, however, that since R&D is always a sunk cost, the same price could well have been arrived at without government subsidies.

The option which faces us is whether or not to establish a "screening committee" to monitor technology transfers solely in order to prevent the USSR from getting "bargains." In considering this option, it is well worth taking account of the probable small magnitude of the gains to the USSR, past U.S. experiences with export controls more rigorous than those of our allies, the inherent difficulties in setting a price for technology and the possible effectiveness of a governmental committee in such a price-setting process, and, finally, the fact that such a committee would be viewed as (and would be) discriminatory by the USSR.

Issues relating to GATT—such as granting MFN status—have been raised above. Clearly, the USSR and the other Eastern nations cannot reciprocate MFN in the traditional way by lowering tariffs—since their tariffs have no impact on internal prices and other real economic magnitudes. On the other hand, reciprocity through commitment to increase imports does simulate part of the real effect of a lower tariff. Furthermore, as noted above, it seems clear that because of evident interest on the part of these nations in Western goods, they will increase imports from the Western nations just as fast as they can augment their hard currency earnings. The West cannot ask more than this.

Of course, MFN means more than just increasing trade by mutual reduction of tariffs. It is also supposed to equalize barriers to trade among trading partners and thereby to eliminate discrimination. On this count, the Communist formula is less satisfactory. True, those Communist nations which are new members of GATT (Poland, Rumania, and Hungary) and participate in MFN arrangements presumably do not discriminate against other Western members of GATT. They are committed to basing their purchases in Western markets on purely commercial considerations. This commitment is inadequate to achieve real nondiscrimination for at least two reasons. First, since a fairly substantial number of the most important East-West transactions are transactions either between governments or between an Eastern government and one or more large Western enterprises and, because these transactions inevitably involve many commodities, it is unreal to expect that each constituent transaction constitutes a purchase in the cheapest market. Second, accession to GATT in no way reduces the discrimination in favor of each others' trade that the Communist nations practice. GATT allows members of customs unions to discriminate in favor of each other and CMEA is a kind of Socialist customs union (although this is denied). However, the degree to which they discriminate in favor of each other in trade is far greater than the discrimination practiced by other customs unions. The reasons for this are partly economic-institutional and partly political. Economically, it is easier for centrally planned economies to deal with other centrally planned economies since, in one large trade agreement, they can each guarantee the other a wide variety of products. This vastly simplifies central planning. Politically, of course, economic interdependence is seen as one of the important ties holding the Communist commonwealth of nations together.

These are some of the major facets of the GATT problem. The United States faces a problem of how to react to a potential Soviet application for membership in GATT. Should we oppose it, favor it, or favor it but with strings attached? At the outset, it must be recognized that past events leave us less than perfectly free to make a decision on matters of principle. For one thing, three Communist nations are already members of GATT. A policy of opposition to Soviet membership or to membership by other Communist nonmembers logically calls for the expulsion of those who are already members. Second, breaches of the spirit and law of GATT principles by Western nations, including the United States, have been fairly common in recent years and have been on the rise as a result of the raw material and energy shortages as well as difficulties with the international monetary mechanism. Since everyone's hands are a little dirty, it is not completely proper to cite dirty hands as a basis of exclusion, particularly when an attempt is being made to clean them. Third, the United States agreed to grant MFN status to the USSR in return for a settlement of the Lend-Lease account, not to mention other commercial arrangements and political concessions relating to freer emigration. Under these circumstances, it would be difficult to oppose Soviet accession to GATT. Fourth, the USSR has already received MFN status bilaterally from most of the advanced industrial nations. Under these circumstances, the Russians lose little if anything by not being allowed into GATT, whereas the Western nations stand to gain from a multilateralization of MFN through GATT by arrangements such as those made with Poland and Romania. Those arrangements commit Poland and Romania to increase their imports from GATT members as a substitute for lowering of tariffs.

In any negotiations with GATT over accession, the USSR would certainly be required, as its MFN commitment, to guarantee that its imports from GATT members rise on a nondiscriminatory basis, along with its trade in general. Every pressure should be brought to bear on the USSR, if not before then after accession, to open its economy still further to East-West trade and to reduce the degree of its discrimination (as the West defines it) against the West and in favor of its Socialist partners. Further, Western GATT members must reconsider seriously the advisability of engaging in larger bilateral agreements with Eastern partners in which the exchange of larger collections of products is settled upon. Granted, the adoption of such state trading techniques does facilitate trade with Eastern state trading nations. It also contributes to discrimination, however, since commercial principles (buying from the cheapest source, selling to the highest bidder) no longer governs the flow of individual products. Does the gain to individual Western nations from such state trading exceed the loss to the same nation (and to the Western trading system as a whole) from having other Western nations engage in such trade?

The United States may soon be called upon to say "yes" or "no" to IMF membership for the USSR and the other Eastern nations. So far only Romania has joined the IMF, so that Eastern involvement is not quite so deep as in the case of GATT. Other factors tend to differentiate the two cases. First, in the case of GATT, the Western nations do not give up anything. As noted, most Western nations had already granted MFN treatment to most of the Socialist nations so that on this count nothing is changed. On the other hand, allowing Socialist nations to join GATT commits them to increasing their trade with the West on a nondiscriminatory (among Western nations) basis, which is all to the good. Membership in the IMF, on the other hand, entitles a nation to three sources of funds: regular IMF credits, a right to share in new issues of Special Drawing Rights (SDRs), and eligibility for World Bank loans. Before one confers such advantages on a new member, it is worth asking what might be expected in return. Unfortunately, it is our opinion that, unlike the case of GATT, the Socialist nations can offer nothing in return for these privileges and stand to gain nothing except financial aid.

There is another economic reason why membership in the IMF should be viewed with considerable caution. As we have noted earlier, the centrally planned economies do not have convertible currencies or meaningful exchange rates. Under central planning with direct controls, they cannot eliminate inconvertibility, meaningfully devalue their exchange rates or eliminate balance of payments pressures. Therefore they cannot even aspire to the international monetary goals of the Western nations, either those evolved at Bretton Woods or those presently being hammered out by the various committees of the major nations and by the IMF. The international monetary system and goals of the Western nations will remain irrelevant to the foreign trade and financial practices of the Socialist nations as long as they do not decentralize their economies as Yugoslavia has done. The political constraints against undertaking such a decentralization appear to be overwhelming for the near future.

The third reason for taking a cautious view toward participation in the IMF is the fact that the international monetary mechanism is presently under enormous stresses and strains and is being laboriously reconstructed. Admitting the Socialist nations to membership at the present time—nations with an alien type of monetary system—would certainly complicate the development of a new framework. Further, admission to the IMF would confer a right to vote—and the USSR would undoubtedly have a large vote—which could complicate the decision-making process without adding a useful viewpoint.

Despite these cautions regarding the relative undesirability on economic grounds of granting membership in the IMF to the Communist nations, it is easy to envisage overriding political considerations relating to détente. Membership of Socialist nations in the IMF, while not desirable, would certainly not seriously hurt the organization. IMF membership does not loom large among the many issues involved in trade expansion.

Note

1. Cited in Joint Economic Committee, U.S. Congress, *Reorientation and Commercial Relations of the Economies of Eastern Europe*, 1974, p. 104.

V

Military Power and Soviet Policy

Thomas W. Wolfe

Introduction

For more than a decade the Soviet Union has been making an extraordinary effort to increase its military power. In an age when the utility of further accretions of military power by states already possessing formidable arsenals of destruction has come to be widely questioned, the Soviet Union has not yet seen fit to slacken its military programs appreciably, either in deference to détente or in connection with various ongoing arms control negotiations such as Strategic Armament Limitation Talks (SALT) and the talks on reduction of theater forces in Central Europe. The outline SALT agreement reached at Vladivostok in November 1974 may signify that an end to the quantitative buildup of Soviet strategic forces is in sight, but as yet neither a completed accord has ensued from the Vladivostok transaction nor have Soviet strategic programs slowed down.

Whatever may have been the impulses which set in motion the Soviet military buildup of the past decade—the "never-again" syndrome generated by the Cuban missile "showdown" of 1962, a Soviet urge to rectify historical military asymmetries and to be recognized as the equal of the United States in the trappings of global power, or simply some more generalized thrust of great power dynamism—the continuing momentum of the Soviet buildup under the détente conditions of the mid-1970s naturally has raised serious questions as to the policy ends it is meant to serve.

Perhaps the questions of most concern to the United States and its allies have had to do with the implications of the Soviet military buildup for the durability

145

of détente. On the one hand, has the Soviet leadership regarded détente and arms control negotiations essentially as tactical modalities to earn a "breathing spell" for the Soviet Union? Once the Soviet military-industrial base has been further strengthened, partly with the help of economic and technoligical transfusions from the West, does the Soviet leadership expect to discard détente for a new phase of systemic struggle in which it can hope to deal with the West from a superior power position?[1]

Or, on the other hand, has the growth of Soviet military power been primarily intended to buttress the USSR's bargaining position on the road to binding agreements with the United States, aimed at stabilizing the overall power relationship between the two? In essence, has the Soviet buildup finally peaked, and are we now witnessing a kind of wrap-up process through which the Soviet leadership hopes to establish a durable détente relationship involving among other things a negotiated status of military equality with the United States?

Obviously, many considerations bearing on such questions as these lie well outside the compass of a chapter intended to address primarily the military and arms control dimensions of Soviet policy. However, it is hoped that in dealing with its particular subject, the present chapter will also be of some help in understanding the wider range of issues that may emerge as the Soviet Union makes its impact felt upon world politics in the next five to ten years.

Factors Influencing the Formation of Soviet Military Policy

It may be useful to open this discussion by sketching briefly some of the salient features of the international and internal environment in which the Soviet Union's leadership finds itself operating today, particularly those features which seem to provide the parameters within which Soviet military policy can be expected to evolve during the next few years.

Significant Changes in the International System

Perhaps the first circumstance to be noted is that the international system of the 1970s is in a greater state of flux than at any time in the post-World War II era. There are differing views as to precisely what kind of a new international order may be emerging, but there does seem to be a general consensus that the world is in a fluid transitional stage from the bipolar politics of the past quarter-century to a more complex and diverse pattern of international alignments.

In this transitional situation, important changes have been taking place in Soviet-American relations, including attainment by the USSR of strategic parity with the United States and the conclusion of the SALT One accords of May 1972. In the words of one of the chief architects of these accords, they could be regarded as a major landmark in the evolution of Soviet-American relations because

For the first time, two great powers, deeply divided by their divergent values, philosophies, and social systems have agreed to restrain the very armaments on which their national survival depends. . . . The final verdict must wait on events, but there is at least reason to hope that these accords represent a major break in the pattern of suspicion, hostility, and confrontation which has dominated U.S.-Soviet relations for a generation.[2]

If the final verdict remains obscure, it is apparent that the two superpowers have a long way to go before fulfillment of the hope voiced by Henry Kissinger. Despite some movement toward accommodation under détente, and some blurring of the familiar lines of bipolar rivalry by the emergence of multipolar politics, the two nuclear superpowers are still locked into a relationship in which they continue to regard each other as dangerous adversaries. To put it another way, the new rules of engagement under which the USSR and the United States are seeking to mediate their overlapping global interests and conflicts are still in the process of being defined.

This process is complicated by the emergence of multipolarity, for as the number of major actors in the international system increases, the superpowers can no longer devise their policies with only each other chiefly in mind, and their ability to control events and hold their alliances together tends to decrease. At the same time, political multipolarity has not yet diluted the dominantly bipolar strategic relationship of the U.S.-USSR, upon which nuclear deterrence essentially rests. The rise of new centers of power, however, will not necessarily have a destabilizing effect on deterrence. Rather, the probability of strategic nuclear war may tend to diminish in a multipolar world in which any one nuclear power will find it more necessary than before to take account of the nuclear potential of third parties.[3]

Along with shifts in the political-military relationship between the superpowers and the emergence of a politically multipolar world, another significant change in the international system today is the growth of economic interdependence and transnational production on an unprecedented scale. Though worldwide economic interdependence is much more marked among non-Communist countries than between the historically autarchical Communist economies and the rest of the world, the interdependence phenomenon has by no means left the Communist camp untouched. The Soviet Union and its East European allies, for example, have not only developed interdependencies among themselves, but they are moving gradually toward more links with non-Communist economies, and toward a greater share of world trade.

At first glance, increasing economic interdependence may appear to portend greater international cooperation, with an implied dampening effect on traditional military rivalries. However, interdependence might prove to have a reverse impact, stimulating a scramble for raw material resources like that maifested during the Middle East oil embargo, as well as efforts by states to export their economic problems to others. Since the Soviet Union is relatively much better off than most Western countries in materials required to support an advanced industrial economy, and hence less vulnerable to raw materials blackmail, the temptation might arise to encourage materials producers to exploit their leverage against the West, with perhaps the implicit promise of political and military protection against reprisals. Such a course, already at least partly foreshadowed by Moscow's egging on of the Arab states in 1973 to apply the "oil weapon,"[4] might hold more appeal should the Soviets conclude that the benefits of economic help and technology transfer expected from the West under détente were not to be forthcoming on a substantial scale after all.

The military implications of a "shrinking world" economic environment are not at all clear, though it might be assumed that the functions of military presence in helping to deny, or alternatively, to assure access to vital resources would take on greater importance. This in turn could have the effect of raising the premium on retention or acquisition of military base rights overseas, even though at the same time military technological trends may act to reduce dependence on overseas bases.

Growth of Soviet Global Aspirations

While the international system has been undergoing changes of the sort sketched above, the Soviet Union's own conduct in the world arena has increasingly reflected its aspirations to play a leading role in global affairs. The Khrushchev era marked the beginning of the Soviet Union's transformation into a global power, in both a political and military sense. Since Khrushchev's ouster in 1964, this process has continued at an accelerated pace, as the regime headed by Brezhnev has sought to generate a military posture suitable to support a widening range of interests abroad. In connection with the globalist trend of Soviet policy, a phenomenon worthy of note is what might be called the great power dynamism exhibited by the Soviet state at the present juncture of its history. It may be argued that the Soviet elite—or, at least, some segments of it among the scientific intelligentsia and industrial managers—has lost its ideological and revolutionary fervor, whatever lip service may be paid to the Marxist-Leninist verities. Nevertheless, it is evident that energy and enthusiasm for pursuing the role of a great power in world affairs is not wanting in the Soviet case. Indeed, the dynamic and rather markedly self-righteous quality that animates the Soviet world outlook appears not yet to have peaked. There is even some sign that ideological fervor may have been rekindled by the Western world's problems in securing access to energy resources, which seem to some Soviet ideologues to have validated Lenin's prediction that the countries of the capitalist system would fall out among themselves over division of the world's basic resources.[5]

With regard to the general influence of ideology upon Soviet policy, the question has often been put in the following terms: Is ideology a potent factor in the policy-making picture, or does it merely provide the ritual dressing or post hoc rationale for decisions based essentially on the perceived "national interests" of the Soviet state? This is a much debated issue which can hardly be settled here, but it does merit brief comment.

Perhaps the main impact of Marxist-Leninist ideology on Soviet policymakers is its contribution to a view of the world in which perpetual systemic conflict is envisaged between the forces of socialism and those of "imperialism." This outlook, rooted in the "class struggle" theory of history, is particularly marked within the Party *apparat*—the real center of political power in the Soviet system.[6] Further, the notion that systemic struggle "cannot be annulled or banned by intergovernmental agreements" runs through the extensive Soviet literature on "peaceful coexistence."[7]

On the other hand, however, the ideological component of Soviet behavior also counsels that the security of the Soviet Union, as the principal Communist state, must be preserved at all costs. This makes for a conservative weighing of prospective gains versus risks in relations with states of the opposing camp and particularly calls for taking care not to provoke a powerful adversary into dangerous reactions.[8]

These countervailing aspects of ideology may help to endow Soviet policy in the international arena with what often appears to be an ambivalent mixture of conflict and cooperation, of pressure tactics alternating with "peaceful coexistence" and détente. But whichever element may be uppermost at any given time, the common denominator in both instances seems to lie in seeking to eliminate or reduce potential sources of threat to the Soviet Union. What might be called, in strategic parlance, a "damage-limiting" philosophy, thus seems to permeate Soviet behavior. As we shall see, this philosophy finds expression in Soviet military doctrine and policy, as well as in Soviet diplomacy.

Whether at bottom such a philosophy owes more to ideological imperatives than to those of Soviet national interest remains a moot question. For that matter, the impulse to limit damage to one's interests is not peculiar to the Soviet leaders; they simply seem to carry it farther than most, as if satisfied only with absolute security. Thus, the really relevant point seems to be that to the extent that negation of potential military and political threats to the Soviet Union involves measures that other states find inimical to their own vital interests, the Soviet proclivity to seek absolute security tends neither to promote global stability nor a fundamental relaxation of tensions within the international order.

The "China Problem"

From the Soviet viewpoint, the so-called China problem has an important bearing on both the Soviet Union's military preparedness and on its interest in political détente with the West and Japan. In a military sense, the unresolved dispute with China means that a substantial share of Soviet military resources must be tied down in the Far East, with Soviet military planning having to take into account a two-front threat—at the USSR's front door in Europe and at its back door in Asia. While the Soviet Union's military preparations in Asia have not been at the expense of its posture in Europe up to now, there is a real question whether the Soviet leadership still feels that the primary military threat to Soviet interests is posed by the Western "imperialist" coalition, led by the United States, or whether Communist China has moved up to the top of the list as a potential threat to Soviet security.

The citing of China as a rationale for a higher level of Soviet military preparation is at least becoming more common in the Soviet Union today, though perhaps the Soviet leaders themselves are not sure whether priority in the allocation of defense resources should continue to be directed in accordance with traditional Marxist-Leninist imperatives against the United States and its allies in the capitalist camp, or whether circumstances now dictate that priority attention be shifted to military preparations against a rival Communist power in Asia. Such a shift would certainly constitute one of the ruder ironies of history.

The Soviet leaders may hope that when Mao passes from the scene the opportunity will arise to patch up Soviet relations with China, but their expectations on this score cannot have been heightened by the Tenth Party Congress in Peking in 1973, when the Soviet Union was again labeled a worse enemy of China than the United States and was accused, moreover, of contemplating a surprise attack against the Peoples' Republic of China.[9] Thus, whatever course Sino-Soviet relations may take in a post-Mao environment, the legacy of "enduring hostility" which Soviet spokesmen anticipate seems likely to counsel against lowering the level of military buildup and vigilance mounted by the Soviet Union in the past few years along its Asian borders.

Politically, Moscow's stakes in the containment of China undoubtedly have been an important incentive for cultivation of détente in Europe and for seeking the cooperation of Asian states like India and Japan. Similarly, the movement toward rapprochement between China and the United States was an important, and some think the dominant, incentive for Soviet improvement of bilateral relations with the United States. However, there seems to be somewhat less Soviet concern today about the Sino-American relationship than several years ago, when many Russians appeared to fear collusion and even a de facto military alliance to encircle the USSR.[a] This more relaxed attitude toward the potential danger that Washington and Peking might team up at Soviet expense has the implication that the Soviets may be led to reappraise to at least some degree their need for U.S.-Soviet détente.

[a]Visiting Soviet lecturers in the United States in 1972-1973 were prone, for example, to stress the collusion theme. But more recent visitors, in light of the fragile progress in Sino-American relations, tend to take the more relaxed view that there are "definite limits" to collaboration between China and the United States.

Economic and Technological Considerations

Although the economic and technological capacity of the Soviet Union to support a modern military establishment of massive size has been demonstrated over the course of time, there is still a wide range of opinion as to what constraints are imposed today upon Soviet military policy by various short-comings in these fields. This is not the place for detailed analysis of the Soviet economy and technological base, but a few observations are warranted on internal problems in these areas and their possible influence on future arms competition with the United States, as well as the extent to which they may help to account for Soviet interest in arms control negotiations and détente.

The performance of the Soviet economy during the past decade or so has been marked by what must seem to the Soviet leadership to be a disturbing loss of momentum, for even though output has increased substantially in absolute terms, the growth rate of the economy has dropped off by almost half from that of the latter fifties.[10] One of the more widely-remarked contradictions to be found in the Soviet economic system pertains to the disparate performance of its civilian and its military-industrial sectors. While Soviet military technology and the defense production sectors of the economy have managed to compete quite successfully with the West, it has become increasingly evident—as Soviet authorities themselves concede—that the Soviet Union is encountering many difficulties in adapting the civilian sectors of its industrial system to the scientific and technical revolution of the modern era. Various reforms under-taken since 1965 to increase productivity and facilitate the introduction of new technology into the civilian sector have as yet failed to resolve Soviet economic difficulties. Occasional bad crop-years have not helped matters.

The prospect that slowdown of growth and uneven performance of the economy would have undesirable consequences both at home and in long-term competition with the advanced industrial systems of the West and Japan seems to have brought the Soviet leaders to the conclusion—not an easy one for the custodians of an autarchically-oriented and ideologically-prideful system—that solution of their economic problems would require greater access to Western industrial technology, management know-how, and development credits.[11] This doubtless was an important factor helping to propel the Soviet Union toward détente and negotiations such as those on the limitation of strategic arms.[12]

What is less clear is whether economic pressures have become an overriding element in the determination of Soviet military policy. Judgment on this issue is made difficult to begin with by the sheer problem of arriving at meaningful figures on the share of Soviet resources devoted to military purposes. Indepen-dent estimates run from 8 to 19 percent at the conservative end of the spectrum to 40 percent or more at the other, while the official Soviet claim comes to about 6 percent.[13] Whatever discount one may apply to such figures, there is some question whether the Soviets themselves, operating with an artificial pricing system and subsidies of various sorts for military goods, actually know what the real costs of their military effort are.[14]

Ample evidence has accumulated that Soviet economic and military planners have been enjoined to find the "optimum congruity" between military requirements and material resources,[15] but just what this optimum may be has never been spelled out. There are doubtless limits beyond which the Soviet leadership would probably begin to find an increased rate of military spending an intolerable brake on economic growth and other needs of their society. Just what these limits may be depends on numerous boundary conditions which can hardly be specified here. But one might hazard a guess that holding an annual military increase somewhat below the overall economic growth rate would be within "tolerable" limits. Most Western analysts today would predict a growth rate in GNP terms of about 4 to 4.5 percent through the remainder of the 1970s.[16] Were the Soviet defense effort to be funded at a rate of increase of only half this much, or even stabilized at something like the present percentage level, it would still reflect a set of priorities placing military claims high on the list.

There is one aspect of the Soviet interest in technology transfer and other economic aid from the West that bears on the level of military effort the Soviet system might be able to sustain. By infusions of outside technology and capital into the civilian sectors of the Soviet economy, resources that might otherwise have to be "borrowed" from the defense sector could be left there, amounting in effect to indirect Western subsidy of the Soviet military economy.

In reporting to the Twenty-Fourth Party Congress in 1971, Brezhnev revealed that 42 percent of defense industry capacity was being devoted to output of civilian goods. Other officials subsequently spoke of plans for further conversion of defense industry production to civilian needs and transfer of some defense Research and Development (R&D) and management expertise to the civilian sector.[17] It is this process for which Western aid to the civilian economy might presumably become a substitute. Whether inputs into the civilian economy from abroad will reach a scale significant enough to give the "military subsidy" issue real bite, however, remains to be seen.

In the technological field, another consideration affecting both Soviet military and arms control policy is how confidently Soviet planners may assess the ability of their military technology system to compete qualitatively with the United States. There seems to be little doubt that the Soviets have a healthy respect for U.S. technological capabilities, and that concern lest an unrestrained American R&D effort should work to Soviet disadvantage has been among the stronger incentives for Moscow's interest in arms control negotiations. Though it goes against the grain for the Soviets to admit in print that the United States is technologically ahead of them, one finds occasional statements suggesting concern that a qualitative "leap" by the adversary could endanger the military balance or that a continued U.S. policy aimed at scientific and technological superiority could "considerably reduce" the value of the SALT agreements already reached.[18]

However, Soviet attitudes toward technological competition are somewhat ambivalent, and one finds on the other hand assertions that the "preferential development of science" and of scientific talent in the Soviet Union to support high-quality military programs is "one of the fundamental elements in military superiority."[19] Similar advocacy of a finely-honed Soviet R&D effort was voiced in 1971 by Colonel-General Ogarkov, then the ranking Soviet military representative at the SALT talks.[20] A "positive" view of the contribution of technology to the strengthening of Soviet military power is a dominant theme in much recent Soviet military literature,[21] while some writers have asserted that the Soviet system is especially well-suited to exploit the emerging possibilities of science and technology in an age when "the scientific-technical revolution is one of the main sectors in the historical competition between capitalism and socialism."[22]

Without laboring the point further, one may say simply that the Soviets would apparently like to constrain the adversary's exploitation of technology while pressing on with their own—an attitude not necessarily confined to their side of the competition.

Soviet Attitudes Toward the Value of Military Power

One would suppose that the way the Soviet leaders feel about the value of military power is germane to the priority they are prepared to give military claims on Soviet resources. It is not an easy matter, however, to determine what the governing attitudes of the leadership are, or how they may be changing as the Soviet Union carves out its place in a world order in which it appears to many observers that only small, nonnuclear powers can any longer afford the risk of war with each other.

As practitioners of power in the Bolshevik tradition, the Soviet leadership can be presumed to have a rather sophisticated sense of the relationship between military and political power. Though the Bolshevik "operational code" hardly neglects the place of armed force in the provenance of power, it does impose a respect for other nonmilitary factors that also count in establishing a favorable "balance of forces" over an adversary. Thus, taken alone, this code would seem to counsel against going overboard in the accumulation of military forces and obligations at the expense of developing and employing other instrumentalities of policy. At the same time, however, another psychology—a kind of addiction to an excess of power—also seems to operate in the Soviet case. This may be what Solzhenitsyn—a perceptive but not unprejudiced critic of the Soviet leadership—had in mind when he said, in his *Letter to the Soviet Leaders*:

Military obligations dictate, you say? But in fact we have only one-tenth of the military obligations we pretend to have, or rather that we intensively and assiduously create for ourselves. . . . For peacetime we armed to excess several times over . . . we maintain this army solely out of military and diplomatic vanity.[23]

One cannot, of course, say with any assurance whether—as Solzhenitsyn seems to imply—a kind of *folie de grandeur* accounts mainly for the Soviet leadership's fondness for massive amounts of military power, or whether this cultivation of power stems from other sources—such as the rude experience of Russian history or some obsessive impulse to acquire "safe margins" of power against potential threats to Soviet security, as mentioned earlier in this chapter. But in any case, it would appear that a psychology involving something more than a refined calculus of the utilities and disutilities of military power helps to shape the attitudes of the Soviet leadership toward its accumulation.

This is not to infer that Soviet military power has tended simply to grow on the basis of the more the better, without thought for its costs or limits. Certainly, there is recognition in the Soviet Union of what has become the accepted wisdom elsewhere—that each increment of military power does not necessarily yield a corresponding measure of security or political advantage, especially in the nuclear age. One may find an articulate Soviet spokesman like G.A. Arbatov, who is both a Party official and director of Moscow's Institute of the USA, observing in the Party journal *Kommunist* that a situation now exists in which "the further accumulation of military power is not accompanied by an increase in political power."[24] It also bears noting, however, that Arbatov does not tell us whether he has in mind a universal phenomenon to which the Soviet Union too is subject, for his reference is to the restraint placed upon the ability of the United States to exploit its power politically, thanks precisely to the "military might" of the Soviet Union.

A somewhat related tendency to exempt the Soviet Union from the disabilities of power suffered by the United States may be seen in Soviet commentary on nuclear war. Even though recognizing the destructiveness of nuclear war and the mutual interest of both sides in avoiding it, Soviet commentators seldom acknowledge that the awesome implications of nuclear war are the same for both parties. Rather, it is the United States for which nuclear war would be "suicide";[25] for the Soviet Union, the script either holds out some vague form of deliverance from the fate befalling the other party, or offers the ritual promise of victory.[26]

Again, this is not meant to suggest that Soviet man takes nuclear war more lightly than others, or that he is in fact confident of emerging the winner. Rather, the point is that *Homo sovieticus* seems to find it necessary, for a combination of psychological, political or other reasons, to leave open-ended the limits beyond which one's power cannot be translated into anything meaningful. Among other things, such a tendency does not readily make for defining clear limits as to how much military power is enough.

Perhaps one of the best illustrations of the "how much" problem can be seen in the case of the doctrine, long dear to the Soviet military, of seeking military superiority over potential adversaries. As many observers have pointed out, this doctrine provides "no clear guide" to the problem of how many and what kinds of forces are necessary,[27] if only because in the last analysis this depends on what military strength the adversary chooses to deploy. But as long as there is a tacit assumption that Soviet security requires a "superior" military posture of some sort, however vaguely defined, the doctrine tends to sanction a rising rate of military preparations. Doubtless it has helped to drive up Soviet force levels, especially over the years in which the Soviets have sought to make up in numbers for qualitative inferiority.

At the same time, the doctrine of superiority has not escaped disparagement in the Soviet Union. In at least some nonmilitary circles, there has been questioning whether "*relative* nuclear superiority" confers any advantage where "the other side possesses *absolute* power which guarantees the destruction of any aggressor."[28] At top levels of the political hierarchy, on the other hand, statements on the superiority issue have tended to take the middle ground, avoiding judgment on the merits or attainability of superiority, but serving notice that the USSR will not permit another power to establish military superiority over the USSR. Brezhnev's words in the spring of 1970 afford a typical example: "We shall answer any attempts by any party to achieve military superiority over the Soviet Union by making the necessary increase in our own military might. . . ."[29]

The Brezhnev formulation is one with which both the Soviet military and the political leadership can probably live comfortably—at least up to some as yet undefined point. From the perspective of the military, as long as the superiority concept is left open-ended, it is a bit like having an unlimited checking account to draw upon to meet new requirements and contingencies that may arise. From the viewpoint of the political leadership, the inherently difficult problem of deciding precisely what is "enough" can simply be postponed. Obviously, in the field of strategic arms, the SALT negotiations have brought closer the time when this open-ended approach may no longer suffice, for there the Soviet Union has agreed that it stands for equality with the United States.

Influence of the Soviet Military on Defense Policy

Such questions as whether a distinct cleavage of views on defense requirements exists between Soviet political and military leaders, and the extent to which the political side of the house defers to military judgment, are matters of perennial speculation in the West. Perhaps the prevailing assumption among Western students of Soviet civil-military relations has been that there are basic institutional differences that sometimes get translated into conflict over policy issues.[30] Some observers go further to argue that top Party and military officials are more or less constantly locked in a sharp internal battle over policy, while a few assert that the Soviet marshals have become so powerful that they are now in fact calling the tune on a wide range of security and foreign policy matters. On the other hand, one may also find a quite contrary set of arguments, essentially to the effect that there is no real dichotomy growing out of institutional or other differences between Soviet political and military leaders, and that the latter continue to be, as they have traditionally been, compliant executors of policies framed by the former.[31]

In the opinion of the present writer, the real situation probably lies somewhere in between. The institutional setting does appear to alter somewhat the perspective from which the political and military leaders, respectively, view defense problems. Rather than a sharp dichotomy between the two groups, however, there seems to be considerable crossing of lines between them, with like-minded factions on both sides of the house tending to cooperate with each other on particular issues. In the past, at least, it would appear that the relationship between the political leadership and the military command has involved essentially what amounts to a division of labor, with the former tending to leave the professional details of security planning, as Kosygin once put it, "to the marshals," while reserving to itself the right of final decision, especially on matters involving large resources or issues of war and peace.

With regard specifically to military influence upon Soviet policy, an empirical judgment would seem warranted that the military establishment—whose head, Marshal A.A. Grechko, has been admitted to the inner sanctum of the Politburo[b]—today enjoys more policy leverage than was the case before Khrushchev left the scene a decade ago. Unfortunately, however, because there are large gaps in our knowledge of the Soviet policy-making mechanism and how it actually works, it is very difficult to determine how military influence makes itself felt and what net weight it does carry in the making of Soviet defense policy. Though one can hardly do justice to this complex subject in the brief space available here, a few salient points can be ventured.

First, the internal environment in which major Soviet military policy decisions are made can perhaps best be described as a closed system of *defense* decision-making within a slightly larger but also closed system of *political* decision-making. The chief actors in the first include both a few top political leaders and higher-ranking representatives of the military and defense-industrial bureaucracies, while the second is largely confined to members of the Politburo and the Party Central Committee's *apparat*. The several organs, both formal and ad hoc, through which military policy issues are mediated between the top level political and military leaders need not detain us here, but perhaps the most

---

[b]Marshal Grechko was taken into the Politburo in April 1973, along with Andrei Gromyko and Yu. V. Andropov, heads, respectively, of the foreign affairs and secret police bureaucracies.

important ones, in addition to a probable subgroup with the "portfolio" for national security matters within the Politburo itself, are the Defense Council or Committee and the Military-Industrial Commission.[32]

Military influence appears to filter through the policy-making system essentially through two mediums—internal leadership politics and bureaucratic processes. Viewed in terms of leadership politics, the situation over the past decade might be characterized as one in which Brezhnev has formed an alliance of convenience with military leaders for support of his internal power position, and in return has been more sympathetic to programs and policies espoused by the marshals than perhaps some of his other Politburo colleagues. Although one may be flirting here with the fallacy of misplaced causality, it can be said that the "test" of this hypothesis is the generally favorable treatment accorded military claims on the budget since the mid-sixties, along with Brezhnev's gradual ascendancy in the collective leadership over Kosygin, customarily pictured as the spokesman for those leadership elements reluctant to divert greater resources from the civilian economy to military purposes. Though variations on this scenario may be played, its central thesis remains that military influence has grown, thanks to the exigencies of internal elite politics.

Viewed in terms of bureaucratic processes and the institutional setting within which defense policy is forged, a somewhat different avenue for the diffusion of military influence is suggested. Inputs of substantive advice from the major bureaucracies provide the basis upon which the chief actors at the top level of the policy-making system reach decisions.[33] Essentially, these inputs must answer three broad types of questions concerning any proposal for a major new military program: (1) Do we have the technology for it? (2) Can we pay for it? (3) Is it important to our security? The top political leadership can turn to nonmilitary bureaucracies for the first two answers. But for the third, it appears that the top leadership can turn for substantive advice only to the bureaucracy whose institutional interests are most at stake in defense policy issues—the military establishment itself.[34] This apparent built-in lack of alternative sources of expert advice on the substantive merits of proposals affecting Soviet security would thus seem, in the absence of overriding objections on technical or economic grounds, to make for a bias in defense policy decisions toward the preferences of the military professionals and their close allies in the defense-industrial ministries.

Having said this, one should note that there are a number of factors at work today that may tend to alter a decision-making pattern biased toward the recommendations of the military. For one thing, the military's virtual monopoly on strategic thought and substantive analysis may be gradually eroding, partly as a consequence of the political leadership's task of sorting out and reformulating the meaning of the physical changes that have taken place in the Soviet Union's power position in the last few years. Secondly, the dramatic and successful effort to catch up with the United States in strategic power may itself tend to dilute the policy consensus within the leadership on which the strategic buildup has hitherto been conducted. That is to say, the overriding imperative to match the United States was an obstacle to any institutional groups outside the military, particularly those competing for resources, which might have sought to question the programs proposed by the military. This obstacle may now become less formidable, and if so, more critical scrutiny of new military requirements may follow.

Thirdly, there is the SALT factor. These negotiations have put the top Soviet leadership and subordinate echelons of the policy-making apparatus through an instructive experience in the complicated business of trying to regulate the size and character of strategic forces. It would seem plausible that the Soviet political leaders' repeated exposure to contentious military issues in the context of negotiations with the USSR's most powerful adversary has made them sensitive to the need for a more balanced base of expert advice than can be provided by the military establishment alone. In particular, the kinds of SALT issues in the in-baskets of responsible Politburo leaders may have prompted the latter to bring some members of the defense-associated scientific community into more frequent consultation, for many of the issues inextricably link technological with strategic-postural considerations. As an afterthought, one might add, however, that it is not altogether clear whether advice from "defense-coupled" scientists would show them to be wholly disinterested parties, or *amici curiae* of the professional military establishment.[35]

Before leaving the question of the respective attitudes of the Soviet political and military leaders toward defense requirements, it may be worth stressing that whatever disagreements may arise between them over particular issues, there are some broad areas in which they seem to share a common outlook. For example, both political leaders and military professionals still seem deeply reluctant in security matters to part with the belief that they can successfully design their own security, and equally reluctant to trust someone else to help look out for it. To the extent that both leadership groups continue to regard as inherently suspect any effort to construct a stable military-strategic relationship with the capitalist adversary on the basis of each side's being solicitous of the other's security concerns, the implications would seem to be that arms control agreements involving deep inroads upon unilateral security planning are apt to encounter what to others may appear to be "unreasonable" Soviet resistance.

With respect to such a policy matter as reconciling the pursuit of détente with a continuing high level of military preparedness, one might suppose that there are some institutionally-seated differences that make themselves felt in the Soviet case. The military establishment probably does not want to see the rationale for big defense budgets undermined by playing down the "imperialist" military threat, whereas some elements of the political leadership and the economic bureaucracy are probably disposed to look more favorably upon the economic benefits of détente and a less demanding defense philosophy. Yet even within the civilian leadership elite, interest in the political and security advantages of a strong military posture seems little diluted by the perspectives of détente, as attested by an arms buildup that has remained largely insensitive to changes in the political environment. To a notable degree, Soviet military might is credited with having made détente itself possible. Indeed, one might venture to say that both the political leadership and the military probably find a rationale that suits both in the following formula, variations of which are frequently to be seen in Soviet media:

The greater the combat might and readiness of the Soviet armed forces and the armies of the fraternal socialist countries . . . the more secure is peace on earth . . . and the broader are the opportunities for consolidating the successes of the policy of peaceful coexistence.[36]

With that, let us turn from this general discussion of factors influencing the formation of Soviet defense policy to some of the specific military programs being pursued by the Soviet Union and the issues they have generated in the present era of détente and negotiations.

Soviet Strategic Programs and Policy in the SALT Era

For more than a decade, the Soviet Union has been engaged in a massive effort to strengthen its strategic posture through expansion of its strategic delivery forces and improvement of its strategic defenses. With the exception of the Soviet program for deployment of ballistic missile defenses, which was halted by the Anti-Ballistic Missile (ABM) Treaty of May 1972, the Soviet Union's unilateral strategic programs have not been greatly affected to date by the various agreements reached in SALT, including the outline Vladivostok accord of November 1974. This has been the case, essentially, because the boundary limits "legislated" thus far in the SALT era have left room for Soviet planners to carry out the successive strategic programs which they evidently have regarded as necessary to provide a prudent hedge against future uncertainty.

A change in this situation may now be drawing closer—provided the Soviet Union decides to sign a full-fledged, ten-year agreement embodying the constraints upon its unilateral strategic programs that were outlined at Vladivostok. But until this happens, the Soviet strategic buildup can hardly be said to have been fundamentally diverted from the track upon which it was set in the mid-sixties prior to the beginning of SALT. Here we shall first cover the main features of the strategic programs undertaken by the Soviet Union and some of the strategic issues raised by them down to the time of the Vladivostok transaction, after which we shall turn to the negotiations in SALT II out of which emerged the November 1974 Vladivostok accord.

Strategic Delivery Forces

As testimony to the value accorded the buildup of Soviet strategic power by the incumbent regime, the successive programs it has pursued without pause for more than a decade tend to speak for themselves. The growth of the USSR's strategic offensive forces since the mid-sixties is illustrated by Table VA-1 in the Appendix, showing an almost fivefold increase in their overall size during the 1964-1975 period.

Land-Based Missiles. The principal emphasis during most of this period was given to land-based Intercontinental Ballistic Missiles (ICBMs) of the Strategic Rocket Forces (SRF).[c] By contrast with the small force of second-generation SS-7 and SS-8 missiles which had been deployed mostly at "soft" or above-ground launch sites prior to 1964, the expanded force of third-generation ICBM launchers was "hardened" to improve its survivability.

The third-generation missile types deployed after 1964 were the SS-9 and SS-11, both liquid-fueled and emplaced in concrete underground silos, together with smaller numbers of the SS-13, the Soviet Union's first ICBM in the solid-fuel category to which the U.S. *Minuteman* belongs. Of the three Soviet ICBMs, the SS-9 proved to be of most concern to U.S. planners, primarily because of its counterforce potential against *Minuteman* launchers and control centers.[37] This heavy Soviet missile was produced in four successive versions, the fourth of which was equipped with a triple Multiple Reentry Vehicle (MRV) warhead. Approximately 290 SS-9 launchers were deployed, about one-third of the number of SS-11s. The latter, about half the size of the SS-9, also went through several modifications, including an MRV version, to improve its accuracy and penetration capability, but it was not considered to have attained a counterforce potential against hard targets.

The Soviet effort to overtake the United States numerically in ICBM forces can be said to have culminated successfully with the SALT Interim Agreement of May 1972—the terms of which conceded the Soviet Union a substantial edge for at least the five-year life of the agreement in both land-based ICBMs and sea-based SLBMs.[d] One might argue that the sublimit of 313 heavy missiles

[c]The Strategic Rocket Forces came into being in late 1959 and early 1960. These forces are described by the Soviet Union as Rocket Troops of Strategic Designation, but are generally known in the West by the shorter appellation.

[d]The Interim Agreement on Strategic Offensive Arms set maximum ceilings of 1,618 ICBMs for the Soviet Union to 1,054 for the United States, and 62 modern nuclear submarines with 950 SLBMs for the Soviet side compared with 44 submarines and 710 SLBMs for the United States. Within the ICBM category, "heavy" missiles of types deployed after 1964 were limited to 313 for the USSR and 54 for the United States. Under a complicated tradeoff formula, the maximum number of SLBMs could be attained only if a prescribed number of old ICBMs were turned in—210 and 54, respectively, in the Soviet and U.S. cases. The net outcome in combined numbers of ICBMs and SLBMs accruing to each side if all options were exercised would be 2,358 for the Soviet Union and 1,710 for the United States.

imposed by the agreement—as well as the curtailment of new silo construction—represented constraints that Soviet planners would not find to their liking, but on the whole it would appear that the quantitative ceilings of the Interim Agreement were probably close to the levels for ICBMs of the SS-9 and SS-11 generation at which Soviet planners had been aiming.

In qualitative terms, the Soviet situation was obviously far less comfortable, for the American edge in Multiple Independent Reentry Vehicles (MIRV) technology and headstart in MIRV deployment conferred substantial advantages upon the United States in accurately deliverable warheads.[e] Since the Interim Agreement established few impediments to qualitative improvement and modernization of ICBM forces on either side, it was to be expected that Soviet strategic planners would next turn their attention in this direction.

What proved somewhat unexpected, however, was the scope and tempo of the follow-on missile programs that unfolded in the Soviet Union after SALT I. In the ICBM field, four new missile systems were found to be in an advanced stage of testing by early 1974, leading top U.S. defense officials to state then that the USSR had entered a new phase of "unprecedented major commitment" to the modernization of its strategic offensive forces on a scale "far more comprehensive than estimated even a year ago."[38] Subsequently, it was disclosed that several additional missiles were under development, although their exact number and other details remain uncertain at this writing.[39]

The four follow-on ICBMs about which most is known are the SS-18, SS-19, and SS-17, each larger than the missile it is likely to replace, and the SS-16, a solid-fuel missile believed to be a land-mobile type. These missiles are notable not only because of their increased throwweight, but also because they are associated with a true MIRV technology that the Soviet Union finally demonstrated in 1973,[40] after earlier MRV programs had failed to close the qualitative gap between the United States and the USSR in the field of multiple reentry vehicles. Except possibly for the SS-16, the new missiles also appear to be linked with a silo construction program that was first identified in early 1972, involving 25 large and 66 smaller silos of new and harder types. Additional construction of such silos, as noted above, was ruled out by the SALT Interim Agreement. However, Soviet planners probably intend to accommodate most of their new ICBMs to old silos of the SS-9 and SS-11 force. This is suggested by Soviet tests of "pop-up" and "cold-launch" techniques, permitting the larger new missiles to be fired from existing holes.[41] Some of the estimated characteristics of these missiles are shown in Table VA-2 in the Appendix.

Among the strategic issues brought into focus by these follow-on systems, the

[e]The situation with regard to numbers of warheads changed markedly in U.S. favor during the two years preceding and the two years following the May 1972 accords, largely as a result of the MIRV deployment programs initiated by the United States in 1970. As may be seen from Table VA-3 in the Appendix, the mid-1974 U.S. combined inventory of some 7,900 warheads and bombs—of which missile warheads accounted for more than three-quarters of the total—compared with an estimated Soviet figure of 2,600, mostly in missile warheads.

central one doubtless was that framed on the U.S. side in terms of the potential counterforce threat that would be posed by improved and more numerous Soviet ICBMs to the prelaunch survivability of U.S. land-based deterrent forces.[42] Coupled with this strategic problem was a concern that the *appearance* of a marked imbalance of strategic forces—no matter what the actual military significance—might have seriously adverse political and psychological effects. Stemming from these twin concerns came the U.S. strategic policy dictum enunciated by Secretary Schlesinger, and paralleling the U.S. position in SALT, that "there must be essential equivalence between the strategic forces of the United States and the USSR—an equivalence perceived not only by ourselves, but by the Soviet Union and third audiences as well."[43]

On the Soviet side, no attempt was made to spell out the strategic rationale behind the new ICBM programs. However, the key strategic decision facing the Kremlin leadership was the extent to which the Soviet Union should go ahead unilaterally to incorporate the new MIRVed missiles into its land-based ICBM arsenal, as against the alternative of trying to reach an agreement in SALT on MIRV without having to accept constraints on the throwweight of Soviet missiles. The implications of the Soviet Union's having opted for the latter course at Vladivostok will be discussed further when we turn specifically to the results of that transaction.

The Soviet capacity to develop more accurate guidance systems for the new family of MIRVed ICBMs was another question of pivotal significance, since accuracy improvements would greatly enhance the potential counterforce threat posed by Soviet strategic forces in the future. By most accounts, it might take the Soviets from six to ten years to match the accuracies of U.S. ICBMs.[44] If so, one implication might be continuing Soviet reluctance to enter agreements that could constrain their chances of catching up with the United States. A second important implication of any difficulties the Soviets might be having in the production of highly accurate guidance equipment was that the counterforce potential of Soviet ICBM forces might evolve at a somewhat slower rate than their numbers and throwweight would otherwise permit—thus stretching out the period in which a counterforce threat to the U.S. *Minuteman* force would have to be taken seriously into account in U.S. strategic planning.

Another issue posed by the Soviet follow-on missile programs was that of land-mobile ICBMs, deployment of which it was generally believed would tend to create strategic instability because of the difficulty of keeping track of them. Although SALT One did not prohibit development of land-mobile systems, the United States had declared in a unilateral statement that it would consider their actual deployment "inconsistent" with the objectives of the Interim Agreement. Since there was a land-mobile version of the new Soviet SS-16, the question arose whether the Soviets planned to deploy it despite U.S. objections. Later, however, Soviet steps in this direction were legitimized, as it were, by the Vladivostok understanding, which permitted either side to deploy land-mobile missiles.

Submarine-Launched Ballistic Missiles. Although land-based ICBMs of the Strategic Rocket Forces were given top priority in the Soviet strategic buildup, a major effort also went into the development of an SLBM force under the auspices of the Soviet Navy. This force entered its first substantial phase of growth following the introduction of the nuclear-powered Y-class submarines in 1967.[45] Roughly comparable to the early U.S. *Polaris*-type submarines, the Y-class was equipped with sixteen tubes for submerged launch of the SS-N-6, a liquid-fueled ballistic missile with a range of 1,300 nautical miles.

By the time the May 1972 SALT accords were signed the Soviet Union had twenty-nine of these submarines in operation and several more in various stages of assembly.[f] It had also begun to build a modified and enlarged version of the Y-class, the *Delta-1* class, the first unit of which was launched in 1972. This submarine carries twelve SS-N-8 missiles with a range of 4,200 nautical miles. In turn, a still larger modification of this class, known as the *Delta-2*, carrying sixteen rather than twelve SS-N-8 missiles, was found to be under construction in 1974.[46] Altogether, by the fall of 1974, around eighteen to nineteen *Delta* units of both types were either built or in assembly,[47] along with the completed Y-class program, which closed out at thirty-four submarines.[48]

One effect of the post-1972 programs was to enable the Soviet Union by about mid-1974, to surpass the United States by a small margin in numbers of operational SLBM launchers (see Table VA-3 in the Appendix). Another effect was to bring the Soviet SLBM inventory fairly close to the "baseline" figure of 740, beyond which it would become necessary to "cash in" older ICBMs or SLBMs in order to move toward the maximum ceiling of 950 allowed the Soviet Union by the Interim Agreement.[g]

Although the replacement issue for the Soviet Union presumably would be eased by the "freedom-to-mix" provision of the Vladivostok understanding, if and when the latter should formally supersede the Interim Agreement, another major question in the quantitative domain would still remain for Soviet planners—namely, whether to move an increasing share of the country's strategic offensive power to sea at the expense of its traditionally-favored, land-based ICBM forces.

---

[f]In May 1972, the Soviets also had nine older H-class nuclear-powered submarines with 3 SS-N-5 missiles each, and some 20 G- and Z-class diesel submarines armed with SS-N-4 missiles. The former were counted under the Interim Agreement, but the latter were excluded.

[g]That is to say, the 210 additional launchers to reach the IA ceiling of 950 SLBMs would come as replacements for old SS-7 and SS-8 ICBMs (which number about 210) or for the 30 SS-N-5 launchers on nine old H-class nuclear submarines, or some combination thereof. If the Soviets wished to retire the nine H-class submarines and replace them with the same number of new Delta-2 class subs (16 tubes) they could do so if they stayed within the overall limit of 62 submarines, but in this case the 144 launchers on the Deltas would be replacing 30 SS-N-5 SLBMs and 114 SS-7 and SS-8 ICBMs. As noted in the text, the complexities of exercising the replacement options would be eased at such time as the Vladivostok provisions might supersede the Interim Agreement. For the United States, incidentally, the replacement issue was less pressing, since the initial Trident program of ten submarines mounting twenty-four launchers each would not reach the deployment stage until after expiration of the Interim Agreement.

Other SLBM issues facing the Soviet Union both before and after Vladivostok involved essentially qualitative considerations. Although the USSR had gotten a jump on the United States by deployment of the 4,200-mile SS-N-8 (the United States would not have an SLBM of comparable range at sea before 1979),[49] it still lagged behind in many qualitative and operational aspects of its SLBM force. This was particularly true in the case of MIRVed SLBMs, which had been widely introduced into American SSBNs since mid-1970, while the Soviet Union had not yet applied its new MIRV technology at sea. Although a MRV variant of the basic launcher aboard the Y-class submarines, the SS-N-6, had been developed, this would still give the Soviets a capability only roughly comparable to that of the U.S. navy's *Polaris* A-3 missile, which was being steadily phased out.[h] An important qualitative decision for the Soviets, therefore, was whether to backfit a missile that was virtually obsolete by American standards, or whether to put their resources into a true MIRVed SLBM, possibly a modified version of the SS-N-8, for deployment in the *Delta*-class SSBNs. Since no program for a MIRVed SS-N-8 had become known by mid-1974, it appeared that the question of how far and how fast to go in attempting to incorporate MIRV technology into the Soviet SLBM force was still a moot issue.

Intercontinental Bombers. The small force of intercontinental bombers operated by the Long-Range Aviation Command constitutes the third element of the Soviet Union's strategic delivery capability. This force underwent no expansion during the post-1964 strategic buildup, remaining at a level of some 140 to 150 heavy *Bear* and *Bison* bombers, of the same vintage as the U.S. B-52, plus about 50 tankers. About two-thirds of this force of long-range bombers is equipped with air-to-surface missiles for "stand-off" delivery of nuclear weapons.

Despite the clear priority given the buildup of its ICBM and SLBM forces, the Soviet Union showed its interest in maintaining a modern bomber delivery capability by bringing out in late 1969 a new supersonic bomber of advanced variable-wing design, the *Backfire*.[50] This bomber, about four-fifths the size of the American B-1, began to enter operational service in 1974 after several years of testing and modification.[51] Uncertainty as to whether the primary mission of the *Backfire* is intercontinental or peripheral, or perhaps for support of naval forces, has persisted since the aircraft first appeared. In the view of U.S. defense officials, the *Backfire* will be capable of intercontinental operations if employed with a compatible tanker force.[52]

Strategic bombers were not included in the SALT Interim Agreement of May 1972, leaving the United States with a numerical advantage of about 3 to 1 in this field. During the pre-Vladivostok phase of SALT II, the Soviets evidently sought to narrow the margin in bomber capabilities by calling for cutbacks in existing U.S. levels and insisting that new U.S. projects like the B-1 be scrapped.

---

[h]The A-3, however, would remain on the ten earliest Polaris boats until these were phased out for Trident.

This approach presumably was closed by the Vladivostok understanding, whose freedom-to-mix provision meant that each side could decide for itself what its bomber levels should be. For their part, Soviet planners faced a decision somewhat analogous to that in the SLBM field—how much of their offensive power should go into bombers at the expense of land-based ICBMs? Judging from the prior pattern of Soviet strategic priorities, a move toward much larger bomber forces would not seem likely, though advanced development programs to keep other options open might be expected.

Strategic Defense Programs

The Soviet Union's dedication to a strategic defense effort substantially greater than that of the United States has long been one of the pronounced differences in the strategic policies of the two countries, reflecting both the disparate nature of the strategic situation in which they have found themselves and differing conceptions as to how best to deal with the problems of security in the nuclear age. Leaving aside the ABM Treaty and its implications for a moment, one may note that the Soviet Union has continued to work steadily at improvement of its strategic defenses since SALT I. This has been particularly evident with regard to programs related to the air defense aspects of the USSR's strategic posture.

In the category of active air defenses, for example, the Soviet Union has continued to deploy such surface-to-air missiles as the SA-3 and the SA-5 to complement an already dense network of older SA-2 missiles for defense against bomber attack.[i] Altogether, though some older SA-2 sites are now being deactivated, the Soviet Union operates close to 10,000 surface-to-air missile launchers of various types for defense against strategic bombers.[53] This is in sharp contrast to the situation in the United States, where the last of the existing strategic air defense missiles (down from a peak of about 2,400 in the mid-sixties) were phased out by the end of 1974.[54]

With regard to the Soviet interceptor force, the other main component of the country's active air defenses (PVO), the overall number of aircraft has declined since the late sixties from about 3,600 to 2,500, but the force is being technically updated by introduction of advanced interceptor types, which now account for half of its inventory.[55] Again, there is a contrast with the U.S. case, where the already much smaller force of strategic air defense interceptors (down to about 400 in mid-1975 from 1,200 in the late sixties) is in the process of being further phased out, while the newest fighters such as the F-14 and the F-15 are earmarked for general purpose rather than strategic defense roles.[56]

In the field of passive defense, an asymmetry of emphasis is also to be seen.

[i]The SA-3 is designed to provide low altitude protection against bombers, while the SA-5, or "Tallin" system, is a long-range, high-altitude system possibly intended to counter missile-launching aircraft before they can reach their target areas.

Whereas the U.S. civil defense program has languished, in the Soviet Union civil defense is still proclaimed to be "an important element of the nation's defensive strength."[57] Indeed, though the ultimate effectiveness of Soviet civil defense measures may be open to doubt, a new phase in a compulsory nationwide program has nevertheless been under way in the USSR, characterized among other things by training for pre-attack dispersal and evacuation of residents of potential urban target areas.[58]

Given the disparity in the weight of the strategic air threat historically faced by the two countries, there had been an understandable logic to the Soviet Union's persistent effort to strengthen its air defenses. As long as there remained some prospect of combining separate air defense and ABM systems into a fully integrated strategic defense system, there was also a further rationale for substantial ongoing air defense programs. On the face of it, however, the logic of continuing to sink massive resources into air defense seemed to have become increasingly dubious after SALT I, for even if a 100 percent effective air defense system were attainable, the yet more formidable problem of defense against missile attack would remain.[j] Seemingly, further prospects of solving this problem were blocked by the ABM Treaty, which ruled out the deployment of nationwide ABM defenses, and thus appeared to leave the country irremediably vulnerable to missile attack.

Implications of the ABM Treaty for the Soviet Strategic Outlook

How and why the Soviet leadership came to sign a treaty so manifestly at variance with previous Soviet policy on ABM is a complex and controversial question.[59] According to one view, the reversal of Soviet policy on ABM which culminated in the May 1972 Treaty was dictated in the main by expedient considerations, such as the economic burden of a major ABM program of questionable effectiveness, and concern that a superior U.S. ABM technology, *Safeguard*, combined with the U.S. lead in MIRV, might place the Soviet Union at a serious disadvantage unless checked. In this view, signing of the treaty did not necessarily reflect any essential change in Soviet dedication to strategic defense; rather, the Soviets may simply have demonstrated inadvertently the high value of ABM in their eyes, for in order to curb the U.S. potential in this field, they were willing to accept constraints on their own.

---

[j]Regardless of the feasibility of ABM defense, there were, of course, other reasons why Soviet planners may have wished to keep up their air defenses, such as being prepared in the event that conflicts should arise in Asia or Europe apart from a direct Soviet-American strategic clash. Uncertainty as to how the SALT outcome might affect U.S. bomber forces could have been another reason. Institutional patterns could also account for reluctance to let Soviet air defense lapse. The point involved here, however, is that while various reasons existed for not dismantling the established air defense structure, the rationale for devoting large new resources to air defense seemed less clear.

Another school of thought holds that something more than mere expediency lay behind the Soviet move, such as a shift of outlook bringing Soviet and American strategic conceptions more into tune. In this view, a strategic relationship based on mutual nuclear deterrence had developed well before SALT began, so that the ABM Treaty itself amounted in essence to both sides having finally agreed to formalize and stabilize this relationship.[60] By so doing, the Soviet side was assumed to have recognized at last the futility of trying to achieve a viable strategic defense of the Soviet homeland, and to have come around to embrace a doctrine akin to the American concept of "mutual assured destruction" as an acceptable basis for maintaining mutual deterrence.

Before going further into the question of whether the ABM Treaty reflected a significant "convergence" of Soviet strategic thinking toward the American outlook, it may be useful to summarize briefly what seems to have been for some years the essential core of difference between the strategic philosophies of the two sides. Perhaps the most fundamental divergence lay in their differing approaches to the dilemma of deterrence versus war-fighting and survival in the nuclear age.[61] In the United States, the prevailing tendency was to resolve this dilemma primarily in favor of deterrence—by maintaining a capability to inflict massive punishment on the society of an attacking opponent, and conceding the other side the ability to do the same. The concept underlying this approach is what came to be known in the American strategic lexicon as "mutual assured destruction," a concept further implying that willingness to accept mutual vulnerability offers the best assurance of strategic stability. Although amended criteria for strategic forces have recently been advanced by U.S. planners, as we shall come to presently, the assured destruction concept remained, at least through SALT I and the first part of SALT II, the central axis of consensus around which major strategic force posture and arms control decisions in the United States were made.

The Soviet Union, on the other hand, while no less dedicated to deterring a nuclear attack, proved notably reluctant to peg its security to a concept akin to that of mutual assured destruction. Rather, Soviet strategic thought was characterized both by resistance to a "deterrence only" strategic posture and by the persistent doctrine that the Soviet Union should seek "balanced forces," backed by an extensive civil defense system, enabling it to wage war and limit damage to the Soviet homeland, thus improving the chances of national survival if deterrence should fail.[62]

The conceptual gulf between these two approaches runs deep. Whatever the shortcomings of the mutual assured destruction concept as an answer to the problem of security in the nuclear age, it does happen to be functionally compatible with both strategic stability and arms control objectives. This is so, essentially, because it is a far less difficult military task to put the opponent's society in jeopardy than to protect one's own. In effect, the knee of the megatonnage-fatalities curve[k] suggests itself as a posturally "sufficient" and conceptually convenient point at which two strategic competitors can come to

---

[k]The "knee" of the curve in question graphically depicts the point at which delivery of additional nuclear weapons ceases to result in any substantial increase in fatalities.

rest—that is, if both accept the idea of living indefinitely with what is customarily described as "the balance of terror."

By contrast, the Soviet strategic philosophy would appear functionally incompatible with finding any clear stopping points and striking an equilibrium. Given the woeful "softness" of populations, a doctrine that seeks substantial survival levels for one's own society in addition to assured destruction of the opponent places before itself seemingly impossible force requirements. As long as this should remain its operational goal, therefore, Soviet doctrine would seem to represent a mandate for endless competition without defined standards of what constitutes enough.[1]

Patently, it would be an exaggeration to assert that Soviet strategic policy has been governed only by this driving doctrinal mandate. Many other considerations and constraints have tempered translation of the doctrine into policy. At the same time, it is worth noting that both the Soviet military and political leaders have had cause for not lightly discarding it. In the military case, the reasons are fairly obvious. Psychologically and institutionally, the military professionals have found congenial a doctrine that justifies generous defense budgets, that stresses the traditional goals of defending the country in the ultimate event of war, and that seems to assign them a meaningful role if such a test should occur.

The outlook of the political leadership, one must assume, has been more ambivalent. Lacking the institutional stakes of the military in the doctrine, Brezhnev and his Politburo colleages probably have been more free to consider the economic and other benefits of a less demanding strategic philosophy. But they too have had their own investment in a doctrinal consensus calling for more than deterrent sufficiency. The strategic buildup of the past decade provides a case in point. Though one may judge that the buildup has still left the Soviet Union well short of an adequate war-fighting and survival posture, its political pay-off can hardly have failed to impress the Politburo. The buildup not only gave the Soviet Union greater room for diplomatic maneuver: more specifically, it "sobered" the American "imperialists," led them to concede that containment of the USSR was a bankrupt strategy, and impelled them to seek settlement of long-standing issues through negotiation instead of confrontation. Thus on both the military and political sides of the house, it would appear that a basic shift in strategic philosophy might not come easily.

To return to the ABM Treaty as an indicator of possible change in the Soviet strategic outlook, one finds little outward evidence of a more receptive attitude toward the strategic notions associated with the doctrine of mutual assured destruction. For example, the renunciation of countrywide ABM goes only part way toward acceptance of this doctrine, which also requires a tender concern for the survivability of retaliatory forces on both sides. On this point, though the Soviets have taken steps to improve the survivability of their own forces, they

---

[1]Compare our previous observations on this point in a slightly different context, p. 154 above.

have never seen fit to eschew measures that threaten the opponent's forces, suggesting a continued belief that deterrence requires more than holding the other side's population hostage. At the end of SALT I, the American side apparently could not persuade the Soviets to go on record that the *mutual* survivability of offensive forces would be good for the security of both parties.[63] Conceptually, the Soviets also have continued to reject the idea of security based on the "balance of terror," a notion inherent in doctrines of shared liability.[64]

As for Soviet military literature published since the ABM Treaty, one finds in it no signs that a new rationale for Soviet strategic forces may be taking shape around a concept like that of mutual assured destruction.[65] On the contrary, military leaders and theorists have continued as before to dwell both upon the importance of strategic defense[66] and upon a prescription for strategic offensive forces that stresses their counterforce mission to "destroy the enemy's main nuclear missile weapons and troop formations."[67]

If the ABM Treaty has stirred up a reappraisal of the pretreaty premises of Soviet strategic doctrine, it obviously is not apparent in the professional literature. Indeed, if any effects of the treaty were to be read into Soviet strategic thinking as reflected in the military writing available thus far, the most likely implication would seem to be that the treaty has given Soviet strategic planners fresh reason for counting upon counterforce systems as the most effective means of carrying out the damage-limitation mission traditionally close to their hearts.

But such contrary evidence as that cited here does not necessarily mean, of course, that the Soviet strategic outlook remains impervious to change. It has been known to happen in the Soviet Union that when established views have been challenged internally, they still are adhered to publicly until a new internal consensus gets thrashed out. Thus it may be that the ABM Treaty and its subsequent 1974 protocol do mark a real watershed in Soviet strategic thinking,[m] and that formal expression of a new doctrinal rationale for Soviet strategic forces simply has not yet had time to catch up. However, if a revised Soviet rationale should be in the making, and if it happens to run along the lines of mutual assured destruction, one must observe that this convergence will have come ironically at a time when the United States chose to modify its own strategic nuclear doctrine in a direction pointing away from its past emphasis on mutual assured destruction alone.

Soviet Reaction to the Schlesinger Strategic Modifications

A perceptible U.S. shift away from the conceptual foundations of mutual assured destruction became manifest in early 1974, when Secretary of Defense

[m]The 1974 protocol to the ABM Treaty restricted even further the permissible limits of ABM deployment, from 200 to 100 launchers on each side.

James R. Schlesinger first advanced a number of amendments to U.S. strategic doctrine and planning. Although our interest here is primarily in the Soviet reaction to these changes, it may be helpful to summarize first the main points of what has become known as the Schlesinger doctrine.[68]

First, there were changes in targeting doctrine designed to "reinforce deterrence" by providing a more flexible range of nuclear options, or, if deterrence should fail, to limit the chances of uncontrolled escalation by being able to respond "selectively" with accurate small strikes against military targets before having to consider the ultimate and increasingly "less credible" option of assured destruction strikes against cities.[69] Resting at bottom on the assessment that the probability of a deliberate, massive nuclear attack was very remote, and that the real problem was to deter lower level provocations that might escalate into general nuclear conflict,[70] this targeting approach also marked an official departure from a four-year-old "self-denying ordinance" against accuracy improvements that would enhance the counterforce capability of U.S. strategic forces.

A second category of strategic adjustments proposed by Schlesinger dealt with force sizing, tying U.S. strategic force levels closely to the criterion of "essential equivalence," according to which the United States would reduce, stay put, or increase its force levels, depending on what the Soviet Union would agree to in SALT and on the further unilateral evolution of Soviet strategic forces.[71] Special emphasis was placed on the point that perceived images of relative strategic power—deriving from such "static" criteria as numbers of launchers, throwweight, megatonnage and warheads—could have an important effect on strategic stability and political behavior, and hence must be taken into account in force planning.[72]

The third element of the Schlesinger approach embraced a number of prudential hedges against "the unknown outcome of SALT II" and especially any attempt by the USSR to achieve a "marked counterforce superiority" by exploiting its large throwweight potential.[73] These included several new R&D projects—among others, a more accurate *Minuteman* guidance system, a higher-yield *Minuteman* warhead, and a terminally-guided MARV for possible retrofit into both ICBMs and SLBMs—all of which would contribute to improved counterforce capabilities against hard targets.[74] Though such measures were intended to signal that the United States was prepared to "match" any Soviet counterforce buildup, it was emphasized at the same time that the United States neither wanted nor was seeking counterforce capabilities of the kind that would be required for a disarming first-strike against the USSR.[75]

As might be expected, the strategic initiatives espoused by Schlesinger in early 1974 did not go unnoticed in the Soviet Union. Visible Soviet reaction was expressed largely on the polemical level, its general themes being that the Schlesinger doctrine sought to revive the "myth" of a Soviet threat in order to justify larger military appropriations, that it was a "bargaining chip" maneuver contrary to the principle of "no unilateral advantage," and that it represented the attempt of anti-Soviet circles to "discredit the policy of détente."[76] Occasionally Soviet commentators also noted that "militarist circles" in the United States professed to be alarmed about "a U.S. lag in the military sphere,"[77] and that these circles were hoping to restore "the lost strategic superiority of the United States by qualitative improvement of weapons."[78]

Up to the time of the mid-1974 Summit meeting in Moscow, there was no public indication that high-level Soviet officials had found occasion to register complaints about the Schlesinger proposals with their opposite numbers on the American side. At the Summit, however, it was reported that Brezhnev objected to the Schlesinger "retargeting program" in strong terms, saying that it implied the possibility of nuclear war and that the United States was seeking a disarming first-strike capability against the Soviet Union.[79] Thereafter fresh criticism of the Schlesinger doctrine began to appear in Soviet media, charging that it was a resort to "pressure tactics" against the USSR.[80]

Perhaps the most explicit criticism came from G.A. Trofimenko, a well-known writer on strategic affairs and a senior member of the Institute of the USA. Writing in the institute's journal for September 1974, Trofimenko said that despite the "unequivocal" repudiation of "use of force or threats of force" in Soviet-American agreements, some representatives of the U.S. military-industrial complex were still resorting to "signalling via threats."[81] An example, he said, was "the excessive publicity given in recent months in the USA to the so-called 'Schlesinger doctrine' on 'retargeting' strategic missiles." Since the "true character" of U.S. targeting is "obviously" a "highly important" military secret, Trofimenko asserted, the statements of Pentagon officials therefore could not be taken to represent "objective information" for the enlightenment of the general public, but rather were a "deliberate attempt to exert psychological pressure on the other side—an attempt to gain, if not direct military-technical advantages, then, at least, conceptual and psychological advantages."

Such an approach, intended to create a "more comfortable position" for the United States in the strategic arms "dialogue" with the USSR by providing "so-called 'bargaining chips'," could not help but undermine the "basic principle of equal security." Further, according to Trofimenko, the possibility of mutually-acceptable arms limitation agreements was undercut when U.S. representatives, "instead of seeking compromises, try to propose to the other side a solution based on a purely American model which answers to traditional U.S. military-technical policy but is radically at variance with the traditions and principles of the other side's military-technical policy."[82]

Notably missing from all Soviet commentary on the Schlesinger doctrine was any direct indication of what impact it might have on the Soviet Union's own strategic policy, or what kinds of strategic measures the USSR might contemplate in return. Given the guarded nature of public strategic discourse in the Soviet Union, such omissions were hardly surprising. However, there was some possibility that the Schlesinger initiatives had become a controversial issue within the Soviet leadership, perhaps giving new edge to an internal debate over strategic alternatives that may have been going on already.

Signs suggestive of some sort of internal controversy involving strategic policy surfaced in late 1973 and early 1974, at which time it became apparent that a muted argument was being waged in the pages of various Soviet publications between two camps which did not see eye-to-eye on questions relating to détente, SALT, and nuclear armaments. One group consisted of writers identifiable as expositors of Brezhnev's détente line, while the other took in a number of military officers writing under the aegis of the Main Political Administration of the armed forces. The "détentist" group could be found arguing that war in the nuclear age was no longer a viable instrument of politics, and that security could not be automatically ensured through further "accumulation of military hardware,"[83] while the military writers challenged the nation that nuclear war would mean the "death of civilization" and that there could be no victor in such a war. Instead, they stressed the need to provide forces "necessary for reliable defense of the motherland," and warned against slowing down Soviet military preparations in a world in which the threat of war still existed.[84]

In many respects, this jousting in print was reminiscent of an earlier debate in Khrushchev's day, which also centered around the code issue of "war as an instrument of politics," and which had reflected strategic policy differences at the top of the Soviet policy-making pyramid.[85] Though one might surmise that the 1974 doctrinal skirmishing again echoed a high-level debate over strategic policy issues of one sort or another, the slender evidence available gave insufficient basis to judge whether the range of debate might have covered widely different strategic alternatives, or whether it was mainly "at the margin" of an internal consensus on what was required for Soviet security—with the differences narrowing down to how much or how little need be conceded for the sake of agreement in SALT with the United States.

In any event, whatever the nature of the debate and the impact on it of the new U.S. strategic approach espoused by Schlesinger, something apparently happened within the Soviet policy-making system during the interval of less than five months between the mid-1974 Summit and the first Ford-Brezhnev meeting at Vladivostok to produce a more appreciable shift in some of the Soviet Union's long-held positions than at any time since SALT II began in November 1972.

SALT II and the Vladivostok Accord

In a broad sense, the deadlock that persisted in SALT II down to the Vladivostok Summit stemmed from the same basic question left unanswered by SALT I: What was to be the future strategic relationship between the two powers? Essentially, this would depend on some combination of "legislated" constraints in SALT and the unilateral strategic programs that each party might choose to pursue apart from SALT. One of the underlying reasons why the negotiations remained at a stalemate was that, despite the rhetoric of "equality" and "no unilateral advantage," both sides were chary in varied degree of sacrificing their unilateral elbowroom. Both were aware that today's contract could be tomorrow's regret—that any comprehensive permanent agreement legislated between them would tend to shape the terms of competition in tomorrow's uncertain world.

Major Issues Left Unresolved by the Mid-1974 Summit

The specific issues over which negotiations came to an impasse during the first two years of SALT II included overall equality in strategic delivery systems, MIRV, and Forward Based Systems (FBS)—together with the problem of combining agreed solutions to these and a number of complex subissues into a comprehensive permanent accord. Space does not permit more than a brief summary of the main points involved.[86]

With regard to overall equality, the attempt to find common ground foundered over the Soviet Union's insistence on carrying over into a permanent agreement its SALT I advantages in missile numbers and throwweight. Rejecting the American formula of "essential equivalence,"[n] the Soviets argued that true "equality" warranted larger Soviet missile forces in compensation for geographic, strategic, and technological asymmetries favoring the United States, including the American advantage in strategic bombers. The throwweight advantage of Soviet missiles versus the U.S. advantage in numbers of warheads (deriving from the U.S. MIRV lead) presented a particularly complicated problem. The nub of the issue was to find a formula that would balance the existing U.S. advantage in warhead numbers (some 6,000 to about 2,000) and the more sophisticated missile and warhead technology of the United States against the greater number and size of Soviet missiles—and which at the same time would take into account the throwweight potential permitting the Soviet Union to wipe out the U.S. lead in numbers of warheads in the years ahead.

From the U.S. viewpoint, an agreement equalizing total permissible throwweight of missiles—after making allowance for bomber payload disparity and the absence of limitations on air defenses—seemed to represent an equitable solution.[87] But for the Soviets, this would have entailed acceptance of fewer launchers in order to stay within a given throwweight ceiling, unless the Soviet Union were to build missiles with less throwweight capacity—a step the Soviets appeared unwilling and perhaps technically unprepared to take. The impasse on

---

[n]The U.S. formula called for approximate overall equality in ICBMs, SLBMs, and strategic bombers, with freedom-to-mix, and with throwweight limits balanced by an allowance for bomber capability.

this issue in SALT II carried over to the related deadlock on how to achieve equitable MIRV limitations.

Basically, the Soviet Union faced the problem in SALT II of stalling off agreements that could curb its freedom to translate its new MIRV technology into deployed forces of MIRVed missiles. The United States, on the other hand, was the initiator of a series of MIRV proposals, each revised in the hope of gaining Soviet approval.[88] A major sticking point was the Soviet position that MIRVed missiles should be limited by numbers rather than throwweight. At the mid-1974 Summit the U.S. side finally yielded on this point, placing still another revised proposal before the Russians. Both sides would limit the number of their MIRVed missiles, but since throwweight was no longer to be restricted, the agreed numbers should compensate for the disparity in throwweight. The proposed figures would allow the United States its programmed total of 1050 ICBM and SLBM launchers, while the Soviet Union would have from 550 to 750 MIRVed launchers. It was also proposed that both sides should begin to phase out some of their land-based missiles with single warheads, as a move toward placing greater reliance on submarine-launched missiles and reducing concern on both sides about a first-strike threat.[89]

The Soviets again turned down this American approach, claiming that it would penalize the Soviet Union, which had chosen to put more emphasis on land-based missiles than SLBMs, and that it would increase the importance of long-range bombers in which the United States had the lead. Brezhnev reportedly set the bottom figure for a negotiated limit on Soviet MIRVed missiles at "about a thousand."[90] Since this was approximately the number the Soviets could be expected to achieve anyway by 1980 under their own unilateral deployment programs, the implication was that the Russians were not prepared to accept any limits on their planned rate of MIRV deployment.

On the FBS issue, the Soviets took up in SALT II where they had left off in SALT I,[91] continuing to insist that American forward-based tactical aircraft capable of delivering nuclear weapons on Soviet territory from NATO airfields or carriers must be taken into prior account in any permanent SALT agreement on strategic arms,[92] notwithstanding the American contention that these were tactical forces committed to the defense of NATO allies, and that the Moscow Agreements of May 29, 1972, specifically recognized that bilateral SALT agreements should not affect obligations "earlier assumed" toward other countries.

In its essentials, the Soviet FBS position called for either withdrawal of FBS or, short of this, for counting FBS in the aggregate total of U.S. strategic forces. The latter would have the effect of reducing by 500 or more the permissible total of American ICBMs, SLBMs, and heavy bombers—the so-called central strategic systems which the United States considered the first order of business in SALT. The alternative Soviet demand for FBS withdrawal was if anything an even more contentious question, for it involved the credibility of standing American commitments to NATO defense.

None of these issues could be resolved at the mid-1974 Summit in Moscow, where, in addition to a few agreements essentially peripheral to the main substantive impasse,[93] the two sides abandoned the objective of a permanent agreement in favor of seeking a ten-year accord to replace the Interim Agreement of May 1972.[94] In appraising the SALT deadlock up to this point, one would be justified in saying that the U.S. side had shown the greater willingness to accommodate its proposals to the objections of the other, though it too was not readily disposed to surrender in the name of equality the several advantages it enjoyed. But if there was an essential distinction between the approaches taken by the two sides, it appeared to lie in the greater degree to which the Soviet Union sought to preserve its own freedom of action, and in its persistent tendency to seek numerical advantages—"compensation" from the Soviet viewpoint—in as many categories of strategic forces as possible.

The Vladivostok Transaction

A basic core of understanding between the Soviet and American sides that laid the groundwork for the Vladivostok transaction apparently was reached during Dr. Kissinger's October 1974 visit to Moscow.[95] What persuaded the Soviet leadership to adopt a considerably less intractable SALT approach than before is still largely speculative. One may choose between two bodies of explanation, the first of which would attribute a Soviet change of mind chiefly to factors inherent in the SALT process and strategic policy, while the second would see the main impetus coming from outside SALT and the strategic domain.

In the first view, the stretch-out of the SALT negotiating schedule arranged at the mid-1974 Summit might be credited with having eased some of the pressure on Soviet planning for rapid deployment of new strategic systems, as Dr. Kissinger had hoped,[96] and thus allowed room to reconcile any differing opinions within the Soviet leadership as to what could be prudently entertained in a new SALT agreement. Or the credit might be assigned elsewhere, for example, to the hard alternatives posed by the Schlesinger strategic initiatives if negotiations should lead nowhere. In the second view, by contrast, the Soviet decision to adopt a less intractable position probably turned essentially on the belief that it was worth paying something in SALT coin to salvage the benefits of détente. In terms of this explanation, the immediate factor abetting such a decision might have been some sort of sobering advice from Kissinger to Brezhnev in October that détente was in deepening trouble and that therefore there had better be some movement in SALT if it were to be rescued.

The brief outline agreement which emerged from the Vladivostok Summit of November 23-24, 1974, committed the two sides to work out during 1975 the details of a new ten-year SALT accord to go into effect upon expiration of the May 1972 Interim Agreement in 1977. Owing to the cryptic nature of the published agreement,[97] most of its specific provisions became known only through later amplifying statements from the American side, leaving a number of ambiguities attributable either to abbreviated disclosure of what had transpired at Vladivostok or to actual lacunae in the understandings reached, or perhaps both.

The main features of the proposed ten-year agreement were: (1) an equal ceiling of 2,400 strategic delivery vehicles for each side, to include ICBMs, SLBMs and bombers, with freedom-to-mix within the total; (2) an equal number of 1,320 MIRVed missile launchers for each side, with no limit on throwweight; (3) land-mobile and some types of bomber-launched strategic missiles permitted to be included in the overall 2,400 ceiling; (4) no constraints on modernization to preclude such measures as accuracy improvements and deployment of new systems still under development like the B-1 and *Trident*; and (5) apparent dropping of the Soviet demand to account for FBS in any agreed aggregate of strategic delivery systems.[98]

In the United States the Vladivostok agreement received a mixed reception, the prevailing sentiment seeming to be that while it had given détente a needed lift, and was better than no agreement at all, it probably did not warrant some of the claims made for it, such as having finally put a "cap" on the arms race. Among the shortcomings of the agreement as seen by its critics were that it not only failed to reduce strategic arms levels but set the overall and MIRV ceilings too high; that it would speed up qualitative competition and boost arms spending; and that by leaving the Soviet throwweight advantage intact, it might stimulate a counterforce buildup that could lead to first-strike capabilities, with a consequent threat to strategic stability.[99]

By contrast with the diverse reaction to the agreement in the United States, it was greeted with seemingly unanimous approval in the Soviet Union, where the Vladivostok Summit was acclaimed as "the most fruitful of the Summits."[100] However, Soviet commentary was confined largely to the political importance of the meeting for its contribution to détente and for helping to guarantee against the outbreak of a nuclear conflict. Military aspects of the agreement were not discussed beyond generalities, and in keeping with customary practice, the Soviet public was left in ignorance as to the specific strategic force levels its government had subscribed to. Some note was taken, however, of criticism in the West that the agreement did not go far enough in limiting strategic arms.[101] Such arguments, according to one commentator, were "false and frivolous," since it should be "clear to everyone that the maximum possible under present conditions was achieved at the Vladivostok talks."[102]

Until the transaction at Vladivostok has been followed up by a full-fledged ten-year agreement, it is probably premature to make any categorical judgments as to its significance. Several of its tentative implications, however, merit some comment.

The high ceilings set at Vladivostok should accommodate most of the new programs the Soviets are capable of carrying out in the next few years. Indeed, though much criticized, the high ceilings were apparently what made agreement possible, as suggested by Dr. Kissinger.[103] However, the proposition that a numbers race was averted because Soviet strategic levels would have moved "substantially higher" in the absence of the agreement,[104] appears somewhat equivocal. Had deployment of new Soviet systems been planned on an additive basis, over and above the existing strategic inventory, this would of course push the aggregate Soviet level well beyond the agreed limit, which it already exceeds by about fifty delivery vehicles (see Appendix Table VA-3). But since the weeding out of older systems also appears overdue anyway, Soviet planners would not necessarily find the Vladivostok "cap" on their overall force level burdensome. In fact, if the Soviets had unilaterally calculated that a much higher force level was needed, it seems not unlikely that Brezhnev would have begun his numbers bargaining at Vladivostok with a correspondingly high bid, which apparently was not the case.[105]

With respect to MIRVed launchers, however, the "cap" claim rests on firmer ground. A bit of arithmetic, using deployment rates given by U.S. defense officials,[106] indicates that in a ten-year period beginning in 1975 the Soviets could deploy 1,900 MIRVed launchers, and that they would reach the permissible level of 1,320 in 1981. Thus, the "cap" constraint would amount to almost 600 launchers—certainly a constraint of some real significance.

In some sense, the essence of the Vladivostok transaction was to forge an agreement conveying the *appearance* of rough equality in rather simplified numerical terms—an agreement that would leave neither party looking like Number Two. Both came out about even with respect to "numerical image." This satisfied one of the main concerns previously voiced by the American side—that a marked asymmetry in the future strategic forces of the two, as measured by "static criteria," might have an adverse political and psychological impact.[107] A second prime U.S. concern centering on superior Soviet throwweight potential was, however, left essentially unassuaged.

From the Soviet viewpoint, leaving the sanctity of throwweight intact was an important gain. During a ten-year period, the Soviet Union could end up with from half to two-thirds more missile throwweight than the United States. Although this might not be translatable into superiority in warhead numbers within the life of the agreement,[o] it would allow warheads of substantially greater yield than those of the United States, and make easier the improvement of Soviet guidance technology, thus helping to compensate for U.S. accuracy advantages. On the U.S. side, the throwweight issue looked somewhat different, depending on who was looking at it. Some critics felt that the throwweight

---

[o]If one uses the estimated number of warheads per missile given for the new family of Soviet missiles in Appendix Table VA-2, and distributes them among a force of 1,300 MIRVed launchers with a sublimit of about 300 for heavy SS-18s, the total number comes out around 7,500-8,000, approximately the same as for the United States. This assumes no great advance in Soviet warhead technology, permitting more warheads per missile, during the life of the agreement.

loophole meant that the U.S. strategic defense problem had been reduced in no "meaningful way" by the accord.[108] Secretary Schlesinger, who had put heavy emphasis on the throwweight issue prior to Vladivostok, appeared to shift ground afterwards, suggesting that the United States could "live with" some differences in throwweight by restructuring its strategic forces to reduce their vulnerability to Soviet missiles.[109] Dr. Kissinger, who once reportedly described the throwweight problem as a "phony" issue, pointed out after Vladivostok that the accord would not preclude the United States from increasing its own throwweight substantially, "if it is judged in our interest to do so."[110]

With or without changes in the throwweight differential between the two sides, however, a major long-term trend "illuminated" by the Vladivostok accord was that with the permissible level of forces and expected improvements in guidance technology, fixed and targetable land-based strategic forces would become increasingly vulnerable, promising to put a high premium on measures to ensure the survivability of the agreed aggregate forces. Given its more diversified strategic force mix, with less of its total strategic capability concentrated in targetable, silo-based forces,[111] the United States would appear to start from a more advantageous position than the Soviet Union with regard to dealing with the survivability problem.

Apparent removal of the FBS roadblock by the Soviet side at Vladivostok would seem to have some interesting implications for the follow-on negotiations. If the Soviets had reassessed the FBS threat against Soviet territory, as suggested by Dr. Kissinger,[112] or had merely been using the issue all along as a device for negotiating leverage, then their dropping of FBS might simply mean that they no longer expected useful mileage out of the issue and would henceforth let it rest. On the other hand, if the Soviets had still felt strongly about FBS, and had only given in because of the urgency of striking a bargain at Vladivostok, then it would seem that the concession might generate internal misgivings about Brezhnev's conduct of the Vladivostok transaction, and that Soviet attempts to hedge on the FBS "give-away" might reappear as the post-Vladivostok negotiations got down to business.[113]

Finally, one might note that the Vladivostok transaction seemed to underscore the intimate linkage between SALT and detente. But this linkage should not obscure the fact that the SALT process has involved something more than service to detente, or vice-versa. SALT also had been driven by what might be termed the unilateral strategic necessities of the two superpowers. In essence, SALT might be seen as an ongoing balancing act between the need for some kind of formal agreement to sustain détente and the need to serve the "strategic necessities" perceived by each side.

What appears to have happened at Vladivostok was an attempt to satisfy the first need through a seemingly simple agreement on numerical ceilings without irrevocable prejudice to the second. The crux of the matter, since the post-Vladivostok negotiations got underway in January 1975, has been whether the balance struck at the Summit would hold up when the two sides tackled the much more complicated task of translating it into a binding ten-year agreement.

Post-Vladivostok negotiations centered on two issues: the U.S. desire to include the Soviet *Backfire* bomber within the Vladivostok 2,400 (missiles plus bombers) ceiling, and the Soviet desire to restrict cruise missiles (U.S.-developed highly accurate air-breathing drones) to a 375-mile range, while the United States insisted on a 1,500-mile range. Behind these were other problems: verification of cruise missile range, for cruise missiles could be tested for 1,500 miles but actually be capable of flying much farther, and their cheapness and great accuracy, which makes them very cost-attractive. The Soviets, one may speculate, intended the *Backfire* bomber as an anti-Chinese and a naval weapon, for they maintain that it is not an intercontinental bomber, and they may well believe or suspect that the United States was seeking its ban on Chinese instigation. Finally, the cruise missile, like PGMs, was another example of U.S. technological superiority, a qualitative factor which, like Soviet quantitative buildup, destabilized the strategic balance. (As to the disputed issue of alleged Soviet violations of SALT I, Moscow has clearly gone contrary to some of the U.S. unilateral declarations made when it was signed, but it is unclear whether the Soviets have violated the treaty itself.)

In Washington Secretary Kissinger appeared more ready to compromise than did the Pentagon. Brezhnev also declared that he would like to have the 2,400 ceiling reduced by a hundred or more, and proposed that two new U.S. weapons systems, the *Trident* nuclear submarine and the B-1 strategic bomber, be banned, in return for (unspecified future) Soviet systems being banned as well. It remains unclear whether or not these negotiations will be successful, and if so when.[114]

Soviet Theater Forces and MFR

Given its position as a great continental power stretching from Europe to the Pacific, it is understandable that the Soviet Union has seen fit to devote a large share of its military resources to ground-air combined forces committed to support of Soviet security and political interests at both ends of the Eurasian continent. Today these theater forces come to slightly more than two million men and some 160 divisions, with supporting tactical air strength of about 4,500 aircraft.[115] When the armies of its Warsaw Pact allies are added, increasing its own forces by about one-third, the Soviet Union's theater force potential looks quantitatively even more impressive, especially in Europe.

This abundant array of theater forces, however, is not a wholly unconstrained asset. The Soviet Union has several thousand miles of borders to secure against potential threats, not the least of which is posed by China—a country against which the joint defense provisions of the Warsaw Treaty itself "cannot be set in motion."[116] Indeed, one of the more striking shifts in Soviet military planning over the past decade has been a substantial strengthening of Soviet theater forces in the Asian regions facing the People's Republic of China, a buildup accomplished not by a transfer of forces from the European theater, but largely by additional mobilization.[117] Today this buildup appears to have leveled off, leaving about one-fourth of the Soviet Union's divisions and tactical aircraft deployed opposite China, somewhat more than half poised toward Europe, and the remainder apparently held as a central reserve.[118]

The possible motivation for Soviet military preparations in Asia, as noted earlier in this chapter, is far from clear. According to some speculation, the Soviet Union has been girding for a military showdown with China, possibly to include "surgical" strikes to destroy China's nuclear capabilities before they reach a level deemed intolerable to Soviet security.[119] A less ominous interpretation is that the Soviet leadership has come to believe that mere political pressure against Peking promises little payoff unless backed by a real flexing of military muscle. In this view, which the present writer finds the more persuasive, one of the powerful constraints against a major Sino-Soviet military conflict is that it might exhaust both combatants and allow third parties to pick up the pieces. Moreover, the unpredictable political and ideological costs of a war between the two leading Communist states would also seem to argue against carrying matters beyond the level of high-powered bluff and intimidation.

The Theater Balance in Europe

Whatever motivation may account for the Soviet military buildup in Asia, the fact remains that most of the Soviet Union's theater forces are still oriented primarily toward Europe. Modernization of these forces to place them on a better footing for either conventional or nuclear operations in the European theater has gone forward steadily since the intervention in Czechoslovakia in 1968, as has the practice of holding periodic joint exercises with other Warsaw Pact forces.[120] Measures to improve the organizational and command structure of the Warsaw Pact also have been carried out, partly in response to internal alliance pressures for reform following the Czechoslovak episode.[121]

By the simpler yardsticks of comparison—numbers of combat divisions, tanks, artillery, aircraft, front-line manpower—the Soviet Union and its Warsaw Pact allies would appear to enjoy a preponderant advantage in conventional theater forces in Europe, as has been the case throughout the postwar period. With the notable exception of NATO's larger arsenal of tactical nuclear weapons and its edge in a few other categories such as total military manpower and numbers of antitank weapons and combat helicopters, NATO comes out on the short side of the purely quantitative comparisons in circulation today. Two such comparisons—one for the overall European theater and the other for the Central Region, which is customarily considered the focal arena between the opposing military coalitions in Europe and which corresponds most closely to the guidelines area for mutual force reductions—are shown in Appendix Table VA-4.

Although Soviet bloc forces enjoy a quantitative advantage in most categories of conventional military power in Europe, as well as being geographically favored by a deep rear and interior lines of communication in contrast to NATO's lack of room for deployment in depth and lines of communication that stretch overseas to the United States, qualitative considerations must of course also be factored into any comparison of the theater balance. Here, one cannot go into the complex business of measuring qualitative and dynamic factors that bear on the relative balance of forces in Europe,[122] beyond noting that there are trends at work which could alter the familiar theater picture of the past. These trends are of both military and political nature.

For example, in the military-technical sphere, there have recently been on the U.S.-NATO side qualitative leaps in antitank weapons and precision-guided air-delivered weapons of various kinds, while on the Warsaw Pact side improvements in armored striking power have been accompanied by creation of a tougher ground antiaircraft environment. It is not easy to sort out what such qualitative changes may do to the theater force balance, or which side they may tend to favor. At first glance, however, the new weapons trends might seem to go a considerable way toward reducing the conventional offensive advantages of the tank-heavy Warsaw Pact forces, although some developments may cut the other way, especially the dense antiaircraft threat against NATO tactical aircraft.

It is turns out that qualitative improvements in conventional weapons technology—perhaps along with some restructuring of NATO forces—do promise to redress some of the imbalance between NATO's posture and the Soviet conventional threat, then the stability of the theater balance in Europe may begin to look less vulnerable to changes in the external strategic equation than might otherwise be the case.

Détente and Mutual Force Reduction Negotiations

In the political realm, the factors that bear most directly on the theater balance in Europe have been the growth over the past four years of a détente atmosphere, accompanied among other things by the opening in 1973 of East-West negotiations on European security and cooperation (CSCE) and the related matter of mutual force reductions. The underlying reasons for the Soviet Union's pursuit of détente politics in Europe cannot be explored here,[123] but the prime issue posed in connection with our subject is whether the Soviet Union now contemplates a more than superficial alteration of its past security arrangements in Europe.

So far as its declaratory intentions are concerned, the Soviet Union has indicated that it is prepared to negotiate a new pattern of European collective security that might eventually involve "the simultaneous dissolution of the North Atlantic alliance and the Warsaw Treaty, or, as a first step, the abolition of their military organizations."[124] On the face of it, the Soviet Union thus appears to stand for measures that would do away with the two-bloc system of military coalitions in Europe and the "legacy" of cold war division between the two halves of the continent. This would, however, entail Soviet acceptance of integrative concepts of the East-West relationship in Europe that are not only at variance with past Soviet practice, but that also run counter to the European agreements thus far negotiated under détente, for these seem carefully calculated to perpetuate the East-West dividing line rather than to erase it. Indeed, Soviet spokesmen have stressed at every turn the central significance of "final recognition" by the West of "territorial changes resulting from the Second World War" and of the "inviolability of the existing borders in Europe,"[125] which seems tantamount to saying that the principle of a divided Europe still informs Soviet policy.

One of the key tests of how far the Soviet Union is prepared to move from past policy and practice lies in the negotiations on mutual force reductions. The Soviet Union, it may be recalled, was in no hurry to get these negotiations underway,[126] acceding only after the Western side insisted that the CSCE must be paralleled by talks on mutual balanced force reductions. However, once the latter negotiations were joined, and after preliminary Soviet maneuvers had succeeded in getting the word "balanced" deleted,[P] the Soviet Union was the first to table a reduction proposal in early November 1973.

The proposed three-stage Soviet plan would begin with a small "symbolic" reduction of men and equipment by the end of 1975, to be followed during the next two years by successive reductions totaling 15 percent of forces on each side.[127] These cuts would affect both "national" and "foreign" forces in Europe, and would be spread across all types of units, including nuclear delivery forces and weapons in the treaty area. At the end of the reduction process, the Warsaw Pact would be left with a continued margin over NATO in the categories in which it had an advantage at the start. The precise terminal margin would depend on what base figures the "equal percentage" reductions were derived from—figures which apparently were not furnished with the Soviet proposal.

By contrast with the Soviet scheme, the proposal offered by the NATO side later in November was built around a "common ceiling" concept of drawing down ground forces on both sides in the guidelines area to a common level of about 700,000. This ceiling, to be reached over a period of several years, would amount to about a 10 percent cut for NATO, compared with 20 percent for the

---

PThe disputed word "balanced" originally reflected NATO's concept that the Soviet side should take proportionately larger cuts "to balance" disparities in force levels and in U.S. and Soviet proximity to the European theater. The title of the talks finally agreed upon is "Mutual Reduction of Forces and Armaments and Associated Measures in Central Europe," which yields the acronymic mouthful: MURFAAMCE. This chapter uses simply MFR.

Warsaw Pact. The first phase reductions would be confined to U.S.-Soviet ground forces, and though involving a similar percentage at this stage, would result in a greater Soviet reduction because of the larger number of Soviet forces in the area to begin with.[128] The NATO proposal, which omits aircraft and nuclear units, would have the effect of cutting back Soviet armored preponderance.[129] Justification of the nonsymmetrical character of the NATO plan was said to rest, among other things, on geography, which would permit the Soviet Union to keep its withdrawn forces nearby in European Russia, while American units would be pulled back across the Atlantic.[130]

Not surprisingly, the Soviet Union has made known its distaste for the NATO proposal, charging that it is a "maneuver" to bring about unequal reductions "at the expense of the socialist states," and that it deals only with conventional land forces, and not critical nuclear units and aircraft.[131] Failure to include "the well-trained West German Bundeswehr" in the initial application of the NATO plan has also been criticized, suggesting that the long-held aim of curbing West German military capabilities is among the more important reasons for Soviet interest in MBFR. By way of undercutting the NATO rationale that mutual force reductions should contribute to stability in Europe by "correcting" present disparities in the threater balance that favor the Soviet side, Soviet spokesmen have argued that "approximate equality" and a stable balance already exist, and hence any reduction agreements should not disturb this "historically-evolved balance of forces in the center of Europe."[132]

In December 1974 NATO endorsed a new U.S. proposal which for the first time included tactical nuclear weapons: withdrawal of 1,000 U.S. tactical nuclear weapons in return for Soviet withdrawal of a tank army: about 1,700 tanks and 65,000 men. The Soviets proposed symmetrical cuts in U.S. and Soviet forces only, as a first stage. Little progress continued to be made in early 1976 in the negotiations, but neither side seemed to want to discontinue them, and at the Twenty-Fifth Party Congress Brezhnev reaffirmed Soviet interest in their success. Their result, however, remained unclear.[133]

On the whole, the Soviet MFR approach appears to involve no basic reordering of security priorities in Europe, nor does it reflect any disposition to embark upon a hasty dismantling of the forward military position the Soviet Union has built for itself in Eastern Europe. Such an approach is probably one which the political leadership in the Kremlin can "sell" without great difficulty to the Soviet military leadership, whose generally conservative instincts might be expected to call into question the wisdom of any more radical reduction scheme. This is not to imply that a marked dichotomy exists between the political and military leaders. Rather, both probably share an interest, perhaps from a somewhat different perspective, in not going too far down a new and untried military security road in Europe.

The central issues for Soviet policymakers in the context of European troop reduction agreements would appear to be: How much military détente can be accepted without either unduly diminishing the Soviet Union's influence vis-à-vis Western Europe or endangering its hegemony in Eastern Europe? To the extent that perpetuation of political détente seems both desirable to the Kremlin leadership and to require some lowering of the level at which the present East-West military relationship is maintained, the Soviet Union may prove willing to reduce its force levels in Europe. But given the long-standing importance in Soviet eyes of having a strong Soviet military presence in Europe, together with Moscow's hard-nosed attitude toward the notion of "balanced" reductions, one may surmise that any agreements the USSR chooses to sign will be such as to permit it to preserve a substantial military foothold in the European arena, no matter what fluctuations there may be in the political climate.

Soviet Naval Power

If it can be said that the Soviet leadership is likely to operate on the traditional assumption that the USSR's interests as a great continental land power call for the continued maintenance of powerful ground-air theater forces in the European and Asian extremities of the Eurasian continent, the situation is somewhat different in the sphere of naval and maritime power. Here, despite reminders from Soviet naval leaders that sea power has played an important role in Russia's history,[134] the Soviet Union itself has only within the fairly recent past set out to challenge the dominance of the seas enjoyed by the Western maritime states, so that the Soviet leadership today faces issues for which the traditional pattern of Soviet military policy provides relatively little precedent.

Before turning to some of these issues, it may be useful to touch briefly on a few highlights of Soviet naval growth under Admiral Gorshkov, who was made head of the navy by Khrushchev in 1955.[135] Since that time Gorshkov has emerged as an eloquent and on the whole, successful advocate of developing an "ocean-going navy" capable of fighting either nuclear or nonnuclear wars and of "supporting state interests at sea in peacetime,"[136] in contrast to a navy whose principal mission previously had been to support the seaward flanks of the Soviet army.

Highlights of Soviet Naval Growth

Perhaps the factor chiefly responsible for what Gorshkov has described as "a new stage" is the development of the navy after he assumed command in the mid-fifties[137] was Soviet perception of a strategic threat from the sea—posed first in the fifties by U.S. carrier strike forces with nuclear-delivery aircraft capable of reaching the Soviet homeland, and in the early sixties by the growing

Polaris SLBM force. Although an imperative to counter these seaborne threats as far offshore as possible seems to have been a major driving force behind the technical evolution and the gradual forward deployment of a "blue-water" Soviet navy, other requirements appear to account for such things as development of an offensive SLBM capability against strategic targets in the United States and for an increasing number of "naval presence" activities in support of Soviet "state interests" overseas.

The latter "flag-sharing" aspect of Soviet naval activity has doubtless brought the Soviet Union some political dividends in such areas as the Mediterranean, the Indian Ocean, and the African littoral, although the actual policy gains of Soviet naval presence to date have probably been somewhat less substantial than pictured in occasional nervous commentary in the West.

One of the salient steps taken by the Soviet naval command under Gorshkov's leadership in the mid-fifties was to opt for a variety of offensive and defensive missile systems which did not require large capital ship platforms, but which could be packaged aboard smaller surface ships, submarines, and long-range, land-based aircraft. This adaptation of missile technology to naval warfare—an innovative move that went far to shape the subsequent development of the Soviet navy[138]—was notable not only for giving the Soviets a formidable anti-surface ship threat against superior Western naval forces, but also for helping to alter Western perception of the Soviet Union from that of a second-rate naval power to a serious competitor.

Along with heightened awareness in the West of the Soviet Union's growing naval capabilities, two opposing schools of thought have arisen in the past few years—one warning with varying degrees of alarm that U.S. naval ascendancy is slipping away, and another which contends that the Soviet navy remains well behind in most categories of naval power.[139] Controversy over this issue tends to thrive on the fact that there are so many asymmetries between the naval forces of the two sides, as well as in the roles they are meant to perform, that it is difficult to set them off against each other in a meaningful way in gross comparisons of the naval balance. In Appendix Table VA-5 may be found a typical numerical breakdown of Soviet-U.S. naval forces as of mid-1974.

On the face of it, the comparison shows the Soviet Union ahead in numbers of surface combatants and submarines, and the United States with a great advantage in aircraft carriers and naval aircraft. The U.S. margin is also substantial in support ships, an advantage partly offset by Soviet use of merchant marine vessels for fleet support, while on the other hand the Soviet Union possesses large numbers of small, fast patrol boats with significant missile firepower which have virtually no counterpart on the U.S. side. In amphibious warfare vessels, numbers favor the Soviets, but their capabilities are largely intercoastal, compared with the global mobility of the U.S. amphibious force.

The comparison involves other force asymmetries also. For example, though the United States has fewer ships afloat, they are generally larger (overall, the

U.S. navy floats twice the gross tonnage of the Soviet navy) and have greater operating endurance. In numbers and range of missiles deployed aboard their ships, on the other hand, the Soviets presently hold a distinct advantage, but this will shrink as the U.S. navy begins to introduce the new Harpoon antiship missile into its surface forces.[140] In short, gross comparisons do not go very far toward measuring the naval balance, for they not only fail to reflect qualitative differences between the two navies that weigh variously to the advantage (or detriment) of each, but they also do not take into account many other pertinent considerations, such as asymmetries in geography, in ties with transoceanic allies, and in relative dependence on overseas commerce and sources of supply, to mention a few.

Not the least of the matters left unilluminated by static comparisons of current naval strength is the direction in which trends of naval development may point. In this regard, it would appear that the Soviet navy today is in transition from a force optimized to exact a high toll from U.S. nuclear-armed naval units at the outset of a general war, and thus to limit damage to the Soviet homeland, to one possessing a better worldwide general purpose naval capability. Though in this process the Soviet Union still seems far from being able to establish long-term control of the sea for itself, it does appear to be increasingly capable of denying such control to others. Needless, to say, this attribute of Soviet sea power takes on additional significance in an age when, as noted earlier, international access to raw materials, especially oil, is becoming increasingly critical to the advanced industrial countries of the West and Japan.

Soviet Naval Policy Issues

At the present phase in the development of the Soviet navy, perhaps the basic issue on the policy agenda is: What share of Soviet resources available to the military establishment ought to be allocated to the further expansion of sea power as an instrument for the attainment of Soviet military-political goals? Given a military structure in which the outlook of ground forces marshals has long predominated, it may be surmised that the naval command has not found it altogether easy to establish a claim to a larger slice of military resources. Indeed, there have been occasional signs of internal debate over the resource issue,[141] and some analysts have suggested that the main point Admiral Gorshkov was seeking to make in his previously-mentioned series of articles on sea power was that the Soviet Union cannot expect to complete the construction of the kind of modern navy which, in his view, it needs, without increasing the navy's relative share of resources.[142] According to other interpretations of the same articles, however, Gorshkov is seen not as an advocate on one side of an unsettled defense debate, but as a spokesman for new program decisions already taken.[143]

Whatever the case may be, probably the single most knotty naval policy issue at stake, at least in terms of the ultimate resource commitments involved, is whether the Soviet Union should attempt to emulate the United States in terms of large carrier strike forces. The Gorshkov articles, incidentally, threw no light on the matter, for carrier programs simply were not mentioned in the series.[144] In the West one finds expert opinion divided on the question, though most students of Soviet naval affairs have consistently felt that the Soviet Union will not set itself such an ambitious goal,[145] if only because its entry into the carrier field was so long delayed.[q] The first two carriers built by the USSR, the *Moskva*-class, are helicopter carriers used largely in an ASW role, rather than strike carriers. A second pair of carriers, the *Kiev*-class, one of which has reached the fitting-out stage, rounds out the carrier construction program to date. Though the *Kiev* at 30-40,000 tons is the largest warship the Soviets have built, it apparently is designed as a platform for V/STOL aircraft and helicopters,[146] and therefore does not appear to be a step in the direction of carrier strike forces along U.S. lines. At the same time, however, the USSR does seem to be gradually moving away from its past dependence solely upon land-based naval air support.

Finally, another set of naval policy issues grows out of the arms control dialogue between East and West. Up to now, most Soviet naval programs have been unaffected by the various negotiations involving strategic or European aspects of the U.S.-Soviet military balance. Only the strategic SLBM component of naval forces has thus far been dealt with in SALT, and the issues before the Soviets in this particular category have been discussed above. But there are other questions affecting naval forces that some members of the Soviet leadership evidently consider ripe for negotiation.

Brezhnev, for example, has reiterated on several occasions, including the July 1974 Summit, that withdrawal of nuclear-armed naval units from the Mediterranean ought to be made the subject of negotiations.[147] From the Soviet viewpoint, such an approach would certainly offer one way to reduce the existing disparity in carrier strength, through negotiated restrictions on deployment of U.S. carriers. What is not clear is where Gorshkov and the Soviet naval command may stand on the issue of extending arms control limitations more widely to naval forces. At the least, such a policy course would probably be difficult for the Soviet admirals to swallow, for it implies that it would be both cheaper and more effective to negotiate mutual restrictions on naval forces than to continue the buildup of countervailing Soviet naval power—a task to which they have thus far dedicated themselves in the evident belief that it serves the best interests of the Soviet Union.

Summary of Salient Military Policy Issues

In this chapter, military policy issues of various kinds have been identified, including those growing primarily out of interaction between the Soviet Union and other major powers, chiefly the United States, and those arising within the

---

[q]The first Soviet carrier, the *Moskva*, designated by the Soviets as an "anti-submarine cruiser" (*protivolodochnii krieser*), was laid down between 1963-1964, and became operational in 1967.

Soviet policy-making system more or less independently of external influences. Here, without trying to catalogue all of the issues dealt with, we shall conclude by summing up briefly what appear to be a few of the more salient issues that emerge from our survey of Soviet military policy.

1. Perhaps the most fundamental military policy issue facing the Soviet Union is whether to pursue a long-term policy predicated upon little or no let-up in military competition with the United States, and therefore dictating a need to preserve maximum unilateral room for decision, or whether to be satisfied with a negotiated relationship of military equality aimed at dampening arms competition with the United States, and requiring acceptance of lasting constraints on unilateral military planning. The record to date would suggest that the Soviet Union at best is moving only slowly and grudgingly in the latter direction against engrained institutional and security attitudes that pull strongly in the other direction.

2. The linkage between détente and Soviet military power underlies the above issue and many others in the domain of Soviet military policy. Without doubt, the Soviet leadership believes that the growth of Soviet military power has made détente possible. What is less clear is how important a role is ascribed to military power as a means of "enforcing" continued détente behavior upon the USSR's political adversaries. To put it another way, the issue is whether the Soviet leadership thinks that a high level of military competition would prove incompatible with a durable détente, or whether it is believed on the other hand that unabated military preparations are required to keep détente on the track. A categorical answer can hardly be given. However, it would at least seem plausible that the Soviet leaders do not care to get caught with their military posture in disrepair if détente should for some reason collapse. This, plus the fact that Soviet security planning must consider other problems besides the power balance with the United States, such as the China problem and the maintenance of Soviet hegemony in Eastern Europe, would seem to put limits on how far the Soviet leaders may consider it prudent to go in slackening their military preparations.

3. In the field of strategic nuclear arms, one of the basic issues is whether to break explicitly with the established doctrinal view that Soviet strategic preparations should not stop at deterrence alone, but should also be directed toward achieving a capability for waging war and ensuring the survival of Soviet society if deterrence fails. To replace this planning rationale with a concept like mutual assured destruction would require parting with the deep-seated notion that the Soviet Union must look out for its own security rather than entrusting it to a contract of shared vulnerability with the adversary. Though signing of the ABM Treaty may have marked a partial step away from traditional Soviet attitudes, it does not appear from the available evidence that the Soviets are ready to embrace mutual assured destruction as the core rationale for Soviet strategic preparations, especially at a time when the United States is deemphasizing its own reliance on this rationale alone.

4. Another basic issue relating to the future U.S.-USSR strategic relationship turns on how confident the Soviets may be about their ability to compete technologically with the United States. This question appears to have been heightened by the Vladivostok accord. During prior phases of SALT, the main feature of the Soviet approach had been insistence on safe margins of force levels as "compensation" for technological and other asymmetries favoring the United States. But at Vladivostok the Soviets seemingly dropped their demands for compensatory numerical margins and FBS withdrawal. This might imply that they have come to feel newly confident of their chances in a stepped-up qualitative race. However, the basis of such confidence is not readily apparent, especially in view of the Soviet lag in critical strategic technologies like guidance accuracy and MIRVed SLBMs. Therefore, the issue would seem to be whether the Soviets look upon the Vladivostok agreement as the starting point for a serious *mutual* effort to mediate and dampen qualitative competition, or simply as a more promising way than their previous approach to constrain U.S. technology while they attempt to catch up.

5. An argument can be made that one effect of bringing Soviet and U.S. strategic forces into approximate numerical balance through the Vladivostok accord may be to provide a long enough "pause" on the same quantitative rung of the competitive ladder to permit working out agreements on other matters such as qualitative controls and force level reductions. Dr. Kissinger, for example, seemed to have had something of this sort in mind when he said that the equal Vladivostok ceilings, even at high levels, should make subsequent reductions easier. However, a catch in this proposition could be the Soviet attitude toward moving down the quantitative ladder. If the high ceilings were what made agreement at Vladivostok possible in the first place, as seems to have been the case, and if the ceilings answered to what Soviet planners consider to be a prudent minimum force level not only against the United States but China as well, then getting the Soviet Union to reduce its forces may prove to be a very stubborn issue.

6. The prospects for regulating qualitative competition and reducing force levels appear sensitive also to what might be called an implied "imperative" to do whatever is permitted by the Vladivostok agreement. Which side is likely to feel more impelled to act on such an imperative is a debatable question. In the U.S. case, concern has been expressed by the arms control community in particular that the Pentagon might try to exceed previously planned U.S. force levels simply to reach the agreed ceilings. For their part, the Soviets could be tempted to develop the maximum counterforce capabilities that high-yield weapons and improved accuracies would allow during the life of the agreement. As noted by Schlesinger and other U.S. officials, a determined Soviet effort to do this could by the early 1980s endanger fixed U.S. delivery systems, while by stressing development and subsequent procurement of such new systems as a larger missile (MM-X) and terminal MARV, the United States in turn could by the mid-1980s threaten the survivability of fixed, targetable Soviet systems. An

important issue for Soviet planners, therefore, if they should happen to give it thought, is whether to embark on a counterforce competition whose end result could be to bring nearer the day when targetable, silo-based systems on both sides would become highly vulnerable—a situation that might well come about eventually in any event through the "natural" growth of strategic technologies.

7. An asymmetry exists in the way the two sides have hitherto planned their strategic forces that could pose some particularly troublesome issues for the Soviet Union in an environment in which the survivability of agreed forces had become increasingly dubious. A large share of Soviet strategic delivery forces consists of targetable, silo-based ICBMs, and likewise most of the Soviet throwweight potential is concentrated in these forces. By contrast, U.S. force loadings—warheads and bomber payload—are spread more widely among diverse systems, leaving only about 25 percent of the U.S. capability in fixed systems, compared with more than 60 percent in the Soviet case. Given this situation, Soviet planners would seem to face major decisions as to how much of their permissible total of delivery forces should be shifted to less targetable SLBM and aircraft systems, or to land-mobile missiles, in order to alleviate the survivability problem. The United States also faces some problems of its own, of course, including the fact that its most accurate systems are the fixed, silo-based ones, and hence disposing of them in favor of SLBMs and aircraft systems might buy more survivability at the expense of accurate counterforce capability, at least in the short run. However, the magnitude of force restructuring required to reduce vulnerability together with the amount of "institutional drag" that would be encountered in doing so, would seem to be considerably more pronounced in the Soviet than in the U.S. case.

8. Although the outline Vladivostok accord itself incorporates no mutually-agreed impediments to the kind of quantity-quality marriage in strategic weaponry that could put the survivability of fixed ICBM forces in jeopardy, unilateral self-restraint might help to head off such a union. In this connection, Schlesinger in his post-Vladivostok annual defense report (February 1975) reiterated that the United States does not want to threaten the survival of the Soviet land-based deterrent and will not try, provided the Soviet Union exercises self-restraint and holds down its own programs. By tying U.S. strategic planning closely to what the Soviet Union chooses to do, Schlesinger in effect has lobbed the ball into the Soviet court, leaving it to Soviet decisionmakers to set the pace of further strategic competition. Whether they should respond by stepping up the pace or by displaying strategic self-restraint is thus probably one of the salient issues confronting the Soviet leadership.

9. With regard to Soviet theater forces, the bulk of which have been oriented toward Europe throughout the three postwar decades, the primary military policy issues facing the Soviet Union might be said to fall into three broad categories. The first concerns the relative priority to be accorded the deployment of Soviet ground-air theater force assets between Europe and its flanks on

the one hand and the Asian territories facing China on the other. Although China has certainly moved up the Soviet list of potential military threats during the past decade, the buildup of Soviet forces in Asia appears now to have leveled off, suggesting that any major shift of Soviet theater force priorities that might require substantial inroads upon the Soviet military position in Europe is not for the time being seen in Moscow as a pressing issue.

10. The second category of issues has to do with the peacetime military posture of the Soviet Union and its Warsaw Pact allies in the present era of détente and East-West negotiations on European security and force reductions. Perhaps the basic issue here is whether the time has come to contemplate something more than superficial alterations in the military security system the Soviet Union has painstakingly built for itself in postwar Europe. Judging from the Soviet negotiating proposals advanced thus far, as well as measures for improving the capabilities of Soviet forces committed to the Warsaw Pact, no substantial loosening of the Soviet military foothold in Europe is under serious consideration, notwithstanding changes in the political climate. However, some lowering of the level at which the East-West military relationship in Europe has been maintained does appear to lie within the range of adjustments the Soviet Union is prepared to make—provided this can be done without essentially weakening Soviet hegemony in Eastern Europe, and without negotiating away the presently favorable balance for the Soviet bloc in exchange for NATO's conception of theater force parity.

11. In the third category of theater force issues are to be found those relevant to the kinds of military operations that would be carried out in Europe in the event of armed conflict. Doubtless, the most critical of these for Soviet military policy is the nuclear problem—how to avoid escalation of conventional operations into nuclear warfare, or failing that, when and under what conditions to make the transition from one to the other. Other issues with large implications for Soviet planning include such questions as whether Soviet forces should be prepared for a short central front campaign or a lengthy war with heavy logistics backup and a requirement for major interdiction campaigns to cut off sea and air reinforcement from the United States.

12. In the naval sphere, apart from such questions as how much of the Soviet strategic delivery capability should be shifted to SLBMs, the salient issues today appear to stem from the transitional stage in which the Soviet navy finds itself. During the past twenty years, the revamping of the Soviet navy centered largely on optimizing it to counter seaborne strategic threats to the Soviet homeland. Today, the navy is in transition from this essentially damage-limiting role to one involving broader, worldwide capabilities. Among the issues that arise in this process are how far and how fast to go in acquiring the kinds of forces, including some form of shipborne aviation, that would permit offensive exploitation of Western dependence on the seas. In turn, the larger issue growing out of the Soviet naval command's advocacy of new transitional programs would appear to

be whether an increased share of resources should be channeled into sea power as an instrument for serving Soviet political-military interests. At this point, it remains unclear whether a basic decision to enlarge the navy's slice of available military resources has already been made, or whether this is still a matter of internal debate.

Some Additional Interacting Factors Bearing on U.S. Defense Policy

Although it has not been the purpose of the present chapter to examine systematically or to pass judgment on the defense and arms control policies of the United States and its allies, certain respects in which these policies are interactive with issues facing the Soviet Union have been noted in the preceding summary. In addition to the considerations already mentioned, there are some other interacting factors that appear likely to have an important bearing on U.S. policy decisions in the national security sphere, and which it may be appropriate in closing to touch upon briefly.

Perhaps the key consideration to be mentioned, at a time when the Indochina debacle and other setbacks have dealt a severe blow to U.S. interests on the international scene, is uncertainty as to how the Soviet Union may assess and act upon the opportunities that the trend of events seems to have unexpectedly placed before it. Whatever U.S. national self-image may emerge eventually from the present American time of troubles, U.S. leaders patently have been concerned by the possibility that the Soviet Union might interpret U.S. difficulties and debates in the aftermath of the Indochina trauma to mean that a slackening of American strength and resolve had set in, which might in turn encourage the Soviet Union to believe that it could safely fish in troubled waters and otherwise exploit détente to its advantage. Something of this sort, for example, seemed to have been very much on the mind of President Ford when he said in his April 1975 State of the World message: "we cannot expect the Soviet Union to show restraint in the face of the United States' weakness and irresolution."[148]

Whether the Soviet leadership in fact believes that the U.S. predicament points toward an unravelling of U.S. national will and confidence, toward an erosion of alliances, and a return to isolationism—all of which could produce a changed Soviet assessment of political opportunities and the relative risks of pursuing them—remains, however, an unknown element of the situation. Until 1975 the Soviets seemed to be maintaining a low profile with regard to trying to profit from recent American reverses[149] but Soviet (and Cuban) involvement in the Angolan civil war (see Chapter IX) was perceived in Washington, although presumably not in Moscow, as contrary to what the United States had seen as the spirit of Soviet-U.S. détente.

In any event, from the official U.S. standpoint, one might expect an assiduous effort to project an image of strength and responsible international involvement, if only to reduce Soviet temptation to exploit trends adverse to the United States. Indeed, President Ford's admonition in his State of the World message that "we will not permit détente to become a license to fish in troubled waters"[150] was coupled to the assertion that U.S. defense measures and alliances would be kept in good repair, in order to counsel continued restraint by the Soviet Union. Similarly, Secretary of Defense Schlesinger later made the point that "valid hopes for détente" would depend on restraint by the other side, which in turn would require U.S. policies assuring "retention of an underlying equilibrium of force in areas of vital importance to the free nations of the world."[151]

However, the need for fresh U.S. exertions in the military sphere in order to maintain a stable balance of forces to insure Soviet restraint and to reassure U.S. allies has by no means gone unchallenged. At first a new debate appeared to be shaping up in the United States around arguments that the loss of Indochina to Communist regimes merely caps a process at work throughout the world in which military power as an instrument of policy has been largely superseded by political, economic, and other nonmilitary forms of power.[152] Notwithstanding the rather contradictory fact that Communist political successes in Indochina rested on long and persistent application of force which finally turned the regional military balance around in their favor, such arguments suggested that U.S. defense policy moves intended to shore up American military power to offset loss of prestige and credibility from the Indochina setback might encounter increasing domestic opposition. But by early 1976 Soviet involvement in Angola and the continuing rise in Soviet military power began to convince even some strong congressional critics of U.S. defense spending that the United States should increase its own defense expenditures, and it seemed likely that this would be reflected in the 1976-1977 defense budget.

The concern felt in the U.S. defense community that it would be the wrong time, in the aftermath of Indochina reverses, to begin slashing the Pentagon budget and retrenching militarily is linked with what has been described as the "crossover" problem with regard to the overall military balance between the Soviet Union and the United States.[153] In effect, the United States is seen as having passed from a long period of military dominance into a short-lived era of parity, which in turn could be transformed into inferiority if increasing Soviet military power were to be combined with declining U.S. force levels and precipitate retrenchment from commitments abroad. Since the United States has never before been obliged to deal with the Soviet Union under conditions in which the latter enjoyed clearcut military superiority, there is naturally a good deal of uncertainty as to how Soviet behavior might be affected if the crossover situation were to become a reality.

In light of the changing international and domestic climate in which U.S.

defense policies and programs have come under intense scrutiny by both friends and adversaries, the role of such negotiations as SALT and MFR in attempting to "legislate" respectively the future U.S.-Soviet strategic balance and the European military balance between the opposing sides has assumed still greater significance than before.

Needless to say, should the negotiations in SALT founder once more after the tentative accord reached at Vladivostok in November 1974, then the worst forebodings of those who fear that intervening events may have altered Soviet interest in regulating the pace of strategic competition could turn out to be justified. On the other hand, should the announced SALT goal of converting the Vladivostok accord into a "final" ten-year agreement equitable to both parties be met, this should to a considerable extent allay concern that American difficulties may have led the Soviet Union to reassess its chances of forging ahead in the strategic arms field against a reluctant competitor. But even if a ten-year agreement on equal numerical ceilings is confirmed in SALT, the question of what constitutes mutual restraint in qualitative competition within such ceilings promises to remain an exceedingly difficult issue to resolve, especially if U.S. defense planners should find themselves restricted by unilateral domestic constraints upon qualitative improvement to which their Soviet counterparts were not similarly subject.

With regard to the negotiations on mutual force reductions in Europe, no measureable effects of American policy reverses in Southeast Asia have as yet become visible in the positions of the NATO and Soviet-bloc sides. When the MFR talks recessed in April 1975 after eighteen months of bargaining, the basic proposals of each side remained essentially unchanged, with the exception of a slight Warsaw Pact concession to permit initial token reductions by the United States and the Soviet Union, provided that all other parties—particularly West Germany—would begin to reduce their forces within six months.[154]

There seems to be little prospect, despite new U.S. and Soviet proposals in late 1975, that the trend of events may prompt the Soviet Union to recognize NATO's contention that an imbalance of conventional forces exists in Europe and should be rectified in any reduction agreement. Rather, as put by a spokesman for NATO, the Soviet side apparently "continues to adhere to an approach that would have the effect of contractualizing the present unequal relationship of ground forces in central Europe, even if at lower levels."[155]

As long as the Soviet stand in the MFR negotiations includes insistence on maintaining what NATO regards as an unequal conventional balance in Europe, NATO planning will continue to face the perennial choice between increasing NATO's conventional strength or relying on the threat of tactical nuclear weapons to rectify the imbalance. The first choice under present circumstances is made more difficult than ever by pressures to reduce NATO force levels either unilaterally for internal economic reasons or in order to get an MFR agreement. The second choice is complicated not only by doubts in many quarters in the

West about the ultimate wisdom of relying on a doctrine of selective use of tactical nuclear weapons, lest actual resort to such a doctrine might escalate into a major nuclear exchange, but also by the possibility that the Soviet Union might again revive its demand for withdrawal of forward-based tactical nuclear systems from Europe when and if a SALT agreement based on the Vladivostok formula is concluded. Although one cannot explore here the full implications of these military planning issues, which are compounded by the increasingly shaky state of NATO's southern flank from Portugal across to Greece and Turkey, it hardly needs saying that the task of maintaining alliance solidarity does not promise to be easy.

Finally, the range of considerations affecting U.S. defense policy in a period of rapid change and potential instability on the international scene goes beyond the problems of maintaining the strategic arms balance vis-à-vis the Soviet Union and the military standoff in Europe. Redefinition of the U.S. security posture in the Pacific, especially if access to bases in the peripheral Asian countries grows more precarious, is one major issue in the offing which could suddenly loom larger should North Korea, for example, seek to emulate the "reunification" example set by North Vietnam. In the Middle East and other potential trouble spots where the existing or projectable presence of American military forces and arms aid have represented an element of the U.S. political "reach" to be taken into account by both friends and adversaries, the constraints on U.S. access arising from political realignments, denial of supporting bases and the like may set new parameters for American security planning. In such circumstances, the basic issue might well come down eventually to whether the bulk of U.S. nonstrategic military forces should be largely withdrawn into a fortress perimeter or restructured along more mobile lines through such measures as increased basing at sea and provision of additional long-range airlift in order to sustain a selective global presence with somewhat less immediate dependence on the network of far-flung bases established in the particular international environment characteristic of the past quarter of a century.

Notes

1. This interpretation of détente as a tactical "breathing spell" preparatory to turning the screws on the West was, it may be recalled, purportedly passed along by Brezhnev to East European Communist leaders in 1973. The authenticity of the report, however, has not been established. See John W. Finney, "U.S. Hears of Brezhnev Reassurance to Bloc that Accords Are a Tactic," *New York Times*, September 17, 1973.

2. Congressional Briefing by Dr. Henry A. Kissinger, office of the White House Press Secretary, June 15, 1972. In *Documentation on the Strategic Arms Limitation Agreements*, Office of Media Services, Department of State, June 20, 1972, p. 35.

3. W.M. Carpenter and S.P. Gibert, *Integrated Global Force Postures: An Overview*, Strategic Studies Center, Stanford Research Institute, Menlo Park, California, January 1973, p. 6.

4. See Victor Zorza, "Arabs Urged by Soviets to Use Oil as a Weapon," *Washington Post*, November 20, 1973.

5. Soviet commentators, for example, have pointed to the energy crisis as a phenomenon indicative of "the sharply increased instability of capitalism," and reflecting "the worsening struggle" among the leading capitalist states for "mastery" of "energy and other resources" belonging to the "developing countries." Boris Ponomarev, Radio Moscow broadcast, January 7, 1974; V. Kudryavtsev, "Behind the Scenes of the Energy Crisis," *Izvestiia*, February 28, 1974; R. Andreasyan, "Oil and the Anti-Imperialist Struggle," *Kommunist*, March 1974, pp. 100-102.

6. Vladimir Petrov, "Formation of Soviet Foreign Policy," *Orbis*, Fall 1973, pp. 819, 831.

7. Professor Aleksandr Logachev, "The Soviet Peace Program and Ideological Struggle of the Two Systems," Radio Moscow, March 12, 1973; V. Osipov, "The Logic of Coexistence," *Izvestiia*, February 17, 1973.

8. Petrov, "Formation of Soviet Foreign Policy," p. 831. See also Jan F. Triska and David D. Finley, *Soviet Foreign Policy* (New York: Macmillan Company, 1968), pp. 434-437.

9. "Chou Says Soviet Is Bigger Threat than U.S. to China," *New York Times*, September 1, 1973.

10. A slowdown in the rate of growth is shown by both official Soviet data and Western estimates. According to the former, it declined from 10.9 percent in the 1950s to a rate of 6.7 percent for the ninth Five-Year Plan period (1971-1975). Western estimates of Soviet GNP generally give a growth rate decline from an annual average of about 6.4 percent in the 1950s to 3.4 percent by the early 1970s. See Abram Bergson, "Soviet Economic Perspectives: Toward a New Growth Model," in *Soviet Economic Outlook*, Joint Economic Committee, Congress of the United States, 1973, p. 40. For other instructive analysis of Soviet economic trends, including the claim on resources of the Soviet military establishment, see the compendium of papers in *Soviet Economic Prospects for the Seventies*, a Joint Committee Print also published by the Joint Economic Committee, Congress of the United States, June 27, 1973.

11. Some analysts argue that periodic transfusions of selected Western technologies have been a logical or rational choice as well as a necessity for the highly bureaucratized and centralized Soviet economic system, which in effect runs best on standard operating procedures in the intervals between doses of innovation from the outside. See Raymond Vernon, "Apparatchiks and Entrepreneurs: U.S.-Soviet Economic Relations," *Foreign Affairs*, January 1974, pp. 253-255.

12. For a fuller discussion of economic considerations as a factor behind

Soviet entry into SALT, see the author's "Soviet Interests in SALT," in William R. Kintner and Robert L. Pfaltzgraff, Jr. (eds.), *SALT: Implications for Arms Control in the 1970s* (Pittsburgh: University of Pittsburgh Press, 1973), pp. 24-28.

13. For example, data published by the International Institute of Strategic Studies give a figure of 7.5 percent for 1973 Soviet defense expenditure as a percentage of Soviet Net Material Product (NMP). The same data, when used with alternative methods of calculating the Soviet defense effort in dollar costs, yield a defense expenditure of $81 to $84 billion, or about 19 percent of NMP of $439 billion. At the other end of the spectrum, a clandestine study produced in Leningrad in 1971 by two pseudonymous Soviet economists gave a range of 30 to 50 percent of the national income going to defense, while the Chinese charged in 1974 that 30 percent of the Soviet state budget was for military purposes, which would come to about 20 percent of national income. By contrast, official Soviet figures for 1974 are 17.6 billion rubles for defense out of a total state budget of 194.1 billion rubles, or 9.1 percent. Using a national income figure of 325 billion rubles (the planned annual average for 1971-1975), the official Soviet claim comes to 6 percent of national income for defense. For sources, see: *The Military Balance 1973-1974*, IISS, London, 1973, pp. 4, 8, 74, 79; Aleksandr Gol'tsov and Sergey Ozerov, *Distribution of the National Income of the USSR*, Leningrad, 1971 (manuscript), pp. 2-3, 7; V.F. Garbuzov, "Report on the USSR State Budget for 1974," *Pravda*, December 13, 1973; AP Tokyo dispatch, "China Asserts Soviet Steps Up Arms Race in Rivalry with U.S.," *New York Times*, April 9, 1974.

14. In this connection, a Czech economist, who directed an official study to determine the real costs of his own country's defense effort in 1969, concluded that in both the Czechoslovak and Soviet cases these costs, which were higher than the official figures, were unknown to the Party leaders. Eugen Loebl, "Russia's Economy," *Interplay*, February 1971, p. 20.

15. See Colonel M. Gladkov and B. Ivanov, "Economics and Military-Technical Policy," *Kommunist Vooruzhennykh Sil*, No. 9, May 1972, pp. 10, 12; Major General M. Cherednichenko, "Contemporary War and Economics," ibid., No. 18, 1970, p. 21.

16. Keith Bush, "Soviet Economic Growth: Past, Present, and Projected," *NATO Review*, No. 1, 1974, p. 23.

17. See Brezhnev's Report to the Twenty-Fourth Party Congress, *Pravda*, March 31, 1971; S.A. Zverev, "The Potentialities of the Sector," *Izvestiia*, July 7, 1971.

18. See, for example: V. Repnitsky, "The Military-Technological Revolution and Inter-Imperialist Contradictions," *International Affairs*, No. 11, November 1970, p. 50; Yu. (V.M.) Kulish, "Strategic Forum: The SALT Agreements," in *Survival*, September-October 1972, p. 214.

19. Colonel V. Bondarenko, "Scientific Potential and Defense of the Country," *Krasnaia zvezda*, August 20, 1971.

20. Colonel-General N.V. Ogarkov, "The Theoretical Arsenal of the Military Leader," *Krasnaia zvezda*, September 3, 1971.

21. Among examples are: Colonel-General N.A. Lomov, chief editor, *Scientific-Technical Progress and the Revolution in Military Affairs* (Moscow: Voenizdat, 1973); Colonel B. Byely et al., *Marxism-Leninism on War and the Army* (Moscow: Progress Publishers, 1972), (in English translation).

22. Colonel V. Bondarenko, "Scientific-Technical Progress and the Strengthening of the Country's Defense Capabilities," *Kommunist Vooruzhennykh Sil*, No. 24, December 1971, p. 9.

23. This letter, dated September 5, 1973, was published by Aleksandr Solzhenitsyn in March 1974 after his expulsion from the Soviet Union. See *Letter to the Soviet Leaders*, translated by Hilary Sternberg (New York: Harper & Row, Publishers, 1974), pp. 35-36.

24. G.A. Arbatov, "On Soviet-American Relations," *Kommunist*, No. 3, February 1973, p. 104.

25. Ibid., p. 105.

26. Representative of statements by political and military leaders on the subject are the following: "Let all know that the Soviet Union will emerge victorious from any war with an aggressor." Party General Secretary L.I. Brezhnev, *Pravda*, November 4, 1967. "Victory in a war, should the imperialists succeed in starting it, will be on the side of socialism and all progressive mankind." The late Marshal N. Krylov, Commander of the Strategic Rocket Forces, *Sovetskaia Rossiia*, August 30, 1969.

27. See David Holloway, *Technology, Management and the Soviet Military Establishment*, Adelphi Papers, No. 76, The Institute for Strategic Studies, London, April 1971, p. 8.

28. G. Gerasimov, "Pentagonia, 1966," *International Affairs*, No. 5, Moscow, May 1966, p. 28. For other skeptical Soviet appraisals of superiority in nonmilitary publications, see: L.N. Ignatev, "Nuclear Weapons and American Foreign Policy," *Voprosy Istorii*, No. 5, May 1971, pp. 86-87; "Observer" article, "A Serious Problem," *Pravda*, March 7, 1970; A.I. Krylov, "October and the Strategy of Peace," *Voprosy Filosofii*, No. 3, March 1968, pp. 3-13.

29. *Pravda*, April 15, 1970.

30. The most thoroughly-documented study reflecting this viewpoint is Roman Kolkowicz's *The Soviet Military and the Communist Party* (Princeton, N.J.: Princeton University Press, 1967).

31. A well-argued case for this view may be found in William E. Odom, "The Party Connection," *Problems of Communism*, September-October 1973, pp. 12-26.

32. The way these bodies operate, indeed, their precise names and membership, are not discussed in Soviet literature. For what might be termed "informed" speculation, see: Holloway, *Technology, Management*, p. 38; John Erickson, *Soviet Military Power* (London: Royal United Services Institute for

Defence Studies, 1971), p. 27; Matthew P. Gallagher and Karl F. Spielman, Jr., *Soviet Decision-Making for Defense* (New York: Praeger Publishers, 1972), pp. 18-19.

33. For discussion of this point, see the author's *Policymaking in the Soviet Union: A Statement with Supplementary Comments*, The Rand Corporation, P-4131, Santa Monica, California, June 1969, p. 10.

34. Although the situation may be changing, such evidence as has been available in the past would suggest that there had not emerged, within the Soviet decision-making system, an informed and independent institutional source of strategic advice and analysis upon which the political leadership could draw. A potential source of such advice has been seen in a few of the research institutes under the aegis of the USSR Academy of Sciences—such as Arbatov's Institute of the USA and Inozemtsev's Institute of World Economics and International Relations, which devote some attention to broad strategic questions. Various knowledgeable scientists with an appreciation of the dynamics of weapons technology and weapons tradeoffs also have been mentioned as alternative sources of expert counsel. However, the patchy evidence available suggests that none of these "outsiders" has been free to encroach upon the traditional province of the military by offering independent judgment on such matters as force requirements, deployments, and basic defense concepts.

35. For comment on the vested interest of a considerable part of the Soviet scientific intelligentsia in a status quo that gives high priority to defense-related research, see the author's "Soviet Interests in SALT," pp. 38-39.

36. I. Sidelnikov, "Peaceful Coexistence and the Peoples' Security," *Krasnaia zvezda*, August 14, 1973. Nor does the contribution of military power to the USSR's global standing pass unnoticed, as the following indicates: "In 1973, Soviet power has grown still mightier; consequently its international authority and influence on the solution of international problems will increase still further," A. Leontiev, "Year of Great Change," ibid., December 31, 1973.

37. See Alton H. Quanbeck and Barry M. Blechman, *Strategic Forces: Issues for the Mid-Seventies* (Washington, D.C.: Brookings Institution, 1973), p. 20.

38. Admiral Thomas H. Moorer, Chairman, JCS, *U.S. Military Posture for FY 1975*, Washington, D.C., 1974, p. 7; *Report of the Secretary of Defense James R. Schlesinger to the Congress on the FY 1975 Budget and FY 1975-1979 Defense Program*, March 4, 1974, p. 45. (Hereafter referred to as *Schlesinger FY 1975 Report*.)

39. John W. Finney, "Pentagon Aides Say Soviet Is Developing New Missiles for Use in the 1980's," *New York Times*, July 26, 1974. This account places the numbers of additional missiles at 10 to 12, including both land- and sea-based types, but it is not clear how many are entirely new or merely modifications of existing missiles.

40. The new Soviet MIRV, unlike earlier Soviet MRV systems, employs an on-board digital computer and a post boost vehicle (PBV) similar to what is

known in the United States as a "bus-type" dispensing system. *Schlesinger FY 1975 Report*, p. 45.

41. John W. Finney, "Pentagon Says 'Pop-Up' Missile Gives Soviet Heavier Warhead," *New York Times*, September 19, 1973; Clarence A. Robinson, Jr., "Soviets Test Cold-Launch ICBM Firings," *Aviation Week and Space Technology*, September 24, 1973, p. 20. See also, "Soviets Test New MIRV Warhead ICBMs," ibid., February 25, 1974, p. 20.

42. Concern that the throwweight advantage of the new Soviet ICBMs might enable the USSR to "develop a clear preponderance of counterforce capabilities" was particularly stressed by Secretary of Defense James R. Schlesinger, who pointed out that the new missiles could give the Soviet Union "10 to 12 million pounds of total ICBM throwweight," compared to about 2 million pounds for the American ICBM force. See his March 14, 1974, testimony in *Hearings Before the Subcommittee on Arms Control . . .* , Committee on Foreign Relations, U.S. Senate, released April 4, 1974, p. 5. (Hereafter referred to as *Schlesinger Testimony, March 4, 1974.*)

43. *Schlesinger FY 1975 Report*, p. 6.

44. See Finney, *New York Times*, July 26, 1974. A noteworthy incidental point bearing on the accuracy issue was the highly unusual "disclosure" by a senior Soviet military officer during the mid-1974 Summit that the United States was underestimating the accuracy of Russian missiles, some of which he said were accurate down to 1/4 mile. Such a departure from the strict canons of Soviet secrecy was unusual. One explanation might be that the Soviets wished to convey the message that withholding technology transfer of items like computers would not really prevent them from fielding accurate missiles. Or, this could have been an indication of a changing Soviet attitude more tolerant of candid two-way discussion of matters like missile accuracy. See Michael Getler, *Washington Post*, July 27, 1974.

45. For more detail on the Soviet effort in the SLBM field, see Thomas W. Wolfe, "Soviet Naval Interaction with the United States and Its Influence on Soviet Naval Development," in Michael MccGwire (ed.), *Soviet Naval Developments: Capability and Context* (New York: Praeger Publishers, 1973), pp. 255-257, 262-265.

46. Moorer, *U.S. Military Posture for FY 1975*, p. 21. See also General George S. Brown, Chairman, JCS, *U.S. Military Posture for FY 1976*, Washington, D.C., 1975, p. 27.

47. Edgar Ulsamer, in *Air Force Magazine*, June 1974, p. 27.

48. See Brown, *U.S. Military Posture for FY 1976*, p. 26.

49. The Trident C-4 missile, expected to become operational in FY 1979, will have a range of 4,000 nautical miles. However, the warhead technology under development for Trident, going beyond MIRV on the C-4 to a more advanced type of multiple warhead, MARV (Maneuverable Reentry Vehicles that can change course on final approach to the target), will be much superior to the

present SS-N-8. See Moorer, *U.S. Military Posture for FY 1975*, p. 9; John W. Finney, "Maneuverable Warhead Being Developed by U.S.," *New York Times*, January 19, 1974.

50. See George Wilson, "Russia Testing New Bomber," *Washington Post*, October 19, 1969; Tad Szulc, "Soviets Said to Fly Big New Bomber; Policy Shift Seen," *New York Times*, September 5, 1971.

51. Moorer, *U.S. Military Posture for FY 1975*, p. 24.

52. Ibid. Reportedly, there are some indications that the Soviet IL-76 jet transport is being modified to serve as a tanker for the Backfire. See Brown, *U.S. Military Posture for FY 1976*, p. 32.

53. Brown, *U.S. Military Posture for FY 1976*, p. 42.

54. Ibid., p. 44.

55. The four most modern interceptors are the YAK-28 (Firebar), TU-128 (Fiddler), SU-15 (Flagon-E), and MIG-25 (Foxbat). The other 50 percent of the PVO interceptor force consists of the SU-11 (Fishpot), MIG-9 (Farmer), and MIG-17 (Fresco). The MIG-23 (Flogger) is also being modified for an air defense role. Ibid., p. 43. See also Moorer, *U.S. Military Posture for FY 1975*, p. 36.

56. Brown, *U.S. Military Posture for FY 1976*, p. 44. These aircraft could be diverted to air defense use, but at the expense of their employment elsewhere in a crisis situation.

57. Major General A.S. Milovidov and Colonel V.G. Kozlov (eds.), *The Philosophical Heritage of V.I. Lenin and Problems of Contemporary War* (Moscow: Voenizdat, 1972), p. 337.

58. See Leon Gouré, *Soviet Civil Defense 1969-1970*, Center for Advanced International Studies, University of Miami, Coral Gables, Florida, 1972, and *Soviet Civil Defense—Post-Strike Repair and Restoration*, June 1973. See also Colonel-General A. Altuaia, "The Main Direction," *Voennye Znaniia*, No. 12, December 1973, pp. 4-5.

59. The Soviet ABM program had its antecedents in the Khrushchev period, but picked up steam about 1964 when work began on the so-called Galosh system around Moscow. By 1967, the first launch positions had been installed. Having taken the historical step of deploying the world's first ABM system, and having laid claim to "solving" the missile defense problem, the Soviet Union was expected to capitalize on its headstart by extending the system to other parts of the country. However, difficulties arose, and in late 1968 work on the Moscow system was suspended, with about 64 of 100 launch positions completed. Although work was resumed in 1971, along with continuing R&D activity, the Soviet leadership evidently decided at some time during 1971 to abandon a long-standing policy of seeking viable ABM defense of the country in favor of mutual limitations on further ABM deployment. A fuller account of the Soviet ABM program may be found in Wolfe, *Soviet Power and Europe*, pp. 186-188, 437-441.

60. See Mason Willrich, "SALT I: An Appraisal," in *SALT: The Moscow Agreements and Beyond* (New York: The Free Press, 1974), p. 264.

61. The discussion here draws in part on the author's "The Convergence Issue and Soviet Strategic Policy," in *Rand 25th Anniversary Volume* (Santa Monica, California: The Rand Corporation, 1973), pp. 137-150.

62. See Erickson, *Soviet Military Power*, pp. 8-11; David Holloway, "Strategic Concepts and Soviet Policy," *Survival*, November 1971, p. 365; Leon Gouré, Foy D. Kohler, and Mose L. Harvey, *The Role of Nuclear Forces in Current Soviet Strategy*, Center for Advanced International Studies, University of Miami, 1974, pp. 71, 77, 94.

63. This point emerged in one of the unilateral statements put into the record by the U.S. Delegation, noting that "an objective of the follow-on negotiations should be to constrain and reduce on a long-term basis threats to the survivability of our respective strategic retaliatory forces." See *The ABM Treaty and Interim Agreement and Associated Protocol*, p. 13.

64. See, for example, N.N. Inozemtsev, in *Pravda*, June 9, 1972. The conception that security can be ensured by a "balance of terror," said Inozemtsev, "has always been alien to our state." See also G.A. Arbatov, "The Impasse of the Policy of Force," *Problemy Mira i Sotsializma*, No. 2, February 1974.

65. A recent thorough survey of the open Soviet military literature dealing with strategic forces may be found in Gouré, Kohler, and Harvey, *The Role of Nuclear Forces in Current Soviet Strategy*. See especially, pp. 77-110.

66. See, for example, General of the Army V.G. Kulikov, "Air Defense in the System for Protecting the Soviet State," *Vestnik Protivovozdushnoi Oborony*, No. 4, April 1973, p. 4. See also Colonel General N.A. Lomov (ed.), *Scientific-Technical Progress and the Revolution in Military Affairs*, Moscow, Voenizdat, 1973 (Translation by U.S. Air Force), pp. 64, 273.

67. That the link between counterforce and damage-limitation has been an explicit one in Soviet thinking, is suggested by the following statement in a Soviet radio broadcast of August 5, 1970, on civil defense activities: "The most effective means of defending the country's population are effective actions aimed at destroying the enemy's offensive weapons both in the air and on the ground at their bases. Missile troops—the new type of armed force—play a major role in the destruction of the enemy's offensive weapons." Cited in Gouré et al., *The Role of Nuclear Forces in Current Soviet Strategy*, p. 110.

68. Fuller treatment of the Schlesinger strategic initiatives and the reaction to them in both the United States and the Soviet Union may be found in the present author's forthcoming study, *Impact of SALT on Strategic Planning and Decisionmaking*, The Rand Corporation, R-1686, Santa Monica, California.

69. *Schlesinger FY 1975 Report*, pp. 4, 5, 38.

70. Ibid., p. 38; *Schlesinger Testimony, March 4, 1974*, p. 55.

71. *Schlesinger FY 1975 Report*, p. 6.

72. Ibid., pp. 28, 29, 43, 44.

73. Ibid., pp. 6, 26, 30.

74. Ibid., pp. 52-55.

75. Ibid., pp. 4, 42; *Schlesinger Testimony, March 4, 1974*, pp. 18-19.

76. For typical commentary along these lines, see B. Svetlov, "Despite the Spirit of the Times," *Izvestiia*, January 4, 1974; A. Platonov and L. Alekseyev, "A Responsible Task," *Pravda*, February 14, 1974; V. Vinograd, "An Increase for the Pentagon," *Krasnaia zvezda*, August 28, 1974; A. Grigoryants, "Those Who Are Against Detente," *Nedel'ya*, No. 35, August-September 1974, pp. 2-3.

77. V.A. Matveyev, "Fresh Gains in the Struggle Against Opponents of Detente," *Za Rubezhom*, No. 22, August 1974, p. 9; Grigoryants, in *Nedel'ya*, August-September 1974.

78. V. Larionov, "Arms Limitation and Its Enemies," *Pravda*, April 7, 1974.

79. See Joseph Kraft, "Letter From Moscow," *New Yorker*, July 29, 1974, p. 70.

80. See, for example, A. Karenin, "On Restraining Strategic Arms," *Mezhdunarodnaia Zhizn*, No. 9, September 1974, p. 19.

81. G.A. Trofimenko, "Problems of Strengthening Peace and Security in Soviet-American Relations," *SShA: Ekonomika, Politika, Ideologiia*, No. 9, September 1974, p. 17.

82. Ibid., p. 18.

83. G.A. Trofimenko, "USSR-USA: Peaceful Coexistence as a Norm of Mutual Relations," *SShA: Ekonomika, Politika, Ideologiia*, No. 2, February 1974, p. 17. For other expressions of a similar viewpoint, see M.A. Milshtein and L.S. Semeiko, "Strategic Arms Limitation: Problems and Prospects," ibid., No. 12, December 1973, pp. 3-12; G.A. Arbatov, "The Impasse of the Policy of Force," *Problemi Mira i Sotsializma*, No. 2, February 1974, pp. 41-47; Aleksandr Bovin, "Peace and Social Progress," *Izvestiia*, September 11, 1973; G.A. Arbatov (ed.), *USA: The Scientific-Technical Revolution and Trends in Foreign Policy*, Moscow, 1974, pp. 69-70.

84. Rear Admiral Professor V. Shelyag, "Two World Outlooks—Two Views on War," *Krasnaia zvezda*, February 7, 1974; General of the Army Ye. Maltsev, "Lenin's Ideas of the Defense of Socialism," ibid., February 14, 1974; Colonel Ye. Ribkin, "Leninist Conception of War and the Present," *Kommunist Vooruzhennik Sil*, No. 20, October 1973, pp. 21-28.

85. For discussion of this earlier debate, see the author's *Soviet Strategy at The Crossroads* (Cambridge: Harvard University Press, 1965), pp. 70-78, and his *Soviet Power and Europe*, pp. 437, 503-509.

86. The discussion hereafter of SALT issues and the Vladivostok accord is drawn from a previously cited forthcoming study by the present author, *Impact of SALT on Strategic Planning and Decisionmaking.*

87. Statement by Paul H. Nitze before the House Armed Services Subcommittee on Arms Control and Disarmament, July 2, 1974. See: "Nitze: 'Essential Equivalence' Should Be Arms Talk Goal," *Aviation Week & Space Technology*, July 22, 1974, p. 43 (hereafter cited as *Nitze Statement, July 2, 1974*).

88. Leslie H. Gelb, "Kissinger Said To Offer Halt on New Missile," *New York Times*, March 31, 1974; ibid., April 12, 1974.

89. Hedrick Smith, "Moscow Sought Parity," *New York Times*, July 9, 1974; Leslie Gelb, "Summit Talk Foundered Over MIRV's," ibid.

90. Kraft, in the *New Yorker*, July 29, 1974, p. 70.

91. See John Newhouse, *Cold Dawn: The Story of SALT* (New York: Holt, Rinehart and Winston, 1973), pp. 174-176.

92. Hedrick Smith, "A Return to Rivalry," *New York Times*, March 24, 1974; Leslie H. Gelb, "U.S. Urges New Arms Talk Approach," ibid., March 3, 1974.

93. These included a treaty on limiting underground nuclear tests; a protocol to the ABM Treaty permitting only a single deployment area of 100 ABM launchers rather than two; an agreement to explore ways of curbing the dangers of environmental modification techniques for military purposes; and two protocols on dismantling and replacement of missiles, confirming procedures worked out by the SCC in accordance with the May 1972 SALT agreements. The latter were kept secret at Russian request. See "Texts of Nuclear Accords and of Joint Statement," *New York Times*, July 4, 1974.

94. John Herbers, "Nixon, Brezhnev Delay Key Curbs on Arms Till '85," *New York Times*, July 4, 1974; Hedrick Smith, "Wait-and-See Summit," ibid.; Robert Keatley, "Moscow Summit Failure To Get Arms Pact Spurs a New Approach for Geneva Talks," *Wall Street Journal*, July 5, 1974.

95. See Leslie H. Gelb, "How U.S. Made Ready for Talk at Vladivostok," *New York Times*, December 3, 1974.

96. Immediately after the mid-1974 Summit, Kissinger expressed the hope that the new SALT schedule might allow negotiating leeway of "about 18 months to gain control of the multiple warheads ... by introducing some stability into the rate and nature of their deployment." See Dr. Kissinger's July 3, 1974 Press Conference in Moscow, text in *State Department Bulletin*, July 29, 1974, p. 210 (hereafter cited as *Kissinger Press Conference, July 3, 1974*).

97. See "Text of the Nuclear Arms Agreement," *New York Times*, November 25, 1974.

98. See "Press Conference of the Secretary of State," Bureau of Public Affairs, Department of State, December 7, 1974; John Herbers, "Kissinger Describes Vladivostok Accord as 'Breakthrough'," *New York Times*, November 25, 1974; Clarence A. Robinson, Jr., "SALT Proposals Facing Hurdles," *Aviation Week & Space Technology*, December 9, 1974, pp. 12-14.

99. See, for example: Editorial "The Vladivostok Accord," *Washington Post*, December 6, 1974; Joseph Kraft, "The High Price of Détente," ibid., November 26, 1974; editorial "New Chance for SALT," *New York Times*, December 26, 1974; Paul Nitze, "Vladivostok and Crisis Stability," *Wall Street Journal*, January 24, 1974; William Chapman, "Senator Jackson Asks Further Arms Limits," *Washington Post*, December 9, 1974; Herbert Scoville, "Moving Backward on Arms Curbs," *New York Times*, December 12, 1974.

100. Editorial, "Great Success of the Vladivostok Meeting," *Izvestiia*, November 27, 1974. See also V. Matveyev, "Developing What Has Been Achieved," ibid., November 29, 1974; "Results of the Meeting of General Secretary L.I. Brezhnev with U.S. President G. Ford," *Pravda*, November 29, 1974.

101. See Yu. Nikolaev, "Vladivostok Meeting: Important Results," *Mezhdunarodnaia Zhizn*, No. 1, January 1975, pp. 7-8.

102. V. Osipov, "Common Sense and Ulterior Motives," *Izvestiia*, December 5, 1974.

103. "Press Conference of the Secretary of State," December 7, 1974, p. 4. Compare also Dr. Kissinger's comment on January 16, 1975, in a TV interview with Bill Moyers, to the effect that those critical of the high ceilings had "never negotiated with the Soviet Union."

104. See "Kissinger Sums Up '74," interview in *Newsweek*, December 30, 1974, p. 29.

105. Reportedly, the overall figure first proposed by Brezhnev was 2,500, reduced to 2,400 in the course of the bargaining. The opening U.S. proposal reportedly was 2,100. See Gelb, in *New York Times*, December 3, 1974.

106. A deployment rate of 200 MIRVed launchers per year was credited to the Soviets by Secretary Schlesinger in testimony in September 1974. For purposes of our arithmetic, a rate of 100 was assumed the first year, and 200 thereafter. See *Hearing Before the Subcommittee on Arms Control . . .* Committee on Foreign Relations, U.S. Senate, September 11, 1974, (Washington, D.C.: Government Printing Office, 1975), pp. 9-10.

107. As noted by Secretary Schlesinger, the agreement also satisfied the congressional guidance laid down at Senator Jackson's behest after SALT I that any new agreement should be based on equal force levels. See *Washington Post*, December 7, 1974.

108. See Nitze, in *Wall Street Journal*, January 24, 1975.

109. See John W. Finney, "Pentagon Chief Sees Pact Leading to Arms Buildup," *New York Times*, December 7, 1974; Michael Getler, "Schlesinger Backs Pact, Sees Some Rise in Arms," *Washington Post*, December 7, 1974.

110. "Press Conference of the Secretary of State," December 7, 1974, p. 2.

111. As pointed out by Secretary Schlesinger, less than 25 percent of the U.S. strategic capability, measured in terms of the numbers of warheads and bombs, resides in fixed ICBMs. In the Soviet case, more than 60 percent is concentrated in fixed ICBMs. See Secretary of Defense James R. Schlesinger, Annual Defense Department Report FY 1976, February 5, 1975, Washington, D.C., p. I-16 (hereafter cited as *Schlesinger FY 76 Report*).

112. See Herbers, in *New York Times*, November 25, 1974.

113. Some slight hint of internal dissatisfaction with the FBS concession was contained in a December 1, 1974 article in *Krasnaia zvezda*, written by Colonel A. Leontiev and entitled "Oil Smells of Blood." The article asserted that forward bases "constitute a source of war danger" and play "a very important role in the plans of Atlantic strategists." See also, "Soviet Military Hints at Dissent on Arms Issue," *New York Times*, December 2, 1974.

114. Leslie H. Gelb, "Another U.S. Compromise Position is Reported Reached on Strategic Arms," *New York Times*, February 17, 1976.

115. *The Military Balance 1973-1974*, pp. 6-7.

116. See Malcolm Mackintosh, "The Warsaw Pact Today," *Survival*, May-June 1974, p. 125.

117. For further details, see the present author's chapter "Soviet Military Policy and Strategy," in Kurt London (ed.), *The Soviet Impact on World Politics* (New York: Hawthorn Books, 1974), pp. 239, 257-258.

118. Moorer, *United States Military Posture for FY 1974*, p. 52.

119. Such speculation has arisen against the background of earlier hints from Soviet sources in 1969 that nuclear attacks against China's atomic installations were being considered. See Wolfe, *Soviet Power and Europe*, p. 259.

120. See John Erickson, "Soviet Combat Force on Continent Grows," *NATO Review*, No. 3, June 1974, pp. 18-21.

121. See Wolfe, *Soviet Power and Europe*, pp. 496-498.

122. For a more extensive discussion of the qualitative aspects of theater force comparisons, see the present author's *Soviet Military Capabilities and Intentions in Europe*, pp. 11-31.

123. For useful insight into this question, see Robert Legvold, "The Problem of European Security," *Problems of Communism*, January-February 1974, pp. 13-33; and William E. Griffith, *The World and the Great Power Triangles*, Center for International Studies, MIT, March 1974, pp. 21-30. See also Thomas W. Wolfe, *Role of the Warsaw Pact in Soviet Policy*, P-4973, The Rand Corporation, March 1973, pp. 1-11.

124. Sh. Sanakoyev, "Peace in Europe and the Confrontation of the Two Systems," *International Affairs*, Moscow, No. 11, November 1972, p. 7. See also Yu. Kostko, "Military Confrontation and the Problem of Security in Europe," *Mirovaia Ekonomika i Mezhdunarodnie Otnosheniye*, No. 9, September 1972, p. 20; N. Kapchenko, "Realistic Path To Ensuring Peace in Europe," *Mezhdunarodnaia Zhizn*, No. 1, January 1973, p. 23.

125. A. Gromyko, "The Leninist Revolutionary Course of Foreign Policy," *Kommunist*, No. 1, January 1973, p. 46; Yevgeniy Belov commentary, Moscow radio, February 15, 1973.

126. For background on Soviet attitudes toward force reductions, see Thomas W. Wolfe, *Soviet Attitudes Toward MBFR and the USSR's Military Presence in Europe*, P-4819 (Santa Monica, California: The Rand Corporation, April 1972), pp. 10-12. For treatment of the issues from the Western viewpoint, see Christoph Bertram, *Mutual Force Reductions in Europe: The Political Aspects*, Adelphi Paper No. 84, International Institute for Strategic Studies, London, 1972; John Yochelson (reprint from *Orbis*, Spring 1973), "The Search for an American Approach," in *Survival*, November-December 1973; Denis Greenhill, in *International Affairs*, January 1974, pp. 1-14.

127. Though the proposals of neither side have been officially published, most of their details have become known. See Richard Homan, "Soviets Leak Troop-Cut Plan," *Washington Post*, November 18, 1973; Andrew Hamilton, "Toward Troop Cuts in Europe," ibid., June 24, 1974.

128. According to the figures on which the NATO proposal was based, the United States provides 28 percent of NATO's ready forces in Central Europe, while the USSR accounts for more than 60 percent of Warsaw Pact ground forces. See "Europe: Mutual and Balanced Force Reductions," in *Foreign Policy Outlines*, Department of State, May 1974, pp. 1-2.

129. Reportedly, the United States—with allied consent—has indicated a willingness to withdraw some nuclear artillery and tactical missiles as an inducement for reduction of Soviet tanks. See Hamilton, in *Washington Post*, June 24, 1974.

130. See Drew Middleton, "West Called 'Not Helpful' in Talks on Troop Cuts," *New York Times*, December 14, 1973.

131. I. Milnikov, "A Responsible Task," *Pravda*, December 17, 1973; Vladimir Komlev dispatch, "West Seeks Unfair Advantages at Vienna Talks," Radio Moscow, December 15, 1973.

132. Aleksandr Urban, "Vienna Measures of Military Relaxation," *Literaturnaia Gazeta* No. 51, December 19, 1973; D. Proektor, "Pressing Problems of Security and Cooperation in Europe: Military Aspects," *Mezhdunarodnaia Zhizn*, No. 5, May 1974, pp. 89-90.

133. Drew Middleton, "U.S. Arms-Cut Idea Is Backed by NATO," *New York Times*, December 13, 1975.

134. The attribution of a strong naval tradition to Tsarist Russia and the assertion that navies "played an important role" in Russian history despite those detractors claiming that "all of Russia's victories were gained only by the army," is one of the recurrent themes in a series of eleven articles by Admiral S.G. Gorshkov which appeared in *Morskoi Sbornik* in 1972-1973 under the title: "Navies in War and Peace." In these articles, Gorshkov also stressed that occasional Russian rulers who neglected "the significance of sea power" paid dearly for their oversight, and he argued, contrary to the known facts, that Lenin advocated a big navy for the new Soviet state. See especially issues No. 3, March 1972, pp. 21, 26; No. 4, April 1972, p. 23; and No. 6, June 1972, pp. 11-21.

135. For Khrushchev's personal account of how he selected Gorshkov to replace Admiral N.G. Kuznetsov, see *Khrushchev Remembers: The Last Testament* (New York: Little, Brown & Co., 1974), pp. 28-33.

136. For more on Gorshkov's successful advocacy of an enlarged role for the Soviet navy in the face of influential critics who argued that in the nuclear age the navy "had completely lost its significance as a branch of the armed forces," see Wolfe, *Soviet Naval Interaction With the United States and Its Influence on Soviet Naval Development*, pp. 8-12.

137. Admiral S.G. Gorshkov, "The Development of the Soviet Naval Art," *Morskoi Sbornik*, No. 2, February 1967, p. 20.

138. Among the best documented accounts of Soviet naval development are two volumes of essays brought together largely by Michael MccGwire. See Michael MccGwire (ed.), *Soviet Naval Developments: Capability and Context* (New York: Praeger Publishers, 1973), and M. MccGwire, K. Booth and J. McDonnell (eds.), *Soviet Naval Policy: Objectives and Constraints* (New York: Praeger Publishers, 1974).

139. See Wolfe, *Soviet Naval Interaction With the U.S. and Its Influence on Soviet Naval Development*, pp. 34-35.

140. Michael Getler, "Navy Seeks More Firepower," *Washington Post*, October 15, 1974. See also Brown, *U.S. Military Posture for FY 1976*, p. 85.

141. A case in point was the reference in a recent book by a Soviet naval officer to Marshal Tukhachevski's assertion, made many years ago, to the effect that the expenditure of a "significant part" of German military resources on the navy rather than the army prior to World War I represented an ill-timed, irrational use of available capital, since the navy could contribute little to Germany's immediate strategic goals. By referring to what he obviously regarded as an outdated historical example no longer applicable in present circumstances, the navy writer can be assumed to have been responding to internal critics of proposed Soviet naval funding. The thrust of his own argument was that "rational" force planning can be facilitated by careful analysis of missions in the light of newly-acquired capabilities of one service or the other. See Captain Yu. S. Solnyshkov, *Ekonomicheskiye Faktory i Vooruzheniye* (Economic Factors and Armament), Moscow, Voenizdat, 1973, pp. 13-15.

142. See MccGwire et al. (eds.), *Soviet Naval Policy: Objectives and Constraints*, Chapter 28.

143. For a presentation of this view, see Commander Clyde A. Smith, "The Meaning and Significance of the Gorshkov Articles," *Naval War College Review*, March-April 1974, especially pp. 19-20.

144. See Smith, in *Naval War College Review*, March-April 1974, p. 28.

145. In this regard, a canvas of the work of twelve Western specialists conducted in 1973 by Robert W. Herrick showed that only two "expected the USSR to construct attack carriers in the foreseeable future," while two hedged on the question. The remainder signified "no." Memo from Herrick to the author, February 1, 1973.

146. Moorer, *U.S. Military Posture for FY 1975*, pp. 69-70.

147. Brezhnev first broached this proposal publicly in 1971. Soviet sources indicate that it was "suggested" at the July 1974 Summit, but that "unfortunately" it was not accepted. See Karenin, in *Mezdunarodnaia Zhizn*, September 1974, p. 21.

148. See text of President's "State of the World" speech before a joint session of Congress, Department of State news release, April 10, 1975, p. 6.

149. See Christopher S. Wren, "Soviet Adheres to Detente Despite Shifts in World," *New York Times*, April 7, 1975.

150. "State of the World" speech, April 10, 1975, p. 6.

151. "Schlesinger Affirms U.S. Vow To Honor Defense Obligations," *New York Times*, April 16, 1975.

152. See, for example, George C. Wilson, "Fallout From Vietnam: Hill Leaders See Challenge to Military Programs," *Washington Post*, April 21, 1975.

153. For comment on this question, see Elmo R. Zumwalt, Jr., "Uncle Sam: No More Mr. Nice Guy," *New York Times*, April 11, 1975.

154. "Talks On Cutting Forces In Recess," *New York Times*, April 20, 1975.

155. Ibid.

Appendix VA

Table VA-1
Growth of Soviet Strategic Delivery Forces, 1964-1975
(Selected Years)

	1964	1970	1972	1974	1975
Intercontinental Ballistic Missiles (ICBM)					
SS-8, SS-8	200	220	210	210	210
SS-9	0	240	290	290	290
SS-11	0	800	970	1,015[a]	1,020
SS-13	0	40	60	60	60
SS-18, SS-19					10[e]
Total:	200	1,300	1,530	1,575	1,590
Submarine-Launched Ballistic Missiles (SLBM)					
SS-N-4, SS-N-5	120	120	30[b]	30	30
SS-N-6	0	160	468[c]	530	540
SS-N-8	0	0	12	100	130
Total:	120	280	510	660	700
Heavy Bombers					
Tu-95 (Bear)	120	100	100	100	100
Mya-4 (Bison)	40	40	40	40	40
Backfire	0	0	0	10[d]	20[d]
Total:	160	140	140	150	160

[a]Increase reflects SS-11 Mod-3s being deployed in new "small silo" types. See Admiral Thomas H. Moorer, Chairman, JCS, *U.S. Military Posture for FY 1975*, Washington, D.C., 1974, p. 18.

[b]Excludes launchers on G- and Z-class diesel submarines, not counted after May 1972 as "strategic missiles." See Moorer, ibid., p. 22.

[c]Does not inlclude launchers "under construction" which were counted in the baseline figure of 740 SLBMs on nuclear submarines allowed the Soviet Union under the Interim Agreement of May 1972.

[d]Role of *Backfire* uncertain. The figures are arbitrary, reflecting estimated start of operational deployment in 1974. See Moorer, ibid., p. 24. The heavy bomber totals exclude about 50 tankers.

[e]Figure arbitrary; reflects reported start of deployment in early 1975.

Source: The numbers in this table, some of which have been rounded off, have been compiled from pertinent issues of *The Military Balance*, published annually by The International Institute for Strategic Studies, London, and from the annual reports and posture statements of U.S. Secretaries of Defense and the Chairman of the Joint Chiefs of Staff.

Table VA-2
Follow-on Soviet ICBM Systems

New Missile	SS-18	SS-19[a]	SS-17[a]	SS-16
Follow-on to:	SS-9	SS-11	SS-11	SS-13
Size Compared to Predecessor	Larger	Larger	Larger	Approx. same
Throwweight compared to Predecessor	One-third more[b]	3-5 times more[b]	3-5 times more	Slightly more
Range (naut. miles)	Over 5500	Over 5500	Over 5500	Over 5000
Estimated Number of MIRV Warheads	5 to 8	4 to 6	4	?
Digital Computer on Board	Yes	Yes	Yes	Yes
Accuracy[c]	?	?	?	?
Type Silo in which Deployable	New large; or SS-9	New small; or SS-11	New small; or SS-11	Possibly mobile
Initial Operational Capability	1975	1975	1975	1975

[a]Whether both the SS-19 and SS-17 will be deployed, or whether only one of these systems will be chosen as follow-on to the SS-11, is not known. If only one is deployed, the SS-19 is considered the most likely candidate. See Moorer, *U.S. Military Posture for FY 1975*, p. 16.

[b]According to unofficial data, the throwweight of the SS-18 is about 15,000 lbs; that of the SS-19 about 6,000 lbs. By comparison, the U.S. *Minuteman III* and *Poseidon* each have a throwweight of about 1,200 lbs. See "The Deadly Calculus of MIRVing," *Newsweek*, July 8, 1974.

[c]No figures on the estimated accuracy of these missiles have been released. However, published accounts from unidentified U.S. sources give the SS-18 an accuracy within 0.5 nautical miles of the target. See *Aviation Week & Space Technology*, September 24, 1973, p. 20. See also above, note #44, p. 200.

Source: The principal sources from which this table is compiled are Admiral Moorer, *U.S. Military Posture for FY 1975*, pp. 15-17; and testimony by Secretary of Defense James R. Schlesinger on March 4, 1974, in *Hearing Before the Subcommittee on Arms Control, International Law and Organization*, Committee on Foreign Relations, U.S. Senate, released April 4, 1974, pp. 5, 33, 43.

Table VA-3
Comparative Level of Strategic Forces Mid-1974 and Mid-1975

	Offensive Forces			
	Operational in mid-1974		Operational in mid-1975	
	U.S.	USSR	U.S.	USSR
ICBM Launchers[a]	1,054	1,575	1,054	1,590
SLBM Launchers[b]	656	660	656	700
Intercontinental Bombers	496	140	498	160
Total:	2,206	2,375	2,208	2,450
SSBN Submarines	41	47-50	41	52-53
Missile Throwweight[c] (ICBM / SLBM)	3.8 mil. lb.	6.5 mil. lb.	(Approximately the same)	
Force Loadings (Warheads & Bombs)	7,940	2,600	8,500	2,800
	Defensive Forces			
ABM Launchers[d]	0	64	0	64[e]
SAM Launchers	261	9,800	0	10,000
Air Defense Interceptors	532	2,600	405	2,500
Surveillance Radars	67	4,000	67	4,000

[a]Excludes launchers at test sites.

[b]Excludes launchers on diesel submarines.

[c]Throwweight figures approximate, as given in Clarence A. Robinson, Jr., "SALT Extension Trades Pondered," *Aviation Week & Space Technology*, May 27, 1974, p. 14.

[d]Excludes launchers at test sites.

[e]Permissible total reduced from 200 to 100 by July 1974 protocol to the ABM Treaty of May 1972.
Source: Table based on *Schlesinger FY 1975 Report*, p. 50; *Schlesinger FY 1976 Report*, p. II-19; Moorer, *U.S. Military Posture for FY 1975*, pp. 20-22.

Table VA-4
Warsaw Pact-NATO Quantitative Comparisons

	Overall European Theater		Central Region	
	Warsaw Pact	NATO	Warsaw Pact	NATO
Troops (combat & direct support)[a]	1,150,000 (485,000 Soviet)	1,113,000 (190,000 U.S.)	800,000 (430,000 Soviet)	600,000 (190,000 U.S.)
Divisions (incl. Div. equivalents)				
armored			26 (14 Soviet)	8 (2 1/3 U.S.)
mechanized			30 (13 Soviet)	11 (2 U.S.)
other			2	2
Total	78 (31 Soviet)	59 (4 1/3 U.S.)	58 (27 Soviet)	21 (4 1/3 U.S.)
Main Battle Tanks (in op. service)[b]	17,600 7,500 Soviet	8,600 (1,350 U.S.)	13,800 (6,850 Soviet)	6,000 (1,350 U.S.)
Artil. Pieces Antitank Wpns.[c]			5,000	1,800 (# favor NATO)
Tact. aircraft	3,600 (1,500 Soviet)	2,800 (300 U.S.)[d]	2,770 (1,250 Sov.)	1,720 (230 U.S.)[d]
Combat Helicop.		(# favor U.S.)[e]		(# favor U.S.)[e]
Tac. Nuc. Wpns.	3,500	7,000	(Approx. same as overall)	(Approx. same as overall)

[a]Ground forces only. About 50,000 air personnel for U.S. and slightly more for USSR in Europe.

[b]Additionally, Soviets reportedly have about 1,000 stockpiled tanks in Europe, while NATO has about 4,000 (of which about 1,300 are U.S.).

[c]Numbers not available. Said to be growing in NATO's favor. See *Military Balance 1973-1974*, p. 90.

[d]There are about 500 U.S. tactical aircraft in Europe, but those based in Britain and with 16th Air Force in Spain not shown.

[e]U.S. has 5:1 margin overall in combat helicopters. Ratio in Europe not available.

Source: Sources for this table include: *Military Balance 1973-1974*, pp. 87-95; Trevor Cliffe, *Military Technology and the European Balance*, Adelphi Paper No. 89. IISS, London, 1972, pp. 26-29; Colonel Delbert M. Fowler, "How Many Divisions? A NATO-Warsaw Pact Assessment," *Military Review*, November 1972, pp. 80-87; Moorer, *U.S. Military Posture for FY 1974*, p. 56, and *for FY 1975*, pp. 58-66; Denis Greenhill, "The Future Security of Western Europe," *International Affairs*, London, January 1974, p. 5.

Table VA-5
Comparative Soviet-U.S. Naval Forces

	Major Surface Combat Ships[a]	
	Soviet	U.S.
Attack carriers	–	15
Helicopter carriers	2	–
Missile cruisers	17	6
Gun cruisers	13	1
Missile destroyers	43	59
Gun destroyers	36	32
Escorts	104	64
Total	215	177
	Submarines[b]	
Cruise-missile subs		
Nuclear	40	–
Diesel	25	–
Total	65	
Attack subs		
Nuclear	30	61
Diesel	150	12
Total	180	73
	Naval Air	
Combat aircraft	715	1,900

[a]Other categories of surface ships not shown include: amphibious warfare ships other than small landing craft—SU 100, U.S. 65; missile patrol boats—SU 138, U.S. 2; gun and torpedo patrol boats—SU 130, U.S. 14; logistics and operational support ships—SU 104, U.S. 156.

[b]Does not include ballistic missile submarines (SSBN). See Table 3, p. 63.

Sources: *The Military Balance 1974-1975*, pp. 6-7, 9-10; Moorer, *U.S. Military Posture FY 1975*, pp. 69-75; Robert Berman, "Soviet Naval Strength and Deployment," in MccGwire et al. (eds.), *Soviet Naval Policy: Objectives and Constraints*, Chapter 22.

VI

The Soviet Union and Western Europe

Robert Legvold

It may have had other storm centers and more dramatic or tragic trials of strength, but the principal theater of the cold war was Europe. The future of no other region mattered so much. The balance within no other region was so carefully calculated, so elaborately constructed, or so constantly exhorted. As its decisive stake, victim, arena, and resource, Europe was the balance point of a bipolar world. Now with that bipolar world disintegrating and the East-West confrontation easing, what place does Europe occupy in U.S.-Soviet relations? How are events in Europe likely to influence our efforts to improve Soviet-American relations? And how are the United States' efforts to improve Soviet-American relations likely to influence events in Europe? How, in particular, is the Soviet reaction to trends within Western Europe and within the Atlantic alliance likely to effect choices open to American policymakers?

The last question reflects a personal analytical bias. We cannot, it seems to me, really understand the challenge that Soviet policy in Western Europe poses for us until we have understood the challenge that Western Europe poses for Soviet policy. Thus, the first two-thirds of what follows deals with Western Europe as a Soviet problem—initially as a conceptual problem, then as a practical one. By conceptual problem I mean the way Soviet leaders worry about developments within Western Europe and in Western Europe's relations with the outside world. By the second I refer to the working objectives that Soviet leaders develop from these concerns, to their strategy for dealing with them and to the mechanisms of that strategy—that is, to the Conference on Security and Cooperation in Europe (CSCE), to negotiations on reciprocal force reductions, to SALT, and to the various forms of bilateral cooperation devised with different West European governments.

Ultimately, however, the United States' interest is in the way the Soviet approach to Western Europe bears on its own policy options. Where can American interests be reconciled in a manner enhancing each side's sense of security, including that felt by the United States' East and West European allies? Where do they remain irreconcilable? Where do they touch upon American efforts to sort out its relationship with Western Europe? And where does the United States relationship with Western Europe impinge on Soviet policy toward America and towards our allies? These are the topics of the last parts of this chapter.

I

The Soviet Union confronts Western Europe in several dimensions. First, Western Europe is an increasingly important element in a swiftly changing international order—what might be called the global dimension. Second, together with the United States, its most powerful nations form the major opposing alliance system—the Atlantic dimension. Third, a critical nucleus of West European states has begun a gradual movement toward economic and political integration—the West European dimension. And, finally, the entire area remains a critical intersection between East and West—the East-West dimension. These "dimensions" obviously overlap—so much so that Soviet policymakers surely do not keep separate their different aspects. But they help us to see a reality in the same way that plastic overlays in an encyclopedia teach us about various systems composing the human body.

The Global Dimension

Like their Western counterparts, Soviet analysts stress the transitional character of contemporary international politics. "By the early 1970s," one of them writes, "the prerequisites for a radical restructuring of the system of contemporary international relations developed on the world scene."[1] Unlike non-Socialist analysts, however, they are not concerned with the geometry of change, the new physics of power, or the shifting psychology of security. They do not think in terms of "muted bipolarity and emerging polycentrism" or of two emerging central balances in Europe and Asia transcended and interpenetrated by the two global powers. Nor do they talk about a world of growing economic and technological interdependence as a non-zero-sum game. Whether the international order is more homogeneous or heterogeneous, more moderate or revolutionary, more diffuse or hierarchical is even less a part of their analysis. To them, this is too ephemeral, an endless shifting of the sands of power.

Their argument is more simple and, despite Marx and Lenin's claimed scientific approach, more normative. They stress not the balance of power but the correlation of forces, history's scorecard; for any Soviet analyst is first concerned with the relative strength or, more precisely, the relative increase in the strength of "positive" or progressive forces. They do not, as a result, simplify change in international politics. Though they maintain and most likely believe that overall trends are favorable, they sense complications at several levels. First, while stressing the growing strength of socialism, now sufficient in some (military) respects "to curtail the aggressive impulses of imperialism," Soviet analysts see this as partially offset by "certain difficulties" that the conflict with China creates for the "world system of socialism" and "the anti-imperialist movement."[2] Second, while exulting over the added momentum that many Third World nations give to the "World Revolutionary Process," Soviet analysts realize that the mixed picture in their part of the world renders the "structure of international relations more varied and confused." Third, although they make much of the "deepening general crisis of capitalism," particularly the mounting tensions among the United States, Western Europe, and Japan, Soviet analysts also acknowledge the underlying cohesion of the "imperialist" world, the continuing global preeminence of the United States and the restraining effects of environmental and technological interdependence.

Because Soviet analysts stress so much the correlation of forces, they are less inclined than Americans to think of West Europe's role in systemic or structural terms. American specialists, none more than Henry Kissinger, deal with international politics as a system, distinguishing one age from another by focusing on the distribution of power, the character of the principal nation-states and the rules of their interaction. Typically, they are today preoccupied with the consequences of a fragmenting system in which Western Europe plays an increasingly important, semi-autonomous, and often competitive role; a world of diverse states at radically different levels of development, with different political orientations, sources of power, and kinds of vulnerability; and, above all, a world that has lost its simple focus, where there no longer is a single, explicit military adversary but rather a host of diffuse, unsponsored, often economic challenges to security. Instinctively American specialists view the problem as one of softening conflicts arising from a shifting distribution of power, balancing the interests and opportunities of major participants, and creating standards, even mechanisms, for addressing security threats posed more by circumstances than by national design. For them the challenge is to cope with the collapse of an international order.

American leaders respond to the problem posed by the Soviet Union's emergence as a global military power by trying to arrange an environment offering diminishing incentives to disruptive behavior. Their natural approach is to manipulate external balances or to present the Soviet leaders with a "calculus of benefits and risks" inducing restraint and thus to try to draw them into constructive participation in international politics.

Given their conceptual bias, Soviet analysts are more inclined to look at Western Europe in strategic terms. For them the critical issues turn on whether imperialism's cohesion and capacity for constraining change are waning, whether the "revolutionary process" in outlying regions is proceeding smoothly, and whether socialism's preferred future appears to be gaining ground more rapidly than capitalism's. They are much less interested in the balance of power (as a system) than they are in the balance of trends (as linear history). It sounds hollow and foreign when now and then the term multipolarity occurs in Soviet publications. This is unnatural language which serves poorly to express their view of West Europe's global dimension.

Soviet analysis starts with the condition of what until recently was called the imperialist "camp." Like Japan, Western Europe is in their analysis the victim of an alliance, trade relations, and political division of labor far out of step with this area's recovered economic strength.[3] As a result, they contend, the capitalist world has become a triangle of discordant interests and open clashes, with the two lesser centers frequently uniting against the United States. The question then raised is whether Soviet leaders regard the triangle of Japan, West Europe, and the United States, about which they write so much these days, as counterbalancing that other less favorable triangle of China, the Soviet Union, and the United States. It would be consistent with a strategic perception of international politics to weigh one triangle against the other and to judge the dangers and opportunities of one partially in terms of trends in the other.

Second, Soviet leaders remain deeply convinced of the United States's determination to dominate its allies and to keep them in the service of American "globalism." They, according to Soviet analysts, are still perceived by the United States "as an instrument of its foreign policy."[4] The more, however, the United States struggles to preserve its influence in Western Europe, to involve this area in its global concerns and to mobilize European resources for its own purposes, the more it undermines the evolution toward a freer international environment.

A freer international environment, however, is not what Soviet writers think advocates of a balance of power system have in mind. One Soviet analyst suggests they assign Western Europe quite another role. First, they want it as a "serious counterweight to the Soviet Union's strength and political influence in Europe and elsewhere;" second, they seek to pit it against Japan, allowing the United States to "arbitrate" their competition; and, third, they are willing to indulge the Chinese who, for their own reasons, wish "to see the European military blocs kept going and the European Economic Community's (EEC's) military-political integration intensified."[5]

The last raises the third Soviet concern: China's relationship to Western Europe. Much as Washington's alleged desire to subordinate Western Europe to American ambitions retains the disadvantages of the Old World for the New, Peking's conception of the New World duplicates the disadvantages of the Old. Indeed, in some respects, it combines the two. On the one hand China imagines

Western Europe to be a critical component in a world of "five power centers" directed against the two superpowers and therefore exhorts European unity, the process of European political-military integration and even the creation of an independent nuclear deterrent. On the other hand it supports a strong NATO and a large American military presence in Europe so that, as Soviet authors quote Chou En-lai, these countries might better "contain" the Soviet Union in the West.[6] For good measure, the Chinese oppose the European security conference and the negotiations on force reductions in Central Europe, warn the Europeans not to be duped by the Soviet policy of détente, and associate themselves with the "revanchist slogans" of a "united German nation" and the "reunification of the German people."

✓

The Atlantic Dimension

Of the dimensions into which I have divided the Soviet perspective on West Europe, the most important is the Atlantic dimension. For not only is this the crucial axis within the imperialist triangle, but it has also been traditionally the United States's main support in the struggle against world socialism. And Soviet leaders still believe that the very essence of American foreign policy is the monumental but hopelessly doomed struggle against "the forces of socialism and the national liberation movement."[7] In this struggle, Soviet analysts say, Western Europe stands as the "second support" of imperialism and serves as the cornerstone of the United States's "global strategy."[8] Atlanticism is the idea and the North Atlantic Treaty Organization (NATO) the instrument by which the United States directs this contribution. Soviet writers do not mean that Western Europe is a kind of semi-passive make-weight of American policy. The "ruling circles" on both sides of the Atlantic, they have always insisted, have an essential, common class interest in "joining their efforts against world socialism."[9] Nor do Soviet analysts mean that the United States does not have other reasons for wanting the Atlantic partnership. It is also, according to them, a way to justify the United States's enormous economic presence in Europe and to ensure its hold over increasingly formidable capitalist competitors. Still, one risks overlooking a basic feature of the Soviet approach to Western Europe if one fails to recognize the importance that Soviet leaders attach to Atlantic cooperation as the key to the United States's global position, its preeminence within the capitalist world, and its struggle against the Soviet Union and the rest of the "Socialist commonwealth."

This remains constant. But beyond this basic conviction there are two important variables: The first is the evolution of the struggle against socialism; the second is the evolution of the ways and means of American domination over its Atlantic allies.

To summarize briefly the first evolution, the Soviet Union in Stalin's day regarded the Atlantic Alliance, and NATO in particular, as an American device for disrupting and then undoing the Soviet Union's wartime gains. Eventually, as the German problem superseded other aspects of the cold war in Europe, Stalin and even more so his successors came to view the Atlantic Alliance in narrower terms: as the basis for Adenauer's rejection of the German Democratic Republic (DDR); for his obstinacy on frontiers and Berlin; for German remilitarization, flirtation with nuclear weapons and adherence to a set of political and economic organizations which in the long run would fall under German domination. In the 1960s Soviet leaders began to divide their emphasis. With attention shifting to conflicts in the Third World, capped by the Vietnam War, Soviet commentary stressed more the dangers of others being dragged into these adventures through alliances like NATO.

The evolution continues. After Brandt's *Ostpolitik* NATO no longer seems so important an obstacle to the consolidation of socialism in Eastern Europe. And after Vietnam it no longer seems so willing to be deployed against, to use the Soviet term, the "national liberation movement." It remains in essence an American instrument for pressing the struggle against socialism and is now viewed as dedicated to five tasks: (1) controlling the pace and nature of détente between West European allies and the East,[10] (2) mobilizing West European support for American involvements elsewhere, though, as the 1973 October War illustrated, with less and less success,[11] (3) conserving more than $20 billion in American investments in Western Europe, (4) counterbalancing Soviet influence in Europe, and (5) deterring positive change in places like Portugal, Italy, Spain, and Greece. But the character of the struggle has grown more remote, in a sense more abstract (resurrecting a "balance of power"), and more indirect (infiltrating the Socialist camp with bourgeois ideas). In short, since détente has turned a rather straightforward contest toward more subtle forms, the challenge of Atlanticism is losing its immediacy and precision.

The other variable is the United States's Atlantic policy. Soviet analysis has always kept close track of the change in style and concept that each new Administration brings to Atlantic relations.[12] Until recently, however, these changes were viewed as marginal—perhaps because Soviet observers actually believed that the real challenges to Atlantic unity were containable. No longer. Since Nixon's first term Soviet analysts have begun to weight seriously the prospect that Atlanticism is collapsing. They pay more heed to the Nixon doctrine of "mature partnership" with Western Europe because they are more impressed by the problems facing the Alliance.

Soviet analysts lump these problems into four basic areas, all of them easily recognized by a Western specialist in Atlantic affairs. First, because of the growing "economic and financial strength of the Western European states," which, Soviet writers say, has created "an objective basis" for improving "their international position in the capitalist world," the Allies now seek to "intensify" their independence from American foreign policy and, when American leaders resist, this produces tension.[13] Second, American involvement in Vietnam did extensive and irreparable damage to the Alliance. In Soviet analysis, not only did it raise again the issue of the credibility of American security guarantees by destroying the domestic consensus supporting a large troop presence in Europe, it also stirred a wariness among Europeans against being drawn into "military adventures and international crises unleashed by Washington in different parts of the world." Third, partially because of Vietnam, they say, but more particularly because of serious social ills at home, the United States appears to others to be in a deep "political-moral crisis." Finally, like many of their Western counterparts, Soviet writers view mounting tensions among allies as the natural consequence of declining tensions between East and West. Détente, they constantly repeat, undermines the cohesion of a partnership built on confrontation.[14]

Together these trends are washing furiously against Atlantic unity. Nixon, they argue, had no choice but to promise to share authority within the Alliance. But all the talk of giving Western Europe greater responsibility within the framework of a "mature Atlantic partnership" and of dividing the burdens of the Alliance more evenly is merely intended to keep things as much as possible as before, only making the Europeans pay more. NATO is still, as far as Soviet observers are concerned, highly valued by the United States in the struggle between "the two world systems" and as a means of "keeping enough levers of influence and key positions in Western Europe to prevent the Western European states from seriously deviating from the orbit of the United States' global strategy."[15] This is how they analyzed the "year of Europe" and the new Atlantic Charter proposed by Kissinger in April 1973. The Americans, they said, were scheming to restore unity to Allied policy-making. Seeing the Common Market distracted by the problems of its next phase and worried about the United States's declining commitment to European security, Kissinger judged this a good moment to shoehorn Europeans into coordinating economic and foreign as well as defense policy.[16]

That Soviet commentators think this is what he was up to proves to them American determination to keep intact a United States-dominated Atlantic partnership. That it was successfully spurned by the West Europeans encourages them to believe in the effort's long-run futility. This is for the long run, however, and, while it colors their assessment of trends in American-European relations more heavily than ever before—the Atlantic Alliance, they believe, may within a generation disintegrate into primitively competitive capitalist centers—Soviet analysts are extremely ambivalent about the interim. However, if over time they see the Atlantic Alliance undergoing striking change, for the present moment they are not so sure that the Alliance's underlying cohesion has been lost. Indeed since the October 1973 War in the Middle East the contrast between the short and the long run has grown sharper for them.

Soviet writers operate with two central assumptions. The first is that

Washington not only has a stake in perpetuating its hegemony over Western Europe but impressive leverage as well. NATO, they consistently argue, is the "main instrument of pressure," both as a mechanism and as a rationale for bringing allies into line. It is in turn reinforced by, they confess, the eagerness of West European leaders to retain U.S. nuclear guarantees and a "large U.S. military presence on the continent." To these factors Soviet analysts add "the ever stronger positions of American capital in Western Europe," the growing influence of U.S. multinational corporations and, significantly, Western Europe's need for American technology to overcome the technological gap created in the 1950s and 1960s.

The second assumption is that leaders of capitalist countries have a "mutual desire to restrain these clashes in the interest of the system as a whole."[17] Thus Yuri Davydov cautions, "In dealing with the increasing tendency toward ever graver contradictions between the USA and Western Europe, one should bear in mind that at the present stage within the present structure of their mutual relations . . . these contradictions cannot go beyond definite limits."[18]

It is in this context that the deepening economic crisis of the Western nations severely complicates Soviet perceptions. Until the October 1973 War Soviet specialists seemed convinced that the United States's grip on its alliance with Western Europe was slipping steadily and irreversibly, despite its means of pressure. In one sense, of course, the bitter explosions occasioned by the war offered Soviet observers vivid evidence of how far that deterioration had already advanced. But there was another dimension to the war and to the oil embargo that followed: Soviet analysts saw as quickly as anyone that the United States had emerged from the Middle Eastern emergency less damaged than the Europeans (or Japanese) and, equally important, less vulnerable to further damage. Thus when Kissinger moved to concert the policies of the major energy consumers in the midst of the oil embargo, Soviet commentators strongly disapproved—presumably not only on behalf of the Arab Organization of Oil-producing Countries (OPEC) countries but also out of the impression that the Secretary of State viewed a common energy front as a convenient way of reasserting American dominance. The February energy conference, they said, quoting Le Figaro, was to proclaim Washington the "oil primate of a 'Western energy directorate'."[19] By exploiting European anxieties over oil, Kissinger evidently intended to accomplish what he had failed to accomplish by exploiting their anxieties over defense.

In the short run they regard this as a miscalculation. The idea of a "common front" foundered under the weight of European timidity and fears, leaving the United States with no means "to ostracize" West European and Japanese "heretics" who "dared, without its blessing, to conclude direct bilateral deals" with oil exporters.[20] Viewed more broadly, however, Soviet analysts are wondering whether events since October have not had a more important effect. Granted the serious economic deterioration throughout the West, is it not clear that the United States enjoys greater economic, commercial, and financial security (and, therefore, power) than its allies, proportionally far greater security than many were arguing before October? And thus the United States again becomes something more than a nuclear superpower among economic equals. Thus, events have also postponed an answer to the most fundamental of Soviet questions, a question that at last they had begun to take seriously: whether the Atlantic bond is breaking and the imperialist camp fragmenting into its constituent parts.

The West European Dimension

Soviet leaders do not like the idea of West European integration. For years they opposed it because they, like American leaders, believed that an integrated Europe would make a stronger and more secure Atlantic Community. From the beginning they regarded the Common Market and its forerunners as simply economic adjuncts of NATO. The United States, they contended, backed the formation, expansion, and full political integration of the EEC, first, because the Common Market would develop the economic potential of NATO's principal European members and, second, because it was to form the "foundation" for a local "military-political bloc aimed against the socialist countries and placed under the direct control of the United States."[21] Despite the growing divergence between the Nine and the United States and despite American apprehensions over West European integration, Soviet observers still tend to emphasize the United States's ability to exploit European integration.

Other trends, however, have emerged to complicate the picture, two of which are particularly important. First, as the weight of the Common Market within the capitalist world has increased, Soviet writers concede that this bloc of states has been transformed from a ward of American trading and investment policies into "one of the world's principal imperialist power centers."[22] Accounting for 42 percent of capitalism's exports (the United States accounts for 13.5 percent) and 32.2 percent of its product (the United States accounts for 40.8 percent), with forty-three million more people and growth rates that were until recently between 50 and 100 percent higher, the Nine represents a significant rival when, as is increasingly the case, its economic interests clash with those of the United States. The statistics are those used by Soviet authors and they appear wherever basic international trends are being considered.

Second, Soviet leaders realize that the integration of Western Europe's most significant economies is now an important reality in Europe. They do not underestimate the enormous obstacles standing in the way of genuine economic and political union and only the West European press outdoes the Soviet press in reporting disrupted timetables, the bickering of members, the hopelessness of the common agricultural program or the dangers of economic recession. But at last they have accepted the Common Market as a reality with which they must come to terms.

When in March 1972 Brezhnev publicly acknowledged the Soviet Union's readiness to live with this group, he did so, as one of his country's leading international affairs specialists explained, because Western Europe had passed a "historic threshold."[23] With British entry into the Common Market Western Europe had escaped the danger of a permanent split. Simultaneously, this enlarged group "had recognized the need to advance to a higher level of state monopolist economic integration." The reference was to the economic and monetary union projected for 1980 but meant more because it accompanied the recognition that a "powerful bloc had been created, possessing the overwhelming part of this region's productive capacity, foreign trade, and monetary reserves."

The economic crisis into which Western Europe and the rest of the industrialized West slid in 1974 led Soviet commentators to ask again whether the EEC was falling apart. Significantly, so far their answer has been, no. "Even if some of the stories of the EEC structure collapse," one of them writes, "the process of integration, objectively necessitated as it is by the development of the productive forces, is bound to go on. It may be retarded or take other forms, but it cannot stop."[24] To underscore the point, Council for Mutual Economic Assistance (CMEA) representatives continue to move toward formal recognition of the Common Market.

Perhaps it is easier for Moscow to come to terms with the reality of West European integration now that the United States must also do so. As a result, however, the questions Soviet leaders face are far more complicated. The issue is no longer integration or not but (1) what kind? (2) how much? (3) of what states? and (4) based on what distribution of power within? From all appearances Soviet leaders are not sure how they want to answer or how to go about promoting their preferences.

On the one hand, they seem attracted to a community strong enough to stand up to the United States and sufficiently advanced to offer the Soviet Union cooperation based on economies of scale. But, on the other hand, not so strong that it approximates China's "intermediate power center" or creates too great a pull on Eastern Europe. To help sort out these alternatives, Soviet spokesmen have begun differentiating between kinds of integration. A degree of economic integration is considered to be all right but any significant gravitation toward political-military integration is condemned. "Little Europe," the term used to evoke the Common Market's worst side, must not evolve toward political supranationalism, military cooperation, or economic discrimination.

The lines, however, are not easy to draw. The process of integration, they know, does not unfold by category or in neat increments. The level of economic cohesion adequate to make Western Europe an effective rival of the United States and a substantial source of capital and technology for the Soviet Union is also a level of cohesion capable of sustaining a political-military bloc. The discomfort Americans feel before the prospect of a West European "Third Force" is only equal to the discomfort Soviets feel over the allure this kind of a Western Europe would have in Eastern Europe. Similarly, the degree of integration necessary to dilute German predominance is a degree of union likely to make it harder for associated and nonmember states to stay out of the Community.

Even more fundamentally, the Soviet dilemma is in the contradiction between its desires for and apprehensions about Western Europe. For, basically, Soviet leaders would prefer to face a Western Europe divided into a loose configuration of "subregions," composed of states dealing for themselves alone, and generously dotted with permanently neutral governments. Given the existence of the Common Market, their instinctive choice is for a slow, ambiguous, troubled, and, ultimately, limited integration capable neither of overcoming the competing foreign and domestic policies of members nor of attracting outsiders. These preferences, for example, are reflected in the strategy adopted toward the Common Market by West European Communist parties at their Brussels conference in January 1974. Parties from countries that have been part of the Community for fifteen years, a Soviet periodical reports, "now seek to end the monopoly orientation of the EEC and to get it reorganized along democratic lines." Those from countries that have recently joined "are working for withdrawal from the Community." And those from associate-member or nonaffiliated countries "are opposing attempts to draw these countries into the sphere of influence of the monopolies dominating the Common Market."[25]

At the same time, a fragmented Western Europe with only rudimentary structures of cooperation must inevitably remain under the shadow of the United States—what Soviet leaders have lamented most for the last twenty-five years. Despite the conflicts between Western Europe and the United States, their greatest concern is still over the ease with which the United States can turn European cooperation to its own advantage. True, American influence over Western Europe has declined markedly in the last decade and, true, the basis for Atlanticism has changed. The Common Market no longer seems so obviously subservient to NATO nor the Western European Union so conspicuously a front organization for American NATO circles. But, according to the Soviet view, American influence remains considerable and most European institutions—particularly those within NATO—continue ultimately to serve American interests.

Thus, for example, the Soviet leaders see the coordination of West European defense as merely increasing these nations' subordination to the Atlantic organization. For example, according to them, the Eurogroup (the ten European members of NATO trying to coordinate their individual Research and Development (R&D), training, logistical, and support functions) simply gives the United States a vehicle for extracting larger European contributions to NATO and for controlling national defense planning. The same thing is true of agencies outside NATO. When the French a year ago supported the Western European Assembly as the most desirable framework for coordinating arms procurement, precisely because it was not a NATO body, Soviet commentators were equally critical: European defense cooperation is, they said, European defense cooperation. "However different the concepts of 'European defense' may be, it can essentially only be an appendage of the Atlantic military machine directed by the Pentagon."[26]

In a way, Soviet leaders react to trends within Western Europe at two levels. At one level, their reaction is primitive, nonstrategic, and fundamentalist. At the other, their reaction is refined, strategic, and adjustable. When the first dominates, the argument becomes simple and self-confident. The general decline in imperialist solidarity together with the gradual improvement in the correlation of forces matter more than specific Atlantic policies or the stages of West European integration. The important thing is that a center of imperialist power competing with the United States has begun to form, which "with time will lead to a significant change in the correlation of forces between the socialist and the capitalist systems in favor of the first."[27] The dangers implicit in West European integration are ultimately put in perspective by the knowledge that "the Common Market is chained to the impossible task of laboring to reconcile irreconcilable interests, of trying to surmount the insurmountable contradictions of capitalist integration."[28]

If their hearts and ideological biases speak to Soviet leaders more or less in these terms, however, their sense of *Realpolitik* has a different effect. For at another level they do think about the implications of a tightly integrated Atlantic Alliance or, in contrast, of Western Europe as a "Third Force," and they worry about trends towards one or the other. If Soviet leaders believed that the middle ground between extremes was great and relatively stable, there would be no cause for concern. Evidently, however, they do not. They seem, in fact, to fear the lingering force of the first extreme and the possibility that, when it collapses, events will move rapidly toward the second extreme. For example, the other reason they object to the Eurogroup is that at some point it may turn "into a Western European military grouping based upon the economic potential of the Common Market."[29] And the primary reason they protest so loudly against Anglo-French nuclear cooperation is because they see in it the specter of an independent European nuclear deterrent, with eventual West German participation and, later, domination.

If this is true, then—Soviet leaders being a cautious group, slightly paranoid, some have argued—the central challenge to policy is easily formulated. The essential defensive purpose of policy is to stabilize the middle ground between these two extremes. How they might hope to go about this and what additional purposes policy may encompass is something addressed in the second part.

The East-West Dimension

How is this West Europe—that now rejects American tutelage, dreams of its own economic/political and perhaps military integration, and speeds far-reaching structural change in the capitalist world—to fit into East-West relations? How will American policies—that supposedly seek to keep this area under American influence and are blessed with considerable means—affect East-West relations? Or, more importantly, how do developments within the rival camp bear on those within their own? After all, Western Europe is important to Soviet leaders not only as the cornerpiece of the United States's global position but also as the setting for their own alliance system in Eastern Europe.

When the present détente gathered momentum five or six years ago, the United States was in no position to play a leading role. Its working relationship with the Soviet Union had seriously withered during the Vietnam War, an effort that was still consuming an overriding share of the American leadership's attention and impeding its freedom to take bold initiatives elsewhere. The primary initiatives, therefore, were West European and, the most important, those of the new German government elected in the fall of 1969. Brandt's *Ostpolitik* gave special meaning to the process of normalizing East-West relations launched by de Gaulle four years earlier. The concessions he offered on frontiers, the Munich agreement, nuclear weapons, and the DDR revolutionized the German problem, opening to grateful Soviet leaders the possibility of at last securing—so far as it was within the gift of the West—the postwar changes in Eastern and Central Europe. As events in Czechoslovakia in 1968 and the Far Eastern Maritime Province in March 1969 had again demonstrated, this was an objective they had every reason to emphasize.

Ostpolitik marked a turning point in postwar relations between East and West in Europe. By offering the Soviet Union its dearest objective directly, that is, legal acknowledgment of the territorial status quo, German policy swept away a whole era of struggling to isolate Bonn and to force the hand of the Americans. No less significantly it reformulated—one would be unwise to say that it removed—the German problem, the fateful core of European politics. West Germany remained preeminent among the Western members of the Atlantic Alliance, but it no longer applied this status to obstructing a general accommodation with the "postwar European reality." It still possessed disproportionate (economic) power within Western Europe. But in the Soviet viewpoint it no longer threatened to match this with nuclear arms. And it still cast a large shadow over its East European neighbors, especially the other Germans, but it no longer sought to drive a wedge between them and Moscow or between the East Europeans and the DDR. In the process, it presented the Soviet leadership with two fundamental challenges that are likely to persist for a long time.

The first is the challenge of drawing the United States into an active role in the politics of European détente. Without American leadership to give sanction and coherence to the West's part in the dialogue, the process of altering the character of relations across the divide will be diffuse and halting. The Soviet Union's efforts to do something about trends in Europe or to effect significant change in the status quo will otherwise forever founder on the chaos and timidity of its West European interlocutors. That is why, when Soviet analysts point to the hostility with which the Nixon Administration first greeted

Ostpolitik, they are reporting no triumph.[30] Détente in this early phase, according to them, was accentuating contradictions within the Atlantic Alliance, inspiring impatient allies to throw off the United States' consecutive lead, and forcing a "Europeanization" of the problem of European security. But, there-fore, so was it generating its own constraints, for, without the American blessing the process could not advance very far. Without the United States there would be no all-European security conference. Without it the vision of East-West economic cooperation would remain spare. And without it détente would have no expression in arms control.

For the same reason, the Soviet leaders had reason to regret the rapid erosion of popular support for the idea of détente in the United States in 1976. Deprived of this reinforcement, the dialogue in Europe grew feeble, negotiations like Mutual and Balanced Force Reductions (MBFR) dilatory, and the mood skeptical. Plenty of reservations, of course, were arising in Western Europe too, but the decisive factor was the Americans. Without them to give order and momentum to NATO's negotiating position in Vienna, or spirit and scale to schemes of economic cooperation, or imagination and leadership to the next steps in the "normalization" of East-West relations, the process faltered.

On the other hand, it was extraordinary to imagine that the United States would serve as the counterpoint providing European détente its coherence. Neither Republican Administration—even while the executive retained control over foreign policy—had any interest in assuming the lead in Europe's diplo-macy. In the brief time between its own original skepticism over German *Ostpolitik* and the later skepticism that its own Eastern policy stirred at home,[31] the Administration never went beyond supporting positions deter-mined in Bonn, Brussels, and Paris.

The proposition was all the more extraordinary in view of the Soviet Union's basic set of assumptions (that the imperialist nations were falling out and American leadership was discredited) and its basic set of objectives (to break the link between American and West European power and to reduce the American hold over this area, admittedly while also averting an acceleration of West European integration.) Perhaps not in a crudely calculated fashion, but in essence nonetheless, the Soviets wanted the Americans to facilitate a process that they, the Soviets, expected would lead to an erosion of imperialist solidarity and the paralysis of alternative forms of union; in the meantime, they counted on them to lend stability and restraint to relations between Eastern and Western Europe.

The second challenge generated by *Ostopolitik* or, more precisely, by the détente that it spurred, was more fundamental and more permanent, for with the fruits of economic involvement came the perils of political penetration. Détente opened the way to levels of cooperation unimagined for twenty-five years; it posed equally unfamiliar threats to the Eastern bloc's carefully preserved insulation. True, détente seemed to end the tendency of Bonn, Paris, and Washington to vacillate between a policy strategy addressed to Moscow and subordinating relations with Eastern Europe and one pressuring Moscow by dealing behind its back with the most receptive of these governments. But in its place the Western powers now deliberately sought to use improved relations to force their ideas, tastes, and practices on the Socialist societies. It was a new and delicate balance that the Soviet leaders were obliged to maintain between interdependence and isolation. Moreover, they soon discovered that pressure in one direction was directly proportional to progress in the other. The active development of East-West relations essential to productive forms of cooperation also intensified the risks of involvement. When those risks were easily managed, as they were in 1975-1976, it was because the process of easing East-West relations had stagnated. And when they succeeded in mustering CMEA, the Warsaw Pact, and other resources to wage the "ideological struggle" made imperative by détente, they discovered that they had no mechanism for defending their societies from another level of contamination, that is, the inflation and the balance of payments problem imported from Western Europe.

So in the East-West dimension the Soviet Union was left with a series of unperceived antinomies: it sought an American investment in a process that it hoped would eventually diminish American influence and deny Western Europe its own; it feared and resisted pressures that could only become more severe the more successful it was in promoting détente's advantages; and to complete the circle, if its own design for Europe were not to flourish, then ultimately there would be no great harm in the failure of American vision. For so long as the United States is disinclined to embrace either the general Soviet approach to European security—that is, "contextual" over "basic" security, something we shall return to later—or its specific proposals in MBFR, CSCE, and on Forward Based Systems (FBS), then the lack of a clear American design for European security is the next best thing. It does not ease the way of Soviet policy but neither does it present the Soviet Union with the problems of an ambitious, alternative conception of European security. Having no conspicuous reason for tampering with the basic structure of European security, Soviet leaders are probably not eager to deal with plans for attacking the underlying causes of West European insecurity, effecting major changes in the nature and deployment of the two military alliances or creating elaborate mechanisms for crisis-management.

Understanding Western Europe's place in a change-swept environment perplexes Soviet observers as much as Americans. They know the rise of Western Europe is portentous; but of what? As both cause and effect in the breakdown of imperialist solidarity, does it, in the most fundamental sense, represent, like the splitting of the atom, matter destroyed? Imperialist power irretrievably diminished through fragmentation? Or, like the cell dividing, is it a reality reproduced and multiplied?—the making of an additional capitalist superpower?

One corresponds to their basic faith—the inherent vulnerability of the opposing world system; the other to their basic fear—the disquieting turns history can yet take. Both, however, are too abstract to occupy the analyst or, even less, the policymaker for very long. They react more normally to the shorter-term ambiguities of trends.

These ambiguities, as I have been suggesting, are, first, the difficulty of knowing whether Western Europe is producing or merely profiting from a more fluid international environment. Second, should Soviet leaders regard the changes forced on U.S. global strategy by intra-alliance dissension as more important than Western Europe's (including the EEC's) continuing susceptibility to American domination? Third, can Soviet leaders still hope to influence integration within the Common Market, or has this process crossed a threshold? Does this process reflect East-West developments, or does it unfold independently of them? Fourth, does the consolidation of Socialist power in East Europe and the regeneration of Socialist economies depend on a gradual but open-ended involvement with the West or does that involvement ultimately threaten the political order in the East? Is the evolution of European events largely a function of a troubled Soviet-American détente or is it semi-autonomous, with a rhythm of its own? Fifth, has *Ostpolitik* removed the German problem as the nexus of European politics, or do Soviet analysts, like some in the West, sense its reappearance in another form as the economic ascendance of the two Germanies places strains on the current distribution of power within Europe's two halves? Finally, is Europe in general a potential source of stability in the tumult of change, or is it subject to its own forms of convulsive change and capable of contributing its own sudden crises to the transition?

II

Formulating the problem posed by Western Europe is one aspect of the problem: doing something about it is another. The policy objectives that Soviet leaders develop in "doing something" should, of course, be influenced by their conception of European trends, but how much they actually are is uncertain when that conception remains obscure. Or its influence may be negative to the extent that conceptual confusion leads to a lack of clarity in objectives.

Traditionally we have thought about Soviet objectives in a region like Western Europe in maximum/minimum terms. Usually, however, this approach has told us more about our fears than the character of Soviet policy. Nowhere is this truer than in the case of Soviet policy in Europe.

Four maximum concerns have from time to time been expressed. The first is whether the Soviet Union *does or does not want the United States in Europe*. This has basically two sides: One, do they hope to eliminate the United States as a counterbalance to their country in Europe (roughly the equivalent of the

Soviet assumption that the United States intends Western Europe as a counter-weight to Soviet influence in Europe)? Or, on the contrary, do they want the United States to remain to contain West Germany or to maintain stability in Western Europe (an assumption of much of the official U.S. assessment of the Soviet approach to MBFR)? Second, do they, in fact, wish to deprive Western Europe of American protection (or break the link to American strategic power)? Or are they more intent on reducing the Atlantic Alliance as an element in the United States's global power?

The second set of concerns involves the Soviet Union's willingness to promote the *fragmentation of Western Europe.* Does the Soviet Union hope to do more than limit the process of West European integration? Does it seek to damage Common Market unity, to harass prospective members and to sabotage the EEC Commission's relationship with the outside world? In short, granted the obstacles, do Soviet leaders nonetheless maintain an active commitment to "rolling back" the process of integration, to reinforcing Western Europe's natural subdivisions, and to spreading neutralism among states on Eastern Europe's periphery?

Finlandization is the third and most famous anxiety. Although a rather shadowy—not to mention invidious—notion, those who use it or fear it have in mind a Soviet ability to command from the rest of Europe the kind of deference paid their interests by the Finns. It conjures up the image of West European governments hastening to Moscow to "buy protection" with major concessions, or, more to the point, of altering their normal foreign policy course out of nervousness over Soviet reaction, or permitting the Soviet Union to meddle in their domestic political affairs—influencing cabinet choices, closing down Radio Free Europe or forcing a limitation of propaganda facilities.[32] It begins as the consequence of trends weakening the Atlantic Alliance or fragmenting West European unity and ends as the principal means for accelerating these trends.

Fourth, there is a deep-seated suspicion that Soviet leaders are eager to see *Communists in West European governments and West European governments Communist.* Whatever their growing differences with West European communism, the suspicion goes, they are committed to getting the French, the Italian, or the Portuguese Communist parties into power. If economic instability in Western Europe grows, the fear is that Soviet leaders may be tempted to exploit it to advance the interests of local Communist parties.

Probably, however, Soviet policymakers regard these as rather impractical inspirations for policy. Not that they have no long-range aspirations or that they would not find a number of these developments congenial. But dedicating policy to such remote goals gets in the way of pursuing other essential short-term objectives. For the policymaker a time-frame is critical. To the extent that dreams touch motivations (marginally), the maximum/minimum perspective is useful (marginally); but it should never take the place of a perspective based on time-frame. Since the policymaker's time-frame is from short range to intermediate range, this is the better basis for judging his objectives.

Short-Range Objectives

In general Soviet European policy has three objectives: to protect Soviet interests in Eastern Europe; to influence developments within the Atlantic Alliance; and to influence developments within Western Europe, and in particular within the Common Market. This is not saying much. Everything depends on what interests are to be protected, what developments are to be influenced, and in what way they are to be protected or influenced.

It also depends on the priority among the general objectives. For years the order of priority appears to have been Eastern Europe, the Atlantic Alliance, and then Western Europe; but lately developments in Western Europe seem to have received a more prominent ranking. Because, however, at different times one objective may be made the means to another, priorities tend to be difficult to distinguish. A good illustration is Soviet policy in the ten years before Brandt's *Ostpolitik*. Throughout much of this period, what may have been a Soviet effort to achieve security in the immediate and narrow sense by protecting the status quo in one part of Europe often seemed to the West to be an effort to achieve change by undermining the status quo in the other part of Europe. As long as the West German government refused any compromise with a divided Germany, Soviet leaders apparently sought to force the issue (1) by compelling its principal NATO benefactors to come to terms with a Socialist East Germany through a direct frontal assault in Berlin crises from 1958 to 1962 or (2) by isolating Bonn, through exploitation of NATO's disarray during the period 1965-1968, in order to diminish U.S. influence in Europe, Bonn's principal support, and in order to draw away important NATO allies like France. But what may have been an indirect strategy, inspired by largely defensive concerns, was not easily distinguished from the more disturbing prospect of Soviet power enthroned in a Europe deprived of all offsetting influences—Atlantic or European.

Similarly, as long as an economically inferior Eastern bloc remained vulnerable to the pull of a vibrant West European market, Soviet leaders had reason to oppose the reinforcement of the Common Market, particularly since they viewed the EEC as a NATO auxiliary and, worse, under the domination of the Federal Republic. But here, too, the Soviet eagerness to protect its empire from the attraction of the Common Market sometimes looked like an unrealistic vision juxtaposing a semi-fragmented collection of West European states to closely disciplined Soviet-East European cooperation.

Today the Soviet Union's approach to its primary objective—that is, reinforcing the stability of Eastern Europe—has become direct. Two concerns dominate short-term policy. The first has been to translate the German treaties into a more comprehensive framework, inducing all of Europe and the United States to accept what the West Germans have accepted. The FRG's willingness to agree to the Polish frontiers, to live with a divided Germany (in the form of "two states within a single nation"), to resolve the issue of the Munich agreement, and to recognize Berlin as outside its sovereignty constituted the heart of a long-sought political settlement. The task these left to the CSCE was

to eliminate the slightest doubts in certain circles concerning the necessity of completing the business of recognition of the inviolability of the border between the GDR and the FRG, in other words, the necessity to invest this recognition with a general European character.[33]

Western specialists occasionally tended to underestimate the depth of Soviet commitment to a general formal acceptance of the territorial status quo. The *Ostpolitik* gave so much and the multilateral process has been so tortured that it was easy to overlook the importance that Soviet leaders attach to its acceptance by all as an essential source of East European legitimacy.

In this respect the CSCE had an absolutely critical role to play. Not only was it the occasion for writing large the settlement worked out with the West Germans and, in the process, for reinforcing their commitment to that settlement, but the Soviet leaders also hoped to use the Conference to do away with the qualification attached by the Germans to the original treaties, that is, the provision for the peaceful change of frontiers. In this they were disappointed. But they did succeed in building about the German treaties a general set of principles which conformed by and large to their conception of East-West relations and which they now offer as a "charter of peace for Europe" and the first major step away from the confrontation by which NATO and the most "aggressive circles" within the West justify themselves.

Second, Soviet leaders seek to expand economic cooperation between East and West Europe as a further reinforcement of the status quo in Eastern Europe. In this case the principal concern is with securing Western capital, technology and markets for the Soviet Union itself. But provided that it can be accomplished without jeopardizing CMEA cooperation and without significantly reorienting East European trade, Soviet leaders want to see their socialist allies included as well. Western Europe is a source of capital and technology that the Soviet Union does not have to spare. Second, Western Europe's competitive markets are also a useful prod to improving the efficiency and quality of East European production.[34] Since the riots in the Polish port cities in December 1970, the potential political fallout from economic failure in Eastern Europe has become an increasingly important concern.

Both objectives, however, carry risks and create secondary tasks. While the "normalization" of East-West relations compels West Germany and its major allies to come to terms with the Eastern status quo, it also exposes the Socialist countries to greater contact with the West. That becomes all the more troublesome when the West tries to exploit this contact to penetrate these societies with bourgeois ideas. As a result Soviet leaders stress that détente requires tighter discipline within the bloc. Similarly, by encouraging or by tolerating larger economic involvement with the Common Market, Soviet policy may eventually stimulate a desire for greater economic—and then political—independence among East European regimes. This may be one of the reasons why the Soviet Union has moved toward acceptance of the EEC, but on a bloc-to-bloc basis; such acquiescence may provide an additional means for controlling East Europe's cooperation with the Nine.

The Soviet Union's second basic objective—to influence developments within Western Europe—is less clear-cut in the short run. For in the short run, the threat of a fully integrated Common Market is not very great and, hence, neither is the pressure to develop comprehensive and detailed policy aims. Still, even the mere threat of integration leaves its mark on policy. Soviet leaders, for example, seem genuinely concerned about inward-looking political or economic groupings in Western Europe. They and the whole of the Soviet press constantly cajole, scold, soothe, and exhort West Europeans in the name of all-European (economic) cooperation. No doubt one of the purposes of détente and such exercise as the CSCE is to keep the Common Market open to the East. Second, while Soviet leaders appear to have accepted the reality of the Common Market, they have sought to avoid extending formal recognition to it as long as possible and have tried to circumvent the common trade policy by negotiating as many last-minute bilateral trade agreements as possible. They have also made an effort to ignore the Community's international role (at the CSCE, for example) as much as possible. Third, they continue to campaign against the Common Market, particularly among the Nordic countries and Austria. "Tying Austria's economy to its West European partners," a Soviet journalist points out, "is fraught with unpleasant consequences," for the crises and economic disruptions of the EEC are passed on to all those who permit themselves to be drawn in.[35] Finally, one cannot mistake their eagerness to impede West European defense cooperation before it begins. Not only is that plain from their treatment of the issue in the press but it also seems to be an aspect of their approach to European arms control.

Deferring discussion of the Soviet Union's Atlantic objectives until this point is not meant to imply that these goals rank last. It is a reflection of basic Soviet ambivalence that neither their behavior nor their commentary indicates which they consider more important—influencing developments within Western Europe or within the Atlantic Alliance. But in either case Soviet objectives tend to be reactive and, more often than not, dependent on developments over which the Soviet Union has little control. This makes it difficult to formulate objectives in concrete policy terms.

For example, the Soviet Union may in fact have specific short-term objectives which are not forced upon it by events, or which are within its control—such as: (1) promoting the withdrawal of American troops from Central Europe or (2) doing away with the so-called forward base systems (FBS) that link West

European defense to American strategic power. But its two most essential objectives are either fundamentally reactive or basically beyond Soviet control. Thus, Soviet leaders may hope to see disagreements within the Atlantic Alliance increase in intensity: it would make it more difficult for these countries to concert their policies in the Mediterranean or on oil; it might, in some instances, smooth the path to Soviet objectives in East-West negotiations and it would, to judge from the Cyprus War, Icelandic fishing quarrels, Maltese conflicts with London, and the Portuguese revolution, help to diminish NATO. But since there is relatively little the Soviet Union can do to ensure that these disagreements occur or to make them worse when they do, it is hard for Soviet leaders to translate them into concrete policy objectives.

Similarly, Soviet objectives in European arms control are also shaped by others, though to a lesser extent. In Vienna, Soviet negotiators may have in the back of their minds reducing forces in a way that would enhance Soviet military power in Central Europe, but they are in these negotiations in the first place because the West insisted. Indeed, the Soviet Union's first objective in MBFR is to make sure that it is not used to ease the problem raised for NATO by the prospect of unilateral U.S. troop cuts.

Intermediate-Range Objectives

When one tries to imagine Soviet objectives in Western Europe over the next ten years—perhaps as long a time perspective as might be asked of policymakers—the picture becomes even hazier. Rather than fixed or coherent objectives, the impression is of a slow, semi-coordinated swirl of apprehensions and hopes. This produces themes but scarcely a comprehensive design for the Europe Soviet leaders would like to see emerge in the 1980s.

In a somewhat schematic fashion, I have divided Soviet preferences into three categories. First, as suggested at the close of Part I, the ambiguities in European trends that stir Soviet ambivalence are, paradoxically, also a critical objective of Soviet policy. Soviet leaders operate with a permanent wariness of the pendulum swinging too far or not at all. It does not matter that they assign a low probability to the political and military unification of Western Europe or to the restoration of an integrated Atlantic Community; they would not be the only leadership to spend time worrying about low-probability outcomes. Moreover, there are lesser variants of each, with higher probabilities. There is, on the one hand, the prospect that the Europeans and Americans will succeed in or be driven to containing their differences and preserving a stronger, albeit looser, but still U.S.-led Atlantic Alliance. On the other hand, there is also the prospect of fairly steady process of West European integration, a cohesive trading bloc which would coordinate foreign policy and cooperate on all military matters, inclusive of nuclear weapons. What the Soviet Union wants is no progress toward either.

Instead, the Soviets would like to see a process of continuous deterioration of Atlanticism and the leveling-off of West European integration. Within what limits, however, they probably are not sure. Since they see no real likelihood of NATO disintegrating within the next decade, Soviet leaders are more apt to think in terms of a gradual, random, unforeseen series of disruptions—such as a Greek withdrawal from the military organization; the recall of forces by the Danes and Dutch; the closing of bases by Iceland; the balking of Germans over use of their airfields, and the inclusion of Portuguese or Italian Communists in governments. It would be significant, they doubtless feel, if this rather haphazard process were reinforced by steadily worsening relations between the United States and the Common Market.

They are also likely to continue pressing for American force withdrawals from Central Europe and to keep the FBS issue alive in some context. Americans delude themselves when and if they think that deep in their hearts Soviet leaders want the Americans in Europe to contain the Germans and to help keep the peace. The most that the United States has a right to imagine is that Soviet leaders do not care to see the Americans leave precipitously because of their fear of the instability that might follow or of the fact that West Germans might feel compelled to make up the difference. Easing American forces out gradually, however, is another matter, one that fits with their undiminished aversion to the linkage of American with West European power.

In the case of the Common Market, Soviet leaders are not likely to have a clear idea of the point where integration becomes intolerable. Obviously there are developments they wish to avoid: the beginnings of Anglo-French nuclear cooperation, greater cooperation within the Eurogroup, the transfer of greater control over trade to the EEC Commission, the strengthening of the Davignon Committee, and the addition of new members. Nor, more fundamentally, does the Soviet Union want the triangle among the Federal Republic, France, and Great Britain to turn into a triumvirate. Soviet leaders have recently shown some concern over the Federal Republic's increasing leverage within the EEC, not so much because they fear an economically ascendant Germany but because of what they see as growing U.S.-German collaboration on the energy question. They want the Bonn-Paris-London triangle to be sufficiently strong to assert its independence from the United States but sufficiently divided to prevent it from overcoming the "contradictions" of integration.[36] And they do not want a single power to dominate the Community, let alone lead it back to partnership with the United States.

The second category into which I have divided Soviet preferences is somewhat more far-reaching and brings us back to the Soviet Union's first concern, the condition of its own alliance system. For years Soviet leaders have advocated dismantling NATO and the Warsaw Treaty Organization or, as a preliminary step, eliminating their military organizations, in effect saying that the militarization of the cold war in the late 1940s was a distortion of the essential competition between the two systems. Socialism, they intimate, would be strengthened by removing this distortion. Removing these two political-military "encrustations" would strike at the essence of Atlanticism (less so the essence of Soviet power in Eastern Europe), it would free the Socialist nations from some of the unproductive burdens of military competition, and it would reduce the most dismaying short-term implications of West European integration. But just as they do not believe in NATO's imminent disintegration, Soviet leaders doubt that the two sides will soon decide to do away with the two blocs. Therefore they must think in terms of gradually building opposition to formal military alliances.

They have not, however, been willing to attack the problem directly by working to reconstruct Europe's underlying military balance. Soviet leaders have been in no hurry to apply to Europe the principle of a "stable balance at lower levels." In part this is because of their caution in the midst of rapidly moving events, in part because of the complexity of the issue, and in part because they link European arms control to SALT. Their commitment to "effective balance"—that is, to preserving the present balance in a modestly reduced form—need not, however, be interpreted as a determination to improve the East's military advantage in Central Europe. It may be no more than a predictably cautious approach to an incipient European détente.

Third, Soviet leaders obviously have some notion of how they would like to see trends develop *within* West European societies. Two developments—the rise of the Left in Southern Europe and the disruption of Western economies—pose for them dramatic but uncomfortable choices. Thus, while the Soviet leaders have from the start conceived of détente as a process leaving room for substantial change (other than in their own camp), neither the prospect of Left-dominated governments in France, Italy, Spain, and, until November 1975, Portugal nor the prospect of considerable economic instability in the West is without severe complications.

Take first the implications of the West's recent economic malaise: the degree of crisis is all important. A certain level of economic difficulty—high rates of inflation and unemployment or even recession—is one thing, offering useful proof that "no measures of a state-monopolistic character can in essence change the cyclical development of the economy."[37] A serious economic collapse, however, is another. No Soviet spokesman embraced the promise of a real depression when the full depth of the current recession was still unpredictable in 1974. On the contrary all seemed to fear it, suspecting that Soviet interests would be damaged. Great economic difficulties might (1) disrupt long-term economic cooperation between East and West, (2) generate dangerous forms of political instability in the West, and (3) prejudice the future of the West European Left. In the last instance, if the bottom falls out, the concern is that Europe may turn not to the Left but to the Right. Then, as one Soviet writer has put it, the "longing" among "certain groups" increases for "a 'strong hand' capable of coming down on the working people."[38]

The question of a lesser level of economic hardship, however, stimulates more ambivalence. Some Soviet leaders, like Boris Ponomarev, maintain that a converging group of crises have made many of the major capitalist societies—particularly, those with strong Communist parties and a rising Left—vulnerable to far-reaching structural change. These interlocking economic, environmental, and social crises, according to this view, create pressure for a reorganization of Western economies (involving greater state control over the "commanding heights" of the economy), a reallocation of resources (involving greater social and less defense spending), a revision of administration (involving greater workers' control over production), and a reassessment of foreign economic policy (involving greater regulation of multinational corporations).

No doubt Brezhnev and most of Ponomarev's other colleagues would like to think that France, Italy, or Japan is susceptible to this kind of change. Even more would they like to think, along with Ponomarev and the analysts who make the argument, that this kind of change is compatible with détente. But evidently their conviction fails them in one or the other respect, for the rest of the leadership has conspicuously refrained from making an issue of the "deepening general crisis of capitalism." Far from suggesting that the West's economic troubles constitute a new Soviet policy front, they have passed them over in virtual silence. Even in his opening speech to the Twenty-Fifth Party Congress, inevitably the occasion for assessing capitalism's underlying weaknesses, Brezhnev put remarkably little stress on the significance of the West's converging crises. Indeed, on the contrary, he said "Communists are far from predicting the 'automatic collapse' of capitalism. It still has considerable reserves."[39] This, however, does not seem to me the end of the issue and we shall return to another side of it in a moment.

The ascendance of the Left in Southern Europe presents choices that are even more basic. On the one hand, two factors sorely complicate the attractiveness of having the Left in power. First, the Soviet leaders apparently worry about the impact that the election of Communist-influenced governments in France or Italy would have on other concerns. Thus they evidently preferred that François Mitterrand not win the 1974 French presidential elections, in part because they feared the effect of the Left's victory on German politics and in part its effect on American and West German foreign policy. Some said that they also mistrusted the PCF's Socialist allies too much to want them in power. Still others maintained that the recession was a poor moment to wish success on the Left. Both in France and in Italy a premature victory in these conditions risked discrediting the Left's program and opening the way to the Right. Whatever the reasons, therefore, the prevailing view in many European circles, some of them Communist, has it that the Soviet Union does not for the moment want the Communists to succeed too grandly. (An increasingly formidable Left is another matter. As a number of Soviet observers have commented, a strong Left out of power constricts the freedom of maneuver of those in power.)

Second, West European Communist parties are themselves striking out on a course unsettling, to put it mildly, to the Soviet leadership. Whether called the *compromesso storico* or "socialism under French colors," the schemes advanced by the Western parties to increase their local acceptance seem to Soviet observers misguided and heretical. The repudiation of the concept of "the dictatorship of the proletariat," the rallying to Western notions of "basic freedoms," and the defense of political pluralism are "opportunism," to use the Soviet reproach, and particularly anathema. Since events in Portugal have drawn sharply the lines dividing the Italians, the Spanish, and, it turns out, the French Communists from the Soviets and like-minded East Europeans, the dialogue has grown harsher. Brezhnev, at the Twenty-Fifth Party Congress, riled by the innovations of the PCF's own recent Congress, publicly condemned "concessions to opportunism," which, he said, "may sometimes yield some temporary advantage, but will ultimately be damaging to the Party." The French, Italian, and British representatives, for their part, promptly repeated from the podium of the Congress their parties' determination to follow an independent course appropriate to the political conditions of modern Western societies. Two weeks after the Congress, Mikhail Suslov, the principal Soviet ideologist, went further in assailing those "opponents of Marxism" who, disguised as Marxists, take what they want from Marx, Engels, and Lenin, use it the way they please, and, in the process, "slander genuine socialism," "emasculate Marxist-Leninist teaching of its revolutionary essence," and "substitute bourgeois liberalism."[40]

On the other hand, as many in the West overlook, the Soviet Union has one essential reason to be interested in the eventual triumph of Western Communist parties and their allies on the Left: by most standards they advocate policy positions more congenial to Moscow than those of the current governments in France, Italy, and Spain. Most outsiders were so preoccupied with Gaston Plissonier's declaration of independence at the Twenty-Fifth Party Congress that they did not notice his criticism of French foreign policy for "returning our country to NATO, promoting the hegemonic aspirations of West German imperialism [a new theme that must have its echo in Soviet thoughts], not taking part in any of the disarmament negotiations, and expressing a readiness to dissolve our national independence in a political-military bloc of 'Little Europe' trusts."[41] Attitudes like these, and they have their parallels in the programs of the most "revisionist" West European parties, are likely to be an increasingly appealing alternative to the policy of existing governments on critical issues from NATO to East-West economic cooperation and from the EEC to arms control.

How the Soviets resolve these fundamental choices will, I think, depend on what the the context of Soviet policy in Europe will bear. If change of this magnitude can be made compatible with détente (and the Soviets have an increasingly liberal notion of what can be) or if détente no longer seems to them worth the sacrifice, they are likely to welcome the idea of the Left in power. Relations between Europe's two communisms are undergoing an indisputable revolution and the adjustment to it will be exceedingly difficult for the Soviet Union. But it will be made, I think, and for pragmatic reasons of foreign policy. In the long run it is likely to turn out to be a poor choice, for gradually it will transform the Soviet Union's own camp as much as it does Western Europe—and it will do so the more rapidly the current "Southern Axis" among the Yugoslav, Rumanian, Italian, and Spanish Communist parties emerges as an axis among states. (But this raises problems of adaptation that in the short run will be far greater for the United States.)

In the meantime there is the problem of the "revolution" in relations between Europe's two communisms. Nothing illustrates better both the change and the Soviet Union's discomfort than the tortured effort to convene a pan-European conference of Communist parties. Admittedly the conference was from the beginning an imperfect recourse. It was originally the PCI's proposal, intended to ease the adjustment of European communism to the contemporary political milieu in Western Europe. This was not a Soviet objective. The Soviet Union was instead looking for an alternative route to an international conference directed against the Chinese, but with little prospect of finding it here. Not that there was anything revolutionary in the Soviet Union's being thwarted by a great many Communist parties opposed to an openly anti-Chinese conference. (This had last happened in 1969.) But the Soviet Union went on to conceive of the pan-European conference as a mechanism for coordinating the behavior of the Western parties—doubtless in orthodox terms—and when this stirred unyielding and ultimately successful opposition, something revolutionary had occurred. The Soviet Union has on occasion failed to get all that it wanted from a gathering of Communists, but never has one been turned against it. This is essentially what has happened in the case of the pan-European conference. First the Soviets were checkmated by the Rumanians, the Italians, the Spanish, and most important the Yugoslavs. Then, when in the summer of 1975 the French joined the other four, they lost entirely. Thus any future conference, far from serving the traditional purposes of Soviet foreign policy, will be Moscow's first major step toward an accommodation with the new world of West European communism.

The accommodation, however, promises to be difficult. The Soviet leadership has not quietly accepted the West European Communist parties' retreat from "proletarian internationalism"—the "holy of holies" in Marxism-Leninism, according to Suslov's Academy speech. Brezhnev at the Twenty-Fifth Congress warned that renouncing proletarian internationalism "is to deprive communist parties and the working class movement in general of a mighty and tested weapon"; it is, he said, to "work in favor of the class enemy." More than anything it inspired Suslov to christen the "struggle against all forms of bourgeois ideology" one of the most important tasks of the "international communist movement." Any compromise, therefore, will be reluctant and constantly retarded by efforts to draw the Western parties back toward orthodoxy.

Returning to the basic issue, in general we would be wise to expect the Soviet Union to support the most radical change to which the West will, in the Soviet estimation, be forced to accommodate. This is the lesson of Portugal (and Angola). If events lead to fundamental change, the Soviets will follow. They are less likely to force events—hence their reluctance to urge a strategy of "permanent revolution" on their Portuguese allies in the spring of 1975. By the summer, however, the confrontation between the Portuguese Marxist-Leninists and the Socialists had created what the Cunhal-Gonçalvez group and, perforce, their Soviet well-wishers took to be a de facto condition of "permanent revolution." In these circumstances the Soviet leaders apparently readily embraced their friends' decision to jettison the "parliamentary road" to socialism and to make the revolution in much the same way that Lenin had in 1917. To come back to the question of the Soviet attitude toward far-reaching structural change in Western societies, the Soviet leaders are likely to behave similarly whatever the occasion. Provided they are not called upon to manufacture or sustain the change and provided that the change is not obviously fatal to other foreign policy priorities, they will be its willing heirs.

The Strategy of Policy

Parts of a basic Soviet strategy have already been implied, but these ought to be spelled out somewhat more explicitly. The term "strategy" is loosely employed because I am really referring to a general approach rather than to a carefully conceived series of steps directed toward a specific goal. Thus the two elements about to be discussed have more to do with the mode of Soviet behavior than with its particular devices.

In this sense the first outstanding characteristic of Soviet strategy is its emphasis on what might be called "contextual" over "basic" security. The difference is in the content that Soviet leaders give to the European part of détente. In Europe the Soviet Union tends to lump all of its initiatives and aims under the single rubric of promoting continental security. But because Soviet insecurity is political, not military, its definition of European security tends to be political rather than military. That is, the Soviet stress on setting down the principles of East-West relations (including the principles of the inviolability of frontiers and nonrecourse to force), on creating permanent consultive organs and on fostering economic cooperation stems from the Soviet Union's primary interest in consolidating the Eastern status quo and controlling the revision of the Western status quo. It is less concerned with remodeling the underlying (military) structure of security. In fact, it clearly feels that the existing military balance ought to be kept intact, if détente is to be safely pursued and Central Europe to be protected should détente collapse. Like France, the Soviet Union believes in "armed détente."[42]

The second noteworthy characteristic of Soviet strategy is its emphasis on security as a process. Most national leaderships deal with détente as a process, but it is somewhat more unusual to define security primarily as a process. In the Soviet view "security should not be regarded as an abstract and static thing in itself, but as a dynamic evolutionary process and a function of the existing and developing internal and external ties."[43] There is obvious good sense in recognizing that security, being a state of mind, cannot be fixed, but the Soviet approach carries this insight to an extreme. It is, as a result, not the end product but the process of building security that Soviet policy seeks to structure—for the same reason that it concentrates on "contextual" security. At the moment, Soviet leaders have no particular reason to labor on behalf of a new European security *system*; their interest is in enhancing the condition of their existing security system.

The Mechanisms of Policy

The Soviet Union has an odd variety of mechanisms for pursuing its policy in Europe. Some are formal, such as the German treaties; some informal, such as a press campaign; some bilateral, such as Brezhnev's summitry; some multilateral, such as the CSCE; some functional, such as agreements on scientific cooperation; some political, such as the public campaign for European security; some narrowly focused; some broadly focused; some desired; some tolerated. A great many are not worth lingering over. Some we should know more about, such as the various nonofficial committees established in Western Europe to mobilize popular interest in the problems of European security. Some we probably cannot know more about, such as the responsiveness of West European Communist parties to Soviet policy dictates (by all indications something that is declining precipitously).

The three that I have chosen to look at more closely—official bilateral contacts, the CSCE, and mutual force reduction negotiations—are those that most impinge on policy. Of the three, the most productive has been the least obtrusive: *the institutionalization of bilateralism*. Using Franco-Soviet relations as the prototype, the Soviet Union has gradually given its relations with all of the major Western powers a formal institutional basis. Though in different sequence for different countries, the principal institutions are: (1) formal trade agreements, (2) general commissions to promote economic cooperation and a range of supporting technical commissions, (3) a set of basic principles to guide relations (in the FRG's case, the 1970 treaties), and (4) regularized summitry. While these measures are obviously the result of a shifting political climate—and not the other way around—they do sharpen, expedite, and, in the case of the trade agreements and basic principles, embody the improvement in East-West relations. Soviet leaders tend to take this process very seriously, for added together these institutions do the lion's share of the work of détente.

If "institutionalized bilateralism" is the most important mechanism of European détente, then the *Conference on Security and Cooperation in Europe* has been its most celebrated. The CSCE was a Soviet invention, designed to promote "contextual security"—and the personification of security as a process. Although once designed to help isolate the West Germans, the Conference eventually became the most versatile mechanism for giving a broad general sanction to the German settlement, for establishing the charter for European détente (the famous ten principles), for promoting East-West economic coopera- tion, for test-flying a set of (carefully circumscribed) "confidence-building measures," and originally for institutionalizing the first permanent multilateral consultation. From the moment the *Ostpolitik* liberated détente, Soviet leaders turned to the Conference as the most suitable means for pursuing the widest range of short-term objectives.

All of this helps to account for Soviet loyalty to a venture that began so inauspiciously and labored so long and painfully. Despite the early shocks of Rumanian independence, the aggressiveness of the neutrals, and the coordinated approach of the Nine, and through the six months of preparatory meetings, the Helsinki Foreign Ministers' Conference, and more than a year of negotiating in three commissions, eleven subcommissions, and a coordinating committee, the Soviet Union doggedly supported the Conference. The Conference produced the first sustained coordination of EEC foreign policy—so effective that the Nine became the primary Western force at the CSCE, and an aggressive one at that. The Conference also gave rise to a variety of cross-cutting alliances, some of which far from respecting the East-West division superimposed a new North- South dimension. And it often forced the neutrals to the side of the Western powers on a range of issues. Still the Soviet Union stood by the Conference.

Whether their efforts were worth it is a matter for time to tell. (The answer, however, is probably going to be considerably different from much of the superficial commentary of the moment that portrays the whole affair as a Soviet con job abetted by poor Western bargaining.) The Soviet Union did achieve a general sanction for the German "settlement" (but without suppressing the qualification on the peaceful change of frontiers); it did secure recognition of its general principles of European relations (but only by yielding on MFN and by promising better commercial information and facilities); and it did succeed in circumscribing the force of the provisions for improved human contact (but only after conceding the provisions in the first place and only in a form that also reaffirms the Soviet obligation under the seventh principle on the "respect for human rights and fundamental freedoms, including the freedom of thought, conscience, religion or belief").

These successes, however, are sufficient to warrant a certain level of Soviet celebration. As was to be predicted, at the Twenty-Fifth Party Congress, Brezhnev and many other speakers cited the CSCE as one of the important fruits of the Soviet Union's "Peace Program." Better than any other event, the CSCE demonstrated the payoffs to an unwavering diplomacy. And better than any other event, it also proved the leadership's excellent grasp of international trends, an ability that Soviet comentary now comes close to arguing enables it to "plan" the evolution of international affairs much as it does the development of the Soviet economy.

By the same token, these successes are sufficient to distress the Soviet Union when the results of the CSCE are disparaged in the West. Ever since Helsinki, the Soviet press has been waging a major effort to restore status to the Final Act, to counteract the suspicion and scorn with which the Conference has generally been received in the West, and to give Western publics the feeling that they, too, have a stake in its results. Soviet commentators have even sought to create the impression that the Final Act, and in particular the basic principles, have a force comparable to international treaty law. In part this is doubtless an attempt to give greater resonance to those features of the Final Act serving their foreign policy objectives. In part, however, it may also be a defensive measure intended to prevent the West from portraying the CSCE as a one-sided Soviet success for which it must pay in the next stages of détente.

The other fundamental point to the Conference is more problematic. The CSCE was after all supposed to be an important first step toward institutionalized relations among European states and hence part of an ongoing process promoted by similar encounters in the future. The Soviet Union had made the idea of follow-up machinery a prominent part of its proposals. And the idea seemed to be a logical aspect of the Soviet conception of détente as a process and this kind of "institutionalized multilateralism" as its engine.

But the Soviet Union never pressed on the issue of follow-up when the decisive moment came. The proposal sponsored by the Eastern countries was conspicuously vague about the formal commitment to regular high-level meetings and seemed designed to avoid such a commitment. This was the major reason that Rumania, Yugoslavia, and Finland objected and introduced their own more explicit proposals on follow-up. Whether because of the inconveniences of Basket III or because of the position of states like Rumania and Yugoslavia, it does appear that the Soviet Union has serious second thoughts about the wisdom of institutions promoting a regular East-West political dialogue. As a consequence, however, the Soviet conception of European détente has become much vaguer and indefinite. Until the Soviet leaders return to "institutionalized multilateralism" or to some substitute for the centerpiece that the CSCE was for Soviet policy in Europe, it will remain so.

The *mutual force reduction negotiation* in Vienna differs from the CSCE in three critical respects. First, it is a Western, largely American-conceived project. Second, it is more narrowly focused and more narrowly constituted: parts of the two military blocs are negotiating a single subject, and although that subject has a large number of elements, the actual talks address only a few of them. And third, it potentially deals with the essence, not the atmosphere of security.

There is a fourth difference that can be gathered from the discussion of

Soviet strategy: because of its origins and its subject, the Soviet approach to MBFR[a] has always had an important defensive quality. As the Soviet Union had "damage-limiting" objectives in the CSCE, it has gains to pursue in Vienna, but by and large these come after its defensive concerns. This is not to deny that the Soviet Union has objectives of its own to pursue. It is clear from the central elements of Soviet proposals and the tenacity with which Soviet negotiators cling to them that, if there is to be a substantial agreement, they expect to achieve three things: (1) to bring the West German Bundeswehr under control, (2) to establish a *droit de regard* over West European defense cooperation, and (3) to influence the pace and timing of American force withdrawals. And as indicated earlier, perhaps they also hope to affect the forward based systems which the Americans refuse to discuss in the bilateral context of SALT. But this is on the assumption that there is to be a substantial agreement, and the discrepancy between the two sides' positions make this improbable.

Thus the Soviet Union is left to labor against the principles of arms control that the West would like to establish for Central Europe, principles that it doubtless regards as directed at altering, not merely reducing, the present balance in this region. In the circumstances, the Soviet leaders probably expect little more than a symbolic accord, but this they would not disdain. For they have made "military détente" the rhetorical focus of current policy and no doubt they would be delighted to have the boost to détente that a symbolic accord might provide.

Reduced to the nub, arms control in Europe raises two critical questions: Is it to be balanced or imbalanced? Comprehensive or limited? Almost all other issues fit within these two questions, including those evoked in SALT and those touching on West European defense cooperation. The problem is that at the moment the Soviet Union perceives the two sides as preferring opposite solutions. The West, it thinks, not only insists on larger Eastern than Western reductions but also on excluding German and other indigenous forces from the first stages of reduction. In short, Soviet leaders see the Western position as concerned solely with disproportionate numbers of their troops out of Eastern Europe. (The West insists that *over time* the two sides do not differ on the issue of which nations are to be included.) As a result there has not been much opportunity to see whether the Soviet Union will compromise on the issue of symmetry if it is reassured on the issue of scope, particularly on the inclusion of the Bundeswehr.

On the surface the differences appear to be considerable: the West seeking to reduce Soviet manpower first. This is to be followed by asymmetrical reductions. When other elements of the balance are raised the West wants to strive for common ceilings. The East has been determined to include the Germans from the start, to get at parts of the forward based systems (eluding

---

[a]Technically MURFAAMCE: Conference on the Mutual Reduction of Forces and Armaments and Associated Measures in Central Europe.

them in SALT), to preclude prepositioning, perhaps to disrupt West European defense cooperation (with the proposals for national subceilings), and ultimately to preserve an "effective balance" that most West Europeans fear is in the Warsaw Pact's favor.[b] But these differences may conceal points of possible compromise. It is not unthinkable, for example, that the Soviet leadership would relent on equal percentage cuts (the inequity of eliminating 15 percent of 100 percent for the FRG and 15 percent of 50-60 percent for the Soviet Union is comprehensible to them), if they were assured that German forces would be included in some fashion. And, if West Germany were included, conceivably they would accept modest asymmetries in the general reductions or agree to confine the first round to ground forces. Or they might be persuaded to relent on national subceilings and symmetrical cuts if the West agreed to negotiate reductions in the number of F-4s and nuclear weapons in Central Europe.

The trouble with this and most other likely compromises is that they beg the critical question of European arms control: how is the underlying balance to be adjusted to preserve Eastern security and reduce Western insecurity? The Soviet leadership, of course, can say, "That's the West's problem." But in the short run a compromise that muddles the answer to the questions of balance and scope is not likely to help either side. For the West it may turn out to accentuate more than soften problems within the alliance. For the East it may turn "armed détente" into an impediment in the search for "contextual security."

III

Ultimately the United States' interest is in how the Soviet attitude and approach toward Western Europe affects the relations between the Soviet Union and America as well as U.S. relations with Western Europe. The answer depends, in part, on one's convictions about the ambivalence that I have attributed to Soviet leaders over what is happening in and to Western Europe: whether one believes they are, in fact, as uncertain as I have argued, or far more single-minded; and, if the uncertainty is granted, whether it will persist should events take a dramatic turn. The last has been downplayed because I suspect, without being able to demonstrate, that Soviet leaders do not know how they would feel should a variety of rather sudden fundamental changes occur (should the Common Market fly apart, the economies of the major capitalist powers collapse, or the Sino-Soviet conflict end). Soviet calculations, as those of others, tend to be behind rather than ahead of events. There is, however, a distinction worth

[b]This confines the issue to Central Europe where apparently both sides want it confined— but we really do not know, having failed to test Soviet reluctance to enlarge the geographical scope when the issue came up over Italy's/Hungary's inclusion. Instead we merely allowed the Soviets to cut the price they felt they had to pay to speed the removal of U.S. troops from the Central European region.

drawing between Soviet interests before and after a crisis occurs. As some aspects of the October 1973 Middle East War suggest, conservatism before the event may turn to boldness after the event. The same may apply to, say, serious economic erosion in the West. The obvious and fundamental point is that the future stability of East-West relations will depend far less on what the United States does do about the Soviet Union than what this nation does about itself.

In assessing the significance for policy of Soviet reaction to Western Europe, a reasonably broad framework is useful. The one used here has three dimensions: The alternative roles that may be conceived for Western Europe in U.S.-Soviet relations, the alternative roles that may be formulated for the Soviet Union in U.S.-West European relations, and the alternative ways in which any of these roles may be developed. The first two involve sets of three alternatives and the last is a continuum between two extremes.

Europe in U.S.-Soviet Relations

Strategies designed at this level rarely exist, but as abstractions they help to characterize a range of actual choice. Allowing for that unreality, the first alternative is to cast Western Europe as a resource or a weight in Soviet-American relations. It is the systemic perspective turned strategic (and the confirmation of deep-seated Soviet suspicions). Accordingly, we would nurture our relations with Western Europe—responding when they sour, capitalizing when they thrive—in order to influence the equilibrium between the United States and the Soviet Union. The primary concern is to ensure a satisfactorily skewed multipolarity—to build safeguards into the balance of power. Reconciliation with Western Europe becomes imperative because the United States needs it to deal with the Soviet Union. Hence, for example, America ought to come to SALT not merely with economic inducements and "bargaining chips," but also with the alliance in vigorous shape. The logic of that imperative is to support Western Europe's political consolidation and desire for independence, to forget about using Western Europe's security dependency as a means of extracting allied concessions in other areas, and instead to satisfy that dependency in the short term while helping to eliminate it in the long term.

The second alternative is the converse. Again, the condition of the United States' relations with Western Europe is featured, but this time for intrinsic, not instrumental, reasons. America's interactions with Western Europe (and with Japan), the argument goes, now constitute the pivot of international relations. These should neither be subordinated or neglected by U.S. relations with the Soviet Union and China, relations that are now of a second order of importance. The United States priority, if we are to have one, must be West-West, not East-West. The importance of East-West relations is not denied, but to the extent that West-West relations bear on them, it should only be to control or soften the side effects of a proper preoccupation with the industrial states of the West (and that part of North-South relations currently so critical to them).

The alternative is that Europe can be largely ignored. In order to get done the job of reconstructing Soviet-American relations, the inevitable, long-term, and basically insoluble conflicts of interests among the Western states must not be allowed to distract the United States. The chore of containing tensions among allies, an elusive and unwieldly process, and the challenge of reinforcing détente, an immediate, accessible opportunity, are separate tracks and should be traveled at different tempos, by different means, and with different expectations of success.

The Soviet Union in U.S.-West European Relations

If we shift our perspective to the Soviet role in U.S.-West European relations, there are again three broad alternatives. The first is to subordinate European concerns to the bilateral relationship. Attention, accordingly, is focused on the most salient aspects of superpower relations, usually meaning the strategic arms race and explosive situations that could draw the two countries toward confrontation. Europe's problems should not be ignored but they emerge primarily as part of a general backdrop to U.S.-Soviet détente and as Europe tends to benefit from that détente. Policy coordination with the West Europeans tends to assume the quality of a gesture, for European roles are secondary and supportive. It is the counterpart of the last alternative: In both, Europe is decoupled from America's preoccupations.

The second alternative makes East-West relations an important part of the solution to West European problems and the solution to those problems an important part of East-West relations. Not only can the Soviet Union contribute to easing the two key problems of security (or insecurity) and Atlantic partnership (or disarray) but, according to this view, it can and should be in on the ground floor. To the extent that frictions among allies are the result of the anxieties of the West Europeans over their long run vulnerability to Soviet power, effective relief can only be had by going directly to the Soviet Union and seeking adjustments in the status quo, particularly in the military status quo, which would reduce these anxieties. This can be done either in the context of U.S.-Soviet relations with close consultation among the allies (benevolent condominium) or in the context of a general offensive in multilateral diplomacy (taking seriously the process of "building all-European security").

The third alternative deemphasizes the importance of the East-West dimension in sorting out Atlantic relations. According to it, this is largely a matter of first putting the Alliance in order and, far from aiding this process, relying too much on East-West relations will only hamper these efforts. East-West relations are still too intractable to be counted upon. Worse, they may simply give the

Soviet Union an opportunity to exploit the discord within the Atlantic Alliance. The root of the problem is thus assumed to lie in other than the East-West dimension. Indeed, even the issue of security is regarded largely as a function of the breakdown of the Western economic order, the United States's psychological disengagement from Europe and the inability of the West Europeans to overcome national parochialisms.

The Range of Choice

How the United States chooses to go about doing what it chooses to do, it seems to me, is better represented by a continuum between extremes than by a specific set of policy choices. There are too many permutations to get involved with specific alternatives. The scale that I have selected runs from the most to the least modest in four categories: (1) objectives, (2) strategy, (3) tactics, and (4) the American role. In each case the extremes are somewhat artificially established; they in fact often overlap. But they are put in these terms to indicate the essential range of choice. The essential range of choice, in turn, is meant to suggest not only ends and means but a way of thinking about ends and means. Finally, I have tried to identify the ways that Soviet perceptions can or should be reflected in the choices we make.

Objectives. It does a certain violence to reality to argue that the extreme forms of objectives are *process* (the way we pursue our aims) on the one hand, and *product* (the aims we pursue) on the other. Process is presumably only the path to product; it is the relationship between means and ends. But where product is hard to achieve, as the ends of international politics often are, process acquires a meaning and virtue of its own. To have process instead of product, of course, is nonsense; that would make the objective of policy only movement with no regard for destination. To have only product is equally preposterous—subordinating everything to a fixed aim and ignoring the effect that getting there invariably has on an objective is a sure guarantee of immobility. But it is not unreasonable to portray one as a function of the other, assuming that at times the concern with process is more important than particular objectives, and that at other times definable objectives become more important than the struggle to realize them. This is not, for example, a bad way to contrast the basic approach to Soviet-American relations of the last two major Republican secretaries of state. Under John Foster Dulles objectives such as ending Soviet domination over Eastern Europe and German reunification overrode any preoccupation with the question of the practical measures by which they might be achieved. (Adenauer's version was reunification before détente.) Henry Kissinger—concentrating on the task of reforming the character of the Soviet-American contest—tends to worry a good deal more about the momentum of relations. A process has been launched and the two sides should take care not to sink it with overly ambitious objectives.

A healthy appreciation of the importance of proceeding a step at a time, of patiently building on each success, and of gradually enlarging mutual confidence is critical to East-West détente. But that can become an end in itself, leaving us without a coherent notion of the kind of world that we are trying to fashion. Many Europeans, who agonize more than Americans about the world that is emerging, fear that too much is already being sacrificed to process.

There are three reasons that their fear has foundation: First, the leaderships of both superpowers, in their eagerness to improve relations, have a tendency to slide around major substantive obstacles. Certainly the current Soviet approach pushes in this direction. Second, this tendency is reinforced by the complexity and intractability of Europe's problems. Anyone whose primary stake is in maintaining the momentum of détente will not relish tackling such problems as long-term crisis management (including Eastern Europe), collective security for all of Europe and comprehensive arms control. Third, when leaderships are harassed by politics at home, they are inclined to reduce the risks in their foreign policy.

Without making the essentially destructive argument that détente must be dedicated to solving problems which have no solution, there is a constant need for orientation. America needs to remind itself of the alternative ways that all-European security might be strengthened, political emergencies handled and arms control made meaningful. The United States should contemplate the long-term implications of Europe's division, of the evolution at work within Europe's two halves, of the role of the two Germanies in their respective camps and in relations between the two camps, of the changing nature of military alliances and of the increasing East-West economic interdependence.

Strategy. As before, the term strategy is used in the nonmilitary sense of a general approach. The continuum extends from a fragmented (or piecemeal) approach to an integral (or systematic) approach. Here, too, either extreme is improbable, but policy strategies do tend to have more of the characteristics of one than the other. Unlike the case in the first category, where the West Europeans are distinguished from the two superpowers in their greater concern over the "product" of European détente, in this instance there is little distinction: None has a particularly integral or systematic approach to East-West relations in Europe.

Both the United States and the Soviet Union claim to have an integral approach. The United States approach used to be known as "linkages," and Soviet leaders maintained that they sought an all-European security system, but linkages were, when still plausible, tactical, and the all-European security system was never a system at all. This makes American and Soviet policy in Europe more compatible; but it does not help to focus the essential interconnections among European problems. The failure is doubtless due to the common stress on process.

The interconnections that the two countries do draw tend to be expediential and fragmentary. The United States did from time to time insist on a loose "parallelism" between the timing of the CSCE and MBFR, but not in their work—even when a logical link existed between the negotiation of confidence building measures in the CSCE and collateral constraints in MBFR. The Soviet Union resists that linkage and, indeed in general, linkage between arms control and the pursuit of "contextual security." Its linkages are *within* arms control. Thus it has long insisted on linking a critical part of the European military balance, the forward based systems, to strategic arms limitation talks but, at the same time, refused to see the link between West European and American security. Both the United States and the Soviet Union underscore the relationship between economic cooperation and détente but each has a different stake in it. Beyond that the two sides do not bother much with the interconnections of problems.

But Europe's problems are profoundly interconnected. The European military balance *is* linked to the strategic balance. American security is linked to European security. European security is linked to the military balance. And détente is linked to European security. So there are deeper interconnections among the CSCE, MBFR, and SALT even when overall policy seeks to avoid them.

If policy were to deal with Europe's problems integrally, the key variable would be MBFR, not as it is presently configured but as a far-reaching attempt to redesign the European military balance (without shirking the link to SALT) and to reorganize the basic deployment of the two military blocs. To say so, however, is to confess the deficiency of a truly integrated policy approach. Even as merely an organizing framework within which more modest initiatives are coordinated, the integrated approach implies a perspective that few leaderships feel is practical, a capacity which few possess for dealing systematically with a broad range of problems, a timeframe within which few care to work, and a willingness to imagine an intricate series of mutual concessions to which few ordinarily pretend.

Tactics. The continuum in this case is more difficult to specify, but degree of centralization is the quality that seems to cut across most basic kinds of choices. To what extent are tactical linkages to be employed? That is, to what extent is the achievement of solutions—as opposed to their content—to be tied together? What degree of consultation and coordination do we wish to achieve with the West Europeans in approaching East-West problems? What degree of concertation do we wish to see them achieve among themselves? And, finally, what role is to be assigned to multilateralism, or is European détente—the CSCE and MBFR notwithstanding—to remain essentially the product of bilateral enterprises?

The American Role. In each of the three previous categories, policy tends toward the low end of the continuum—subordinating outcomes to process, fragmenting rather than integrating problems, dealing with them piecemeal rather than systematically, and by decentralized rather than centralized "tactics." The same is true in this instance: American policy tends to react rather than lead. Of the four basic aspects of policy this is the one that most pleases the West Europeans. It is the aspect that least pleases the Soviets, who would like to see the United States whip the Allies into line on several issues (a paradox of the basic Soviet attitude toward Atlanticism).

This leads us to the crux of the problem of choice in our policy toward Europe. Although an obvious oversimplification, by and large the Soviet Union has had a higher stake in the current orientation of American policy than has Western Europe in all but the fourth category. (The second category, that of strategy, is somewhat problematic because it is uncertain how integrated an American strategy the West Europeans want and how resistant the Soviet leadership would be to one that was more integrated—though they are not likely to develop their own first.) As a result the Soviet-American détente has been strengthened, but it is doubtful that either Atlantic relations or European security has been equally strengthened, if at all.

The alternatives, however, are not clear and where they are the choices are not easy. Since American policy is not alone in its basic orientation, logically the way to turn European détente into a genuine search for security is for the United States to take the lead. But in doing so, ironically, it risks damaging Atlantic relations. If, instead, it merely concentrates on satisfying the European concern with "product" and on reinforcing consultation, it does no service to U.S.-Soviet relations and probably none to European security. And if it comes to the aid of European security with a truly integrated approach, at least initially it is likely to complicate both Atlantic and East-West relations.

In a nutshell, we face three fundamental choices over the next decade: First, in the degree to which the United States views East-West relations as a route to the solution of our intra-alliance problems and the condition of our alliance as an important factor in East-West relations; second, the extent to which this nation is prepared to take the lead in developing a coherent strategy for addressing the European dimension of East-West relations; and, third, the value which America assigns to a new and sturdier system of security for all of Europe. All of them are difficult.

Notes

1. A. Stepanov, "Soviet Foreign Policy and the Restructuring of International Relations," *International Affairs*, no. 1 (January 1974), p. 5.

2. Yu. P. Davydov, "Doktrina Niksona—Krizis globalizma," in Yu. P. Davydov et al., *Doktrina Niksona* (Moscow: Izdatelstvo Nauka, 1972), pp. 9-10.

3. This is a common theme in a great range of Soviet literature. For one directly related example see D.E. Melnikov, "Zapadnaya Evropa v mirovoi politika," in D.E. Melnikov (ed.) *Mezhdunarodnye otnosheniya v Zapadnoi Evrope* (Moscow: Izdatelstvo "Mezhdunarodnye otnosheniya," 1974), pp. 18-23.

4. Y. Davydov, "USA-Western Europe: A 'New Relationship,' " *International Affairs*, no. 1 (January 1974), p. 37.

5. Ibid., pp. 37-38. Davydov heads the section specializing in U.S. relations with Europe in the Institute USA.

6. Y. Agranov, "Peking's Great-Power Policy and Western Europe," *International Affairs*, no. 4 (April 1974), p. 24.

7. Anatoli A. Gromyko, "Amerikanskaya vneshnaya politika," *SShA: Ekonomika, Politika, Ideologiya*, no. 4 (April 1972), p. 44.

8. Ye. N. Novoseltsev, "SShA: Zapadnaya Evropa—'zreloe partnerstvo'," in Davydov, *Doktrina Niksona*, p. 168.

9. Davydov, "USA-Western Europe," p. 36.

10. Novoseltsev, "Zreloe Partnerstvo," p. 171

11. Davydov, "USA-Western Europe," p. 35.

12. One of the more impressive recent reviews is A.I. Utkin, *Tsentry sopernichestva: SShA i Zapadnaya Evropa* (Moscow: Isdatelstvo "Mezhdunarodnye Otnosheniya," 1973), esp. pp. 9-49.

13. Novoseltsev, "Zreloe Parnerstvo," p. 166.

14. O. Bykov, "Kuda vedut 'neoatlanticheskie' puti?" *Mirovaya Ekonomika i Mezhdunarodnye Otnosheniya*, no. 6 (June 1974), p. 31.

15. Novoseltsev, "Zreloe Parnerstvo," p. 168.

16. For a concise and reasonably comprehensive statement of an argument made many times over, see A. Volgin, "Atlanticheskoe nastuplenie Vashingtona," *Mirovaya Ekonomika i Mezhdunarodnye Otnosheniya*, no. 5 (May 1974), pp. 76-80.

17. Davydov, "USA-Western Europe," p. 40.

18. Ibid.

19. Vladlen Kuznetsov, "Washington Oil Talks," *New Times*, no. 8 (February 1974), p. 10.

20. Ibid.

21. V.S. Shein, "SShA-EEC:Uzel protivorechii," *SShA: Ekonomika, Politika, Ideologiya*, no. 1 (January 1973), p. 62.

22. Ibid.

23. Nikolai Inozemtsev's speech to the September 1972 Varna Conference in "Les rélations internationales en Europe dans les années 1970," in *Europe 1980* (Geneva: A.W. Sijthoff, 1972), p. 129. Brezhnev's comment was in his address to the 15th Trade Union Congress, *Pravda*, March 21, 1972, p. 2.

24. Yuri Shishkov, "The Malaise of the Common Market," *New Times*, no. 44 (November 1974), p. 20.

25. Yuri Pankov, "For Peace and Social Progress in Europe," *New Times*, no. 8 (February 1974), p. 5.

26. V. Kuznetsov, " 'European Defense' Again?" *New Times*, no. 49 (December 1973), p. 11.

27. S.P. Madzoevskii, " 'Treugolnik' London-Parizh-Bonn," in Melnikov, *Mezhdunarodnye Otnosheniya*, pp. 152-53.

28. Commentary, "Bonn Veto," *New Times*, no. 40 (October 1974), p. 17.

29. Shein, "SShA-EEC," p. 65.

30. As one Soviet observer noted, the Administration dragged its feet, warning that unilateral efforts to improve relations with the Soviet Union would prove "illusory," run the risk of creating "friction among allies," and be used by the other side as "a weapon in the political war." See Novoseltsev, "Zreloe Partnerstvo," p. 172.

31. After the May 1972 summit in Moscow, Soviet commentators implied that the United States had at last caught up with the West Europeans. As one of them reported after the summit, now the ground has been cut out from under "the opponents of relaxed tensions . . . between the FRG and the socialist countries," who "before were able to speculate on a certain ambiguity and contradictoriness in Washington's attitude." See Ye. N. Novoseltsev, "Sovetsko-Amerikanskie peregovory v verkhakh i Evropeiskaya bezopastnost'," *SShA: Ekonomika, Politika, Ideologiya*, no. 12 (December 1972), p. 44.

32. See Walter Laqueur, "The Fall of Europe?", *Commentary* 53 (January 1972): 33-40.

33. V. Romanov, "The Basis of Lasting Peace in Europe," *International Affairs*, no. 3 (March 1973), p. 15.

34. One Western expert has written of the Czechoslovak stake in trade with the West: "Czechoslovakia did not want excessive integration to hinder its growing trade with Western markets—its main source of advanced technology and a highly useful medium for 'verifying' the technological standards and quality of Czechoslovak exports." See Z.M. Fallenbuchl, "COMECON Integration," *Problems of Communism* (March-April 1973), p. 37.

35. Valery Begishev, "Austria, Crossroads of Europe," *New Times*, no. 14 (April 1974), p. 16.

36. For a fairly sanguine assessment that this is about where the triangle is, see S. Madzoevskii, "V 'treugolnike' London-Parizh-Bonn," *Mirovaya Ekonomika i Mezhdunarodnye Otnosheniya*, no. 10 (October 1972), pp. 39-60, and the same author's " 'Treugolnik' London-Parizh-Bonn," cited earlier, pp. 120-152.

37. N. Inozemtsev, *Pravda*, August 20, 1974, pp. 4-5.

38. Lev Bezymensky, "Whose Hour in Western Europe?" *New Times*, no. 37 (September 1974), p. 8.

39. *Pravda*, February 25, 1976, p. 4.

40. See the report of his speech to the Academy of Sciences in *Pravda*, March 18, 1976, p. 2.

41. *Pravda*, February 29, 1976, p. 8.

42. The phrase is Michel Tatu's.

43. M. Dobrosielski, "Peaceful Coexistence and European Security," *International Affairs*, no. 6 (June 1972), p. 35. Dobrosielski is the director of the Institute of International Affairs in Warsaw, but the journal is Soviet and so, unquestionably, is the view.

VII

The Soviet Union and the Middle East

Oles M. Smolansky

Pursuit of Soviet Interests in the Middle East[a]

Moscow's 1955 entry into Middle Eastern politics was based on the growing might of the USSR and reflected Khrushchev's determination to compete with the United States on a global scale. The move was conditioned by such primary motives as military strategy, politics, economics, transportation, and communications and was only secondarily influenced by the Russian Empire's traditional and well-known preoccupation with the region situated along its southern border. It should also be noted that Communist doctrine, although it supports it, has not been the determining factor in Moscow's policy in the Middle East and elsewhere in the Third World. While the Kremlin has traditionally had a rather inchoate attachment to the idea of undermining the economic and political stability of the West by detaching from it its "vast colonial hinterland," actual Soviet involvement in the affairs of the developing countries soon exposed the limits of Marxism-Leninism as a diagnostic and prognostic "science." Indeed, the instances in which ideological orthodoxy has had to give way in the face of political reality are so numerous as to admit of no other conclusion.

---

[a]The region referred to as the Middle East in this chapter is arbitrarily divided into three geographic subdivisions—the eastern Mediterranean, the Persian Gulf, and the Arabian-Red Seas area—in which the USSR, over the years, has exhibited considerable interest. Among the states currently receiving Moscow's attention are: Egypt, Syria, and, lately, Libya; Iraq and Iran; People's Democratic Republic of Yemen (PDRY) and Somali Democratic Republic (Somalia). It should be noted, however, that the analysis of Soviet policies in the Middle East will of necessity occasionally spill over into some neighboring regions, such as the Maghrib, the Indian subcontinent, and others.

In contrast, there can be no doubt that a general concern for military-strategic considerations, i.e., the national security of the USSR and the possibility of
its being threatened from the Middle East and the surrounding territories, has
been an important element in shaping the Kremlin's attitude. American actions
of the late 1940s and early 1950s—such as the attempts to set up regional
defense organizations and above all the permanent stationing in and near the
Mediterranean of U.S. naval and air power—could not but be interpreted by
Moscow as potential threats to Soviet security. This made it imperative to the
Kremlin leaders to try to neutralize the U.S. military and political presence in
the Middle East and the eastern Mediterranean, even at a time when the advent
and growing sophistication of nuclear weapons and delivery systems were bound
to make many traditional strategic concepts obsolete. Thus, since the early
1960s Washington has no longer thought it necessary to maintain a large-scale
U.S. military presence on the Middle Eastern and North African land mass, as
was shown by its acquiescence in the closing of U.S. air bases in Morocco, Libya,
Saudi Arabia, and Pakistan and its removal of Jupiter missiles from Turkey and
Italy. In contrast, until July 1972 the Soviets were increasing their conventional
military presence in the area. This seeming paradox can be explained by the fact
that in the 1960s the United States improved its qualitative position in the
region by the introduction into the Mediterranean of *Polaris* submarines capable
of hitting a wide range of Soviet targets.

Primarily in an attempt to neutralize both the U.S. Sixth Fleet and *Polaris*,
the Kremlin in the early 1960s decided to deploy a naval squadron (*eskadra*) in
the eastern Mediterranean. For this force to represent a credible deterrent,
however, since the Soviet navy had no aircraft carriers and only a rather
primitive seaborne resupply and maintenance system, Moscow needed to acquire
naval and air facilities in the region. This alone would account for Khrushchev's
and Brezhnev's persistent efforts to establish close working relations with a
number of Arab states, above all Egypt, Syria, Algeria, and, more recently,
Libya.[b]

Not much headway was made in Algeria, where Ben Bella was replaced by
Boumédienne in June 1965, nor in postrevolutionary Libya. Egyptian and, it
appears, some Syrian facilities became available after 1967, but the Soviet
highwater mark was reached between 1970 and 1972 when de facto Russian
naval and air bases were established in Egypt.

On balance, while military-strategic considerations explain much of Moscow's
post-Stalin policy in the Middle East, the considerable outlay of resources and
prestige involved has not netted the Russians significant military advantages.
Their capacity to neutralize the Sixth Fleet and *Polaris* remains questionable, the
more so because since they lost their Egyptian bases they cannot provide air
cover for the *eskadra*.

Another major Soviet objective in the post-1945 period was to weaken

---

[b]The schism with Albania in 1960 lost Moscow its access to the Valona naval base.

Western (and particularly U.S.) *political* positions in the Middle East. Outwardly, as American influence there continued to decline, the USSR seemed to be making impressive gains, especially among the region's "progressive" states, such as Egypt, Iraq, Syria, Algeria, South Yemen (PDRY), Sudan, and Somalia. Moscow also normalized relations with Turkey, Iran, Tunisia, and Morocco and established correct relations with Kuwait.

It is often overlooked, however, that the decline of U.S. influence—reversed dramatically, though perhaps only temporarily, after the 1973 Yom Kippur War—was not so much the result of Soviet efforts as it was of Washington's continuing inability to combine its staunchly pro-Israeli stand with close working relations with the Arab states. The USSR, to be sure, has done its best to exploit this U.S. predicament to its advantage. Even with this built-in advantage, however, Moscow's political gains in the area have not been nearly as impressive as is commonly believed in the West.

For example, Sudan's President Jaafar al-Numayri, who in the late 1960s had shown great interest in cooperating with Russia, abandoned this line in the wake of the abortive 1971 attempt by local Communists to overthrow his regime. Moreover, some leading Arab "radicals," among them Libya's President Muammar Qadhdhafi, have openly criticized Moscow for its failure to force Israel to abandon the Arab territories occupied in 1967. This, coupled with Qadhdhafi's antipathy to Communist ideology, has been one of the reasons why he has persistently refused to establish close links with the USSR. (Libya's recent rapprochement with the Soviet Union appears to be a tactical move intended to strengthen Qadhdhafi's hand in his continuing feud with Sadat and, conceivably, to forestall a possible future Western attempt to seize Libyan oil fields.) Moreover, even where the Kremlin appeared to have won "steadfast friends," its long-term tangible benefits have often been far from clear. For example, Iraq's desire to cooperate with Russia is understandable in the light of Baghdad's frequent isolation from its neighbors as well as its determination to play a leading role both in the Arab world and the Persian Gulf. Nevertheless, Iraq's pursuit of its own interests does not always correspond to Soviet policies and, therefore, makes its current Ba'thi leadership rather unreliable. Syria, governed by another antagonistic branch of the Ba'th, falls into a similar category.

Soviet relations with Turkey and Iran, while outwardly cordial, have remained cool, for apprehensions about the Kremlin's ultimate intentions are a deeply ingrained tradition in Ankara and Tehran. The recent rapprochement between Turkey and the USSR-a result of Ankara's disenchantment with Washington's stand on Cyprus—is not likely to dispel the ancient Turkish fear of Russia. Moscow's efforts in the Arab West (the Maghrib) have led to limited economic and military cooperation with Algeria and Morocco but the Kremlin's attempts to obtain naval facilities there have so far been unsuccessful.

The most serious blow to Moscow's position and prestige in the area was delivered by President Sadat, who in July 1972 ordered the eviction from Egypt of most Soviet military personnel. Cairo's action underscored Russia's inability to control the Egyptians in spite of the latter's military and economic dependence on the USSR and forced the Kremlin to recognize that it could not base a credible military posture in the eastern Mediterranean on Arab support. The move also nullified some of the gains made in the Soviet attempt to neutralize the U.S. strategic preponderance in the Mediterranean. Moreover, many of the political advantages Moscow secured in the Arab East after 1967 have virtually evaporated, as demonstrated by the efforts of Egypt, Sudan, northern Yemen, and, more recently, also Iraq and Syria, to improve relations with the West.

In short, in terms of political as well as military-strategic interests, the USSR has relatively little to show for its substantial investments of resources and prestige in the Middle East. The only exceptions to this conclusion are the PDRY and Somalia, where some initial successes have been achieved. But these countries' relative closeness to the USSR is dictated at least in part by the fact that no other great power (except China) has shown any interest in coming to their assistance and that their main antagonists—Saudi Arabia and Ethiopia, respectively—have traditionally maintained close working relations with the United States.

Economically, the Middle East is of some importance to the USSR, which over the last decade has become the major purchaser of Egyptian cotton and Iranian natural gas. Nevertheless, neither product constitutes an important Soviet national interest: natural gas is useful but not indispensable to the Soviet economy, and cotton has been imported primarily because it is Egypt's main export item. It has been accepted not because of need but in partial payment of Cairo's immense purchases of Soviet weapons and industrial equipment.

The most important economic aspect of the Middle East is, of course, its enormous petroleum resources. It must be noted at the outset that the USSR does not at present rely on Middle Eastern or North African petroleum nor is it likely to develop such a dependence in the current decade. The view that Moscow is determined to remain self-sufficient in energy production is supported by Brezhnev's efforts to secure large-scale Western capital investments to develop Soviet oil and natural gas reserves and by the Kremlin's recent far-reaching decision to increase sharply domestic production and consumption of abundant coal, a move which is clearly designed to spur economic growth and to free additional quantities of petroleum for export to Western Europe.

What will happen in the 1980s and beyond is unclear. Most Western experts expect that for a number of reasons, including geography, logistics, and shortage of equipment and capital, the Soviet Union will eventually have to become a net importer of petroleum. If so, the Kremlin might one day decide to establish a major economic foothold in one or several oil-producing countries of the Middle East. But to do this, the Russians would have to overcome some important political and technical problems, including their relatively limited petroleum processing capabilities. They will also have to continue abiding by the normal rules of international commercial transactions. Indeed, the Soviets may well find it in their long-range interest to temper some of the cleverness in international commerce which they have demonstrated in recent years. This cunning has earned Moscow substantial economic profits but also much ill-will in such oil-producing nations as Iraq and Iran which are determined not to be bested in future transactions.

Finally, the Middle East has long served as an important trade, transportation, and communications center, linking Europe, Asia, and Africa. While in many ways it has retained this traditional role, the technological revolution of the past three decades has reduced its former significance. The closing of the Suez Canal during the 1967 war is a good illustration. Whereas before the June conflict the waterway was considered indispensable for international trade, most of its former users adjusted readily to the new situation.

In the late sixties and early seventies it was widely assumed in the West that, among the great powers, the USSR would benefit most from the Canal's reopening. This, the argument ran, would greatly facilitate the flow of Soviet supplies to North Vietnam and also ensure a larger and therefore more effective Soviet naval presence in the Indian Ocean. It is evident, in retrospect, that the first assertion was largely unfounded, for enough Russian supplies reached Hanoi to be a major factor in North Vietnam's 1975 victory. As for the second supposition, there can be no doubt that the task of moving Soviet naval vessels into the Indian Ocean has been greatly facilitated by the reopening of the Suez Canal in June 1975. At the same time, it should be noted that a modest Soviet naval presence in the Arabian Sea has been maintained since 1968 and that, so far, there has been no dramatic increase in its size.

In any event, because of its geographic proximity to the Middle East, the USSR depends on the region's important waterways—particularly the Turkish Straits and the Suez Canal—much more than the United States. However, to conclude that this leads to a more "aggressive" Soviet policy in the Middle East or the Indian Ocean is to miss a significant point: to pursue its objectives in these regions the USSR needs and relies on a state of relative peace. For in war both waterways can easily be blocked, and the consequences of impaired access to the Mediterranean and the Indian Ocean would be infinitely more serious for Russia than for the United States.

In summary, an examination of Moscow's post-Stalin policy in the Middle East reveals that military-strategic motivations have far outweighed economic considerations. It should be added that the initial reasons for the Soviet "offensive" have since been reinforced by the resultant "vested interests," which prompted the USSR to try to protect and preserve its Middle Eastern gains. On balance, it appears to this writer that the advantages secured have not offset the liabilities incurred in the process of extending Soviet participation in the affairs of the area. However, judging by their determination to "hang in" in the Middle

East in the face of all adversities, this view is clearly not shared by the majority of the Kremlin leaders.

The Current Situation

In the latter half of the 1960s, after an enormous investment of resources and capital, the USSR finally achieved nuclear parity with the United States. The international recognition of this accomplishment allowed the Kremlin for the first time to contemplate seriously the advantages of a "real détente," i.e., a process of superpower accommodation in which the Soviet Union could deal with the United States from a position of approximate equality. In addition to a general awareness of the catastrophe which a nuclear war would represent, the desirability of a new departure in Soviet-American relations was also dictated to both Moscow and Washington by a number of other factors, ranging from strategic and international considerations to domestic politics and economics.[c]

The Arab-Israeli Sector

In the early 1970s, the superpowers thus appeared intent on limiting the nuclear arms race, normalizing their political and economic relations and lowering tensions in some of the globe's critical trouble spots. Moreover, in the case of the United States, the mounting pressures of the Watergate scandal limited Nixon's effectiveness in dealing with foreign policy matters that did not require immediate attention and in 1972-73 the Arab-Israeli conflict fell into this category.

As it turned out, Brezhnev, in an important departure from Moscow's previous position in this matter, was willing to cooperate with his "partner in détente." In addition to the general considerations alluded to above, his outlook was also influenced by the decline of Russian influence in Egypt, which in July 1972 culminated in the elimination of the Soviet bases there, and his apparent realization that the Mediterranean and the Middle East had lost much of their former military-strategic significance. Finally, in 1971-1972, Syria showed no inclination to subordinate itself to Soviet wishes, the Kremlin's willingness to scale down its involvement in the Arab-Israeli sector becomes quite understandable.

The shift in Moscow's attitude became discernible in late 1972 and 1973. Whereas prior to that time the USSR had accepted the Arab right to use "all means necessary" to regain the territory lost in 1967, Soviet official statements issued in 1973 (particularly during Brezhnev's visit to the United States) emphatically insisted that this be achieved "by peaceful means." This implied that the Kremlin was prepared to acquiesce in the existing status quo.

---

[c]This theme is developed more fully elsewhere in this volume.

It is hard to tell what course history might have taken had it not been for two major, unrelated events which profoundly changed the situation in the Arab-Israeli sector. The first was the Egyptian-Syrian decision to attack Israel, and the second was the resignation of President Nixon, one of the main architects of U.S.-Soviet détente.

The October War was caused in part by the Arabs' realization that they could not count on the superpowers to change significantly a status quo unacceptable to them. They proved correct in their calculation that a major war would restore the Middle East as the "number one" item on the international agenda and would bring the superpowers back, *but on opposing sides.* Political competition between Washington and Moscow in the Middle East was thus resumed. After the cease-fire on the Egyptian front had been effected, largely through the efforts of Secretary Kissinger, President Sadat, apparently persuaded of Washington's willingness (its ability was never in question) to work for a solution acceptable to the Arabs, began to reestablish close political and economic cooperation with the United States. Given the Soviet military and political backing of Cairo after the outbreak of the October War, Egypt's attitude must have enormously upset Moscow, but, since there was little the Soviets could do about it, they reacted simply by sharply reducing their military aid and by adopting a cool attitude to Sadat's initiative and Kissinger's attempts at mediation.

Thus, Moscow's negative attitude toward Kissinger's "step-by-step" diplomacy was conditioned by the actions of both Egypt and the United States. Given Sadat's preferences, it is easy to understand his desire to reassert Cairo's independence from the USSR at a time when he seemed convinced of Washington's determination to achieve a breakthrough in the Arab-Israeli impasse, as well as his failure to appreciate the intricacies of American politics which led to Nixon's resignation. It now appears, however, that, barring some new and decisive initiatives by the Ford Administration, Sadat may well have overplayed his hand. Even though relations with the United States are cordial and large amounts of money have been channeled to Egypt by a number of Arab oil-producing countries to strengthen its economy and to facilitate arms purchases from other (mainly West European) sources, the Egyptian armed forces remain heavily dependent on continued deliveries of Soviet spare parts and, even more significantly, they have been trained in the use of Soviet, not Western, equipment. Large-scale infusion of Western weapons systems into the Egyptian military establishment would result in a major logistic dislocation which is bound in the near future to affect adversely the country's ability to wage a major war. Given these basic facts, and the growing Egyptian uncertainty concerning U.S. intentions, it was therefore no surprise that despite the periodic propaganda blasts by both sides, Sadat unsuccessfully felt out the USSR in search of a degree of political rapprochement and of new weapons. It is equally significant that Moscow declined to rush to Sadat's assistance, as evidenced in part by its refusal to resume large-scale arms shipments to Egypt and to place a moratorium on the enormous debt owed by Cairo to the USSR. (The Syrians, in contrast, encountered no such difficulties.) Viewed in this light, the Soviet behavior clearly reflects both Moscow's unwillingness to break with Egypt—still the leading Arab state—and its determination to keep applying pressure on Cairo to lessen its reliance on the United States and to reestablish closer relations with the Soviet Union.

But although neither Moscow nor Cairo probably wanted to break with each other, the break occurred, symbolized by Sadat's March 1976 denunciation of the Soviet-Egyptian friendship treaty, his allegation that Moscow had prevented India from supplying Egypt with Soviet-type spare parts, and his canceling the facilities the Soviet navy enjoyed in Egyptian ports. He did so shortly after he made a tour of the Arab oil states in the Gulf, from which he reportedly returned with aid pledges of $1 billion, probably in part to buy Western arms. Yet to reequip the Egyptian armed forces with them will be a long and costly process, and at least in the election year of 1976, it hardly seemed that Sadat would get too much of a *quid pro quo* from Washington very soon.

Another reason for the Kremlin's position has been the attitude adopted by the United States. The post-October War cease-fire and disengagement agreements were worked out by Secretary Kissinger, Presidents Sadat and Asad, and the Israeli government without prior consultations with the USSR and outside the framework of the Geneva peace conference, convened by Washington and Moscow in December 1973 to help negotiate a settlement between Israel and its Arab adversaries. In Moscow's eyes, the United States was thereby reaffirming its determination to ignore the legitimacy of both Soviet interests in the Middle East and of active Soviet participation in the region's affairs—principles which the Kremlin has been promoting and Washington has refused to accept ever since Moscow's entry into Middle Eastern politics in 1955. Détente or not, this state of affairs is not likely to be tolerated by any Soviet government, no matter how seriously it may wish to improve its relations with the United States. (Indicative of the Kremlin's attitude have been, among other things, the concerted but abortive attempts to reconvene the Geneva conference in the wake of Kissinger's temporary failure in March 1975 to negotiate the second disengagement agreement between Egypt and Israel.)

The exclusion of the USSR from the major negotiations among the United States, Israel, and the Arabs goes a long way toward explaining Soviet policy in the aftermath of the October War. The Kremlin must have felt helpless and frustrated. It had no leverage in Jerusalem and its ability to influence both Washington and Moscow's Arab clients was severely limited. To add to the Soviets' discomfort, Sadat had decided actively to seek a resolution of the Arab-Israeli conflict through close cooperation with the United States and in total disregard of the USSR.

Discouraged as the Russians undoubtedly were, even in this "dark hour" they were not prepared to abandon the stage and thus to leave the United States to exploit the Arab-Israeli problem to its own advantage. Lacking other viable options, Moscow first of all reaffirmed its commitment to peace in the Middle East. It also attempted to regain a measure of Arab good will and confidence by insisting that lasting peace could be achieved only by the satisfaction of all the "legitimate" Arab (including Palestinian) demands, above all Israel's return of the territories occupied in 1967.

At the same time, in an obvious attempt to ensure that it would not be excluded from future negotiations, the Kremlin insisted that peace talks be conducted at Geneva, where as a cochairman it could count on playing a prominent part. The Soviets also showed renewed interest in the Palestine Liberation Organization (PLO), with which they had maintained limited relations since the late 1960s. Moscow sensed correctly that in the Palestinian issue it had a trump card (not a "time bomb," as some observers maintain) which could be played when the USSR needed to exert pressure on a negotiating process from which it had either been excluded or over which it had little control.

Soviet insistence on the inclusion of the Palestinian problem in the agenda for Israeli-Arab peace talks was an ingenious move which in the end (if it ever comes) could pay handsome political dividends. However, given the vicissitudes of Arab politics, Moscow's stand is not without disadvantages. It may be realistically assumed that the PLO also regards its Soviet "connection" as a trump card to be played in its negotiations with the Arab governments, the United States, and Israel but to be discarded any time it suits its preferences.

Last but not least, as already indicated, the Soviet Union endeavored to improve relations with Syria. In the late 1960s-early 1970s, Damascus, like Cairo and Baghdad, exhibited a lively interest in maintaining economic cooperation with and in securing large-scale military, technical, and financial assistance from the USSR. But, in contrast to Egypt and Iraq, Syria refused to conclude with the USSR a Treaty of Friendship, designed to establish close political cooperation between them. This pointed display of independence was due to Asad's determination not to tie himself too closely to any outside power and to Moscow's reluctance to press Damascus on an issue which the latter regarded as an outward appearance of subordination. The result was a considerable cooling of Soviet-Syrian relations, which, paralleling the developments in Egypt, prevailed until October 1973. The situation which the USSR and the United States encountered in Damascus after the war, however, differed from the Egyptian scene in a number of important ways. The most significant one was probably the degree of caution, sometimes bordering on mistrust, with which Asad received Kissinger's proposals for a cease-fire and a troop disengagement. Initially, the Syrian president reluctantly agreed to go along with Washington and Cairo. However, even he did not believe that Israel will voluntarily evacuate the entire Golan Heights area, a move which Damascus regards as a prerequisite to peace between Syria and Israel. Asad's subsequent intransigence, which markedly contrasted with Sadat's pro-U.S. stand, necessitated increased reliance on the USSR, whose military and political assistance he needs to enable Damascus to deal with Jerusalem from a position of relative strength while the major problems remain unsolved. As a result of its opposition to the second Israeli-Egyptian disengagement agreement, Syria has been the beneficiary of large-scale Soviet military support. It has also thereby improved its position in the Arab world, especially with the PLO. Its position has also been improved by its mediation of the Lebanon Civil War, its consequent current predominance there, and its rapprochement with Jordan.

Yet while Asad's caution has given the Soviet Union another card in the superpowers' diplomatic poker game in the post-October Middle East, it is questionable whether the Kremlin has thereby gained much additional leverage in Damascus. The Syrians are extremely sensitive about any real or potential infringement on their sovereignty and independence. In addition, like Egypt, their position has been significantly strengthened by the flow of funds from the oil-producing states to pay for the arms purchases from the USSR.

In short, and contrary to some Western opinion, the USSR is not now in a position either to afford or to deny to the Arabs an opportunity to negotiate with Israel. The acceptability to the countries directly involved of the various peace provisions will ultimately determine the success or failure of future negotiations. Should the Arabs, by whatever means, resolve their differences with Jerusalem, the Russians will not be able to prevent them from signing a peace treaty. They simply do not have that kind of "clout" in either Cairo or Damascus, and their recent emergence as a "protector" of the Palestinians is not likely to change this state of affairs.

It was precisely the realization on the part of the Kremlin that it was being excluded from the real negotiating process between Israel and the Arabs which prompted Moscow to reassert its political presence by increasing its military supplies to Syria (while severely limiting arms shipments to Egypt), by backing the PLO, and by insisting on peace talks at Geneva. How much the USSR will succeed in restoring a measure of its influence in the Arab East, however, depends largely on the ability of the United States to deal effectively with the individual Arab leaders and to tackle the problems which divide the Arab states and Israel.

At the time of this writing it appears that Secretary Kissinger will not be able to settle the major differences separating Israel and its Arab neighbors and that the problem of peace will eventually be entrusted to the Geneva conference. This turn of events will present the USSR with an opportunity either to contribute to or to impede the resolution of the Arab-Israeli impasse. Which course of action the Kremlin will take remains to be seen, but there are some reasons to believe that its role might turn out to be a constructive one.

Persian Gulf

Moscow's interest in the Gulf has been conditioned by the same three types of considerations (military-strategic, political, and economic) which have motivated its policies elsewhere in the Middle East. Specifically, Soviet security concerns have been generated by the often denied but, to Moscow, very real possibility of the deployment of U.S. strategic nuclear submarines in the Indian Ocean. The Soviet naval presence in the Arabian Sea, in the general proximity of the Gulf, was probably conceived in part as a response to this strategic problem. (This subject will be discussed in greater length in the next subsection.)

In the late 1960s, the exclusivity of what was becoming, after the announcement of Britain's intention to withdraw from the Persian Gulf, a U.S.-USSR "dual domain" was broken by the appearance of Communist China. In the emerging triangular relationship all three powers were initially pitted against each other. Only in the 1970s, as a result of the U.S.-Chinese rapprochement, did Peking shift from its previously inflexible hostility toward both superpowers to a primarily and more pronounced anti-Soviet stand. Peking therefore backed Iran—a country supported by the United States—in its efforts (directed in part against the USSR) to establish itself as the leading military power in the Gulf. Locally, Iraq has been the only Gulf state willing to establish and maintain reasonably close ties with the Soviet Union. In the late 1960s and early 1970s the "progressive" Ba'thi regime was opposed by the conservative, monarchist regimes of most of the Gulf states, among them Iran and Saudi Arabia, and was therefore politically isolated from its neighbors. Because of the perennial quarrels between the Iraqi and Syrian branches of the Ba'th, relations between Baghdad and Damascus have also been strained. Since Iraq has been the traditional rival of Egypt for leadership of the Arab East, Baghdad desperately needed a powerful outside backer capable of delivering political, military, and economic support.[d] Because the "progressive" nature of its regime made intimate relations with the Western powers impossible, Iraq's choice was limited to faraway, economically weak China or nearby, powerful Russia. It was not a difficult decision to make, and the Iraqi Ba'th found in Moscow a patron more than mildly interested in a client-state with access to the Persian Gulf.

The Soviet attitude was conditioned by Iraq's geographic location, its important petroleum reserves, and its determination to play an active role in Gulf and general Middle Eastern politics. Cooperation between the two countries has expanded continuously since the late 1960s, as shown in part by the conclusion in 1972 of a Treaty of Friendship patterned on the Egyptian and Indian models. It is probably no exaggeration to say that until recently Iraq,

[d]Regional and international considerations were reinforced by domestic problems, particularly the regime's protracted inability, until 1975, to "solve" the Kurdish problem.

along with the PDRY and Somalia, has been one of Moscow's most valued clients in the Middle East. Nevertheless, the problems which the Russians have encountered in Baghdad illustrate the tenuousness of Soviet-Arab relations. The local Ba'th is ideologically opposed to communism. It is also determined to preserve Iraq's independence and pursue a foreign policy of which the Kremlin occasionally disapproves. (A good example is the question of the future settlement of the Arab-Israeli conflict. While the Russians are prepared to guarantee the security of the Jewish state, the Iraqis oppose any solutions which would entail recognition of Israel's right to independent existence.) The Iraqis are equally intent on conducting their domestic affairs in accordance with their own wishes, as shown by their war against the Kurds, which the Russians initially opposed and worked hard to prevent. (The Soviet reluctance to support Iraq's military action against the Kurds is explained by the additional leverage on Baghdad which the war provided for the USSR.) Nevertheless, while many of these and other problems have occasionally strained Moscow-Baghdad relations, the USSR has invariably stopped short of an open break, because such a turn of events would not only further weaken Russia's total position in the Middle East but also jeopardize its access to Iraqi oil and eliminate any meaningful Soviet presence in the Persian Gulf.

However, to keep its positions in Baghdad, the USSR has had to pay a price elsewhere, not only in Cairo and Damascus but also in the Gulf itself. Soviet support of Iraq has heightened the already considerable suspicion about Moscow's intentions on the part of the region's conservative regimes. This is especially true of Iran (prior to its March 1975 agreement with Baghdad) and Saudi Arabia, which effectively dominate most of the Gulf. The resulting mistrust and occasional overt hostility has not, however, prevented increasing economic and limited military cooperation between Moscow and Tehran[e] or Soviet establishment of normal diplomatic and economic relations with Kuwait.[f] Otherwise, however, the Kremlin has made no significant inroads into the Persian Gulf, for Saudi Arabia, Bahrayn, Qatar, the United Arab Amirates (UAA), and Oman have refused to have any but the most superficial dealings with the Soviet Union.

Moscow's difficulties have been exacerbated by endemically unstable local conditions. The most obvious example has been the war in the Dhufar province of Oman, where local security forces, supported by the British and the Iranians, have been battling Marxist-led rebels, supplied by the PDRY, Iraq (until March 1975), and the USSR. Although the Soviets had nothing to do with the outbreak of the uprising and have been able to do little to prevent the rebels from

---

[e]The latter has been purchasing Soviet armored personnel carriers and artillery. Most observers believe that the Shah's main objective is to impress the U.S. Congress, where there has been criticism of his arms purchases, with his ability to purchase weapons from the USSR.

[f]According to hitherto unconfirmed reports, Kuwait has also purchased large quantities of modern Soviet weapons.

apparent defeat, the Kremlin did become involved. Its decision was caused by its traditional distaste for political conservatism, which the Sultan of Oman personifies, and by the fact that Peking had initially chosen to demonstrate its commitment to world revolution by backing the Dhufari rebels. Under the circumstances, the Kremlin could do no less. (It is indeed ironic that because of their rapprochements with Iran and the U.S. the Chinese have in the meantime discontinued their support and left the Russians "holding the bag.") Whatever its motivations, Moscow's involvement has reinforced the reservations and apprehensions of those who, like the Shah, do not object in principle to maintaining correct working relations with the USSR. Moreover, now that Saudi Arabia and the PDRY have recently resumed diplomatic relations, another indication that the rebellion has failed, one may speculate how long the Soviet and Cuban presence in Aden will remain.

Even a cursory examination of the immensely complex political picture in the Gulf, of its tangled rivalries and ancient feuds, reveals a volatile, potentially explosive area which, while attractive to the Kremlin because of its economic and strategic importance, presents the USSR with virtually insurmountable political problems. Since Soviet foreign policy under Brezhnev has been marked by realism, relative restraint, and awareness of the dangers which beset any ambitious outsider, it may be predicted that in the near future, barring totally unforeseen developments, the Kremlin will abstain from active, large-scale participation in the affairs of the Persian Gulf, except in Iraq. Even there the fragility of Moscow's position is underscored by Baghdad's reported refusal to allow the establishment of a Soviet naval and air base at Umm Qasr; by the March 1975 Iraqi-Iranian treaty settling most of the major differences which in the past had separated the two states; and by Iraq's subsequent espousal of the Shah's call for the removal of all "foreign presence" from the Gulf.

The economic importance of the Persian Gulf is obvious. Some two-thirds of the world's proven oil reserves lie under the sands of its riparian states or under its waters. Most industrial and developing nations rely on petroleum as their chief source of energy and could not survive economically if the flow of oil were long interrupted. Moreover, the vast amounts of hard currency accumulated as a result of recent increases in the price of oil and available for large-scale investment and purchases abroad have further enhanced the economic significance of the Gulf oil-producing states.

Given these elements of the situation, the USSR's geographic proximity to the Persian Gulf, the strong likelihood that it will eventually become a net-importer of petroleum, and the fact that units of the Russian navy make occasional calls at Umm Qasr, it has become popular in some Western circles to point to the danger of aggressive Soviet designs in the Gulf. Such allegations are almost surely unfounded. In view of the Western dependence on Gulf oil it is unrealistic to expect the USSR to undertake overt military action in an effort to gain access to or effectively interfere with the flow of petroleum in the Persian

Gulf itself or elsewhere on the high seas. Whether or not the Soviet navy could do so, it must be obvious to the Kremlin that such aggression would produce resolute U.S. countermeasures. The risk of a nuclear confrontation between the superpowers would thus be raised to an unacceptable level, and no rational Soviet leader would therefore seriously consider taking such steps. This means that the USSR will have to secure what oil it needs and can get by peaceful means. Russian cooperation in the development of Iraq's North Rumaila oil fields may indicate how the Soviets are planning to do so.

Moscow's stand on some of the petroleum-related issues which have dominated the headlines in the post-October 1973 period—namely nationalization of Western oil companies, the embargo, and the rising price of petroleum—have often been cited as additional causes for alarm. The Kremlin has in fact long used the oil companies as a convenient "whipping boy," by pointing out to the Arabs that they would not achieve "real independence" until they expropriated these large foreign enterprises. Since most petroleum-producing states have been nationalizing the companies, there is a natural tendency to tie these measures to Soviet exhortations. The evidence suggests, however, that there is no connection between them. The Arabs (and other producer-governments) are pursuing their own interests, and Moscow's prodding and stated preferences have had no direct influence on them. Nor have the Soviets directly benefited from the actual or proposed nationalizations of Western oil companies. If anything, control over extraction, refining, transportation, and marketing of petroleum by Middle Eastern producers is likely to bring them into direct competition with Russia, which now supplies some 15 percent of the oil consumed in Western Europe. Resale of Iraqi petroleum (bought under the terms of previous agreements for approximately $1.80 per barrel) in European markets in the wake of the embargo netted the Soviets, according to Arab sources, over $3 billion, but has also generated significant Arab, and particularly Iraqi, resentment.

The problems of embargo and of high and rising oil prices fall into a different category. The USSR has openly supported both actions and many analysts explain its position as another manifestation of a Soviet desire to weaken the "capitalist" West. There is of course much truth in this assessment: an economically weaker West is likely to be more amenable to Moscow's political pressure and wishes for broader economic and trade relations. The actions of the oil-producers have also enabled Russia to expand its own exports and, much more importantly, to charge its customers current market prices. The Soviets have thus substantially increased their hard currency reserves, and therefore can more easily afford to buy badly needed agricultural products and industrial commodities from the West. On the negative side, the recent increases in the price of petroleum have raised the prospect of considerable outlays of hard currency by the Soviet bloc to pay for purchases of Middle Eastern oil by the countries of Eastern Europe. Be that as it may, the evidence suggests that the Soviet role in these developments has been an indirect one. The mere presence of

Russia, with its declared interest in the Middle East, has probably helped to restrain those Western circles which might otherwise have seriously considered taking immediate punitive steps to deal with what to many was an intolerable situation and has no doubt emboldened the producers to adopt a relatively rigid attitude vis-à-vis the consumers.

In short, contrary to Western fears, the Kremlin's prospects for dominating the Persian Gulf do not appear particularly bright. However, in light of the fact that the Russians' major objective in the region appears to be the much more modest one of assuring themselves of a voice in those regional affairs that might affect their broader interests, Moscow's position as a relatively detached but powerful neighbor is not a totally unenviable one. One of its specific interests in the area appears to be the use of Iraqi port facilities to help maintain a Soviet naval squadron in the Indian Ocean. This same objective has also probably motivated Russian activities in yet another area, the littoral states of the Red and Arabian Seas.

The Red-Arabian Seas Area

Most of the emphasis in this chapter has been on the Arab East and the Persian Gulf, traditionally the main areas of extensive Soviet activity in the Middle East. However, since the late 1960s—and the process has accelerated since 1972—Moscow's attention has shifted southward toward the Red and Arabian seas, in part in order to establish a Soviet naval presence in the northwestern part of the Indian Ocean.

Initially the USSR showed interest in most of the independent states of the region: Sudan, Ethiopia, and Somalia on the African side and the two Yemens on the Arabian peninsula. For a number of reasons, such as the abortive 1971 Communist coup in the Sudan, the internal instability and, prior to the 1974 coup, the basically pro-Western orientation of Ethiopia, and the emergence of a conservative, pro-Saudi regime in northern Yemen, Soviet options and opportunities in the area have been significantly reduced. On balance, however, these developments may have been a blessing in disguise, allowing the USSR to concentrate its attention on the PDRY and Somalia, which can meet most of Moscow's present military and political requirements in the northwestern Indian Ocean. The political radicalization in both of these states, which has brought to power groups outwardly committed to the transformation of their societies on the basis of "scientific socialism," has played handsomely into the Kremlin's hands. Coupled with the relative political isolation of both countries, their official leaning toward the Soviet brand of Marxism-Leninism has produced a degree of intimacy in their relations with the USSR unmatched anywhere else in the Middle East.

Moscow has underwritten a large program of military aid to each, designed to strengthen their armed forces and to embrace the expansion and modernization of existing and the construction of new naval and air facilities. The latter, many Western observers fear, are intended for use by the Soviets as well as for domestic forces. Military assistance has been supplemented by badly needed economic, technical, and financial aid and by high-level visits among Soviet, Yemeni, and Somali dignitaries. (A Treaty of Friendship between the USSR and Somalia was signed in June 1974.)

The reasons for Soviet interest in the northwestern Indian Ocean can also be conveniently classified as military-strategic, political, and, to a much lesser degree, economic. As to the first, since the emergence of *Polaris* as an effective U.S. nuclear delivery system, the Russians have shown considerable anxiety about its possible presence in the Indian Ocean generally and the Arabian Sea in particular. (This subject has received periodic mention both in the Soviet press and in the speeches of political and military officials.) There is certainly a rational basis for such fears: the Arabian Sea is an ideal deployment area to reach Soviet and Chinese targets. Moreover since the early 1960s the United States has taken a number of steps to establish the capability to deploy *Polaris* and *Poseidon* submarines in the Indian Ocean. Among them have been the construction of radio and communications centers in northwest Australia and Ethiopia and the December 1966 agreement with Great Britain which provided for the building of another communications center at Diego Garcia in the Chagos Archipelago. (The latter has since been expanded to include naval repair and other facilities.) In February 1975, British naval and air facilities on the island of Masira, situated in the Arabian Sea off the coast of Oman, were made available for American use.

Supporters of American policy have disputed the view concerning Soviet anxiety about U.S. intentions, claiming that there is no "permanent" deployment of *Polaris-Poseidon* in the Indian Ocean and that given the present limitations of antisubmarine warfare (ASW), a Soviet naval presence in the Arabian Sea will not make much difference anyway. Neither of these objections appears persuasive. U.S. nuclear submarines do occasionally cruise in the Indian Ocean, but this is not the real issue. What is significant to the Kremlin is that they could be introduced into the area at any time; and that the Indian Ocean remains a logical place to deploy them in times of severe superpower crises. The second point is more difficult to refute. Nevertheless, the United States and the Soviet Union are spending a great deal of time, money, and resources on ASW research. Admittedly, thus far success has proved elusive. However, the Soviet efforts to establish a network of naval and air facilities necessary to maintain existing ASW capabilities, to conduct oceanographic research, and to engage in other activities related to the task of keeping a permanent naval presence in that part of the world would alone justify to Moscow the expense of establishing close working relations with Somalia and the PDRY. Moreover, an existing naval force with well-established support facilities also makes sense tactically, i.e., any breakthrough in ASW technology could be operational that much more quickly.

The Soviet naval units have also promoted the political interests of the USSR in the Arabian Sea and elsewhere in the Indian Ocean. One of the main centers of Soviet competition not only with the United States but even more with Communist China has been the Indian subcontinent, an area outside the scope of this chapter. It should be noted, however, that there also military-strategic considerations have been reinforced by political ones.[g]

The decision to establish a Soviet naval presence in the Indian Ocean may also reflect the Kremlin's ambition to reach qualitative naval parity with the United States as well as the determination of the Soviet naval command to gain a "place in the sun" in the country's armed forces hierarchy. The Indian Ocean, which connects the Pacific and the Atlantic, was therefore a logical place to establish a Soviet naval presence, especially since Moscow had previously done so in the Mediterranean.

The relatively modest Soviet naval force in the Arabian Sea presents no real threat to vital Western interests. Even when reinforced occasionally by detachments from the Black Sea or Pacific fleets, it is still inferior to U.S. carrier task forces which can be dispatched to the Indian Ocean from the Seventh Fleet, as happened during the 1971 Indian-Pakistani war. The Soviet fleet cannot deal effectively with *Polaris* and *Poseidon* submarines. Politically, the Soviet naval presence can be and occasionally has been used to help exert pressure on a client-state (as in the case of the Iraqi-Kuwaiti border dispute of 1972), but the effectiveness of "flag-showing" exercises in the modern world is a matter of some debate. It is equally unlikely, to repeat, that it would be used to interfere with the flow of Persian Gulf petroleum.

In any event, the Russians seem firmly entrenched in Somalia and the PDRY and could theoretically use these positions to expand Soviet influence into neighboring countries. How realistic this prospect is, especially in the light of what has transpired in recent years in the Sudan and northern Yemen, is debatable. (At the time of writing the political situation in Ethiopia remains sufficiently confused to prevent meaningful analysis.) The only thing that can be said with certainty at this juncture is that the Kremlin seems intent on strengthening its positions in the Indian Ocean in general and the Red-Arabian Seas area in particular and that in the process it has acquired in the latter region two additional clients, with all the advantages and liabilities that such an arrangement entails. Moscow's efforts have not gone unnoticed in Washington, and it may be assumed that the Indian Ocean will emerge as another major arena of U.S.-Soviet competition.

The Changing Middle East and U.S. Policy Options

Three basic options are open to the United States in its attempts to deal with the Soviet presence and policies in the Middle East: unilateral

[g]Soviet economic activities along the Indian Ocean perimeter, also outside the scope of this chapter, have been extensive in India, Iran, Bangladesh, Somalia, and the PDRY.

action, continued competition, and efforts at mutual accommodation and cooperation in selected problem areas.[h]

Unilateral Withdrawal or Intervention

Unilateral disengagement is, justifiably, the least popular among the American public as well as decisionmakers, and in vogue only at the extremes of the country's political spectrum. It represents in part a revulsion against the Vietnam War on the one hand and against the alleged inability of the government to deal "decisively" with communist aggression on the other. To both extremes, the U.S. experience in Southeast Asia could easily be repeated in the Middle East with the result that at best the United States would be drawn into the agony of another Vietnam, and at worst it could face the possibility of a nuclear war with the USSR.

In any event, of the three major options mentioned above unilateral withdrawal is the least likely to be considered seriously by any U.S. government. Given the realities of Soviet-American competition in the Third World as well as the vital Western interest in Middle Eastern petroleum, it must be dismissed on several counts. It would not contribute to the maintenance of general peace and international security; it would leave the states of the area open to Soviet manipulation and pressure, thus jeopardizing vital economic interests of the non-Communist world; and it would mean U.S. abandonment of a major military, political, and economic investment. As long as the superpowers continue to compete, such a course of action would be both irresponsible and dangerous.

Not directly affecting any vital interests of the USSR but of utmost concern to the West as well as to the petroleum-producing states is the exact opposite of withdrawal—unilateral intervention by the United States to seize control of the oil fields of some Arab country or countries. Since veiled threats to use force under certain, albeit very remote, circumstances (i.e., to avoid the "economic strangulation" of the West) have been made by President Ford and Secretary Kissinger this alternative must be considered a potential policy option. There can be little doubt that such an action would make oil available to Western consumers even in the face of threatened Arab sabotage: fires can be extinguished, wells can eventually be restored to normal production, and desert areas can be reasonably effectively sealed off against would-be saboteurs. But this drastic course is not likely to be taken except as a last resort. Its moral and legal consequences aside, in my view such unilateral U.S. intervention would constitute a colossal political blunder. Since force is not likely to be used against Iran

---

[h]The likelihood of a total settlement of all the outstanding U.S.-Soviet differences in the Middle East is extremely remote. Therefore, while technically a fourth "option," it is omitted from this discussion.

or pro-Soviet Iraq, its use elsewhere in the Gulf would result in eliminating from power some pro-U.S., anti-Soviet, and anti-Communist Arab regime or regimes (Saudi Arabia is most prominently listed as a likely target), in antagonizing *all* the Arabs for a long time to come, and in giving the USSR an unprecedented opportunity to fish in troubled waters—a temptation no Kremlin leader would be likely to resist.[i]

Superpower Competition

This option not only describes the current state of superpower relations in the Middle East and elsewhere but also enjoys widespread support in the American public and some influential interest-groups in Washington—and, for that matter, Moscow. Some of its underlying assumptions and ramifications therefore deserve to be considered in detail. To begin with, it has been argued above that some of the fundamental presuppositions on which the official U.S. view of the Kremlin's interests and capabilities in the Middle East has been based are erroneous and that others have been overtaken by events. We may now reexamine this assertion by juxtaposing (1) America's own interests and capabilities in that region (as currently defined and implemented by Washington) and (2) Moscow's ability to affect them in a decisive or even a major fashion.

It is generally believed that the United States is preoccupied with the Middle East for a number of military, political and economic reasons.[j] The main ones are: petroleum, political stability, in the region as a whole and in the Arab-Israeli sector in particular, and apprehension about the extent of Soviet penetration and Moscow's ultimate intentions in the area, which is considered vital to the security of the Western world.

The main point about the relation of the USSR to Middle Eastern oil is that Moscow's ability seriously to interfere with its production, processing, transportation, and marketing is extremely limited. While the Soviets have encouraged the Arabs to nationalize the Western companies and to impose and prolong the embargo, the actions of the petroleum producers were not, as noted, a result of the Kremlin's exhortations. There is no reason to believe that this state of affairs will change in the foreseeable future.

Roughly the same conclusion applies to the problem of present and future political stability in the Middle East. Here one must distinguish between states where the USSR has acquired some political and economic influence and those which have refused to have any serious dealings with Moscow. Looking at the

[i]Until recently Libya looked like another possible intervention locale. But the recent introduction, as a result of the 1975 Soviet-Libyan arms deal, of hundreds of Soviet military advisers has made such an undertaking too risky to contemplate.

[j]A purely humanitarian concern is undoubtedly a factor, too, but because of its inherent vagueness and questionable effect on decision-making, it will be omitted from this discussion.

first category, and admitting for the sake of argument that the Soviets may be inclined to interfere in the domestic affairs of such countries as Egypt, Syria, Iraq, and others, years of experience have no doubt taught the Russians at least one important lesson: this is a risky and treacherous path to follow. Given the relative instability of Arab politics, any possible short-range gains from such "meddling" are not only bound to be temporary but may also be confidently expected to cause a counter-reaction in the country in question and among the Kremlin's other clients. Moreover, Moscow as a rule has attempted to work *through*, not against, the regimes in power. Needless to say, none of the above precludes the possibility of occasional Russian intrusions into the domestic politics of client-states, but to base U.S. policy on the assumption that this is the rule and not the exception in the Kremlin's behavior in the Middle East is to miss a very important historical lesson.

Turning to the second category of states, those which refuse to have any extensive contacts with the USSR, it may be assumed that some elements in Moscow are awaiting the overthrow of the traditionalist monarchies and their replacement by "progressive" regimes, which would mean a serious political defeat for the United States. Moreover, "progressives" would be more likely to establish and enlarge relations with the USSR and its satellites. But no matter what it wishes, there is little evidence to suggest that the Kremlin is in fact trying to subvert or overthrow traditionalist regimes. The Dhufar rebellion is the only known exception to this rule and even in this instance Moscow's involvement seems to have been undertaken with something less than joy and anticipation.

In short, whatever its preferences and expectations, the USSR seems to have approached the problem of political "de-stabilization" in the Middle East with relative caution. Washington's apprehension about Moscow's willingness and, for that matter, ability to effect such changes and to use them to its advantage has been exaggerated.

Much the same also applies to Soviet-U.S. naval competition. The conditions which influenced Washington's original decision to establish a naval presence in the Mediterranean no longer exist. Their place has now been taken by what may be called "vested interests" (and since the introduction of the Soviet squadron there this is true of the USSR as well) and by a number of generalizations used to justify the American position.

Thus there are frequent references to Russia's threat to NATO's "southern flank," its possible ambition to assist in the annihilation of Israel, and, generally, its desire to take over not only all of the Middle East and North Africa but Europe as well. What such views omit, however, is that any of these actions would bring the USSR into a direct military conflict with the United States and no serious-minded Soviet leader would therefore entertain them as viable options. As for NATO's "southern flank," the main threat to the alliance's effectiveness stems not from Russia but from its own members, as has been demonstrated by the latest Cyprus crisis and the domestic disarray in Italy and

Portugal. Neither the Sixth Fleet nor the *Polaris* force is equipped to deal with these internal political problems of the Western camp.

A more serious argument concerns the value of the Sixth Fleet and the *Polaris* submarines as an important strategic factor in the overall nuclear balance between the United States and the Soviet Union. While the combined capacity of these components of America's nuclear arsenal should not be underestimated, in the total nuclear equation they are an auxiliary force, ranking far behind the land and sea-based (*Poseidon*) ICBMs. Washington's capacity to deliver devastating nuclear strikes against Soviet territory would therefore not be significantly affected by an inability to attack enemy targets from the eastern Mediterranean.

Turning to the Arab-Israeli sector, it is equally questionable whether a physical U.S. presence in the Mediterranean is essential to insure the preservation of Israel, a goal to which the United States is clearly committed. If kept sufficiently supplied with military hardware, the Israelis give every evidence of being able to protect their own national security.[k] Of course, they could not do so if confronted directly by the USSR, but, primarily for the same reasons that an anti-NATO move seems improbable, a major Soviet military action against Israel is hardly within the realm of the possible.

To conclude, competition has not been without some advantages for both Washington and Moscow. For example, the latter has used the extensive U.S. presence in the Middle East as an excuse for, as well as an instrument of, its own penetration of the area. Conversely, the United States has been able to capitalize on the resulting fears of the conservative and/or anti-Russian and anti-Communist regimes to strengthen its own position, particularly in the "Northern Tier" states (Turkey, Iran, and Pakistan) and in the Persian Gulf. On balance, however, the superpowers' gains appear to have been offset by their liabilities. The extensive investments in money and/or prestige in such potentially highly explosive problem areas as the Arab-Israeli sector, the Persian Gulf, and Cyprus notwithstanding, the United States and the Soviet Union, while demonstrating a certain capacity to "manage" crises initiated by local participants, have consistently been unable to prevent them. In the resulting tension and wars the superpowers have faced the danger—however slight—of losing control and of embroiling themselves in a nuclear confrontation which neither side seeks or desires. By their presence and maneuvering they have also incurred the displeasure of a number of Mediterranean and Indian Ocean states, which resent the expansion of U.S. and Soviet influence and competition in their respective regions. Last but not least, the initial American military and political predom-

---

[k]The uncertainties of Portuguese politics have raised the question of the availability of the Azores Islands—an important refueling and maintenance base in the October 1973 arms airlift to Israel—and thus of American ability to deliver arms in time of another Middle Eastern crisis. While the denial of the base would constitute a major logistical problem, it is doubtful that it would make it impossible for the United States to assist Israel effectively, but given denial to the United States of the use of West European airbases for this purpose, it would be very difficult.

inance in the Middle East has not blocked either Soviet penetration of that area
or the establishment of a Soviet naval presence in the Mediterranean and Arabian
Seas. Conversely, the Kremlin, in spite of strenuous efforts, has failed to
neutralize the American underwater nuclear delivery systems operating in the
Mediterranean and capable of deployment in the Indian Ocean, or to weaken
decisively Washington's positions in the Middle East.

Accommodation and Cooperation

This option constitutes neither appeasement of or capitulation to the USSR nor
is it a panacea for all the manifold and complex international problems of the
Middle East. Instead, based on the recognition of the Soviet presence in that
region, this option implies internationalization and perhaps even institutionalization of some aspects of superpower rivalry in those carefully selected conflict
areas where objective preconditions for a mutually acceptable compromise
appear to be present. Among such preconditions are the following: the problems
involved affect the perceived interests of the superpowers and have led to a
stalemate or have reached a critical stage; there is reason to believe that the
parties to the dispute do not oppose or are actually interested in a peaceful
settlement of the conflict; and such a resolution would not affect adversely any
vital superpower interests. The best and perhaps the only example of a Middle
Eastern problem which meets all these requirements is the Arab-Israeli dispute.

A critical point in Israel's relations with its neighbors was reached during and
after the October 1973 war. As a result, Jerusalem, Cairo, Amman, and to a
lesser extent Damascus now appear to favor a peaceful settlement on terms
acceptable to them. There is no need to belabor the issue of superpower
involvement and Washington's long-standing desire to settle the conflict by
peaceful means. The big question mark, therefore, remains the attitude of the
USSR which, in the past, has used the Arab-Israeli dispute to strengthen and
enlarge its own positions in the Arab world.

However, some emerging trends make the prospects for a peaceful settlement
more hopeful. In the 1970s the Soviet stand on the Arab-Israeli problem has not
been nearly as inflexible as is commonly believed. Thus, as noted, in his 1972
and 1973 dealings with Nixon, Brezhnev agreed to the president's suggestion to
place the Arab-Israeli problem on the "back burner" in the obvious expectation
that future attempts to settle the issue would be undertaken jointly by both
superpowers. In so doing, the secretary-general clearly demonstrated his willingness to seek a resolution of the conflict, provided the USSR could play a role
commensurate with its superpower status and equal to that of the United States.
That nothing tangible emerged from this promising initiative cannot be blamed
exclusively on the Kremlin.

At present, there appear to be several specific reasons why the Kremlin may no longer be interested in maintaining tension and may go along with efforts to resolve the Arab-Israeli dispute.

1. General proliferation of weapons in that sector, including the introduction of medium-range ballistic missiles. This qualitative change in the balance of power between Israel and its neighbors has made "management of tension" a highly risky undertaking and increases the possibility of superpower involvement in any future Israeli-Arab confrontation.

2. Even if one discounts the possibility of another war, the current state of constant tension, marked by periodic two-way raids across the Israeli borders, pits the superpowers against each other politically. This situation has already adversely affected U.S.-USSR relations, or, to be more precise, the views of many in the West as to the genuineness of Brezhnev's commitment to détente.

3. The Kremlin might also like to see the conflict resolved lest constant political turmoil lead to further radicalization of Arab politics. This argument conflicts with the view of many Western observers, who maintain that radicalization is precisely what Moscow desires. However, the opposite may be true, as evidenced by Brezhnev's efforts to maintain close working relations with Syria and, to a lesser extent, Egypt (whose leaders are "radical" only with regard to Israel) and, in the context of Palestinian politics, to back Arafat against the Popular Front and other genuine radicals. This position is understandable: most of the "real" radicals are pro-Chinese in their philosophy and outlook, and the last thing Russia wants in the Arab East is the proliferation of pro-Peking sentiments.

4. Finally, being relatively realistic, the Soviet leaders are under no illusion as to the usefulness of their Arab "connection." They know that the USSR cannot easily control its clients and, for this reason, must regard their mutual relations as a "marriage of convenience" to be broken whenever circumstances so require. (Needless to say, this attitude is shared by the Arabs.) This point enables the Russians and the Arabs to be reasonably flexible in their dealings with each other.

It would thus appear that the time is now ripe for the resolution of the Arab-Israeli impasse, that most of the local actors appear willing to search for a formula which would be acceptable to them, and that the USSR is likely to go along with efforts at peaceful settlement, provided that its interests and right to be a full participant in the negotiations are recognized by Washington. Is it, therefore, advisable for the United States to continue searching for a solution through bilateral negotiations with Israel, Egypt, and Syria? Or should an attempt be made to transfer these efforts to Geneva, where the USSR would play an equal role as cochairman? Views on this subject have differed widely, not only in Washington and Jerusalem but also in Cairo and Damascus.

The latter course has much to recommend it. The limitations of the "stage-by-stage" approach have become all too painfully obvious. Not only has the second Egyptian-Israeli disengagement agreement seriously weakened President Sadat's position in the Arab world, but it has also raised the hope of millions of Egyptians for an early improvement in their living standards—an expectation which Sadat may not be able to meet because of the staggering problems facing his country's economy. Political and economic stagnation is likely to lead to his removal from power, a turn of events which would constitute a serious setback for U.S. policy in the Middle East. In contrast, the internationalization of the Arab-Israeli problem might not only offer a better chance of short-term success but is also essential for long-term peace and stability in that sector.

Deliberate exclusion of the USSR from efforts to establish peace between Israel and the Arabs may lead to Soviet attempts to sabotage them through the use of the Palestinian issue and exertion of whatever influence Moscow has in Egypt and Syria not to settle for anything less than complete satisfaction of all Arab demands. This is serious enough but is only half the story.

In approaching the Arab-Israeli problem, it is important to distinguish between a peace treaty and a meaningful and durable peace. The difficulties inherent in attempts to negotiate the former are very serious indeed. However, even if a peace treaty is eventually signed, the question of *real* peace will remain. Without Russia's cooperation this issue will remain unsolved and will lead inescapably to more, and more serious, trouble in the future.

A document certifying that peace has arrived after decades of bloodletting can be a worthless scrap of paper, as evidenced by developments in "postwar" Vietnam. There is no reason to assume that the Israelis will entrust their destiny to a piece of paper or that the parties concerned will not *have* to reassure themselves against all possible future contingencies. This means, above all, that their military establishments will have to be kept in a state of relative preparedness and will have to be equipped with modern weapons. In other words, the Arabs and the Israelis will continue to need great power support. Unless there is a previous understanding between Washington and Moscow, the latter's opportunities to fish in troubled waters will be almost limitless. In short, an agreement with the USSR is a *sine qua non* for the establishment of a durable peace in the Arab-Israeli sector; and to be effective it will have to embrace not only a superpower guarantee of the sovereignty, security, and territorial integrity of all parties concerned (including the Palestinians) but also a formal undertaking by all great powers to regulate arms supplies to this area. Recognition of Soviet political "parity" in the Middle East, one may well think, is a small enough price to pay for support in attaining these important objectives.

It could of course be argued that the legitimization of Moscow's presence and influence in the Middle East is bound to affect negatively the vital interests of the United States and of the region's pro-Western or "neutralist" governments. U.S. recognition of Moscow's "political parity" could be interpreted by the conservative and moderate regimes as a sign of indecision and vacillation in the face of the continuing Soviet pressure. Washington's international credibility, severely strained by the Vietnamese fiasco, could sink to new depths. This, in turn, could undermine the positions of moderate leaders, such as President Sadat and King Husayn, who seem to prefer a peaceful resolution of the Arab-Israeli conflict through cooperation with the United States (and exclusion of the USSR). Finally, a U.S. decision to compromise with the Soviet Union might strengthen the hand of those in the Kremlin who have long advocated an active Soviet policy in the Middle East by demonstrating that unceasing political pressure on the "capitalist" world does indeed pay off in the long run.

These are serious and weighty arguments. Nevertheless, it seems to this author that the major gain—settlement of the Arab-Israeli conflict—is likely to outweigh the short-range liabilities. In the long run, the possible resolution of one of the region's major political problems is bound to strengthen the moderate and conservative elements in the Arab world, for it would severely curtail the effectiveness of the radicals. Internationally, it would greatly decrease Egyptian and Syrian dependence on the USSR, a turn of events bound to please most Arabs as well as the Western powers because it would significantly reduce Moscow's opportunities to benefit from anti-Western feeling in the area.

In short, this writer believes that more can be gained by the United States in the Arab-Israeli sector through cooperation with than by opposition to the USSR, since the course which Moscow will follow will to a considerable extent depend on Washington. None of this means that all U.S.-Soviet differences in the Middle East can be resolved in the near future or that no competition—military and political—will remain. (This is particularly true of the Arabian Sea area.) But if superpower rivalry in the Arab-Israeli sector could be significantly reduced, an explosive time bomb would be defused and chances for a potential military confrontation between the United States and the Soviet Union would be greatly reduced. Such a development could only benefit all concerned.

Among other problems to which the principle of limited accommodation and cooperation might apply in the decades to come are the continuing superpower naval rivalry in the Mediterranean and the Indian Ocean and the ever-growing influx of ultra-modern weapons into the Middle East. Solutions to these problems which would be mutually acceptable to Washington and Moscow are probably not presently available. What if anything is done in the future will depend in part on the general progress (or the lack of it) of détente, the ability of the West to cope with its serious economic difficulties, and events in the Middle East over which the superpowers have traditionally exercised only limited control. It is not impossible, for example, that armed to the teeth, some Persian Gulf states might one day drift into a major war, confronting the United States and the Soviet Union with a situation not entirely dissimilar to the Arab-Israeli conflict of today.

Although for the sake of convenience options two and three have been discussed separately, there is no reason why some of the alternative courses of action suggested in them cannot be pursued simultaneously. More specifically, while agreeing to disagree in some problem-areas—such as the Persian Gulf and the Arabian Sea—where competition has not yet reached crisis proportions, the superpowers can attempt to negotiate in the Arab-Israeli sector, where tensions may once again approach a flash point in the not too distant future.

In the meantime, following its own unsuccessful attempts in the spring of 1975 to persuade the Arabs to iron out their differences and to present Israel and the United States with a united Soviet-Arab "front" at Geneva, the Kremlin has adopted a cautious "wait and see" policy. Publicly it insists that a resolution of the conflict can be undertaken only within the framework of the Geneva conference, in which the PLO must participate as an "interested party"; that, in exchange for Arab recognition of its right to exist as an independent state, Israel must abandon all the territories occupied in 1967; and that the "national rights" of the Palestinians must be recognized and guaranteed by all concerned. At the same time, the USSR has kept its other options open: in December 1975 Gromyko agreed to hold bilateral consultations with the United States regarding the resumption of the Middle East talks but refused Kissinger's proposal to convene a preparatory meeting of the original participants of the Geneva conference which would have excluded the PLO.

This Soviet position rests on an appreciation of the fact that chances for a major U.S.-sponsored breakthrough in the Middle East appear very small indeed in 1976. President Ford is not likely to antagonize the politically influential pro-Israeli segment of the American electorate in this election year, while it makes little sense for Jerusalem to make major concessions to what may well be a lame-duck administration. Since the pressure to produce a settlement is on the United States, Israel, and Egypt, the USSR may be expected to bide its time and await future developments. The only way for it to be excluded from the final settlement would be for Washington to apply sufficient pressure on Jerusalem to comply with Arab demands for the evacuation of the territories occupied in 1967. Since, as noted, in 1976 such an initiative is highly unlikely and since the future of American politics will remain clouded for the remainder of this year, the most prudent course for the USSR to follow would be simply to wait while reaffirming the "principled" Soviet approach to and stand on the settlement of the Arab-Israeli conflict. Not surprisingly, that is precisely what Brezhnev did in his February 24 speech before the Twenty-Fifth Party Congress.

VIII

Soviet
Policy
in
Asia

Thomas W. Robinson

The General Setting of Soviet Foreign Policy in Asia

The Soviet Union, geographically part of Asia since its formation (and before, considering the Soviet Union spatially continuous with Tsarist Russia), has been an Asian power of consequence since the 1920s, when it seized Outer Mongolia from China, and particularly since the late 1930s, when it forcibly turned back Japanese probing of the Siberian border. Recent Soviet concern with Asia dates, however, only from the end of World War II, the Communist rise to power in China, and Khrushchev's "forward" strategy in Asia. Since 1950 Asia has become an arena for Moscow's global competition with the United States and, later, for regional competition with China. Therefore, Soviet Asian policy is influenced by more than Russian history or anti-American cold war policies. It is in fact, the product of three sets of factors: historical determinants, domestic priorities, and global and regional political-economic relationships.

History continues to shape Soviet policy toward Asia. Until very recently, circumstances allowed the Russian-Soviet nation-state to give little emphasis to Asia, which made it possible to concentrate attention on Europe geographically and the United States strategically. These two areas posed the most serious threats to Russian security (the only exception, aside from China very recently, being Japan in the early part of the twentieth century) and it was in Europe, not the United States, that Soviet leaders saw anti-capitalist revolutionary potential. The Soviet Union, therefore, like Russia before it, faced West out of necessity and opportunity. When the West was preoccupied at home or in colonial areas, the Soviet Union, like its Russian predecessor, could live in relative peace. This was the situation during most of the nineteenth century and between the two world wars. When Western expansion was not possible in colonial regions, or when the European balance of power broke down, Russia (or the Soviet Union) became involved in European affairs. Twice during each of the last two centuries Russia became involved in Western wars—Napoleonic expansion and the Crimean War in the nineteenth century and the two world wars during the twentieth century. When the West was weak, Russia attempted to expand geographically or to recoup losses suffered from previous Western incursions, as at the ends of the Napoleonic era and of the two world wars. Throughout, a weak and divided Asia was not a factor in Russian policy.

Several times before 1950, however, Asia did play a major role in Moscow's calculations, all because of the rising power of Japan. In 1905 a weak Russia was defeated by a strong Japan—the first time that Russia had to fight in Asia. At the end of World War I, Japan temporarily occupied portions of Siberia. In 1937 a militaristic Japan probed the Soviet-Chinese border to test Soviet strength and resolve. And in 1945 a strong Soviet army, fresh from victory over the Nazis, pushed out the Japanese forces occupying Manchuria, thus paving the way for Chinese Communist occupation of important regions of northeast China. All four instances gave rise to the operational rule, in the Soviet mind, to be cautious, indeed, suspicious, of any strong Asian power and to neutralize that power in order to concentrate on more important European problems.

After 1950, however, the Asian situation changed fundamentally. Japan, the only historical threat to Russia, was critically weakened by the war and temporarily withdrew from conducting an active foreign policy. Its place was taken by the United States, who, allied with and occupying Japan, posed an even greater threat by virtue of its global posture and nuclear weaponry. China, historically weak, quickly recovered its strength through reunification under a Communist government. It was therefore natural for the Soviet Union to ally with Peking to balance the American-Japanese combination, thus preserving the Asian status quo and permitting Moscow to maintain its predominant interest in Europe. Later, however, Japan recovered its economic strength and China, disillusioned with the overly-close Soviet tie, broke away from it. This presented Soviet decisionmakers with the unprecedented danger, made worse after 1969 by the emerging Sino-American proto-coalition, of facing simultaneously three powerful and unfriendly states in Asia. For the first time, therefore, the condition of a relatively quiescent Asia as a requisite for an active policy elsewhere was not met and Moscow therefore had to divide its attention between Europe and Asia.

For Moscow other factors have also changed, some partially compensating for but others aggravating these unprecedented developments. Positively, Soviet power has grown so enormously that by the 1970s it could begin to challenge the United States in distant parts of the globe. This meant that despite Chinese unfriendliness and continued Japanese alliance with America, the Soviet Union could play an active role, particularly in South and Northeast Asia, where access was not blocked overland by China or by sea by the United States. From the mid-1950s, therefore, Moscow could afford to conduct its Asian policy without total reliance on European events. But this newly-developed ability was balanced by the necessity to confront the United States strategically everywhere and regionally in Europe and the Middle East, thus preempting energies and attention that might have made for greater Soviet involvement in Asia. Since the beginning of the cold war the Soviet Union has had to give priority to competing with the United States and maintaining its newly-won empire in East Europe. Even so, the Vietnam War, Soviet support of India, and the anti-Chinese Soviet military build-up in Siberia demonstrated that Moscow now could act in Asia as well when she so chose.

In evaluating the contribution of historical factors to current and future Soviet Asian policy, equal weight should be given to relative Soviet noninvolvement in the area, and to the fact that the current unprecedented situation undermines the determinative character of the past. The Soviet Union today must play a balance of power game in Asia, given Chinese, Japanese, and American power there. Moscow also finds that she can do so, albeit not as effectively as in Europe and the Middle East. Soviet decisionmakers nonetheless still remember past "lessons," however inapplicable they are today. One such "lesson" is that strong indigenous states (principally Japan, but now China as well) are a danger to Soviet security and cannot be trusted, even in alliance. Another is not to enter a Far East war with an opponent fighting at or near his home base, unless a deliberate buildup of Soviet force has previously occurred. A third is to avoid conflict when more important—e.g., European or global—matters demand attention. A fourth is to promote security through expanding Soviet-controlled territory (or, more likely, controlled by a malleable local government) whenever the principal opponent(s) in Asia are temporarily weak, usually as the result of war. Finally, history shows a Russian propensity to compromise with or neutralize a strong opponent by settling outstanding disputes or by pointing to common extra-regional dangers.

While history thus continues to affect Soviet policy, domestic limitations shape Soviet Asian involvement even more. Several basic characteristics of the Soviet Union limit or channel its involvement in Asia. Most Soviet populations, agriculturally productive land, and industry are in European Russia. The Soviet Far East is quite distant from Moscow and connected to it only by a thin and easily-interruptable line of communication. Siberia is still largely empty space, populated by a hardy few mostly located south of the Trans-Siberian railroad and quite close to the Chinese or Mongolian borders. The area is rich in natural resources and has an increasingly large industrial base, but the center of gravity of the Soviet Union will remain west of the Urals for the foreseeable future. So long as Siberian weather patterns, locations of transportation routes, population levels, and industrial trends continue along their present course, it is doubtful whether Soviet policy toward China or even Japan can be much more than defensive in character. Environmental limitations in Soviet Central Asia are less severe, but even there much of the land is marginal, lines of communication to South and Southwest Asia are thin and difficult, the population is largely minority peoples whose loyalty to Moscow is not total, and local industry is not so concentrated or so highly developed as in European Russia. The multinational character of the Soviet Union, half of whose population are non-Great Russian minorities often divided from their national brethren in South and East Asia, gives a defensive tone to Soviet policies toward states bordering on Soviet Central Asia.

Other domestic factors concern political and economic development and the status of the Soviet Communist party in the eyes of the people. Since the Bolshevik Revolution, the overriding tasks of the Soviet Communist party have been to forward the socio-political integration of the Soviet peoples; to develop the national economy in the most expeditious but still Socialist manner (even at the expense of consumer desires and the most rational mode of economic organization and productivity); to convince the population that the Party deserves to continue its overall leadership role and to retain its monopoly on ideology. The Party has succeeded, more or less, in all these respects, but the passage of time, the more advanced nature of the economy, and the increasing sophistication of some sectors of the population are precipitating major social changes. These threaten to undermine the Leninist character of the Party and to convert its leadership into a group more interested in preserving its own power and privileges and in enhancing bureaucratic socialism than in reinvigorating Marxist ideology and carrying out idealistic notions of social, if not political, democracy.

Many realize that the Party must reassert its control over negative trends and turn them in directions more compatible with its interests and goals. The resulting preoccupation with domestic affairs affects the attention which Party leaders give to foreign relations and dictates that as far as possible they be so managed as to give the Kremlin the greatest possible domestic freedom of maneuver. For this reason, as well as for others more strictly concerned with foreign policy, the Party pursues détente with the West; caution in the Middle East, where local conflicts could quickly lead to superpower confrontation; and balance of power politics as the best safeguard from military attack and for access to the "Third World," where today's important radical movements are found. In Asia this gives more impetus to Soviet policies of détente toward Japan; "correctness" combined with strength toward China; engagement with South Asia through support for India; and in Southeast Asia encouragement—to the extent possible consistent with its own military noninvolvement—of violent communist-led revolutionary movements.

Global security relationships, especially with the United States and China, are a third factor influencing Soviet Asian policy. Since the dawn of the nuclear age in 1945, Soviet decisionmakers have had to calculate every policy change from the viewpoint of the danger of nuclear war with the United States. Since Moscow's overriding interest from that time on has been to prevent nuclear destruction of the Soviet homeland, all other aspects of policy have become secondary, sometimes negotiable issues, despite their intrinsic importance under other circumstances. It is true that the fear of nuclear attack has gradually lessened and that other aspects of Soviet policy have correspondingly (although never totally) freed themselves from this constraint. This includes portions of Soviet Asian policy, especially after Moscow and Washington signed the nuclear test ban treaty in 1963 and the two superpowers subsequently negotiated a series of arms control measures.

Nonetheless, the freedom of maneuver for Soviet policy in nonnuclear matters is very limited: any issue, if it touches vital American, Soviet, or Chinese interests can be infused almost instantly with a nuclear content, however remote initially from strategic nuclear matters. The Soviet Union therefore must exercise caution in Asia even when dealing with nonnuclear states or nonmilitary issues. The best recent examples of this are Soviet policy toward Southeast Asia when America was intensely involved in the Vietnam conflict and Soviet policy toward China during and subsequent to the 1969 border crisis. As nuclear weapons spread to other Asian states—at present to India, but potentially also to Japan, South Korea, Taiwan, Pakistan, and Iran—Soviet policy must become increasingly circumspect. On the other hand, to the extent that arms control measures make the use of nuclear weapons less likely, Soviet Asian policy will have relatively greater freedom to pursue its goals. But given the increasing probability of nuclear proliferation and the ever-greater difficulty, therefore, of achieving meaningful arms limitation agreements, it seems likely that the nuclear weapons question will continue to limit Soviet behavior in Asia.

Global competition with the United States and China has nonnuclear dimensions that would continue even were nuclear weapons somehow to vanish. The very existence of that competition would bring the Soviet Union into direct conflict with the United States or China, if they did not also possess nuclear weapons. But the presence of nuclear weapons raises the stakes so high that an upper limit, albeit undefined and varying with the issue, if imposed on conflict, limiting its slowing down Soviet reaction time to other states' policy initiatives, and making minor issues more urgent. Nuclear weapons, therefore, limit nonnuclear conflict, but also infuse a military dimension into questions that initially have no such component. Like strongly-held ideologies, nuclear weapons penetrate other spheres at will and substitute their own standards of judgment for more traditional modes of conflict management.

The ideological factor is the last, although far from the least important, domestic element in forming Soviet Asian policy. It influences policy in three ways. First, Marxism-Leninism in its current Soviet version is a filter through which definition of all state interests must pass. Secondly, among other means, the Soviet Communist party seeks through ideological appeal to justify its continued monopoly of power over every sphere of domestic life. Categorizing the external world in Marxist-Leninist terms is one means of making good this claim. Third, because the Party wants to avoid domestic challenges to its supreme position, it portrays its foreign policy as the continuation of its domestic program and conducts its foreign relations, even with regard to seemingly nonideological matters, with an eye to their effect upon the Party's domestic status. It is true that in any concrete foreign policy situation ideology takes second place to practical goals and methods, and conflicts between ideology and "power" are usually resolved in favor of the latter. Nonetheless, the Party seems increasingly concerned about the declining degree to which the Soviet population supports Party initiatives for ideological as opposed to material or national interest reasons, and about the domestic effects of external criticism—especially from America and China—of the quality of its rule at home. Because it seeks to insulate domestic developments from the changes sweeping the external world, the Party is hypersensitive to attempts by foreign powers to involve themselves, even if only as critics, in Soviet domestic life.

The international component of Soviet ideology influences Soviet Asian policy directly. Stemming from the Leninist theory of imperialism, it categorizes major Asian trends in optimistic terms and, through addenda to the original formulation, explains why non-Communist Asian states achieved independence from Western colonialism and today pursue nationalistic policies that seem not to make them candidates for early communization. True, latter-day Leninist theory seems merely to rationalize these developments and not to influence policy determination greatly. Thus, such concepts as the "two-stage revolution," the "non-capitalist (but also non-Socialist) path," countries non-Socialist but "oriented toward socialism," "state capitalism," and "national democratic states" have been promulgated to explain why mixed socialist-capitalist neutralism, not communism, is the main current in the Third World. Soviet ideology also tries to show that the trend of events, despite appearances, if toward eventual socialization of the means of production under a bona fide (i.e., Soviet-oriented) Communist party. Despite these problems, theory does supply much of the vocabulary of intra-elite communication in Moscow concerning policy toward neutralist Asian states and it does influence the range of choices which Soviet decisionmakers feel are open and the probability they assign to alternative future developments. Hence ideology should not be discounted even when calculating probable Soviet short-term policies, while in the medium and long terms it exerts an important influence.

With regard to the seven Asian Communist states (six, if one counts North and South Vietnam as one state), Moscow adopts a different ideological position, since these states are within the "movement." It therefore assesses their policies in terms of their adherence to or deviation from the "true" Marxist-

Leninist course. But in contrast to the Soviet ideological stance towards non-Communist states, intra-movement ideological pronouncements tend to be very closely connected with "national interest" policies. The clearest example is the mutual reinforcement of these two aspects of Sino-Soviet relations since 1956. Soviet policymakers formulate policies toward other Asian Communist states and nonruling parties partially in terms of "proletarian internationalism"; approve the foreign policies of the other partners in the same terms when those policies accord with Soviet interests; categorize, by reference to the storehouse of ideological sins, policies not favorable to Soviet national or ideological interests; evaluate in similar terms the domestic policies of ruling and nonruling Asian Communist parties; and declare, if the occasion arises (as it might well with China), when and why a given Party has departed so far from the Soviet-established norm that it must be excommunicated from the "movement." Soviet ideological policy toward Asian Communist parties is not mere verbal window-dressing: a large percentage of the space in Soviet Asian policy journals and books is devoted to ideological matters, while Soviet policymakers talk as if ideological questions are important policy determinants and in many instances bend their policy decisions to accord with ideological norms. To be sure, nonideological matters are also important in Soviet relations with Asian Communist parties. But in contrast with Moscow's posture toward non-Communist states, the ideological factor within the "movement" is much more keenly felt and thus exerts more weight on Soviet policy toward Asian Communist parties.

A third set of factors influencing Soviet Asian policy is the regional international political setting in East, Southeast, and South Asia and its relationship to the two central global relationships: the strategic Sino-Soviet-American triangle and the economic triangle between the developed West—including Japan—, the non-Asian Socialist "commonwealth" headed by the Soviet Union, and the developing Third World, particularly the oil-exporting nations of the Middle East. Important intraregional political relations are bilateral: Sino-Soviet, Soviet-Japanese, and Soviet-Indian, as concerns Moscow; American relations with China, Vietnam, and India; and Sino-Japanese matters. But since the 1960s Moscow's Asian regional policies have greatly depended upon the global strategic triangle. Thus the changing status of Sino-Soviet, Soviet-American, and Sino-American competition has influenced the degree of Moscow's interest in and accessibility to Asia. During the early and mid-1950s, when China and Russia were friendly, the Soviet Union had access to the East Asian heartland. Because this also meant Soviet-American and Sino-American estrangement, Moscow had difficulty establishing intensive contacts with Japan, Southeast Asia, and India. After 1963 Soviet-American relations turned reasonably good, Sino-American ties remained poor, and Moscow's relations with China deteriorated, leading to Soviet exclusion from China itself and also from non-Communist Southeast Asia and, as a consequence, precipitating Soviet interest in improving relations with South Asia. When Sino-American relations improved after, and as a result of, Sino-Soviet military clashes in 1969, Russian interest in Japan and India increased, and it found access to Southeast Asia somewhat easier. While many other specific factors helped to determine Soviet policy, changing relations among the three major world powers are an important influence on Moscow's willingness and ability to involve itself in Asia.

The global strategic triangle is also important because it siphons off energies and attention that Moscow could otherwise invest directly in Asia. The Soviet Union must allocate a substantial portion of its available power to global competition with America and China. While the forms, kinds, and totality of Soviet power have risen vastly in the quarter-century since World War II, American power has increased as well and the residue of Moscow's own energies left over to pursue Asian goals has varied widely. The interrelated factors of global tripolar competition and relative Soviet and American power have dictated much of the level and kind of Soviet involvement in Asia. Thus, even though the Soviet Union showed great interest in South Asia from 1954 on, it was unable to make major investments in the area: the disparity between its power and that of the United States left little over for improving relations with "developing" countries, and the gross level of Soviet power was still far below the level where it could afford major involvement in those areas. Later, after the mid-1960s, the absolute level of Soviet power increased and Soviet-American competition became less critical as détente gathered momentum. Moscow's ability to involve itself in Asian matters correspondingly rose, and although the Vietnam conflict took up much of this, once direct great power participation in that war was past, the Soviet Union could increase its involvement greatly in Northeast, Southeast, and South Asia. The new security relationship with India, based on the Friendship Treaty of 1971, and the slowly emerging economic ties with Japan, keyed to a raw materials-industrial products exchange, show the Kremlin's unprecedented ability to back its political goals with the full panoply of policy instruments.

The growth in power of the other two members of the strategic triangle has powerfully influenced Moscow's participation in Asian affairs, particularly as concerns China after the late 1960s. The outbreak of border violence triggered major Soviet troop transfers to the Chinese frontier which, in conjunction with the end of the Vietnam conflict, led to wholesale changes in the Far Eastern military balance of power and to the political earthquakes of Sino-American détente, the Nixon "shocks" administered to Japan, and Soviet-sponsored Indian hegemony on the subcontinent. These developments might have occurred in any case, but their rapidity came in part from Chinese recovery from the Cultural Revolution and from the removal of the Vietnam albatross from around the American neck. The Soviet Union henceforth was "locked in" to intensive contact with Asia.

International economic relations historically have been of little concern to

Moscow, given its generally autarchic economy, relatively low level of international trade, and nonparticipation in capitalist international institutions. Recently, however, major world economic changes have materially affected Soviet economic policy toward Asia. One change is the increasing interpenetration of the economies of the capitalist West, including Japan, through multinational corporations and international monetary arrangements. The resultant increased rate and sophistication of technological progress in the West puts pressure on Soviet industry to modernize itself faster. Higher levels of Soviet trade with the West ensue as Moscow seeks to avail itself of the new technology. Because Japan is an important exporter of technology and finished industrial goods and because she desperately needs convenient and plentiful sources of raw materials, a natural (if still potential) confluence of interests exists with the Soviet Union, which needs Japanese goods and technology and which has in Siberia the resources the Japanese desire. And because of the competition with China for Japan's favor, Moscow has a political reason for improving its economic ties with Japan. Similar interests exist between the Soviet Union and the United States, although distance, geography, and politics have brought fewer results.

In Soviet economic relations with "developing" Asian states, such as India, the opposite tends to emerge: the Soviet Union can supply them with needed industrial goods (and to some extent agricultural products) in exchange for primary products and consumer goods. Here also, however, political criteria tend to govern the level of trade. The Soviet government has shied away from close economic ties with non-Socialist Asian states or with economies linked with the United States. This has reduced Soviet trade in Asia to an artificially low level, since most states in the region fall in one of these two categories. Since China is also a political opponent, trade with Peking has also fallen to low levels. One result of détente with the United States, however, is a rise in Soviet trade with Asian states associated with the West, while estrangement from China has led to more trade with China's Asian opponents.

The second economic triangle, between the developed West as a whole, the Soviet-led "Socialist commonwealth" (but not including China), and the resource-exporting Third World (particularly the Middle East), closely reflects the present political division of the world and hence appeals to Soviet policymakers as a way of categorizing international economic relations. Moscow can claim, with justification, membership along with the United States in both the strategic and economic triangles, can assert a natural economic and political harmony of interests with the Third World against the West, and can claim that the other economic triangle—comprising the United States, Europe, and Japan—is only one element in the larger whole. Soviet policy has not yet gone to these lengths— Moscow is still reacting cautiously to the precipitous economic and political changes resulting from the 1973 Organization of Petroleum Exporting Countries (OPEC) escalation of oil prices—but it seems likely that it will do so. The implications for Soviet Asian economic policy vary with the region under consideration and with Moscow's political relations with the United States and China, which are discussed below. Suffice it to say here that there are many contradictions between Soviet economic and political policies, that they are usually resolved in favor of political primacy, and that, given the importance to Soviet policy of relations with the United States, China, and the Middle East, Moscow's Asian economic policy is more likely to depend on global strategic and economic developments rather than on trends within Asia.

All of these factors—historical, domestic, and global—produce the general character of Soviet Asian policy. In addition, however, there are certain structural characteristics of Asian politics as a whole that, because they have not existed heretofore in their present combination, give a unique cast to the current situation. Because the rapidly increasing power of China has made global strategic politics triangular and because all three members of the strategic triangle are physically present in Asia (even the United States, which through Hawaii, Alaska, and its ties with Japan, Taiwan, and the Philippines, is an Asian territorial state), Asia is the geographic core of the triangle. Only in Asia, principally Northeast Asia, do all three have vital territorial interests. Asia is not the center of world politics; the European-Middle Eastern arena is, and only the Soviet Union and the United States are critically involved there. But given the territorial propinquity of the three major powers in Asia—and given the presence of the world's third economic power, Japan, adjacent to all three strategic nuclear states—Asia occupies an unprecedented place in world politics.

Three other factors add to the situation. First, the United States has committed itself to playing a major role in Asia. This contrasts with the past, when the United States, while never adopting the current European-style isolationist policy toward Asia, did vary the degree of its involvement and sometimes did not protect its Asian interests with the requisite means. There seems little likelihood that America will again voluntarily withdraw from Asia to the point where it need not be considered a major element in regional politics. As a global power, in competition with Russia and China, America must remain involved. Second, for the first time all the major Asian states are strong and active. Not only are America, China, and Russia all at or near the peak of their historic power, but Japan (despite its lack of a strong military and a nuclear capacity) and India (despite its domestic problems) are actively involved, simply because of their domestic strength (economic in Japan's case, military in India's). With the exception of Burma and Bangladesh, Asia is today composed of relatively strong states pursuing active foreign policies. Many of the suggestive parallels with the past thus no longer hold, although it remains true that to the extent that political relationships are determined by *relative* power status, past patterns may persist. Barring civil war, nuclear war, or major economic disaster, each of the major states of the area will continue to pursue activist policies. As a result, Soviet Asian policy will face conditions different from the past.

Third, the range of substantive issues at stake in Asia is also unique. There is the question of how to fit the enormous growth of Chinese economic and military power since 1950 into the overall framework. There is the issue of how to adjust to the newly active and permanent presence of the Soviet Union itself, which in the past was overcome by the combination of distance, the blocking effect of Chinese and South Asia geography, and the lack of available Russian resources. There is the problem of how to accommodate a now-nuclear India within the Asian strategic framework and, more importantly, how to prevent (if that is called for) or arrange for (if it seems wise) a nuclear Japan. There is the persistent problem of the divided states: Korea, and (to some extent) China itself. Can they be reunified without renewed war, and if not, can the continuation of the unnatural division be mitigated on the personal if not the political and economic levels? Finally, there is the increasingly important problem of how to industrialize and modernize Asian states while at the same time solving problems of energy and resource allocation, increasing food production and limiting population growth, and constructing a new and viable framework of international economic institutions.

The growth of Soviet power in the last thirty years has been so great that hardly a problem of international concern in Asia can now be settled without Soviet participation or without taking Soviet interests into account. But the concomitant growth of Japanese, Chinese, and American power has limited the effect of Soviet influence, and the quadrilateral nature of regional Asian politics (Japan is the fourth power in Northeast Asia, India in South Asia) has produced local balances of power that have so far severely limited Moscow's successful pursuit of its goals. In Northeast Asia, China has linked itself, albeit tentatively and in no formal manner, with Japan and the United States to render nearly stillborn Moscow's efforts to increase its influence in that region. In South Asia, China and the United States (and also Iran) have found a common interest in opposing expansion of Soviet involvement in the subcontinent, even though Moscow's ties with New Delhi are formalized by the new Friendship Treaty and neither Peking nor Washington possesses great influence in the Indian capital. But the Chinese military threat, the necessity for India (and Bangladesh) to accept continual emergency shipments of grain from the United States, and American-Chinese-Iranian protection of Pakistan balance the new Soviet involvement.

In Southeast Asia, the situation remains complicated despite the end of the Vietnam War and the associated conflicts in Cambodia and Laos. Here too, increasing Chinese and residual U.S. power greatly limited the degree of Russian penetration. The Soviet Union does have two ways of influencing Southeast Asia: the strong desire of the Vietnamese Communist regime not to become a Chinese satellite and the advantages of maritime-based trade, through which Moscow can increasingly appeal to indigenous regimes. Ultimately, however, the Soviet role in Southeast Asia depends on the sufferance of Peking and Washington as well as on events and attitudes within the region itself. As

Peking's power grows, Hanoi will increasingly be less able to maintain its autonomy, whenever Peking chooses to exert pressure. Presuming the continuation of Sino-Soviet discord, Moscow will thus be ever less able to intervene in favor of any pro-Soviet forces in the Vietnamese capital. And although some perceive that the Soviet Union now possesses a navy nearly the equivalent of the American navy itself, insecure lines of communication and the lack of attack carriers limit Soviet ability to protect its merchant marine in any major crisis. Thus, Soviet economic ties with Southeast Asia depend on the strength of Sino-American détente.

In all three regions of Asia, therefore, increasing Soviet involvement is being met with American and Chinese countermoves (even if indirect and often for quite different reasons), while Japan, which would otherwise have much to gain economically from closer Soviet ties, remains suspicious of Soviet intentions and is deterred by anticipation of negative Chinese and American reaction. Since the smaller Asian states tend to follow the American or the Chinese lead, the current situation is not favorable for a startlingly larger Soviet role in Asia.

Sino-Soviet Relations: The Key to Soviet Asian Policy

While many factors contribute to Soviet attitudes and policy toward Asia, Moscow's relations with the other global power, the United States, and its relations with the other major regional power, China, form the core of Soviet Asian policy. At present, however, Sino-Soviet relations form the most important of the three bipolar sides of the global strategic triangle, since détente, the term best descriptive of contemporary Soviet-American and Sino-American relations, depends primarily upon continued ideological and organizational disagreement, personal enmity, political hostility, and military confrontation between Moscow and Peking. Were either power to modify its bilateral relations and hence its policy toward the United States, the entire structure of international politics, as well as of Soviet Asian policy, would change as well. Given the dependency of international politics and the Soviet Asian policy on the nature of the strategic triangle, and the unstable nature of Sino-Soviet relations, extremely important modifications in either could result even from relatively small changes in Soviet or Chinese policies toward each other.

The present situation is made up of several elements, of which the most important is the military confrontation along or near the Sino-Soviet border. With over fifty divisions, a huge store of conventional and nuclear weapons, and a well-developed logistic infrastructure, the Soviet military can wreak tremendous damage upon almost any series of Chinese targets, occupy important parts of China if not all centers of power, and inflict very high casualties on any Chinese force confronting it. The Chinese have equivalent numbers of troops, an increasing quantity of modern arms and supporting equipment, a nuclear strike potential that will soon be able to reach the entire Soviet Union and can already destroy several Soviet Siberian and Far Eastern population centers, and an army and a populace that would make long-term Soviet occupation of large areas possible only at very high cost. The military situation is thus a stand-off and should continue so for the foreseeable future, barring unforeseen technological breakthroughs, massive new deployments, or conscious, erroneous, or irrational decisions to initiate military action.

A second element is the ideological differences between the two Communist capitals. These gestated for a long time (even before the Chinese Communists came to power in 1949), developed and came into the open in the late 1950s and early 1960s, and have been a major factor ever since. While details need not detain us, each Party spends much time and energy discrediting the ideological and organizational claims of the other and pointing to the purity of its own policy. Soviet and Chinese policies and interests are thereby skewed away from a wholly "rational" direction. These questions also affect Soviet and Chinese willingness (or reluctance, as the case may be) to provide material aid to, or support the domestic programs and foreign policies of, third countries. Further, they may modify or eschew policies which in the absence of the ideological dispute they would otherwise consider. For instance, the Soviets occasionally seem anxious to call an international Communist conference to read the Chinese out of the movement and appear willing to make concessions to East European and some nonruling parties if they attend the meeting and follow the Soviet lead. For their part, the Chinese use every forum possible to attack the Soviets, and their pronouncements always contain references to points of ideological and organizational differences, a good example being the anti-Soviet emphasis in Chinese speeches at the 1974 international population conference at Bucharest. Thus American policy toward Moscow and Peking must constantly consider how any initiative would be accepted ideologically in the two capitals.

A third element concerns personalities: the fact that some Soviet and Chinese leaders do not like to deal with their counterparts in the other country. This is particularly true of Mao Tse-tung himself, who has long held personally negative views of the Russian leadership, but it is also evident with many Russians. Much of the latter-day difficulties between the two parties and states can be traced to this element in Mao's personality; hence, some change in Chinese policy after the Party chairman dies, is probable. But the longer the present enmity continues, the more Soviet and Chinese decisionmakers will regard the other side as deficient in personal and national character, and the more difficult it will therefore be, to improve their relations in the post-Maoist period. The Soviets have allowed this to affect their official dealings with the Chinese less than have the Chinese, but even in Moscow there is a pronounced anti-Chinese atmosphere that stems as much from personal dislike of the present Chinese leadership as from disagreement with Chinese political and ideological inclinations.

A final element in contemporary Sino-Soviet relations is the historical legacy and the political policies that flow from it. Moscow-Peking ties are poor because past relationships have been poor. Trade, after having been almost totally ended, continues at an artificially low level. Cultural exchanges and movement of persons, having stopped, remain at a near-standstill. Suspicions as to motives, having been aroused, find confirmation whether or not facts support them. The longer present circumstances continue, therefore, the more difficult it will be to change.

What are some alternative future developments in Sino-Soviet relations that might affect Soviet-American relations and hence the fundamental character of international politics? In the short run, it seems likely that not much will change and that the relative freedom of action the United States now enjoys will continue. The reason, aside from the four factors outlined above, is that Mao Tse-tung personally determines the Chinese policy of enmity with the Soviets. As long as he is alive, there is little probability of any major change. But Mao is now quite elderly and may pass away at any time or become so enfeebled as to be effectively removed from having a major voice in new policy initiatives. The short run may thus indeed be short, although even three or four years can characterize a political era. But for the time being Sino-Soviet relations, and hence much of Soviet-American and Sino-American relations, depend upon the heartbeat of Mao Tse-tung.

Thereafter, three possibilities seem likely. The first is that the present relationship will endure with little modification. Patterns and habits having been ingrained, policies, to the extent that they accord with basic Soviet and Chinese interests, would continue. Attempts might be made to patch things up, much as after Khrushchev's fall in 1964, but would fail when both sides conclude that differences were too fundamental for post-Maoist decisionmakers to solve. Given the absence of Mao's personal imprint on Chinese policy (as well as, for that matter, of Chou En-lai's), however, Sino-Soviet relations would not get progressively worse. A de facto agreement could emerge preventing further deterioration in relations. Although no improvement would thereby come for some years, Moscow and Peking could count on a no-war no-peace scenario. Trade levels would remain low, military confrontation persist, diplomatic relations continue frosty, and the atmosphere of personal dislike and suspicion of motives endure. It is possible, under these assumptions, to imagine a modest slackening of tensions after Mao's passing. Marginal issues, such as the level and severity of mutual criticism or the lack of cultural or tourist connections, could be settled. The atmosphere would thus improve somewhat. But an agreement to disagree on ideological issues or to refrain from competing for the loyalty of foreign Communist parties or developing states would not be possible, nor would there be settlement of the border problem or mutual thinning out of troops along the boundary. Realizing anew the depths of their differences, the Soviets and the Chinese would return to their old habits and gird for a long, although not necessarily violent, struggle.

The second and third possibilities would probably occur, if at all, once the preliminary stages of the above procedure were completed. In the second case, Soviet and Chinese decisionmakers, gathered to sound each other out, would discover to their surprise that Mao's death had cleared the atmosphere and that the Chinese were now willing to talk in substantive terms and desirous of settling fratricidal ideological disputes. The border question, at the heart of the present difficulties, would be quickly solved. (The question can be solved now and only Chinese, i.e., Mao's, intransigence has prevented it.) A new and large trade agreement would be signed, cultural delegations and the flow of information increase, propaganda levels lower, and a commission be convened to discuss outstanding ideological questions. Such an outcome might require changes in the Soviet leadership, for some in the Brezhnev group seem committed to an anti-Chinese line.

The Soviets are trying to set the stage for such a massive improvement in their ties with Peking, so that when the opportune moment comes they will not have burned their bridges to the Chinese and made rapprochement impossible. Despite its occasionally stringent nature, the volume and tone of Moscow's propaganda is much less than it could be; their forebearing attitude in connection with Chinese spy charges and the seizure of a Soviet helicopter crew is calculated to encourage a more moderate Chinese attitude; and their general posture is one of disappointment at Chinese actions coupled with a wait-and-see attitude. Soviet policy, despite the military buildup and calls for an anti-Chinese Asian collective security system, thus hopes to set the stage for a post-Maoist rapprochement.

The third possibility would also occur at the end of a relatively short post-Maoist period of mutual testing. This time, however, Soviet and Chinese leaders would conclude that, because previous attitudes and policies persisted, each must gird for the worst. The military buildup would therefore resume and possibly even accelerate, and the Soviets would attempt to isolate China from possible allies and free themselves for military action. Border incidents and propaganda attacks would become more severe and more frequent, and a general atmosphere of fear and paranoia would grip both capitals. The stage would be set for Sino-Soviet war.

Third party involvement in a Sino-Soviet military conflict, if it did occur, would depend on its geographic extent, level of casualties, and type of weaponry used. Limited to nonnuclear land engagements causing relatively light losses in the border provinces only, such a war probably would not draw in outside parties, either to protect themselves and their interests or to support one of the two contending sides. At the other extreme, a conflict involving all forms of armaments, including nuclear, and inflicting high civilian as well as military casualties, could involve other states, not only East European Communist countries, but—in the (probable) event that China were the losing side or in the (even more probable) situation of lethal nuclear fallout settling upon Far Eastern and North American countries—the Western community as well. In any case, war between China and Russia would change the international political landscape immeasurably and disfigure Soviet and Chinese foreign policies, and hence world politics as a whole, for many decades.

It is useful to assign probabilities of outcome to each of these alternatives, and to evaluate them in terms of American interests and options. Events are influenced by a myriad of factors, not the least important of which is the order in which things happen. But it is possible to assign different likelihoods to the three possibilities (realizing that these are points along a spectrum of futures) based on the current situation, trends likely to move in some regular manner, and "feel" for the manner in which the various factors might fit together at a given moment.

To this writer, it seems probable that the third alternative, Sino-Soviet military conflict, will not occur. The risks for both sides are too great. The military balance is moving toward equality as Chinese nuclear and conventional levels increase. The time for a successful Soviet "surgical" strike on Chinese nuclear and rocket facilities has long passed; the Chinese will always have enough deliverable warheads left to destroy one or more Soviet cities, a risk unacceptable to the Kremlin. The rigidity that even low-level military conflict would give to every other aspect of Soviet and Chinese foreign policies is in itself probably too high a price to pay for winning a few battles. (A war, given the nature of the Soviet and Chinese nations, would never be "won.") On the other hand, military conflict could be initiated in circumstances similar to Soviet-American nuclear confrontation: a wildly irrational decisionmaker; misinterpretation of radar images, malfunction of early warning systems, and other such technical causes; or a political crisis coupled with military threats that might trigger military preemption.

If military conflict is increasingly unlikely, implications follow for the other two alternatives. An increasingly stable Sino-Soviet military balance may permit Soviet and Chinese decisionmakers to devote more attention and military might to other areas and situations. For the Soviet Union, this might mean increased willingness to involve itself in the Middle East, in an oil crisis-induced depression *cum* civil disruption in Italy, or in the coming Yugoslav succession crisis. Another possibility would stem from Soviet-Chinese efforts, once it became clear that the balance of forces between them had become stable, to come to some arms control agreement, thus enhancing the safety of the balance. Force reductions would provide both states with additional military force for use or potential use elsewhere. It might be possible to couple Soviet-Chinese reductions with East-West force reductions in Europe, depending upon the Soviet-American political atmosphere. In any case, a decrease in the probability of a Sino-Soviet military clash would free both parties for more active roles elsewhere and would remove one of the current bases of détente in Soviet-American (and Chinese-American) relations. The trade-off would thus be a reduction in Sino-Soviet tensions, with the resultant gain of having to worry less about Sino-Soviet war, in return for declining Soviet and Chinese propensities to continue the current emphasis upon "peaceful coexistence" with the United States and its allies.

Continuation of the first alternative, the status quo of frozen relationships, near-zero contacts, and mutual antagonism seems likely as long as Mao is alive and not totally retired from political activity. Mao will not live forever, however, and senility or even political pressure may force him to retire before his physical demise. He does appear to have succeeded in "vaccinating" the Chinese polity against the Soviet revisionist virus, and no Chinese leader now will publicly advocate mitigating the conflict with the Russians, much less setting it aside entirely. Nonetheless, all three recently-deposed Chinese military leaders (P'eng Teh-huai, Lo Jui-ch'ing, and Lin Piao) were accused of advocating just such a course, as was Mao's first-designated successor, Liu Shao-ch'i. Therefore, pressure for revision in Sino-Soviet relations will probably arise again. Without Mao to stop it, pressure to prolong current policy will decline, while, as we note below, the forces favoring Sino-Soviet rapprochement will probably increase.

The one "objective" (i.e., nonpersonality dependent) factor that favors current policy on both sides is the increasing relative power of China. Unless a combination of natural disasters and maladministration throws China off its present course of major yearly increases in industrial and military production, with the resultant ability to conduct a more active foreign policy, China is likely to close the gap, albeit slowly, between itself and the Soviet Union. Perceiving this, Soviet decisionmakers may opt not to seize the opportunity of détente or rapprochement with Peking but instead to prolong or even to intensify confrontation. This would be a major policy change for the Soviets, who currently maintain a watchful policy of waiting for Mao's demise, but it is possible that they may give up hope for improvement, especially if the post-Maoist group were disinclined to settle outstanding disputes with the Soviet Union.

The final alternative, détente, seems to be the most probable Sino-Soviet future. The current confrontation is in one sense ideologically "unnatural," for despite major differences of emphasis and priority and a long history of dispute, the conflict is an internecine one. Soviet and Chinese Marxists continue to hold in common important tenets of the faith, while their differences largely concern how to deal with the United States and its allies. Moreover, as Chinese society modernizes and industrializes, social disparities between the two countries (one reason for Chinese criticism of Soviet policies) will be mitigated. Soviet-style revisionism as a method of organizing society is the probable future for China, a fact that Liu Shao-ch'i clearly perceived and attempted to act upon. There will be other Liu's—Chinese modernizers—in the future.

The legal and procedural issues in the border negotiations are soluble at any time. The differences concern ownership of riverine islands, the boundary location at a number of other places including the Ussuri and Amur river dividing line, and the question of Soviet admission of the "unequal" nature of the pre-1971 border treaties. None but the ownership of the major island fronting on Khabarovsk is other than a minor issue, and that is soluble once the Chinese agree to cede their claim in return for Soviet claims to other islands amounting to approximately the same area. Once Chinese negotiators receive the go-ahead from the Chinese Politburo, a new agreement can be signed. The way will then be open to agreement on border military dispositions as well as talks on trade, cultural and intellectual contacts, and ideological differences.

Whether, and to what extent, détente thus defined becomes rapprochement will depend upon political imponderables in the Soviet Union and China and upon the policies of other states, especially the United States. This brings into focus American interests and options as concerns Sino-Soviet relations. First, it would be disastrous for the United States again to have to face a united Sino-Soviet bloc, this time immeasurably stronger than in the 1950s. Second, it follows that the United States has no interest in the solution of outstanding Sino-Soviet differences, unless major war between the two Communist giants would thereby be averted or unless resolution of differences was made part of, or led directly to, compensatory settlement of Soviet-American and Sino-American differences. Such a settlement could well involve Sino-Soviet-American nuclear and conventional arms control and disarmament; the overall Middle Eastern power distribution as it relates to energy and to Soviet, American, and possibly Chinese involvement in that region; and solutions to such "supranational" issues as environmental quality, world food production and distribution, and inflation. With regard to Sino-American relations, agreement would have to be reached on the Taiwan issue and hence the locus of the American embassy in China; some trade-off of American Far Eastern bases versus Chinese involvement in "national liberation movements" in Southeast Asia; a joint pledge to work towards peaceful solution of the Korean question; and possibly some *modus vivendi* in Southeast Asia.

Third, the United States is interested in the evolution of the domestic character of Soviet—and Chinese—societies in a more open, liberal, and democratic direction and would like to see the Sino-Soviet relationship not hinder those developments. Fourth, and most importantly, the United States is interested in a Sino-Soviet relationship that will maximize Washington's freedom of action in regard to the two Communist states and with respect to third states, regions, and issues. This means that America would not favor trends tending to reunite Moscow and Peking on the basis of an anti-American platform; that Washington would approve Sino-Soviet détente only if it measurably increased the probability of solution of "supranational" problems *and* bilateral Soviet-American and Sino-Soviet issues; and that the United States would seek to link Sino-Soviet rapprochement to an overall East-West settlement. In all these instances, the American interest indicates continual and close involvement in changing Sino-Soviet relations, seeks to triangularize bilateral Sino-Soviet developments inimical to its own policy goals, and attempts to adjust bilateral Soviet-American and Sino-American relations to compensate for—or even to preempt—renewed Sino-Soviet closeness.

Since prospects for a general international settlement are not good, it follows that the United States must try to forestall major changes, either meliorative or war-threatening, in Sino-Soviet relations, or to couple support of Sino-Soviet détente with further progress on important bilateral issues between Washington and the two Communist capitals. What options, keyed to the three alternative Sino-Soviet futures, does the United States possess in this regard or what options could it generate? With regard to the first alternative (no basic change in Sino-Soviet relations), perseverance with current policies is probably desirable, with perhaps some minor modifications. American policy has been to "treat the Soviet Union and China equally." This in practice means leaning to the Chinese side, since the United States had no dealings with Peking for so long, since China needed support during the post-March 1969 period of overt Soviet military threat, and since the Soviet Union is the greater military threat to the United States. If it desires to continue the present Sino-Soviet relationship, however, the United States might not wish to lean too far, lest the Soviet Union feel that it was being used in détente by Peking and Washington for their own ends. Thus, for instance, the granting of most favored nation status to China as means to promote rough trade equality might be withheld for a relatively short time until the Soviet Union is accorded the same treatment. Or conversely, Washington might feel that rising Soviet power requires leaning farther toward China to counterbalance it.

Another topic is progress on Strategic Arms Limitation Talks (SALT), Mutual and Balanced Force Reductions (MBFR), and related disarmament and arms control issues. Questions concerning any future Chinese participation are now turned aside by both delegations; i.e., the Sino-Soviet arms question and the emerging Chinese nuclear threat to the American homeland are separated, in public, from the Soviet-American talks. It is questionable how long this separation can continue, for at some point the Chinese nuclear force will become large and sophisticated enough to enter more than marginally into Moscow's and Washington's strategic calculations. To assure continual American progress with Moscow in this area, it might be useful to raise the question of bringing the Chinese into the various talks, noting that increasingly little time remains wherein separate Soviet-American agreements can be worked out. The implied alternative is initiation of Sino-American disarmament talks, which is to Moscow's disadvantage under current assumption, while the gain would be an earlier and perhaps more advantageous Soviet-U.S. agreement. On the other hand, any Soviet-American agreement that frees the Soviets to deal forcibly with the Chinese would destabilize the Sino-Soviet military situation and might contribute to eventual Sino-Soviet military conflict. In any case, fitting the Chinese into the overall strategic equation is an intricate and delicate process that must be initiated soon.

One way to buttress the status quo is to stress the Sino-American side of the triangle. One way to encourage the Soviets to intensify Soviet-American détente is to show steady progress in settling issues separating Peking and Washington. This is very difficult with respect to recognition, since it is tied to the question of the future of Taiwan. The United States may lack motivation to recognize Peking fully since it may consider it has done that for all intents and purposes in the liaison offices agreement and since the "evolution of forces" on Taiwan seems to be pointing toward eventual de jure or de facto political and economic independence from the Mainland. However, given Peking's dissatisfaction with the present arrangement, Washington might find it advantageous to propose full recognition and place a consulate-general, or even a Japanese-style trade office, in Taipei instead of a full embassy. On the trade question, the Chinese may change their minds as to the desirability of a large volume of exchange of goods if the balance continues to be one-sidedly in favor of the United States. To build the present temporary level of relations into a permanent factor in Sino-American relations and to forestall major improvement in Sino-Soviet trade, it might be useful to consider granting the Chinese most favored nation status. Finally, one factor in Sino-American relations capable of careful modulation is cultural exchanges, transportation routes, and tourism. While it has usually been China who has rejected American proposals, the United States does possess some cards, some of which could be used in a Soviet-American context. For instance, increased American tourism in China would help balance Sino-American trade and might prompt Moscow to increase the quality of their tourist services to Americans. Exchange of technical delegations and technical information with China where no such agreements with the Soviet Union exist might help Soviet-American negotiations in other areas. These examples show that changes in Sino-American relations will influence the Soviet-American relationship and that if American policy is to continue détente with Moscow, utilizing the Chinese connection, i.e., providing examples of American interest in prolonged détente with Peking, might prove quite helpful.

The second alternative Sino-Soviet future, détente leading to rapprochement, is difficult for the United States to deal with because most of the factors in its favor are beyond American control. So long as relaxation of tensions does not set the stage for a wholesale restructuring of relations between Moscow and Peking, Sino-Soviet détente would not necessarily be contrary to American interests in constructing a peaceful world and in solving "supranational" problems. Even with rapprochement, taking certain steps would encourage Moscow and Peking not to change their current, if separately motivated, orientation toward Washington of cooperation and joint solution of bilateral differences. The United States could continue to work with the Soviet Union and China on common problems but could hint that Sino-Soviet rapprochement might end or curtail mutually beneficial Soviet and Sino-American programs. A distinction should be made between generally beneficial marginal adjustments in the Sino-Soviet relationship (such as reducing the probability of major war through arms control measures) and major improvements (such as settling outstanding ideological differences or solving the border question *in toto*) that might prove detrimental to the United States. Having little to fear from the former, Washington could contribute to making Sino-Soviet (indeed, Sino-American) military conflict less probable, for instance, by transferring technology to the Chinese for a modern satellite-based early warning system against possible Soviet missile attack. This would also improve U.S. security vis-à-vis the Soviet Union by making Moscow less likely to launch a nuclear attack. As solution of "supranational" problems emerges as a central American interest, the United States might wish to contribute to working out new international institutions and mechanisms structured to make it easy for the Soviets and the Chinese to support them separately.

Thorough-going rapprochement would be contrary to American interests. Perhaps the only workable long-run policy to avoid it is to set up in the short term so many points of contact, joint ventures, and exchange programs that Moscow and Peking would be increasingly less tempted to cast off the Americans in favor of renewed 1950s-style ideological militancy, and be more inclined to continue along the current path of separately-developed bilateral ties with Washington. This is easier said than done because Chinese and Soviet goals are often at variance with American interests. Nonetheless, the United States does have several advantages. Russia and China desperately desire American technology, trade, and managerial skills. Building Soviet-American and Sino-American trade into a permanent and important factor in the planned economics of the two countries would help to continue good relations, and implied threats of greatly curtailing such programs would help convince Moscow and Peking not to carry rapprochement too far. While tourism, exchanges, and trade can be shut off almost instantly by either communist power, and should therefore not be counted on greatly to forestall major rapprochement, patterns once set up are broken only with difficulty. The same can be said for purchasing Chinese and Soviet raw materials, especially oil, to the extent that such commodities are available and are compatible with American policies of energy self-sufficiency.

In order to forestall rapprochement, the United States ought not to try to interfere overtly in the internal affairs of either Russia or China. There are short-term gains to be obtained from tying liberalization of American trade policy to liberalization of Soviet (and perhaps Chinese) emigration policy, but in the longer run Soviet (and perhaps Chinese) decisionmakers will become more and more resentful. Short-term gains are likely to backfire in the long run. In a post-Maoist situation, when the Soviets and some Chinese will argue strenuously for rapprochement, items such as the emigration issue, a relatively small matter in other situations, might be magnified many times.

Another area where the United States could build safeguards against anti-American rapprochement is strategic arms control. The Chinese factor is an under-the-table element in Soviet-American negotiations, not only because the Chinese refuse to begin such talks but also because the Chinese nuclear force is still too small to enter greatly into the calculations of the two sides. Because the time wherein this latter situation will continue is decreasing, the United States might well advise the Soviets of the necessity to come to a bilateral agreement speedily. Any such agreement would have to take Chinese reactions into account, in that the current atmosphere of lessened Sino-American antagonism would best not be clouded over by a Soviet-American strategic arms limitation agreement obviously disadvantageous to the Chinese. A point may also come when American interests (i.e., the size of the Chinese nuclear force) will dictate opening separate negotiations with the Chinese or pressing the Soviet jointly to invite Peking to participate openly in the negotiations. The results, *if* agreements were signed, would presumably be the same, but the probability of agreements emerging at all would be vitally affected by the manner in which they were arrived at. To prevent major Sino-Soviet rapprochement, Washington should keep the Chinese reasonably well informed as to American thinking while Soviet-American negotiations proceed (thus enhancing Chinese trust and "educating" Peking in the terminology of this field) and use the possibility of parallel Chinese-American negotiations to convince the Soviets to come to an early agreement.

The best of all possible worlds for the United States would be to sign a significant and realistic agreement with the Russians that recognized the Chinese component, tacitly or explicitly, and then to sign a similar agreement with the Chinese (although details would be different). If this were done before the prospect of major Sino-Soviet rapprochement increases greatly, Washington would possess separate binding agreements with both Moscow and Peking, safeguard the general strategic balance, promote all-around arms control, and minimize the desirability of Soviet-Chinese cooperation at its own expense.

A final area for forestalling Sino-Soviet rapprochement aimed at Washington concerns China's attempts to satisfy its national goals in Asia, to the extent they are consistent with American interests. China will be less interested in Moscow's blandishments if the United States continues to show interest in, and ability to aid, Peking in attaining long-sought goals. China's Asian interest is threefold: recovering Taiwan, providing for national security and economic development, and increasing her influence in surrounding regions. It is exceedingly difficult to satisfy Peking with regard to the Taiwan issue. Nonetheless, despite the evolution of the political and economic situation on Taiwan leading it even farther from reunion with the Mainland, one useful option would be to continue perceptible progress in upgrading relations with Peking and, by implication, lessening ties with Taipei, but in no case attempting to freeze the new status quo in some legal manner. Aside from upgrading the liaison office in Peking to embassy status (which implies full recognition) and downgrading the Taipei embassy to the consulate level, Washington could persist in decreasing the number of American military personnel on Taiwan. Both measures assume Peking's continued adherence to those clauses of the Shanghai Communiqué concerning nonuse of force in the Taiwan straits area.

Washington could sign an agreement with Peking concerning no first use of nuclear weapons, or indeed, give its blessings to proposals that non-Soviet Asian states, including China, sign some form of collective nonaggression agreement. Chinese desires to increase its influence in East, Southeast, and South Asia, so long as Chinese actions are nonviolent, are probably not inimical to American interests and could well be entertained. There is, further, no reason why China should not establish diplomatic ties with all the states of Asia and increase its levels of trade and cultural exchange. Such developments would tend to improve Sino-American trade imbalances, limit the spread of Soviet influence, and open China further to the beneficial influences (in American, if not Maoist eyes) of closer contact with foreign, especially Western, cultures.

We come, finally, to the alternative of deteriorating Sino-Soviet relations leading ultimately to war. While, as noted above, this prospect is increasingly unlikely, the situation could change were the military balance to move increasingly in Soviet favor or were Moscow's efforts to isolate China, diplomatically and militarily, to be more and more successful. The United States has options in each contingency. Active pursuit of strategic and conventional arms control measures contribute to a stable military balance. If Peking appeared to be in acute need of military hardware to stave off imminent Soviet attack, the United States could supply arms to China. Washington could, within legal limits and in accord with American interests, transfer some kinds of military technology to China, just as it could exchange strategic raw materials with Peking. More indirectly, the United States could adopt as a guiding diplomatic principle not to enter into agreements with the Soviet Union, or otherwise accede to Soviet efforts, which were obviously intended to isolate China diplomatically. For instance, during negotiations with the Soviets on European security and force reductions, the United States would wish to avoid allowing Moscow to greatly augment its troop strength against China. Following Soviet agreement mutually to withdraw troops from Central Europe, America and China might also jointly oppose Soviet-sponsored "collective security" arrangements in Asia that did not include both Washington and Peking.

As China grows stronger, however, and can increasingly counter the Soviet threat with her own power, the risk of Sino-Soviet war declines and with it American leverage in the Sino-Soviet relationship and in other arenas of world politics. At some juncture, Chinese strength will be great enough to retaliate with nearly equal effectiveness against most Soviet military initiatives. At that point, and probably long before it the risk of a Sino-Soviet war will decline significantly. Sino-Soviet options relevant to the United States will then be reduced to the choice between continued dispute and limitation of the level of differences through détente or rapprochement. Which way China will turn and what freedom the United States will have, in the superpower triangle, in other geographic areas, and with regard to important substantive issues, will depend on the imponderables: the timing and specific situations. But it will also depend on American actions taken ahead of time.

Two things seem clear whatever the details. One is that even a limited Sino-Soviet combination would be disastrous for the United States. This would be especially so in an era, as many presume the world is now entering, of American-led international cooperation and institution-building. The other is that the Soviet Union and China are rapidly increasing their power to project their influence in distant regions, while the United States, beset with internal difficulties and declining relative power abroad, will be increasingly ill-equipped to deal with a massive display of Soviet power or, in Asia, of Chinese power. The United States will therefore all the more need reliable allies in every area of the world. So long as the United States can maneuver between Russia and China to secure its own goals, American interests elsewhere will be safeguarded. But were Soviet and Chinese power to be ranged against the United States, together or separately, American abilities to build that "new world" of which it dreams will be severely limited. If joint search for new solutions and new institutions is to be the operative principle of American foreign policy, a major share of Washington's efforts must go to assuring, as a safeguard, the continuation and the expansion of the Western alliance, to integrating the Soviet Union and China, on a separate and piecemeal basis, into the new global system, and above all to discouraging Moscow and Peking from reuniting to fight a new cold war against the West.

Soviet Policy Toward Northeast Asia (Japan and Korea)

Soviet policy toward Northeast Asia centers on Japan. It derives from the historical background and domestic political factors mentioned, in the first section of this chapter and depends as well on global-regional relationships with the United States and China. With respect to Japan Moscow pursues the following goals. First, strategically, it attempts to loosen the bonds of the Japan-American Defense Treaty, which during the 1950s and early 1960s converted an otherwise demilitarized Japan into a *place d'armes* for potential American use against Soviet territory and discouraged Tokyo from major rearmament. Drawing Japan away from the United States while simultaneously preventing Sino-Japanese rapprochement remains the principal Soviet strategic-military interest in Northeast Asia. Moscow seeks to avoid having to face an unfriendly and armed Japan, prefers to see Tokyo unattached to either of Moscow's opponents in the global strategic triangle (and still weak militarily), and wishes ultimately to transfer Japanese political-military dependence to itself.

A second goal is economic. Noting Japan's near-total dependence upon external sources of raw materials and energy, perceiving the enormous productivity and scope of Japanese industry, and conscious of the underdevelopment of Siberia and its richness in natural resources, Moscow keenly wants an economic alliance between the two countries. Japanese industrial products, technical know-how, and capital would be exchanged for Soviet raw materials and energy so as organically to link Eastern and Pacific Russia with Japan. The purpose is as much political as economic, for a Japan economically tied to Russia would be less tempted to resume its historic course of military encroachment upon Russian territory, need less to retain close economic ties with America, and be less tempted to move into the Chinese economic embrace.

A third goal is political. The Soviet Union wishes to see Japan end its close ties with Washington, thus aiding Moscow's drive to break up the American-centered alliance system in Asia. On the other hand, the Kremlin does not want Japan to fall into Chinese hands or, worse, to add China to the Japanese-American alliance system, even if only informally. As long as Sino-Soviet enmity and Soviet-American global competition continue, Japan retains the option to go nuclear or to vastly increase her conventional forces, and Japan tends, as at present, to become more of a free agent in the Northeast Asian balance of power structure, Japan will be the center of Northeast Asian political maneuvering and Moscow will have to compete for her allegiance. Since Japan also wishes to attain *its* own economic and security goals, and assuming only marginal change in the current Asian political situation, Moscow will be unlikely to wrest Japan from her American tie. A close Chinese-Japanese connection appears equally unlikely as long as there is no radical shift to the left in Japanese domestic politics. A rational Japan would seek to balance between Moscow and Peking while retaining a generally pro-American stance, including retention of the Defense Treaty with the United States. Japan is pursuing such a policy at present. Moscow must thus be content to be one supplicant for Japanese favors.

Serious obstacles impede major improvement in Soviet-Japanese relations. The Soviet Union consistently scores lowest in public opinion polls in Japan, reflecting events at the end of World War II and historic Japanese suspicion of communism and of Russian intentions in the Pacific. There are major territorial differences between the two states, particularly about ownership of the four lower islands in the Kuriles chain, which have been in Soviet hands since 1945. Since 1955 Japan has pressed for their return, despite the fact that Tokyo formally renounced ownership of them in the San Francisco Peace Treaty of 1950. In recent years, Moscow has held out the prospect of possible return of at least of some of these four islands in order to induce large-scale Japanese investment in Siberia. While "real" Soviet intentions with regard to the islands are unclear (Moscow refused to consider Japanese Premier Tanaka's overtures in this regard during his visit in 1973 and Soviet Foreign Minister Gromyko was equally adamant during his 1975 Tokyo visit, largely because the question is closely tied to the Sino-Soviet border issue), it is doubtful that major changes in Soviet-Japanese relations can occur without agreement on this issue.

The economic question has two parts. There is the problem of fisheries, which, because prime fishing grounds are located near the disputed islands, has led to Soviet seizure of many Japanese vessels and therefore continuing friction. There are also disagreements over the exact terms of exchange between prospective Japanese investment in Siberia and Soviet shipments of raw materials. These include whether, and to what extent, the United States would join the venture and thus share the risk with the Japanese (and the abrogation of the Soviet-U.S. trade treaty therefore makes large-scale investment in Siberia less likely); the mode and timing of Soviet repayment of Japanese loans; the problem of very high Soviet investment requests (several billions of dollars); and the very long lead time before Siberian oil and other raw materials would be forthcoming.

Despite these obstacles, Soviet-Japanese relations could improve greatly were Soviet and Japanese policymakers to deem it worth their while. That depends not only on the solution to these problems (which in reality are negotiable "bargaining chips" to the Russians) but on the overall character of international politics in Northeast Asia, that is, on variables external to Soviet-Japanese relations. These include American-Japanese relations, Sino-Soviet relations, and Japanese domestic political changes.

Recent Japanese-American relations have been strained, although the framework of joint military security, mutual economic benefit, and political cooperation remains. In all three dimensions, however, Japan continues to move away from a relationship of intimacy with and dependence upon the United States toward greater autonomy and freedom in its international relations. Politically, America will cease to be the center of Japanese attention as Japanese regional and global concerns challenge the presumption that major policy changes must be first cleared with Washington. Economically, while heavy reliance on America as a source of raw materials and a market for finished goods will continue, Japan will increasingly diversify away from the United States in both respects. In the security area, as a result of American and Asian regional pressure, and the consequences of Vietnam, Japan will probably feel compelled to contribute more heavily to its own defense and may even feel the need to join a regional security organization, as long as the latter does not overtly threaten China or the Soviet Union. The real choice for Japan is whether it wishes to continue to purchase security protection through the American Treaty and hence to avoid remilitarization and/or the nuclear option; or whether its desire to free itself from excessive dependency upon America requires redefinition of its security interests and heavy rearmament. The long-term answer will be found in Japan's grand reassessment of its ties with Washington (which is presently a controlled if not an entirely rational process) and in changes in Chinese attitudes toward Tokyo, Sino-Soviet relations, and South Korea.

The future also depends heavily upon developments between Moscow and Peking. The previous section set forth three post-Maoist alternatives: continuation of the status quo, military conflict, and either détente or rapprochement. If the Moscow-Peking standoff continues, Tokyo can continue to move away from Washington while maintaining its principal alliance with the latter, balance politically between the two Communist capitals, and broaden its sources of supplies and markets. The Defense Treaty with Washington would probably be retained as insurance, but there would be little pressure for Japan to increase force levels or develop nuclear weapons. If a Sino-Soviet détente developed, Japan might continue to import Soviet and Chinese oil and other raw materials. But the drift away from America would probably halt as Japan sought to guard against rapprochement between the two Communist states. Depending on her reading of the international "atmosphere," Tokyo might augment the Self-Defense Forces and even look more closely at the nuclear option. Sino-Soviet rapprochement, on the other hand, would force Japan back into closer ties with the United States, as the pre-split world political situation would tend to reemerge. Under such circumstances, Japan would have little opportunity for economic diversification, the United States might insist that it share the Asian defense burden against the renewed Communist "threat," and perhaps pressure would build up within Japan to go nuclear. A Sino-Soviet war would also push Japan back toward the United States and, depending on the course of the conflict, would tend to draw America and Japan into a common defense arrangement against the Soviet Union. Internal pressures of nuclearization would probably rise greatly, depending on whether nuclear weapons were used in the Sino-Soviet conflict.

Since continuation of the existing situation or Sino-Soviet détente seem the most likely alternatives, and presuming that Japanese options in the security, economic, and political arenas depend heavily on Sino-Soviet developments, Japan could well continue its present Soviet policies with a reasonable prospect of success, particularly in the economic field. Tokyo and Moscow could proceed with joint ventures in Siberia, the Kuriles problem could be considered on its merits, and relations in general could improve. The less likely contingencies of Sino-Soviet rapprochement or conflict, however, would short-circuit contemporary trends in Soviet-Japanese developments in all three fields, although Soviet-Chinese military conflict might force Moscow to be more forthcoming on the islands question and, to the extent possible in the face of wartime needs, on Japanese development of Siberia. In general, however, these unpalatable futures would skew Soviet-Japanese relations away from its present direction.

Foreign policy questions are a central issue in Japanese domestic politics and parties and factions, and exert much more influence over politics than seem warranted by Japan's relatively favorable position in Asian and world politics. External developments, over which Japan has little control, thus are more important to internal political trends than in many other countries and often demand as much political attention as domestic questions, over which the parties do have some control. Foreign policy issues are often catalysts for leadership changes in the Liberal-Democratic party and are the central means by which the

Japanese Socialist and Communist parties attack the government. It is therefore impossible to discuss alternative domestic political futures in Japan without introducing the foreign policy variable at the outset. The major questions relate to what kind of ties Tokyo should maintain with Washington, particularly whether the Security Treaty should be retained; what China policy Japan should pursue; and what economic policies the country should adopt in face of the oil crisis and other problems of raw materials supply. Soviet policy, by comparison, rates relatively low on the scale of Japanese domestic political concerns, principally because of general agreement (except for the Moscow-oriented faction of the Japanese Communist party) that the Soviet Union, while the presumed "enemy," is not an immediate security threat; that little overall economic progress can be made with Moscow until the Kuriles dispute is settled; and that Asian regional relations with Moscow are the responsibility of the Americans operating on the global level. Thus Soviet-Japanese relations probably will continue not to be the occasion for the resignation of a prime minister, of factional conflict within the Liberal-Democratic party, or of major Socialist and Communist attacks upon Conservative rule.

Future ties between Tokyo and Moscow depend upon continuity and change in the internal Japanese political and economic order. Three major alternatives exist: movement to the political right; continuation of Liberal-Democratic (i.e., conservative) rule; and replacement of the present government by a coalition of leftists. Barring world economic collapse, there is small chance of rightward movement. That would mean Japan-centered nationalism, a highly active and even aggressive foreign policy, remilitarization and probably nuclearization, anti-foreignism and a neo-colonial search for economic dependencies. The most probable future is continuation of Liberal-Democratic domination in Tokyo. But while this might provide short-term policy stability, it would not necessarily lead to solution of Japan's problems or to long-term continuity in Soviet-Japanese relations. If the Liberal-Democrats were indeed able to master Japan's social and economic challenges, renew their ranks, and broaden their electoral base, and if there were no further external "shocks," the degree of national unity that could result might set the stage for a creative expansion of the Japanese role in Asian and world affairs. By contrast, lack of dynamic Liberal-Democratic leadership, for whatever reason, could lead to higher levels of popular dissatisfaction and intraparty disputes, and these in turn might result in transfer of power to an unstable Center-Left or Center-Right coalition unable to take decisive action. Somewhat less likely—but equally important—is a movement leftward. The probability of such an eventuality depends largely on intra Liberal-Democratic party factional struggles, on electoral judgment of conservative success in dealing with outstanding issues (mostly economic), and the resultant strength of the non-Communist Left.

Continuity in Japanese foreign policy is thus based in the domestic political sphere upon the quality and longevity of Liberal-Democratic rule in Tokyo.

Were that to be materially affected, through foreign events or the cumulation of domestic trends, radical changes in foreign policy orientations could result. Such trends exist today. One issue is whether the ruling party can effectively meet the dual challenge of rapid inflation and demands for major changes in social structure. If a serious depression were to hit Japan, perhaps through no fault of the government party, voters might blame the Liberal-Democrats and turn to some coalition (*if* it could be formed) of the two Socialist parties and Komeito. Another equally likely possibility could be the breaking up of the conservatives themselves, given their factional nature and their lack of a nationwide grassroots constituency, and formation of an alliance between some Liberal-Democrats and elements of the Socialist left. Were trends to move in either of these directions, and the conservatives (or at least the mainstream faction) to fall from power, Japanese foreign policy could be very different. The Japanese Socialist party, the Komeito, and the various Communists have all pledged to denounce the Security Treaty if they ever were to gain office. Given the ideological nature of their viewpoint and the length of time they have made this promise, they would no doubt do so. The Left has also promised to greatly improve relations with China, which together with cutting the bonds with Washington would fundamentally reorient Northeast Asian international politics. While these developments do not seem likely today, they are not out of the question. Even though the pressures of the international economic situation, together with possible changes in Sino-Soviet relations, might establish fairly narrow limits beyond which a new coalition could proceed only at its peril, governments often act contrary to the interests of the states they represent. Soviet policymakers would probably feel they had little choice, under such circumstances, but to gird militarily for the worst, cease economic cooperation with Japan, and attempt to work out a Soviet-American "containment" agreement to limit the scope of a new Sino-Japanese coalition.

Fortunately, many factors would forestall or mitigate political division of Northeast Asia into Sino-Japanese and Soviet-American camps. A more important issue, perhaps, is the circumstances under which Japan might develop a strategic nuclear force or even a local defense force based on nuclear warheads. The conservative government has kept this option open by presenting a number of conditions (which amount to escape clauses) under which it signed the Non-Proliferation Treaty, and has not yet pressed for the Treaty's ratification by the Diet. Moreover, although the Left does not now oppose the government's policy of "three nonnuclear principles"—neither to produce, possess, nor admit nuclear weapons into the country, the Socialist parties and the Komeito have stated that they would not close the door to the nuclear option were changed international circumstances to warrant it. There is thus some unity of views across the Japanese political spectrum concerning nuclear possibilities, summarized as an agreement that no overt moves will be taken unless the external situation forces Japan to depart from its present policy of abstention. But the various escape clauses in the Treaty itself (publicly noted by the Japanese government) and the multiplicity of "changed international circumstances" that could be used as an excuse for nuclearization make it entirely possible that *any* future government in Japan could decide in favor of it. The Soviet Union can, of course, influence that decision by not drastically revising its course of détente with the United States, separation from China, and rapprochement with Japan. A *major* change in any of these relationships, however, could set off a train of events in Japan leading eventually to nuclearization—although it is very unlikely that the Japanese would seize upon nonfundamental international political or economic changes as an excuse for going nuclear. The point is that Japanese warnings over this issue could limit the lengths to which Moscow can go in revising its own policies toward America, China, and Japan.

The Korean question is the other significant issue that affects Soviet Northeast Asian policy. Given the disparity in power between the two Koreas and the four major regional states, inter-Korean developments ought to be closely controlled by the overall balance of power. This theoretically correct statement accords reasonably well with the policies of the four extra-Korean states, all of whom recognize the dangers of renewed conflict. But the stalemate between the North, supported by China and the Soviet Union, and the South, supported by the United States and implicitly by Japan, is tentative internationally and unstable locally. Internationally, weakening post-Vietnam American resolve could lead to a corresponding decline in Soviet and Chinese propensities to hold back the North Korean leadership from launching a new invasion, just as an indication (to be sure, difficult to conceive under any realistic scenario) of declining military support for Pyongyang could lead to an adventurous military policy by a Seoul government desperate to recoup a deteriorating domestic political situation.

Locally, the balance between North and South Korea is unstable. While open to interpretation and composed of a large number of factors, the military balance seems to be inclining seriously toward the North, as both Russia and China compete for Kim Il-Sung's favor through supply of arms. This is distressingly similar to Hanoi's ability to arm itself for war in the South by playing Peking and Moscow off against each other. Of equal seriousness, the disparity between democratic pretentions and autocratic repression by the Pak Chung Hee government in Seoul, coupled with continued armed subversion from the North, could engender a degree of political instability in South Korea that the North might misinterpret as an ideal opportunity for invasion. Were this to develop in an atmosphere of uncertainty over the American commitment to defend the South (possibly exacerbated by public unwillingness to defend an unpopular Seoul government), together with Sino-Soviet rapprochement or successful Hanoi-style efforts by Kim to commit Moscow and Peking separately to back renewal of the war, the result could be a tragic rekindling of the conflict.

These international and local possibilities define the three courses open to

Soviet policymakers regarding Korea: support of the status quo, i.e., militant Northern confrontation with the South, but short of war; support for gradual North-South rapprochement; and backing a new Northern invasion of the South. The first two options require Moscow to influence Pyongyang to move in the opposite direction from what it desires and therefore requires holding out additional inducements or threatening to withhold, or actually doing so, present or future benefits. This means promising additional economic aid or withholding delivery of military supplies. Moscow's policy in either situation is governed more by its relations with Peking and Washington than with Pyongyang. Furtherance of the Sino-Soviet stalemate, for instance, together with détente with Washington and continued American support for the Republic of Korea, incline Moscow toward inducing Pyongyang to modify its attempts to sew discord in the South, if not encouraging Kim to sit down with Pak at a Korean love-feast. If the Sino-Soviet situation were to change in the direction of détente or even rapprochement, Moscow's policy toward Pyongyang would depend on whether its relations with Washington remained within the détente framework or whether there was a renewed bipolar tendency. The former, associated with Sino-Soviet détente, would make possible a coordinated carrot-and-stick policy by the two major Communist powers and the United States to force the Korean disputants to modify their total enmity. The latter, following from Sino-Soviet rapprochement, would probably lead to renewed Soviet-Chinese support for a forward North Korean policy reminiscent of the early 1950s and fraught, therefore, with extreme danger. In these and other instances, however, Soviet policy depends on factors over which it has only partial control: developments in the Korean peninsula, relations with Peking (which, as noted in the previous section, greatly depend upon events in China), the course of détente with Washington, and, were Tokyo to adopt an independent and active posture on the Korean question, domestic changes in Japan.

The multitude of factors and processes constituting the new structure of international politics in Northeast Asia present no clear and simply described set of alternative future regional arrangements. However, one can sketch the range of policy options open to Soviet decisionmakers and draw conclusions as to desirable policy options and instrumentalities available to the United States as it confronts a more active Soviet Union in this area. A prudent, state interest-centered policy would include the following particulars. Presuming that relations with China will not improve, that détente, even of a residual sort, with the United States will continue, and that Japanese politics will not move drastically left or right, Moscow's most important goal would be to forestall or discourage, through positive economic and possibly even territorial incentives, the formation of an anti-Soviet Japanese-Chinese coalition or, worse, a regional agreement between Japan, China, and the United States. Second, given Soviet memories of an aggressive Japan, the Kremlin must do all it can to prevent Tokyo from rearming and must especially discourage the Japanese from acquiring nuclear weapons. Moscow must convince Tokyo that the Soviet Union is neither a strategic nor a tactical military threat. In Soviet eyes, this means including Japan in a regional "collective" security arrangement, relying upon the United States to keep the Japanese satisfied within the Security Treaty, and influencing the Japanese left to work against remilitarization. Economically, Moscow wishes so to enmesh the Japanese in joint ventures in Siberia and to offer them so much petroleum and other raw materials that the Japanese economy will become ever more dependent, even if only partially, on Soviet raw materials. The trouble is that all these means of policy are weak reeds for Moscow since all depend on the cooperative or separate efforts of groups over whom Moscow has no real control. Moscow seems however, to have no other choice, given the absence of more effective instruments.

With respect to North Korea, under the same three assumptions just noted, Moscow would be wise to persist in discouraging Kim Il-Sung from violent military acts against the South, thus promoting Soviet-American détente. At the same time, however, to compete with Chinese influence in Pyongyang, the Soviet Union must continue to supply North Korea with military hardware, aid its economy, and verbally to cater to Kim's desire to take advantage of potential disorders in the South. A basic and inherently unresolvable contradiction thus exists in Moscow's North Korean policy which, given Soviet behavior in similar situations, will probably lead to the Russians incorporating both aspects within a single whole.

Ideological goals and means are not included in this version of a "prudent" Soviet policy. Ideology is, to be sure, not absent from Soviet motivational patterns or even from policy considerations. Moscow is, for instance, more in tune ideologically with leftist Japanese parties than with the conservative government and, given the persistence of Marxist thought patterns in the official Soviet mind, Moscow would like to create economic and political difficulties for the Liberal-Democrats. But Soviet influence over the Japanese left is limited and an ideologically-based policy toward Japan would leave Moscow open to American changes of a Soviet policy of selective détente. Moscow probably also favors substantial North Korean subversive efforts in the South, given that the Republic of Korea is allied with capitalist America and is ruled, in Russian eyes, by a combination of military and economic repression based on bourgeois class imperatives. But the costs are too great, again because such actions would cut one pillar away from détente with the United States and rekindle cold war passions in the West. Thus, because of the American presence in Japan and Korea and because of American global power (one of the initial reasons for a détente policy), the ideological element normally although decreasingly associated with Soviet foreign policy is severely limited, if not totally absent.

Presuming that these three assumptions continue to reflect international political reality, Soviet policy may continue as in the past. If it changes, it will do so not because of deliberate policy initiatives for long-term ideological reasons but as the result of reacting to events and policy departures adopted by states and parties independent of Moscow. Even if one varies the assumptions and presumes détente or rapprochement with China, Soviet policy would not change drastically nor have any significant additional freedom of policy initiative. If there were closer Sino-Soviet ties, for example, Japan might feel compelled to consider more carefully whether to invest heavily in Siberia and constrained to increase its armament. Both would represent heavy defeats for Moscow, but they would not necessarily replace the present policy of positive inducements with one emphasizing negative sanctions. Indeed, the latter would drive the Japanese even more quickly back to the Americans. Moreover, depending on how far Sino-Soviet détente proceeded, Soviet competition with Peking for more trade with Tokyo and for influence over the Japanese Left might continue. Only a major Sino-Soviet rapprochement would change Soviet policy toward Japan significantly, for it would force international politics back into the cold war bipolar mold. Given Japanese economic power and military potential and past Soviet-Japanese history, Moscow might not be willing to restructure its ties with Peking so drastically. Thus, paradoxically, Japan's relative autonomy within the Northeast Asian political system, its continuing ties with the United States, and its potential for playing a more active military role in Asia may all limit an eventual Sino-Soviet rapprochement.

One important conclusion stands out for future American policy in Northeast Asia toward the Soviet Union. By firmly supporting Japan and South Korea, economically, politically, and militarily, by encouraging them to deal with the Soviet Union, North Korea, and (in the case of Japan) China from domestic strength, and by providing a crucial element of strategic and economic stability, the United States channels Soviet policy into peaceful courses, forces Soviet policymakers to adopt an incremental and reactive approach, and points out to Moscow the undesirability of relying heavily on ideology in its short-term policy. The importance of maintaining formal security relationships with both Japan and South Korea seems apparent, as well as of cooperation with Japan to weather severe economic storms. More social discontent in Japan and South Korea would seem to be contrary to these ends. A Conservative party "drift" in Japan that might split the electorate between a strong Left and a strong Right would probably rigidify Soviet policy toward that country, as do repressive political practices in South Korea.

The dangers to American interests with regard to Japan and Korea are obvious: world economic collapse leading to a possibly fascist Japan; conservative inability to solve Japan's increasingly serious social problems leading to Liberal-Democrat downfall, a leftist government, and denunciation of the Security Treaty; reignition of the Korean conflict, partially caused by politically-induced disorders in the South; and, most importantly, reestablishment of Sino-Soviet ties of such warmth as to reverse Soviet-American and Sino-American détente and replace emerging multipolarity with renewed cold war bipolarity. But with the partial exception of Sino-Soviet changes and Moscow's role in inhibiting or encouraging a militant North Korean policy toward South Korea, the Soviet Union can influence these trends only marginally. Hence, American policymakers, concerned about a more active Soviet role in Northeast Asia, might give more priority to solving these problems than toward being overly concerned with possibly dysfunctional Soviet initiatives. Soviet power is growing rapidly in Northeast Asia, but Moscow can grapple with the issues in the region only indirectly and only through refraining from using its new strength.

Soviet Policy in Southeast Asia

Southeast Asia differs from Northeast Asia in several respects which affect Soviet behavior. No indigenous state can play a central role in world politics, although one regional state, Vietnam, threatens to dominate the area. The number of states is large (ten); there has been active Communist-non-Communist military conflict in nearly all of them; all (except perhaps Singapore) are economically underdeveloped; all except Thailand share a colonial past; and most are under military rule. Because of their proximity to the southern Chinese border, all regional states must take account of Peking's policy, especially when China is militarily strong and politically united. Until very recently the region could ignore the Soviet Union, whose interest went largely unnoticed and whose presence was not generally felt. Because of United States control of the seas, American territorial interests and nearby military bases, and cold war fears of Chinese intrusion, Washington, not Moscow has gained easy access to the region. Although Moscow can reach Southeast Asia from the Suez Canal or overland through East and South Asia, its degree of involvement is subject to the grace of China and the United States (and even Japan, were she to build a strong navy). This, together with Moscow's European and global strategic orientation, has meant that the Russians have lacked experience in Southeast Asian affairs. They entered the scene only in the mid-1950s and in earnest only in the 1960s.

Once they graduated from observer to participant status, however, Moscow quickly increased its involvement there. Particularly during the Khrushchev era, the Kremlin emphasized the presumed harmony of interests between the Soviet-led Socialist countries and the Third World. For a variety of reasons, the Soviets initially concentrated on two states, Indonesia and Burma. But the Sukarno-Indonesian Communist party fiasco of 1965, the increasing isolationism of Burma, the Soviet break with Peking, and the Vietnam War combined to forestall or render stillborn most Soviet initiatives in the region, cut off land access, and skewed Soviet concern from winning friends and influencing people to defense of a fellow Communist state from "imperialist" attack. By 1970, the Soviet Union had very little to show for its large investment in economic and military aid, propaganda, and policy attention. The 1970s showed no extensive

Soviet military or political presence in the region, no local Communist party or other "national liberation movement" responsive to its call, no client state, low trade levels, and no active program of economic aid. Its position twenty years after its first foray was therefore still weak, although, given its increasing power and continued interest (only whetted by the violent exacerbation of the Sino-Soviet conflict and American military withdrawal from Indo-China), Moscow could hope that things might improve. It therefore began a new campaign, which because of the more open atmosphere of global multipolarity and China's reemergence from its Cultural Revolution cocoon, augured reasonably well for the future.

All three of Moscow's goals in Southeast Asia reflect the Kremlin's difficulties in moving into the region and its more demanding concern with the strategic triangle. The first goal is to demonstrate its superpower status. The Soviet Union wishes to be accepted as a participant in all sectors of Asia, not just the Northeast, and wants its efforts in such areas as increased trade with, and establishment of a maritime presence in Southeast Asia to be understood as powerful instruments to that end and not to be ignored by anyone. Moscow has not yet been able to give definitive proof of the extent and permanence of its involvement along these lines, an indication of the high "start-up" costs of this venture. Second, the Soviet Union feels it must carry global competition with the United States and China into this region as well as others. Thus Moscow wants to reduce the American presence in Southeast Asia and to "contain" the spread of Chinese influence there as elsewhere. The danger, as the Kremlin sees it, is that Southeast Asia might become an arena for joint Sino-American competition, but with an unwritten agreement that both keep the Russians out. Soviet policy must forestall this eventuality, through constantly inserting itself into the interstices created by American-Chinese actions, appealing to local states (Communist and non-Communist alike) to maintain their independence from these two external powers through leaning toward the Soviet Union, and thus creating a Southeast Asia balance of power wherein Moscow can play the role of balancer. Two related subsidiary goals are: to prevent the resurgence of such an important Japanese role in the area that Moscow would find even less room for maneuver; and, in an era of Sino-Soviet differences, to lead local Communist parties and other radical movements away from Peking and back to Moscow. The third goal, also stemming from the Kremlin's role as a global power, is to ally the Socialist countries as a group (excluding China, for the moment) with most of the developing nations of the Third World. Southeast Asia is a crucial laboratory for showing this to be a workable arrangement benefiting both sides.

Merely listing these goals shows that even after Vietnam, Southeast Asia is not now of prime concern to Moscow, that its involvement is subject to more important aspects of Soviet policy elsewhere, and that the likelihood of attaining them depends critically upon the attitudes of local regimes, the United States, and China. Soviet policy, like that of every state, must adjust to the existing historical and political situation. But in Southeast Asia the decolonialization process, Chinese ability quickly to maximize its role, the Vietnam War and the Sino-Soviet split, and the Sino-American détente have all made so difficult Soviet attempts to exert influence that most of its efforts have not been worth their investment price. The Soviet Union has thus had little freedom to choose the time, place, or manner of its involvement. Khrushchev originally chose Indonesia and Burma because they were the only non-Communist regional states both decolonialized and not then in the American alliance system. Even with them the Soviet role depended on the fluctuations of their internal politics. In Indonesia, Moscow maximized its influence in the early 1960s but lost its advantage when Sukarno (and the Indonesian Communist party) turned to the Chinese as a counterweight and was excluded completely when he fell from power in 1965. In Burma, much propaganda, aid, and "friendship" missions came to naught because the Burmese government, despite its superficial Socialist attributes and its designation by Soviet ideologues as a "national democratic state," isolated itself from all external influences, whether from Moscow, Peking, or Washington.

Chinese and American activities in the region also heavily determined Soviet interest and investment. The pronounced Soviet activity in the mid-1960s was more a reaction to the stepped-up Chinese role in Indonesia and Indo-China than it was part of the Soviet drive in the developing world. And Moscow's failure to appeal effectively to local regimes as a convenient (i.e., powerful but distant) counter to Peking stems not merely from their leaders' fear of Chinese displeasure but also from their suspicions that Soviet intentions were not totally pure. Were China not so close and Russia not so far away, this might not have been the case and China might not have outdistanced the Russians in trade, aid, and military assistance in Southeast Asia. Peking thus determines much of the degree of Soviet success or failure in the region. It was, for instance, China that beat the Russians in the race for Sukarno's favor after 1963; it was China that made the better appeal to Sihanouk after his ouster from Cambodia in 1971 (the prince was in Moscow at the time and decided to set up his government-in-exile not in the Soviet capital but in Peking!); and it was Peking's public support for North Vietnamese military involvement in the South (together with great amounts of military aid, large numbers of paramilitary Chinese workers sent to the North, and broad utilization of South China as a secure base area for Hanoi) that first brought the Russians into the conflict and then set boundaries, along with the American military offensive, to their involvement.

The Vietnam War drew the United States into its near-disastrous military and economic role in the South and the combination of tactical military require-ments and hardware with which to wage it assured that the rest of Indo-China would eventually become involved. It was American participation that broad-ened Soviet participation: only then could Moscow influence Hanoi, through supply of critically needed war supplies, and thus demonstrate to Washington that the war could be settled only with Soviet cooperation. But Soviet participation had to be channeled through the North Vietnamese, and the Americans dominated the situation elsewhere in nonneutralist Southeast Asia. Hence, the war brought few long-term gains to Moscow. However, the end of intensive American participation did not spell the end of enhanced Soviet influence, because Hanoi found leaning toward Moscow was necessary to maintain its balance between the two major Communist powers and because only Moscow had the economic wherewithal to assist in reconstructing North and South Vietnam. Hanoi also feared that a vastly stronger China, combined with a Soviet propensity to switch its attention and resources away from Southeast Asia in its new global competition with the United States, would lessen Soviet interest. Hence, it held out inducements to Moscow.

The possibility in Russian eyes of joint Chinese-American condominium over Southeast Asia, the product of Soviet-induced Sino-American détente, also induced the Russians into the region. Moreover, greater Soviet accessibility stemmed as well from the more open, multipolar character of international politics and declining fears of military Chinese involvement. Even before the end of the Vietnam conflict, indigenous states tended to welcome a marginal Soviet presence, because they knew that Moscow was still weak locally and because Soviet activity could be closely controlled by their own acts and by the balance of power within the strategic triangle. Relative weakness thus had its advantages for Moscow—the Russians were not widely feared, their very novelty engendered curiosity, they posed no immediate threat to any regional state, and (other than providing military support for Hanoi) they were not involved in intraregional rivalries. Thus Soviet policy in the 1970s was as constrained by processes and policies over which they exerted no control as during the previous two decades.

The Soviet role in Southeast Asia, as distinct from its interest in the area, has therefore been determined by facts and forces over which it can exert little control: distance; more demanding resource and policy commitments to competition with America and China; Chinese land proximity and American maritime primacy; the Sino-Soviet split; and differing regional ideas as to how the area should be governed. Current Soviet policy toward several of the indigenous states, its posture concerning regionwide issues, and its proposals for addressing Asian economic and security problems as a whole all show, however, that the situation is changing, if still marginally. Moscow demonstrated through its actions in the Indo-China War that its interests must be taken into account. Despite the break in land access due to the conflict with China, the Russians proved they could resupply Hanoi with war materials; with the accelerating growth of the Soviet navy, they could do so again, even against American maritime opposition. Moscow has also shown new interest in the Philippines and Thailand, America's closest allies in the region: a trade agreement was signed with Thailand and in 1972 the Philippines sent the president's wife, Imelda

Marcos, to Moscow two years before her visit to Peking. Malaysia has become the object of much Soviet attention: several new large-scale economic aid projects have been started; the Soviets annually purchase a significant percentage of Malaysia's rubber output; and Malaysia seems willing to play ball with Moscow politically, expressing approval, for instance, of the Soviet collective security proposal, and seems to want to use Soviet influence in Southeast Asia to balance Peking. Singapore continues to receive several hundred Soviet merchant-men each year and allows Soviet ships to be repaired at its shipyards. Although Soviet relations with Indonesia still have not recovered from the attempted Communist coup of 1965, Indonesian debts to Moscow have been rescheduled and a Soviet deputy foreign minister visited Jakarta in 1974 to express his support for the Indonesian position on closure of ocean spaces between islands in the Indonesian archipelago. Finally, with regard to Cambodia, the Russians seem willing to take the low road and have recognized the new government in Pnom Penh even though their influence there is nil.

While this is not a catalogue of a successful policy, the overall Soviet position has improved notably compared with what it was a few years earlier. Moscow's basic strategy favors quiet diplomacy, trade and aid, and low-keyed persuasion. Because it has no major economic or territorial interests in the area (unlike, in its eyes, the Americans or the Chinese), Moscow declares that it can be trusted to pursue a policy advantageous to the region as a whole. Its collective security proposal, although not greeted with shouts of approval (indeed, most states in the area have reacted with confusion and suspicion), is at least being kept alive as one alternative form of regional security. Moreover, Moscow has professed at least some interest in supporting the principle of regional economic organization. Although it has attacked the Asia and Pacific Council (ASPAC) and remains ambivalent about the Association of Southeast Asian Nations (ASEAN), it supports the Economic and Social Commission for Asia and the Pacific (ESCAP), probably because, being a United Nations organ, it is susceptible to some Soviet direction and substitutes the one-nation one-vote principle for weighted voting arrangements. Finally, the Soviet navy is making its presence felt in Southeast Asian waters, a trend that will accelerate now that the Suez Canal has been re-opened and as the Soviet ship-building program produces increasing numbers of capital ships, especially aircraft carriers.

Although Moscow's Asian collective security proposal has received little Southeast Asian support, it might yet obtain a receptive hearing were the Russians to explain more clearly what they had in mind or were changed conditions to warrant greater interest. The form such a system would take seems reasonably clear. Patterned after the Soviet-Indian Friendship Treaty of 1971, the "system" would actually be a network of bilateral treaties, take the Soviet definition of "peaceful coexistence" as its operative principle, provide for arms limitation and perhaps even nuclear-free zones and encourage expanded trade and cultural relations. The Russians have in mind a gradual *process* of working collectively with Asian states to enhance all-around security. Although it would ultimately include China and Japan, it would take the place of existing military treaties in Asia as a whole. Russian purposes are threefold. First, the Soviet Union wishes to construct a *cordon sanitaire* around China. (Since China vehemently opposes the scheme, a system including all Asia states but Peking would be indistinguishable from an anti-Chinese alliance). Second, Moscow wants to fill the void it expects to be left by gradual American withdrawal from Asia and hopes to replace the American alliance system with one of its own. Finally, the Kremlin seeks to forestall new Asian security groupings that might exclude itself but include China. Despite the vagueness of Soviet pronouncements on the subject, two things seem clear: the Brezhnev-proposed system has nothing in common with traditional definitions of "collective security" ("collective defense" seems to be a more accurate term), and its time has not yet come in the eyes of Southeast Asian statesmen.

If the above reasonably accurately represents past and present Soviet positions in Southeast Asia, what of the future? As in Northeast Asia, much depends on developments over which the Russians have little or no control. And as before, many of the same factors are at work: the policies of indigenous states, particularly Vietnam; the course of Sino-Soviet relations; and the fate of Soviet-American détente. While it is impossible to forecast future policy choices for all ten Southeast Asian governments (and even if we could, they would probably not amount up to an integral whole), several regionwide trends seem apparent. First, the possibility of a rekindling of the Indo-China War is real as the Lao Dong-Viet Cong-Khmer Rouge-Pathet Lao attempt to expand, gradually but forcibly, into adjacent areas. The 1973-1974 "truce" in Vietnam was no more than that and ended because the Communists believed they had the requisite military means, because the United States was unwilling to respond in kind, and because their opponents, having been weakened through attrition, were unable to respond. Similar conditions in Thailand may produce similar results. Second, barring a major oil price roll-back, the area could gradually divide into beneficiaries of high raw materials prices (principally Indonesia and Malaysia, but possibly including Thailand) and the rest, who will become increasingly less well off by comparison. Third, a gradual multipolarization of regional politics could emerge to the extent that the Soviet Union were able to improve its situation being first content as balancer between America and China but later graduating to a status equal to the other two), and to the extent that local political divisions become more complex. In the latter instance, three possible groupings stand out: Communists (Vietnam, Cambodia, and Laos); a non-Communist coalition (Malaysia, Thailand, Indonesia, Singapore, and the Philippines); and the one hermit (Burma). Local and strategic groupings could unite, in the sense that local Communists probably would incline toward China (Hanoi possibly to Moscow, Pnom Penh to Peking), and local non-Communists toward the United States. Burma would have to hope for the best.

These possibilities depend, however, on continuation of the present division between Moscow and Peking and on prospects for further Soviet-American détente. As noted in the section above, this is only one of four possible outcomes. If Sino-Soviet détente replaced Sino-Soviet separation, the framework within which the above trends are projected would be distorted and the trends correspondingly skewed. For instance, détente would probably increase the chances of new Communist-non-Communist fighting in the region: Hanoi would tend to fear American intervention less, since Moscow and Peking now would more likely respond with "united action" to American threats of renewed intervention. Détente could also free Soviet and Chinese oil resources to rescue oil-poor have-nots in Southeast Asia, thus measurably enhancing their influence in those countries and even utilizing the oil weapon to force the United States (and even Japan) out of the region. Finally, détente between the two major communist states would tend to halt the trend toward multipolarity in Southeast Asia.

Sino-Soviet rapprochement would lead to severe modification of the three trends noted above and pose a serious danger to peace throughout the region. Sino-Soviet war, on the other hand, would so draw Soviet and Chinese resources away from the region that the local Hanoi-centered Communist military movements might find themselves facing their American-backed opponents without the traditional support of the two Communist giants. They might then opt for a truce, adopt the "peaceful path" to socialism, or even slowly decline in effectiveness. But since the scale and duration of Sino-Soviet fighting would heavily influence long-term prospects, the effects in Southeast Asia of such an eventuality are very difficult to foresee.

The prospects for Soviet-American détente also heavily condition Southeast Asian futures and Soviet policy. However, a prior consideration is that Soviet-American détente itself was endangered by Soviet support for North Vietnamese violations of the Paris agreements and conquest of South Vietnam; thus, at least one regional event could alter global Soviet-American relations. In the short run, Soviet-American relations were not as affected by the manner in which the war ended as by the subsequent freedom of movement elsewhere which it provided both to Washington and to Moscow.

Soviet policy in Southeast Asia will be visibly affected also by whether overall détente with Washington continues and on what basis. Continuation of one set of trends—slow but steady progress on arms control, steady American investment in Soviet industrial development, supply of grain in times of poor harvest, and a modicum of political and cultural contacts—would give Moscow the room for maneuver it desires in Southeast Asia and probably lead to its becoming a major participant in regional trends. America would in this scenario, countenance a more intense Soviet involvement on grounds that it was both innocuous and controllable. Presuming that Sino-Soviet relations remained bad, continued Soviet-American détente could lead to parallel efforts to counter the Chinese presence in Southeast Asia. On the other hand, curtailment of détente over such issues as the Soviet arms buildup and negative American assessment of the overall advantage of détente to the two sides could lead to resumption of overt Soviet-American rivalry in the region over such questions as Soviet arms supply to Communist Indo-China, naval maneuvers and base rights, and competition for purchase of the region's raw materials.

American policy choices in Southeast Asia vis-à-vis Soviet policy there are necessarily complex. Under present circumstances, Washington has little to fear from greater Soviet involvement in such areas as trade, shipping, and economic aid. There is, to be sure, the problem of Soviet supply of war materials to Hanoi for subversion of Thailand and Malaysia. A critical measure of détente, in fact, should be the lengths Moscow is willing to go to induce Hanoi to refrain from new ventures or from stepping up its present backing of Vietnamese-Khmer Rouge-Pathet Lao military activities outside of their respective states. Unless the United States makes clear its militant opposition to major changes by force in the post-Vietnam status quo, the Kremlin may feel it can with impunity increase its support beyond that minimally necessary for Hanoi's defensive safety. Just as in the Middle East, continued Soviet support for nonviolent resolution of local conflicts appears to be a condition of prolonged détente. This not only means constant checking on Soviet performance but also support for local governments and groups opposed to Communist expansion.

Aside from the military question, there is little reason why Moscow could not be allowed to increase its activity in Southeast Asia. Some Soviet energies would probably go to counter the Chinese, which would assist American efforts to resist what could become a major drive for regional influence. Some of the rest could assist local produce. As Southeast Asia industrializes, her peoples will be less tempted by—or less driven into the arms of—communism, which depends for success on ever-worsening economic and political conditions. Thus to the extent that an increased Soviet presence contributes to stability in both these spheres, it serves American interests. Washington has little to fear from a Southeast Asian situation in which all three global powers operate with relative equality. It would provide enough freedom of maneuver for local regimes to contribute to their overall betterment and it could avoid confrontations in which no alternatives other than fighting presented themselves.

Tolerating a larger Soviet role in Southeast Asia implies that the United States remains willing to make major investments in this critical area, that it stands ready to defend its remaining allies by force if need be, and that it is willing to make the expenditures necessary to play the multipolar balance of power game. Encouraging further Soviet entrance into the region presumes that Washington needs assistance in maintaining the status quo there (or arranging systemic changes only in a relatively slow and orderly manner), in two senses. First, when American resources are spread ever thinner and when demands at home are rising ever more quickly, it is useful to share the burden of regional peace-keeping and economic development with the Soviet Union, so long as no irreversible changes detrimental to American interests take place. Second, in an era when China is likely to become a much more influential force in Southeast Asia, possibly the equivalent of the United States itself, it is useful for Washington to balance it with the resources of another state, particularly those of the Soviet Union that the United States can monitor and, to some extent, control and even interdict if need be.

American interests seem to favor supporting the gradual establishment of a multipolar political system in Southeast Asia, in which America, China, and Russia would compete for the favors of local regimes, in which security within present boundaries is the *sine qua non* of regional international relations, and in which the local balance tends to move in tandem with the global strategic balance among the three and with the global economic balance between the American-led West, the Moscow-led East, and (possibly) the China-led Third World. Current Soviet goals seem to fall within these parameters, and thus no critical reason exists why Moscow could not play a greater role in Southeast Asia and contribute at the same time to American goals in the region.

Soviet Policy in the Indian Subcontinent

The Soviet position in, and attitude toward, the Indian subcontinent is fundamentally different from that toward East, Northeast, and Southeast Asia. Soviet access is direct and, despite natural barriers, relatively easy. There are no territorial disputes between Moscow and any of the eight states of the region, thanks principally to the nineteenth century British policy of protecting India by establishing buffer states whose boundaries were, for the most part, clearly marked out. As in colonial times, the region is dominated by one state, India, to which Moscow devotes most of its policy attention. In the mid-1960s the Soviet Union replaced the United States as the principal external power active in the region, and today is India's security guarantor against China and Pakistan. The subcontinent is the worst off of the four Asian regions: no state is economically developed and the entire region is beset with population, food, political, and social problems that are together nearly impossible to overcome. Despite India's explosion of a nuclear device and its predominant military position, neither it nor any other regional state poses any credible security threat to Soviet territory. The Soviet Union, involved in South Asia from nearly the beginning of its existence, since 1954 has consistently devoted to South Asia a high percentage of its entire investment in the developing world. Finally, the region is the only non-Chinese area of Asia where American influence is not paramount.

Soviet goals concerning South Asia stem directly from this environment, from Moscow's broader strategic objectives, and from the circumstances in which the Russians find themselves elsewhere in Asia. The Kremlin's most important purpose is to assure that the subcontinent will not be utilized by any power, internal or external to the area, as a staging ground for operations against Soviet territory. Land operations are hardly likely in an era of massive Soviet strength and of completion of the decolonialization process, but air or missile attack is within the realm of the possible. Thus the Soviet Union desires above all to keep America and China, the only two relevant states, out of South Asia. Having satisfied this aim, the Soviets can then work toward converting South Asia into a Russian sphere of influence. Their principal means is to be India's security guarantor and even to stand ready to be the neutral mediator of intraregional disputes. The Soviet-Indian Friendship Treaty is the symbol of the former and the Tashkent Agreement of the latter.

Once these two purposes are satisfied, Moscow can turn to more specific goals. One is to move the nations of the subcontinent, generally through alliance with the ruling elite (but depending also on mass pressure from below, when and to the extent that it is available), slowly toward the Russian understanding of Socialist, and ultimately Communist, rule. This seems a distant goal at best, given the lowly status of local Communist groupings and the strongly anti-Communist sentiments of the ruling elite of all regional states, to say nothing of the imposition of authoritarian nationalist rule in India. Nonetheless, the situation could change radically and rapidly were deteriorating economic conditions to generate armed political movements dedicated to overthrowing the established order.

The other Soviet purpose is to use South Asia as a jumping-off place for more direct access to Southeast Asia and as a staging area for outflanking China. A China threatened on three sides by Soviet power could hardly think of conducting an adventurous policy along the Sino-Soviet border or elsewhere in Asia. Were Soviet power ranged along China's borders in that manner—from Vladivostok to Gilgit to Burma—China would be "contained" in Asia and Russia could correctly claim to be the greatest power in Asia. Such an outcome is highly unlikely under present or foreseeable circumstances, but the Soviet drive for establishing a "collective security" system could provide a near-term substitute.

The remaining Soviet aims vis-à-vis South Asia are means to serve the above four goals. One is to be able to point to South Asia to demonstrate the benign nature of Soviet policy in Asia as a whole. To this end the Soviet Union invests a large percentage of its economic and technical aid budget, devotes much diplomatic activity, beams a considerable percentage of its propaganda and gives a relatively high proportion of her non-Middle Eastern military assistance to South Asia, principally to India. In addition, Moscow annually purchases as much of the region's industrial raw material produce as it can absorb, signs trade and barter agreements for large dollar volumes, gives as much agricultural aid as her own agrarian base will allow, and sends and receives numbers of cultural, educational, and tourist groups, again principally to India. Finally, Moscow seeks to utilize the subcontinent as a naval way-station between Suez and Singapore and to establish its newly-felt maritime strength by establishing a permanent Indian Ocean presence.

The first of these goals is already in hand and the Soviets are well along toward the second. The Soviet-Indian Friendship Treaty of August 1971 is essentially a security alliance that, despite its title, compromises Indian freedom of action and places Moscow, of the outside powers, in a preeminent position. By its provisions India may not ally with other states in manner incompatible with its spirit of Soviet protection; it may not sign agreements directed against Moscow; and must consult Moscow whenever any attack or threat of attack occurs, so that joint action may be taken. The treaty does not limit Indian freedom to enter arrangements with other states—the Indians even anticipate some *modus vivendi* with China—but it is a definite limitation upon New Delhi and is the primary vehicle for turning South Asia into a Soviet sphere of influence. Because India is now supreme on the subcontinent and because Soviet influence, combined with Sino-American opposition to the Gandhi government, has effectively eliminated Peking and Washington as serious competitors, the Soviet Union now has a position of unprecedented strength in the region. When coupled with a cautiously friendly attitude toward the Pakistan remnant and approval of India's own protectorship over Sikkim, Bhutan, and (to some extent) Nepal, Moscow is in as solid a position as any external power could be to have a major voice in future South Asian affairs.

India knows this and, with some reservations, approves it. It was, after all, the Soviet Union that equipped the Indian military, built a large share of India's heavy industry, bought Indian industrial produce and raw materials to provide short-term markets, and supported New Delhi in such international fora as the United Nations. Moreover, there is room for still greater Soviet involvement in India. Moscow can encourage New Delhi to tie the Indian economy to its own through coordinated five-year plans; push India into stronger declaratory statements against American and Chinese policy in South Asia; "suggest" that India reduce educational and cultural ties with the West; press the Indian leadership to nationalize Western-owned enterprises in the country and adopt other economic measures moving the Congress party leftward; obtain basing rights (or at least repair and refueling rights) for the expanding Soviet Indian Ocean navy and urge the Indians to help promote Moscow's Asian collective security proposal.

Neither China nor America has influence in India anywhere near to that of Russia, nor can they move India quickly away from Moscow. Nonetheless, major obstacles impede further movement in Moscow's direction, and the Kremlin's influence in New Delhi may have peaked. The principal limitations come from the Indian leadership itself. Jealous to guard its new power and aware that the Soviet Union is not expending huge sums merely as India's disinterested benefactor, the Congress party shows signs of discomfort as the Russian bear-hug tightens. What opposition there is to Mrs. Gandhi, although cowed, is basically anti-Soviet, which may also inhibit Indian cordiality toward the Soviet Union. India is also aware that it has lost considerable status in the Third World by trying to divorce her pretentions to leadership of the nonaligned states from its obvious lack of neutrality and its dependence on the Soviet Union. Moreover, New Delhi worries, rightly, that its value to Moscow might quickly decline in the wake of a Sino-Soviet détente. Finally, India knows that the Soviet Union neither has the agricultural surpluses to feed the increasingly large multitude of the hungry throughout the region, nor will go on indefinitely funding (and refunding) the large Indian repayments debt to Moscow.

The United States, principally, and China, secondly, of the external actors, can, if they wish, bail New Delhi out of its excessive reliance on Moscow. Only the United States can supply the food and other economic assistance necessary and counter the Soviet drive to enhance its security position in South Asia and in the Indian Ocean. Only China can lessen its border conflict with India, the chief reason for India's security tie with Moscow in the first place, first, as it has, by normalizing relations and then by resuming border negotiations. The Indian position itself has also strengthened and could lead eventually to declining dependence on Moscow. The most obvious example is its acquisition of an initial nuclear capability. New Delhi has also required a significant conventional weapons production capability, lessening its need to purchase military hardware from the Russians. Moreover, the Emergency Decrees give New Delhi new ability to address Indian domestic socioeconomic problems with greater probability of success. Finally, with Pakistan reduced in territory through the secession of Bangladesh and the danger of a two-front war consequently eliminated, India's need for Soviet military support is considerably reduced.

India wants to dominate the subcontinent, and this accords perfectly with short-term Soviet goals. But to buy back its own independence from Moscow, New Delhi may have to take out insurance, if it is offered, with Washington and Peking. India would like to be able to control Chinese and American advances so as to maximize its benefits from both (political in the case of China, economic in the case of the United States) and then to use them to blackmail the Soviets into agreeing to further Indian political domination of adjacent regions and to give India more financial and economic aid. The Indian leadership might thus bring the Americans and the Chinese back into the picture.

Would the two powers understand and cooperate with Indian attempts so to use them? India is now the prisoner of Chinese hostility and American indifference, and both powers see advantages in prolonging their estrangements from New Delhi. Aside from their differing abilities to influence Indian policy directly, each can indirectly pressure the Indians. Both can continue, and even increase, their support for Pakistan, and both can become more involved in Bangladesh (America positively by providing food and other assistance and China negatively by stepping up its support for local radicals). This would be the easier because the new rulers in Dacca are much less pro-Soviet and pro-Indian than the late Sheikh Mujibur Rahman was. The United States can continue to "punish" Indira Gandhi for her own anti-American and domestic authoritarian policies by changes in aid policies and symbolic diplomatic coldness. This would tend to drive India even further into the Soviet embrace, to be sure, but New Delhi might fear that this would irreversibly compromise its independence and would surely end its regional supremacy. India may therefore be concluding that it should compromise with the Americans, the Chinese, and the Pakistanis rather than sell itself further to the Russians. The unpalatable alternative would be the reestablishment of a balance of power on the subcontinent—a Soviet-Indian combination against an American-Chinese-Pakistani grouping. While the latter has shortcomings (principally Pakistani weakness), the possibility of such a split is a danger that India seems not to wish to confront.

Three other complicating factors could influence developments. One is strategic rivalry between the United States, the Soviet Union, and China, particularly for using the Indian Ocean as a station for nuclear missile submarines. The Soviet Union and the United States also seem determined to station surface warships there. The opening of the Suez Canal will accelerate this process by the Soviet Union. Both seek base rights in the littoral states or on mid-ocean islands to support their respective fleets. With the advent of American Trident nuclear missile-firing submarines, nuclear warheads can be fired from the Indian Ocean at comparatively short range at most Soviet territory, overflying South Asia en route. As the United States develops Diego Garcia as a base, the Soviet Union undoubtedly will seek similar facilities on the East African coast or in India itself. Under present plans, neither state will emplace large fleets in the Indian Ocean, although even the presence of aircraft carriers, along with nuclear submarines, might be taken by India, Pakistan, or Iran as a security threat. To the extent that the American fleet adds protection to Pakistan, it will become a part of the overall military balance of power in South Asia. Given Indian sensibilities, New Delhi is then likely either to grant base rights to the Soviets or to augment its own fleet in the Indian Ocean—or, more likely, do both.

The Soviet-American naval arms race which is beginning in the Indian Ocean thus could lead to a greatly augmented Soviet presence there and further compromise Indian sovereignty. Seemingly little can be done about this. The United States and the Soviet Union are not about to agree to stay out of the area. The United States views the global strategic equation as in need of balance by new American nuclear submarines in the Indian Ocean. Because the Soviet-Indian alliance has tipped the balance so seriously against Pakistan, Washington may feel that Pakistan needs the protection that a surface fleet, a quick and convenient means of changing the balance of power, could provide.

A second factor may enter the South Asian balance of power. Iran is significantly increasing its military and economic power in the region. Like American and Chinese policy, Iranian interests with India and the Indian Ocean naval situation center on opposition to Soviet expansion. In addition, however, Iran feels a religious affinity for Pakistan and for that and ethnic reasons (Baluchis in both countries) it desires to preserve that state from further territorial losses to India. This interest too, it shares with America and China. The Shah, moreover, has used his new-found economic power to gain influence in New Delhi, as was shown by his visit to the Indian capital in 1974, and elsewhere in South Asia. Although Iran is currently, like India, asserting a greater degree of regional autonomy against all three of the outside big powers, there is a pronounced anti-Soviet (and, to some extent, pro-American) bias in Tehran's attitudes, born of historic Iranian suspicions of Russian intentions and concern in the future over excessive Soviet economic and political influence in New Delhi and potential Soviet military threats from the Indian Ocean. Given the oil price/international finance crisis, the Shah holds important economic cards with which he can spread Iranian influence, preserve Pakistani autonomy, and limit Soviet power in the subcontinent, and he can exchange some of those cards with the United States for military chips. The Shah has granted India large-scale, low-interest credits for Iranian oil, for which he undoubtedly expects to obtain a political *quid pro quo*: the limitation of Soviet influence in India. Moreover, the rising power of the Iranian navy will within five years become a major factor in the Indian Ocean. The Shah plays a cooperative game with the Indian prime minister because they share interests vis-à-vis the outside world and because economic power often counts more heavily these days than does an equivalent investment in military hardware. This will probably continue for the foreseeable future, but at some point in the growth of Iranian power, Tehran's economic and security interests may diverge from those of India. Kremlin policymakers may then find themselves forced into a closer embrace with New Delhi than even they would like, as Iran, Pakistan, and China (and perhaps the United States) gradually form an anti-Soviet *entente*.

The third factor is China and future Sino-Soviet relations. The second section of this chapter has shown that the prospects for change in these relations are great, principally with respect to détente and/or rapprochement. If either were to occur in the post-Maoist period, the South Asian situation could change considerably. Détente would dampen Soviet enthusiasm for investing so much of its energies in India, since Moscow's anti-Chinese motivations would have decreased. Chinese support for Pakistan would correspondingly diminish. Sino-Indian relations might or might not change, depending on the nature of the post-Maoist regime and the degree to which détente approached rapprochement. While the resultant interstate relations in South Asia would not necessarily return precisely to their pre-Sino-Soviet split status (Soviet interest in India antedated the split, and the growth in India power has made it unlikely that Moscow and Peking could push New Delhi around at will), there would probably be a tendency for Russia and India to fall apart and for India and America to reestablish closer ties.

These new factors could operate simultaneously in the coming years, since none depend upon the prior occurrence of the others. Moreover, all would change the present situation, now dominated by the Soviet-Indian alliance, toward more closely balanced relations and toward recovery of American influence in the subcontinent. Thus, *if* it be judged that American interests should center on opposing Soviet security overlordship in South Asia *as a whole*, stationing an American fleet in the Indian Ocean and encouraging the build-up of Iranian military power are two ways of doing so. On the other hand, American interests could also concentrate on maintaining good relations with India, on helping to establish peaceful relations between India and Pakistan, and on removing excess Soviet influence from the subcontinent in the process. If so, the United States should then try to construct an overall regional balance of power which, while in the short-run one-sidedly in favor of India, would give America continued access to the vast majority of the subcontinent's population.

The United States possesses unique economic instruments to influence South Asian outcomes, ones which can outdistance Soviet military advantages. In food, technology, organizational skills, capital, and certain types of industrial goods the United States holds a comparative advantage over the Soviet Union, and India desperately needs them all. No good reason exists why these instruments should not be utilized to counter Soviet primacy and at the same time to encourage India to concentrate its energies on solving its and its neighbors' problems. The United States has three choices in its South Asian relations with the Soviet Union. It can abandon the area to Moscow, which will then maximize its advantage and pursue the entire range of its South Asian goals. Or the United States can counter Soviet primacy indirectly by stressing the importance of the military balance of power and therefore—in cooperation with Iran and possibly China—shore up Pakistan as a partial counterweight to India. Or Washington can compete directly with Moscow for India's favor by using economic instruments to better the lot of the Indian people (as well as those of other South Asian nations), and thus transfer Soviet-American competition from the military-political to the socioeconomic realm. Which choice America adopts cannot be determined by Washington alone. Much depends on Indian attitudes (which in turn are closely related to India's domestic, political, and economic problems), on the security-related actions China takes in support of Pakistan, and on Iranian military and oil price decisions. If the United States wishes to recover its primacy in India, lost to Moscow for nearly a decade, it will have to appeal to New Delhi on more positive grounds than is now the case. This would mean essentially that Washington would have to favor the third choice.

Conclusion: Policy Options for the United States

Paradoxically, it is both easier and more difficult for the United States to deal with the Soviet Union in Asia than in other regions. It is easier because most

Soviet-American issues are of comparatively little concern to Asia, because Soviet-American rivalry is expressed more directly in, and is of greater relevance to, other geographic regions, and because natural barriers and the policies of local states provide little room for political-military maneuvering of either superpower. It is more difficult because both states find themselves in policy straitjackets in Asia, for different reasons, and policy options for both are correspondingly narrowed. Moreover, for the United States as well as the Soviet Union, most policy-relevant trends and events are not in their own hands, so that their actions tend, even more than usual among states, to be reactive rather than initiative in character.

Both states, further, must derive their Asian policies from the character of their own bilateral relations, particularly in the strategic nuclear realm, and from the structure of and changes in the global strategic and economic triangles. The geographic loci of the economic triangle are external to Asia (the strategic triangle lacks a geographic center), and although Japan and China (and, to some extent, India) are increasingly powerful, all three are regional military powers and only Japan is a global economic power. These factors, plus Moscow's geographic, ideological, and cultural distance from Asia, constrain the Soviet Union to play a much less active role there than she would like. Ordinarily, these same elements would allow the United States to exercise significant influence in Asia. This was the case even after the 1949 Communist seizure of power in Peking. But the Vietnam War and its domestic American sequel meant a reversal of this trend, while China's reemergence onto the world scene, Japan's enormous increase in economic power, the oil crisis, and the failure of successive American governments to solve endemic socioeconomic problems at home all placed major constraints upon America's Asian activities. Given that neither Japanese nor Chinese power and activism is likely to decline in the foreseeable future, or that Vietnamese communism is likely to acquire benign, nonviolent characteristics, or that Soviet initiatives in other regions will be backed with declining military and economic power, American ability to influence the course of events in Asia is likely to remain lower in the near future than at any time since the late 1930s.

It follows that, so far as Soviet-American relations in Asia are concerned, American options are limited to means by which Washington can restrict the increase in Soviet influence there, either by cooperating with other Asian states, by attempting to stretch out or delay inevitably developments or, finally, by using its available power at carefully chosen critical junctures. Fortunately, the natural difficulties that Moscow encounters in Asia make it possible for Washington to think realistically in such terms—which are, by contrast, increasingly less possible in Europe and the Middle East, and in the strategic realm. America's basic policy vis-à-vis the Soviet Union in Asia must therefore be to neutralize Soviet initiatives, to avoid participation in conflicts that would siphon off power and attention from other arenas of Soviet-American competition and to seek agreements with regional powers to hold Moscow at a distance.

Essentially, this means American participation in regional Asian balances of power as a marginal but occasionally important participant, i.e., as a balancer in the traditional sense. The only exception concerns the continuation of the American nuclear umbrella over America's Asian allies, principally Japan and South Korea, and the prolonged presence of American ground troops in South Korea. Absence of either would cause such sharp and disastrous changes in the overall Asian balance of power as to invite, respectively, Japanese nuclear armament and rekindling of the Korean War.

Within these constraints, the United States possesses a number of general options in Asia with respect to the Soviet Union. Since China and Japan are the two states to whom Washington must pay the most policy attention, possible policy departures concerning other states depend on what can be done in Sino-American and Japanese-American relations. With respect to China, the most important U.S. goal is to forestall or mitigate Sino-Soviet rapprochement. Recognition, trade, and agreement on the status of Taiwan are the main means, short of military support in a Sino-Soviet war, to that end. For Japan, economic support, particularly the supply of critical raw materials, reassurance on military questions, and encouragement of Liberal-Democratic intra-party reforms (so as to prolong conservative rule in Tokyo) are the important items. In both cases the critical choice for the United States is whether it will be able to find the will and the patience *not* to make major changes in its current policy or, to put it more positively, whether Washington can change the details and instrumentalities of policy to bring about a continuation of present trends. Since the latter all point to minimization of the Soviet presence in Asia, options such as these will probably remain the basis of Washington's Soviet-related China and Japan policies as long as the Soviet Union continues to be America's principal global opponent.

Relatively little change in relations among China, Japan, America, and the Soviet Union in Asia means that options for Washington policymakers will derive from small variations in the status quo among these four states or from other, separate issues. On the Korean peninsula, aside from the troop question, there is the problem of how to prevent further deterioration of the political situation in the South from affecting the military balance with the North. The policy instruments for the United States are unchanged: military aid, the threat of troop withdrawal, and the effect of public (principally congressional) opinion on Administration attitudes. The choice is whether Washington will utilize these means to encourage the Pak regime in Seoul to modify its incipient totalitarianism in favor of a reasonable degree of democracy or whether it will close its eyes to the situation until changes can be made only with very great difficulty. One choice that America might wish to consider is whether, and to what degree, to move into a more direct diplomatic relationship with North Korea, an option the timing of which is not unrelated to American involvement in the future course of the Pak regime.

Southeast Asia, as we have noted, can still be partially isolated from the Soviet Union, and therefore only Vietnam's desire to keep free of Chinese overlordship while simultaneously pursuing its goals in the rest of Indo-China provides easy entry there for Moscow. The principal choices for the United States are whether to conspire, in effect, with China to keep Moscow out of the region, or to cooperate with Peking and others to minimize Soviet influence, or whether, carefully and selectively, to encourage an enhanced but peaceful Russian role. So long as the overall politico-military balance between Communist and non-Communist states in Southeast Asia is not definitively settled, which is to say for the foreseeable future, it may be wiser for the United States to help keep the Russians out of the area, for aside from innocuous trade and maritime activities, Moscow's principal role is that of main arms supplier for Vietnamese-supported insurgencies. However, were the overall balance of power within Southeast Asia as a whole to move in favor of a unified Communist Indo-China allied, as seems inevitable, with China, then it might be useful for Washington to encourage a greater Soviet presence in order to multilateralize the balance of power. This presumes, of course, that the present level of Sino-Soviet enmity will persist which, as was discussed, is not probable. If there were more than a minimum rapprochement between the two Communist states, the choice for Washington would be whether to increase massively its own support of the remaining non-Communist states, principally Thailand and Malaysia, or whether to write off the region entirely. Having failed to support non-Communist governments in South Vietnam and Cambodia, the United States still need not be forced to cross that bridge if it can successfully discourage Sino-Soviet rapprochement.

If Hobson's choices abound in Southeast Asia, they are fortunately absent in South Asia with respect to Soviet-American relations. There the question is how to recoup the situation, i.e., to establish a more evenly balanced Soviet-American presence in New Delhi. The choice for Washington is whether to work through India or to form some loose coalition of lesser local power—principally (and almost solely Pakistan)—and outside anti-Soviet powers—America, China, and Iran. It is probably easier, and surely safer, to emphasize the former, especially since the security of local non-Indian states can probably still be assured and access to the region's most powerful and populous state would thereby be obtained. Trends, indeed, point in that direction and American policy instruments would seem to be effectively used if channeled through New Delhi rather than directed against it. A security guarantee for Pakistan can probably be accomplished by a minimal arms transfer to Rawalpindi and trust in Indian unwillingness to go no further in dismembering Pakistan. A more critical policy question is what to do about the large Soviet naval presence in the Indian Ocean that is sure to come now that the Suez Canal has been reopened. The United States would seem to have little choice but to emplace a sizable force of its own in the area and to step up its cooperation with Iran, and even China, to balance the size of the Soviet fleet, even though this might partially alienate India. Perhaps matching the American force structure strictly with that of the Soviets, and assuring the Indians that the American fleet's purpose is strictly to counter the Soviet presence, will reassure Indian sensitivities at least partially.

On the whole, future Soviet policy toward and presence in Asia should not be difficult for the United States to handle as compared with problems of Soviet-American relations in the Middle East and Europe. To be sure, Asia cannot avoid becoming an arena for Soviet-American global competition, increasingly more so in the future than now. But Asia need not become a problem for Soviet-American relations, the linch-pin of the present global political system, that threatens to precipitate changes for the worse between Washington and Moscow. The future of Soviet-American relations in Asia thus depends largely upon the course of events within China, over which the United States has very little control. In that regard, the critical policy question for America is how to maintain and improve its anti-Soviet proto-coalition with Peking and what to do to prevent China, if it again allied with the Soviet Union, from becoming once again America's principal Asian enemy. If the latter were to transpire, Asia, now fortunately (but perhaps temporarily) a zone of quasi-peace, would become the focus of a new series of violent conflicts in which the United States probably could not help but be a major participant and in which even the American territorial homeland might as a result be subject to devastating attack. That contingency the United States must work hard to avoid.

Soviet Policy in Africa and Latin America: The Cuban Connection

William E. Griffith

Africa

Until recently Soviet policy in Africa[1] could best be viewed as only one aspect, and not the most important one, of Soviet policy in the underdeveloped world. The Middle East and South and Southeast Asia clearly had priority for Moscow. In the 1950s and 1960s Khrushchev hoped that such radical "national demo-cratic" regimes as those of Ben Bella in Algeria, Nkrumah in Ghana, Sékou Touré in Guinea, and Modibo Keita in Mali would follow the same path which he also hoped that Egypt, Indonesia, and India would: toward gradual, peaceful transition to Communist rule. In Africa three other specific factors encouraged an active Soviet policy: competition with the Chinese, the West's support of, or at least lack of opposition to, the white minority regimes in southern Africa, and the few African Communist parties.

In the 1960s the Chinese saw Africa as the most favorable terrain for Maoist revolutionary movements. Peking devoted much time, men, and money to furthering them there and to supporting such national liberation movements as it could attract in whole or, by splitting them, in part, on an anti-Soviet, anti-Western, anti-white, black nationalist platform. This spurred on the Soviets to compete with the Chinese in the continent. Indeed, by the late 1960s the Soviet Union probably saw China, not the United States, as its main enemy in Africa.

Even before that Moscow had realized the anti-Western and pro-Soviet potential of the black African struggle against the white minority regimes in the

Portuguese colonies, Rhodesia, and South Africa, which generated frustration and radicalism to their north and thus helped to turn a few African states, and most liberation movements, toward the Soviets for military and economic aid.

The few indigenous Communist parties in Africa, notably in South Africa, Algeria, Egypt, and the Sudan, were solidly pro-Soviet, but as in the Middle East, they were small, largely European in orientation and sometimes in composition, and, therefore, of little help to Soviet policy. The radical black African regimes, to say nothing of the conservative ones, opposed them. Thus, Khrushchev understandably gave priority to support of black nationalist movements.

The initial Soviet efforts in black Africa, in the 1950s and 1960s, largely failed. Post-colonial black African nationalists were suspicious of the Soviets, as they were of all other foreigners. Moscow understood little about black Africa and made major blunders in dealing with it. In the first great East-West conflict in black Africa, in the ex-Belgian Congo in the 1960s, Soviet arms support to Lumumba and later to Gbenye and Soumaliot could not counterbalance American aid to the Congolese victors: Kasavubu, Adoula, and finally Mobutu. The Soviets also suffered a major defeat in the Sudan in the early 1970s, when Nimeiry largely destroyed the large, pro-Soviet Sudanese Communist party. The other major Soviet defeats in Africa were the military coups which overthrew Ben Bella, Nkrumah, and Keita, for their military successors rejected pro-Soviet for non-aligned policies.

It thus seemed that while the Soviets might gain some influence in black Africa by giving indispensable arms aid to the African struggle against European colonialism, they were likely to lose it again after independence was achieved. Moreover, continuing French influence in the francophone African states, British in Nigeria and Kenya, and American in Zaire and Ethiopia seemed likely to perpetuate Soviet losses.

The Soviets could console themselves that the Chinese had done no better. The initial Chinese attempts to support and train African guerrillas to overthrow some black African governments boomeranged against them. Only in Tanzania, where the Chinese financed the Tanzam railway to transport landlocked Zambian copper to Dar es-Salaam rather than to the Portuguese ports in Angola and Mozambique, did the Chinese seem to have some hopes for the future.

So Moscow and Peking turned to the guerrilla movements directed against the "white redoubt": continuing white minority rule in Angola, Mozambique, Guinea-Bissau, Rhodesia, and South Africa. Many leaders of these movements were products of areas of long European colonization, notably in Angola and South Africa, and were therefore ideologically Europeanized and often, like the Soviets, Marxist and multiracial in orientation. This was particularly true of the Soviet-aided MPLA in Angola and the African National Congress (ANC) in South Africa, both of whose leaderships contained many Marxists. The MPLA leadership was primarily composed of urbanized, assimilated (*asimilado*) intellectuals, many of them mulatto. Some of them had ties with the Portuguese Communist party and had absorbed pro-Soviet Marxism in Lisbon and Paris. The ANC leadership was made up, in part, of black members of the multiracial South African Communist party, many of whose leaders were whites. Moscow therefore naturally supported the MPLA when in the early 1960s it began guerrilla war against the Portuguese. Moreover, the MPLA had only a minority (Mbundu) tribal base, which made it the more dependent on Soviet assistance to compete with the combination of the (Bakongo-based) FNLA, supported by Mobutu, and the (Ovimbundu-based) UNITA.

In part because of Sino-Soviet hostility, but primarily because of tribal rivalries and the issue of multiracialism versus black nationalism, all the southern African liberation movements split except for the PAIGC (Guinea-Bissau) and Frelimo (Mozambique).[a] Chinese aid usually went to the black nationalist splinter groups FNLA and UNITA in Angola, ZANU in Rhodesia, SWANU in Nambia (Southwest Africa), and PAC in South Africa, who were prepared to oppose their pro-Soviet competitors of the larger, older, often mulatto or multi-racial groups, which the Soviets continued to aid and influence. As the 1975 Angolan civil war showed, they had an increasing capability, much greater than the Chinese, to aid them with arms, money and in Angola with Cuban troops.

The Soviets (and the Chinese) also profited from the perception by most black African leaders that the West, and particularly the United States, supported, or at least did not oppose the white minority regimes. U.S. desire to keep its air base in the Portuguese Azores, British investment in South Africa and unwillingness to crush the white rebellion in Rhodesia, British and French arms sales to South Africa, and the lack of any significant Western support for these guerrilla movements left them no choice but to rely on Soviet and to a lesser extent on Chinese support. Moreover, in the early 1970s Washington incorrectly estimated that white rule in all of southern Africa would last for a prolonged period and adjusted its policies accordingly. (The fact that some of the black African leaders also thought so, and, therefore, reciprocated South Africa's recent détente policy toward them, did not help the U.S. position in most of black Africa.)

Such was the situation when the 1974 coup in Lisbon and the departure of the Portuguese from Africa threw southern Africa into flux and Angola into civil war. The result by late 1975 was a major Soviet (and Cuban) victory and an American defeat in Angola, whose consequences have already been global with respect to Soviet-American détente. The MPLA victory in Angola was due to massive Soviet arms aid and above all the some 12,000 Cuban troops.

The Soviet Union and Latin America:
The "Cuban Connection"

Until Fidel Castro took power in Cuba in 1959, Latin America had been an exclusive U.S. sphere of influence. The main Soviet concern there had been to sup-

---

[a]The small COREMO split-off from Frelimo was of little political importance.

port and guide the Latin American Communist parties.[2] European in formation and membership, they ranged from minor sects in Central America and Andean states to minority but mass-based parties in developed, European-settled Argentina, Uruguay, and especially Chile. Traditionally pro-Soviet, they remained revolutionary in theory but became "coalitionist" in practice. Because they despaired of soon coming to power in a continent largely, and after 1945 increasingly, under authoritarian, right-wing military rule, they usually tried to enter coalitions with democratic or authoritarian regimes in order to share in their power and spoils. Indeed, after 1945, this was one of the reasons why they were increasingly challenged in Latin America by the "Jacobin Left"—radical, revolutionary, violence-oriented Marxist rural and urban guerrilla movements led largely by university students of upper middle-class origin.

Fidel Castro and his Cuban guerrilla movement shared with the Jacobin Left a fanatical hatred of the oligarchy which dominated Latin America and of what they saw as its demeaning, corrupt subordination to U.S. power and profits. Castro came to power largely because of the incompetence and corruption of his opponents and the illusions of his liberal democratic supporters. He was above all a radical, anti-American *caudillo*, and far less a disciplined Marxist-Leninist. But his hatred for the United States, his determination to revolutionize Cuba, and his continental and global ambitions—Cuba has always been too small for him, as Yugoslavia has been for Tito—made him seek protection from Moscow against U.S. hostility. His continental ambitions made him support Jacobin Left guerrilla movements in Guatemala, Columbia, and Venezuela. He, thereby, clashed with the Soviet-supported Latin American Communist parties, which until the early 1970s he rejected as reformist, and with the Soviet desire for détente with the United States, to which Moscow intermittently gave priority over support for him. Moreover, *Fidelista* ideology—guerrilla struggle as the origin of a true Communist party, moral instead of material incentives, and unconditional hostility to the United States—all of which Moscow rejected, challenged Soviet ideological primacy.

Castro was pleased by, and indeed probably requested, the 1962 Soviet installation of missiles in Cuba and he deplored Khrushchev's humiliating withdrawal of them. Thereafter, Soviet-Cuban relations were strained. Almost all of Latin America came under the rule of right-wing military dictatorships. The 1964 replacement of Goulart in Brazil by anti-Communist, pro-U.S. military authoritarianism and Brazil's subsequent rapid economic growth and global ambitions were major blows to Moscow and Havana. Uruguay also became a military dictatorship and it and Paraguay became Brazilian satellites. Argentina fell into near-chaos and its Communist party was far outnumbered by the Peronist unions and Jacobin Left terrorists; neither was pro-Soviet.

The greatest defeat for Brezhnev and Castro, however, was in Chile. Both had strongly supported Allende, but Moscow and the Chilean Communists had urged him to moderation while Castro urged him to extremism. Allende, politically indecisive and economically an inflationist populist, vacillated and was overthrown by a right-wing military coup. (U.S. covert support of his opponents played only a minor role. Allende's inflationist populist policies turned the middle class against him and, as with Goulart in Brazil in 1964, his toleration if not encouragement of subversive activity in the military spurred on the military elite to overthrow him.)

Yet Castro, always pragmatic, did not stop trying to expand his influence outside Cuba. He only changed his tactics, to work with, rather than in opposition to, Moscow and to work with established states and national liberation movements, rather than to try to subvert them. He still intends to play a major and, he hopes, a greater role as a Socialist model for, and a leader in, the Third World, and thereby eventually to substitute his influence for U.S. influence in the Caribbean and the rest of Latin America.

Castro took over the Soviet policy of improving relations with the Latin American states. In 1974-1975 he had some success in this respect, notably with Mexico, Peru, and Panama. Moreover, the trend toward radicalization in some Caribbean states, notably in Jamaica and Guyana, favored some Cuban influence there. Moscow probably viewed this favorably because it fitted its purpose simultaneously to pursue Soviet-U.S. détente and to increase Soviet influence in Latin America.

The Cuban expeditionary force was not only the decisive factor in the 1975 MPLA victory in Angola but it also marked the renewal of U.S.-Cuban hostility and a new, major strain on U.S.-Soviet détente. Castro sent troops to Angola in my view for four reasons: his rapprochement with the Soviet Union in domestic and foreign policy; his determination to play a regional and global role; his desire thereby to make himself more important to, and less totally dependent on, Moscow; and his hope so to raise his prestige thereby that he can intensify his renewed drive for influence in Latin America.

Nor was 1975 the first year that Castro sent troops to Africa or elsewhere. Since the early 1960s small detachments of Cuban troops have been stationed in Guinea, where they serve as Sékou Touré's pretorian guard; in Congo-Brazzaville, from which in mid-1960s Che Guevara unsuccessfully tried to reignite the crushed Gbenye-Soumaliot rebellion against Mobutu; in Syria, where in 1973 there were some 3,000 Cubans; in Guinea-Bissau, where some Cubans fought with the PAIGC against the Portuguese; and in South Yemen, where a few Cuban troops and Cuban pilots backed up the unsuccessful Soviet- and South Yemen-supported and armed Dhofar rebellion. The Cuban military intervention in Angola was thus not Castro's first, but it was by far his most important and decisive one to date.

The 1975 Angolan Civil War

The coming to power in Lisbon in 1974 of Gen. Spínola and thereafter of the leftist MFA military soon brought Portuguese evacuation of its African colonies:

Guinea-Bissau, Mozambique, and Angola. Moscow's years of unsuccessful aid to African guerrilla movements were beginning to pay off. Guinea-Bissau and Mozambique became independent under united, anti-Western, but not primarily pro-Soviet guerrilla leaderships. Indeed, Frelimo in Mozambique was probably influenced more by China than the Soviet Union. But in the 1975 Angolan civil war Soviet arms and Cuban troops brought victory to the pro-Soviet MPLA.

In mid-1974, after the Lisbon coup, the Chinese gave considerable arms aid to Holden Roberto's FNLA, whose guerrillas they had been training in Zaire. The Soviets, after a few months of giving no aid to the MPLA, then torn by factional strife, by late 1974 responded with increased assistance to the MPLA. Thus, the Sino-Soviet conflict, not Soviet-U.S. rivalry, probably precipitated massive Soviet intervention in the Angolan civil war. The United States reacted to the Soviet move by beginning covert aid to the FNLA via Zaire. The Chinese withdrew, correctly realizing that they could not match Moscow's aid to the MPLA and perhaps fearing that they would appear too associated with South Africa.

After independence the MPLA beat off the FNLA threat to Luanda from the north, with the help of Cuban troops who began to arrive in Angola, first in Cuban and then in Soviet transport planes. In October 1975, the South African military intervened covertly to support UNITA, which the MPLA was threatening, and came close to Luanda from the south, only to be beaten off by Soviet-armed Cuban troops. Thereafter, FNLA and UNITA resistance rapidly collapsed and the Soviets, the Cubans, and the MPLA were triumphant.

The long-time Soviet large-scale involvement in Angola had four causes. The first was the long-time Soviet support of the MPLA. The second was rivalry with China. The third was rivalry with the United States. The fourth was Soviet policy in Portugal, which had strongly supported the Portuguese Communist party, with which most of the MPLA leadership had long been associated, and whose defeat in August 1975 probably intensified Soviet intervention in Angola.

The Soviets probably correctly estimated that after the Vietnam War and Watergate, U.S. public and congressional opinion would stop U.S. covert aid to the FNLA and that Washington would not suspend the SALT negotiations or grain sales to Moscow because of Soviet activity in Angola. They also correctly estimated that most black African leaders hated and feared South Africa more than the Soviet Union, and that those such as Angola's neighbors, Zaire and Zambia, who could not long or publicly endorse South African military aid to UNITA. The Soviets also correctly estimated that South Africa would not fight on alone once the United States backed out. Finally, Moscow saw that an MPLA victory in Angola would make Rhodesia and Namibia much more vulnerable to guerrilla warfare, if hardly at first to conventional attack; and that against their white minority regimes Soviet and Cuban aid would be essential, black Africa could not oppose it, and if the United States did oppose it, or supported the whites, Soviet political gains would likely be even greater. Soviet calculations in

Angola have so far proven correct. They may well not have been all that precise—Moscow has had long experience in exploiting targets of opportunity—but the size of the Soviet-Cuban operation in Angola hardly indicates total improvisation.

It is now clear that Moscow, Castro, and the MPLA held most of the cards in Angola. Because the MPLA was multiracial in orientation, urban, *asimilado*, and partly mulatto in leadership, and largely Marxist in ideology, the leftist Portuguese military favored it over what they saw as the racist FNLA. Because the FNLA was supported by Zaire and the United States and UNITA by South Africa, and because the MPLA was tribally in a minority, only Soviet arms and Cuban troops could prevent its otherwise certain defeat. When the South African spearhead nearly captured Luanda in mid-1975, it became clear that Soviet small arms aid alone would not be enough to save the MPLA from defeat, let alone to give it victory: trained combat troops to man heavier weapons were also required. Castro was ready, willing, and able to send them and Moscow provided airlift to transport them.

Moreover, because of its minority tribal position, its partly mulatto and largely Marxist leadership, and the threat to it from South Africa and perhaps from UNITA insurgency against it, the MPLA is not likely soon to dispense completely with the Soviet and Cuban presence. Indeed, Moscow is likely to develop naval facilities in Angola. Thus as long as any white minority regimes remain in power in southern Africa—and South Africa is likely to remain dominated by its white minority for some time to come—Moscow can probably correctly expect to increase its newly-won influence in Angola and to gain influence elsewhere in southern Africa.

In sum, the United States could not have come out ahead of the Soviet Union in Angola without major U.S. arms aid to the FNLA and UNITA and, in addition, large-scale South African troop involvement, for only that could have defeated the Soviet-armed Cubans. But given such South African involvement, even if it could have continued this policy in the face of domestic U.S. opposition, the Soviet Union could only gain. Thus, for the United States, Angola was a "no-win" situation.

However, for Moscow and Washington, Angola and the rest of the "white redoubt" will probably remain unique because of the racial element involved. There the United States will hardly compete with the Soviets to aid the black guerrilla movements, to whom the Soviets and the Cubans will probably again be necessary to defeat the whites. But as the near-crushing of the Soviet-armed Dhofar rebellion with the aid of Iranian troops demonstrated, just the opposite of Angola was occurring elsewhere, and in a more strategically important area: in Dhofar Western proxies beat Soviet ones. Angola, therefore, may well forecast what will happen in Rhodesia, in Namibia, or perhaps even eventually in South Africa, but it hardly foreshadows what will happen in the rest of the underdeveloped world.

Notes

1. See Volume X in this series, Helen Kitchen (ed.) *Africa: From Mystery to Maze*, and notably John Marcum's chapter in it, "Southern Africa after the End of Portuguese Rule," his "Lessons of Angola," *Foreign Affairs* 54, 3 (April 1976): 407-425, and his *The Angolan Rebellion*, vol. 1 (Cambridge, Mass.: The MIT Press, 1967.) I have benefitted greatly from many discussions with Prof. Marcum, from my travels in Africa in 1962, 1963, and 1970, and from comments on an earlier draft of this chapter by Prof. Marcum and by my MIT colleague Prof. Robert Rotberg.

2. Edward Gonzalez, "Castro and Cuba's New Orthodoxy," *Problems of Communism* 25, 1 (Jan.-Feb. 1976): 1-19; Edward Gonzalez and David Ronfeldt, *Post-Revolutionary Cuba in a Changing World*, RAND R-1844-ISA, Dec. 1975. I am grateful to my Fletcher colleague Prof. Ernst Halperin for comments on an earlier draft of this section and for many discussions on Latin American communism.

X

Moscow, Washington, and Eastern Europe

Robin Alison Remington

The nature of this analysis differs radically from those dealing in depth with different aspects of the Soviet system and their relevance for U.S. policy. That difference is rooted in long standing American foreign policy priorities, so aptly underlined by President Ford's first "plain talk" with the nation in which he referred to our relations with West Europe, Japan, Latin America, China, and the Soviet Union, but not to East Europe. His address demonstrated a certain continuity of U.S. policymakers, attitudes epitomized by Cordell Hull's wistful aside in his memoirs that if Great Britain and Russia would only decide on what to do about the East European states, Washington would gladly agree.

Despite this reluctance to have a coherent East European policy, East-Central Europe continues to intrude into other vital areas of American national interest. This area, involving eight countries—Albania, Bulgaria, Czechoslovakia, East Germany (DDR), Hungary, Poland, Romania, and Yugoslavia,—1,264,438 square kilometers, and a total population of 113 million, in postwar years has systematically been an element of U.S.-Soviet relations, affected Washington's dealings with West European allies, influenced NATO policies, and increasingly become a consideration vis-à-vis the Middle East.

With the cold war bipolarization of the 1950s, Hull's desire to avoid the complications of relating to East European nations directly had become a

My writing of this chapter benefited greatly from the general research assistance of Rada Vlajinac of the MIT Center for International Studies and in the section on the DDR from David Alan Kahn's research using West German sources. I am also indebted to our editor, William E. Griffith for his comments, particularly concerning Soviet-German relations.

convenient policy simplification symbolized by "roll-back" and "liberation." East-Central Europe, with the exception of East Germany and to some extent even there, was perceived as an adjunct of U.S.-Soviet hostilities: an area that could be treated as a unit, important as a potentially vulnerable pressure point to be utilized during confrontation with Moscow. This is not to say U.S. policymakers did not have a genuine interest in "democratization"/"liberation" of East Europe. It is rather to point to the simplicity with which that policy was understood. The object was to "crack" the Soviet bloc, with an implicit assumption that once Moscow's hold weakened (or if an East European Communist regime fell) more liberal, pluralistic (axiomatically more desirable) substitutes would arise.

The complexity of international politics in the 1960s, when the bipolar international system began to fade into infinitely more fluid, decentralized patterns, the implications of "peaceful coexistence" as translated into détente, and intra-bloc conflicts between the Soviet Union and its "satellites" have all worked to erode the underlying assumption of grey, Stalinist uniformity throughout East Europe. Stalin died in 1953. With him died whatever validity there may ever have been for Washington's East European policies based on the concept of collective treatment.

In short, this kind of chapter is difficult, if not impossible, to write without falling into the pitfall of oversimplification. For if East Europe can no longer be realistically treated as "an area," the chapter itself is committed to an analytically unreal task.

To try to overcome this dilemma, it focuses primarily on three countries chosen for their strategic importance to Washington and Moscow alike: Yugoslavia, East Germany, and Poland. Other East Central European states are emphasized only to the extent that their domestic and foreign policies interact with those of these three states, or in cursory references to key developments that should be watched by those attempting to map future contingencies.

Yugoslavia

Yugoslavia differs from the two other East European countries forming the core of this analysis in three salient respects. First, the nature of its unknowns. Second, the significance of political outcomes there for the future of European security. And third, the greater extent to which the United States has both held and pursued positively-defined policy objectives vis-à-vis Yugoslavia over time.

Recent international developments have escalated concern about that pivotal question of contemporary European politics—after Tito, what? The Turkish intervention in Cyprus with its wake of violent Greek anti-Americanism and the decision of the new Greek government to move away from NATO while simultaneously legalizing the Greek Communist party for the first time in twenty years have obvious military-strategic implications. For our purposes not the least of these is the extent to which these events magnify the geopolitical significance of Yugoslavia for those charged with maintaining and/or securing the balance of power in Europe.

Physically, ideologically, even economically, Yugoslavia has been the dividing line between East and West. Since 1948 both blocs have de facto adjusted to a "nonaligned" Yugoslavia, despite sporadically intense maneuvering to "tilt" Belgrade to one side or the other. A Yugoslavia solidly integrated into the opposing bloc would be most likely unacceptable to both Washington and Moscow, particularly in view of the relationship of the Adriatic coast to the ever-present possibility of rising tensions in the Mediterranean.

At present the Soviets give every sign of being aware of the American nervousness on this matter and of not being anxious to exacerbate it. The USSR is also no stranger to Yugoslav touchiness at outside interference. Not surprisingly, when Brezhnev personally dismissed the "Brezhnev doctrine"[a] as a "Western fabrication" in September 1971, Moscow and Belgrade have emphasized the harmony and "normalization" of Soviet-Yugoslav relations. Economic contacts increased. Tito received red-carpet treatment on his trip to the Soviet Union in June of 1972, the order of Lenin, and a Soviet Marshal's sabre. The Western press spoke of a Yugoslav-Soviet honeymoon, speculating that Yugoslavia might be lured into the Warsaw Pact even before Tito died. Given the extent that the Yugoslav leader was careful to keep his options open both to the West and even further east, in the form of increased trade with China, it seems evident that such rumors of his sliding gently back into the Soviet fold were exaggerated.

Recently escalated polemics against "cominformists" (a catchall term for a variety of pro-Soviet factions in Yugoslavia) indicate that the Yugoslav leadership remains sensitive to Soviet meddling. Indeed, Dr. Vladimir Bakarić, a vice president of the collective state presidency and member of the LCY presidium, went so far as to attack such groups for being "instruments of alien influences whose political line amounts to compelling Yugoslavia to join the Warsaw Pact" (Tanjug, October 21, 1975). Whether or not Yugoslav anti-cominformist activity is a cause or symptom of strain with the Soviets over differing interpretations of the proposed pan-European conference of Communist parties, Soviet-Yugoslav relations have deteriorated publicly during 1975. Nor did the November 27, 1975 *Pravda* article claiming that "conspiratorial sectarian groups" in Yugoslavia represent "no one but themselves" and blaming "reactionary circles" in the West for inventing anti-Yugoslav activities in order to discredit the USSR settle the

[a]Generally referred to as a doctrine of "limited sovereignty" in the East, this was an *ex post facto* rationalization of the use of Soviet troops to force Czechoslovakia back to a more orthodox road to socialism in 1968, on the grounds that within the socialist commonwealth "sovereignty" must be viewed as a class rather than a national attribute, i.e., Moscow reserved to itself the right to use military means when developments within any socialist country damaged either its own socialism or, in the Soviet view, the basic interests of other socialist countries.

matter. When Yugoslav Foreign Minister Miloš Minić visited Moscow (December 8-11, 1975), the article undoubtedly did smooth his discussions there. This was shown by the successful conclusion of simultaneous economic talks in Belgrade, during which it was agreed that Yugoslav-Soviet bilateral trade is to increase by 150 percent over the next five years. The new agreement has been described by the Yugoslav press as "the largest ever."

Yugoslavs may well view such economic carrots with a cynical eye in light of the rocky implementation of their 1972 agreement with Moscow. Tentative statements of "full unanimity of views" notwithstanding, Yugoslav decision-makers are keenly aware of the extent to which continued perceived Yugoslav instability invites interference from at least "some forces" in the Soviet Union. Significantly, trials of "cominformists" continue, as do closer Yugoslav relations with China despite current tensions with Albania. To understand this apparently contradictory situation, it must be seen in the context of ongoing political turmoil in Yugoslavia.

The Yugoslav state has suffered from political hypertension ever since December 1970 when President Tito decided to stage-manage his own succession via the constitutional amendments of 1971. The attempt failed. The amendments, originally put forward to insure a smooth transition—to solve the question of "after Tito?"—became the vehicle of both national (ethnic) demands and a republican (regional) challenge to the central Party authority of the League of Communists of Yugoslavia (LCY). In the ferment that followed, it almost seemed that the state, indeed the Party itself, was "withering away." Ethnic tensions, a deep-rooted historical danger to the unity of the Yugoslav state, skyrocketed.

The situation peaked in December 1971 with the fall of the Croat Communist leadership following the Zagreb student strike. Tito himself attacked the strike as counterrevolutionary and justified the measures taken against the Croatian League of Communists as necessary to avoid civil war. Although the most visible consequence of that crisis has been leadership changes in Croatia and maneuvering to prevent reincarnation of ancient ethnic antagonisms, with a liberal-dogmatic cleavage that cut across ethnic considerations, at bottom the issue is one of organizational reconsolidation, by which Tito is determined to make the Party respected again, even if that respect is based on fear.

This attempt has continued to convulse Yugoslav political life. Nor did the apparent pause following the oft-postponed Tenth Party Congress, held in May 1974, necessarily mean that the process had come to an end. It is too soon to tell. What is evident is that the organizational changes of the Tenth Congress are a radical departure. They provide potentially valuable clues to future power configurations.

In second-guessing tomorrow, however, it is worthwhile to keep in mind some milestones along the way. In the Balkans things are so often not what they seem. The hypothesis that rather than having tightened control at the top, as most commentators supposed at the time, the Second LCY conference in January 1972 transferred actual power down to the fifty-two member Central Committee (then called Presidium) where such historical figures as Kardelj, Bakarić, and other republican party leaders retained membership, seems to be supported by the manner in which Tito returned to his somewhat sidetracked recentralization in December 1972. It was in a tactical alliance with the otherwise powerless Executive Bureau that Tito forced the issue. On September 18 he and the Executive Bureau sent a letter to LCY base organizations outlining measures that "must be taken resolutely and without vacillation" to increase the unity and efficiency of the party. The letter was sent without the approval of the Presidium (Central Committee). Endorsement by the larger body came only *after* the forced resignations of the chairman and secretary of the Serbian League, Marko Nikezić and Latinka Perović, and then only *after* heated debate within the Serbian Party. The reshuffle in Serbia was not the end of the matter. "Resignations" of reputedly "liberal" republican leaders (at least with respect to the economy) took place in Slovenia and Macedonia as well.

There is no doubt that this campaign paralleled credit negotiations in Moscow. As one could say in the jargon of the participants, it was no "accident" that the credit negotiations, begun on September 20, were translated into a signed agreement on November 2, almost immediately after the Thirty-Sixth LCY Plenum's somewhat lukewarm support for the tasks outlined by the Tito-Executive Bureau letter. Nor should one be surprised at the virtually simultaneous (November 1) *Pravda* article commenting favorably on Tito's handling of the struggle against nationalism.

After all, there is no reason to assume that even when on its good behavior Moscow would consider it out of order to use economic leverage to encourage internal changes that would not only tie Yugoslavia more closely to the East financially but also move the Yugoslav party itself down the road of Socialist acceptability from the Soviet view. Nor would Tito feel the slightest compunction about getting as much as he could in economic side benefits for changes which he wanted in any case. Although possible Soviet influence on what will be an important part of Yugoslavia's industrial infrastructure, particularly in the less developed regions of the country (mainly Bosnia), is a potential problem, Yugoslavs are not unsophisticated about such matters, particularly in view of the history of broken promises and paper credit that did not turn into dinar or rubles, nor do they lack experience in balancing between Moscow and other options. The deeper result was that the drive to recentralize the Party produced major social, political, and economic side effects, some of which may have delayed fuses in terms of their impact on Yugoslav society.

First, the "reform" virtually wiped out the entire middle generation of modernizing leaders (Tripalo, Dabčević-Kučar, Perović, and Kavčič in Slovenia), who had secured their republic bases after the fall of Ranković in 1966. These men and women, despite their differences, knew each other, were able to work together, and indeed had developed a kind of mutual trust. Ironically, in the spring of 1972 some people in Zagreb appeared more worried about the possible fate of Nikezić than did many in Belgrade. They felt he understood the position of the northern, more industrialized republics and at least could be bargained with. He had an intangible goodwill that has all too often been disastrously lacking between Serbs and Croats in their bloodstained past. It is not impossible that the new leadership of the Serbian party can build it. To date it is not clear whether that is a priority for them.

Secondly, since 1971 the role of the army as a political actor until and potentially after Tito's death has become much greater. It has often been overlooked that the importance of Ranković's fall in 1966 was not limited to the Party. Aleksandar Ranković was not only the head of the security forces, a secretary of the Party, and Tito's then most likely successor. He was also permanent president of the Veterans Union. Until his disgrace a virtually symbiotic relationship existed between Party and army. The most well-known veterans were at the same time the most prominent members of the Party. Politically reliable veterans almost automatically held top posts in the administrative, security, and economic structures. After his departure, if not by any means solely because of it, the symbiosis was sharply curtailed.

By 1967 army budgets were being questioned. In 1968 the invasion of Czechoslovakia, a highpoint of national unity, also strengthened those who wanted self-management to apply to the army. The strategy known as general people's defense made territorial defense units "co-equal" with the army. The problem with this strategy is that professional and nonprofessional soldiers frequently do not mix well. For to my mind the question that is usually asked, will the military intervene in politics when Tito goes, has long been the wrong question.

There is not a little evidence that the military is up to its neck in a perhaps uncoordinated but nevertheless active intervention in two of the most important political questions in Yugoslavia today:

1. In what way are conflicts at the highest level resolved?
2. What will be the future nature of the Yugoslav party itself?

With respect to the first question, one must remember that in December 1971 Tito referred to the duty of the army to defend socialism internally as well as at its borders. Even more crucial are the signs that it may have been individual if not collective intervention by members of the armed forces that led Tito to resolve the Croat crisis in a fashion that many Yugoslavs, even outside Croatia, considered to have been "using a sledgehammer on a walnut." Army inputs were also involved in the forced resignation of the Serbian party chairman in 1972. According to a *Politika ex post facto* analysis (March 16, 1973), "veterans accepted the [Tito's] letter with the greatest enthusiasm. They are supporting the party without reserve. Their faith in the party now is again confirmed." There is some reason to think that this "faith was confirmed" with the aid of the then chief of military counterintelligence, General Ivan Mišković, who reportedly played a major role both in the events in Croatia in 1971 and during the maneuvering that led to Nikezić's resignation.

Such support (what I have called elsewhere subliminal intervention) may be instrumental in determining the scope of current Party reforms. It could have a potentially decisive impact on just what kind of Party Yugoslavia is left with when Tito goes. The nature of that Party and its links with a genuine constituency or the lack of them will in turn determine the extent to which the Party will have to rely on the army as a factor in domestic security.

The rising importance of the army in politics appeared in sharp relief at the Tenth Congress of the League of Communists of Yugoslavia, held in Belgrade on May 27-30, 1975. On the eve of the Congress, May 17, General Franjo Hrljević, an active duty army general—a Croat from Bosnia—was appointed head of the State Security Service (UDB). This meant that the civilian security service, removed from army control in 1946, was back in the hands of the military.

At the Congress itself twenty-one generals and other high-ranking officers of the Yugoslav army became members of high Party bodies, a tremendous increase in the number of military figures at the top level of the Party. This meant fifteen top-ranking army figures in the new Central Committee, six officers in the Party control and statutory commissions, plus another army general, Dr. Vuko Goce-Gucetić, as the new public prosecutor.

Thus it becomes ever more clear that the popular dichotomy between army and Party, as to which will be *the* controlling force in post-Tito Yugoslavia, is a false one. The imagined military coup, in which the army would throw a debilitated Party out, is more and more out of phase with reality. At present there is good reason to doubt that the military leadership sees any particular incompatibility between its aims and those of the Party. A more accurate view might be that the top-ranking military considers itself a righteous defender of the correct and proper Party line; an attitude indicated by the results of the Tenth LCY Congress.

Third, since 1971 not only the Party but the entire social fabric of Yugoslavia has existed in a state of turmoil. The best minds and an exorbitant amount of energy went into drafting the constitutional amendments of 1971, which have for all practical purposes gone on the rubbish heap of history. Then came the task of drafting and debating the new 40,000 word constitution, passed in February 1974. All of this was accompanied, even after Tripalo and Nikezić left the political stage, by a kind of pseudo-revolutionary hysteria in which the criminal code was changed so that "enemies of the revolution" could be suitably punished. Intellectuals who disagreed were attacked as "anarcho-liberals" and economic doubters pushed aside or harassed as "technocrats." In the meantime the actual economic problems of the country must continue to wait while all enterprises and institutions rewrite their internal laws to make them conform—to the extent that anyone understands what that means—with the self-management provisions of the new constitution. This in a state with a reported 32 percent inflation rate.

Fourth, the method of solution has a built-in problem. To whatever extent the stability of Yugoslavia depends on a general belief that an independent Yugoslav foreign policy can survive his death, resolution of differences by direct intervention by Tito himself weakens the country's chances. The situation is past the point where having Tito intervene to "save" the country has any utility. He cannot contribute to the myth of his own indispensability without doing active harm.

If, as this author is inclined to believe, those Yugoslav economists who insist that the "national" manifestations of 1971 were to a large extent the result of economic scarcity interacting with differing levels of developments throughout the country are correct, the current political reshuffling will not only not solve the national question: it runs the danger of its long-run intensification. The roots of the matter are economic. A Yugoslavia that lacks economic stability lacks a fundamental ingredient for political stabilization. Forbidding expression of grievances does not solve them.

Since 1949 U.S. policy has been dedicated to the idea that maintaining "Tito's Yugoslavia" as a viable alternative to the Soviet model in Eastern Europe was in the U.S. interest. Such a policy had a price tag: "viable" meant economically as well as politically. The Yugoslav Emergency Relief Act of 1950 involved large-scale U.S. economic and military aid. At this time U.S. policy towards Yugoslavia had a certain straightforward quality. Once Washington accepted that the Soviet-Yugoslav dispute was not a trick or a myth, then U.S. support for Tito potentially weakened Moscow's hold on the Balkans and even its organizational maneuvering in the United Nations. To be anti-Soviet, an axiom of U.S. policy during the height of the cold war in the 1950s, made financial support of Tito logical.

But the complexity of politics in the 1960s and 1970s has weakened the logic of the decision to "keep Tito afloat." Although Khrushchev's attempt in the late 1950s to use persuasion to bring Yugoslavia back into the bloc did not wholly succeed, it did bring about a temporary rapprochement that included reassessment of U.S.-Yugoslav relations from Belgrade's perspective. Yugoslavia rejected U.S. military assistance in 1957. U.S. economic assistance—except for surplus agricultural products—ended in 1960, partly as a result of U.S. domestic factors leading to an overall reassessment of such aid.

Throughout the early 1960s there was a marked decline in U.S.-Yugoslav bilateral relations. "Correct" Soviet-Yugoslav contacts played a substantial role in worsening Sino-Soviet differences. Yugoslav trade actions with West Europe increased. Belgrade's policies heavily emphasized influence in the nonaligned Third World. But after the 1968 Soviet invasion of Czechoslovakia, Yugoslav and

U.S. policies once more shifted toward parallel paths. Yugoslav nonalignment seemed to give way to an emphasis on Europe rather than being primarily a tactic for influence building among developing nations in the Third World.

But European security Yugoslav style is not the same concept that is talked about in Washington or Moscow. At the core of Belgrade's policy toward European negotiations, notably the Conference on European Security and Cooperation (CSCE), is the assumption that new names for the old Europe will not do. A Europe with less ideological divisions but one in which spheres of influence have replaced camps, client states are the "satellites" of yesterday, is not a Europe in which Belgrade can feel secure. Détente in central Europe while tensions escalate in the Mediterranean is a deep Yugoslav fear. It leads to Yugoslav demands that *all* European states should have a voice in any restructuring of the political status quo, and that superpowers should at least begin thinking about dissolving the military blocs rather than institutionalizing them still further through the Mutual and Balanced Force Reductions (MBFR) negotiations, which some Yugoslav scholars cynically describe as a means of maintaining superpower monopoly of European problem-solving. To whatever extent, as some of its participants have indicated, the CSCE has been primarily a victory for the policies of "the Nine,"[b] these Yugoslav goals have been achieved, which is not to say that in the actual negotiations Belgrade was the most forceful in pushing them. In part because of domestic turmoil, Yugoslav follow-through clearly lagged behind initiatives from Bucharest on such matters.

Realistically, a clash of Yugoslav-U.S. interests on specific issues in Europe can be expected. Even more, Belgrade's attempt to retain at least a foothold among the Third World nonaligned may cause sharp discrepancies between Belgrade and Washington's views, particularly towards the Middle East. Despite the improvement in the bilateral relationship since 1968, symbolized by former President Nixon's visit to Yugoslavia in September 1970, the 1971 exchange of military delegations, and Tito's trip to Washington in October-November 1971, and the Overseas Private Investment Corporation's (OPIC) extension of guarantees to cover investment of private U.S. capital in Yugoslavia in February 1972, and culminating in the January 1976 agreement to resume U.S. arms sales to Yugoslavia, there remain ongoing conflicts of national interests and interpretation of international crises. Witness the subsequent delay in arms talks.

Such differences are to be expected. The danger for the United States lies in oversimplifying Yugoslav foreign policy, e.g., in assuming that Soviet-Yugoslav cooperation during the 1973 Middle East War was primarily the result of Soviet influence rather than of Yugoslavia's special relationship with Egypt and other parts of the Arab world. In short, a Yugoslavia treated as ever closer to the Soviet bloc can be expected to gravitate in that direction.

---

[b]"The Nine" originally meant the 1965 sponsors of a resolution in the UN General Assembly to promote good neighbor relations among European states with different social and political systems—Austria, Belgium, Bulgaria, Denmark, Hungary, Sweden, Finland, Romania, and Yugoslavia. Subsequently joined by the Netherlands, this group stayed in touch and to a considerable extent coordinated their European security initiatives.

Moreover the danger of a solution that pins faith on the army to maintain control after having purged first Croat nationalists and then Serb "chauvinists" from the LCY in order to rid the Party of factionalism is that despite its carefully patterned ethnic diversity at the top, to a large percentage of those Yugoslavs who are not Serbs the army, not Nikezić, *is* the incarnation of Serb hegemony. Although estimates vary, in late 1971 a conservative one (that of Dr. Bakarić) was that 70 percent of army officers were Serbs. Nor would this appear to be compensated for by the new ethnic composition at the top of the Party. The nationality composition of the 205 top functionaries after the May 10, 1974 Party congress included 87 Serbs and Montenegrins (the latter, although they have a separate republic, speak Serbian and are considered by many other Yugoslavs to be the most orthodox of Serbs), as compared to 56 Croats and Slovenes, representing the interests of the northern, more industrialized sectors of the country.

There is little likelihood that given the history of Soviet-Yugoslav relations, a post-Tito Party dominated by the army would have strong enthusiasm for the restrictions involved in any formal liaison with the Warsaw Pact. Such a Party would be likely to maintain an independent Yugoslav foreign policy, which the United States would sometimes find to its liking, sometimes not. Its most serious problem would be the question of internal measures necessary to maintain control in face of what might well be escalated level of terrorist violence either at the time of or shortly after Tito's death. Even if a major tightening did not recreate the intensity of conflict of interwar Yugoslavia, it could risk weakening mass support for Party and army alike until Yugoslav self-managing socialism, as an alternative to the Soviet model in Eastern Europe, had little to fear from Soviet attack because it had already been eroded from within.

This is not to say that there is anything which the United States can or should do to directly influence Yugoslav internal politics. It is rather to make the point that the army may or may not view itself as neutral and Yugoslav in its role in and outside the Party. How it views itself in some cases, will be less important than how it is viewed by the non-Serbian nationalities and indeed how it behaves.

The DDR

Ironically, U.S. and Soviet policy towards East Germany has had a fundamental common denominator, Washington and Moscow alike have tended to view their relationship to East Germany in light of their policies towards the other, larger half of the German nation, the Federal Republic of Germany (FRG). Today for Washington the critical issue is to what extent U.S. policy towards the Honecker regime should be a function of U.S.-West German relations, to what extent a corollary of détente with Moscow, and to what measure a reaction or interaction with DDR policy towards the United States. The first two considerations amount to deciding whether relations with Moscow or Bonn have priority for U.S. national interests.

In the third dimension, any attempt to evaluate the DDR's foreign policy of either today or tomorrow must show some sensitivity to the fact that that policy is rooted in the East Germany of yesterday. For twenty-six years Walter Ulbricht personified the East German Communist party (SED, Socialist Unity party), from May 2, 1945 when he marched into a devastated Berlin in the uniform of a full colonel of the Red Army until his replacement as first secretary of the SED by Erich Honecker on May 3, 1971. Those years left their mark on the Party, on the people it governed, and on his successor. Honecker was a member of the SED Central Committee and a candidate member of the Politburo in 1950. By 1958 he was a member of the Politburo and a secretary of the Central Commmittee. His career flourished in Ulbricht's shadow. His perception of policy options is undoubtedly influenced, not only by twenty years of participation in the highest circles of party decision making, but also by Ulbricht's political style.

Walter Ulbricht did not have a pleasant reputation. He has been described as blunt and taciturn, a tough practical politician without a kind word for anyone. Whatever the accuracy of that description, it is probably as accurate as the theoretical assumption that leaders as political actors are formed by their circumstances. Ulbricht and his Party were operating with maximum restraints and minimum resources.

Propelled into power by Soviet troops, he and they controlled the smaller, truncated "other" Germany. His political survival depended on Soviet support. Even his economic viability was being destroyed by the heavy reparations flowing from the Soviet Occupation Zone into the Soviet Union to rebuild war-shattered Russian industries. "Proletarian internationalism," the euphemism for Moscow first, demanded the gutting of whatever industrial infrastructure remained in East Germany. Unpopular with those he purported to rule, his economy raped by his only political allies, considered a puppet leader of a nonstate by the West, Ulbricht was in no position to cultivate political charm.

The Soviet Occupation Zone declared itself the German Democratic Republic in 1949. In West Germany mapmakers continued to label the area *Mitteldeutschland* ("Middle Germany"). To most of non-Communist Europe it became, and for many remains, East Germany. Nor was Soviet support unequivocal. Although never taken seriously in the West, in 1952 Moscow did propose discussions on the issue of a unified, neutralized Germany. When the GDR participated in the founding of the Warsaw Treaty Organization, late as 1955, it did so as a second-class member. Ulbricht's speech to the founding meeting reserved the right to withdraw in the event of a future "unified democratic Germany." The East Germans sat in the Political Consultative Committee set up at that meeting, but they were conspicuously absent from the Joint Command of the Armed Forces until 1956.

None of the above is likely to have given a sense of security to Ulbricht or the other SED leaders, struggling with the tasks of postwar consolidation and economic reconstruction. They were a "provisional" government, destined at least in one Soviet version to be token partners in a reunified demilitarized Germany. They were potentially expendible cards in a game for much higher stakes. That is, to everyone except themselves.

Given this scenario, Ulbricht's emergence as the most loyal of East European sycophants during the cold war years of the 1950s should be no surprise. If, as the saying went, a cold in Moscow produced a sneeze in Bulgaria, it meant simulated pneumonia in East Germany. The cold war gave Ulbricht and the SED the territory they pretended was a state. It gave them political life as something other than phantom émigrés of the international Communist movement, living in Moscow and fed by, feeding upon, and serving Soviet interests. There can have been no rejoicing in the SED as the total hostility of the 1950s deescalated into a "limited adversary relationship" between Moscow and Washington in the 1960s. Although by this time the SED had Moscow and the Warsaw Pact firmly committed, on paper, to the concept of two German states, normalization in Europe spelled danger on two fronts: political survival and success in what had to be their primary concern, domestic control. That cold war tensions declined was the central issue for the USSR, the United States, and the majority of East European states, to whom a more relaxed political climate in Europe opened new political, economic, and cultural possibilities. If it must happen, *how* was the crux of East German nightmares. They had little to gain—economically they had long benefited from a special arrangement with West Germany and thereby with the Common Market—and they had a state to lose.

In my view the impression that Ulbricht operated only as a loyal reflex of Moscow's wishes was at least partially·incorrect even in the mid-1950s. This is not to say that the leader of the SED was in any sense anti-Soviet: quite the reverse. That was a period when the interests of both parties appeared and were virtually identical. If anything it was Ulbricht who used his time to the best advantage. For while Moscow was convulsed by the power struggle after Stalin's death, destalinization, upheavals in other East European states, followed by a conflict of increasing intensity with Peking, the SED quietly built up its image as Moscow's unshakeable, indispensable, and loyal ally. In return it did not do badly. Those turbulent years saw:

1. Soviet commitment to two German states.
2. Moscow and Warsaw Pact support for building the Berlin Wall in 1961, necessitated by mass refugee flight to West Berlin.
3. A firming up of bilateral treaty commitments.
4. Virtual control over East European (if not Soviet) relations with West Germany, which did not crack until Romanian recognition of Bonn in 1967.

There were signs even before the late 1960s that Ulbricht followed Moscow "blindly" only on safe roads that he wanted to travel. His method of "destalinization" in response to Soviet pressure for reform and collective leadership was to purge possible groups of challengers to his authority. First to go were high level bureaucrats demanding more flexibility in party affairs, then a group of economic planners centering around heavy industry. Two members disappeared from the Politburo as did four of the six secretaries of the Central Committee. All this, done with dispatch, was not something that, after the repercussions of its pressure for imitation of the new Soviet model in Hungary and Poland, Moscow was likely to challenge. Nonetheless the maneuver demonstrated the nature of Ulbricht's loyalty as well as his understanding of tactical timing. It also cast into sharp relief a fact of intrabloc politics often missed by western analysts. Ever since Stalin's death East European conformity has been a sporadic, not a consistent priority in the Kremlin.

The underlying Soviet axiom has been gradually changing from "say as I say and do as I do" to "say as I say and do as you like as long as you do it quietly and keep the domestic scene under control." Unfortunately for Ulbricht, by 1969 he was being pressed by the Soviets for actions, not words. Former West German Chancellor Willy Brandt decided that the road to improved, i.e., speaking, relations with the other half of Germany led through Moscow and moved steadily in that direction. This chapter is far too brief to detail that process. The salient point for our purposes is that Soviet pressures for normalization intensified and became explicit. The SED was pushed into "inner German" talks, Poland fell away and began negotiating the Oder-Neisse border with Bonn despite evident DDR trauma at seeing its carefully constructed formula of a package deal disappear, and the 1970 nonaggression treaties were signed with no clause providing for full de jure recognition of the DDR.

By now it is commonly agreed that Ulbricht balked. He managed to delay the process, yielding on one point, stalling, even hinting by his pointed lack of a ritual attack on China at the Soviet Twenty-Fourth CPSU Congress in March 1971 that if pushed to the wall the DDR might join Albania in dramatic, public defiance of Moscow's wishes. His replacement as first secretary of the SED by Erich Honecker (in which the Soviets quite probably were not uninvolved bystanders) came just one month later. It is useful to remember that when Ulbricht stepped down that May, the first wave of Western political analysis was not one of surprise. Soviet-East German "differences" had been so esoterically handled that even the most avid followers of intrabloc tensions were divided not so much on the content of such "differences" in 1969-70 as on their very existence. Ulbricht's resignation as first secretary of the SED was initially interpreted as a clever maneuver to insure that he controlled the choice of his hand-picked successor. Not an unreasonable assumption, but one soon abandoned when Ulbricht did not speak at the SED congress at the end of June.

Honecker himself criticized the former first secretary for a style that had not paid sufficient attention to the norms of collective leadership. His lavish praise of the Soviet Union included hints of minor conciliation on Berlin. The speculation that has now become part of standard interpretations on the fall of Ulbricht became Soviet-centered.

Moscow got rid of Ulbricht because he had become a stumbling block on the road to détente by his footdragging on Berlin. The logical corollary was that with the new DDR leadership it would be a much smoother road ahead. At a minimum one can say that it was in Soviet and perhaps even East German interest to have the West think so. One should, nonetheless, be cautious about assuming that Honecker's behavior while consolidating his new position said much about how far he can be pushed to deviate from the SED conception of their vital interests. Undoubtedly he was more vulnerable to Soviet pressure than his predecessor, for while he is a respectable member of the SED apparat of long standing, he does not have Ulbricht's prestigious record in the international Communist movement. Still, Honecker did not speak on the side of moderation in 1969-1970. Although Moscow might well have been more willing to come to an agreement over his head than they would have been while Ulbricht was in power, agreements in principle requiring client state implementation often prove harder to put into practice than anticipated.

Honecker's foreign policy constantly reiterates the need for closer DDR-Soviet relations, involves demonstrative praise for Soviet initiatives, and on the surface appears to be a model of accommodating Moscow's wishes. Officially it rests on the five point "peace concept" set forth in June, 1971:

1. Willingness of the DDR to participate fully in a European Security Con-ference.
2. Willingness to become a member of the UN and its special agencies.
3. Willingness to establish relations with all countries.
4. Willingness to establish relations with the Federal Republic of Germany according to international law.
5. Willingness to normalize relations with West Berlin on the basis of the special political status of the city (not belonging to the Federal Republic) in order to aid the cause of détente in Central Europe.

The important thing about such principles is that they are broad enough to sound conciliating, but vague enough to allow maximum latitude in actual behavior.

The Berlin accords of September 1971 were finally signed without open DDR dissatisfaction. Still, "technical" delays over translation and obvious reluctance to begin a bilateral relationship with Bonn (without which the Berlin agreement would have become scraps of paper in the dead letter office of political settlements) signalled continued SED reluctance to compromise on the core of

West German *Ostpolitik*, inner-German relations. Take, for example, point four of the above program. There was nothing new in East German willingness to establish relations with West Germany based on international law, which was another way of continuing to press for de jure recognition by the FRG: one step further than the Brandt formula of "two German states, one German nation."

Nor did the May 1973 declaration by the then DDR Foreign Minister Otto Winzer, that the Party must become "fully conscious of new conditions and opportunities for political and economic relations abroad," result in radical departures from former policy. The "new" goals articulated by SED Politburo member Hermann Axen in 1973 were:

1. Strengthening the power, unity, and international influence of the socialist community; strengthening and deepening the brotherly bonds with the Soviet Union; continued improvement of coordination in foreign policy of the national of the Socialist commonwealth; and perfecting cooperation with Warsaw Pact and the Council for Mutual Economic (CMEA) Assistance.
2. Strengthening cooperation with "nationally liberated" countries and with national liberation movements.
3. Establishment of the principle of peaceful coexistence with capitalist states and the development of mutually beneficial relations with them. Stable political and economic ties should be developed with these countries, with whom the achievement of peaceful coexistence is particularly important.
4. The fight against the aggressive policies of imperialism, in order to assure world peace, collective security in Europe and Asia, and international disarmament.

"Inner-German" relations (providing the FRG was not singled out as an example of aggressive imperialism, under point four) would fall into point three, as would bilateral U.S.-DDR relations. The key phrases of point three are "mutually beneficial" and "stable political and economic ties." For no one can doubt that any contacts which the SED felt would destabilize their domestic situation would be excluded as *not* beneficial. This leads us to the source of the current problem.

Honecker inherited a resource base infinitely greater than that which Ulbricht took over in 1945. Today the DDR is one of the ten most industrialized nations, it has achieved United Nations membership, recognition of its statehood from 111 nations—including U.S. recognition on September 4, 1974, and equal participation in international negotiating forums such as that of the Conference on Security and Cooperation in Europe. The difficulty is that despite these foreign policy successes, despite the appearance of domestic harmony with virtually flawless law and order, a steady trickle of young East Germans still run away, at great risk to their lives, to West Germany. The Berlin Wall constructed in 1961 saved the bulk of the DDR's labor force. It may have drained the will to leave from the majority of the population. Yet that small stream of those who continue to flee raises disquieting questions.

A state is a state not just when it is recognized from the outside. It is a state when it has acquired authority as well as power to coerce. And in the DDR, the "leading party," all efforts to establish that authority notwithstanding, has no secure index of success. Honecker and his corulers do not know what would happen if the Wall were taken down. What they suspect does not lead to any desire for increased contact with the West. For although the East German standard of living is the highest in the Socialist world, it still does not compare favorably with the Federal Republic whether the issue is butter, or freedom of speech and thought, or options for political participation for those who care.

Moreover, in the struggle to achieve legitimacy based on something other than Soviet troops, the New Economic System introduced in 1963 brought with it not only economic successes but created precisely what it had been designed to avoid, more potential demands on the political system. The NES required, or to be more exact expanded, one layer of East German social stratification—the technical, bureaucratic elite of scientists, managers, economists, and engineers. This is not to say that these individuals are or were "in opposition" to the Party. Rather, authority based on economic successes brings organizational trade-offs. Once created, a large technical, bureaucratic elite, with privilege and prestige, can easily develop a craving for enough power at a minimum to try to structure its own environment to protect those privileges.

The alternative to built-in opposition is cooptation. In the DDR this has led to increased representation of technical elites within the highest state and Party bodies: the Council of Ministers, the Central Committee, and even marginally the Politburo. This might bring pressure for another, "different" kind of Party, in which individuals with a different conception of means and even ends might play the leading role. To assure that such experts remain sufficiently "red" is a high priority of the party. To move too fast too close to the Federal Republic could sabotage that objective. Keeping technical-managerial room for maneuver limited in a situation where 70 percent of DDR trade continues to be with CMEA, in the context of ever closer ties with the "Socialist community," makes organizational-bureaucratic sense. In short, while the overriding objective of East German foreign policy has been to achieve recognition and thus upgrade its international status, that goal was always tempered by an awareness of potentially dangerous domestic repercussions.

As East German foreign policy has been more successful, its emphasis on domestic success as well became greater. The delicate balance between these considerations was well demonstrated by the sudden flare-up of tension over Berlin in July 1974. Apparently without complete bureaucratic coordination, Bonn decided that among the least threatening of possible projects to pin down its interpretation of its legal position under the Berlin Agreement would be to set up a Federal Environmental Protection Office in West Berlin.

From July 25, when a law establishing such an office was passed, until mid-August the DDR delayed traffic on the transit routes to West Berlin, querying travelers as to their place of work. Pointedly, one employee in the environmental office was refused right of passage. On July 29 Washington broke off talks on establishment of diplomatic relations with the DDR, and a State Department spokesman saw that successful conclusion of the negotiations depended on a "satisfactory" settlement of the situation.

Diplomatic relations with the United States were an East German foreign policy priority. Nonetheless, the intensity with which the SED fears increased contact with the other half of Germany resulted in a policy that those involved must have known would damage the chances for, or at best delay, the desired recognition by the United States. Throughout August the situation improved, with the result that U.S.-DDR relations were established in September 1974. Such a resolution can rightly be seen from the U.S. side as a one-shot victory. Whether due to Washington's stand or to intervention from Moscow, the East Germans abandoned harassment of the transit routes and thus tacitly accepted the West German *fait accompli*.

Yet the U.S. action may or may not have been politically wise. What else, thereafter, did Washington have that East Berlin wanted? Or, to be more accurate, wanted enough to respond to pressure in the event of another, perhaps more sensitive incident? The degree of DDR "misbehavior" that it would take for Washington to withdraw recognition would, one assumes, be considerably greater than intermittent transit harassment. Might it have been better to let the two German states plus the Soviets sort out the matter, in conjunction with a U.S. statement that overall U.S.-DDR negotiations would hang fire not only until this "situation" was satisfactorily settled but until there was a satisfactory built-in procedure for taking care of future trouble? The question is hypothetical, and any other policy may not have been possible. Indeed, the State Department handling of the issue may as well have been taking advantage of increased tension to appear in the eyes of the American public to have "gotten something" for an act it intended to agree to in any case.

My purpose in emphasizing the incident is more general. Now and for some time to come, bilateral relations with the United States are likely to be rather far down on the Honecker leadership's foreign policy goals and priorities. Given the domestic situation in East Germany, the evident decision to tie the country ever more firmly into CMEA (the Soviet-dominated Council on Mutual Economic Aid) as protection from anticipated West German pressure, and the restatement of collective responsibility for protecting Socialist gains (i.e., the Brezhnev Doctrine) in the October 1975 Soviet-DDR Friendship Treaty, U.S. room for maneuver is limited. There are marginal economic possibilities, particularly in terms of products that can not be gotten in the East, such as electronic components, computer technology, etc. IBM and Honeywell may find the DDR an interesting and interested market. Such licensing agreements as that allowing the Pepsi Cola Company to build a plant in the East German seaport of Rostock may become more common. However, the likelihood of increased receptivity to cultural or political exchange or easier access for Western scholars as a spinoff of such economic contacts is slim.

This is not to imply that such economic proposals should not be systematically suggested. It is rather to underline my opinion that it would be more a matter of keeping direct channels of communication open for the future than of current concrete agreements. If DDR political behavior in the Ulbricht and Honecker eras is a clue to political futures, then of all East European countries the DDR is the place to expect, consistently, not only two but three and four steps back for every step forward.

Poland

Strategically, Poland is the Soviet Union's most important buffer, Moscow's military line of no retreat. Politically, Warsaw has managed to operate alternately as an exception and as a pacesetter. It kept "anti-Titoist" purging to a minimum in the carnage that followed the 1948 Soviet-Yugoslav break. It made peace with the peasantry, which left 85 percent of the country's agriculture in private hands, thereby avoiding the battle over collectivization that so tore the fabric of social toleration and human values in the USSR and its other East European allies. Out of the officially recorded losses of World War II, in which 220 out of every 1,000 Poles died, the subsequent de facto civil war between the Communist government and anti-Communist partisans, and the barely avoided war in 1956 between Poland and the USSR, eventually came a *modus vivendi* with Polish Catholicism and the intellectual community. The extent to which both groups have continued to have active political inputs can be seen in the changes in the text of the new Polish constitution which resulted from massive public pressure from the Church and Polish intellectuals alike. The changes, which removed several provisions which would have formalized Poland's subordination to the Soviet Union, showed that the leadership would make significant concessions to public pressure, which thus remained an important factor in Polish political life.

If the importance of Warsaw to Moscow were not itself sufficient reason for special attention to U.S.-Polish relations, the Polish-American lobby, more than eight million strong, and like so many other U.S. ethnic minorities increasingly concerned with its ethnic heritage, adds an important domestic consideration to Polish-American relations.

Since 1970 Poland has in my view given at least the appearance of having moved steadily in directions compatible with U.S. interests. Although some anti-Semitism remains, Polish Jews are allowed to depart freely for Israel, and scant attention is paid to the tendency of many to go instead to Western Europe or the United States. Despite continued jamming of Radio Free Europe broadcasts and overt support for a hardline stance on "basket three" in the European Conference on Security and Cooperation (free exchange of people and ideas) in practice exchange of scholars is quietly encouraged. Bureaucratic red-tape notwithstanding, American scholars operate in Poland in larger numbers and with greater freedom of movement than any other East European country. Their ability to do so is more endangered by the projected cut-off of PL 480 "counterpart" funds, scheduled to end within three years, than by Polish lack of cooperation. Polish scholars come to the United States to study and teach not as political émigrés but as colleagues in good (if uneven) standing in their Polish universities. With direct Polish flights from Warsaw to New York, Polish tourism in the United States has shot up dramatically. In short, whether the measure is domestic autonomy, standard of living, or the visible symbols of "liberalization" as understood in the West, Poland could be classified as a nonproblem, as doing as well as could be expected.

But in my view such optimism ignores the complexity of post-Gomulka Poland and the fragility of Gierek's consolidation, should his economic success prove temporary promise rather than substance.

Edward Gierek came to power in December 1970 in the wake of food riots in the Polish coastal cities of Gdańsk and Gdynia, and Szczecin, faced with a declining economy and work-stoppages that continued into January-February of 1971, when the textile workers of Łódż struck with demands for higher pay and better working conditions. Domestically he was, without a consolidated power base, coping with a volatile situation which could have escalated into a general strike while the strength of Gen. Moczar's potential "Partisan" challenge to his control of the Party remained unknown.

Internationally, Moscow had no reason to object to or wish to sabotage Gierek, and if anything probably preferred his to Moczar's "nationalist" orientation. Nonetheless, this was the first test of the "Brezhnev Doctrine." At least in principle, the possibility did exist (publicly supported by both East German and Czech sources) of using the military option retained in the *ex post facto* Soviet justification of intervention in Czechoslovakia. Or as with Dubček, the Soviets could have proclaimed correct "noninterference in Polish internal affairs" until conditions deteriorated to such an extent that only forceful intervention, and perhaps not even that, would have stemmed the downhill slide. It is doubtful that Moscow dismissed the contingency of using troops without taking into calculation the historical likelihood that no matter what the odds the Poles would fight. That the Kremlin opted for sufficient economic aid to allow Gierek time to pull the country back together speaks volumes not only about Polish-Soviet relations but also about the new sophistication of the Soviet role in East European crisis management.

Historically, for Russia Poland has always been more than only a foreign policy issue. During the spring of 1971 Poles visiting Kiev spoke of an upsurge of enthusiasm for Polish culture and even language in the Ukraine. Such domestic-foreign policy linkages are extremely difficult to document. But one thing is certain: the Soviet leadership did allocate the equivalent of $100 million in hard currency to stabilize Poland. And they did so when Gierek was sponsoring not only economic reform but "rejuvenation" of the Party, negotiations, even compromise, with the Church, and a quiet, systematic attempt to bring what had been one of the most oppositional elements in Czechoslovakia—the intéllectuals—into the process of reform via working groups in the Polish Academy of Sciences.

Buying time with economic reforms, perhaps the most important of which was the end of compulsory agricultural deliveries, designed to provide incentives for increased food production, Gierek gradually outmaneuvered the Moczarites, replaced many of the Gomułka holdovers, and put together his own leadership. This group is conspicuous for its youth. In 1975 Gierek was fifty-nine and the average age of full Politburo members was fifty-one and of Politburo alternates and Central Committee secretaries forty-five. The Polish leadership is one of the youngest not only in East but in West Europe as well.

It is also marked by a variety of unknowns. During their consolidation of Gierek's and incidentally their own power, the leadership appeared marked by unity and direction. Economic reform had first priority. As the standard of living rose, giving even more visible evidence of the Party's leading role in what for the rioting workers of 1970-71 was the crucial issue, talk of Party rejuvenation began to disappear. Although still in theory willing to work with the Church, "working with" became more ambiguous. The bulk of the demands published during or immediately following the December events remained unmet. The Party has at least verbal doubts about the Church hierarchy's dedication to détente and points to organizational concessions on such matters as the number of seminaries and recently ordained priests (currently reportedly 800, second only to Italy in Europe). As one highly-placed Polish source put it, "there is no problem with the church as long as they realize who are political leaders of the nation."

Reports of the various intellectual task forces are coming in and have been met with a variety of responses. Much of the educational reform program put forward by a working group headed by the internationally-known Polish sociologist Jan Szczepański has been adopted in principle. Implementation is slow and not only as a result of official unwillingness. The Church, and indeed in rural areas many parents as well, has been bitterly opposed, particularly to the boarding school aspect of this reform. There have been rumors of rural riots, with some speculation that an attempt to push through its less palatable aspects envisioned would run into the kind of opposition not seen since the Polish peasants successfully resisted collectivization.

There also appears to have been considerable pressure on intellectuals for ideological uniformity. But it is so diffuse and erratic in nature that it is not clear whether this is a planned retrenchment, similar to that which Gomułka gradually brought about after the transient victories of 1956, or the reflection of power struggles within the intellectual/academic community itself, struggles that reflect strong diversity of views on this matter by respective political patrons.

This brings us to one of the most sensitive unknowns about Gierek's youthful leadership group. The summer of 1974 witnessed the downgrading of one of his apparent favorites, Franciszek Szlachcic, a move ratified by Szlachcic's disappearance from the Polish Politburo elected at the Seventh Congress. What united those who opposed Szlachcic, other than fear of his growing influence with Gierek, is not evident. That Gierek himself was either unable or unwilling to save his protégé may indicate a much more collective leadership than most outsiders have been willing to consider in reality in today's Poland.

This is not to imply that Gierek's control is slipping. He is naturally less popular than when he came to power. Those who come in on reform platforms with great expectations for change on the part of constituencies divided on the question of priorities inescapably disappoint some while satisfying others. On balance, economic successes have bought the Gierek government a good deal of political credit. Moreover, his cultural—if not political—nationalism also mobilizes support untapped by Gomułka.

For example, the decision to rebuild the Warsaw royal castle is an important indicator of the regime's relationship to the nation. It symbolized the dedication of Communist Poland to the nation's history and tradition. The significance of the decision to rebuild the castle is more psychological than economic. It did involve allocating resources that certainly Gomułka had never been willing to commit to remind the Poles of their non-Communist past. More importantly, however, it showed Gierek's willingness to mobilize Polish national consciousness, and his attempt to make visible, or more cynically, to create an implicit unit of values between the Polish Communist leadership and the Polish people that goes deeper than the tokenism often attributed to East European independence.

This stress on Polish national goals in the context of Poland's solidarity with the "entire Socialist community," was a keynote of the Gierek's closing speech to the December PUWP Congress. According to the *Trybuna Ludu* (December 9) text, the following highly patriotic reasons were among those given for why an "independent and secure Socialist state" should be considered the best of futures by all Polish citizens:

During a long historical period, the Polish nation was deprived of sovereignty over its own country, for which it struggled with utmost self-sacrifice. . . .

It was not until the creation of the socialist Polish state, . . . that advantageous conditions were established for an all-out dynamic development. . . .

Everybody, every time, everywhere must serve the interests of our state, must strengthen it, and must prevent any possible harm from being done to its power and authority.

None of which is to say that there will be a break in Polish-Soviet relations.

Despite warnings of bourgeois attempts to use ideological penetration and economic levers (a sure sign of concern at the extent of Polish economic dealing with the West) to weaken the unity among Socialist states, Brezhnev warmly praised Poland's "impressive progress" in recent years in his speech to the Congress. Moreover, the Soviet leader upgraded Gierek to "an outstanding figure of People's Poland, the Socialist Community, and the International Communist Movement." His emphasis was all on Polish successes, successes that had even greater significance because they "had not been achieved under normal conditions."

In short, Warsaw wants, and sees no reason why Poland cannot have, the best of several worlds: close ties with the Soviets, increasing bilateral political-economic-cultural contacts Westward, and the option to explore the limits of its common interests with such East European mavericks as Romania and Yugoslavia. To date this policy has had considerable payoffs and minimal costs. From the Polish perspective, its economic component is most crucial.

Here there is material basis for Warsaw's optimism. Poland has good energy and raw material resources. Major new coal discoveries near Lublin can hopefully be translated into Western credits to be paid for in coal. Nonetheless, higher prices for Soviet oil will cancel out at least part of this advantage and make Warsaw more vulnerable to political pressure from Moscow. (Even so, Poland, because of its coal, is less economically and politically vulnerable to rising Soviet oil prices than are Moscow's other East European allies.) The fall of Brandt made the success of negotiations linking West German credits to the repatriation of ethnic Germans more tenuous. Schmidt has dealt harder with Warsaw than Brandt did.

While the average Pole was economically better off than before 1970, in May and June of 1974 and in the spring of 1975 the government again faced serious meat shortages and growing restiveness. That in 1974 the situation was resolved apparently by releasing supplies set aside for foreign markets says a good deal about the regime's order of priorities or, perhaps, survival instincts. Yet in order to maintain or increase the current standard of living Warsaw desperately needs more capital. It is not clear how serious the current shortage is. Unless it is absolutely necessary to act, the government will most likely try to wait it out.

Gierek tried to compensate for all this during his October 1974 visit to the United States. The *New York Times* headline, "As Gierek Visits U.S., Poland Basks in Stability and Economic Prosperity," was a flattering overstatement of his domestic situation.

Good will aside, Gierek came to Washington looking for money. The view that he was acting as Brezhnev's "alter ego" is absurd. Poland does not benefit from U.S. funds channeled to Moscow. He went home without having achieved the dramatic expansion in U.S.-Polish commercial relations forecast by a Warsaw delegation visit to the United States in May 1974. The consequences of that failure are unclear, for without forward economic momentum Gierek's Poland could easily backslide into political turmoil. Should that happen, mediating specific internal consequences or even contenders would be difficult. The impact of any major change in Poland would not be limited to Poland's borders. There would be repercussions throughout East Europe, in the Soviet Union itself, and potentially in East-West relations.

Finally, although this author agrees that fundamental changes will not take place in Eastern Europe without the prior acceptance of the Soviet Union, Moscow's view is something that can and has changed over time and is subject to influences coming from East Europe. In Communist as well as non-Communist systems nothing succeeds like success.

Hungary

Of the remaining East Central European countries most relevant in area considerations and policy decisions in Washington, Hungary is at the top of the list both for political and economic reasons. In the context of future developments the "Hungarian way" has come to mean many (if not all) things to all factions in East Europe.

First, out of the ravages left by the failure of the Hungarian revolution of 1956, the new government, led by János Kádár slowly, methodically established order, consolidated power, and moved to bind the wounds of its embittered society by gradually ending the post-1956 terror. By 1961 Kádár—still thought of by many as a Soviet puppet or at best an unscrupulous opportunist—had quietly put forward a slogan with wide-reaching implications: "Whoever is not against us is with us." The importance of this formulation for Hungary, for other East European countries, and indeed in the long run for relations between Moscow and the Soviet Union's smaller Warsaw Pact allies is often underrated.

In Hungary itself, that slogan signaled an end to terror and the beginning of the apparently bitter economic struggle of the early 1960s that culminated in the formal introduction of the Hungarian New Economic Mechanism (NEM) in 1968. It signified not only the regime's willingness to accept less than total political commitment, but also thereby strengthened the hand of reformers anxious to bring home, or in other instances reengage, Hungarian technical expertise to reknit the nation's socioeconomic fabric. In Poland a similar philosophy, if unarticulated, has marked Gierek's dealings with the Polish workers and intellectuals alike. It is an as yet still ignored precedent that could be drawn upon by Husák in Czechoslovakia. And at the "bloc" level, Moscow's toleration (on occasion amounting to support) of NEM can be seen as the extension of Kádár's formula to at least the economic arena, when it comes to that difficult process of setting boundaries for acceptable vs. unacceptable deviations from the increasingly ambiguous norm of "correct" domestic construction of socialism.

The Hungarian party's method of coping with the political side effects of NEM, one carefully *not* claimed to be a model for anything, has to some extent been just that. In the ever-delicate balance of attempting to nurture technocrats who are both "red" and "expert" without slipping into the "red or expert" dilemma, Kádár rejected reducing the Party to a mediating coordinating role. While in principle maintaining its ideologically crucial "leading role," the Party has nonetheless recognized three types of legitimate interests interacting in Hungarian society—the interests of the state (considered to represent the people), individual interests, and group interests. Again, although this formulation stops far short of formal acceptance of socialist pluralism or of allowing "interest groups" (as understood in the West) to organize, it has in practice been remarkably similar to both Polish post-1956 attitudes and the recent behavior of Warsaw vis-à-vis the Polish population. In short, economically and even politically Hungary has inconspicuously retained fragments of the doomed Czechoslovak 1968 experiment.

Despite the New Economic Mechanism's evident economic success, with the Hungarian growth rate documented at 6-7 percent in 1973, a definite rise in the standard of living, etc., there is a deep-rankling problem that threatens to become worse. If it does, it would certainly have an impact on other economic reform attempts in East Europe, most likely in the Soviet Union as well. This is the unforeseen, or perhaps ignored, result of building in wage egalitarianism as a fundamental expectation of the Hungarian working class. Politicians, with Emerson, frequently see foolish consistencies as the hobgoblins of small minds, and, in this case of economic productivity also. Yet to be told that you never had it so good, even if accurate, is less effective in a situation where one sees that others (others that one has been carefully taught to consider as having no more just demands on social resources than oneself) have it eight to ten times better.

Thus since 1972 the Hungarian leadership has primarily struggled not with direction of the economy but with how to handle what has been correctly identified as a new brand of "workers opposition" to precisely the social-political spinoffs of economic successes.

The most recent, still tentative resolution of these dilemmas at the March 1974 Plenum of the Hungarian Central Committee showed the persuasiveness of such opposition at the highest echelons of the Party. The Central Committee conceded that it was necessary to "develop a network of well thought-out measures" for increasing worker influence on *all* spheres of life. It identified the still low educational level of the working class as a priority problem for educational policy. Most important, the personnel changes announced added up to a major setback for powerful advocates of economic reform such as Rezsö Nyers who was removed from the Secretariat, while cultural reformer György Aczél was shifted from the Secretariat to a less important post as deputy chairman of the Council of Ministers.

This is not the first time that such proletarian demands from below have had their impact on East European economic and political development. Precisely this social sector, fighting to preserve, and when possible to increase, its piece of the pie, undermined the Yugoslav economic reforms of 1961 and 1965. Czechoslovak traditions of wage egalitarianism were at a minimum influential in preventing the economic reforms of 1964 from being implemented. This in turn resulted in the worsening economic situation that eventually contributed to Novotný's 1968 downfall. And, in all fairness one must admit that had the experiment in "socialism with a human face" not been aborted by military intervention, it might have lost much worker support along the way when euphoria declined and the costs of Šik's economic overhaul became more inescapable to those inevitably most affected.

Political infighting in Budapest will undoubtedly continue. Whether the decision is to continue with the reform, to table it due to undesirable political consequences, or (most likely) a compromise slowdown, Kádár's position has already been weakened by the decline in influence of two of his closest supporters and the evident lack of enthusiasm for his admitted successes through NEM. The eventual outcome will influence economic contingency planning of other East European regimes and even in Moscow. Its very existence strengthens the hand of conservative forces skeptical of the possibility of achieving a viable blend of economic modernization, political toleration, and Marxist-Leninist social values.

For the most part these are complexities that U.S. policymakers should be aware of in attempting to plan for future East European options. It is not a drama in which Washington has or should expect to play a direct role. The State Department does have an offstage yet direct interest in these events particularly as they are reflected in Hungarian cultural policy toward American scholars. For with Budapest as with Belgrade it is necessary to decide where to draw the line. Hungarians have a right to decide who shall be allowed to do research in their country. What Washington must decide is whether the conditions under which such research is conducted and/or whether U.S. scholars involved need work under constant harassment or fear of expulsion is also a Hungarian decision or something that must be worked out jointly. Despite Kádár's efforts to keep Hungarian foreign policy reassuringly in line with Soviet preferences, however, the very nature and mechanics of the internal reforms are reflected in foreign economic relations. In a state that depends on foreign trade for almost 40 percent of its national income, such linkage was inevitable. Likewise there are unavoidable consequences for Soviet-Hungarian relations with potential spinoffs re Budapest and Washington.

Even before the recent energy crisis, Hungarian economic planners gave priority to getting long-term guarantees of raw materials from the Soviets that Moscow simply did not want to give. Soviet refusal to be pinned down in turn added to the difficulties of Hungarian planning, increasing the temptation to look elsewhere. as a corollary, within the joint councils of CMEA, Budapest has consistently put forward proposals compatible with the Hungarian NEM but more radical than the Soviets are currently prepared to see implemented, such as enterprise-to-enterprise cooperation bypassing the role of the Socialist ministry.

Indeed, the "market approach" fundamental to Hungarian reforms has had a significant impact on Hungarian desire for economic relations with the West and its flexible approach to such dealings. Soviet increases in intra-CMEA oil prices hit Hungary hard, given the country's shortage of other energy resources, harder than other East European states. Budapest is certainly thereby more vulnerable to Soviet pressure. It may also be more tempted to look West economically. If so, this could in turn result in an easing of cultural tensions. It could also make the Hungarians more dependent on Soviet credits and consequently more sensitive to Soviet cultural wishes.

During the long, hot summer of 1968, the Czech journalist Ludvík Vaculik poignantly, prophetically wrote, "By winter we shall know everything." Certainly Brezhnev's praise for Polish economic progress at the PUWP Seventh Congress must have echoed hopefully in Budapest. In the Hungarian case too, time will significantly increase the knowledge available to help in the frustrating task of predicting policy-making variables salient for the 1970s.

The Balkans

Under pressure of lack of space and the logic of this particular approach to the topic at hand, for our purposes the Balkans include Romania, Bulgaria, and Albania. This is not to ignore the vital nature of Soviet-Yugoslav policy for that area, nor to dismiss the relevance of Moscow's attitudes toward such "western" Balkan nations as Greece and Turkey. It is simply an artificial device to stay within the constraints of the project at hand.

Romania

The importance of being Romania has for so long been an accepted fact of eastern intra-alliance politics, security in the Balkans, and the increasing independence of small, medium-sized European states as political actors in Europe that it need only be underlined, not explained. For years Romanian political maneuvering has involved trade-offs which led to speculation that Bucharest was "returning to the Warsaw Pact fold."

Such speculation tends to ignore several facts of Soviet-Romanian political life. First, Romania always stressed its Warsaw Pact membership, even if sometimes it was a member of dubious standing. Secondly, Romanian manipulation of its stance within the alliance in order to buy space for independent policy elsewhere dates back to at least the early 1960s, and there is some evidence that it had begun in the mid-1950s. Soviet troops left Romania in 1958. Their withdrawal followed intense, submerged jockeying throughout 1957 and early 1958, involved a Romanian visit to China at a time when the Sino-Soviet conflict was perhaps the best kept international secret of the decade, and evidently had not been on Moscow's mind at the time of the signing of the Soviet-Romanian bilateral treaty on the stationing of Soviet troops on Romanian soil in April 1957.

Recently there has been a seeming contraction of earlier Bucharest demands for abolition of military blocs, on restructuring of the Warsaw Pact, and even, for the first time in eleven years, on Warsaw Pact maneuvers on Romanian territory. Romanian forces participated in a joint staff exercise with Soviet and Bulgarian officers in February 1973. Bucharest has become more cooperative in CMEA. Moreover, Ceauşescu was pointedly present, not absent, from summer meetings of Communist leaders in the Crimea in 1972 and 1973.

These events must be seen in the context of overall Romanian political-organizational maneuvers. There has been no decline in Bucharest's studied neutrality on Sino-Soviet issues. Unlike with the other East European countries, the Soviets do not have a stranglehold on Romanian energy resources. Romania produces 70 percent of its crude oil consumption and does not depend on the Russians for natural gas. Therefore Soviet economic pressure for political profit is less possible to apply. Romania continues to try to diversify its economic dependence on other socialist countries, so that current Romanian trade with other CMEA member states is estimated to be only 46 percent of total Romanian foreign trade. Maintaining opportunities for such diversification thus helps Bucharest's freedom of maneuver.

Above all, Ceauseşcu's good behavior within the Warsaw Pact has paralleled highly unpalatable Romanian initiatives from Moscow's view (sometimes from Washington's as well) first at the preliminary negotiations in Helsinki and then at the actual Conference on Security and Cooperation in Europe (CSCE) in Geneva. Romania was the guiding spirit behind the unity of "the Nine" (small West and East European states) during CSCE. This unambiguously public break with the "solidarity" of "jointly coordinated" Warsaw Pact policy was more than a minor source of irritation to the Soviets, despite their studied casualness about it. It would be a miracle if this had not intensified Soviet pressure on Romania to conform in other respects. Given past patterns, that the Warsaw Pact institutional mechanism proved to be a vehicle both of pressure and tacit compromise should not seem strange. After all, what is to be gained by verbally pushing for dissolution of blocs when there is the opportunity for helping to restructure the international environment in the direction of that goal?

This brief attempt to demonstrate that politically the Romanian position in the Balkans has continued on its by now normal zigzag path is not to say that there will not be a time, indeed perhaps in the not distant future, when the whole process could be thrown radically out of joint: particularly in light of the implications of the recent restatement of the Brezhnev doctrine in the Soviet-East German Treaty of Friendship. So much depends on Yugoslavia. Ceauşescu is working against time. When Tito goes, his vulnerability will increase, no matter what happens in his neighboring and until now natural Yugoslav ally. Seen in this light, sustained U.S. interest in Romania has more than a small role in strengthening a development that we did not create but one which we have certainly perceived as favorable.

Bulgaria

Sofia has long been Moscow's mainstay in the Balkans, because of Bulgaria's strongly felt pan-Slav and pro-Russian traditions, and because Bulgarian nationalism has focused on its Balkan neighbors, thereby making Soviet support a crucial element of Bulgarian security. The tendency to conclude that this stable interaction of Soviet-Bulgarian interests will continue is great. There are no significant signs to the contrary, despite weak indications of an increasing Bulgarian Balkan identity. Throughout the 1960s Sofia rather uncomfortably participated in the movement for Balkan cooperation and attempted to "normalize" relations with Greece and Turkey, while Zhivkov reportedly even almost included a call for a meeting of Balkan leaders to make a common declaration on security in April 1971. There is no reason to assume that these moves signified so much as an anti-Soviet quiver.

Yet there is a potential Bulgarian-Soviet difference that might be of serious magnitude. It too is tied to the fallout of post-Tito Yugoslavia. In the Balkans the Macedonian question is never dead, nor does it to any real extent "fade away." Bulgarian-Yugoslav tensions over "their" or "their neighbor's Macedonians" have long been seen as a barometer of Soviet-Yugoslav relations. In the past, such interpretations left little to quibble with. But by the early 1970s it was increasingly unclear who was pressing whom for what.

If we recall a certain sequence, the future appears still more cloudy. In September 1971 Brezhnev went to Belgrade to take another of those famous Soviet "one step forward" on the road to rapprochement with Yugoslavia. He went at a time when a number of already agreed upon Yugoslav-Bulgarian treaties remained unratified because of Yugoslav insistence that its version be in Macedonian, one of the official languages of Yugoslavia. (Macedonian is a language not recognized by Bulgaria.) From Belgrade Brezhnev went to Sofia. Not until November was the first of these treaties ratified by the Bulgarians. Perhaps a coincidence. Perhaps he did not really want Belgrade to think Soviet desire for rapprochement extended to putting pressure on the most loyal of Moscow's allies. Perhaps not.

Let us look briefly at a possible scenario. Tito dies. The Yugoslav Communist party, with the army as its "leading force," remains officially nonaligned but is toying with the idea of informal contacts with the Warsaw Pact forces, along the lines of current Yugoslav liaison with CMEA. Moscow would be most unlikely to want to discourage such a hopeful development, particularly if it were paralleled by internal tightening of Yugoslavia in a manner that is already taking place and that reduced the potential attractiveness of "self-managing socialism" as an alternative to the Soviet model in East Europe.

Then there is the question, tactfully or bluntly, directly or indirectly put: What about Macedonia? What if the Yugoslav price were "closer" ties—in the cultural sector for instance—with Bulgarian Macedonians whom Bulgaria considers Bulgarians? Under Todor Zhivkov, it is easy to say so what? However, there was that mysterious Bulgarian attempted "coup" in 1965. At the rate of recent turnover of East European leaderships, it is hard not to speculate that Todor Zhivkov is at least potentially facing younger challengers, who would consider such a move both a heavy-handed provocation and an ideal moment in which to change the guard.

This is all highly speculative. But in the past ten years changes that would have been unthinkable have taken place with more than minor regularity. In 1957 it would have been hard to imagine Albania as a Chinese island of influence in the Balkans.

Albania

Nevertheless, by 1961, precisely as a result of an earlier Soviet-Yugoslav flirtation, Moscow and Tirana were vindictively attacking each other in intra-party meetings and soon severed formal diplomatic relations. Chinese support for Hoxha's regime helped greatly to bring the Sino-Soviet dispute into the open. In 1968 Albania denounced the Warsaw Pact as a "treaty of slavery" and formally withdrew from the alliance, despite the fact that institutionally the Warsaw Pact was not involved in the intervention with Czechoslovakia, nor has its political consultative committee in any way registered approval of the use of troops to "resolve differences" among member states.

After the intervention Tirana did move to improve relations with other Balkan states, even—ironically—its former *bête noir* Yugoslavia. Yet the Sino-American thaw has placed the Albanian regime in an increasingly untenable position. Given Albania's blood-feuding approach to its differences with the Soviet Union, ideologically based on rejection of Soviet revisionist contacts with U.S. "imperialist warmongers," to see Chinese revolutionary purity on a downhill slide in the same direction is a political liability of the worst kind. It is one thing to be two million Albanians and 800 million Chinese against the world. It was another to be two million Albanians allied to Peking during times when Chou En-lai told East European newspaper correspondents that "distant waters do not quench fire," August 1971.

Moreover, to see China abandon the line that has provided massive justification of Albanian internal dogmatism makes other problems for Tirana. The tensions have been most recently manifested in the first purge of a high Party official since the early 1960s, with the disappearance of Beqir Balluku as Minister of Defense in mid-July 1974. An event that only became public in October 1974, it has been followed by other leadership changes.

Such tensions can be expected to intensify. Albanian reluctance to follow Peking's lead, or even to moderate its polemics against the evils of U.S. imperialism during China's "normalization of relations" with the West, has been combined with the fact that Tirana has become a Mecca for the most fanatic Marxist-Leninist splinter groups, thereby implicitly criticizing Mao's self-proclaimed role as the guardian of international Communist ideological correctness. On the whole, Peking has refrained from public signs of annoyance. However, for the first time since the Chinese began in the 1960s to foot the bill for the Albanian budget, there have been signs that Peking's economic assistance to Tirana is not a sure thing. Given the uncertainty of internal Chinese developments following Chou En-lai's death in 1976, very little about Peking's future policy can be counted on. Should the Chinese withdraw or even seriously cut their economic support, Hoxha would be in deep economic trouble, with resultant divisions of opinion on how to handle the crisis.

This is not to imply that there is necessarily anything that Washington can or should do about Albania other than keep an eye cocked toward upcoming developments. The United States has removed the restriction forbidding Americans to travel in Albania. The Albanian government has made quite clear that, with minor exceptions for U.S. citizens of Albanian descent, it wants no part of better political relations or tourism. It is doubtful that even the temptation of Tirana's Adriatic ports would lure Moscow into fruitless guerrilla conflict at high cost for low gain. Nonetheless, as with Bulgaria, the most delicate question is what will be the role of Albanian-Yugoslav relations in the post-Tito period? For in Europe, out of roughly 3.3 million Albanians, 1.3 million live in Yugoslavia, centered predominantly in the Kosovo and scattered in Macedonia and Montenegro. If their population rate continues at the 29 percent ratio of from 1961 to the early 1970s, by 1981 they will form the third largest national group in the Yugoslav state. They are currently pushing for and have achieved de facto republican status. The question is whether that will be enough.

Given the current Albanian regime there is no doubt that Albanian-Yugoslav leaders in the Kosovo prefer to work to maximize their influence and options within Yugoslavia. Yet Hoxha will not live forever. Indeed with the third consecutive shakeup of high-level Albanian Party and government leadership in the summer of 1975, it seems increasingly evident that Hoxha, like Tito, is strenuously trying to control the outcome of a succession struggle already underway in Tirana. It is a process undoubtedly intensely followed by Yugoslavs concerned with the implications for Albanian domestic and foreign policy.

In the meantime, it appears that trials of "cominformists" have extended to the Kosovo. There are strong and increasing cultural ties between Tirana and Priština, the Kosovo's capital. One should not rule out the possibility that Balkanization in the future may break the patterns of the present. The perceived threat of Yugoslav-Albanians opting for their theoretical right of self-determination may have an out-of-proportion influence on internal power struggles within Yugoslavia. They have made vast strides in moving from second-class citizens to participants in the Yugoslav political community. With luck these will have been successful by the time of reckoning. Only policymakers who count on luck gamble with the most fickle charmer of history.

Czechoslovakia

Even in 1976 it is still depressing to write about Prague. Husak continues to hold the line—a relatively moderate centrist paradoxically kept in power by the same forces that invaded to insure that Czechoslovak socialism would return to a more orthodox path. Moscow destroyed the core of the experiment of the Prague spring. Yet Soviet troops now remain in part to prevent the recapture of power by dogmatists who would have been flushed out of the political process had the Dubček regime succeeded from reaping the benefits of their victory. All that is left of the intended reform is the demand that ranked seventh on the Czech list of priorities—Slovak autonomy. Indeed, Slovak participation in central organs of state power has increased, as has the level of ethnic bitterness within this multinational state.

From abroad dedicated Czech and Slovak émigré groups work to keep the sparks of 1968 smouldering both within and outside of Czechoslovakia, with so far only marginal results. Internally there are no signs of Kádárization, although Husak has managed to prevent the massive use of terror. It is hard to imagine that there will be much change soon in any direction. Émigré activity will continue. Husak will stay in power as long as his Soviet support lasts, which in turn will hinge on the international atmosphere as much or more than on Czechoslovak domestic developments. The bulk of the Czech, if not of the Slovak, nation will remain on its historic path of passive internal emigration.

Prior to intervention there might have been at least indirect moves from Washington that would have helped Dubček keep afloat. After the Nixon administration had made clear by 1971 that the developing Moscow-Washington "special relationship" would admit no impediment from such awkward moments in the past, it is doubtful that any acceptable, subtle shifts in U.S. policy toward Czechoslovakia will have supporters, opportunities, or in the unlikely event of either or both, success in the near future.

On balance East Central European nations remain as they have been poetically described, "Eagles in Cobwebs," the objects rather than key actors of international politics. Paradoxically, in the arena of intra-Communist politics this is less true than in the world at large. This brings us briefly to the institutionalization of Soviet-East European relationships within the Warsaw Treaty Organization.

The Warsaw Pact

May 1975 marked the twentieth anniversary of the Warsaw Pact alliance, which according to Brezhnev's address to the CPSU Twenty-Fourth Party Congress in March 1971 acts "as the main center for coordinating the policies of Communist states in Europe." Whether or not such coordination is enough from the Soviet view, it undoubtedly exists and has been most evident in the coalition's systematic campaign for a European Security Conference. Reactivated in the mid-1960s, its success added stature to the Warsaw Pact as a part of Soviet policy and an actor in European politics. This reflects on Soviet-East European relations outside as well as within the alliance. For unlike the stereotype of superpower-client state interactions, these are not perceived by the participants as a one-way street.

Take, for example, the Polish attitude. In foreign policy Gierek has consistently emphasized alliance with Moscow, loyalty to the Warsaw Pact, and a basic unity of views. This does not mean the Polish leadership considers itself a satellite. Far from it, Poles dislike the implications of the "client-state" label. Rather, what is freely admitted to be a political necessity, "close" relations with Moscow, is simultaneously seen as the prime channel for maximizing Polish influence not only within the Eastern alliance but also in European politics as well.

In considering the evolution of Soviet attitudes toward European security it should be recognized that many of these initiatives, dating back to the Rapacki Plan of 1957, came first from Warsaw. In the late 1950s and even throughout the 1960s this was assumed in the West to be "socialist division of labor" on the foreign policy front. Today it would be naive completely to dismiss such an assumption. It would be equally foolish not at least to consider the possibility that while these Polish moves were never made "against" Moscow and quite obviously would not have gotten off the ground without Soviet backing, they may well have been outgrowths of genuinely-held Polish policies that won rather than mirrored Soviet support.

In short, the April 1974 restatement of the WTO political consultative committee that the alliance remains willing to dissolve its organizational structure into a collective European security system notwithstanding, there is no reason to think that even Romania—and Bucharest has been *the* most vocal supporter of abolition of military blocs—in reality wants to see the Pact go. Romanian freedom of maneuver, so evident in foreign policy since the mid-

1960s, would have been perceptably more difficult without the possibility of organizational trade-offs within the WTO. Just as the joint alliance can be an instrument for pressure on less powerful members, it also makes possible potentially greater East European inputs in the "coordination" of communist policy in Europe. As Malcolm Mackintosh has pointed out, the reorganization of the Joint Command in 1969 and the creation of a Military Council was a concession to pressure from the smaller member states, and for the East Europeans, despite continued Soviet dominance, is a considerable improvement over the situation that existed before 1968. This military upgrading has been paralleled by more high level bilateral consultation among members and greatly expanded representation at political consultative committee meetings.

Of course the Soviet Union could invade Romania or any other East European country if it decided to do so. Still, even in 1968 Moscow's intervention in Czechoslovakia came only after months of agonizing reappraisal. The costs of such intervention for other Soviet policy objectives are continually rising. Invasion is always an expensive, unpredictable solution with less than satisfactory results.

The Soviets will increasingly be faced with situations where Moscow accepts a wider diversity of domestic/foreign policy behavior in East Europe, resorts to economic blackmail, or invades to get artificial conformity to an ever more fuzzy Soviet model. Given these choices not dissolution but conflict containment, which amounts to an ongoing struggle on the Soviet side to translate its power into influence and East European attempts to transform the formal rules of the alliance into political reality, is the most likely future scenario for the Warsaw Pact.

European Communist Conference

Another arena of inter-Party maneuvering which has taken on increasing importance for Yugoslav and Romanian politics since 1973 has been the drawn out "preparations" for a European Communist conference. These two ruling parties have been joined by the Italian and Spanish Communist parties, and at the end of 1975 by the French Communist party as well, in a "southern axis" whose procedural victories at 1974 preparatory meetings in Warsaw and Budapest and 1975 meetings in East Berlin effectively blocked substantive support for Soviet objectives. Once decisionmaking by consensus had been agreed to, those parties pushing for the lowest common denominator of agreement had virtual veto power.

Soviet relations with the West European Communist parties are treated in the chapter on the USSR and Western Europe elsewhere in this volume. Certainly the coordinated opposition of these West and East European Communist parties to Soviet policy on the conference reinforced Yugoslav and Romanian resistance and influenced and, at least as long as the negotiations went on, also made it more difficult for Moscow to pressure Belgrade and Bucharest in other respects. Indeed, the 1975 Yugoslav denunciations and trials of "cominformists" were probably in part intended to put pressure on Moscow with respect to the conference as well as elsewhere, and at least in part they succeeded.

By November 1975 the Soviet leadership must have decided to abandon their original hopes for a positive pan-European conference prior to the February 1976 CPSU Twenty-Fifth Party Congress. An East German compromise draft statement (their third version) that had led to optimism about some possibility of a final draft was replaced by what the Spanish delegate called "a document of an 'ideological type'." He pointedly referred to "certain parties" with plans for conferences in the near future that had changed their line on an early pan-European conference, now preferring to have it postponed.

The Soviet shift, although certainly unexpected, might have its own political logic. A sudden push for a strong communique containing "some obligations for all parties" might have succeeded. It would not have been the first time that Moscow had won by changing the ground rules of an inter-Party meeting at the last minute. If it failed Brezhnev had no document to present to the Twenty-Fifth Congress, but a weakly worded document from his perspective might have been worse than none at all. His passing reference to the significant role of regional Communist conferences in his report to the Central Committee put these meetings firmly in the context of the long-sidetracked Soviet aim for a world Communist conference.

Conclusions

The critical U.S. choice is whether or not to have a specifically East European policy or to view East Europe as an adjunct of Soviet-American relations, or in the case of the DDR, U.S.-West German relations. Once this underlying policy decision has been made, political options vis-à-vis these countries will expand or contract depending on fundamental economic choices. How much, if any, economic aid will Washington give Eastern Europe to prevent a narrowing of East European political autonomy due to deepening dependence on Soviet energy resources? The time has passed where "collective treatment" is at all helpful in answering such a question.

Specifically with respect to the three countries forming the core of this analysis, the following issues are central. Washington must decide whether or not maintaining a nonaligned post-Tito Yugoslavia is important for U.S. foreign policy. If so, how should this concern be made clear to Moscow publicly or privately? If not, Washington should understand that the result may be a major change in the European balance of power.

This author assumes that U.S. policy toward post-Tito Yugoslavia will be based on a number of preferences, some of which may be incompatible. A minimum objective is to avoid civil war, not solely in order to prevent Moscow from taking advantage of such a crisis but also because the threat of that conflict spreading first within the Balkans and perhaps to other parts of Europe as well is a danger to everyone. The Cypriot crisis was largely limited to Cyprus, but nonetheless its political and economic aftermath had major repercussions for Europe as a whole. A sudden outbreak of fighting in Yugoslavia might be much more difficult to contain and its political consequences considerably more drastic.

Given this policy goal, U.S. policy has an overall interest in Yugoslavia's economic and political stability. This stability at present requires accepting the League of Communists of Yugoslavia as a positive integrating factor. For of all the organizational upheavals of the past few years, and indeed to some extent as a result of them, the Party remains the one unifying force within the country. With the increasingly visible role of the army at the highest level of the Party, any idea that to support the army is in some sense supporting an alternative to the Party is starkly unrealistic. To support the army with funds, weapons, or training facilities in the United States is to support the most cohesive faction within the LCY, not an eventual substitute for the Party. It is in this context that the January 1976 U.S. decision to renew arms sales to Yugoslavia must be evaluated. Moreover, it should be kept in mind that although the Yugoslav armed forces are dedicated to the territorial integrity of a sovereign Yugoslavia, their ideological preferences are not intrinsically anti-Soviet or unpleasing to Moscow.

The events of the last five years indicate that the army representatives in the Party should be placed toward the dogmatic end of any continuum of opinion on such matters as inner-Party democracy, inputs from below, and what is loosely defined as "liberalization." Since 1974 these issues have centered on harassment of the Marxist humanist *Praxis* group of professors. Despite a temporary improvement that summer, by 1975 their position had sharply worsened. U.S. policymakers should be prepared for a contingency in which the apparent choice is between a stable *or* liberalizing post-Tito Yugoslavia.

Although undoubtedly academic freedom of access is a higher priority for scholars than politicians in either the United States or the East European countries involved, within Eastern Europe this issue has a broader political significance as well. Not only has position on cultural-academic exchanges proved to be an index of attitude towards the overall question of relations with the West, but the extent to which such changes operate smoothly also provides a clue to the domestic balance of liberal vs. dogmatic forces. Thus the 1974 expulsion of some American scholars from Yugoslavia presents a preview of difficulties the United States may face in the future.

Research in Yugoslavia by foreigners is under ever more strict control. Proposed research must be approved by a military committee within each republic to assure that it does not endanger the nation's security. This is a difficult if not intrinsically unreasonable restriction on academic collaboration. To expel American citizens on unspecified charges and without giving either the individuals involved or the U.S. embassy in Belgrade evidence of wrongdoing is another matter. If the option of a clear U.S. policy on the ground rules of cultural collaboration and its interaction with other spheres of U.S.-Yugoslav relations is not taken, the implicit conclusion is that it is in the U.S. interest not to rock the boat while Yugoslavia becomes an increasingly closed society both in terms of its own citizens and foreign access.

In sum, there is (and in the future will be even more so) a need for hard choices and considered trade-offs. On the most fundamental level, it is correct to think that a stable post-Tito Yugoslavia is desirable from Washington's perspective, whether the criteria is politics, economic, or security. Yet in the history of American foreign policy, opting for the appearance of stability has had its drawbacks that in some cases amounted to opting for an illusion that bought only time and future trouble.

As to East Germany, there will continue to be two major areas of U.S.-DDR tension. Despite the improvements in transit traffic between West Berlin and West Germany, it will remain a barometer of the DDR's sense of threat, and "difficulties" in it will recur at any time Honecker feels he is being pushed too far too fast. There is little that the United States can do about this directly, but indirect pressure via Moscow will probably help as it has so often in the past. Moreover, West German economic relations with the Soviet Union and Eastern Europe will continue to provide a disincentive for harassment of West Berlin transit traffic.

Another important problem for DDR foreign policy is mutual force reduction in Central Europe. Any U.S.-USSR agreement on force reduction in the two German states will be viewed with great apprehension in the DDR. The key area where Honecker has not been repeating with enthusiasm, and in some instances not even repeating, Brezhnev's statements on "jointly coordinated foreign policy" has been troop reductions. For even as the unlikely removal of the Berlin Wall, which would cause a desperate, if esoteric, battle between the Soviets and their East German ally and would undermine the essence of SED internal security, any withdrawal of Soviet troops, the buildup of DDR forces notwithstanding, might be similarly, if less seriously perceived in East Berlin, unless, as Moscow and East Berlin hope, it so limits West German forces as to override East German fears.

Has the transition from Brandt to Schmidt changed this scenario? Brandt led West Germany not only with personal charisma but down a well-plotted road toward a very different kind of relationship between the two halves of "the German nation." He was therefore particularly dangerous to his East German opponents. His successor Helmut Schmidt has given priority to domestic and West European and Atlantic policies over *Ostpolitik*. He has been considerably tougher on the Berlin issue. This has two contrasting implications for the DDR, first, positive: a declining sense of threat from Bonn; but second, potentially negative: the need to look for other economic options, for lower Bonn priority for *Ostpolitik* can mean a less advantageous East-West German economic "special relationship." The latter may mean more bilateral U.S.-DDR economic agreements. Also, given the reported rise in Soviet oil prices to the DDR, the East Germans may be forced to diversify their trade patterns, which would have a potential spillover into U.S.-DDR relations even if the last U.S. commodity Washington is likely to be willing to see flow into East Europe at the present time is oil or related sources of energy.

Further should there be a major economic recession in Western Europe, the DDR would undoubtedly be hurt by it, but much less so than Western Europe. Controlled prices, regulated rents, and full employment would cushion ordinary citizens for more than in a market society. Defecting West would therefore be much less appealing, and the more stable the DDR would become. In short, ironically, the worse things are in the West, the better are the chances for East-West German contacts.

With respect to Poland, if one assumes that Gierek with luck and limited inputs of capital can continue on his present path, any serious deterioration of U.S.-Polish bilateral relations is unlikely. The sorest point, Radio Free Europe broadcasts and Polish jamming of them, have been lived with for long enough to ignore them unless more basic problems arise. One critical choice for U.S. policy is whether these broadcasts should be continued to Poland and the other East European countries or not, and to what extent they should or should not reflect U.S. government policy.

Poland, Yugoslavia, and Romania are East European states to which the United States has granted most favored nation (MFN) status. Another critical choice, therefore, is whether MFN status should be granted to other East European states; if so, to which ones; and for what reasons. Is Washington most concerned with degree of foreign policy autonomy from the USSR, degree of domestic political liberalization, both, or the advantages of removing former trade restraints in this region for the American economy. In short, is the criteria for MFN status to Eastern Europe going to be economic or political?

There is however, a more serious decision for Washington policymakers. Seeing Gierek as Brezhnev's "alter ego" requires or at least indicates one kind of policy. Viewing Warsaw as a political-ideological broker between Washington and Moscow suggests another strategy. Zvi Gitelman has demonstrated the diffusion of political innovation from Eastern Europe to the Soviet Union in the case of Yugoslavia, Czechoslovakia, and Hungary. His basic thrust might be applied with even greater results to Poland. For if Socialist pluralism and an increasingly tolerant intellectual climate can develop in the shadow of Soviet nervousness, in my opinion it will happen in Poland. Here in particular the much criticized Western recognition of postwar East European borders and the current political status quo in the Helsinki European Security Agreement of 1975 may contribute not only to Gierek's freedom of maneuver in dealing with Moscow but also to his willingness to tolerate the emergence of a legitimate, if limited, pluralism. (Or to put it another way, rather than abandoning East Europe, détente may make Communist leaderships more vulnerable to social, economic, and over time even political pressures from below.) Take for example the compromise changes in the Polish draft constitution that occurred between its proposal at the December Party Congress and its presentation in the Sejm in February 1976 after two months of open, vocal objection by Polish intellectuals and the Church hierarchy.

Such an evolution would not be a result of U.S. policy but of Polish political culture interacting with Marxist goals. Not that Washington's policy choices will have no influence. At the moment the most concrete choice appears to be in the direction of retarding, perhaps unwittingly, pro-Western forces. If PL 480 counterpart funds are cut off as scheduled, systematic collaboration between Polish and American scholars will become more difficult to finance, and the political position of those in the Party and academic community who view such contacts with suspicion will be strengthened. The policy choice should be made with an awareness that it is a political, not merely an economic issue.

It is true that the energy crisis and the increasing price of Soviet oil to other CMEA members is an additional lever for pressure for political conformity should Moscow decide to turn that economic screw. Nonetheless East European states are endowed with different raw material resources and differing degrees of determination to look for other political options. This situation graphically demonstrates the pitfalls of "collective treatment." If these countries are defined as ever more closely tied to Moscow due to their energy needs, without exploring to what extent they are willing to look elsewhere, they will probably become so. That in turn is a U.S. policy choice. Are we willing to pay, through aid or credits, for example, and if so how much, and to which countries, to strengthen the possibility of autonomous policy initiatives in Eastern Europe?

In sum, it is useless to think in broad outlines about areas that are very different and where U.S. interests are not the same. In this writer's view the "main danger" for U.S. policy in Eastern Europe is that of self-fulfilling prophecies.

XI

The Industrialization of Eastern Europe and East-West Trade

J.M. Montias

Whether a nation emancipated itself from Nazi occupation by its own resistance, as Yugoslavia and Albania did, or whether it was chiefly or entirely liberated by the Soviet army, as in the rest of Eastern Europe, its new rulers belonged to a revolutionary elite with virtually no links to past governments or indeed to the dominant society of the prewar period. Integral in their rejection of the conservative or bourgeois principles that had held sway before the war, committed to fundamental restructuring of their country's social and economic systems on the basis of the abolition of private ownership of the means of production, and bent on rapid industrialization on the pattern of the Soviet Five Year Plans, they did not hesitate to remove every human obstacle to the realization of their projects.

Because the imported new elites, many of whom had spent years of emigration in the Soviet Union, had only tenuous links with the past, they could afford to be extreme in the pursuit of their goals. They avoided the compromises that homegrown leaders, with stronger domestic roots, would have been forced to make. Leaders such as Ana Pauker and Rudolf Slánský, whatever may have been Stalin's suspicions, were untainted by petty nationalism and unwavering in their devotion to the Soviet conception of proletarian internationalism. Only Tito and Gomułka, who had spent the war years in their home countries and were less alienated from traditional society than the camp-followers of the Soviet army, succumbed to the temptation of gaining wider support by espousing nationalist causes.

In retrospect, it is remarkable that Stalin's appointees in Eastern Europe, without compromising their aims, were able to elicit the cooperation of such a large segment of the domestic intelligentsia in carrying out their economic policies. Their notable success in manipulating the technical and scientific intelligentsia to their purposes was due to the fact that these two sets of people, however divided they might have been on most political issues, shared similar views on the necessity for rapid industrialization and for strengthening the defense of their countries.

The catastrophic effects of the worldwide depression of the thirties were vividly remembered in the area, particularly in Poland and Czechoslovakia, which had suffered more than most of the nations of Europe. The failure of the go-it-alone, beggar-my-neighbor policies practiced throughout the interwar period enhanced the attractiveness of engaging in mutual aid and cooperation with the Soviet Union and the fellow-captives of the area. The memory of prewar military weakness, induced by the lack of industrial capability, coupled with the fear of German revanchism, also helped to dispel any latent opposition to the nationalization of industry and to the rulers' economic plans. The new rulers therefore had no difficulty inducing the engineers, the technicians and the scientists, who had been schooled before the war, to train numerous new cohorts of skilled personnel. They did so in the old universities, which were expanded or reconstructed to meet the swollen demand for their graduates.

Cooperation between old and new elites led to their interpenetration. The postwar history of Eastern Europe chronicles the gradual transformation of the governing group—in part through personal conversion, in part through the promotion of a new breed of men—from Soviet loyalists to national Communists, eager to exploit all the possibilities of domestic progress, subject to the restraints imposed by Soviet pressures and by their desire to retain power at almost any cost. Proletarian internationalism, once an overriding objective of alienated rulers, has become an obligation which must be more or less faithfully heeded by rulers, most of whom have reached some sort of an accommodation with their own subjects. At present, of course, Erich Honecker of the German Democratic Republic (GDR), János Kádár of Hungary, Todor Zhivkov of Bulgaria, and Gustav Husák of Czechoslovakia must be more forthcoming in response to Moscow's pressures than Edward Gierek or Nicolae Ceauşescu, but the difference is more in the extent and diligence of compliance than in the spirit, which, irrespective of bargaining power, distinguishes sharply between "us and them." This is not to deny that the weaker a Party chief's domestic power base happens to be, the more he must rely on the Soviet Union for support and the more zealous he must be in meeting Soviet demands. (In the years following a Soviet invasion, as in Hungary after 1956 or Czechoslovakia after 1968, Party leaders were weak domestically because their collaboration with the occupant alienated the population; their very weakness compelled them to cling the more tightly to the force that propped them. It took nearly a decade for Kádár to work his way out of this maze, which still holds Husák captive.)

Whether or not these speculations on the primary motivation of East European leaders are well founded may have a critical bearing on the choice of options open to the United States in dealing with Eastern Europe. We shall come back to this theme in the closing pages of this chapter.

For the last quarter of a century, every East European country, irrespective of its initial level of development, of its degree of political allegiance to Moscow, or even of the extent of centralization or decentralization in the management of its economy, has been engaged in rapid economic development centered on the expansion of heavy industry. Electric power, metallurgy, engineering, and military hardware received the highest priority for investments and skilled manpower in every East European economy in the 1950s; chemicals and electronics moved to the top of the priority list in the 1960s and early 1970s.

These investments created significant new capacities in heavy industry. To cite only one indicator of industrialization, electric power produced per inhabitant just before World War II was less than 75 kwh. in Bulgaria, Romania, and Yugoslavia, approximately 100 kwh. in Poland (in prewar borders), and 160 kwh. in Hungary, which may be compared to 114 kwh. in India in 1972. In recent years Bulgaria has been producing more electricity per capita than Italy (2,590 kwh. versus 2,374 kwh. as of 1972). Poland and Romania produced more than 2,000 kwh. of electricity per capita and Hungary and Yugoslavia more than 1,500 kwh. in 1972, which was about the same as Italy in the mid-1960s. Czechoslovakia's production of electricity per capita, already on a par with Holland in 1938, had grown tenfold by 1972 (a rate of growth, incidentally, which was neither more nor less than Holland's.)

Consumer goods industries, while not so neglected as in the first spurt of postwar growth, have rarely been at the forefront of the planners' attention: they were almost always edged out by heavy industry in the competition for the scarcest human and material resources. Nevertheless, even they made substantial progresss, at least after 1955. More households are now equipped with a television set and an electric washing machine in Czechoslovakia and the GDR than in France. The possession of refrigerators in these two countries is perhaps what it was in France around a decade ago. Hungary and Poland are only five years or so behind the more advanced Socialist countries in the availability of these household goods. Ownership of private automobiles in Czechoslovakia and the GDR has been growing rapidly although it still lags quite a bit behind Western Europe. In the GDR, for instance, the number of registered automobiles per 100 persons in the total population—8.2 in 1972—was about what it was in France in the late 1950s. In all these respects, the Balkan countries are still severely retarded. In Yugoslavia, which leads Romania by a number of years in this respect, there were still only 4.5 registered cars per 100 persons in 1972.

Thanks to moderate increases in farm output and, in the cases of the more developed countries of the area, to growing imports of foodstuffs, East European levels of food consumption are now fairly respectable, both in quantity and nutritive value. Meat consumption per capita, which is highly correlated with the overall quality of food consumption, is about on the same level in the GDR as it was in the Federal Republic of Germany in the early 1960s; in Poland meat consumption per capita is approximately as high as in Denmark and substantially higher than in Norway; and Bulgaria and Spain are more or less keeping abreast, both lagging a couple of kilograms behind the Soviet Union (as of 1971).

Average rates of growth of total national product give some idea of the rapidity of the overall development realized since the war. According to Western estimates, GNP rose at approximately 4.5 to 5 percent per year in the period 1950-1970 in the GDR, Hungary, Poland, Czechoslovakia, and Yugoslavia and at 6-7 percent per year in Bulgaria and Romania. (Soviet rates of growth during the same period probably were slightly in excess of the first group.) Per capita figures of national income provide a rough measure of the final result of this record of growth. At 1967 prices, net domestic product per capita in the immediate prewar period was about $300-350 in Bulgaria and Romania; in 1972 it was estimated to have reached $1,400-1,500 for the former and $1,200-1,300 for the latter. In Poland, Hungary, and Czechoslovakia, domestic product per capita roughly tripled between 1937-1938 and 1972 (from circa $470 to $1,500 for Poland, from $600 to $1,700 for Hungary and from $900 to $2,500 for Czechoslovakia). There are no precise comparable figures for 1938 in the case of the German Democratic Republic, but there is some reason to believe that the increase in aggregate product from 1938 to the early 1970s was approximately on a par with Czechoslovakia's. To put these figures in perspective, we may observe that the Ivory Coast in 1971 had about the same per capita product as Bulgaria and Romania before the war, while Portugal in the late 1960s was on a level with Hungary in 1938. In the early 1970s, per capita product in Bulgaria and Romania had caught up with Ireland (circa $1,300), while Hungary's per capita product nearly matched Italy's (circa $1,700).

If we compare the growth of Eastern with Western Europe, we have to conclude that both sides of what used to be called the Iron Curtain made out approximately as well. Compared to the very mediocre performance of Europe as a whole in the period 1918-1939, both Socialist and market economies have grown very rapidly indeed.

The productivity of labor and capital has also improved in the two parts of Europe, without any marked disparity in the final record. In a test case of the impact of system differences on productivity carried out in East and West Germany, it has been shown (by Peter Sturm) that the economies of scale which the Federal Republic's economy enjoys by virtue of its greater size are sufficient to explain the entire difference in productivity per unit of combined labor and capital inputs between the two Germanies. Differences in the degree of efficiency between market and centrally planned systems, if they exist at all, are hard to pin down statistically. One area where they are still salient, however, is in foreign trade, where inefficiencies complicate the problems that all Socialist nations face in attempting to export high-quality manufactures to the West at a reasonable domestic cost.

To claim that an economic system is "centrally planned" says very little about the extent to which concrete and detailed allocation decisions are made by central authorities and transmitted through commands to enterprise managers, as in the classic Soviet model of the early 1950s. Even Yugoslavia has a central plan. Yet, ever since the early 1950s, Yugoslav enterprise managers have been free of detailed controls by higher authorities and current production decisions are made essentially in response to market demands. Since the mid-1960s, even investment decisions in Yugoslavia have been largely decentralized, and the central (Federal) plan has been degraded virtually to the status of a macroeconomic forecast. None of the East European countries have traveled anywhere as far on the road toward decentralization. All have retained the administrative apparatus—from branch ministry to directorate or association—which functions, or at least is empowered to function, as a transmission belt for conveying the orders of central authorities all the way down to the enterprise and plant; this is in contrast to Yugoslavia where this apparatus was dismantled in 1951 and 1952. The Hungarian leaders instituted a New Economic Mechanism in the 1960s, which combines elements of central planning with fairly extensive autonomy for enterprises. The higher authorities in Hungary coordinate the decisions of their subordinates when informal contacts between producing and consuming enterprises do not achieve desired results. The balancing of supply and demand through freely enacted price changes still plays a subsidiary role in this coordination process. The Poles have also granted greater autonomy to the managers of enterprises but without allowing for price-setting by enterprises; the balancing of supply and demand through prices is even more limited in Poland than in Hungary. There is no evidence so far that decentralization of input, output, or investment decisions has had a dramatic effect on growth or on productivity anywhere in Eastern Europe. The experience of Czechoslovakia in the early 1960s, when national income declined or stagnated for about three years, proves, if anything, that a combination of decentralizing reforms with overly ambitious investment plans can have disastrous consequences. The Polish strategy of the Gierek years aiming at the "dynamization" of foreign trade—allowing exports and imports to determine patterns of domestic production rather than letting them be determined as residual elements of supply and demand—seems to have had a more positive effect on growth and efficiency than any institutional reforms. This point touches on long-run problems of East European foreign trade that appear to be more fundamental than internal reforms for the continued success of economic development in the region.

When small nations pursue a Soviet strategy of industrialization, they eventually confront serious balance-of-payments problems. As they develop, their industrial plant must absorb increasing quantities of liquid and solid fuels, metallic and nonmetallic ores, rubber, cotton and wool, which, in part or in whole, must be imported from abroad. Concentration on heavy industry and the lack of sufficient incentives to plant managers to cut down on the intake of material inputs result in higher levels of raw materials consumption than in a market economy. In 1972, for instance, Bulgaria consumed approximately as many tons of fuel, expressed in coal equivalents per capita, as did France with a national product per capita about twice as large as Bulgaria's, Czechoslovakia consumed 26 percent more, relative to its population, than the Federal Republic of Germany, which is still several years ahead of Czechoslovakia in its development. Countries at a relatively early stage of Soviet-type industrialization, such as Bulgaria, Romania or Poland in the 1950s, may export a greater value of raw materials and semi-fabricates at world prices than it imports but, after a few more years on the same track, they are certain to run up a substantial import surplus in these groups of commodities. As a typical example we may cite Poland, which, in the period 1953-1955, still exported about $100 million more in fuels, raw material and semi-fabricates than it imported; by 1970 its imports of these goods exceeded exports by $600 millions (in current U.S. dollars). More advanced countries such as Czechoslovakia and the GDR, which were already running large deficits in this trade group in the 1950s, could not prevent the gap from widening further in the 1960s and early 1970s. For these industrialized countries, the difficulty was compounded by the necessity of financing imports of foodstuffs, which, by the late 1960s, had risen to a level greatly in excess of the value of exports in this category. (The deficit in foodstuffs amounted to nearly $1 billion for the GDR and $600 million for Czechoslovakia in 1971).

To finance these deficits in raw materials and foodstuffs, at least in the absence of very large credits from foreign partners, export surpluses in manufactured goods had to be achieved. By the early 1970s all the countries of Central and North Eastern Europe were earning such surpluses, primarily by selling more machinery and equipment abroad than they bought, but also, particularly since the mid-1960s, by running excess balances in trade in manufactured consumer goods, imports of which were pared down to the bone. The Balkan countries including Yugoslavia are somewhat exceptional in that they have been financing their relatively moderate deficits in raw materials with net exports of industrial consumer goods and foodstuffs, while their deficit in machinery and equipment has, in part, been covered by foreign medium- to long-term credits and in part by "invisible earnings" from tourism. They are, however, rapidly moving toward an overall balance in their exchanges of manufactured products.

To any nation's export surplus in manufactured goods, there must correspond a deficit in trade in these goods for at least one partner. Among the members of the Council for Mutual Economic Assistance (CMEA), only the USSR was capable and willing to absorb the Eastern European economies' mounting surpluses in manufactured exports and to provide in exchange the millions of tons of iron ore, petroleum, ferrous metals, and other materials needed to keep their chimney stacks smoking.

Armaments stood out as the only major group of manufactures in which the Soviets generated a surplus—selling about three times as much to their partners in CMEA as they bought from them in the late 1960s. But this was not nearly enough to balance their deficit in trade of civilian manufactures vis-à-vis CMEA. In 1969 the Soviet Union bought $4.3 billion worth of manufactures of all types from CMEA members, $2.1 billion in excess of the manufactures which were sold to them. Even this great deficit fell short of the Soviet surplus of $2.4 billion in the raw materials and foodstuffs categories. The difference (about $0.3 billion) must have been financed by net capital exports to the European Socialist countries, including credits extended to Czechoslovakia in the wake of the invasion.

This pattern of trade has been tolerated by the Soviets for many years, but with increasing reluctance. As Soviet publicists have reiterated, raw materials are very expensive to produce and to transport to the borders of Eastern Europe; production and transportation costs have been growing in recent years as ores and fuels have had to be extracted in ever more remote districts of Soviet Asia. At the same time, the costs of substituting domestically produced manufactures for East European imports has been declining. Soviet economists state that, in the case of many types of machinery and equipment imported from Eastern Europe, it is much less costly to produce an imported item domestically than to extract the raw materials needed to pay for its importation. This argument appears to have some merit. In any event, the pressure exerted by the Soviets to reduce their deficits in exchanges of manufactured products is also motivated by their desire to move toward a structure of foreign trade more in keeping with their status as an industrialized nation. Only underdeveloped economies, after all, submit to large deficits in their trade in manufactures.

To help defray the high investments costs bound up in developing natural resources in Soviet Asia, several East European states, including the GDR, Czechoslovakia, and Poland, have been induced in the last few years to contribute equipment on long-term credit, which the USSR will eventually repay in the form of raw-material exports to its creditors. In the period 1971-1975, East European credits for the development of Soviet resources came to about $1 billion; they are expected to increase by at least 20 percent in the next five years. Bulgaria's contribution, which was of the order of $100 million in 1975, was slated to triple in 1976. According to one Polish source the low interest rates East European exporters of capital obtain for their loans—much lower than world levels, in contradiction to the principle that world prices are supposed to be the basis for transactions within CMEA—discourage them from extending new credits.

Exchanges with the West, which average about a third of the value of the trade turnover of the East European members of CMEA, also play a crucial role for the Socialist economies. Imports of machinery and equipment from Western Europe—and to a growing extent from the United States—make an essential contribution to the modernization of East European industries, particularly in electronics and in other branches where research and development expenditures are a large part of costs. Imports of machinery and equipment from developed capitalist countries, as a percentage of total imports in this category from all countries, ranged from a low of 12 percent for Bulgaria in 1969 to a high of 45 percent for Romania in 1971 and 1972. Czechoslovakia, which depends critically on such imports from the West for bridging the technological gap which still separates it from the most developed countries, imported three-quarters of its machinery and equipment, including armaments, from CMEA and other socialist countries and only a quarter from the West in 1972. The bulk of Yugoslav machinery imports, by contrast, originated in the West, although the share of CMEA as a supplier of these goods was expected to increase significantly according to the long-term agreements signed with CMEA members in the early 1970s. Consumer goods from the West are only imported in small volume by CMEA members—they represented less than 10 percent of the value of imports from developed Western nations for any member in the early 1970s—but they do add an appreciable element of quality and variety to the assortment available in retail shops. Finally, many types of raw materials and foodstuffs unavailable or very scarce in the Soviet bloc are procured from the West.

The pattern of exchanges of CMEA countries with the advanced free-market economies is characterized by a net export balance in raw materials, semi-fabricates, and foodstuffs and a net import balance in manufactures. The net drain on supplies of primary products aggravates the scarcity of these goods in the CMEA area. Because raw materials and foodstuffs are in deficit supply in CMEA and because they can fairly easily be sold for convertible currencies in the West, they are frequently called "hard goods," in contrast to most middling-quality manufactures produced in the area, which are termed "soft."

The GDR is the only exception to the pattern of net exchanges of hard goods for high-quality Western manufactures. Thanks in part to its special arrangements with the European Economic Community via the Federal Republic of Germany, it succeeded as early as 1970 in achieving a small export balance in its trade in manufactured goods with the developed market economies.

There is statistical evidence to support the hypothesis that the share of the West in an East European nation's imports of manufactures depends positively on the value of primary products it has available for export (to East or West). Other things equal, then, as its deficit in raw materials and foodstuffs deepens in the course of its further industrialization, it will become increasingly difficult for an East European economy to raise the share of the West in its imports of manufactures. The pattern of East European industrialization, with its heavy dependence on raw materials, may force CMEA members to trade chiefly with each other, irrespective of their primary allegiance to the Soviet bloc per se. Although Western credits and improvements in the quality of East European manufactures available for sale in the West will tend to mitigate the adverse effects of mounting deficits in raw materials and foodstuffs, the economies of Eastern Europe are likely to remain basically dependent on the Soviet Union as a source of primary products and as a market for their manufactures.

The events of the years 1973-1974—the oil crisis, two-digit inflation in key countries in the West, the balance-of-payments difficulties besetting the members of the European Economic Community, and the stringency of credit on world money markets—have further strengthened the hand of the USSR in dealing with its East European allies. Yugoslavia's economy has also been weakened and is more vulnerable to Soviet pressures than before.

With the partial exception of Romania and Hungary, which produce 70 and 20 percent respectively of their total consumption of crude oil, the East European states are almost totally dependent on imports of oil for the high and growing quantities they consume. In addition, all but Romania are becoming dependent on imports for a part of their natural gas consumption. The Soviet Union presently exports over 55 million tons of crude oil a year to Eastern Europe—a little above 10 percent of its total production—and 5 billion cubic meters of natural gas (as of 1973). These imports represented about two-thirds of total East European consumption (80 percent of imports) and a tenth of gas consumption. From 1971 to 1974, the price the Soviets charged for their oil was around $18 a ton, on the basis of long-term contracts, which was roughly comparable to the price prevailing in world markets in the early 1970s. The price of Soviet gas deliveries to Czechoslovakia and Poland was approximately 50 cents per 1,000 cubic meters, a shade below the price charged by the Dutch in their deliveries to Western Europe. The immediate impact of the threefold increase in world prices of oil that hit the Western world in the last quarter of 1973 was confined to the supplies which the East Europeans had to buy outside the Soviet bloc. Thus the initial increment in foreign currency expenditures, expressed on a yearly basis, may have been in the neighborhood of $0.7 billion, a fairly moderate sum in terms of total East European exports to the West, which were in excess of $6 billion by 1973.

A higher hurdle must be jumped now that the Soviet Union has begun to jack up its prices for oil and gas. Even though the CMEA agreements were supposed to be running until January 1, 1976, it was recently reported that the prices of Soviet oil deliveries to Hungary and the GDR for the entire year 1975 were raised to about $6 per barrel, or $25 more per ton than the price the East Europeans had been paying so far. It was announced in 1975 that raw material prices in CMEA trade would be based on a moving average of world prices of the preceding five years. This means that the Eastern European economies can expect to bear the full brunt of world increases in petroleum prices by the end of the decade.

Already in 1976, prices of Soviet oil sold to Hungary were slated to rise to $7.2 a barrel. Assuming that approximately the same price was charged throughout the CMEA area, we infer that socialist Eastern Europe will have to pay an additional $2 billion a year for its oil (on a total import volume of 60 million tons). If gas prices were raised in the same proportion, another $0.4 billion would have to be transferred to the Soviet Union above present levels. The total increase of $2.5 billion in the yearly bill for Soviet fuels would amount to nearly a quarter of total East European exports to the Soviet Union, exclusive of Yugoslavia, as of 1973. This is by no means a negligible burden. The Soviet Union, moreover, cannot be expected to increase its deliveries of oil at anything like the high rates of the early 1970s. By 1980 it is anticipated that the East Europeans will have to get some 40 percent of their oil from Iran and the Arab states, presumably at world prices. This might add another $1.5 billion to their import bill (over and above present purchases of Middle-Eastern oil at world prices).

An aggravating factor in the situation from the East European point of view is that it may become more difficult for them to earn foreign-currency rubles to pay for Soviet oil, to the extent that large-scale increases in Soviet purchases of manufactures from the West displace supplies from other sources, including principally Eastern Europe. The Soviet negotiators in CMEA, conscious of their dominant bargaining position, have successfully opposed East European efforts to increase the prices of their manufactured exports, particularly in the case of the products of light industry.

The different states of Eastern Europe suffer to a varying extent from the consequences of the oil crisis. Romania, with its highly developed petrochemical industry, may gain almost as much from the increased prices of its exports as it loses by having to import close to a third of its consumption at world prices. Poland produced nearly 160 million tons of coal in 1973 and exported 37 million tons at prices that were at least 50 percent higher at the end of that year as they had been in 1970. Increased export prices for bituminous coal make up only in part for the much higher bill the Poles will have to foot for liquid fuels. Czechoslovakia, the GDR, Hungary, and Bulgaria are a good deal worse off than Poland and Romania. Bulgaria, in particular, has gone further than any other member of CMEA in converting its furnaces from coal to oil, which made up 46 percent of its total fuel consumption in 1970, compared to 10 percent in Poland, 17 percent in Czechoslovakia, and 29 percent in Hungary. It must now pay a high penalty for its success in adapting to what used to be the cheapest source of energy.

Yugoslavia imported 8.3 million tons of crude oil in 1973, 27 percent of which were supplied by the Soviet Union. Assuming that Soviet prices remained unchanged and that all imports from the Middle East were made at world prices in 1974, the import bill would have risen by $410 million or 22 percent of all Yugoslav exports in convertible currencies (at 1973 levels). If Soviet prices were raised to world-market levels, this would add another $110 million a year to Yugoslav payments to the Soviet Union or 13 percent of total exports to the CMEA area (also at 1973 levels). Extraordinary increases in oil prices have already contributed to a serious deterioration in Yugoslav's terms of trade. In the first nine months of 1974, import prices rose by 26 percent. The prices of manufactured products on which Yugoslavia depends for its exports rose minimally. (In mid-1974, Yugoslav attempts to raise prices of buses and parts sold to Poland—an important item of export—met with a rebuff when the Poles decided to pull out of the market.)

The recession in the countries of the European Economic Community has induced retrenchments in imports from outside the area that have hurt Eastern Europe's agricultural exports, which, in better times, encountered the least resistance in penetrating Western markets. Hungary and Romania were dealt the first blow when, in early 1974, the EEC placed an embargo on meat exports to members of the Community. The adverse effect of this move on Hungary was mitigated by the Soviet Union's order for 60,000 head of cattle that were to be paid for partly in rubles, partly in convertible foreign currency. The part paid in rubles will merely add to the substantial debt the Soviets have run up in their clearing account with Hungary. (Large surpluses in trade with the USSR have for years been accumulated by small East European countries including Hungary; their inability to erase these balances is due in part to Soviet unwillingness to deliver more raw materials and foodstuffs, in part to their own reluctance to increase their purchases of the middling-quality manufactures the Soviets are able to offer over and above long-term agreements.) The embargo, on balance, will probably have an adverse effect on Hungarian interests, not only because it will presumably entail some shortfall in earnings in convertible currencies compared to a situation of normal exports to the West but because the Soviet Union will presumably expect to gain some advantage, political or economic, for bailing out its ally. We have a precedent here in the case of Bulgaria which increased its short-term indebtedness to Western creditors so much in the mid-1960s, that, according to some reports, Zhivkov was forced to apply to Moscow for a gold loan to meet Bulgarian obligations. The result was a precipitous decline in imports from developed market economies, apparently at Soviet urging, from a high of $408 million in 1966 to $260 million in 1969. The *quid pro quo* the Hungarians will have to offer in exchange for Soviet aid may also entail a curtailment of imports of manufactured goods from the West. A graver prospect is that they may be obliged to place a tighter rein on intellectual discussions at home and further dilute their economic reforms, which have already retrogressed significantly from the degree of decentralization they had achieved in the early 1970s.

Yugoslavia is especially vulnerable to the deteriorating economic situation in Western Europe on account of the 800,000 or so Yugoslav workers, employed chiefly in Germany, Belgium, Holland and Switzerland, whose remittances represented a quarter of all Yugoslav foreign-currency receipts and paid for 30 percent of the entire import bill in 1972. Growing unemployment in EEC countries, particularly in Germany, will necessarily bring about some loss in these *Gastarbeiter's* jobs and cause a loss in Yugoslavia's foreign-exchange receipts, not to speak of the problem of reintegrating a number of these former emigrants into the Yugoslav economy.

If Western credits could flow to Eastern Europe as freely as they did in the late 1960s and early 1970s, the impact of the inflation and recession in the West would not be as serious as it is. But several of these countries, including particularly Romania and Yugoslavia, are gravely overextended. Toward the Federal Republic of Germany alone, their principal creditor, they each owed in the neighborhood of 2 billion DM or nearly $900 million at the end of 1973. Romania had considerable difficulty renegotiating its outstanding debts to Germany in 1974-1975 before it could draw on new lines of credit. United States banks, which rapidly increased their business with Eastern Europe in the early 1970s, have been chary of late of getting more deeply involved in financing Eastern Europe, even on a short-term basis. At least one large U.S. bank ceased to extend short-term credit to Yugoslavia in mid-1974.

In sum, the events of the last two years have strengthened the USSR and weakened Eastern Europe. The Soviets have reaped enormous gains on world markets as a result of the sharp rise in the free-market prices of gold, platinum, diamonds, petroleum, and other primary commodities that they export; they gained from the sale of arms to the Arabs after the Arab-Israeli war of October 1973; they succeeded by their judicious and timely purchases in the United States in moderating the drain on their foreign-exchange reserves of their substantial grain purchases. Their position would have been stronger if it were not for the heavy purchases of wheat and corn in the United States, made necessary by the poor harvest results of 1975, which must be depleting the foreign exchange reserves accumulated by the Soviet Union in the previous two years. Nonetheless, their foreign-exchange and gold reserves must still be at or near their all-time high—a not inconsiderable advantage in the economic negotiations with the United States and other Western powers. By contrast, the reserves of the East European states are strained, and the prospects of obtaining large amounts of private credit are poor. Recent hints in the Soviet press suggesting that the disparity between levels of living in the USSR and in Eastern Europe ought to be reduced—to the advantage of the Soviet population—appear both ominous and realistic in view of the recent changes in the balance of economic power in the Socialist commonwealth.

Before delving into the options open to the United States, it may be useful to summarize recent trends in the evolution of this country's trade-and-credit relations with Eastern Europe. The upsurge in U.S. commercial exchanges with Eastern Europe is relatively recent. Throughout the 1960s U.S. exports to Eastern Europe, exclusive of Yugoslavia, stagnated at a level between $100 to

$150 million a year, roughly 1 to 1.5 percent of the combined imports of these countries. U.S. imports from Eastern Europe, partly as a result of the granting of Most Favored Nation status to Poland in 1963, quadrupled between the beginning and the end of the 1960s. The net effect of the two trends was to shift the balance of trade from a U.S. surplus of $60 million in the early 1960s to a deficit of $73 million in the period 1968-1971. The great leap forward came in 1973, in the wake of the détente in U.S.-Soviet relations. U.S. exports to Eastern Europe in that year rose to $605 million, more than twice the level of 1972. A projection based on the first nine months of 1974 suggests they may rise to $900 million for the year.

Inasmuch as most of this spectacular expansion in exports was financed by U.S. government and private credits, imports could not be expected to, and in fact did not, rise to nearly the same extent. Imports from Eastern Europe actually rose from $224 in 1972 to $300 million in 1973, leaving the United States with a surplus in commodity trade with Eastern Europe of a little more than $300 million in the latter year, over half of which were financed by credits. Exports of manufactures contributed much less, and exports of foodstuffs much more than their initial shares to the upsurge in trade. This was in marked contrast to the tripling in U.S. exports of manufactures to the USSR from 1972 to 1973, which raised their share from 15 percent to 21 percent of total U.S. exports to the Soviets. East European importers of American manufactures, particularly of machinery and transport equipment, are still only a fraction of what they would be if this country's share in East European imports from Western industrialized nations were as high as one would expect from the share of the United States in the total imports of manufactures by Western industrialized nations. Calculations based on U.S. Department of Commerce "middle-level" projections indicate that actual imports of U.S. machinery and equipment by Eastern Europe in 1973 were about one-fifth of their expected level based on these "normal" shares. U.S. exports of machinery and equipment to the Soviet Union, on the other hand, came to perhaps two-thirds of their expected level.

The reasons for the unwillingness or inability of Eastern European buyers to import manufactures from the United States are not altogether clear, but one reason must surely be that the East European states are less able than the Soviet Union to generate a large volume of freely convertible currencies with which to finance the portions of their deficits not covered by credits. However that may be, there is every indication that the United States will have an important role to play in the next few years as a supplier of foodstuffs to Eastern Europe and as a source of credit-financed high-technology goods, provided at least that détente is not interrupted. This double role opens a number of options for U.S. policymakers.

The choices before U.S. policymakers in dealing with Eastern Europe turn critically on their perception of the goals and strategies pursued by East European leaders. It was argued earlier that these leaders were increasingly

motivated by national purposes and less concerned with proletarian internationalism, which some observers would regard as little more than a code name for
Soviet interests. Policymakers who see the Party chiefs of Eastern Europe, with
the possible exception of Tito and Ceauşescu, as mere satraps of Moscow, bent
on making their maximum contribution to the military-economic power of the
Soviet bloc, would look at the options confronting them in a very different light.
There would be no obvious reason, for example, why they should wish to treat
the East European states with special consideration or discriminate in any way in
their favor, relative to the Soviet Union. Indeed, the logic of this approach might
even be pushed so far as to suggest that Eastern Europe should be discriminated
against in order to bring about popular dissatisfaction and increase the probability of riots and rebellions that would weaken the Party leaders' hold over their
subjects and undermine the power of the Soviet bloc. This is indeed an
option—familiar to Americans from the history of the 1950s—but one which I
believe to be based on a misperception of the present objectives, attitudes, and
degrees of popular support of East European rulers.

A strategy more in keeping with my image of these rulers would use
economic policies to attract and conciliate them to the broad interests of the
United States in détente, political stability, and worldwide economic progress.

Several East European nations have already helped to create a propitious
climate for international détente, the most conspicuous case being Romania's
mediating role in the rapprochement of the United States with China. Poland has
from time to time been a useful intermediary in U.S. relations with the Soviet
Union. Yugoslavia so far does not seem to have been invited to intervene in U.S.
negotiations with Egypt and the Arab world, but there is here a potential
catalyst for peace in the Middle East that may some day be drawn upon with
profit. Neither can one totally ignore what might crudely be called the civilizing
influence of Eastern Europe over the Soviet Union: its potential in the long run
for bringing about peaceful internal change in the manner in which Soviet
subjects are governed and in which the Soviet economy operates. The East
Europeans may exert such an influence in many ways but perhaps most
effectively by displaying successful examples of Party-supervised liberalization in
their political and economic spheres. Domestic relaxation in the Soviet Union, in
turn, could be expected to have favorable repercussions for the West in the realm
of Soviet foreign policy.

The United States of course need not have a uniform policy toward Eastern
Europe. An important option lies in differentiating among the East European
countries (particularly in the concessions on trade and credit the U.S. government might confer on them) according to the degree to which they may be
willing to cooperate with the United States in solving international problems or
for any other purpose. This line has been followed, with limited success, in the
preferential treatment of Poland in the late 1950s and early 1960s and of
Romania in recent years. It is perhaps opportune at the present time to consider

the option of improving political and economic relations with all East European countries, though not necessarily at the same pace.

Aside from the political advantages of conciliating the East European states, the United States, if my image of essentially peaceful East European intentions is correct, stands to gain more than it might lose from the continued industrialization of Eastern Europe. The nations of this area are small but reliable trade partners, whose imports are less likely to be affected by a recession or by a sudden attack of protectionism than the imports of many of our Western partners. (The curtailment of Western imports by an East European importer due to unanticipated balance-of-payments difficulties, as occurred in Bulgaria in 1966-1967, may perhaps be averted by sympathetic U.S. or international monetary actions, including the extension of temporary credits to meet the emergency.) The greater the economic potential of these countries, the more they can contribute to America's welfare by selling it the goods they produce with a comparative advantage in exchange for agricultural products and various chemicals, machinery and equipment items, and means of transportation in which the United States enjoys an advantage. The net effect on employment of expanded trade with Eastern Europe is probably beneficial, although a precise prediction of this effect cannot now be made. (In any event, the direct impact on the United States economy of expanding trade to its full potential cannot be very large, considering that the combined national products of the East European countries do not exceed 25 to 30 percent of U.S. GNP.)

One should not overlook the potential benefits of East European industrialization to the underdeveloped market economies, particularly in view of the specialization of East European industry in the production and export of capital-intensive engineering products that are not too demanding in skilled personnel for their operation, such products being essential to the development of the industrially retarded nations. In the end, every country, including the United States, stands to gain from the abundance and relatively low prices of machinery and equipment in world markets and from the industrial progress of developing countries which they will help make possible. Ideally, one might wish to foster triangular exchanges, whereby the United States would export increasing quantities of highly sophisticated equipment to Eastern Europe, while Eastern Europe expanded its exports of relatively simple engineering products to the developing nations.

Given these various options, what are the instruments available to decision-makers in the U.S. government to pursue the objectives they will have selected? They are few in number and generally self-evident in their application: (1) Most-favored-nation status may be extended to all East European states, irrespective of whether or not MFN is finally granted to the Soviet Union. (2) Exports to Eastern Europe may be facilitated by abolishing licenses for all goods except for specifically designated strategic items. (3) The U.S. Export-Import Bank may be instructed to support with liberal credit facilities the expansion of American exports to Eastern Europe. (4) These East European states not now members of the International Monetary Fund—Romania and Yugoslavia are at present the only members—may be encouraged to join the organization and to take advantage of its short-term credit resources to help solve their balance-of-payments problems. In certain cases, it might be mutually advantageous for the United States to enter into bilateral agreements with East European partners that would promote trade by providing a measure of long-term security for buyers and sellers and by improving the information available to both parties about the quantities and specifications of exportable goods. Finally, consideration might be given to new legislation or to the revision of Internal Revenue Service regulations that would ease the burden of taxation on American businesses participating in co-production or other cooperative agreements with East European enterprises.

But these are mere details of implementation. The critical choice, which requires a judicious assessment of the present situation in Eastern Europe, is whether the United States wishes to aid or to hinder the further economic development of individual East European states or of all these states together. An important consideration in this choice should, in my view, be the weakened economic position of Eastern Europe vis-à-vis the Soviet Union and the opportunities this may provide for Soviet power to curb the relative autonomy won in recent years by most East European countries and to draw Yugoslavia— independent but deeply divided by its conflict of nationalities—into its sphere of influence.

XII

The Soviet Union and Eastern Europe: Recommendations for United States Policy

William E. Griffith

The basic policy issue in Soviet-American relations is *not* détente as such, which the American and Soviet political elites will probably, and in my view correctly, continue to find useful to their interests. For there is no theoretical or practical alternative to détente except cold war, which is risky and mutually counter-productive, or war itself, which would destroy civilization as we know it. Thus, the issue is a cost-benefit one: How can the U.S. best simultaneously manage conflict, competition, and limited and, hopefully, cautiously increased coopera-tion with the Soviet Union? And it is an issue of priorities: What priority should the United States give to its relations with the Soviet Union in contrast to priorities for energy, trade, monetary, Middle Eastern, and food affairs, and relations with its allies?

There are in my view three major American policy options toward the Soviet Union. The first is to give overall priority to bilateral cooperation with the Soviet Union, primarily with respect to strategic weapons, with the aim of transforming the conflictual relationship into a cooperative one. The second is a balance of power policy, particularly with China, in order to limit the conflict relationship with the Soviet Union, but with the expectation that the Soviet-U.S. relationship will remain primarily one of conflict and that the United States should concentrate on getting as much out of détente as it can without endangering its continuation. The third, which complements the second but in the short run is contrary to the first, is to give priority to its relations with its allies and to energy and Middle Eastern problems over relations with the Soviet Union. This would mean that in a Soviet-U.S. issue involving the interests of

Western Europe or Japan, the United States would give priority to maintaining good relations with them even if this made Soviet-U.S. agreement more difficult.

In my view the United States should give first priority to the third alternative, and second priority to the second. The first, whose goal might eventually be reached as a result of priority for the third and second, should not be given priority in the near future, for it fails to understand that for Moscow, and therefore for Washington, détente is political competition.

The U.S. should therefore downgrade its present priority for its relations with the Soviet Union. Why?

First, U.S. relations with the Soviet Union are now relatively stable, or where they are not, notably in the Middle East and southern Africa, the major U.S. problems cannot be solved by cooperation with the Soviet Union. Second, the Soviet Union has as much interest in strategic arms control as the United States has, and with respect to the qualitative arms race and nuclear nonproliferation it probably has more, because of the U.S. technological advantage and because with the exception of India new atomic powers would probably not be pro-Soviet. (On the contrary, the two major potential atomic superpowers, Japan and Western Europe, are likely to remain anti-Soviet.) Third, the interrelated problems of energy and the Middle East critically affect the U.S. domestic economy as well as its foreign policy and therefore the United States should give them priority. The final and most important point is that downgrading the priority for U.S. relations with the Soviet Union is the best way for the United States to carry them on effectively. For the continuing U.S. conflict relationship with the Soviet Union will largely center in exactly those areas, Western Europe, the Middle East, China, and Japan, which are anti-Soviet, and in the improvement of whose relations with the Soviet Union the United States has little interest. Therefore, U.S. priority should be for improving relations with Western Europe and Japan, and for coordinating with them U.S. policies toward the Soviet Union. The second alternative, a balance of power policy, especially vis-à-vis China, can effectively be combined with the third, but certainly not with the first, for good U.S. relations with China put pressure on Moscow simultaneously to improve its relations with the United States.

This does not mean that the United States should abandon détente with the Soviet Union. On the contrary, this policy offers, in my view, the best way to carry it on. For Moscow, détente means strategic arms control, conflict management, access to Western and Japanese technology and credits, and stabilization and if possible widening of its sphere of influence plus gradual, controlled destabilization of those of its opponents. For Moscow sees itself not as a saturated power but as a successfully expanding one.

U.S. public opinion should free itself from the illusion that East-West détente means international stability. Moscow has always said that it means continued political and para-military struggle below the level of Soviet-U.S. war. The Soviets declare themselves determined and proud to engage in this struggle. In it, as in the military balance, the United States will abandon the struggle or accept inferiority in it at its peril. True cooperation with the Soviets, as opposed to limitation of the conflict relationship, will not soon come, and illusionary pursuit of it in the short run will imperil its eventual attainment. The United States should therefore control transfer of technology, credits, and grain to the Soviet Union, its relations with its allies and China, and such joint projects as in space to help to limit Soviet expansionism and favor détente.

A more difficult policy issue, because of the Soviet and U.S. domestic factors involved, is that of U.S. involvement in Soviet internal affairs. The argument that the United States should link exports of grain and technology to the Soviet Union with Moscow being forthcoming on arms control, Middle Eastern, and southern African issues seems to me convincing—despite the views to the contrary of many U.S. businessmen and farmers. The U.S. debate will probably continue to center on whether or not they should also be linked with Moscow's permitting free emigration, particularly of Soviet Jews, and decreasing its repression of intellectual and nationalities dissidence.

Three preliminary points should be made on this issue. First, in our increasingly transnational world all nations will influence each other more and more, intentionally or not. U.S. jazz and casual clothes have probably had more mass influence in the Soviet Union and Eastern Europe than have any other aspects of U.S. life. Second, through the broadcasts of the Voice of America and Radio Liberty, particularly by the latter's rebroadcast of Soviet dissident material, the U.S. is actively influencing Soviet public opinion, just as the Soviet Union similarly tries to influence U.S. public opinion, and the United States should continue to do so. For, third, while the Soviet Union refuses to agree to the entry of Western ideas and information into what it regards as its sphere of influence, it openly asserts and covertly pursues what it calls "the intensification of the international class struggle" throughout the world, including within the West. For example, the recent covert Soviet financing of the Portuguese Communist party has been greater than the overt financing of the Portuguese Socialist party by West European social democratic parties, and the Soviet Union committed much more money and arms aid to Angola than did the United States.

The policy issue is therefore *not* whether the United States should or should not try to influence Soviet internal affairs—unless one believes, as I do not, in unilateral ideological disarmament. The United States should strive for propaganda parity with the Soviet Union, for Moscow will not, and cannot without changing its system, accept mutual ideological disarmament. Moreover, there is a direct connection between internal liberalization in the Soviet Union and Soviet foreign policy. For the secrecy and repressiveness of the Soviet regime, as long as it continues, will prevent Soviet public opinion from moderating expansionist Soviet foreign policy interest.

The principal specific issue is, then, not whether political struggle will continue but what should be the U.S. policy priority in the payoffs which it wants to get from Moscow in return for food and technology transfers, limitation of armaments, and not allying with the Chinese. In my view they should be primarily, although not entirely, in Soviet foreign, not domestic policy. The payoffs will be limited anyway, and the U.S. needs all that it can get from the Soviet Union in strategic and conventional arms control, in the Middle East, and elsewhere. Moreover, liberalization in the Soviet Union will be at best very slow, and in the short run the United States can count on little of it no matter what U.S. policies are.

American traditions and the nonconformist conscience, however, will prevent Washington from long or successfully carrying out a policy of *Realpolitik*, whether or not one may think that it should. It therefore behooves any American government, for this reason as well as in the pursuit of propaganda parity, to make clear its disapproval of Soviet ethnic and intellectual repression, including the imprisonment, consignment to insane asylums, and refusal to allow to emigrate of Soviet dissidents, whether Great Russian Jewish, or from the other Soviet nationalities.

These general policy recommendations will neither end nor work against Soviet-U.S. détente. They are, rather, proposals for a realistic policy of parity in détente. They offer, in my view, the best prospects for containing the expansion of Soviet influence, for gradual improvement of Soviet-American relations, and, we may hope, for the eventual moderation of Soviet policy.

In the *military field* the United States should insist on overall equivalency with the Soviet Union of strategic weapons and therefore reject a policy of minimal deterrence. Toward this end, the United States should use its qualitative superiority. It should for strategic and moral reasons continue the "Schlesinger doctrine" and reject MAD. Because the Soviet Union has at least as much if not more incentive to conclude further SALT agreements as the United States does, the United States has no reason to make unilateral concessions to do so. Nor, therefore, should SALT be decoupled from other Soviet-U.S. policy issues.

The United States should continue to resist pressure for unilateral U.S. troop reductions in Europe. To forestall them and to cement détente in Central Europe, the United States should actively pursue and institutionalize the Vienna force reduction negotiations. It should continue to insist on overall equivalency in reductions, which it should define as asymmetrical reductions in both Soviet land forces and in American tactical nuclear ones. It should make no concessions to the Soviet attempt to use MFR to get a hand on the West German Bundeswehr. It should compensate for the recently increased Soviet conventional superiority, particularly in tanks. Since in Europe the United States is likely to remain inferior to the Soviet Union in conventional ground forces, it should continue to compensate for this by qualitatively notably better military technology, precision-guided munitions (PGMs) such as "smart bombs" and "smart shells," by tactical nuclear weapons, and by continuing to refuse to exclude their first use in an initially conventional East-West conflict in Europe.

As to the issue of West Europe and Japan becoming nuclear powers, the Soviets will do all they can to prevent what would be a major change in the East-West balance of power to their disfavor. Whether Japan will go nuclear within the next two decades or so is unpredictable. Western Europe is unlikely to, if only because this is implicitly excluded by the 1970-1973 German settlement. Should either or both seem likely to do so, however, the Soviet Union will certainly attempt to persuade the United States to join with it to prevent it. While nuclear proliferation is contrary to U.S. interests, it is likely to occur. Moreover, any U.S. attempt to prevent Western Europe or Japan from going nuclear, particularly in open or tacit collusion with the Soviet Union, would have a disastrous effect on U.S. alliance relationships. The United States should, therefore, neither favor or oppose Western Europe or Japan going nuclear. Rather, it should adopt an attitude of benevolent neutrality, including making it clear that if it did occur the United States would be prepared to give technological assistance in return for coordination of nuclear planning. With respect to the Chinese nuclear force, the United States would have an interest in aiding it if the Soviet Union were to take a more hostile attitude toward the United States, or in order to deter a threatening Soviet attack on China.

Soviet-American naval competition is likely to intensify. Moscow will continue to use Soviet naval power against Peking as well as Washington. The policy issue is whether the United States should maintain its present naval superiority over the Soviet Union or accept parity or Soviet superiority. Russia has always been primarily a land power. The United States, like Great Britain, has traditionally been a sea and air power, and in the post-Vietnam War era it has wisely reverted to this tradition. Contrary to the Soviet Union, U.S. allies and their sources of raw materials and energy are across the seas. Furthermore, the United States can only strategically compensate for Soviet ground superiority and thereby assure rough overall military parity by having a superior navy. Washington should be prepared to negotiate on naval limitation with Moscow, but it should accept naval parity only in the—very unlikely—event that Moscow would accept ground force parity as well.

With respect to *Sino-Soviet relations*, the United States should continue its present policy of "active nonalignment" between the Soviet Union and China, balancing between them and holding over the head of each its option to ally with the other. The United States has to be more interested in its relations with the Soviet Union than in those with China because Moscow is a far stronger and therefore more dangerous global opponent than Peking. But it does not follow that it therefore needs to have better relations with Moscow than with Peking. (The post-1971 U.S. move toward China improved, not worsened U.S. relations with the Soviet Union.) On the contrary, with Soviet power growing and U.S. public will in foreign policy crippled, Washington should further improve its relations with Peking in order to deter Mao's successors from moving back toward Moscow and to put pressure on Moscow to limit its expansionist policies.

A major Sino-Soviet rapprochement would be a disaster for the United States because it would deprive Washington of this possibility. One of the most important tasks for U.S. foreign policy vis-à-vis the Soviet Union, therefore, is to do what it can to insure that Mao and his successors remain hostile to Moscow. That the Soviet Union will resist this policy, and that for a time it may worsen Soviet-U.S. relations, is true. But it is not decisive, for improvement of U.S. relations with China, in contrast to allying with China against the Soviet Union, will in the long run make Moscow less hostile to the United States as well.

In the *Middle East* the United States should also use its relations with the Soviet Union with respect to food and technology sales and to China in order to influence Moscow to limit its competition there with Washington. But it should not, in return for Moscow's cooperation, favor a greater Soviet role in the Middle East than the limited one which Moscow now has, for Moscow can neither decisively aid nor prevent an Arab-Israeli settlement: only the United States, the Arabs, and the Israelis can do that. Its achievement, which in my view can only be done by a combination of persuasion and pressure to get Israel to withdraw to the 1967 boundaries (with minor rectifications) in return for U.S. and international guarantees of its and Arab security, will sooner or later be an absolute precondition for preventing another Arab-Israeli war. The prevention of such a war should in my view have major priority in U.S. foreign policy, primarily to avoid the casualties, destruction, oil production limitation, and U.S. alliance crises it would cause, but also to prevent a revival of Soviet influence in the Middle East. Soviet losses in the Middle East have been so great, U.S. interest in limiting their influence there seems to me so clear, and the Soviets can and will do so little for settlement and stability in the area, that the United States has no interest in centering its policy there on cooperating with Moscow toward an Arab-Israeli settlement.

In *South and Southeast Asia*, Soviet-American competition will be primarily naval. There is little or nothing that the United States realistically can, need, or should do to try to reacquire predominant influence in India, with whose intractable problems Washington can well afford to watch Moscow grapple. (However, the United States equally has no reason not to reciprocate any Indian moves to improve relations with Washington.) The United States should look favorably on the anti-Soviet aspects of the policies of Iran and Pakistan, and it should base its policies in South Asia on a close relationship with Iran. In Southeast Asia the most effective U.S. policy vis-à-vis the Soviet Union is to maintain close ties with Indonesia and Australia and to contribute to Sino-Soviet rivalry in the area.

Africa for the United States is strategically a land mass blocking air flights and making difficult sea access to the Middle East. The United States therefore has an interest to prevent the establishment of Soviet military or naval bases there. Africa also has significant natural resources: for example, Nigeria is now the second largest exporter of oil (after Canada) to the United States. Finally, the views of twenty-six million American blacks will become increasingly influential in Washington. The Soviet (and Cuban) victory in Angola has highlighted the issue of U.S. policy toward the Soviet presence in Southern Africa.

U.S. policy in Angola failed in 1975 because U.S. analysis there was wrong, most of all in not understanding that any U.S. policy parallel with that of South Africa could only aid Moscow and hurt Washington, because it would push most black African states away from Washington and some toward Moscow. A successful U.S. policy vis-à-vis the Soviet Union in Africa must therefore first of all be a successful U.S. policy *in* black Africa.

An effective U.S. policy vis-à-vis the Soviet Union in Africa thus requires clear, complete U.S. political dissociation from the white minority regimes in Southern Africa, condemnation of their rule in Rhodesia and Namibia and demands for immediate black majority rule there, and condemnation of apartheid in South Africa. It should also include economic aid and technical assistance for those black African states now most menaced, notably Zaïre and Zambia, but also for Angola and Mozambique. The United States should offer to recognize Angola, as it has Mozambique, for there is no better alternative, and wait patiently for them to respond. The United States should continue to condemn the Soviet (and Cuban) presence in Angola, but not expect Angola to expel them or the other black African states soon to demand it. Rather, the United States should make clear to Moscow that it will retaliate against the Soviet Union for its actions in Angola in areas of its own advantage and choosing, by cutting back on technology transfer to the USSR and improving our relations with the Chinese, and that if Moscow continues, in southern Africa or even more elsewhere to act as it did in Angola, the United States will help Peking to improve its defensive military potential against the Soviet threat to its borders.

Unless and until all of southern Africa comes under black majority rule, the United States can at best limit its losses there. U.S. public and congressional opinion will neither probably aid the black guerrilla movements nor force major changes in Pretoria's policies, while the Soviets will continue arms aid to the guerrillas, whom South Africa will for some time at least successfully resist.

Finally, the United States should make clear to Moscow that its aid and encouragement to Castro's involvement in Africa and in Latin America, if continued, will move the United States even further away from them and toward the Chinese; that the United States will move against Castro by further economic sanctions; and that if Castro tries to send troops anywhere in Latin America, the United States will blockade Cuba and, insofar as the Soviets are involved, begin even stronger U.S. retaliatory measures against the USSR than those outlined above.

Eastern Europe

In Eastern Europe the most important U.S. policy question is to what extent the United States should give it significant priority in its foreign policy at all. Should it regard Eastern Europe as a low-priority area? Or should it try to contribute to liberalization and autonomy in Eastern Europe, in order to lower Soviet influence there, because of a spill-over effect that this would have in the Soviet Union, or for its own sake? And what varying degrees of emphasis should it give to liberalization and to autonomy?

In my view the United States should follow a policy of peaceful engagement in Eastern Europe,[1] utilizing détente with the Soviet Union and with the East European states so as to encourage more national autonomy and internal liberalization there, without attempting to encourage them to break with the Soviet Union or to overthrow domestic Communist rule, because either or both would only again bring in the Red Army. The United States should encourage national autonomy from the Soviet Union in Eastern Europe as the Soviet Union encourages autonomy from the United States in Western Europe, but also, again like the Soviet Union, it should work for controlled, not uncontrolled change. The United States should have as one of the major aims of its European policy to encourage the reunification of Europe, but this must be pursued primarily by Western Europe, with American help.

The United States should also try to aid domestic liberalization in the Soviet-controlled area of Eastern Europe, in a carefully limited and controlled fashion, in order to further national autonomy, because it would encourage sentiments favorable to the West, and because of the traditional commitment to it of the United States and particularly of its millions of citizens of East European descent. It should therefore maintain Radio Free Europe, including its broadcasts on internal East European affairs. It should use food, trade, and technology for linkage purposes to pursue both of these.

Regionally, the major defensive U.S. interest in Eastern Europe is the preservation of the national independence of Yugoslavia and Romania. It should therefore regularly make clear to the Soviet Union that Soviet interference with, or invasion of, either or both would not only mean the end of Soviet-U.S. détente but make likely a Sino-U.S. military alliance against the Soviet Union. It should make clear its commitment to the unity, territorial integrity, and independence of Yugoslavia (and Romania) and its rejection of separatist movements among nations of Yugoslavia. Yet this should not mean that the United States should remain silent with respect to the limitations on freedom in both countries. Again, pure *Realpolitik* will not work because it is against U.S. traditions.

The U.S. should pursue policies of détente, improved relations, and trade and cultural exchange with the other East European countries. This should be particularly emphasized with Poland, the most important Warsaw Pact East European state, a country from which the ancestors of so many Americans came, and in the recovery of 1919 of whose independence the United States was so instrumental.

East Germany presents a special issue to U.S. foreign policy. West Germany, the most important U.S. ally in Western Europe, regards it as one of the two German states in one German nation and therefore claims a special role toward it. Moreover, the United States is committed, and should remain so, to U.S. troop presence and military guarantee of West Berlin, and it has a major troop commitment in West Germany as well. It follows that Washington should continue to follow and support West German policy toward East Germany, since if it does not it will imperil, to no advantage, its key alliance with Bonn.

The Soviet Union's maintenance of its hegemony over most of Eastern Europe by presence or threat of its military power, not by genuine alliances, is potentially one of its weakest foreign policy positions. The United States has no interest to encourage rebellions in Eastern Europe, for it has no interest to risk war with Moscow to prevent the Red Army crushing them. But neither does it have any interest in aiding Moscow to consolidate Russian hegemony over Eastern Europe. U.S. traditions and national interest join to reject such a policy, and by measured but clear and regular declarations, Washington should make clear that it does.

The policy proposals recommended here are neither simple nor short range. They run against the impatience, the optimism, and the simplistic moralism so characteristic of much of the American tradition. Their realization will be made difficult by congressional antipathy to the Executive and by the demobilizing effects of détente on U.S. public opinion. They will compete for attention with other foreign policy priorities and with pressing U.S. domestic problems. But I do not share, and indeed I regard as historically quite unjustified, the current cultural pessimism of some intellectuals about the American future. The Soviet Union is exactly what most of the world now sees it to be: a retrogressive, bureaucratic, repressive, and therefore unattractive model of political, economic, and social development. Its rising influence is a result of its military power and that alone. When adequately informed and intelligently, firmly, and cour-ageously led, America has responded to far greater challenges before than it faces from Moscow today and will face tomorrow. I have no doubt that it will do so again.

Note

1. Zbigniew Brzezinski and William E. Griffith, "Peaceful Engagement in Eastern Europe," *Foreign Affairs* 39, 4 (July 1961): 642-654.

Index

About the Authors

WILLIAM E. GRIFFITH is Ford Professor of Political Science at Massachusetts Institute of Technology and Adjunct Professor of Diplomatic History at The Fletcher School of Law and Diplomacy, Tufts University. Among his major works are: *The Sino-Soviet Rift* and *Sino-Soviet Relations 1965-1967*. He is the general editor of the MIT Press series, Studies in Communism, Revisionism and Revolution, of which there are twenty-one volumes to date. His *The Germanies and the East* will soon be published. His major fields of expertise include Central and Eastern Europe, Sino-Soviet relations and the Middle East.

SEWERYN BIALER is director of programs at the Research Institute on International Change of Columbia University and teaches comparative politics in Columbia's Department of Political Science. His publications include the book: *Stalin and His Generals* and numerous articles on Soviet politics.

PETER REDDAWAY, senior lecturer in Political Science at the London School of Economics, was educated at Cambridge University, Harvard, Moscow University and the London School of Economics. In addition to contributions to *The Times* (London), *The Observer* and *The New York Review of Books*, he is closely associated with the journals *Index on Censorship*, *Religion in Communist Lands* and *A Chronicle of Human Rights in the U.S.S.R.* He is the author of several books including *Uncensored Russia: The Human Rights Movement in the Soviet Union* (1972). In 1973-74 he was a junior fellow of the Research Institute on Communist Affairs at Columbia University.

JOSEPH S. BERLINER, professor of economics at Brandeis University and associate of the Russian Research Center, Harvard University, is an expert in the economics of socialist countries. He is a past president of the American Association for the Advancement of Slavic Studies, and is currently the president of the Association for Comparative Economic Studies. He has authored the following books: *Factory and Manager in the USSR* (1957), *Soviet Economic Aid* (1958), *Economy, Society and Welfare* (1972) and *The Innovation Decision in Soviet Industry* (1976).

FRANKLYN D. HOLZMAN is professor of economics at Tufts University and its Fletcher School of Law and Diplomacy. A research associate of the Russian Research Center, Harvard University, he is particularly known for his expertise in the fields of socialist economics and international economics. His recent books include *Foreign Trade Under Central Planning* (1974), *Financial Checks on Soviet Defense Expenditures* (1975) and *International Trade under Communism: Politics and Economics* (1976).

THOMAS W. WOLFE is a senior staff member of The Rand Corporation and a member of the faculty at the Institute for Sino-Soviet Studies at George Washington University. A retired military officer and former air attaché at the United States Embassy in Moscow, his area of expertise is Soviet and East European affairs, with a speciality in defense policy and related foreign policy activities. He wrote *Soviet Strategy at the Crossroads* (1965) and *Soviet Power and Europe: 1945-1970* (1970). His next book will be *The SALT Experience*.

ROBERT LEGVOLD is associate professor of political science at Tufts University. He is primarily interested in Soviet policy in West Europe, particularly in the problem of European security, and in Soviet perceptions of the shifting military balance between East and West. He is the author of *Soviet Policy in West Africa* and a forthcoming study of *Soviet Policy in France, 1958 to Present.*

OLES M. SMOLANSKY is professor and chairman of the Department of International Relations at Lehigh University. A 1972-1973 senior research fellow in the Research Institute on Communist Affairs and the Middle East Institute, Columbia University, his major interest is Soviet policy in the Middle East. He is the author of *The Soviet Union and the Arab East under Khrushchev.*

THOMAS W. ROBINSON is associate professor of political science at the University of Washington and at the Institute for Comparative and Foreign Area Studies there. Previously associated with the Council on Foreign

Relations and the Rand Corporation, he has also taught at Dartmouth, Princeton, the University of California at Los Angeles, and the University of Southern California. He specializes in Chinese politics and foreign policy, Soviet foreign policy, Sino-Soviet relations and international and strategic relations. He is the author of *The Cultural Revolution in China, Forecasting in International Relations* (with Nazli Choucri), and his forthcoming works include *Lin Piao: Chinese Military Politician* and *Chinese Foreign Policy*.

ROBIN ALISON REMINGTON is associate professor of political science at the University of Missouri (Columbia) and a research affiliate of the Massachusetts Institute of Technology Center for International Studies. An exchange scholar at the Belgrade Institute of International Politics and Economics during the academic year 1970-1971 and a visiting scholar associated with the Warsaw Institute of International Affairs, spring 1971 and 1974, Professor Remington is the author of *Winter in Prague: Documents on Czechoslovak Communism in Crisis* (1969) and *The Warsaw Pact: Case Studies in Communist Conflict Resolution* (1971), and is a member of the executive council of the American Association for Southeast European Studies.

J.M. MONTIAS is professor of economics at Yale University. He specializes in East European economics and in theoretical and empirical problems of comparisons of economic systems. He has consulted extensively with United Nations organizations. Professor Montias has written *Economic Development in Communist Rumania* and has in press *The Structure of Economic Systems*.

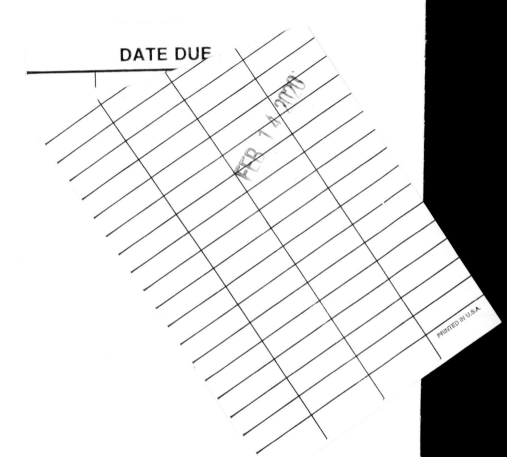

DATE DUE

FEB 14 2020

PRINTED IN U.S.A.